ALL AFIRE TO FIGHT

ALL AFIRE TO FIGHT

The Untold Tale of the Civil War's

Ninth Texas Cavalry

MARTHA L. CRABB

POST
ROAD
PRESS

AN AVON BOOK

AVON BOOKS, INC.
1350 Avenue of the Americas
New York, New York 10019

Copyright © 2000 by Martha L. Crabb
Interior design by Kellan Peck
ISBN: 0-380-97794-X

Library of Congress Cataloging in Publication Data:
Crabb, Martha L., 1928–
All afire to fight : the untold tale of the Civil War's Ninth
Texas Cavalry / Martha L. Crabb. —1st ed.
p.   cm.
Includes bibliographical references and index.
1. Confederate States of America. Army. Texas Cavalry Regiment, 9th.
2. United States—History—Civil War, 1861–1865—Regimental histories.
3. Texas—History—Civil War, 1861–1865—Regimental histories. I. Title.
E580.6 9th.C7   2000   99-42903
973.7'464—dc21   CIP

First Post Road Press Printing: January 2000

POST ROAD PRESS TRADEMARK REG. U.S. PAT. OFF. AND IN OTHER COUNTRIES, MARCA
REGISTRADA, HECHO EN U.S.A.

Printed in the U.S.A.

FIRST EDITION

QPM   10   9   8   7   6   5   4   3   2   1

www.avonbooks.com/postroadpress

Contents

CONTENTS

MAPS

Illustrations

FOREWORD

My interest in the Civil War began unexpectedly when an injury forced me onto the couch for a week. The only book in the house I hadn't read was a book club selection I'd failed to return: Bruce Catton's *Grant Moves South*. I opened the book convinced I would soon be bored. I couldn't put it down.

Having read American history all my adult life—an interest I inherited from my father—I began studying the war that saved our country from disintegration, reshaped it forever, and proved to the world that free men could rule themselves.

Twenty-five years later, I set out to write a thirty-page story about two great-uncles, Reuben and Jesse Rogers, who served in the Ninth Texas Cavalry. My research led to the Research Center of the H. B. Simpson History Complex at Hillsboro, Texas. The material in the center quickly persuaded me I should tell the stories of the Rogers brothers and their comrades whose dedication to duty compelled them to ignore death and disease, hunger and exhaustion, for four years.

The Ninth and three other North Texas and East Texas cavalry regiments—the Third, the Sixth, and the First Texas Legion (also known as the Twenty-seventh)—were brigaded together early in the war. The men soon came to view the four regiments as a single unit, known later in the war and to history as Sul Ross's Texas Brigade. *All Afire to Fight* is the story of these Texas cavalrymen. Because the words of those who helped make history have an immediacy that no retelling can attain, this book tells the Texans' stories as often as possible in their own words, found in letters, diaries, journals, memoirs, family stories, county histories, unpublished U.S. Archive records, and the *Official Records*.

Although many of these rambunctious, independent young men had been in the Lone Star State only a few years, all proudly considered themselves Texans and strove to live up to the state's reputation for bravery and self-reliance. They brought with them into the Civil War the famous heritage of the Tennessee militia and the Texas Rangers, two groups of daring men who were the most efficient—and the most deadly—military units of their times.

Across the Civil War West from Indian Territory to Arkansas, Mississippi, Tennessee, Alabama, and Georgia, the Texas cavalrymen fought cold and hunger as well as Yankees. They would have been naked except for clothing they captured or their families sent from home. Their government in Richmond, never able to grasp the importance of the West, neglected them and refused many of them furloughs during their entire service. Their reputation for courage and reliability often kept them in action until they were staggering with exhaustion.

After the war, their brigadier general, Sul Ross, was twice elected governor of Texas by the largest pluralities in the history of the state. He was the best known and most popular Texas citizen during the last quarter of the 1800s. Sul Ross University at Alpine honors this worthy soldier, statesman, and educator. Still, the stories of these brave men and their leader have never before been told.

George "Gris" Griscom, first an orderly sergeant and soon adjutant of the Ninth, was present every day of the regiment's three years and nine months of Confederate service. His diary provides a daily chronology of the regiment that would be impossible to reconstruct from official documents. The diary also helps fix times and places of events described in other sources. I couldn't have written this book without Griscom's diary and the other collections at the H.B. Simpson History Complex.

These stories of the Ninth Texas Cavalry are incomplete because only a few men left records of their time in service. Some were too busy, others were disinclined to write during or after the war. Certainly, the rascals and the illiterate, the embittered and the deserters, and the men whose experiences were too disturbing to put on paper left no letters, kept no diaries, wrote no memoirs. Also, courtesy and customs of the 1860s discouraged writers from describing their undesirable comrades. Neither did I tell every fact or every story. A book can be too long. And research must stop, a difficult task for me because the hunt is always more fun than the trophy.

Without the Texas cavalrymen's valor and dedication to duty I would have had no tales to tell. Without the expertise of three gracious gentlemen, who guided me through the processes of transforming a manuscript into a book, the Texans' stories would still be untold. Words are inadequate to express my appreciation to freelance editor Jerry Gross of Gross Associates; Clyde Taylor of Curtis Brown, Ltd.; and Stephen S. Power, who heads the Post Road Press imprint at Avon Books.

My special thanks to Peggy Fox, director of the H. B. Simpson History Complex Research Center, for her invaluable help, and also to the staffs of the Killgore Memorial Library of Dumas and the Amarillo Public Library for their assistance. I am indebted to Patti Darnell for her research at the Dallas Public Library, where she is a volunteer.

I gratefully acknowledge my debt and sincerely thank many friends and relatives, and my fellow Civil War buffs, some of whom I have never met. Their suggestions and comments encouraged me and improved the stories of my cavalrymen. Several people read the entire manuscript: my daughter-in-law Janet Crabb, my brother Delbert Lewis, writing friend Louise George, and Civil War buff William P. Banks Jr. My twin, Mary Griffin, patiently read the book aloud to me chapter by chapter and coerced me, as sisters do better than others, into deleting much fascinating information that did not belong in these stories. Her ear for cadence also improved the writing.

My special thanks to James Dark, Ron Moore, and Denny Hair, Civil War buffs scattered across Texas, for sharing their detailed knowledge with me. I am indebted to my writing group, Coleman Ward,

CALENDAR OF EVENTS

August 1861–October 28, 1861
Chapter 1: All Afire to Fight

August 20	Quayle's Mounted Riflemen left Fort Worth
October 2	Ninth [Sims's] organized
October 14	Ninth inducted into Confederate service
October 28	Regiment started to Arkansas to join Brig. Gen. Ben McCulloch

October 29, 1861–January 9, 1862
Chapter 2: Yankee Indians

November 11	Ninth ordered to report to Col. Douglas H. Cooper in Indian Territory (present eastern Oklahoma)
November 19	Battle of Round Mountain
December 9	Battle of Bird Creek (Chusto-Talaah or High Shoal)
December 26	Battle of Chustenahlah
January 9	Ninth left Fort Gibson, Indian Territory, for Arkansas

January 10–February 16, 1862
Chapter 3: The Seat of War

January 12   Ninth arrived at Van Buren, Arkansas
January 15   Ninth reached winter quarters on Horsehead Creek

February 17–April 16, 1862
Chapter 4: A West Point General

February 17   Ninth Texas ordered to northwestern Arkansas
February 26–
March 1   Maj. Sul Ross's raid into Missouri
March 3   Orders classifying Sims's regiment as Ninth Texas
              Cavalry; Maj. Gen. Earl Van Dorn reached Strickler's
              Station
March 7–8   Battle of Pea Ridge or Elkhorn Tavern
March 17   Ninth Texas arrived at winter quarters on Horsehead
              Creek
March 28   Col. Thomas Churchill's cavalry started for Missouri
April 14   Churchill's Cavalry arrived at Des Arc, Arkansas; Ninth
              and other Texas cavalry regiments dismounted

April 16–September 3, 1862
Chapter 5: Infantrymen

April 18   Ninth arrived at Memphis
April 26   Ninth arrived at Corinth, Mississippi
May 9   Battle of Farmington
May 10   Reorganization under Conscription Act
May 29   Retreat from Corinth
June 8–
September 3   Infantry training

September 4–December 7, 1862
Chapter 6: Cannon Fodder

September 7   March to Iuka, Mississippi, began
September 19   Battle of Iuka
October 3–5   Battles of Corinth and Hatchie Bridge
October 23   Reorganization

December 8, 1862–January 7, 1863
Chapter 7: Horses! Horses!

December 8   Horses arrived from Texas
December
15–27   Holly Springs Raid

January 8–May 22, 1863
Chapter 8: Glorious Tennessee

January 8   Brigade began march to Tennessee
February 28   Arrived at Spring Hill, Tennessee
March 5   Battle of Thompson's Station
May 7   Van Dorn assassinated
May 18   Reorganization by promotion up the ranks
May 19   Siege of Vicksburg began
                 Brigade started to Vicksburg

May 23–December 16, 1863
Chapter 9: Guard Duty

June 3   Brigade reached Canton, Mississippi
July 1   Skirmish at Messenger's Ferry, Queen's Hill
July 4   Vicksburg surrendered
July 14-20   Raid behind Sherman's lines
August 18   Brig. Gen. John W. Whitfield resigned

August 28–
September 4   Fifty men deserted
December 16   Col. Sul Ross assumed command of Texas Brigade

December 17, 1863–May 14, 1864
Chapter 10: A Texas Ranger

December 17,
1863–January
20, 1864   Expedition to Gaines Ferry
January 28–
February 7   Fighting gunboats on the Yazoo River
February 8–28 Expedition to Meridian
March 5   Battle of Yazoo City
April 4   Took up line of march to Alabama
April 27   Encamped at Tuscaloosa, Alabama
May 9   Received marching orders to Georgia
May 14   Arrived at Rome, Georgia

May 15–August 11, 1864
Chapter 11: Stalling Sherman

May 17   Battle of Rome
May 25–27   Battle of New Hope Church
June 27   Battle of Kennesaw Mountain
June 30   Last extant roll of Ross's Brigade
July 5   Ninth Texas crossed the Chattahoochee
July 17   Gen. Joseph Johnston replaced by Gen. John B. Hood
July 20   Battle of Peach Tree Creek
July 22   Battle of Atlanta
July 28   Battle of Ezra Church
July 28–30   McCook's raid on the Macon & Western Railroad

August 12–October 24, 1864
Chapter 12: Paying the Piper

August 18–20	Kilpatrick's Raid on the Macon & Western Railroad
August 31	Battle of Jonesboro
September 1	Fall of Atlanta
October 24	Began march to Alabama

October 25–December 27, 1864
Chapter 13: Riding with Forrest

November 18	Forrest's cavalry began Tennessee Campaign
November 30	Battle of Franklin
December 7	Forrest's Battle of Murfreesboro
December 15	U.S. supply train captured near Murfreesboro
December 15–16	Battle of Nashville
December 27	Tennessee Campaign ended

December 28, 1864–June 1865
Chapter 14: Duty Done

December 31	Brigade reached Iuka, Mississippi
January 12	Brigade headquarters at Corinth
January 13	Hood resigned
mid-February	Ross's headquarters at Deasonville, Mississippi
February 20	Half the brigade furloughed
April 9	Robert E. Lee surrendered Army of Northern Virginia
April 26	Joseph E. Johnston surrendered Army of Tennessee
May 4	Richard Taylor surrendered Department of Alabama, Mississippi, and East Louisiana
May 15	Brigade signed paroles at camp near Canton, Mississippi

ORGANIZATION AND COMMAND

—November 11, 1861—

COMMAND OF THE WEST–Gen. Albert Sidney Johnston
DEPARTMENT OF INDIAN TERRITORY–Brig. Gen. Albert Pike
Col. Douglas H. Cooper, commanding

- **9th Texas Cavalry–**
  Col. William B. Sims   Indian regiments and battalions
  Lt. Col. William Quayle
  [known as Sims's or state designation
  of 4th Texas Cavalry]

—January 1, 1862—

COMMAND OF THE WEST–Gen. Albert Sidney Johnston
ARKANSAS COMMAND–Brig. Gen. Ben McCulloch

1ST BRIGADE   2ND BRIGADE
Col. James M. McIntosh   Col. Louis Hébert

- **3rd Texas Cavalry–Col. Elkanah Greer**   - **Whitfield's Battalion Texas Cavalry**
  Lt. Col. Walter P. Lane   **Col. John W. Whitfield**
  [Greer's or South Kansas-Texas]   11th Texas Cavalry–Col. William C. Young

- 6th Texas Cavalry–
  Col. B. Warren Stone
  Lt. Col. John S. Griffith
- 9th Texas Cavalry–
  Col. William B. Sims
  Lt. Col. William Quayle
  [Sims's or 4th Texas Cavalry]
Bennett's Co. Lamar Co. Texas Cavalry
  Capt. H.S. Bennett
1st Arkansas Mounted Rifles
  Col. Thomas J. Churchill
2nd Arkansas Mounted Rifles
  Col. James M. McIntosh

Lt. Col. James J. Diamond
  [Young's or 3rd Texas Cavalry]
3rd Louisiana Infantry
5 regiments Arkansas infantry
Brooks's Battalion Cavalry
3 artillery batteries

—March 17, 1862—

COMMAND OF THE WEST–Gen. Albert Sidney Johnston
after April 6–Gen. Pierre G.T. Beauregard
TRANS-MISSISSIPPI DEPARTMENT–Maj. Gen. Earl Van Dorn
ARMY OF THE WEST–Maj. Gen. Earl Van Dorn
Adjutant–Col. Dabney H. Maury

FIRST DIVISION–Maj. Gen. Sterling Price

1ST BRIGADE
Col. Henry Little
★★★

2ND BRIGADE
Col. Louis Hébert
- Whitfield's Texas Legion–
  Col. John W. Whitfield
★★★

3RD BRIGADE
Lt. Frank C. Armstrong, inspector-
general
★★★

4TH BRIGADE
Brig. Gen. Martin Green
★★★

1ST CAVALRY BRIGADE
Col. Elkanah Greer

2nd Arkansas Cavalry
- 3rd Texas Cavalry–
  Lt. Col. Walter P. Lane

2ND CAVALRY BRIGADE
Col. Thomas J. Churchill

- 6th Texas Cavalry–
  Col. B. Warren Stone
- 9th Texas Cavalry–
  Lt. Col. William Quayle
11th Texas Cavalry [Young's]

—July 3, 1862—

DEPARTMENT NO. 2–Gen. Braxton Bragg
ARMY OF MISSISSIPPI–Gen. Braxton Bragg

ARMY OF THE WEST–Maj. Gen. Sterling Price

FIRST DIVISION–Brig. Gen. Henry Little

1ST BRIGADED
Col. Elijah Gates
★★★

2ND BRIGADE
Brig. Gen. Louis Hébert

- Whitfield's Texas Legion–
  Col. W.J. Whitfield
- 3rd Texas Cavalry–Col. R.H. Cumby
  Lt. Col. Hinchie P. Mabry
3 Arkansas & Louisiana infantry regiments

3RD BRIGADE
Brig. Gen. Martin E. Green
★★★

SECOND DIVISION–Maj. Gen. John P. McCown

1ST BRIGADE
Brig. Gen. William L. Cabell
★★★

2ND BRIGADE
Brig. Gen. Thomas J. Churchill

THIRD DIVISION–Brig. Gen. Dabney H. Maury

1ST BRIGADE
Col. T.P. Dockery
★★★

3RD BRIGADE
Brig. Gen. Charles W. Phifer
★★★

2ND BRIGADE
Brig. Gen. J.C. Moore
★★★

- 6th Texas Cavalry–
  Col. L.S. "Sul" Ross
- 9th Texas Cavalry–
  Lt. Col. Dudley W. Jones
3rd Arkansas Cavalry
2 artillery battalions

—October 3, 1862–Battle of Corinth—

ARMY OF WEST TENNESSEE–Maj. Gen. Earl Van Dorn
PRICE'S CORPS OR ARMY OF THE WEST–Maj. Gen. Sterling Price

FIRST DIVISION–Brig. Gen. Louis Hébert–Brig. Gen. Martin E. Green
Texas cavalry regiments dismounted

1ST BRIGADE
Col. Elijah Gates
★★★

2ND BRIGADE
Col. W. Bruce Colbert

- 1st Texas Legion–
  Col. John W. Whitfield
- 3rd Texas Cavalry–
  Lt. Col. Hinchie P. Mabry
4 other regiments
2 batteries

3RD BRIGADE
Brig. Gen. Martin Green–
Col. W.H. Moore
★★★

4TH BRIGADE
Col. John D. Martin–
Col. Robert McLain
★★★

MAURY'S DIVISION–Brig. Gen. Dabney H. Maury
Texas and Arkansas cavalry regiments dismounted

PHIFER'S BRIGADE
Brig. Gen. Charles W. Phifer

- 6th Texas Cavalry–
  Col. L.S. "Sul" Ross
- 9th Texas Cavalry–
  Lt. Col. Dudley W. Jones
3rd Arkansas Cavalry
Stirman's Sharpshooters
[some men from 9th Texas]
McNally's Battery

MOORE'S BRIGADE
Brig. Gen. John C. Moore

2nd Texas Infantry–
Col. Wm. P. Rogers
★★★

CABELL'S BRIGADE
Brig. Gen. W.L. Cabell
★★★

CAVALRY CORPS [mounted]
Brig. Gen. Frank C. Armstrong

Slemons' Cavalry
Wirt Adams' Cavalry

CORPS OF DISTRICT OF MISSISSIPPI–Maj. Gen. Mansfield Lovell
★★★

CAVALRY BRIGADE [mounted]
Col. William H. Jackson
★★★

—October 20, 1862–Reorganization after Battle of Corinth—

DEPARTMENT OF MISSISSIPPI AND EASTERN LOUISIANA–Lt. Gen. John
C. Pemberton
ARMY OF THE WEST–Maj. Gen. Sterling Price

BOWEN'S DIVISION–Brig. Gen. John S. Bowen
★★★

MAURY'S DIVISION–Brig. Gen. Dabney H. Maury

• 3rd Texas Cavalry–Col. Hinchie P. Mabry
• 6th Texas Cavalry–Col. L.S. "Sul" Ross
• 9th Texas Cavalry–Lt. Col. Dudley W. Jones
• Whitfield's Texas Legion–Col. John W.
  Whitfield
2nd Texas Infantry
13 Alabama and Mississippi regiments and
battalions

—December 20, 1862–Holly Springs Raid—

COMMAND OF THE WEST–Gen. Joseph E. Johnston
DEPARTMENT OF MISSISSIPPI AND EAST LOUISIANA–
Lt. Gen. John C. Pemberton

CAVALRY CORPS–Maj. Gen. Earl Van Dorn

TEXAS BRIGADE
Lt. Col. John S. Griffith

• 3rd Texas Cavalry–
  Lt. Col. Jiles S. Boggess
• 6th Texas Cavalry–Capt. Jack Wharton
• 9th Texas Cavalry–
  Lt. Col. Dudley W. Jones
• Whitfield's Texas Legion–Col. Edwin
  R. Hawkins, Lt. Col. John H. Broocks

UNBRIGADED UNITS

8 regiments
4 battalions
Roddey's command

—March 31, 1863—Battle of Thompson's Station—

COMMAND OF THE WEST—Gen. Joseph E. Johnston
ARMY OF TENNESSEE—Gen. Braxton Bragg

FIRST CAVALRY CORPS—Maj. Gen. Earl Van Dorn

FORREST'S DIVISION—Brig. Gen. Nathan Bedford Forrest
★★★

JACKSON'S DIVISION—Brig. Gen. William H. Jackson

<u>WHITFIELD'S BRIGADE</u>
Col. John W. Whitfield

<u>ARMSTRONG'S BRIGADE</u>
Brig. Gen. Frank C. Armstrong

- 3rd Texas Cavalry—
  Maj. Absolom B. Stone
- 6th Texas Cavalry—
  Col. L.S. "Sul" Ross
- 9th Texas Cavalry—
  Lt. Col. Dudley W. Jones
- Whitfield's Legion—
  Lt. Col. John H. Broocks
Capt. Houston King's battery

3rd Arkansas Cavalry
4th Mississippi Cavalry
Sanders' Battalion Cavalry
Jenkins' Alabama Cavalry Squadron

—August 22, 1863—

COMMAND OF THE WEST—Gen. Joseph E. Johnston
ARMY OF MISSISSIPPI AND EASTERN LOUISIANA—
Lt. Gen. William J. Hardee
CAVALRY IN MISSISSIPPI—Maj. Gen. Stephen D. Lee

JACKSON'S CAVALRY DIVISION—Brig. Gen. William H. Jackson

<u>1ST BRIGADE</u>
Brig. Gen. George B. Cosby
★★★

<u>2ND BRIGADE</u>
Brig. Gen. John W. Whitfield

<u>ROSS'S BRIGADE</u>
Col. L.S. "Sul" Ross

1st Mississippi Cavalry—
Col. R.A. Pinson

- 1st Texas Legion—
  Col. Edwin R. Hawkins
- 3rd Texas Cavalry—
  Lt. Col. Jiles S. Boggess
- 9th Texas Cavalry—
  Lt. Col. Thomas G. Berry

- 6th Texas Cavalry–
  Capt. Peter F. Ross

[Col. D.W. Jones on leave Aug. 11–Sept. 19, 1863]

Clark (Missouri) Battery, Capt. Houston King

—November 1863—

DEPARTMENT OF MISSISSIPPI AND EASTERN LOUISIANA–
General Joseph E. Johnston
CAVALRY IN MISSISSIPPI–Maj. Gen. Stephen D. Lee
★★★

JACKSON'S DIVISION–Brig. Gen. William H. Jackson

1ST BRIGADE
Brig. Gen. George B. Cosby
★★★

ADAMS'S BRIGADE
Brig. Gen. Wirt Adams
★★★

2ND OR TEXAS BRIGADE
Col. Hinchie P. Mabry

- 1st Texas Squadron–
  Capt. R.W. Billups
- 3rd Texas Cavalry–
  Lt. Col. Jiles S. Boggess
- 6th Texas Cavalry–
  Maj. Jack Wharton (detachment to Ross's Brigade)
- 9th Texas Cavalry–
  Col. Dudley W. Jones

—February 20, 1864—

DEPARTMENT OF ALABAMA, MISSISSIPPI AND EAST LOUISIANA–
Lt. Gen. Leonidas Polk
CAVALRY CORPS–Maj. Gen. Stephen D. Lee

JACKSON'S DIVISION–Brig. Gen. William H. Jackson

1ST BRIGADE
Col. Peter B. Starke
★★★

ADAMS'S BRIGADE
Brig. Gen. Wirt Adams
★★★

FERGUSON'S BRIGADE
Brig. Gen. Samuel W. Ferguson
★★★

2ND BRIGADE
Brig. Gen. L.S. "Sul" Ross

• 1st Texas Legion–
Col. Edwin R. Hawkins
• 3rd Texas Cavalry–
Col. Hinchie P. Mabry
• 6th Texas Cavalry–
Col. Jack Wharton
• 9th Texas Cavalry–
Col. Dudley W. Jones
Missouri Battery–Capt. Houston King

—June 10, 1864–Georgia Campaign—

ARMY OF TENNESSEE AND GEORGIA CAMPAIGN–
Gen. Joseph E. Johnston
ARMY OF MISSISSIPPI–Lt. Gen. Leonidas Polk
after June 14–Lt. Gen. Alexander P. Stewart

JACKSON'S CAVALRY DIVISION–Brig. Gen. William H. Jackson

1ST BRIGADE
Brig. Gen. Frank C. Armstrong

6th Alabama Cavalry
1st Mississippi Cavalry
2nd Mississippi Cavalry
28th Mississippi Cavalry
Ballentine's Mississippi Cavalry

3RD BRIGADE
Brig. Gen. Samuel W. Ferguson

2nd Alabama Cavalry
12th Mississippi Cavalry
56th Alabama Cavalry
Miller's Mississippi Cavalry
Perrin's Mississippi Cavalry

2ND OR ROSS'S BRIGADE
Brig. Gen. L.S. "Sul" Ross

• 1st Texas Legion–
Col. Edwin R. Hawkins
• 3rd Texas Cavalry–
Col. Jiles S. Boggess
• 6th Texas Cavalry–
Lt. Col. Peter F. Ross
• 9th Texas Cavalry–
Col. Dudley W. Jones

ARTILLERY BATTALION

Croft's (Georgia) battery
King's (Missouri) battery
Waties' (South Carolina) battery

—July 31, 1864–Atlanta Campaign—

ARMY OF TENNESSEE–Gen. John B. Hood

CAVALRY CORPS
Maj. Gen. Joseph Wheeler
★★★

MARTIN'S DIVISION	KELLY'S DIVISION
Maj. Gen. William T. Martin	Brig. Gen. John H. Kelly
	★★★

HUMES' DIVISION–Brig. Gen. William Y.C. Humes

HARRISON'S BRIGADE	ASHBY'S BRIGADE
Brig. Gen. Thomas Harrison	★★★

3rd Arkansas Cavalry
4th Tennessee Cavalry
8th Texas Cavalry
11th Texas Cavalry

WILLIAMS' BRIGADE
★★★

JACKSON'S DIVISION–Brig. Gen. William H. Jackson

ROSS'S BRIGADE	ARMSTRONG'S BRIGADE
Brig. Gen. L.S. "Sul" Ross	Brig. Gen. Frank C. Armstrong

- 1st Texas Legion–
  Col. Edwin R. Hawkins
- 3rd Texas Cavalry–
  Col. Jiles S. Boggess
- 6th Texas Cavalry–
  Lt. Col. Peter F. Ross
- 9th Texas Cavalry–
  Col. Dudley W. Jones

1st Mississippi Cavalry
2nd Mississippi Cavalry
28th Mississippi Cavalry
Ballentine's Mississippi Cavalry
Escort, Co. D., 2nd Mississippi Cavalry

FERGUSON'S BRIGADE
Brig. Gen. Samuel W. Ferguson

2nd Alabama Cavalry
12th Mississippi Cavalry
56th Alabama Cavalry
Miller's Mississippi Cavalry
Perrin's Mississippi Cavalry

—August 1, 1864–Georgia Campaign—

- 9th Texas Cavalry–Lt. Col. Thomas G. Berry
Col. Dudley W. Jones wounded, on medical leave

—September 3, 1864–Georgia Campaign—

- 9th Texas Cavalry–Capt. Hamilton C. Dial
Col. Dudley W. Jones wounded, on medical leave
Lt. Col. Thomas G. Berry, killed
Maj. James C. Bates, wounded, on medical leave

—November 18, 1864–Tennessee Campaign—

ARMY OF TENNESSEE–General John B. Hood
CAVALRY CORPS–Maj. Gen. Nathan Bedford Forrest

BUFORD'S DIVISION
Brig. Gen. Abraham Buford
★★★

CHALMERS'S DIVISION
Brig. Gen. James R. Chalmers
★★★

JACKSON'S DIVISION–Brig. Gen. William H. Jackson

ROSS'S BRIGADE
Brig. Gen. L.S. "Sul" Ross

ARMSTRONG'S BRIGADE
Brig. Gen. Frank C. Armstrong

- 1st Texas Legion–
Col. Edwin R. Hawkins
- 3rd Texas Cavalry–
Lt. Col. Jiles S. Boggess
- 6th Texas Cavalry–
Col. Jack Wharton
- 9th Texas Cavalry–
Col. Dudley W. Jones

1st Mississippi Cavalry
2nd Mississippi Cavalry
28th Mississippi Cavalry
Ballentine's Mississippi Cavalry
Escort, Co. D., 2nd Mississippi Cavalry

—January 15, 1865—

DEPARTMENT OF ALABAMA, MISSISSIPPI AND EAST LOUISIANA–
Lt. Gen. Richard Taylor
CAVALRY CORPS–Maj. Gen. Nathan Bedford Forrest
***

ROSS'S BRIGADE
Brig. Gen. L.S. "Sul" Ross

- 1st Texas Legion–
Col. Edwin R. Hawkins
- 3rd Texas Cavalry–
Lt. Col. Jiles S. Boggess
- 6th Texas Cavalry–Col. Jack Wharton
- 9th Texas Cavalry–Col. Dudley W. Jones

—March 15, 1865—

DEPARTMENT OF ALABAMA, MISSISSIPPI AND EAST LOUISIANA–
Lt. Gen. Richard Taylor
CAVALRY CORPS–Lt. Gen. Nathan Bedford Forrest
***

ROSS'S BRIGADE
Col. Dudley W. Jones

- 1st Texas Legion–
- 3rd Texas Cavalry–Maj. Absolom Stone
- 6th Texas Cavalry–
- 9th Texas Cavalry–
Lt. Col. James C. Bates

CAST OF CHARACTERS

CREED, AUGUSTUS R. "GUS"—Company A, Ninth Texas Cavalry. Born 1835 in Missouri and moved to Tarrant County, Texas, about 1858. After the war he married Reuben and Jesse Rogers's oldest sister. Gus was farming in northern Tarrant County when he joined Quayle's Mounted Rifleman, the militia company that became Company A, Ninth Texas Cavalry.

CREED, GEORGE W.—Company A, Ninth Texas Cavalry. Gus Creed's younger brother.

DUNN, JOHN S.—Company A, Ninth Texas Cavalry. Born December 12, 1843, in Texas. When he was thirteen his family moved to Grapevine in Tarrant County. John had four older brothers and six sisters. He quit school to join Quayle's Mounted Rifleman.

DUNN, SOLON—Company A, Ninth Texas Cavalry. Older brother of John Dunn; born in 1834 in Alabama. When he was five his parents moved the family to Texas. Solon kept the first store in Grapevine and served as postmaster. He had been married three years when the war began.

GARRETT, DAVID G.—Company E, Sixth Texas Cavalry. Born in Gallantin, Tennessee. He and several young men came to Texas together to make their way in the West. David purchased land in Cedar Grove, Kaufman County. He and Mary "Mollie" Gibbard were engaged when he left to join the cavalry. David's letters to Mollie and her family indicate he had a good education.

GRISCOM, GEORGE L. "GRIS"—Company D, Ninth Texas Cavalry. Born in 1837 in Pennsylvania. When he was ten his family moved to Petersburg, Virginia, where they became friends with the Robert E. Lee family. Gris received a good education and had many friends and relatives in Virginia. He went to Texas when he was twenty and was in Dallas by 1859. Gris was present for duty every day of the Ninth's existence and kept a diary of the regiment's activities.

JONES, DUDLEY W. "DUD"—Company I, Ninth Texas Cavalry. Born in 1842 in Texas. His wealthy family made their home at Mount Pleasant, Titus County. When the war started Dud quickly returned home from Columbia, Tennessee, where he was attending Maury Institute. He joined the Titus Grays, which became Company I.

KEEN, NEWTON A.—Company C, Sixth Texas Cavalry. Born in 1845 in Indiana. His family moved to Dallas County, Texas, the next year. Newt began hunting when he was six, and could ride any animal, wild or tame, when he was fourteen. By then he was doing a man's work. Newt's mother died when he was seven, and his father died six years later. When the stepmother drove all the Keen boys out of the house, Newt, age fourteen, went to live with his Keen grandparents on their nearby farm. He was attenting school when war fever swept northern Texas.

ROGERS, REUBEN—Company A, Ninth Texas Cavalry. Born November 11, 1840, near Springfield, Missouri, and moved to Texas in 1858. Reuben lived four miles south of Grapevine with his father, stepmother, five brothers, and three sisters. The family farmed and raised stock.

ROGERS, JESSE—Company A, Ninth Texas Cavalry. Born July 11, 1844, a brother of Reuben. Jesse left school to join the Texas cavalry.

ROSE, VICTOR M.—Company A, Third Texas Cavalry. Grew up in Victoria, Texas, home of his wealthy family. In May 1861 he left Centenary College and boarded a steamer headed up the Red River to Texas. On board he met Col. Elkhanah Greer, who was returning from Richmond with his commission and authority to raise a regiment of cavalry in eastern Texas. Victor joined one of the ten companies that were formed into Greer's Regiment, later known as the Third Texas Cavalry.

ROSS, LAWRENCE SULLIVAN "SUL"—Company G, Sixth Texas Cavalry. Born September 27, 1838, in Iowa Territory. A few months later the elder Ross moved his family to the Republic of Texas. Ten years later the Rosses established their home in Waco, McLennan County. Sul graduated from Wesleyan University at Florence, Alabama, in July 1859. A captain in the Texas Rangers when the war began, he resigned but was soon appointed aide-de-camp with the rank of colonel by the governor of Texas, Sam Houston. Sul, hoping for action with the Confederate army, declined Houston's offer in order to join a cavalry company his older brother Peter was raising.

SPARKS, A. W.—Company I, Ninth Texas Cavalry. Born in 1841 in Alabama. His family had lived in Titus County for several years when A.W. left school to join the Titus Grays, one of ten militia companies that formed the Ninth Texas Cavalry.

SPARKS, JOHN N.—Company I, Ninth Texas Cavalry. John was A. W. Sparks's older brother, born in Alabama in 1836. When the war began he was a wagoner in Titus County, Texas.

CHAPTER 1

ALL AFIRE TO FIGHT

August 1861–October 28, 1861

Reuben Rogers crept down the ladder from the loft and out of the house in the dead of night. He slipped past a row of young bois d'arc trees to the corral to saddle a horse. Reuben had made up his mind and would argue with Pa no longer. He stuffed a couple of changes of clothes into his saddlebags and tied a coat and blanket behind the cantle of the saddle. Murmuring to the horse, Reuben took the reins in one hand, a shotgun in the other, then led the animal down the lane and onto the road before mounting.

It was August 1861. The moon, low on the eastern horizon, cast shadows through the warm night air of Tarrant County, Texas. Reuben rode past the small log church of Minter's Chapel, a few miles south of Grapevine, before turning toward Fort Worth, fifteen miles southwest. When the tension in his broad shoulders began to ease, he relaxed in the saddle and pushed up the wide brim of his hat with two strong fingers.[1]

Reuben and his friends, Gus and George Creed, had talked for months of nothing but war—the excitement, the arrogant Yankees, Fort Sumter, Bull Run. As the furor in Texas had escalated during the past year, logic had degenerated into rage and near hysteria. People in north-eastern Texas blamed abolitionist plots for an unusual number of fires that burned businesses across the region—even though most blazes were started by sulfur matches self-igniting when temperatures rose as high as

114 degrees. Old men declared that a fire-red comet, which lighted the northeastern sky through the summer and early fall of 1860, was an omen of bad luck, an indisputable sign of war. Around the Capitol in Austin and in town squares across the state, cries of "Secession! Seces-

Capturing U.S. Army Headquarters in San Antonio

sion!" were heard. Passions had exploded through the fall of 1860 and into the winter, forcing suspected abolitionists to flee or be hanged. Texas seceded March 2, 1861. By late summer the Confederate government had elected Jefferson Davis president, established its capital in Richmond, Virginia, and won its first encounters with the U.S. Army.[2]

Reuben and the Creed brothers learned of the Confederate victory at Wilson Creek, near their old Missouri homes, in mid-August. The glorious news spread an epidemic of war fever across Texas as surely as a contaminated well spreads typhoid. In this first major battle west of Virginia, the Confederates killed a Federal general and sent the Yankees scampering north. Young men across the Lone Star State were soon "all afire for a chance to fight."[3]

Many joined the army seeking adventure; others were compelled by duty. A. W. Sparks, a student from Titus County, knew he had to fight for Texas or "pull his freight" as a traitor, a thought he "could not entertain for a moment." He "could see no honorable course for Texas men but to stake their lives, their liberty, their all for Texas." Another Texan said those who refused to join "ought to live in the swamps of Arkansas the balance of their days without ever seeing the face of a woman."[4]

Men all over the state dashed off to enlist after the battle of Wilson Creek. Many were fearful, not of war but of missing a chance to fight. A sixteen-year-old from Dallas County wrote:

Civil War fever was a high tide and sweeping everything before it. And having little sense, and no war sense at all . . . the 18th day of August 1861, I was on horse-back and sworn into the service for one year. . . . It was with a light heart I rode away from the land of peace and plenty to that of blood and trembling under the shock of battle.[5]

While the frenzy had built, Reuben had thought of his Rogers ancestors, who had always fought for their land and their beliefs. Grandpa Rogers marched into Alabama with Gen. Andrew Jackson during the War of 1812, and *his* pa made gunpowder for the Patriots during the Revolution. Reuben was determined not to miss his chance. When he reached Fort Worth he enlisted in Quayle's Mounted Riflemen, a cavalry company being raised in northern Tarrant County.[6]

The Mounted Riflemen were commanded by Judge William Quayle, a Grapevine resident who was raising the company in and around Fort Worth. Reuben had met the judge, an Englishman and former sea captain who had migrated to Texas for his health. Quayle had purchased a large tract of land, which he worked with slaves. An educated man, he had been elected district judge, then district clerk. Quayle was an ardent secessionist and well-known in the area. His reputation as an upright man of means drew into his company men from Fort Worth, Grapevine, Birdville, and the surrounding area. Quayle was typical of men who gained authority to raise companies and regiments early in the war. His experience as a ship's captain, giving orders and disciplining men, enabled him to quickly organize his company.[7]

Gus and George Creed, Reuben's neighbors in Missouri and now in Texas, also joined Quayle's Mounted Riflemen. The three knew several of their new comrades, but it had been only three years since their families had migrated to Tarrant County—not long enough to know the names of all the people and horses and most of the dogs in the area. However, they were not the only newcomers. The first Tarrant County settlers had arrived in the Grapevine area less than two decades earlier.[8]

Fort Worth, a busy frontier settlement of about 350 souls, was the

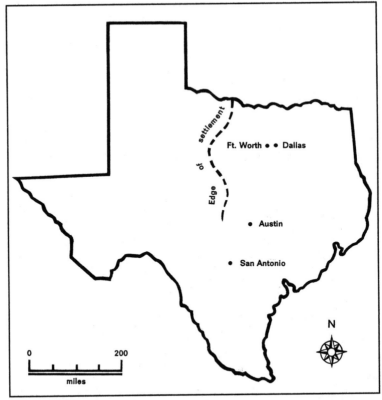

Texas—1860

largest town in the county, with a doctor, a lawyer, and a blacksmith. A teacher held school on the second floor of the Masonic Building. The town saddler, an ex-soldier, bent over his bench long hours each day. The village had grown up in and around the quadrangle of the abandoned log fort on the Trinity River. A few stores, a wooden courthouse, a flour mill, and a couple of saloons served the surrounding area.[9]

Reuben, Gus, and George marched with the Riflemen to Fort Worth's public square the morning of August 20. The company contained 93 privates, 3 lieutenants, 5 sergeants, and 4 corporals—105 men and boys. Captain Quayle sat his splendid horse with pride and assurance, his lithe frame erect, his brown eyes missing nothing. His troopers were mounted on an assortment of fine horses, Indian ponies, and Texas mustangs, even a few mules. The men wore semi-uniforms of jean fabric in varying shades of blue. Broad-brimmed Texas hats shaded their eyes. Each man was armed with a long gun and a six-shooter or two.[10]

Wagons and horses jostled for space around the square. Politicians, families, and friends, nearly the entire population of Tarrant County, crowded the wooden porches and spilled out onto the dusty streets. All had come to see their boys off to war. Grapevine residents cheered for Reuben Rogers, the Creed brothers, and the other Riflemen. Widow Elliston of Birdville grieved when her high-spirited sixteen-year-old son, Mark, rode by. Smithfield residents had no trouble spotting big A. M. Hightower, a six-foot, three-inch Scots-Irishman who wore a size-thirteen shoe.[11]

When the ceremonies began, a hush fell over the crowd. The soldiers swelled with pride and anticipation. Their families felt happy and proud, but also apprehensive; wives and mothers dreaded the anxiety and loneliness they knew lay ahead. A few older men in the square knew what war was about. It had been forty-five years since the War of 1812 but only fifteen years since the Mexican War. Yet this war seemed so right, so necessary—and most people were convinced it would be short.

When the speeches were finished, pretty, young Martha Quayle, the recent bride of Captain Quayle's brother, came forward carrying a folded flag. Looking over the Riflemen, she spotted her own brother. She began:

> *Gentlemen of the Grapevine Volunteers. Our once happy and prosperous country is now shaken from the center to the circumference with the horrors of civil war. War under any circumstance is to be deplored, but the present more than any that the annals of history give us an account, for it is brother against brother, and a blind and maddened fanaticism warring against our peculiar institutions, and even the privacy of our domestic hearths is threatened. I beg leave to present you on behalf of the Ladies of Grapevine the Flag of our Country, of which any patriot may well be proud; and committing it to your charge we feel well assured that it will be protected and defended . . . ever remember that you are protecting the wives, mothers and daughters that have a right to claim protection at your hands . . . may that God, whose Eye is over all his works, protect you. . . .*

Captain Quayle accepted the rectangular silk banner. The ladies had stitched together a field of one white and two red stripes with a blue canton containing a circle of white stars.[12]

When the ceremonies ended the Riflemen mounted, marched around the square, and rode out of town, their new Confederate Stars and Bars fluttering in the breeze. An uproarious crowd of proud men, tearful women, and wildly cheering boys watched the Riflemen descend

the high bluff, splash across the Trinity River, and strike out northeast through green prairies. Everyone was proud of this first company to leave the area and the first cavalry company to leave Tarrant County.[13]

First Flag of the Confederacy

The rambunctious horsemen bounded across sparsely settled countryside for several days. In a holiday mood, they rode seventy miles to Sherman, a town of four or five hundred people, two or three stores, and a one-horse mail. A dozen more miles north Quayle's company reached Camp Reeves, nestled in a lush grove near the Red River. Tents of other companies were scattered among the oaks at this camp of instruction, which had been established by the state of Texas for volunteer cavalry companies.[14]

Another band of Tarrant County men arrived early in September. Wealthy Fort Worth merchant M. J. Brinson had raised a company of seventy men around Johnson's Station (modern Arlington). The two Tarrant County companies and eight others recruited in North and East Texas were gathering to form a regiment of Texas State Cavalry.[15]

Sgt. George "Gris" Griscom of Brinson's company began keeping a diary. He noted the green troopers' activities: "We lay in camp drilling and sparring—going home occasionally and finally moved about two miles to Brogden Springs," nearer the Red River, the boundary between Texas and Indian Territory. The companies camped below the springs in a stand of trees.[16]

Titus County's A. W. Sparks, who was determined to "pull his freight" in this war, had left college to enlist. He described the recruits' equipment:

There were rifles, flint and steel, but most were full stock percussion muzzle-loading machines that had been used for killing bear, deer and other wild animals. Double-barrel shotguns were the favorite. A few pistols were in the command, and were in great demand by the officers. Each soldier carried a huge knife, usually made from an old mill file, shaped by the blacksmith and ground according to the fancy of the owner.

Another veteran remembered that "some of the knives were three feet long and heavy enough to cleave the skull of a mailed knight, through helmet and all." The horses were a fair average of Texas mustangs, but a few had strains of noted blood. Clothing was light, unsuited for hard service, but most of the new cavalrymen wore tall boots made of Texas tanned leather. A large flap on the front of the boots protected the rider's knees. Blankets often were pieces of carpets taken from floors.[17]

On October 2, all ten companies had arrived and the regiment organized. In both the Federal and Confederate volunteer armies, newly organized regiments elected their regimental officers, and each company elected its captain, lieutenants, and noncommissioned officers. Men campaigned for rank in the manner of political candidates, openly soliciting votes and working behind the scenes. The man who had secured official authority to raise the regiment usually won the colonelcy. Likewise, the man who had raised a company generally was chosen captain. Choosing officers often was more of a popularity contest than a question of selecting the most capable individuals.[18]

A prosperous merchant-planter from Red River County, William B. Sims, was elected colonel of the new regiment. William Quayle was elected lieutenant colonel. Quayle's Mounted Riflemen chose as their captain thirty-two-year-old Sgt. Thomas G. Berry, from Grapevine Prairie, in northeastern Tarrant County. Unlike other officers in the newly formed regiment, Tom Berry had neither wealth nor slaves, but his fairness, integrity, and sound judgment were evident to all.[19]

Both the Union and Confederate armies used letter designations for companies. A regiment contained ten companies, A through K. All skipped the letter *J* because in the script style of the times, *I* and *J* often were written alike. Perhaps *J* also was considered unlucky—a jinx, a Judas.

The captains drew lots for company letter designations. Berry drew an *A,* and the Mounted Riflemen became Company A of Sims's Texas Cavalry, Texas State Troops. M. J. Brinson, elected captain of his company, drew a *D.* George Griscom, age twenty-four, was elected orderly sergeant of Brinson's company. Gris's responsibilities included forming the company for drill or battle, distributing forage and rations, and keeping company rolls and books. Having grown up in Virginia, where his family counted the Robert E. Lees among their friends, Gris was better educated and more cosmopolitan than most of the new cavalrymen. His family was one of many divided over the question of secession—one brother fought for the Union, another with the Confederacy.[20]

The men regretted giving up the unit names they had chosen at the beginning of recruitment: Quayle's Mounted Riflemen of Tarrant County, the Titus Grays of Titus County, the Cypress Rangers from Cass County; as well as their identifying colored stripes or badges: The Titus Grays wore a blue stripe on the shoulders of their shirts, The Cypress Rangers a black stripe; the company from Lamar County, a yellow stripe. Company affiliation was important. Companies were identified by county, and members came from the same surrounding area and often were kin. Thus, a real camaraderie quickly developed among the men—or boys, as they were usually called.[21]

Throughout the Confederacy privates were called "boys" despite their actual age. To be sure, many *were* boys. John Sloan of Company C was only thirteen, and several of his comrades were sixteen. A few men were old enough to be grandfathers. A "boy" in an East Texas cavalry regiment was sixty-three. Nevertheless, most men in Company A were neither children nor graybeards. Half were in their early twenties, three fourths between eighteen and twenty-seven. The teenagers would survive hard field service well enough, but men over forty soon discovered they could not withstand the hardships of campaigning.[22]

The officers, mostly men of property and education, were older than the privates. Average age of the regiment's sixteen officers was thirty-four; one was fifty-three. At nineteen, Lt. Dudley W. "Dud" Jones was the youngest. None were professional soldiers. Three were lawyers, two were merchants, one was a district clerk, and several were farmers. Another was a broker, and Dud Jones was a college student.[23]

The 1860 census reveals that three out of four white men in Texas farmed. As might be expected, farmers and farmers' sons made up the

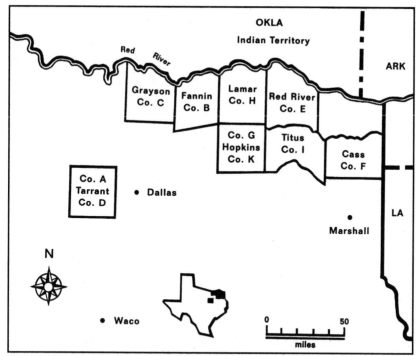

Northeastern Texas
Home Counties of Ninth Texas Cavalry
(1860 County Boundaries)

majority of the regiment. Others lived in small towns scattered across the area. None were city boys because there were no large towns in northeastern Texas, much less cities. Only 2,000 persons lived in Dallas, and the largest town in Texas, San Antonio, had a population of only 8,235. Within the counties furnishing companies to the regiment, Sulphur Spring, in Hopkins County, was the largest town, with a population of about 2,500.[24]

October 14, two weeks after the regiment organized, Col. William C. Young arrived to muster Sims's Regiment into Confederate service for twelve months. Governor Edward Clark had commissioned Young, a Mexican War veteran, former U.S. marshal, and colonel of a recently organized cavalry regiment, to induct four cavalry regiments of northeastern Texas men into Confederate service. The new regiment was also known as the Fourth Texas Cavalry, but was designated the Ninth Texas Cavalry, C.S.A., a few months later. (To avoid confusion, the regiment name used here will be the Ninth Texas Cavalry from the date of muster.)[25]

The muster-in rolls made that day are the earliest documentation of the men's service. Official records show eighty-two men and four officers enrolled in Company A. Several men had joined the company at Camp Reeves, while a dozen or more had gone home when they discovered living in a tent at a camp of instruction was often dirty, boring, and confining. The rolls noted each man's company affiliation; his name, rank, and age; plus the distance he traveled to rendezvous and the value of his horse and horse equipment. Although the companies had been recruited during the summer and fall in eight different counties by ten different men, the muster-in rolls state that all joined for duty and enrolled on October 14, 1861, at Camp Reeves and that all were enrolled by Col. William C. Young, C.S.A.[26]

The muster-in roll of Company A included Pvt. Reuben Rogers of Grapevine, age twenty. Reuben's horse was valued at $120, his horse equipment at $18. Although it was eighty miles from Grapevine to Camp Reeves, the roll noted that all men in the company traveled 150 miles to rendezvous, an arbitrary number chosen by Colonel Young. The men were reimbursed ten cents a mile for travel.[27]

The new soldiers, like all Confederate cavalrymen, furnished their own horses, horse equipment, arms, and clothing. Eighteen-year-old Alex Anderson rode into Camp Reeves on a nag worth $60, while John Estill of Grapevine proudly sat his splendid mount valued at $150. Most men in the company rode good horses, ranging in value between $100 and $125. According to the 1861 tax rolls, the average Tarrant County horse was worth $40.[28]

Horse equipment included a saddle, a bridle and halter, and a forty-foot rope with an iron picket pin. A. W. Sparks's horse, Old Napoleon, was a large black gelding valued at $100. A.W.'s rawhide skeleton saddle was worth $25, and his saddlebags $4. His other equipment consisted of two blankets worth $7, a bridle he valued at $2, and a common double-barrel shotgun, $25. A.W. stuffed into his saddlebags underclothing, four shirts, and four pair of drawers worth $8. He valued his coat and pants at $16, his boots at $6, and a canteen, a cup, a knife, and a belt at $3, for a total value of $196, which he considered a fair average for Texas cavalry privates. This initial cost of equipping a cavalryman made that service unavailable to poor men or their sons.[29]

Although the government was responsible for furnishing clothing and personal weapons, at the beginning of the war it fell to the men to supply their own, as A.W.'s list of items he brought with him shows. If a man's horse died or was captured, he was afoot until he could purchase another, impossible on a private's pay. Captured horses were issued on rare occasions, but families often furnished money to purchase remounts.

Company and regimental equipment and supplies for newly raised Texas regiments came from several sources. The state of Texas furnished limited numbers of arms, wagons, mules, tents, and other small equipment from the captured U.S. arsenal at San Antonio. Families and patriotic men of means supplied companies raised in affluent East Texas. Counties usually furnished some equipment for companies raised within their jurisdiction. For instance, in September 1861, Hopkins County issued $5,000 in bonds to furnish blankets and camp equipment. Two months later, Hopkins County commissioners agreed to borrow $1,209 from the school fund to buy clothing and equipment for their volunteers. Companies G and K of the Ninth were among the companies raised in Hopkins County.[30]

A Texas cavalry company officially contained 115 men—a hundred privates, a captain, a first lieutenant, a second lieutenant, three third lieutenants, and nine noncommissioned officers. Ten companies constituted a regiment. Each regiment required several mule- or horse-drawn wagons to carry food and forage, cooking utensils, tools, ammunition, medical supplies, tents, and extra clothing—all the gear necessary to keep the men in the field.[31]

The new cavalrymen camping at Brogden Springs lacked equipment and had no transportation—wagons and draft animals—but they were now members of the Confederate States Army. When the company rolls had been taken and Colonel Young had finished his official duties, Colonel Sims, a large, fine-looking gentleman, reviewed his troops and addressed them in his "foghorn voice": "We are soldiers enlisted for the war, and from [this] day we will regard war, civil war, as our profession, and in life it is the duty of every man to study, to understand his profession. . . ." Sims also said his purpose was to make the men into effective soldiers. His dedication to duty plus his "noble nature" won the men's respect.[32]

Soon after the regiment was inducted into the army, Brig. Gen. Ben McCulloch, commanding in Missouri and Arkansas, ordered the Ninth

Texas to join him as quickly as possible. While the regiment waited for equipment and transportation, the men drilled and trained their horses, always under the watchful eye of the colonel. For mounted drill, Sims formed his ten companies of about eighty men each into two battalions. Maj. Nathan B. Townes, a thirty-four-year-old lawyer from Lamar County, drilled one battalion, and William Quayle, now lieutenant colonel, the other. Quayle's experience at sea had quickly earned him recognition as the best military man in the regiment. He rode the most valuable horse in the company he had recruited and was an excellent horseman, an enviable accomplishment in the 1860s. Quayle's battalion consistently was best in drill.[33]

Townes and Quayle had their hands full corraling eight hundred wild frontier boys mounted on the same number of wilder horses. The horses laid back their ears and bucked when the bugles blew. Galloping in rank, they shied and threw their riders. Herded together, they kicked and bit to establish dominance, while the boys strutted and bragged for the same purpose. The sea captain and the lawyer must have felt as though they were trying to train a herd of buffalo.[34]

Volunteers, whether Union or Confederate, men or horses, were notoriously independent. At this point in their army careers the boys wanted to be soldiers, but they resented curtailment of their liberties. They had yet to learn that *soldier* and *freedom* are antonyms. The officers were as green as the men and had more to learn if they were going to be effective. Only a competent captain could transform raw recruits into a good company; only a capable colonel could create a valuable regiment.

The horses, the men, and the officers began to learn. The horses became accustomed to strange noises and smells. In a couple of weeks most no longer feared the bugle, but it took longer for some to become accustomed to gunfire. A few never did. The boys learned to get up and to go to bed, to form and to dismiss, to mount and to charge, by fife and drum or by bugle call. Fifes and drums were of little use to mounted men galloping after an enemy. The new soldiers began learning their duties and the precise maneuvers of cavalry. They also learned to stay awake standing night guard and to hold their tongues when given orders.[35]

The officers strove to discover their responsibilities and to learn the intricate procedures and commands. A cavalry tactics manual published later in the war contains 340 pages of minute detail that each officer was required to know. Service and tactics manuals, however, were scarce at Camp Reeves, and the few available were likely copies of U.S. Army infantry manuals. The lawyers, merchants, and farmers laboring to learn to be cavalry officers studied by candlelight when they could borrow a book.[36]

Both the men and the officers were introduced to military law and discipline, especially trial by court-martial. Soon after the regiment was organized, a man accused of stealing was tried by court-martial at the headquarters tent. Found guilty, he was dishonorably discharged. A soldier wrote:

> . . . *to the music of the fife and drum [he was] marched through all the camps to the outer guard line, where he received his belongings and departed, never to return. . . . Never before had I seen a man so debased. His face was covered with that shame that cannot be transferred to paper. It was hideous . . . he was even too low in manhood's scale to be killed by the country's enemies.*[37]

Later in the month the regimental adjutant was accused of abolitionism and bigamy, abolitionism being the more serious. Gris noted in his diary that while the officers debated the sentence in the privacy of the headquarters tent, "the boys *en masse* took him out and hanged him and gave his outfit to a poor boy, a member of the same company." A short time later a "worthless character" who had attached himself to Company D was caught near camp in the act of raping a married woman. The boys again snatched the prisoner from the guards and "hanged him to a tree until he was dead," A.W. wrote. "No tears were shed at his burial. His outfit was distributed among the most needy of the company." The young men in the regiment were "greatly influenced by these events." They had discovered that disgrace and death were the penalties for disobeying orders, and to them, disgrace was the more severe.[38]

The recruits soon learned that other offenses were punishable by death. During organization of the regiment, the long, tedious Articles of War were read to the assembled men. Both the officers and the men learned that sleeping on sentinel duty, disobeying a lawful command, assaulting a superior officer, misbehaving in the presence of the enemy, or corresponding with or giving information to the enemy could result in being shot. Minor offenses brought punishment of fines, extra duty, hard labor, or more often, physical punishment such as carrying a heavy log all day, standing on an empty barrel for hours with a bottle in each hand, or carrying a pack filled with fifty pounds of rocks.[39]

After the bigamous, abolitionist adjutant was hanged without benefit of court-martial, Lt. Dud Jones, the nineteen-year-old college student, was appointed adjutant. Jones was a fine-looking young gentleman with a quick mind and a rich family. The 1860 census shows young Dudley W. Jones owned twenty-two slaves and property valued at $26,000 in his own name. Officers in the Ninth owned an average of seven slaves and $17,000 in property. Nevertheless, Jones's appointment derived from his competence as well as his wealth and position.[40]

Two weeks after the muster rolls were made, Colonel Young managed to arrange for enough wagons and mules to supply transportation for the new regiment. On October 28, Company A mounted and splashed across the Red River near what is now Denison and followed Captain Berry northeast into Indian Territory, present eastern Oklahoma. Quayle's Mounted Riflemen were finally on their way to join Ben McCulloch in Missouri, the seat of war. The delicious aroma of autumn saturated the air as the company rode through stands of oak and hickory alternating with open meadows. The boys frolicked through the unsettled countryside, hunting game and camping on clear streams. They "were off to see the elephant."[41]

CHAPTER 2

YANKEE INDIANS

October 29, 1861—January 9, 1862

Capt. Tom Berry and his eighty-five new cavalrymen pointed their horses north from the Red River. Sixty miles up the road they stopped at Boggy Depot, where they would rendezvous with the rest of the regiment. The depot was a stage stop and Indian trading post at the junction of several old roads, including the famous road from Fort Smith, Arkansas, to Texas and on west to Santa Fe. Another road went north to the Creek Indian town of North Fork Village, then to Fort Gibson and on into Missouri. When the Butterfield Overland Mail Line's stage-coaches stopped at Boggy Depot on their way to San Francisco in the 1850s, travelers complained that the small house, proudly called a hotel, provided meager services.[1]

Boggy Depot was not new to Reuben. Three years earlier he had driven one of the family wagons from his home just north of Springfield, Missouri, to Fort Smith and on to Texas. His father had moved the family to the Lone Star State when arguments over slavery intensified in Missouri. The war his pa had anticipated had started, and conflict in the border state of Missouri had already turned bloody.[2]

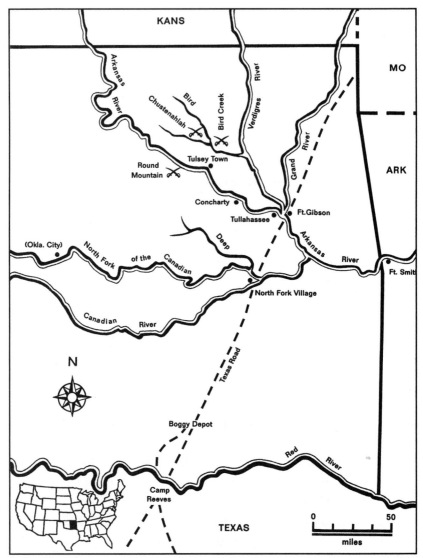

Indian Territory
(Oklahoma)

It was now November, and Reuben knew that Missouri still had a star in the flags of both the United States and the Confederate States. Missouri was one of three important border states Jefferson Davis coveted and Abraham Lincoln felt he had to save for the Union. Missourians could not decide which flag to fly. The armies would.[3]

Reuben and the Creeds looked forward to seeing their relatives and eating a home-cooked meal in Missouri. Reuben must have wanted to gallop up to his grandfather's house to show off his weapons and his cavalry horse. A warrior at heart, Grandpa had fought the British and the Creek Indians with Andrew Jackson's army during the War of 1812. During the recent battle of Wilson Creek, Grandpa had danced a jig when he heard the distant boom of cannon thirteen miles to the west. A grandson said, "I had to chase the geese away so the patriarch could hear the cannonading better. It was a sound which pleased the old veteran mightily."[4]

When Sims's ten companies, about seven hundred men, reached Boggy Depot, the regiment formed as best they knew how and strung out on the road. The ragged column of new soldiers displayed all the colors of the rainbow, gaudy shawls and handkerchiefs, Indian trade goods purchased at the post. The horseman marched north in column of fours toward Fort Gibson, deeper into Indian Territory.[5]

The fourth day, and sixty-five miles out of Boggy Depot, the regiment forded the shallow Canadian River and rode into North Fork Village in the evening. A few years earlier a traveler had described the Creek town as a dense settlement between the Canadian and the North Fork of the Canadian. It was Monday, November 11, Reuben's twenty-first birthday.[6]

The men were feeding their horses that evening when a courier trotted into camp with a dispatch for Col. William B. Sims. The message changed the regiment's orders. Sims was instructed to join Col. Douglas H. Cooper, commanding Confederate Indian forces in Indian Territory. Cooper and his Indian regiments were retreating before a superior force of Federal Indians and would continue to fall back until reinforced. Reuben would have to put off seeing Grandpa.[7]

Indian Territory was occupied by the Cherokee, Choctaw, Chickasaw, Creek, and Seminole. During the 1830s, these tribes had been forcefully removed from their homes in the southeastern United States and settled on unoccupied lands west of white settlement. Because of their close association with the white man over several generations, the tribes had adopted many customs and institutions, as well as vices, of the whites. Most tribal leaders were part white, educated, and spoke English. Many sent their children to school, wore white man's clothing, and owned black slaves.[8]

The practice of enslaving captives was common among American

Indians long before Columbus. In the South, the Indians easily slipped into the Southern system of black slavery and brought it with them to Indian Territory.

In addition to other white customs, four of the five tribes modeled their governments on those of the states. Because these tribes had adopted the white man's ways, they came to be called the Five Civilized Tribes, a term still in use. And indeed, they were civilized when compared with the nomadic, warlike buffalo hunters of the Great Plains. Each of the Five Tribes occupied a delineated territory and operated under its own laws and government, and so came to be known as a nation—such as the Cherokee Nation, the Creek Nation—a term also still in use.

During the summer and early fall of 1861, the Five Tribes, like the Missourians, argued and fought among themselves over which flag they would fly: the Stars and Stripes or the Stars and Bars.

The Upper Creek and Lower Creek had fought on opposite sides during the War of 1812 and had become bitterly divided into two warring factions long before their 1836 removal to Indian Territory. The Upper Creek's old chief, Opothleyohola, derisively called "Old Gouge," settled his people on the Canadian River. The Lower Creeks located north on the Arkansas, putting the Lower Creeks to the north and the Upper Creeks to the south. The two groups finally were moving toward a common government when the Civil War again split the Creek Nation.[9]

Opothleyohola, by then in his sixties, remained loyal to the Union, although he had fought the United States in the War of 1812. He was a revered leader and the richest man in the Creek Nation. The Lower Creeks, led by Daniel and Chilly McIntosh, were pro-Confederate. The animosity between Opothleyohola and the McIntoshes was of long standing. In addition to being hereditary enemies, Opothleyohola's followers had beheaded Daniel and Chilly's father in Georgia in 1825.[10]

Early in the war Cherokee council chief John Ross, a wise and influential leader, struggled to remain neutral and abide by treaties with the United States. Other Cherokees openly supported the South. By the fall of 1861, Confederate pressure and propaganda had persuaded John Ross that the Cherokee Nation had no choice. Ross reluctantly declared allegiance to the Confederate States of America. With his course set, he labored to unite his people and the other Indian nations with the Southern cause.

The Seminole, tenacious fighters who had been dragged forcefully from their Florida homes in the mid-1840s, were not yet securely settled in Indian Territory when the war began. They too attempted to remain neutral but eventually followed the Cherokee and Lower Creek.

The Choctaw and Chickasaw never doubted where their allegiance lay. Douglas H. Cooper, their Indian agent, was a determined secession-ist, as was their oldest and most influential missionary. Moreover, the Choctaw and Chickasaw, whose lands lay directly across the Red River from the Lone Star State, were swayed by Texas propaganda. Both nations proclaimed for the South two months before the first shot was fired at Fort Sumter.

A major source of pressure and propaganda that swung the Chero-kees, Lower Creeks, and Seminoles to the Confederacy was Albert Pike, an eccentric Little Rock, Arkansas, lawyer and passionate Rebel. Pike, only ten years younger than Opothleyohola, had fought in the Mexican War but had no other military experience.[11]

The War Department commissioned Pike a brigadier general and gave him command of the newly created Military Department of Indian Territory because the Indians trusted him and because he had fought in the Mexican War with Jefferson Davis. Also, Pike had often represented the nations and recently had settled an old Choctaw claim against the Federal government that won that nation nearly $3 million.

Late in the fall of 1861, Pike had traveled to Richmond to visit President Davis and to report his success in keeping the nations in the Confederacy. Pike left Indian agent Douglas H. Cooper, by then a colo-nel in the Confederate army, in command of the unstable situation in Indian Territory.[12]

Cooper believed the presence of Unionist Creeks threatened peace and unity in the territory. He also feared a slave uprising among the hundreds of blacks in Opothleyohola's camp. A Texas colonel wrote the War Department in Richmond suggesting Cooper drive out Opothleyo-hola to prevent the Five Tribes "from being trifled with by the Federals." All the Southern states refused to tolerate Union sympathizers, and there was reason for concern in Indian Territory. Each nation already had raised and equipped regiments of mounted riflemen, but all were not sure where their allegiance lay. The colonel of a Cherokee regiment and many of his men had objected to the alliance with the Confederacy and continued to waver. Certainly, the McIntosh brothers needed little incentive to attack their hereditary enemy. Cooper had set out to neutralize Opothleyohola, the "arch old traitor" in Cooper's mind.[13]

Opothleyohola and his Upper Creeks, firmly refusing to change allegiance, considered the Confederate tribesmen traitors. When Cooper and his Indian regiments threatened the Upper Creek settlement, Opothleyohola and his people loaded their wagons with food, clothes, furniture, and household goods and started north toward Federal protection in Kansas. Fifteen hundred warriors protected their families and seven hundred black slaves.[14]

Cooper had led the Choctaw, Seminole, Lower Creek, and Cherokee battalions and regiments against Opothleyohola in order to "compel submission to the authorities of the nation or drive him and his party out of the country."[15]

Into this caldron of mixed emotions and loyalties, anger and blood lust, rode a single Confederate cavalry regiment: the Ninth Texas.

Sims, at the Creek town of North Fork Village, read Cooper's order for assistance and called his officers to their first council of war on November 11. Of course, the privates knew something was brewing, and every man in the regiment felt a tingle of excitement long before receiving orders.[16]

Before daylight the next morning, fifty men from each company, five hundred troopers, headed northwest with ammunition and two days' rations in their haversacks. Lt. Col. William Quayle led the marching column while Sims remained with the support and the wagon train.[17]

Quayle's men halted a few minutes at noon to eat their small rations, fill their canteens in the creek, and feed the horses a handful of corn. The men rode steadily through the afternoon, often slowing to ford streams single file at buffalo crossings. A traveler had described the area a few years earlier as "a wild vacant country, dreary but for its beauty with here and there at long intervals a hut or wigwam." When the sun set on the horsemen, it had already been a long day. The men were worn and hungry—"wolfish," as they would have said. The horses were tiring. Pushing on another ten miles in the darkness, the column finally reached Cooper's camp at 10:00 P.M. They had ridden sixty-five miles.[18]

The Texans had grown up on horseback, but sixty-five miles in a single day tested their endurance, to say nothing of their horses'. Only Texas Rangers, who pursued the Comanche across West Texas, could have considered the day ordinary.[19]

When the cavalrymen arrived at Cooper's encampment, they marched through the Indians' camps amid "extravagant demonstrations of joy." The Indians shouted and "fired a grand salute," which the Texans "returned with about the same unmilitary regularity." The tribesmen danced until nearly morning. Finally, the regiment bivouacked.[20]

The Texans dragged their weary bodies out of their blankets the next morning and surveyed the huge encampment of over eight hundred Indians. The only white faces were a Texas cavalry company of a hundred men serving as Cooper's escort, Capt. Otis G. Welch, commanding. The McIntosh brothers were there with their Creeks—Col. Daniel N. McIntosh with his First Creek Regiment, Lt. Col. Chilly McIntosh with his Creek Battalion. The rest of the force contained six companies of Cooper's First Choctaw and Chickasaw Regiment and Seminole chief Maj. John Jumper's Creek and Seminole Battalion.[21]

The Ninth Texas came under the command of an experienced officer for the first time. Col. Douglas H. Cooper, an impressive Southern aristocrat of forty-five years, outranked Col. William Sims because Cooper's appointment predated Sims's. Cooper had a broad forehead, deepset eyes, and the bearing of authority. He had grown up in President Davis's home state of Mississippi and had been captain of a company in Colonel Davis's Mississippi Rifles during the Mexican War. Cooper and Davis had remained friends, a distinct advantage in obtaining Confederate commissions.[22]

The first morning under Cooper's command, Quayle's cavalrymen were issued flour, cornmeal, raw beef, and unshelled corn. They were ordered to cook six days' rations and shell the corn for their horses. The pans, kettles, and ovens were far off in the wagon train. The boys looked at the issue and wondered what to do, but they set about their tasks.[23]

Each trooper chose his own method. Some built fires and baked their unleavened mixtures of cornmeal and water on hot rocks or in the ashes. Others made hoecakes by flattening the cornmeal mixture on a board and tilting the board up toward the fire. When the cake was brown, it was flipped and browned on the other side. The inexperienced cooks seared their fingers and smoke blew in their eyes. The cornbread crumbled and burned. The boys made their flour into thick dough, twisted it around a stick, and baked it over the coals. It was hard as flint. They roasted the beef over the flames. While waiting for the food to cook, they shelled the corn. The unfamiliar tasks took all day.[24]

In the evening the Texans watched the Indians prepare for battle and realized, to their astonishment, that the ceremony was as serious to the tribesmen as prayer was to Christians. The Texans could not understand a word spoken, but A. W. Sparks later heard a translation and related the scene in his memoirs of the Texas cavalrymen. After the Indians assembled, a warrior rose and spoke:

"Friends, Opothleyohola, one of our race who has been honored and loved by his people, has become mad with his brothers. . . . We offered to meet him as a friend and brother, but he turned his back on us, then we sent him a white flag but he painted it red, a sign of war, and sent us this." The speaker held a huge club . . . shaped like a chicken's head. It was covered with blood and had hair in its bill. This scene was met with screams and gobbles which lasted for some minutes, when a few guns were fired and silence was restored. The speaker went on: "What does this mean? Ask the old men who have lived beyond the Great Water [the Mississippi River] and they will tell you it means WAR! It means that they will kill our children, it means that they will burn our houses, it means they will take away our squaws, it means they will drive off our cattle, and when we have grown weak for want of food they will hunt us down in the mountains and scalp us like wolves." Here the speaker again [was] drowned in a series of yells. The glimmer of the low campfires made the painted bodies of the Indians look like demons rising from the infernal regions. . . . The orator resumed, "Let us paint our faces, a sign that we look no more upon the squaw until her enemies are no more. . . ." At this juncture a ring was filled with painted Indians, all marching in a side-like manner, stepping high and fast, while they chanted a strange song.

Delighted with the performance, many Texans joined in the dancing.[25]

Most of the boys had never seen anything like this, although many had grown up hearing Indian stories. Reuben's Grandpa Rogers grew up on the exposed and dangerous East Tennessee frontier when every man kept his rifle constantly within reach, when every woman knew each trip to the spring could be her last. Moreover, when the Rogers family moved to Tarrant County, soldiers had abandoned the log post of Fort Worth only six years earlier, and white settlement reached but a short distance west. Beyond rampaged the Comanche, the scourge of the Great Plains. Comanche depredations had terrified the Texas frontier for 140 years and would for 15 more. In Tarrant County, Reuben and the other men new to the Texas frontier surely had absorbed some of the Texans' well-justified fear and hatred of Indians.[26]

The Tarrant County boys had given no thought to being scalped when they joined the cavalry. They anticipated fighting Yankees in far-off places, not feathered tribesmen three hundred miles from home. But soldiers, which they were quickly becoming, go where they are ordered.

Early Friday morning, November 15, shrill bugle notes exploded into the darkness. The Texans pulled on their boots and hurried to the picket lines to feed the horses, then breakfasted on rations cooked the day before. When the bugler sounded Boots and Saddles, each man saddled his horse and strapped on forty loads of shot and powder, his arms, a peck of shelled corn for his horse, blankets, a canteen, a tin cup, and his half-cooked or burned rations. Each man wore a blue-and-red string tied around his left arm. The string was the Confederates' badge, to be worn by both Indians and Texans. The strings had been passed out earlier with firm instruction to wear them and to let no Indian or white man pass without one. The Federal Indians, the Texans were told, would wear corn shucks in their headdresses or plaited in their hair.[27]

Five hundred Texans formed and waited. Horses snorted. Leather creaked when the men shifted in their saddles. Odors of leather and animals mingled with smoke from a hundred campfires. The Texans watched in amazement as Cooper's warriors marched by in column of twos. The Indians were armed with old muskets or shotguns, but many had only bows and arrows. They rode small ponies and were dressed in

"garb ranging from a common gent's suit to a breech clout and blanket."
All wore the blue-and-red string. Their faces were painted, each warrior
after his own design, but most commonly three lines of deep red from
the edge of the hair down the forehead and meeting between the eyes
with a large red spot on each cheek. Others had painted red circles
around their eyes, making "many hideous looking faces" to the Texans.
If the designs denoted rank or had other meaning, Quayle's men failed
to discover it.[28]

Many tribesmen wore head coverings of animal skins—bear, calf,
buffalo, or cougar. Others wore a single feather from an eagle, a turkey,
or a buzzard. An old warrior, clad in only a breechcloth, leggings, and
moccasins, marched by on foot carrying a long full-stocked rifle. A four-
foot peafowl feather in his hair trailed down his bare back. The Texans
named him "Old Pap." He spoke only one word of English, *no,* and
answered "No!" to anything said to him.[29]

The sun was well above the horizon when the Ninth Texas formed
behind Cooper's escort and the warriors. All 1,400 men rode northwest
up the Deep Fork of the Canadian in search of the old Creek chief who
refused to swear allegiance to the Confederacy. The country was rough;
the riding was hard. The column passed a few deserted log cabins with
rail fences and patches of grain. They found corn for the horses, but the
men had only their rations.[30]

They struck Opothleyohola's trail leading north the next day. The
shrewd old Creek had burned the prairie and destroyed the country along
his path, leaving no grass for the cavalry horses. The following day Cooper's command pushed on and bivouacked at Opothleyohola's abandoned
camp. Animal bones, cold campfires, and hoof prints of large numbers
of cattle, sheep, and horses littered both sides of the creek for more than
a mile. The trail to the northwest was as wide as a stage road.[31]

The fourth day out, November 18, the command took the trail at
first light. All day and long after dark they rode across burned prairies.
The men had eaten their six days' rations, and there was nothing for the
horses. Hunger gnawed at the bellies of both men and animals the next
morning. A.W. said he was hungry enough to eat a dead dog. But they
saddled up and pushed across the Red Fork of the Arkansas with the
rest of the column. Fortunately, they soon came upon a herd of cattle

left behind by the Union Indians and made for themselves a noon meal of fresh beef.[32]

Late in the afternoon the advance spotted camp smoke and enemy scouts along Round Mountain Creek, west of the junction of the Cimarron and Arkansas. Cooper ordered Quayle to charge the Indian encampment with Companies A, D, and I. The detachment galloped across an open prairie toward wisps of smoke drifting from trees along the creek. Riding into the timber, they wondered what they were getting into, but the enemy camp was deserted. Back on the prairie, they spotted enemy scouts ahead. Quayle, erect in the saddle, his full beard and dark hair flying in the wind, galloped at the head of his detachment toward the Indians. The Texans marveled at an enemy scout mounted on a white horse. The man was setting fire to the prairie while riding at full gallop— "by some means of magic," A.W. thought. The chase continued five miles. Opothleyohola's men suddenly emerged from the trees along the creek and began firing balls and arrows. The battle of Round Mountain opened.[33]

Most of the Texans were familiar with the acrid smell of gunpowder, but few had been in a firefight. This time they knew the bullets were directed at them. A Texas cavalryman described his first time under fire: "Bang went the gun, and it gave me the shivers all over for it was the first gun I heard fired in the war. . . . The roar and crack of the gun had a far different meaning than one [fired] in time of peace." Another said, "I felt very much like shooting after I was shot at."[34]

Capt. Charles S. Stewart and his Company I were leading the advance when the firing started. Spurring his famous bay, Stewart raced toward the Indian on the white horse. "Away we went," A.W. remembered, and "my heart swelled that Old Napoleon kept a close second to Captain Stewart's noted bay." Fifty yards from the creek, a volley of balls and arrows crashed into the Texans from the enemy, hidden behind the bank of the creek. Distracted by the warrior on the white horse, Stewart, an old Indian fighter who should have known better, had led his company straight into an ambush. "Left into line!" he roared. The men formed, and fired several shots before falling back. A.W. was riding side by side with Stewart when the captain yelled, "Form on me, boys!" and tumbled off his horse, dead. Two buckshot in the left of Stewart's head "threw a large wad of his brain" onto A.W.'s sleeve and coat collar. Company I wheeled and rejoined the rest of the detachment.[35]

Quayle's men tried to make a stand, but the Indians flanked them. The Texans fell back and fired again. The Indians then ran the Texans into "a place where we had no chance to dodge," Ben Vines of Company I wrote home a week later. "I continued discharging my gun as fast as I could load until I had shot eight times and I think that my old musket called several of them," Ben added. The sun disappeared below the horizon and darkness had closed in before Quayle ordered Stewart's men and the other companies to fall back to the main command. The troopers gladly turned their horses.[36]

Cooper later reported that "during the retreat a constant fire was kept up on both sides. Many of the enemy were killed, and on our part one officer and four men [were killed] and one man wounded."[37]

By the time Quayle's men fought their way back to the main column, it was exceedingly dark. The enemy attacked in force. The Confederates dismounted and held off several confused attacks on the prairie, in timber, around a house, even in a swamp. In the dark the men aimed at the flashes of enemy guns.[38]

Eerie shadows created by many small prairie fires danced through the tall grass. An Indian captain reported that the prairie "was burning very rapidly, and I may have taken the motion of the grass for men." Ben Vines "was taking good aim by the fire lights from their guns" as bullets whistled around his ears. It was impossible to tell which men wore blue-and-red strings and which had cornshucks in their hair.[39]

Suddenly, yells from the Choctaw and Chickasaw, which the Texans had learned to recognize, signaled victory. "The fight was called off, our regiment to the bugle call and the Indians to a peculiar whoop," A.W. wrote. The enemy had withdrawn.[40]

Cooper later reported: "Our men escaped mainly in consequence of being dismounted and by firing either kneeling or lying down." Gris Griscom attributed part of the Texans' success to Lt. Dudley Jones, the Ninth's young adjutant. During the worst fighting, Jones formed the regiment into a hollow square, the formation in which a body of infantry is drawn up to resist a cavalry charge.[41]

The regiment staggered back half a mile to the river, where thirsty men and animals gulped water. The horses grazed the dry grass, where it was not burned, but the men had nothing to eat. They collapsed on the ground, too tired to move. Behind the security of a strong guard, which no Texan or Indian could breach without the password *Texas,* they slept the deep sleep of exhausted young men but remained under arms—their boots on, their guns by their sides, their horses saddled.[42]

The killing had started, and the meaning of war changed for the Texans that November evening in Indian Territory. A.W. fell asleep smelling blood and brains on his sleeve. Others remained alert on the picket lines. What they felt, only a combat veteran would know.

Indian Territory would hold no fond memories for Company A's Hardy Holman, from Birdville. His horse had died on the march, he had lost his saddle and all of his gear, and he had been wounded.[43]

John Friend, of Company A, was seriously wounded. Four men in the regiment had been killed, including old Captain Stewart and a boy of sixteen. The six Texas casualties were from companies A, D, I, and C. The combined losses of Cooper's escort and the three Indian regiments were only three men killed and two wounded at the battle of Round Mountain, revealing which units did the most fighting.[44]

Cooper claimed the "enemy loss to have been about 110 killed and wounded" and that Opothleyohola's forces were "variously estimated at from 800 to 1,200 Creeks and Seminoles and 200 to 300 negroes."[45]

Long before daylight the next morning, the men shook thoughts of yesterday from their minds and prepared to move out. They were back on the battleground expecting to fight again when the sun cast its first rays over the winter landscape. Opothleyohola's camp was deserted.[46]

The Confederates found the chief's carriage, fifty yoke of oxen, a herd of sheep, over a hundred starving ponies, and twenty modern wagons branded "U.S." The wagons were loaded with what the Texans called "plunder"—provisions, equipment, household goods. One contained food, salt, sugar, and coffee. The men were famished, but the wagon of food was burned. It had been poisoned with strychnine and left for bait. The Texans collected trophies of buffalo robes, tanned bear and wolf hides, and other curiosities. They rounded up the Indian ponies and part of the stock, then burned everything else. They also took a number of prisoners, who were turned over to Cooper's Indians. Later in the morning the hungry men butchered several animals and bolted half-cooked, unsalted meat.[47]

"We gathered up the wounded and dressed their wounds and buried their dead among our own," A.W. remembered. The Rebel dead had been scalped, except Captain Stewart. "Some we found had been tortured to death with fire, others shot," Gris wrote, and added, "Our Creeks took some scalps, the first I ever saw." Another Ninth Texas cavalryman wrote his father two weeks later that "two men taken prisoner the evening previous [were] tied and beaten to death."[48]

The men of Company I searched the entire field that morning for their captain, whom they had trusted and loved "like a child loves his father." They finally found him only a hundred yards from the enemy camp.

> His body was stripped . . . and acorns were arranged in a line upon his naked body—more like the work of children at play than the acts of warfare. We wrapped him in a blanket and placed the body on a horse and conveyed it several miles from the spot where he fell and under cover of darkness we made a grave with only our hack knives.

The somber young men covered the grave with stones and burned brush over and around it to hide "all signs of a grave where we left him."[49]

The command buried the rest of the dead, as Gris reported, "on a pretty spot near the Red Fork of the Arkansas in a grove of black Jacks firing the usual salute over their graves & feeling for the first time as one does when leaving comrades slain on the field."[50]

The next morning the Ninth Texas cavalrymen mounted their tired horses and rode down Red Fork to the Arkansas with a detachment herding the captured ponies at the rear of the column. They followed the river southeast in search of their wagon trains, where meat, biscuits, and salt waited. Unrelenting cold rain drenched the hungry men as they trudged over burned prairie. Often there was no road or trail. The severely wounded were jerked and bounced along the rough trail on horse litters. Hardy Holman, slightly wounded, could ride. Several men who had broken out with measles slumped in their saddles. At night comrades made rude shelters for the sick, caring for them as tenderly as they knew how.[51]

Food and forage were difficult to find. At deserted houses the horsemen found a few hogs, cattle, and goats, which they ate without salt or bread. At a homestead they found a few potatoes and a small amount of wheat in the sheaf. Each man received a handful of wheat. They rubbed out the grain in their palms and ate it raw. The longer they chewed the more glutinous it became, but it "tasted fine for it was the only bread" they had eaten for four or five days. John Friend could not chew raw grain or tough beef half broiled over an open fire. His jaw was broken. His messmates found a cooking pot and made broth for him.[52]

The evening of the fourth day on the trail, Quayle's hungry, dirty men reached their train at Concharty, a small Creek town at a wide bend of the Arkansas. Concharty was about forty miles upstream from Fort Gibson.[53]

Quayle had sent an advance to tell Sims to have his men start cooking. "I was hungry and it [was] the want of salt that gave me the most annoyance," A.W. said. When the famished troopers reached the train, "a great heap of biscuits lay in the pan and the skillet was heaped with good brown slices of pork," but to their dismay each man was ordered to eat only one biscuit and one slice of meat, then feed his horse five ears of corn and water him at the river, three hundred yards distant. The men then could have seconds, and again feed and water the horses. After wolfing down their meat and biscuits soaked in salty grease, they hurried to feed and water the horses so they could eat again. Far into the night throngs of men led their mounts to the river and rushed back. "On the fourth biscuit I had enough, thank God," A.W. said.[54]

A.W., Gris, all the hungry men ate and slept, then ate and slept again all the next day. The following day the regiment moved down the Arkansas a few miles to the Presbyterian Tullahassee Mission, where the sick and wounded found shelter. Several more men came down with measles.[55]

John Friend, Hardy Holman, and the other sick and wounded sighed with relief when they crawled onto cots in the imposing three-story brick mission building. They were exhausted and they were in pain. Each longed for home and tender female hands. Regimental surgeon James E. Robertson did what the state of medicine made possible, but good food provided by orchards and prosperous farms surrounding the mission must have aided the men's recovery more than pills and potions.[56]

Farms near the mission supplied abundant forage for the horses as well as food for the men. The Texans, starved for anything fresh, gorged on apples from nearby orchards. But as soon as they were rested and fed, they became bored and "wished for a more active life."[57]

Cooper granted their wish. Saturday, November 30, he ordered the Ninth Texas to again join him in pursuit of Opothleyohola. The available force of the regiment marched away from the comforts of Tullahassee, leaving behind a hundred men sick with measles. This time the Texans took their supply train.[58]

The weather turned bitter cold the day they set out, riding northwest. Troopers blew on their fingers and wiggled their cold toes in colder boots. Icy air stung their faces. More men came down with measles, and soon the sick outnumbered the well. At the Creek village of Tulsey Town (Tulsa), the trains turned back to the mission, loaded with the sick; the Ninth was down to 260 horsemen. Six days after leaving Tullahassee, the Ninth joined Cooper's command of 780 men and Col. John Drew's First Cherokee Mounted Rifles of 480 men. Fortunately, the Indian regiments had their trains with them.[59]

Several nights, cold rain poured down on the men as they slept on the ground. The morning of December 8, they dried their blankets over blazing logs and fired their guns to check for moisture, stalling movement of the command until midmorning. When scouts found Opothleyohola's forces on Bird Creek at noon the next day, the column halted. Late in the day a scout came in with information that the Creek chief had two thousand warriors painted for a fight and was planning a night attack. When Drew's Cherokees heard the news they were panic-stricken. They scattered into the woods, leaving their tents standing, and in many instances even their horses and guns. A detail from the Ninth, Company A and part of Company D, was sent to the abandoned Cherokee camp to retrieve the equipment. Gris led the detail warily through darkness, expecting to be attacked at any moment, but safely reached the Cherokee camp. They struck the tents, loaded the camp gear into the abandoned wagons, and reached their own camp at 2:00 A.M. without seeing an enemy. Behind a heavy guard, they remained under arms the rest of the night.[60]

The Confederates, obviously outnumbered, marched back down Bird Creek the next morning as a feint and in search of a better defensive position. The Ninth Texas formed the rear guard, protecting the precious Cherokee wagons. A few miles down the creek, Opothleyohola's men attacked the rear of the Ninth. Galloping to the rear, Cooper ordered Sims to divide his regiment. Quayle advanced with Company A and detachments from several other companies, a hundred men in all. Heavy firing quickly exploded into their ranks. The men charged the enemy over and over, sometimes mounted, other times on foot. Gun smoke soon swirled in the cold air. Finally, the detachment formed with the rest of the command and continued fighting—"at close quarters and . . . with great fury," according to Cooper. Four hours after the first volley, the enemy disappeared into the darkness.[61]

Gris was impressed that "the gallant Colonel Cooper was ever present when the bullets flew the thickest." Fifteen years earlier, during the Mexican War, Cooper, then a captain, witnessed unusual courage. He fought in two major engagements commanded by Gen. Zachary Taylor, whose unassuming courage impressed everyone. Jefferson Davis, West Point trained and hungry for glory, led Cooper's company and the rest of the Mississippi Riflemen with ability and courage.[62]

On Bird Creek, Cooper counted his losses—fifteen killed, thirty-seven wounded. He estimated the enemy's loss at near five hundred, obviously too high. Again, Texas Companies A and D suffered, losing two killed and six wounded. A.W., whose company had no casualties, later wrote that at the battle of Bird Creek "our sufferings were not so severe for we could well care for the wounded." The Cherokee wagon train contained food and cooking utensils as well as tools and ammunition.[63]

Colonel Sims reported about late in the battle: "I ordered my men to fall back [and] mount their horses, after which we made a charge and succeeded in getting our wounded men off the field."[64]

Colonel Sims, of Red River County, and Colonel Quayle, of Tarrant County, were from North Texas, where the last Indian raids had taken place fifteen years earlier. Had they lived on the far western edge of settlement in the Lone Star State where the Comanche and Kiowa regularly raided, they would have known before their *first* battle with *any* tribesmen to get their wounded off the field.

The Ninth and the rest of the Confederate force withdrew and bivouacked for the night. Sitting around their fires that evening, the men refought their second battle. They had survived and now felt like veterans, but the thought of killing another man did not sit easy on the conscience.[65]

The weary Texans rolled in their blankets when tattoo sounded. The physical and emotional efforts of battle had exhausted them. Every muscle in their bodies ached. While they slept, the temperature plunged and snow began to fall. The snow was three inches deep by morning.[66]

A.W. would have been glad to sleep in the snow, but he was on duty. He tramped around and around all night, guarding forty Indian prisoners huddled on the smoky side of a roaring fire. The prisoners were turned over to the Rebel Indians the next morning. A.W. wondered what happened to them. He later wrote, "Whether they were executed or [turned] loose I never knew, but this I do know, we had no prisoner returned to us."[67]

The next morning Cooper ordered the Ninth to escort the wagon train loaded with sick and wounded to a homestead that was serving as a camp. The regiment set out across the snow-covered landscape while the rest of Cooper's men investigated the battlefield and buried the dead. At the homestead, the Texans found three deserters, two from Colonel Drew's regiment and one who had deserted from Young's Eleventh Texas Cavalry at Boggy Depot. Sims immediately convened a court, found the three guilty, and hanged them on the spot.[68]

While the Ninth escorted the train east, several companies scouted ahead but found none of the enemy. On Friday, December 12, the column again reached the comforts of Tullahassee Mission, where the sick and wounded found shelter.[69]

The regiment set out east the next morning down a narrow dirt road cut through dense stands of oak and hickory. Late in the afternoon the comforting aroma of wood smoke drifted through the cold air. The smoke curled from stone chimneys of substantial log homes. The Stars and Bars, floating over a two-story building of mottled brown stone, was a welcome sight. This was Fort Gibson, long famous, now the new Indian Department headquarters. To the east behind the post's stone buildings stood the dilapidated old log fort, its cottonwood palisade weathered and leaning like an ancient warrior with arthritis. The fort had been established by frontier-famous Col. Matthew Arbuckle in 1824 to protect Indian settlers from the warlike Osage. It had been abandoned for four years when Confederate troops reoccupied it two months before the Ninth Texans arrived.[70]

Sims led his regiment along a dirt street toward the two-story stone building. The dirty, bearded horsemen sat up straighter in their saddles when ladies appeared on their porches to wave white handkerchiefs. When the U.S. Army had abandoned the fort in 1857, it was ceded to the Cherokee and a town had developed around the old compound. To the Texans, most inhabitants were "mixed blooded people and were well educated, and many seemed wealthy."[71]

Sims took command at Fort Gibson, the Cherokee Nation's main supply depot as well as department headquarters. The only habitable structure at the old fort was the two-story stone structure, originally the commissary. Across the street, an incomplete two-story stone barracks lacked a roof. The original log fort, several hundred yards behind the commissary, was used as a depository for stores.[72]

Fort Gibson stood on the east bank of the Grand River a couple of miles above its confluence with the Arkansas. The river was Fort Gibson's connection to Fort Smith and the world. When Colonel Arbuckle was scouting for a fort site at the head of navigation on the Arkansas, he failed to find a good boat landing. Searching up the Grand, though, he discovered a rock shelf that made for an excellent natural one. Keelboats and steamboats, tied to iron rings anchored in the rock shelf, soon were unloading men and supplies, missionaries and visitors to the fort.[73]

The post came to be known as the graveyard of the army. During its first dozen years 6 officers and 293 men died there, most from malaria, then known as bilious fever. Low and swampy, the area was a perfect breeding ground for mosquitoes. When the U.S. Army finally understood quinine's specific qualities, which civilian doctors had known for several years, duty at Fort Gibson ceased to be a death sentence.[74]

The Ninth camped near the clear-running Grand. When the wagon trains arrived the next day, Dr. Robertson established a hospital in the garrison buildings for 250 sick and wounded. A trooper recalled:

Quite a number of Cherokees lived in or about the Fort . . . and their generosity was never surpassed by any people, especially in the care of our sick. The measles was a terror in the regiment and many were sick and the burial service was of daily occurrence.[75]

Often the Stars and Bars flew at half mast, and funeral processions made their somber way to the burial ground southeast of the fort. The men of Company A trudged to the cemetery to bury comrades three times during the last half of December. Again, Fort Gibson was living up to its reputation as a graveyard.[76]

The Texans felt they had returned to civilization after six weeks in the field. There were stores, substantial houses, women, and children. The Texans explored the old fort, listened to speeches, and watched Indian sham fights and war dances.[77]

The old stockade fascinated Gris and A.W. It was built in a square, oriented roughly north and south, with the main gate on the east. The boys inspected the remnants of the original oak palisade and wandered around inside the connecting log rooms that formed the fort's perimeter. The musty smell of old wood and longtime occupation wafted up from well-tramped dirt floors. There were no exterior windows that would allow entry of hostile Indians—or fresh air. A.W. was impressed with the "nice hewn logs" and the single "small door made thick and heavy." Gris noted that Fort Gibson had consisted at one time of two good blockhouses and plenty of quarters but had gone to ruin.[78]

Perhaps they imagined the post when humble soldiers and proud dragoons fed their mules and curried their horses, when Indians crowded around the gate to trade, when travelers filled the few empty rooms. The Texas Road from Missouri led through Kansas, then followed the Grand River south to Fort Gibson and on to Texas. A frontier historian wrote:

For many years an amazing number of emigrants, freighters and traders going to or returning from the then unknown country beyond Red River passed over this road . . . [and] noted the neatly whitewashed blockhouses and palisades of Fort Gibson.[79]

Fort Gibson was the best known fort in the Southwest. Sam Houston, artist George Catlin, and author Washington Irving had enjoyed the fort's hospitality. Famous and soon-to-be famous soldiers had served at the post or passed through on their way west: Gen. Henry Leavenworth, Col. Henry Dodge, Col. Stephen Watts Kearney, Capt. B. L. E. Bonneville. During the Civil War, decisions made by West Point–trained officers who knew Fort Gibson before 1860 would decide the fate of the Ninth Texas Cavalry. These officers included Lts. Jefferson Davis, Samuel R. Curtis, James M. McIntosh, and John Bell Hood; Capt. Earl Van Dorn; and Cols. Joseph E. Johnston and Robert E. Lee.[80]

Now the Ninth Texas would remain there until equipment, rations, and orders arrived. In addition, Cooper, realizing he needed help to deal with Opothleyohola and his warriors, had written Ben McCulloch's headquarters in Arkansas, requesting reinforcements. With little else to do but stand guard and feed the animals while they waited, the Texans loafed around camp watching Indian sham fights and war dances or slipped off to hunt squirrels and wild turkeys in the river bottom.[81]

Friday, December 20, reinforcements trotted in from Arkansas. The colonel of the Second Arkansas Mounted Rifles rode at the head of the relief column. He wore a full beard and sat his horse like a professional soldier. He had graduated from West Point twelve years earlier and recently had resigned his captain's commission in the First Cavalry to serve the Confederacy. The colonel's name was James M. McIntosh, and he was a white man, not an Indian. He was unrelated to the two Lower Creek colonels, Daniel and Chilly McIntosh, but Cooper would find all three of his Colonels McIntosh equally impossible to deal with.[82]

Riding into Fort Gibson that day, Col. James M. McIntosh must have thought of other times he had been at the old post. When he was ten, his father commanded Fort Gibson. Before the war, Colonel McIntosh had served on the frontier, including Indian Territory.[83]

McIntosh reached Fort Gibson with battalions from five Texas cavalry regiments, 1,600 men in all. Cooper, camped with his Indian regiments twenty miles north at Choska, had not been notified that McIntosh was coming. When Cooper reached Fort Gibson that Friday to make a speech, he was surprised to find James McIntosh impatiently waiting. After a short discussion between the two colonels, McIntosh announced that he was going after Opothleyohola immediately. He rode out of Fort Gibson with 1,380 men, leaving a small battalion with Cooper. The professional soldier had no intention of waiting for Cooper to gather his forces.[84]

Before returning to Choska with his escort and Maj. John W. Whitfield's Battalion, Cooper ordered the Ninth Texas and Col. John Drew's First Cherokee Mounted Rifles to join him in a few days. Most of Drew's men had returned to the regiment after deserting at Bird Creek. Col. Stand Watie commanded the other Cherokee regiment, the Second Cherokee Mounted Rifles. Both regiments impressed the Texans. One Texan recalled that Stand Watie's regiment was a

> *fine looking body of men . . . they were of Indian blood, but if they differed from any other regiment in soldierly appearance, I could not detect it, so different were they from the other Indian soldiers that I had met. Col. Drue also had a regiment of Cherokee Indians which were unlike Stanwats' [Stand Watie's] . . . they all appeared to be full-bloods.*

Drew's Regiment of 1,214 men contained no whites. A Texas officer observed that Colonel Drew's Regiment was made up of "the finest set of warriors that can be found anywhere," and predicted, "They will make their mark wherever they come in contact with the enemy."[85]

Watching the goings-on at Fort Gibson, the men in the Ninth knew their days in camp were numbered. In any army, news and gossip flash through camp like a turpentined cat, as the Texans would have said. But with the weather getting colder by the day, warm tents and loafing around camp seemed more pleasant than prospects of again chasing the old Creek across icy streams and through burned prairies.

Another cold front slipped down from the north Sunday, December 22. Sleet peppered the tents and was changing to snow when Company G rode in from Arkansas with twenty days' rations. Plump flakes fell softly and built up on the guards' hats and the horses' backs before turning to slush on the ground. It was a good evening to sit by the fire, but there were chores to do. Tomorrow the regiment would march.[86]

The Ninth rode north fourteen miles that Monday and camped with Cooper's men. Tuesday, Cooper led his regiments and the Texans seventeen miles northwest in the direction of Tulsey Town. They bivouacked in a grove of trees on a beautiful little stream. It was Christmas Eve 1861.[87]

After mounting the guard that evening, "quite a number of the soldiers, considering the holiday season, decided that we would celebrate . . . and in a noisy manner proceeded with the hilarities of the wild and wooley soldier," A.W. wrote. Sims "at once sent us orders to retire without further noise. This order was received with great protest. Not even free on Christmas." The men sent a delegation to the colonel asking to be allowed "a little recreation, as it was Christmas." Sims was "reclining before his campfire, half dressed and wrapped in a blanket, with saddle, sword and pistols within easy reach, while his famous horse stood munching only a few yards from his bed. A change was noted from the fine cultured citizen of a few months ago to the professional warrior." When the boys asked to be allowed to celebrate, Sims "arose to a sitting position on his couch" and answered:

No! Sons, No! Remember you are soldiers, and I, as your commander, have promised to keep you at all times in a manner that you shall be able to render to your country the most effective service, and while we rejoice with the season, we must make no demonstration, for we are in the front of a savage enemy and know not when he may strike at us. No! Go to your beds and sleep and husband your energies for the hard service that is yet before us.

The camp quieted down.[88]

Gris wrote in his diary that the column remained in camp Christmas Day, waiting for the Cherokee teamsters, who had again deserted. Another Texan said the column failed to march that day because Cooper and his Indians were drunk. Gris lamented that "nothing around reminds us of the day unless that we lay over and do not move." Yet, the men must have found some pleasure in sitting around their fires in a beautiful grove cut by a clear-running stream.[89]

McIntosh's Texas cavalrymen did not delay. The day after Christmas they found Opothleyohola's encampment on the heights of Chustenahlah, in the Osage Hills, twelve miles north of Tulsey Town. McIntosh formed his men for the attack, the Third Texas Cavalry in the center flanked by the Sixth Texas Cavalry and the Eleventh Texas Cavalry.

McIntosh ordered the Third to attack straight up the steep slope. Commanding the regiment, Lt. Col. Walter P. Lane, a tough old veteran of San Jacinto who never underestimated his own ability, ordered his men to dismount and tighten their saddle girths, then told them that the quicker they got among the Indians the fewer empty saddles they would have. "We went up the hill like shot out of a shovel," Lane wrote, "and in a moment were amongst them before they had time to reload their guns." McIntosh reported that "one wild yell from a thousand throats burst upon the air and the living mass hurled itself upon the foe. The charge at the commencement of the battle was splendid; none more gallant was ever made."[90]

Col. John S. Griffith, commanding the Sixth, watched the Third's charge for a few moments, then led his regiment up the mountain before receiving orders. The Indians tried to make a stand, but the Texans were on them so fast they were forced to retreat—but not before they riddled Griffith's uniform with bullet holes and shot off a tuft of his whiskers. Eight Texans were killed, thirty-two wounded.[91]

McIntosh's troopers chased the fleeing tribesmen, picking them off one by one. The affluent and civilized boys and men from East Texas had become hardened to the killing. A Texan later said, "I took the scalp of two Indians that day; that was all that I had time to fool with." Another wrote after his first fight:

> It is strange how blunted are our sensibilities amid the perils of war. Those who were the most sensitive at home are perfectly callous on occasions of this kind. Men ride over the battlefield and laugh at what would once shock them.[92]

Victor M. Rose, of the Third Texas Cavalry, an eighteen-year-old college student from Victoria County, later described the campaign from the view of a private. After pursuing the Indians "far into the inhospitable plains" to the wild and beautiful mountain brook of Chustenahlah Creek, the Texans marched slowly up to the base of the mountain. At the order to charge, "a thousand excited horses plunged madly up the steep ascent, and a thousand rifles poured such a leaden hail into the ranks of the astonished and terrified Indians that no effort was made to hold the works."[93]

John Miller, of the Sixth, wrote that after the battle

we followed the defeated Indians about fifteen miles, till they took refuge in a dense cedar-break when we abandoned the pursuit. When we returned to the battlefield, the horrors of war were glaringly pictured to our view, when we saw women and children, whose camp had been destroyed, hovering together, and freezing in the snow, while 'round them lay the bodies of children, and mothers with babies still clasped in their arms, frozen to death by the pitiless storm. Heirlooms, cherished by their Tribes for centuries, were left and lost forever, crude musical instruments, and primitive weapons of war, a Bible printed in the Creek language. The Indians were attacked in their camp, and many of their women and children were left behind.[94]

John found a silver medal struck in commemoration of the peace treaty between the Creek and the British in 1694. John approached a woman, "tall, majestic, defiant; the very embodiment of Stoic Heroism," but when he gave her the Bible and the medal, "the sternness of her face was changed to smiles of gratitude." The medal, from "the Great Father across the sea," was a treasured heirloom passed down by the woman's ancestor, an ancient chief. The woman offered John a twenty-dollar gold piece, but his "conscience could not take her gold."[95]

Rose listed the prisoners and property taken after the battle of Chustenahlah, also known as the battle of Patriot Hill:

Two hundred and fifty women and children; forty or fifty negroes; five hundred head of ponies; seventy or eighty wagons; one hundred head of beef cattle, five hundred head of sheep, ten thousand (more or less) dogs; buffalo robes, beads, belts and other trinkets too numerous and too infinitesimal to name.[96]

McIntosh took part of the property with him, including 190 sheep that he drove back to Fort Gibson.[97]

The Ninth Texas and Cooper's regiments, hurrying along behind McIntosh, reached Tulsey Town the day of the battle. That evening they cooked four days' rations and cleaned their guns in preparation for action. They planned to leave their trains at the Creek village and "start again for Old Gouge." They knew nothing of the battle.[98]

The following day they set out northwest to join McIntosh, whose "well-appointed command was too fast for mine," Cooper later complained in his report. Couriers soon met Cooper with information that McIntosh's brigade had already scattered Opothleyohola's people. Cooper was angry with McIntosh for failing to wait until the two could cooperate. The men in the Ninth were disappointed, having been "anxious to be concerned in it," but it was too late.[99]

McIntosh and his men, astride captured Indian ponies and leading their warhorses, hurried back to Fort Gibson. They left the sheep and rode on to Arkansas, where the horsemen returned to their winter quarters, scattered across the northwestern part of the state. Victor Rose wrote: "In the case of the Third regiment, the boys were glad enough to return to their comfortable quarters and resumed the social duties and pleasures that had been so unceremoniously broken up by the late call to arms."[100]

After meeting McIntosh's victorious column north of Tulsey Town, Cooper was determined to accomplish something. He led his command northwest. Baffled by the terrain and the cagey old Creek, Cooper went on hunting for scattered enemy over rough mountains. The weather was pleasant when the command rode up Bird Creek and crossed the big bend of the Arkansas, but their rations had given out. Again, men and horses alike were hungry. In a few days another winter cold front swooped in, dropping the temperature and blowing sleet from low, dark clouds. The column hurried toward the protection of a timbered creek.[101]

During the day and through the night sleet and freezing rain continued to fall. Ice half an inch thick accumulated on the soldiers' guns and the Indians' bows. Most of Cooper's tribesmen had "no more apparel than would cover one-half the naked body," and many were bareheaded. Old Pap's ice-coated peacock feather sagged down his bare back. There was no game, nothing but ice, wind, snow, sleet. Cold and hungry, the men were blind to the beauty of the country. "The fatiguing scout," Cooper noted, was made "over exceedingly rough and bleak country, half the time without provisions, the weather very cold, during which one man was frozen to death."[102]

Finding the earth covered with sleet the next morning, Cooper decided to return to his trains, and marched down the Arkansas. After four
days with nothing to eat, the soldiers butchered a few Indian ponies.
The roasting meat reeked like a sweaty horse but tasted fine—and it
filled the men's empty bellies. In a better humor the next day, they
marched through what Gris called "beautiful valleys." The column finally
reached Tulsey Town, where their trains waited with full rations of bread
and coffee.[103]

The horsemen rode into Fort Gibson three days later, on Tuesday,
January 7, 1862, two weeks and a new year after setting out. Through
the years, columns of dragoons and trains of immigrants had found food
and shelter at the fort, and the Ninth Texas troopers surely sighed with
similar relief when they rode their weary horses through town to their
camps.[104]

Several men had ridden north from Texas to join the regiment during
its time in Indian Territory. Six men joined Company A, according to
the November–December 1861 company muster roll, taken December
31, 1862. The Ninth Texas reported an aggregate of 713 officers and
men with 677 present. By the last day of the year, Colonel Sims and a
few men had been granted leaves and furloughs to go home for a few
weeks, again leaving Lieutenant Colonel Quayle in command.[105]

While Gris and the other company orderly sergeants were taking
their rolls, regimental adjutant Dud Jones saw that his paperwork was in
order. At the same time Tom Berry signed for Company A's share of
the available small equipment:

*11 axes, 3 ax handles, 6 hatchets, 1 pick, 1 pick handle, 9 spades, 4
frying pans, 5 tin pans, 5 spoons, 5 tin plates, 40 pounds Castings
[lead to mold bullets], 5 wooded buckets, 7 haver sacks, 10 tents, a
lantern and a Sibley stove.*

Four frying pans, five tin spoons, and a single lantern did not go far
toward supplying Berry's eighty or more men.[106]

Surgeon Robertson's hospital was nearly empty by the time the regi-

CHAPTER 3

THE SEAT OF WAR

January 8–February 16, 1862

The men of the Ninth spent a day getting ready to travel. They repaired their gear, greased the wagon wheels, packed their equipment. Wednesday morning, January 8, 1862, they joked and laughed as they saddled their horses and fell into column. With "great rejoicing," they marched east on an old road that followed the Arkansas River. They camped that night on the Illinois River, a clear-running tributary to the Arkansas, and on another beautiful stream the next night. A tent, a full stomach, and a cup of hot coffee improved the scenery.[1]

Sunday, Quayle and his 650 wild Texas boys crossed the Arkansas two and a half miles below Fort Smith and rode into Van Buren. It had been ten weeks since they had been in a white town.[2]

They surveyed the village as they marched along the dirt street, the farm boys and planters, merchants and lawyers sitting their horses with the assurance of veterans. Officers squared their shoulders and tried to look professional. After all, they were not a pack of ragtag recruits; they had spilled the enemy's blood. It did not matter that their foe had worn buckskins instead of blue or that he had no cannon; blood was blood.

Reuben and his friends Gus and George Creed were feeling their oats, as they would have said. For three and a half months they had been cavalrymen; they had taken part in three campaigns, fought two battles, and won. They had survived bullets and arrows, cold and hunger, had seen men shot, scalped, burned, hanged, and frozen to death. Now they were cavalrymen, the army's elite. Best of all, they had proved to themselves that they were men.

Fort Smith, Arkansas

In Van Buren, the Texans thought of little but celebrating. This was their kind of town, stocked with food and whiskey, full of Rebel sympathizers and pretty girls. The cavalrymen reveled in the return to their own kind, marking their lost Christmas with whiskey, noise, and merriment. Many got roaring drunk despite heroic efforts of their officers—at least, *some* of their officers.[3]

Colonel Quayle herded his riotous band through Van Buren to a Dr. Throuston's residence. They camped near the medical laboratory where the doctor compounded patent medicines commonly used as far away as Texas. A "wag" in the regiment suggested the men were "not drunk but effected by the medicinal powers of the nearby medical laboratory." Either way, it was a couple of days before the powers dissipated and everyone's head cleared.[4]

Colonel Quayle and Adjutant Jones attended to their official duties at Brig. Gen. Ben McCulloch's Van Buren headquarters. Jones turned in his muster rolls, which noted the regiment's strength on December 31. Quayle received permission to furlough an officer and two men from each company. The two officers learned that the regiment was assigned winter quarters on Horsehead Creek, fifty-five miles east, on the road to Clarksville and Little Rock.[5]

Quarters of other cavalry regiments raised in North Texas and East Texas were scattered along the Arkansas River valley between Fort Smith and Horsehead Creek. These were the regiments that had supplied detachments for the force Col. James McIntosh had led into Indian Territory a month earlier.

The Sixth Texas had built its quarters a couple of miles from the mouth of Big Mulberry Creek where it empties into the Arkansas, six miles below Van Buren. The Eleventh Texas was quartered a few miles up Mulberry Creek. Victor Rose's Third Texas had built its "shanties" six miles farther east in a sweet gum grove at the confluence of Frog Bayou and the Arkansas.[6]

When Quayle and Jones returned from headquarters, the Ninth marched. As the horses' hooves bit into the frozen, rutted roadbed, the men rode cautiously, concentrating on the road to prevent their animals from slipping. Reuben and several friends still felt the effects of Van Buren's "top bug juice," as they called it. They slumped in their saddles while the teetotalers smirked.[7]

In two days the regiment reached Horsehead Creek, seven miles west of Clarksville and three miles north of the Arkansas. They found stables and cribs of corn for the horses, but nothing for the riders. In the cavalry, however, horses took precedence over men. The troopers watered their animals at the creek and began setting up camp in a clearing. When they discovered they were on the Slidell Place, they named their encampment Cantonment Slidell.[8]

The next morning officers laid off the campgrounds and assigned sites by company. Each captain divided his company into groups of twelve or so men, called a mess. Each mess would build its own cabin, "as fancy as inclination suggested."[9]

The cavalrymen began cutting and hauling logs, a familiar task to most. Several messes purchased roofing boards from local residents. The mess to which A. W. Sparks and his brother John had been assigned constructed a snug cabin "six feet high to the eaves and covered with split boards on ribpoles, held in place by other poles for weighting down the roof." They gathered rocks and mixed mud for a fireplace. At the back of the cabin they built a scaffold bedstead from wall to wall the full width of the house. Saddles, feed, and other supplies were stored on the dirt floor under the bed. The two carpenters in Company A surely helped each mess in the company build a sturdy cabin, or at least offered advice.[10]

The weather was pleasant, but in a couple of weeks winter rolled in again like an uninvited guest. Cold rain turned to sleet, then snow. When not on duty, the Texans hovered near roaring fires in their well-chinked houses. A.W.'s and John's mess slept snug and warm, piled together in their common bed like a litter of huge puppies. Gris, remembering icy nights in the field, wrote that he was "much more comfortable than rolled in a blanket in the snow or even [in] a tent."[11]

John Hudgins was relieved to be in a warm cabin instead of rolled in a blanket on the cold ground because he was ill, miserably ill. He lay in the cabin built for the sick and wished for his father's prayers. Perhaps John dreamed of his mother and murmured her name, but she had been dead three years that month. John's friends did what little they knew to do. Dr. Robertson came when he could, but part of the time he, too, was sick.[12]

Measles had continued to rampage through the regiment and was treated with alcohol and a tea made of spice wood. Dysentery weakened many others. Each morning at ten o'clock sick call, Robertson dispensed three small opium pills to each dysentery patient as was commonly pre-scribed. To A.W., the doctor "appeared to be greatly surprised when the disease did not respond to his treatment."[13]

The sick took Robertson's pills and tried their own remedies. A pamphlet on soldiers' cures published later in the war declared that keep-ing the body clean prevented fevers and bowel complaints. Another treat-ment for intestinal problems was hot tea made from the bark of slippery elm, sweet gum, willow, or dogwood.[14]

Everything failed young John Hudgins. He died January 29, 1862, at age eighteen. When John's friends gathered to bury their comrade, they were far from a church or a cemetery, far from the comforts of parents and friends. The men dug a grave a short distance from camp, perhaps a spot selected for a cemetery. Chaplain T. A. Ish, of Tarrant County, said a few words and read from the Bible before the men lowered the shrouded body into a solitary soldier's grave. Death, bold as he was in the mid-1860s, was becoming too familiar.[15]

The sick men in the Third Texas on Frog Bayou were more fortu-nate. All officers and many privates had brought their black body servants with them into service. The blacks cooked and washed, took care of the horses, tended the sick. Also, Col. Elkanah Greer's wife, children, and more servants had returned with him from leave in December. Mrs.

Greer's "angelic ministrations at the bedsides of sick soldiers" earned her the lasting devotion of her husband's men. Mrs. Greer's practical home remedies and tender care surely had more effect than the doctor's narcotics.[16]

Epidemics of mumps and measles had started among the Texas regiments in the fall. A trooper had written home in December that 350 men in Greer's regiment were sick with measles. The disease continued to spread for several months. The March–April 1862 Company A, Ninth Texas, muster roll noted that during the past two months seventeen men had missed duty because of illness and two had died. The January–February roll, which failed to survive, certainly would have named others. Among those missing duty in Company A were Gus Creed and Hardy Holman. Army life had not been easy for Hardy—he had been wounded at Round Mountain and his horse had died. But Hardy was tough, and he would stay.[17]

At Cantonment Slidell, the Texans not sick with flu, measles, or dysentery found little to complain about. There were plenty of rations, and the men were comfortable in their cabins. They loafed around camp after feeding the stock and mounting the guard. Victor Rose, snug in his shanty at the Third's camp, recalled "a life of pleasure and social dissipation in the fashionable circles of Frog Bayou." A Sixth Texas cavalryman, in quarters a few miles up the Arkansas, wrote home that he was well and that "the Confederacy has fed & clothed me well up to this date."[18]

The privates in the Ninth Texas, from a less affluent part of the state than the Third Texas, did their own washing and took turns cooking, new experiences for most. Only a few cowboys who had batched and frontiersmen who had been on Indian campaigns knew anything about preparing food. Cooking was women's work, beneath male dignity except as an alternative to starvation. But they did their best with rations of cornmeal or flour, beef or pork, salt, coffee, sugar, and molasses issued by mess. The commissary department occasionally furnished fruits and vegetables when they could be obtained, but not in Arkansas in the winter. In addition, the men supplemented their rations with canned foods purchased from a stock of goods a Dutch sutler kept in a nearby shanty.[19]

During the war peddlers and sutlers appeared, seemingly by spontaneous generation, anytime and anywhere an army camped. From the backs of wagons or in temporary sheds they peddled food, pants, shirts, hats, belts, tobacco, soap, stationery, books, newspapers, candy, cards, dice, and trinkets—anything to make a profit, which, of course, was their sole motive. The Dutchman, however, pushed the profit motive too far. When the troopers tired of his "extortioning," they threatened to hang him come morning. To emphasize their feelings, they piled fifty condemned wagons around his shanty with the obvious intent of setting them afire, "causing the old fellow to leave in haste the next morning."[20]

Tormenting the sutler sparked some fun, but the idleness and routine soon became boring. The boys stirred up mischief, hunted bear and turkey along the river bottom, organized war dances, and raced their horses, a favorite pastime with cavalrymen. They tried the speed of some of the Arkansas stock, to their sorrow. A little gray horse belonging to a local "hayseed" beat one of the Ninth's best horses, likely Maj. Nathan B. Townes's famous piebald or Colonel Quayle's valuable horse.[21]

Colonel Sims returned from Texas in the middle of February. The boys greeted him with a serenade and a whooping war dance, then fired their guns by platoon, thunderclap after thunderclap, until the entire countryside was alarmed. Sims and others coming from home brought clothing and recruits, food and mail. The boisterous greeting was for coats and cakes, news and friends, as well as the colonel.[22]

During the regiment's time in Arkansas men continually rode in from Texas to join brothers, cousins, friends. The veterans, feeling their importance, replied to the recruits, eager questions with "an air of freezing indifference." But one veteran evaded answering when asked how many men he had killed.

"Did you ever kill *one?*" the recruit insisted. "Did you ever shoot one, and see the blood spout out—see it, yourself?"

"It is better," the veteran replied, "to be in doubt whether we ever killed *one,* than to have the conscience tormented with the belief that we killed them all."[23]

Men who came north to join Company A included Solon Dunn, older brother of John; Alva Knight, older brother of Sam; and J. Amos Burgoon, one of Reuben's kinsmen. Sixteen men's names appear for the first time on the March–April 1862 Company A muster roll, the next extant roll after the regiment left Fort Gibson. The other nine companies also increased by about the same number of men.[24]

The mail Sims brought was the first the men had received since leaving Texas. The soldiers savored their letters, reading them over and over. Mail was a touch of home, a thread back to those they loved—"white winged messengers," as one trooper fondly called his letters. A Louisiana private wrote his wife, "I never have any enjoyment only when I hear from some of you."[25]

The Civil War letters of David Garrett, Company E, Sixth Texas Cavalry, were saved by his family and his fiancée. David received his first letter after being away from home six weeks. He wrote his sweetheart immediately: "Mary, your kind letter was perused with much pleasure but while reading it[,] it was with some difficulty that I suppressed my feelings, & prevented a tear to fall from my eyes." By the time the men in the Ninth Texas received mail from home, they had been away four to five months.[26]

U.S. mail ceased, of course, when a state seceded. The Confederate Postal Department gradually established service, but the only mail moving between Texas and Arkansas in early 1862 was hand carried—or, more correctly, horse carried. Mail to and from Fort Worth, Birdville, Johnson Station, and Grapevine was by courier until after the war, when U.S. postal service was reestablished. Throughout the war, Texans wrote families and friends, often having to wait months to dispatch their letters until someone was going to Texas. When a man left to go on furlough or army business, he was loaded down with mail. When the traveler returned, he was equally laden.[27]

On Horsehead Creek, the men soon tired of writing unanswered letters or racing their horses, and they began to look for other entertainment. Some rode into Clarksville to have a drink and flirt with the girls. Others saddled their horses and rode west along the Arkansas valley, often as far as twenty miles, to visit friends and relatives in the other Texas regiments.[28]

Besides visiting, Company A had guests. Reuben's father, Mack Rogers, arrived from Tarrant County. He had forgiven Reuben for sneaking off in the night like a coyote from the chicken house. Reuben was his eldest son, and Mack had come to bring his blessings. Mack came from a long line of frontiersmen willing to fight for what they believed, and he believed in the South's right to secede. He owned no slaves, but his frontier heritage of independence and self-sufficiency led him to support States' Rights.[29]

Mack brought news and family gossip, plus a wagon loaded with food, clothing, and supplies. He might have come with his brother-in-law, Amos Burgoon, and other recruits from around Grapevine. Perhaps he brought a couple of his younger sons or a father or two of other men in the company. He would not have come alone.[30]

After Pa left, Reuben was enjoying Sunday's leisure in his warm cabin on February 16, when a courier from Van Buren headquarters trotted into camp. Everyone quickly learned that Brig. Gen. Sterling Price's Missouri Confederates were fleeing into northwestern Arkansas with a large and determined Union force harassing their rear. Price and his army were a few miles inside Arkansas at Elkhorn Tavern, on Telegraph Road. The old inn lay no more than seventy-five crow-flying miles north-northwest of Cantonment Slidell. The Ninth Texas was ordered to meet Brig. Gen. Ben McCulloch near the tavern at once.[31]

It was the middle of winter, and a bad winter at that. Not one of the Confederate generals who soon would be embroiled in a bloody conflict had had the least idea the bluecoats would venture a winter campaign. But the U.S. commander in southwestern Missouri, Brig. Gen. Samuel R. Curtis, refused to be intimidated by cold winds and icy roads.

Curtis, a fifty-seven-year-old Iowan, had his headquarters at the railhead of Rolla, Missouri, halfway between Saint Louis and Springfield. Curtis had set out to challenge Sterling Price's Missourians, cozy in their winter quarters around Springfield. The Union general hoped to gobble up the gray army, or at least keep the men too busy to move east and reinforce a Confederate force building to challenge Gen. Ulysses S. Grant.[32]

Samuel Curtis was a complex Victorian gentleman with the methodical precision of the engineer he was. Tall and heavily built, Curtis wore a ruff of cheek whiskers framing his narrow lips. He looked more like a sedate businessman than a capable soldier. He had graduated from West Point in 1831, then served a year in Indian Territory, but it would be fifteen years before Curtis served a few months in the Mexican War; most of the thirty years since his graduation he had practiced law and engineering. When the Civil War began Curtis was a U.S. congressman, but soon his West Point training and past active duty brought out the latent warrior in the old man.[33]

The Confederate generals in Arkansas, their two armies, and all the cavalrymen camping and tramping around Arkansas were about to find out how much of his West Point training Samuel Curtis remembered after thirty years.

One of the Confederate generals in Arkansas was Sterling Price. Known to his men as "Old Pap," Price was an impulsive, charismatic Missouri politician. His only military experience was as a regimental colonel serving in Santa Fe and on a short campaign into Mexico during the Mexican War. Price was a large man, six feet two, and heavy. He had a shock of receding gray hair but wore neither mustache nor whiskers, uncommon in the 1860s. One of his men wrote: "His figure was portly, striking and noble; the countenance exhibited marked intelligence, and wore a genial expression, while his manner was . . . courteous, dignified and impressive."[34]

Price had raised his army of Missouri militia to protect their state from Union occupation. In January 1862, the Federals held Saint Louis and eastern Missouri, but Price and his Confederates controlled western Missouri. They were lounging around their winter quarters when the Yankees appeared. Price, knowing he was outnumbered, began falling back. Curtis followed. By mid-February both armies had reached northwestern Arkansas.[35]

Price had collected massive military stores in warehouses at Springfield. When Curtis came marching down the road with 12,000 men and fifty cannon, Price hauled away everything he could find transportation to carry. According to Victor Rose, the Missourian's train was "the most multitudinous and variegated wagon train ever concentrated on the continent. Every specie of wheeled vehicle from the jolting old ox-cart to the most fantastically painted stagecoach" creaked and rumbled down the rutted road.[36]

Price started out with forty-seven guns and 8,000 men, many of them veterans of the battle of Wilson Creek. But the blue cavalry constantly harassed him over the hundred miles rough roads between Missouri and Elkhorn Tavern. By the time he reached Arkansas, he had lost one gun and his back trail was littered with broken-down wagons, pots and pans, dead and dying mules, and hundreds of sick and worn-out men.[37]

Brig. Gen. Sterling Price

Rain, snow, and bitter cold had tormented men and animals alike. One morning a Missouri State guardsman was so cold he felt he was dying. His clothes were frozen on his body, his feet so swollen he could barely stand. When ordered to fall in he said, "Oh, God, Colonel, shoot me, if you will, but don't ask me to fall in." The guardsman rode a caisson south.[38]

When Price's men dragged into Cross Hollow south of Elkhorn Tavern, everyone was exhausted and harassed, particularly Price. His temper did not improve when Brig. Gen. Ben McCulloch stomped into his tent. The two men were opposites. McCulloch was a soldier; Price was a politician. McCulloch was taciturn; Price was volatile. The Texan lived quietly and frugally; the Missourian reveled in good food and genial company.[39]

To make matters worse, Price needed McCulloch's cooperation to face the Federals, but the unclear command situation had created nearly ruinous dissension between the two powerful leaders of their states. Neither had the confidence of the War Department, essentially Jefferson Davis, because neither had been trained at West Point. Consequently, Davis would grant overall command to neither. McCulloch could issue no orders to Price, nor could Price command McCulloch; Price could only plead and rail, and railing at Ben McCulloch was not a good idea. Yet, the two were forced to cooperate.[40]

Ben McCulloch was a famous and ferocious frontiersman and Texas Ranger, an authentic Texas hero before 1861. As a young man he had followed his friend Davy Crockett to Texas and fought side by side with

Sam Houston in the Texas war for independence. Later, McCulloch won fame as a Ranger on the Texas frontier and in Mexico during that war. Pragmatic old Ben had spent much of his life in the saddle with a pistol in each hand, a shotgun in his saddle scabbard, and a Bowie knife in his belt. He was an outstanding Indian fighter and a dead shot. His courage has been described as a complete absence of fear. Fighting Indians and renegades along the Texas frontier had taught the Ranger to strike like a bullet, suddenly with no warning, and then to ask questions. Merely to state that Ben McCulloch was tough is an insult both to him and to the English language.[41]

Brig. Gen. Ben McCulloch

McCulloch, in his mid-twenties when he entered Texas, was fifty when the Civil War began. Early in the war he was placed in charge of troops in Texas. A few months later he was commissioned a brigadier general and assigned command in Arkansas. He and Price had barely managed to cooperate long enough to win the battle of Wilson Creek. Now, Price was begging McCulloch to help him again.[42]

Sterling Price and Ben McCulloch, different as they were, had two things in common: The Southern cause held both their hearts; and both held the hearts of their men. Soldiers love generals who look after them and respect them. And most of all, they love the ones who lead them to victory, which Ben and Old Pap had done at Wilson Creek.

War departments also favor generals who win, but in Richmond, Price's and McCulloch's bickering had become a scandal. President Davis, concentrating on the Union army across the Potomac, finally glared west and decided to end the bickering by appointing a major general to command in Arkansas. Davis mulled over his cadre of West Point favorites and asked Henry Heth and then Braxton Bragg to go to Arkansas. Both turned him down. Davis then chose Maj. Gen. Earl "Buck" Van Dorn, West Point 1842, a flamboyant, egotistical professional with a glittering prewar reputation. Van Dorn was a soldier from the tips of his polished

CHAPTER 4

A WEST POINT GENERAL

February 17–April 16, 1862

Maj. Gen. Earl Van Dorn reached Little Rock January 28, 1862, two weeks after his appointment as commander of the Trans-Mississippi District. He charmed the capital elite for a week, then sped off to the far northeastern corner of the state to plan his spring campaign against Union-held eastern Missouri. With heart and mind focused on the glory of taking Saint Louis, Van Dorn gave little thought to what was happening in northwestern Arkansas.[1]

A week after the Texans on Horsehead Creek learned that Sterling Price had fallen back to Arkansas, an express rider galloped into Van Dorn's headquarters with the news. Van Dorn reported to the War Department in Richmond: "For reasons which seemed to me imperative I resolved to go in person and take command of the combined forces of Price and McCulloch."[2]

Impetuous as always, Van Dorn boarded a steamer the next day. He took only his manservant and a native guide. That evening the steamer tied up at Jacksonport, on the White River, where Van Dorn's adjutant, Col. Dabney H. Maury, caught up with him. The party spent a day preparing to ride horseback across northern Arkansas. Van Dorn mounted his black thoroughbred mare the next morning and headed out. He set a fast pace. The four men rode long hours in biting cold but slept in feather beds at convenient farmhouses when night came.[3]

Maj. Gen. Earl Van Dorn

When the party reached a particularly swift stream, they improvised a raft. The unstable craft tipped during the crossing, dumping Van Dorn into the icy water. He laughingly swam ashore and only partially dried his clothes before remounting. That night Van Dorn developed a cold and fever. Unwilling as he was to admit it, at forty-one he was past the age of quick recovery. When he rode into Van Buren a week after learning of Price's retreat, he was feverish and miserable.[4]

On Horsehead Creek, the Ninth Texas cavalrymen knew nothing of Earl Van Dorn or Samuel Curtis. The regiment was ordered to march north and that was that. The men scurried around the rest of the Lord's Day getting ready for their first blind date with the Yanks. The men checked their equipment and packed a few wagons. They would travel light.

Monday, February 17, the available force of six hundred started for the Boston Mountains, which rose between them and Elkhorn Tavern. Col. William Sims and Lt. Col. William Quayle rode with the regiment. Maj. Nathan B. Townes remained at winter quarters in command of enough men to mount the guard and tend the sick.[5]

Reuben surely was among the six hundred. He was present for duty on every extant company muster roll, and he rode a good horse, judging from the listed values of horses in his company. Nevertheless, no record exists of the men who rode north from Horsehead Creek that Monday morning.[6]

The Ninth bivouacked between Mulberry and White Oak Creeks the first night out. A layer of ice covered the ground the next morning.

The men brushed snow from their clothes and turned up their collars. Freezing rain continued all day until ice coated everything—the mens' beards, their clothes, the saddles, the covers of the few wagons they had brought along to haul ammunition and supplies. Men and animals struggled over steep, tortuous mountain roads. A veteran later wrote:

On either side of the road, the precipitous mountains rose hundreds of feet overhead, while giant icicles hung . . . from the overhanging rocks like huge stalactites, and glistening in the bright rays of the cold winter sun [they] looked like suspended spears of giants.[7]

The Ninth bivouacked that night on the West Fork of the White River near Fayetteville, a pleasant village of two thousand and the major forward supply depot for the Confederates in Arkansas. When a howling winter storm rolled in during the night, Gris, shivering in what he considered northern cold, thought of "the peaceful semi-domestic scenes" back on Horsehead Creek.[8]

Other Texas cavalrymen also left their warm cabins and hurried north. Newton Keen's and David Garrett's Sixth Texas, in quarters on Mulberry Creek, received orders to march the day the Ninth moved out. Newt was an orphan who had lived with his grandparents a few miles north of Dallas. He had eagerly ridden off to join the Sixth when it formed. Newt's and David's colonel, B. Warren Stone, described their trip in his report:

In six hours my men were in the saddle, train en route, ammunition distributed, and the march begun. I made 20 miles that day and encamped on the north side of Boston Mountains. At daylight the following morning the troops were on the move. Receiving orders during the day urging me forward, I hastened, fed my stock by the roadside, and made a march of 54 miles to Cross Hollow, where we arrived at 10 p.m., through continuous rain and sleet and Egyptian darkness.[9]

Cross Hollow, site of a large cantonment, lay sixteen miles north of Fayetteville on Telegraph Road. The telegraph line from Missouri ended three miles inside Arkansas at Elkhorn Tavern, a two-story, weather-boarded, log building painted white, and surrounded by a large

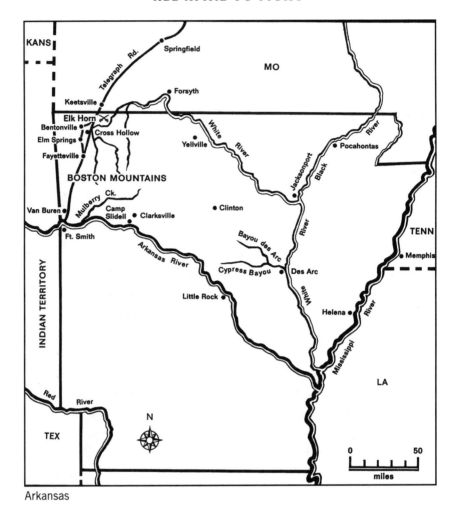

Arkansas

clearing; however, the road continued on south as a narrow, rutted trail cut through dense woods. It crossed Little Sugar Creek, three miles away, then wound its way to Cross Hollow and passed through Fayetteville. From Fayetteville it continued south, climbed the Boston Mountain, then plunged down to Van Buren, on the Arkansas. Although the telegraph line barely reached into the state, the road all the way to Van Buren was known as Telegraph Road—or occasionally, the Wire Road.[10]

Little Sugar Creek cuts through the Ozark Plateau from east to west. The ground rises to the north and forms a broad plateau named Pea Ridge because wild peas grew on its slopes. Atop Pea Ridge and west of Elkhorn Tavern, a sandstone escarpment, Big Mountain, rises several hundred feet. Dense timber alternated with small prairies. High ridges and deep gorges made travel difficult, but a few primitive roads cut through the trees connected homesteads scattered across the rough countryside.

When Newton and David rode their tired horses into Cross Hollow with the Sixth Texas at ten Tuesday night, hundreds of fires reflected on the snow-covered ground. Ben McCulloch's Texas and Arkansas infantry and Sterling Price's Missourians, exhausted by forced marches, hovered near their campfires.[11]

The two testy generals met at Price's headquarters tent to discuss how their combined forces could drive the Yankees back beyond Springfield. The Texan pointed out that Cross Hollow was a poor place to make a stand. The Missourian disagreed. Ben wanted to move farther south to better defensive ground. Old Pap wanted to fight here and now. McCulloch suggested that a move south to Boston Mountains would stretch the Federals' two-hundred-mile supply line, perhaps to the breaking point. Price thought differently. The long-standing difficulties between the two flared, and, it was said, McCulloch cursed Price. Three-fourths of the senior officers supported McCulloch, but the council of war broke up without a decision. Late in the night, when a civilian brought news of threatening Federal movements, Price grudgingly gave in.[12]

The two armies set out the next morning, slogging along Telegraph Road. Thousands of shoes and hooves soon pounded the ice-coated road into a mire. Behind the columns of men and wagons rose thick, curling volumes of smoke and a lurid glare of flames. Stone's Sixth Texas, having survived the "Egyptian darkness," had been left to burn the log buildings and follow as rear guard. Late in the afternoon both armies halted near Fayetteville to bivouac near the Ninth's encampment.[13]

Night came early under a leaden sky. As the temperature dropped, Price's and McCulloch's men built fires and cooked supper. Infantrymen and cavalrymen alike slept rolled in their blankets on the damp ground. The tents had been left at winter quarters.[14]

In Fayetteville the next day the Confederates salvaged what they could of the food and ammunition stored in the town before torching the large wooden storehouses and heaps of flour and bacon. Several city blocks burned to the ground. The armies marched south from the town toward the Boston Mountains, as McCulloch had insisted. The Missourians' long retreat from Springfield finally halted at Strickler's Station, a stage stop for Butterfield Overland Mail coaches. The cavalry regiments followed the infantry, scouting and occasionally skirmishing with a few Yankees.[15]

During the next few days the Ninth learned of skirmishes and heard about casualties, and they knew a battle was brewing. They waited. One evening the troopers cooked five days' rations of bread on sticks. The next morning they moved out but were ordered back before making contact with the enemy. Another day they received orders to be ready to move at the sound of the bugle. The men impatiently waited all day. No orders came.[16]

McCulloch took advantage of the lull to reorganize some of his forces. Brig. Gen. James M. McIntosh, who had been promoted after leading the Texas cavalrymen after Opothleyohola in December, was placed in command of a cavalry brigade made up of five regiments—the Ninth Texas, Elkanah Greer's Third Texas, B. Warren Stone's Sixth Texas, William C. Young's Eleventh Texas, and the First Arkansas Mounted Rifles, 3,747 men in all.[17]

Another cavalry unit, Whitfield's Battalion, Col. John W. Whitfield, commanding, had been dismounted to serve as infantry. Four of the Texas units—the Third, the Sixth, the Ninth, and Whitfield's Battalion—came together for the first time in northwestern Arkansas. The regiments had been formed and mustered into Confederate service near the same time. Most of the men were from North Texas or East Texas, and many were kinsmen or knew one another. During the next year they came to look upon the four regiments as a single unit. They were brigaded with various regiments at different times and their officers changed, but the men rode, marched, and fought side by side for the next three years and three months.[18]

Victor Rose served with the Third. Newton Keen, David Garrett, and Maj. Lawrence Sullivan "Sul" Ross served with the Sixth. Reuben Rogers, Gus and George Creed, A. W. Sparks, and Gris Griscom served in the Ninth. H. McBride Pridgen was a private in Whitfield's Battalion.[19]

The troopers immediately learned to depend on one another—and on Maj. Sul Ross of the Sixth Texas. McCulloch dispatched Ross on a raid behind Federal lines to reconnoiter, destroy stores, and do what he could to disrupt Curtis's supply line. Ross's detachment of 557 men contained ten companies, including three from his Sixth Texas and two from the Third. From the Ninth Texas, Ross took Capt. James English's Company I and Capt. Thomas Berry's Company A. Again, no record of the men who went on the raid survives.[20]

McCulloch chose Ross to lead the raid because the twenty-three-year-old had successfully led two raids behind Federal lines for McCulloch in the fall. The Texas general also knew Ross's reputation as a daring captain of Texas Rangers. When the Civil War began, the Texas Rangers were the best armed and most effective mounted force in the United States. Their endurance and physical courage were legendary. Like their Tennessee militia ancestors, the Ranger force evolved on a bloody and hazardous frontier from harsh necessity.[21]

Sul Ross grew up on that dangerous frontier. His tall, handsome father, Shapley Ross, was a tough and respected Indian agent and Texas Ranger. Shapley passed on to his sons his rare courage, upright honesty, and dedication to what he viewed as right.[22]

Sul learned to control his fear early in life. When he was six a band of Comanches came to the Ross home. While some of the Indians held the family hostage, Sul led others to the garden so they could help themselves to corn and melons. The warriors taunted the child, pinching his bare legs and whipping him with arrows. Shapley had told his children never to show fear around Indians because the tribesmen respected courage and were less likely to kill those they respected. Sul refused to flinch when the Comanches tormented him. The child returned to the house with blood running down his legs but a composed face. The Comanches took their loot and rode off.[23]

Maj. Sul Ross was a tall, slender young man with a modest manner and solemn blue eyes. He rode a good horse and carried a double-barreled shotgun in a saddle scabbard, a knife and a holstered six-shooter on his belt. His pistol could have been a Colt Navy or perhaps a .44-caliber Colt Army Model 1860, the handgun most often used during the war and the overwhelming choice of Southern officers and cavalrymen.

The Colt 1860 was the most effective military pistol of the time, and Sul knew how to use it.[24]

Ross led his column north from Strickler's Station on February 23. The hard riding Texans headed toward Missouri. They passed east of the enemy, who invariably called them Texas Rangers, then swung onto the Telegraph Road. They galloped into Missouri and on toward Keetsville, a small town seventy miles in Curtis's rear.[25]

If Reuben rode through the stark winter landscape with the raiders, he no doubt thought of his old home, a few more miles northeast near Springfield. Telegraph Road was familiar ground to him. It was the road the Rogers family had traveled from Reuben's birthplace to frontier Texas. For Reuben, Missouri seemed more like home than the log house in Tarrant County with its new bois d'arc fence and unbroken black prairie. Reuben had been nearly grown, eighteen, when he parted with his cousins and friends, and with Grandpa. Reuben wanted to tell Grandpa about fighting the Creeks in Indian Territory, and he wanted to hear the old man's stories of fighting the same tribesmen during the old man's war. Perhaps Reuben longed to visit the little Watts family graveyard, where his mother lay buried beneath the trees.[26]

Newton Keen was not thinking of home when he entered Missouri. He had joined the cavalry for adventure, and this was his first chance "to see the pictures of inside war scenes." Newt left an account of the Keetsville raid. It was a four-hundred-mile round-trip, and the troopers rode day and night. Tuesday, February 25, Ross's men halted for twenty minutes just south of Keetsville, then formed in column of fours and marched toward the village. After sunset, Major Ross, Newton Keen, Will Beeming, and another man rode side by side at the head of the column.

"Halt, who goes there?" a Yank called out.

"Friend," the Texans answered.

"Advance, friend and give the password."

Beeming rode to "within ten feet of the sentinel and shot him down." At the "crack of the gun" the Texans spurred their horses to a full gallop.[27]

They stormed into Keetsville. When they reached five sutlers' wagons parked for the night, they drove off the guards and burned the wagons. Newt described the scene:

There were some three hundred Yankees in the town and near so many of us, but we so utterly surprised them that they ran in every direction. . . . I charged up and down the street and fired my gun and whooped and yelled hardly having sense enough to know what I was doing, but it sure was war.

Newt said he had no more sense than to have "run right into one hundred [Yankees] as quick as one."[28]

The Federals took shelter in houses and formed behind fences. Ross dismounted his men and, as he would write home a few days later, "after a hard contested fight . . . drove them from house to house, until they finally broke in wild disorder" and "made good their escape leaving behind them 25 dead, and all their property and effects." The fight had lasted only a few minutes. The Texans captured sixty cavalry horses, many mules, and eleven prisoners without losing a man.[29]

After about an hour the column galloped out into the darkness, herding their astonished prisoners mounted bareback on captured horses. Fighting Indians had taught Ross how to escape pursuit. The command rode all night and had breakfast thirty miles from the field of battle the next morning. Newt felt sorry for the prisoners because "their old Yankee horses" seemed "to trot about straight up and down, and it is rather wearisome to maneuver thus all night on the bare back of a horse." After breakfast the Texans "fixed up some pads for them."[30]

Ross and his men then swung east around the Union army. The terrain was rugged, the riding hard. To avoid enemy cavalry sent in pursuit, the column was forced "to take to the mountains on White River, and run the gauntlet all the way back, traveling day and night for 36 hours without eating anything but turnips," according to Ross.[31]

The men were so exhausted the major had to "ride along and appeal to them nearly all the time, to hold on a little longer and we would be inside our line, and cheer them up by telling them we would meet scouts or pickets of ours very soon." Two men who lagged behind were captured. When the column finally reached its own lines, the men "fell by the roadside worn down with fatigue and loss of sleep."[32]

Ross was unaware that Col. Grenville Dodge, commanding a Federal force east of Telegraph Road, had learned of the raiders' presence as they hurried south near Dodge's position. Not knowing what the horsemen were up to, Dodge withdrew west and joined other Federals at Cross Hollows.[33]

Later in the war, after Confederate commanders learned how to effectively use mounted forces, McCulloch would have sent most, if not all, of McIntosh's horsemen north to cut Curtis's supply lines. Had the Federals' source of food, fodder, and ammunition been severed, they would have had to retreat. The old engineer knew this, and he worried about it. But the war was new in February 1862, the command situation in Arkansas was a miserable mess, and no one had enough experience to comprehend the possibilities. Obviously, Ross's presence accidentally spooked Colonel Dodge.

It was Saturday, March 1, when Ross and his "wearied, conquering heroes," as his colonel called them, reached their camps near the other troops at Strickler's Station. Newt still sympathized with the Yankee prisoners. He felt that "by the time they made the two hundred mile trip they felt[,] about the middle between head and foot[,] most miserable."[34]

McCulloch praised Ross for "his dashing gallantry and skillful conduct throughout the affair." Colonel Stone lauded the young Texan, stating he could not

> too highly estimate the chivalry and gallantry of this intrepid, daring knight, nor too highly appreciate the prudence and administrative ability of this officer, who, although but a boy, has won imperishable honors as an officer in the border warfare of Texas on repeated occasions, meeting, as he has now done, the full appreciation and admiration of our executive [Governor Sam Houston], and securing his fullest confidence. It is with pride that I thus bear testimony to the distinguished merits of my brave major, L.S. Ross.[35]

It wouldn't be the last time Ross would distinguish himself.

Near the time Companies A and I rejoined the Ninth after their dash north, Major Townes and a detachment of about seventy-five men—furloughed men and others who had recovered from measles or dysentery—from winter quarters joined the regiment. They brought recruits, clothing, letters, and packages from home. Men continued to trickle in from Texas. Shortly after the seventy-five arrived from

Horsehead Creek, another group of recruits and furloughed men reported, bringing "clothing &c from home." The "&c" included a fine pound cake for Gris, which he shared with his entire company.[36]

The day Gris shared his cake, Sims received orders officially classifying his regiment the Ninth Texas Cavalry. Counting the near six hundred who had marched from winter quarters ten days earlier, the regiment's strength was close to seven hundred. Company A's aggregate was very near a hundred.[37]

The recruits arrived just as another cold front slid down from the north. It rained, then snowed and turned painfully cold. Winter was in no hurry to give up its grip on northwestern Arkansas. Men sat for hours in the cold while others picketed and patrolled. Horses stamped their feet and blew steam from their nostrils. When night came, the cavalrymen built fires and huddled behind logs with their saddle blankets for cover.[38]

Major General Van Dorn and his escort rode into the Confederate camp at Strickler's Station Monday, March 3. A forty-gun salute, the proper number for a major general, echoed through the snow-covered mountains. The handsome, flamboyant major general reined his splendid black mare to a stop in front of McCulloch's spartan headquarters. Resplendent in a gold-embroidered blue coat and dark blue pants tucked into his blackened cavalry boots, Van Dorn shook hands with his old friend, Ben McCulloch. The Texan wore his usual civilian clothes—he fought in three wars without ever wearing a uniform. Van Dorn wore all the flash and glitter allowed, which included four Hungarian loops of gold braid extending from the elbow to the cuff of his tunic, a wreath containing three gold-embroidered stars on each side of his collar, and two one-inch gold strips decorating the outer seam of his pants.[39]

"Soldiers: Behold your leader! He comes to show you the way to glory and immortal renown," Van Dorn began an address to the assembled crowd. Many cheered, but the Texans reserved their applause. It was Old Ben they trusted to show them the way. The dashing dandy from Mississippi, despite his reputation as a fighter, would have to prove himself.[40]

Gris, Reuben, Gus, and George had not been in Texas long enough to know Van Dorn's reputation as a soldier, but Newton and David undoubtedly knew. Ben McCulloch and other Texas officers not only knew Buck Van Dorn but had served with him. Elkanah Greer had fought with the Mississippi Rifles at Monterrey, Mexico, where then-Lieutenant Van Dorn served on the staff. McCulloch and his Texas Rangers had led Gen. William J. Worth's column in the attack on Monterrey. Van Dorn had watched from a distance when Ben and his fearsome band slashed their way through the Mexican Lancers. McCulloch might not have noticed the young lieutenant, but Buck could not have missed the Texas Ranger at Monterrey. In early 1861, Van Dorn, in command of the Confederate military in Texas, and McCulloch, in charge of the Texas military, worked together from their separate headquarters in San Antonio.[41]

Sul Ross also knew Van Dorn. When Major Van Dorn was stationed in Texas with the Second Cavalry in 1858, he added to his Mexican War fame with a successful campaign against the troublesome Comanche known as the battle of the Washita. Sul Ross, home on vacation from college and then a captain in the Texas Rangers, commanded 135 friendly Indians on the expedition from North Texas into what is now southwestern Oklahoma. Three days after Sul's twentieth birthday the soldiers found the Comanche village and attacked. The troopers killed most of the warriors, scattered the women and children, and burned the camp. An officer was killed, and several troopers were wounded. Both Van Dorn and Ross were shot. An arrow pierced Van Dorn's left wrist and lodged deep in his arm near the elbow. Another arrow entered his abdomen near the navel and exited on his right side. A Comanche arrow struck Sul Ross in the shoulder. He slumped in the saddle. Before he could reach for the arrow, a .58-caliber Springfield ball slammed him in the chest, blew its way through his body, and came out between his shoulder blades. Neither man could be moved for five days. They lay in the open, protected by a single post oak. Finally, the cavalrymen loaded the officers on mule litters and took them south to a base camp. From there, a rider dashed to the nearest fort for help. Van Dorn and Ross were praised and acclaimed—Van Dorn across the nation and Ross across Texas—for their "Glorious Victory Over the Comanches." Five weeks later, Van Dorn was back on duty. Ross recovered in a few weeks and returned to college in Alabama; he graduated in the spring.[42]

At Strickler's Station, Van Dorn stood near the fire with hunched shoulders. His old wounds ached and he was sick. But Buck never let anything get in the way of his quest for glory. The Yankees were close by, and if he dawdled Curtis might slip away. Van Dorn asked a few questions and ordered the army to move come sunup.[43]

Tuesday morning, March 4, Price's and McCulloch's infantry set out with three days' cooked rations, one blanket each, and a small wagon train. In the lead, the cavalry "took up the line of march in the hardest kind of a snow storm and moved northward about 12 miles." Gris's captain reported that their company's forty-eight mounted men made a forced march all day. Behind the horsemen, infantrymen fought their way step by step into the howling storm. That evening the army reached Fayetteville, where it had been a couple of weeks earlier. Sims's men made camp four miles north of town. The weather turned viciously cold.[44]

The commanding general and his staff had started that morning with Price's column. Van Dorn ducked his head as he rode into the blizzard, but he was so ill he could barely sit his horse. After an hour he could ride no longer. He crawled into an ambulance and covered himself with blankets. When night came, he found a warm house in Fayetteville while his men spent the night on the field with no shelter, where "anything like sleep was out of the question," a soldier said.[45]

Reveille blasted through the frosty air long before daylight. Men rose stiffly. Tramping around in four inches of wet snow, they fed their horses and boiled coffee. At first light, McIntosh's cavalrymen mounted and rode north through Fayetteville ahead of the infantry. A shroud of snow-flakes covered charred buildings in the once-pretty town.[46]

From Fayetteville, McIntosh led his horsemen north on the Benton-ville Road, which ran nearly parallel to the Telegraph Road, west of it by six to eight miles. The infantry, tired and footsore from yesterday's march and a sleepless night, fell far behind. A small wagon train of ammunition and a few supplies, sufficient in Van Dorn's estimation, brought up the rear.[47]

The Ninth Texas cavalrymen saw only what was in their immediate front. They passed some scorched mills their forces had burned on the retreat ten days earlier. In the afternoon the clouds broke and welcome rays of sunshine warmed the men's backs and spirits. The cavalrymen remained in their saddles all day and made camp that evening with the army at Elm Springs, midway between Fayetteville and Bentonville.[48]

Haggard infantrymen staggered into camp. They had marched twelve punishing miles with rifles, blankets, and haversacks slung over their shoulders. Ominous clouds once again hung overhead. Under the darkening sky, infantrymen built fires and boiled cornmeal in water, hardly sufficient food for the weather and the wear, but all the commissary department had managed to supply. Snow began to fall and continued all night. When exhaustion overcame cold, the soldiers slept by fits and starts. Miserable as they were, the infantrymen were warmer than many cavalrymen. When camped together, the infantry guarded camp during the day, the cavalry at night. A couple of miles beyond the circle of fires, Sims's men watched and listened for Yankees while snow stacked up on their hats and shoulders.[49]

The Ninth guarded camp only a few hours before the army lurched to its feet. Victor's Third Texas trotted north at 3:00 A.M., leading the Ninth and all the cavalry toward Bentonville, another dozen miles north. Scouts had reported several thousand Yankees, commanded by Brig. Gen. Franz Sigel, in and around the town. Infantrymen stumbled along behind, dazed from cold, hunger, and exhaustion. Van Dorn later complained in his report that he "endeavored to reach Bentonville by rapid march, but the troops moved so very slowly." He had slept warm, eaten a hot breakfast, and was riding.[50]

McIntosh halted the cavalry on a highland prairie two and a half miles from Bentonville. Waiting for the infantry to come up, he and Van Dorn conferred. The Texas troopers had a clear view of the town, where smoke was rising from several buildings. The Federals had set fire to a portion of the town and were destroying their supplies. A.W. watched Sigel's infantry march through town and out onto the Camp Stephens Road, leading east. Camp Stephens Road intersected Telegraph Road where it crossed Little Sugar Creek.[51]

A.W. saw "the forces of Gen. Sigel with uniforms and glittering arms as they moved from Bentonville." The Confederates had no uniforms. Moreover, they carried an assortment of arms, whatever they could obtain. A.W. continued watching, "and while thinking of their grandeur," the Texans received orders: "Forward! Quick time, march!"[52]

Van Dorn had ordered McIntosh to swing the Texas cavalry around the town, then dash east until he was ahead of Sigel. McIntosh then would get back on the Camp Stephens Road in front of the enemy column and be waiting in ambush when the Yankees appeared. McIntosh was sure his horsemen could move fast enough to get in front of Sigel's foot soldiers, but no one had reconnoitered the route. Other Rebel forces moved east across a prairie to intercept the enemy.[53]

The Texans trotted out of town. When they turned north they came to the edge of the prairie and entered a dense oak and hickory forest. Three thousand cavalrymen formed in column of fours and funneled onto a narrow road that fell off into the breaks of Little Sugar Creek. Colonel Greer, whose Third Texas was in the lead, later reported, "Owing to the broken, rocky and mountainous character of the country north of town, and the absence of a road leading to the Camp Stephens Road," the rapid move to cut off Sigel slowed to a crawl. On their right was a mountain the entire length of the brigade, and Camp Stephens Road was on the other side. The cavalry was hemmed in.[54]

The horses slowed to a walk in the rough, rocky gorge. Both men and animals were worn out. They had been on the move almost constantly for more than forty-eight hours, without decent food and with practically no rest. The men's hands and feet were numb from cold. The horses were in no better condition. Some of the men were walking, leading their horses "to get warm by exercise" when enemy cavalry suddenly appeared at a crossroads sixty yards in their front. "Bang! Bang! went the guns." Two men at the head of the column tumbled off their horses, killed instantly. "Forward! Front into line! Charge!" rang down the line. McIntosh had led his men into an ambush. The impetuous general drew his sword and yelled at his bugler to sound the charge. "A deafening roar of artillery, and rattling of musketry greeted the charging column, and minnie balls, grape and canister chorused through the air."[55]

In the van, the Third Texas fell into disorder. Horses reared and snorted. One man was thrown. Another's horse became unmanageable and ran straight toward the Yankees. Farther back in the column, the Ninth fired at anything blue. "Amid a shower of balls," McIntosh "grasped the flag, and waving it over his head, implored the men to rally for another charge." Greer reported that "the enemy proved to be in strong force in the hollow . . . 4,000 or 5,000 strong, composed of infantry, cavalry and artillery." Actually, there were about six hundred.

After two attempts to charge, the Texans were forced to retire to the right on the mountain.[56]

They stopped on the steep slope to catch their breath. The horses' sides heaved as they sucked in air. Stephen M. Hale, a brave old frontiersman from Greenville, Texas, and captain of Company D, Third Texas, "stood up in his stirrups, tears trickling down his snow-white beard," and roared, "This here regiment are disgraced forever! I'd a ruther died thar than to a give arry a inch!"[57]

The colonels and captains sorted out their scrambled forces. They found horses for the dismounted and tended the wounded. The man whose horse had run away with him and another who had been bucked off came in riding double. Considering the ambush, it seemed a miracle to Greer that his losses were so low. The Third lost ten killed and twenty wounded. The Ninth, farther back in the column, suffered only one man wounded and three or four horses killed.[58]

McIntosh gave up his sweep to reach Camp Stephens Road and ordered the brigade to fall back to Bentonville. The cavalrymen urged their tired mounts back up the rocky road to the prairie. Off to the southeast, artillery rumbled. Other Rebel forces had made contact with Sigel. From Bentonville the cavalrymen turned onto Camp Stephens Road and rode east to join McCulloch's division. They reached Camp Stephens, on Little Sugar Creek, late in the day and bivouacked with the army.[59]

Newton Keen, riding toward Camp Stephens that evening with the Sixth, saw a wounded Yankee,

> *close by the side of the road. He lay with his head up against a tree, and was suffering much. He was a young, smooth-faced boy about 18, and real good looking, and I thought he might have a mother and brothers and sisters[,] but then I thought all these amount to nothing in war. The friendliest and most faithful watchers he had in his last hours were the little twinkly stars above him. The unseen Eternal God may have had a covey of unseen angels keeping watch, and when his spirit was freed from mortal clay it went sweeping[,] in company with angels[,] up to the Throne of God to live and sing far above the roar and clash of war and death.*
>
> *That youthful boy as he lay beside the tree in his lonesomeness*

made an indelible picture on my mind which has never been erased. Just a little further on lay a blue coat cold in death[,] torn and rent by a cannon shot[,] and close by lay two horses mangled in death by grape shot. The sun was sinking low in the west and a great battle was expected next day and many a soldier boy expected his last night's sleep but for some cause I seemed very much unconcerned.

Newt was two weeks past his seventeenth birthday.[60]

Greer reached Camp Stephens, seven miles from Bentonville, late in the evening, his men and horses exhausted from exposure and cold. Again, snow began to fall, and there was nothing to eat for man or beast.[61]

Other Texas cavalrymen, riding toward camp that evening, passed their old comrades in arms from Indian Territory. Van Dorn had ordered Brig. Gen. Albert Pike, the fat, old, eccentric lawyer commanding in Indian Territory, to hurry to northwestern Arkansas with his Indian regiments. Pike had grumbled and complained—the Indians "refused to march until they were paid" and, "as by their treaties, could not be taken out of the Indian country without their consent." And Pike, by his own admission, was "entirely too corpulent to ride long on horseback." In addition, the old lawyer chafed at being under Van Dorn's command. The two had violently disagreed in the past and mutually detested each other.[62]

Pike and his nine hundred Indians, John Drew's and Stand Watie's Cherokees, camped west of the main army. Victor described the tribesmen as "all painted, in conformity to the horrid custom of their people." Victor was among the Third Texas cavalrymen who had dashed into Indian Territory with McIntosh back in December. A Missourian who had never seen the Cherokee regiments remembered his first sight of the tribesmen:

They came trotting gaily into camp yelling forth a wild war whoop that startled the army out of all its propriety. Their faces were painted for they were "on the warpath." Their long black hair qued in clubs hung down their backs, buckskin shirts, leggins, and moccasins adorned with little bells and rattles, together with bright colored turkey feathers fastened on their heads. . . . Armed only with tomahawks and war clubs [they]

*presented an appearance somewhat savage, but they were mostly Chero-
kees, cool and cautious in danger, active and sinewy in person, fine
specimens of "the noble red man."*[63]

The Confederate army—Price, Pike, and McCulloch—gathered
along the south side of Little Sugar Creek near Camp Stephens that
night. It was Thursday, March 6. Price's army consisted of 6,818 men
and eight batteries of light artillery. McCulloch commanded 4,637 infantrymen, 3,747 cavalrymen, and four batteries, a total of 8,700 men and
eighteen guns. Van Dorn later reported the whole force under his command at about 16,000 men. During the entire war, no other Confederate
commander entered battle with such superior numbers.[64]

Three miles to the east, on the north side of Little Sugar Creek, Curtis's
blue-clad soldiers watched the Rebels gathering. Since leaving the railhead at Rolla seven weeks earlier, their numbers had dwindled to 10,500.
In addition, their quartermaster and commissary, Capt. Philip H. Sheridan, had barely managed to keep them fed and had failed to keep them
shod. Many were barefoot and others shivered in threadbare pants. Hauling clothing, ammunition, food, and fodder two hundred miles over
primitive roads taxed even Sheridan's driving energy.[65]

A.W. did not see the barefoot Federals. He saw only that they were
"magnificently equipped, and abundantly provided with all the murderous machinery of war."[66]

Curtis had concentrated his army on the imposing bluffs of Little
Sugar Creek overlooking the Telegraph Road crossing. They waited
behind breastworks of black jack logs. The old West Pointer methodically
saw to the details of his position and communications, and especially his
vital wagon train. He knew tomorrow the guns would roar.[67]

Earl Van Dorn reported that the enemy, about 20,000 strong, "waited
in their strongly entrenched camp." Van Dorn was not about to throw
a hastily assembled and untried army against prepared fortifications. In
conference with McCulloch and McIntosh, who knew the area, the
major general made other plans. He threw out pickets and bivouacked

as if for the night, then began a move around the Union army. Van Dorn planned to take Price's Missourians and march eight miles around Big Mountain, which rose behind Elkhorn Tavern, then come down Telegraph Road from the north and strike Curtis's rear at daylight before the Federal knew what was happening. McCulloch's men would stop on the south end of the escarpment, west of Curtis, and attack from there. Van Dorn shared this information with only his staff, Sterling Price, and Ben McCulloch. He pointedly ignored Albert Pike.[68]

A surprise, two-pronged attack such as Van Dorn planned is difficult to bring off. The men marching around the enemy must move swiftly and silently to surprise the foe. Both wings of the army need to be in place at the appointed time. Both should attack at the same moment—a great deal to expect with no reconnoitering and a hodgepodge army that was already starved and exhausted.

Van Dorn knew he had to hurry. Staff members galloped from camp to camp with orders. At eight that evening Price's weary infantry—they had marched nineteen miles at double-quick that day—got to their feet. They started on the roundabout march ahead of McCulloch's men, who had the shorter distance to go. Greer's Third Texas took up the line of march before their wagons had all arrived, leaving the men with nothing to eat after the hard day's march. The Ninth saddled up at midnight and formed in column but waited an hour or so before moving out. Everyone knew that in a few hours the battle would begin. To no one's surprise, snow began to fall and continued all night.[69]

Sul Ross, riding with his Sixth Texas, worried not for his own safety but for the army. A week later he wrote his father-in-law in Texas:

> Every half mile I saw the Infantry in squads of 50 and 60, and even more lieing on the roadside, asleep, and overcome with hunger and fatigue. Then it was my spirits began to fail and I trembled with fear at the result of an engagement . . . when our best men—those upon whom we must rely in Battle, were lieing Exhausted on the roadside, unable to reach the Battle field.[70]

The rapid march Van Dorn planned had gotten off to a slow start. A short distance out of Camp Stephens, long columns of infantrymen slowed when they reached Little Sugar Creek. A single narrow bridge of rails spanned the icy stream. Morning had dawned fair and clear before all the infantry passed and the cavalry could cross. (In the usual order of march, the mounted men take the lead to reconnoiter and clear the way for the men on foot, but Van Dorn had ordered the Texas and Indian cavalry to bring up the rear.)[71]

The bridge was not the only obstacle. Van Dorn later reported that he "hoped before daylight to reach the rear of the enemy. Some obstructions, which he had hastily thrown in the way, so impeded our march that we did not gain the Telegraph road until 10 a.m. of the 7th." Curtis's troops had been in the area a couple of weeks, certainly long enough to throw up all manner of obstructions on the surrounding roads. Felled trees slowed the infantry's passage to the north.[72]

The Ninth Texas was the last regiment in McIntosh's column, with the Indians following. Many tribesmen had blackened their faces with charcoal, a sign they were suffering from hunger. They had not eaten in two days.

North of Little Sugar Creek, Sims's men marched and countermarched with the brigade for several hours. The men had no idea where they were going or what lay ahead, but neither did their colonels. At 11:00 A.M., Price opened "the ball by a brisk cannonading." The cavalrymen then moved toward Elkhorn Tavern. Cannon fire echoed across the ridges from the east in long, deep, rolling sounds like distant thunder. Van Dorn and Price had finally reached Telegraph Road, where they found Curtis's blue-clad soldiers waiting with their rifles loaded and their cannon charged. During the night, Curtis, having become convinced that Van Dorn had moved to attack his rear, had ordered a change of front.[73]

McIntosh's brigade of five regiments, a mile and a half west of Elkhorn Tavern, marched along a road in column by regiment. When the horsemen entered a small prairie about 250 yards across, "smoke rose and there came a rumbling noise like the heavens had split open, and a whistling noise like a square plantation tumbling through the air." Shells from an enemy battery a hundred yards to the right fell among the horsemen. A Federal infantry regiment wheeled into line with the artillerymen. McIntosh rode to the head of the column and, waving his sword, ordered the regiments to form for the charge.[74]

Sims threw out a squadron to protect the Ninth's flank and swung the rest of his men into line. The regiment's colors, carried by Hyram Duff, rippled in the sunshine. The other Texas regiments formed right of the Ninth, Pike and his Indians to the left. Adrenaline surged through every vein. Five bugles from five regiments pierced the air. "Charge! Charge!" Sims yelled.

"The heavens resounded with the tramp of warriors' steeds." The horses leaped an eight-rail fence and jumped a ditch. Company K, the center and guide of the Ninth, led the regiment straight toward the battery of four brass howitzers.[75]

Cavalry Charge at Pea Ridge

Rebel yells rent the air. Cherokee war whoops shrieked above the cannon's roar. Frenzied horses laid back their ears and ran full out. Three thousand madly charging cavalrymen "swept over the field, in the midst of a tempest of iron hail, the thunders of artillery, the yells of the combatants, and the groans of the dying and wounded." Smoke and the rotten egg smell of black powder filled the air.[76]

The Ninth's Company K reached the guns and planted the first flag on the enemy battery. The Cherokees were close behind, firing guns and arrows. Yankee gunners managed to fire only a round or two before they broke. "In an instant our gallant columns were pouring a destructive fire in the face of the enemy, and at once they abandoned their guns," Colonel Stone reported. A Union soldier said, "Men and horses ran in collision, crushing each other to the ground."[77]

The Federals, completely overwhelmed by the yelling, slashing horde, fled or surrendered. One threw his hands up and ran to a man in Company K. In the seething mass of screaming men and horses, the Texan failed to understand the Yankee's actions. The Texan slammed the man in the head with the butt of his gun and "prostrated him with his dead comrades."[78]

In less than ten minutes the horsemen silenced the guns and scattered the enemy. "The iron dogs of war are hushed," Victor wrote. "The

Stars and Stripes go down, and the Stars and Bars of the South waves in triumph."[79]

The troopers were intoxicated with success. Pike reported that "around the taken battery was a mass of Indians and others in the utmost confusion, all talking, riding this way and that, and listening to no orders from anyone." The Indians "straddled the guns and rode them in joy over our victory." In the chaos, the Indians also "shot arrows as well as rifles, and tomahawked and scalped prisoners," Curtis reported. Van Dorn admitted that the bodies of dead Yankees were "shamefully mangled." A Federal colonel reported that many were "pierced through the heart and neck with knives." When Federal artillerymen managed to throw a couple of shells onto the field, the Indians scattered into the woods.[80]

Silent cannon were glorious trophies, but when the big guns "spoke" the Indians' tribal concept of bravery allowed them to get out of harm's way. In no way were they cowards. Their customs were different. Likewise, scalping and mutilation of dead enemies' bodies were deeply set in their culture. Indian and American concepts of warfare held nothing in common.

After the elation of victory subsided, the men of the Ninth realized Sims's right sleeve was soaked with blood and his arm hung lifeless by his side, shattered by grapeshot. When the colonel, protesting all the way, was taken to the rear, command of the regiment passed to Quayle.[81]

Quayle and the men began looking for their comrades among the two hundred or more wounded and dead. To their horror they found over a dozen of theirs dead and two dozen wounded. They gathered up the wounded and re-formed by company, dismounted. The men led their horses and a few animals from the captured battery to the rear and tied them to trees. When the thrill of victory ebbed, the men realized they were exhausted. Fear, excitement, and the exertion of battle after thirty-six hours in the saddle left no one unaffected. Some sat silently, a few laughed and joked, others could not stop talking—normal reactions to intense stress.[82]

Sounds of battle rolled in from around Elkhorn Tavern, to the east. The Texans soon began to wonder why they were idle, why they received no orders. At sunset the distant cannonading ceased, and the Ninth fell back a mile. Officers reported their losses—thirteen killed, seven mortally wounded, seventeen wounded, and three missing, a total of forty, and fifty or more horses. No one in Company A was killed, but four were wounded. Company K, the center and guide that morning, suffered twenty-three casualties, more than half the regiment's total.[83]

That day the flag of Company K became the colors of the Ninth Texas Cavalry. A.W. wrote, "We dressed upon it, we carried it, we loved it, and we never lost it." It was "a small brownish red silk flag, in the center of which was a crescent moon and thirteen five-pointed silver stars. It was trimmed with silk fringe

Flag of Company K, Ninth Texas

and was attached to a dark mahogany colored staff with a gilded spear head at the top." Later the other companies furled their flags and sent them home.[84]

During the afternoon the Texas cavalry colonels had become concerned over their lack of orders, and had wondered what to do. Stone kept his Sixth Texas in position and impatiently waited for orders. Greer remained "on our side of the field, anxiously awaiting orders." Late in the afternoon, he reported: "I went in person in search of Generals McCulloch and McIntosh. I soon met with the staffs of the two generals, who informed me that each one of them was dead, and that I was the senior officer on the field," but no one had notified him that he was in command.[85]

Shortly after the cavalrymen had taken the battery, General McCulloch, with his adjutant by his side, had ridden his handsome red sorrel forward to reconnoiter. His Maynard carbine, black velvet suit, and high boots covered with woolen netting attracted an Illinois company's attention. The Yankees steadied their rifles on a rail fence and fired. A bullet pierced the old Ranger's heart, and four others struck the sorrel.

Ben McCulloch died instantly, "embalming his country's cause with his blood, and depriving his admiring soldiery of their military chieftain and idol," Stone reported.[86]

When James McIntosh was informed of McCulloch's death and that command had passed to him, he drew his sword and galloped off at the head of the Second Arkansas Mounted Rifles, the wrong place for a division commander. Within minutes a bullet had struck McIntosh in the heart. In another few hours McCulloch's infantry commander, who had not been informed that command had passed to him, was captured. Van Dorn's right wing was leaderless, leaving the Texas cavalrymen to wait in ignorance.[87]

It was evening before the men of the Ninth learned what had happened. At 10:00 P.M., Quayle met in a log house with Greer and the other officers who could be found to decide what to do. Later they withdrew to the main road, half a mile to the rear, and sent a courier to Van Dorn for instruction. The men unsaddled and lay down on the muddy ground.[88]

The Cherokees had scattered west toward home. Stone and his Sixth had ridden off toward Camp Stephens to guard the wagon trains, a prudent move. Many infantrymen had drifted away or been captured. An hour after midnight the Ninth resaddled and took up the line of march with Greer and the few remaining men left after yesterday's disasters. Greer reported his effective force at not more than three thousand men. Another colonel wrote that his men were "almost exhausted by fatigue, loss of sleep, hunger, after 3 days and nights of forced marching and a day's action." Infantrymen were "staggering with fatigue and half dead with cold and hunger."[89]

Cold wind moaned through the trees as the weary men and animals made their way north around Big Mountain. Stars sparkled in an obsidian sky. The column finally halted on Telegraph Road a mile west of Price's infantry. At sunrise, deep-toned thunder from forty cannon roused the men from their stupor. The Ninth Texas and the rest of Greer's men waited impatiently in line of battle, again wondering what was happening beyond their view.[90]

Two hours later the cavalrymen were ordered to move back a mile and form on the sides of the road but to keep off the road and out of the way of the infantry. As the regiments "passed slowly by no indication of alarm or knowledge of defeat could be discerned," a colonel wrote. Eventually it dawned on everyone that their army was retreating. Pike later accused Van Dorn of leaving two thousand men without notice of the retreat.[91]

While the Texas cavalrymen were guarding the roads for the infantry, word came down the line of the Third Texas for the man with the fastest horse to deliver a message to Van Dorn. Pvt. Douglas Cater reported to Colonel Greer, who handed Cater a folded paper and sent him on his way. With the road full of retreating infantry, Cater took to the brush. After a hard ride he found the general's staff and gave the message to Col. Dabney H. Maury, Van Dorn's adjutant. A smile broke out on Maury's face as he read the message. He refolded the paper and handed it back to Cater, saying, "Tell him to keep it." Cater stuffed the paper into his pocket and started back at a gallop. Puzzled by Maury's flippant answer to what he thought was important news, Cater pulled the paper from his pocket and read: "General, I have captured three barrels of whiskey. What shall I do with it." Cater angrily tore the message to shreds and threw it to the ground. "I didn't take any message back," he said, but "went in search of my company," and "the boys had a good laugh at my expense."[92]

The Confederate army was in full retreat. The Ninth bivouacked that night under the full moon and threw out a heavy picket line. Without their train, they had nothing to eat, nothing to feed the horses. Officers walked the picket lines to keep the exhausted guards awake.[93]

"The whole command stampeded & scattered all over the mountains," David Garrett wrote home two weeks later. For the next four days his regiment "had nothing to eat but a little fat pork, [and] we travelled night & day, all our men were worn out, a great many have taken sick since the fight." Newton remembered, "We then beat a retreat back to the Arkansas, while the rain, sleet and snow came down in floods." Sul Ross wrote his wife, "My blankets were left and at night I would lay three fence rails down on the ground, & wrapped up in my Saddle Blanket, and try to sleep." General Curtis reported, "The foe scattered in all directions." The Yankees later crowed that they had run Van Dorn "out of Arkansas and clean on to Memphis, Tennessee."[94]

The Ninth, serving as rear guard for the infantry, climbed the steep road to the top of the Boston Mountains, constantly watching for enemy cavalry. None appeared. They found a little cornmeal at a gristmill, but nothing else. Tuesday, the famished men reached the Third's winter quarters on Frog Bayou, where a detachment of their train joined them, but the wagons carried no food.[95]

By Thursday, March 13, Van Dorn had reached Van Buren and was firing brusque orders to his exhausted regiments. On Frog Bayou, men coming in from Van Buren brought news of other regiments and Colonel Sims's serious wound. Cold rain peppered down. Half the men were sick, the rest were weak from hunger and exertion. During the entire campaign Van Dorn, who slept in warm houses, remained unconcerned about the physical condition of his men or his animals.[96]

The Ninth Texas cavalrymen started east toward their winter quarters. They stopped a few days at the Sixth's camp on Mulberry Creek, where they found corn for the horses but little for the men to eat. From there, Quayle led the regiment thirty-one miles east through the town of Ozark and on to Horsehead Creek. They arrived Monday, March 17, a warm, sunny day, a month after the courier had arrived with orders to join McCulloch near Elkhorn Tavern.[97]

Everyone was tired and disgusted to the point of anger. Colonel Quayle, A.W., Gris, and every trooper in the Ninth Texas knew the Confederate army had been whipped while the Texas cavalrymen idled away the afternoon awaiting orders. Ben McCulloch, their hero and division commander, was dead. James McIntosh, their brigade commander, was dead. William Sims, their regimental colonel, could lead them no more. The men had starved and frozen, ridden day and night, used up their horses, lost forty men and their colonel. All for nothing. It was hard to remember the pride they had felt in Indian Territory.[98]

Men in the other Texas cavalry regiments were as irate. Newton Keen wrote, "General Van Dorn was perhaps the only man in the army that was whipped." Victor Rose wrote, "The soldiers, every one of whom felt that the beaten enemy was not entitled to possession of the field" and "the men had been defrauded of their well-earned dues." David Garrett wrote that "both sides were whipped." Sul Ross said, "We whipped ourselves."[99]

Pvt. McBride Pridgen of Whitfield's Battalion had a good reason to be angry. He said, "By the gods! We whipped them! We butchered them! We exterminated them! And I don't believe there was but one man escaped to tell the tale, and *he* stole my blankets." In the heat of battle, Pridgen had laid down his huge, gray, double blanket with his name embroidered in scarlet worsted in one corner, his prize possession. When Pridgen returned to retrieve the treasure, a Yankee had carried it off.[100]

The officers, who knew more of what had happened, were madder than the privates. They blamed Van Dorn for losing a battle he should have won. Albert Pike, in three lengthy reports, pointed out that he was not informed of the battle plan, he received no orders or messages, he could find out nothing, and "the infantry had marched 60 miles in 3 days, had been on foot all the previous night [and] had no food or water." Four months after the battle, Pike was still mad. He wrote his superior that Van Dorn "ran away, ahead of his army, at 10 o'clock in the morning. He says so himself. He left half his army behind, without notice of his retreat. General Van Dorn's report is, as another officer has said, 'true until you get to the forks of the road, and all false afterward.' " It was well into April before all the Texas colonels forced themselves to write reports.[101]

Van Dorn's report further infuriated Pike and the Texas colonels. The major general blandly wrote that "a series of accidents entirely un-foreseen and not under my control and a badly disciplined army defeated my intentions." He complained that "the troops moved so slowly" and that "some obstructions, which he [Curtis] had hastily thrown in the way, so impeded our march," but "our loss was not heavy . . . not being more than 800 or 1,000 killed and wounded and between 200 and 300 prisoners." Furthermore, "the officer in charge of the ordnance supplies could not find his wagons." The officer knew where the ord-nance wagons were. They were exactly where Van Dorn had ordered him to park them. The general then glibly wrote, "I was not defeated, but only foiled in my intentions."[102]

The Texas troopers, green as they were at judging generals, knew the Confederates had fought well and that Van Dorn was responsible for what had happened. What they failed to realize was that Samuel Curtis remembered a great deal more of his West Point training than Earl Van Dorn recalled. Gen. Richard S. Ewell, who had served with Buck Van Dorn in the Lone Star State, said that in Texas Van Dorn "had learned all about commanding fifty United States dragoons and had forgotten everything else."[103]

★   ★   ★

Van Dorn, at his headquarters in Van Buren, kept his couriers busy with strings of orders and instructions. On March 17, he reorganized his Army of the West, as he named the forces. The Sixth, Ninth, and Eleventh Texas, and Col. Thomas J. Churchill's Arkansas regiment were assigned to the Second Cavalry Brigade, commanded by Churchill. The new brigade formed a reserve under the immediate command of Van Dorn. The general had plans for the cavalrymen.[104]

At Cantonment Slidell, the Texans pondered what they had learned about war during the battle of Pea Ridge. They were thankful to again have a roof over their heads, and they soon caught up on sleep, but food was scarce. The horses fared better on an abundance of corn.[105]

In a few days Churchill rode in with the rest of the Second Cavalry Brigade. Van Dorn had ordered Churchill to take up a post at or near Horsehead Creek and prepare for an expedition back across the Ozark Mountains. Churchill was ordered

> to proceed as rapidly as possible to Forsyth [Missouri], on White River. You will march without tents and with only sufficient wagons to carry the rations of your men. You will leave the wagons at Forsyth, march upon Springfield by forced march, and endeavor to capture and destroy the stores of the enemy at that place. . . .
>
> After accomplishing all you can against the enemy in that vicinity you will rejoin your wagons and proceed by the quickest and best route to Pocahontas [in northeastern Arkansas].
>
> The quartermaster and subsistence department will furnish such funds as you may require of them for purchase of your supplies of forage, subsistence, store, &c., and such other supplies. Send your baggage to Jacksonport . . . a proper guard with it. It is expected that you will be ready to march on this expedition by the 23rd instant.
>
> You will please take every pains to insure absolute secrecy as to the object and destination of your command.[106]

For ten days the Ninth prepared to take up the line of march. The horses needed at least that long to rest and get back into condition after a month-long campaign. The men shoed the horses, cleaned their weapons, checked their equipment. Amos Burgoon and the other teamsters repaired the wagons and harnesses. Friday, March 28, Quayle's men rode away from their snug winter quarters and away from the little graveyard where their dead lay. Churchill led the column through Clarksville and turned due north into the foothills of the Ozark Mountains. Each company took only one wagon to haul cooking utensils, a few tools, a little food, and fodder. As ordered, they would purchase supplies along the way.[107]

The Ninth's regimental wagon train, properly guarded and laden with the sick and wounded, moved east on a road leading toward Jacksonport, the steamboat landing in eastern Arkansas where Van Dorn had begun his ride across the state. The cavalry brigade would meet the train at the river port. Van Dorn planned to assemble his army at Pocahontas and strike out for Saint Louis in April. Churchill's cavalry raid on Curtis's supplies was to hold the Federals in southwestern Missouri.[108]

On the first day's march from Horsehead Creek, Churchill's men and wagons crossed a peak of the Ozarks and wound their way down into a narrow, fertile valley, crossing a small creek "a 100 times during the day's march." They bivouacked on the mountain, seventeen miles out of Clarksville. The wagons lagged behind. The riders fed their horses a bit of corn, but the men laid down on the ground with empty stomachs.[109]

They started crossing the main mountain chain the next day. Horses and wagons plunged down Bear Creek's deep gorge and climbed out along an almost perpendicular, zigzag road, "it requiring the whole of each company to assist their respective wagons up the steep—& they have 6 mules each & *contain only* cooking utensils," Gris wrote. They bivouacked in the Buffalo Creek valley. The next day the column passed through Jasper and marched across broken and barren county.[110]

The sixth day out from Horsehead Creek the brigade left the wagons and rode north into Missouri. They stopped for the night on the south bank of the White River, opposite the village of Forsyth. The "river [was] so swollen by the late rains as to be swimming," Gris wrote in his diary.[111]

If Reuben was with the riders, he thought of home, only twenty miles north, half a day's ride. He surely considered how he might wrangle a day's leave to visit Grandpa and other members of the large Rogers clan living close by. But first the brigade would have to find a way to cross the flooded White River. Reuben must have rolled in his blanket on the muddy ground that night and wondered if he dare dream of home.

Morning brought the answer. The cavalry raid was canceled, and the command was ordered to Des Arc, Arkansas, two hundred miles southeast on the White River. The column mounted and rode back into Arkansas. That evening they reached their train.[112]

Horses and wagons slogged across Arkansas in constant rain that turned the primitive dirt roads to quagmires. Several nights Amos

and the other teamsters found nothing to feed their animals. Mules, with stronger hindquarters and more stamina than horses, stood up better under the rough work and irregular feed than the cavalry mounts. Nevertheless, during their six months in the army, the horses—as well as the men—had either toughened up, died, or

Wagon Train Bogged in the Mud

been abandoned.[113]

Cowboys and Horse Indians took strings of five to eight horses per man on extended trips or campaigns, but a cavalryman rode the same mount day after day. Animals could stand hard service for a few days, but they could not carry a man or pull a wagon day after day without food and rest. They would quit.

The cavalrymen rode through Yellville, Burrowsville, and Wiley's Cove. Six days out of Forsyth, they crossed a chain of mountains and camped near Clinton, where the roads worsened. Amos and the other teamsters fought to keep the train moving. They double-teamed and cursed at the tops of their lungs through bog after bog but fell farther and farther behind the mounted men. Several nights the teamsters surrendered to the mud and camped alone.[114]

Churchill decided to leave the train to come on as it could and ride on to Des Arc. The cavalrymen cooked two days' rations and moved out. Rain poured down. Twenty miles from Des Arc they swam the horses across flooded Cypress Bayou. Twelve days out of Missouri, they reached Des Arc.[115]

It was there that Gris, A.W., and the rest of the Ninth Texas learned Van Dorn's new plans for them. If they had been disgusted with the general after Pea Ridge, now they were appalled and enraged. Van Dorn had ordered the Ninth and his other Texas, Arkansas, and Missouri cavalry regiments dismounted and shipped to Mississippi as infantry.[116]

Infantry! Infantrymen walk. In frontier Texas, a land of horses, no man walked when he could ride, and only the lowest classes had nothing to ride. Most of the Texas recruits came from the middle and upper classes of Texas society. The governor of Texas, when badgered by Richmond for infantry regiments, had replied:

The people of Texas . . . live on horseback, and it is with great aversion they enlist in the infantry. Cavalry, efficient cavalry, can be obtained from this State almost to the extent of the male population, but infantry is difficult to furnish.[117]

For the Texans, who had flocked to join the cavalry "this order [was] a breach of faith, totally at variance with [their] contract."[118]

A member of the Third Texas expressed his feeling about walking after the battle of Wilson Creek. Pvt. B. L. Thomas, a Texas Irishman, said he "would rather suffer crucifixion, head down, than be left afoot in Missouri."[119]

Cavalrymen were the army's privileged. Horses gave them freedom that men on foot lacked. On horseback, soldiers were free to forage for themselves and their horses; free to visit towns, where there were whiskey and girls; and free from charging cannon with a bayonet.

If cursing could kill, Van Dorn would have been in his grave. He assured the men they were temporarily dismounted and would have their horses back as soon as the "nature of the service" would admit. The Texans swore, but they submitted.[120]

Men from each company were assigned to take the horses back to Texas. Lt. James W. Calloway commanded Company A's seven-man detachment. A.W. rode with the men from Company D. Each man led a string of saddled horses, riding one horse and guiding the leader of the others. Tuesday, April 15, 1862, the column started west toward Little Rock, where they would cross the Arkansas and ride southwest to the Red River and into Texas. The ex-troopers of the Ninth Texas Cavalry (Dismounted) sullenly watched their horses head toward home.[121]

CHAPTER 5

INFANTRYMEN

April 16–September 3, 1862

The Ninth Texas Cavalry (Dismounted) crowded aboard the steamer *Star Victoria*, which was secured to the wharf at Des Arc, Arkansas. It was noon, April 16, 1862. Teamsters helped load the regiment's wagons and mules and the officers' horses. An hour later the *Star*'s steam whistle bellowed through the damp air as the heavily laden vessel eased into the White River's muddy current and moved downstream toward the Mississippi, more than a hundred miles south.[1]

Other steamers followed, loaded with men and equipment of the Sixth Texas, the Eleventh Texas, and Churchill's Arkansas Cavalry. Newton Keen described his trip:

The river was at full tide and . . . its banks were overflowed. There was about a 1,000 men on the boat. It was the first time I had ever been on a boat. This was a magnificent large one. The water swept it across a curve and it ran against a large pecan tree some two foot through. I thought sure it would break the great boat into two pieces, but to my astonishment the tree bent . . . and [the boat] dragged itself through the boughs of the tree. My mind caught the idea of great force and power. I went down into the engine room and saw the ponderous machinery and heard the throb and beat of the mighty power and force which propelled the great ship of a boat through the waters. . . . The great boilers were heated by wood, and we often landed for the purpose of taking on wood. . . . The wood was all split and 4 feet long, stacked along on high points. It was surprising to see how quick a dozen Irishmen could load a ship with wood.[2]

Memphis, Tennessee

Boatmen tied the *Star Victoria* to a landing at dusk. It began to rain and the sky was dark as a wolf's mouth. Packed onto the decks, the boisterous crowd of young men joked and jostled through the night. With the first glimmer of dawn the *Star* cast off and got under way. When she passed another steamer, the boys shouted and cheered.[3]

The *Star* steamed out into the Mississippi and turned north toward Memphis at 3:30 in the afternoon. The huge river was out of its banks from recent rains. Residents in small skiffs paddled around houses that were filled up to the windows. The Texans watched as a woman and three children paddled around the edge of the timber in a small skiff. Other residents cheered the soldiers from the second floors of their flooded homes.[4]

The *Star*, slowed by the powerful current, steamed north through the night. By dawn she had passed Helena, and shortly after noon she tied up at Memphis, more than a hundred miles above the mouth of the White. Marching down the gangplank in a downpour, the soldiers marveled at the busy wharf. Army teamsters helped wrestle the mules and wagons off the boat, then hitched up their teams and loaded the drenched baggage. The regiment marched two miles to the eastern suburbs of the town to make camp.[5]

During the next few days the young Texans gawked at the big-city sights. Memphis, with a population of close to 25,000, "was the greatest and largest city" Newton had ever seen. Standing on the wharf watching blacks drag goods and merchandise to and from the boats fascinated Newt. At a bank in the city, he exchanged a twenty-dollar Confederate bill for a five-dollar gold piece and five silver dollars, the last gold or silver coins he would see until after the war. Newt spent a few cents on fish, the thing he enjoyed most in Memphis.[6]

The Texans relished the novelties of the busy river port, but war news ricocheting around the city disheartened them. Confederates had lost the battle of Pea Ridge in March—which they needed no one to tell them about—the battle of Shiloh April 7, and the struggle for Island No. 10 the next day. The U.S. Navy was bombarding forts guarding New Orleans, and the U.S. Army was in front of Richmond. Names of generals unknown to the Texans filled the papers. One whose name they heard for the first time would become indelibly imprinted in their memories: U. S. Grant.[7]

The Ninth Texas and Gen. Earl Van Dorn's other regiments had been hurried east four hundred miles to reinforce the Confederates gathering to face Grant's army, camped a hundred miles east of Memphis on the Mississippi–Tennessee border. While Van Dorn's men had struggled across Arkansas's muddy roads, Confederate commanders had attacked Grant near the little log meetinghouse of Shiloh in what turned out to be the first truly bloody battle of the Civil War. The butcher's bill—as the more callous called the casualty totals—amounted to 23,741, nearly 500 more than in all previous American wars combined: the Revolution, the War of 1812, and the Mexican War.

The Confederates left the field to the Union after the battle of Shiloh and stumbled back to Corinth, where they began fortifying the vital railroad junction and nursing 8,000 mangled men. The wounded filled makeshift hospitals in Memphis, Chattanooga, Corinth, and Okolona; some were cared for in private homes scattered across the entire area. Sul Ross wrote his wife from Memphis that the town was full of Shiloh's wounded.[8]

Three men from Company A, including Amos Burgoon, added to the medical burdens in the city. The three were left at an overcrowded

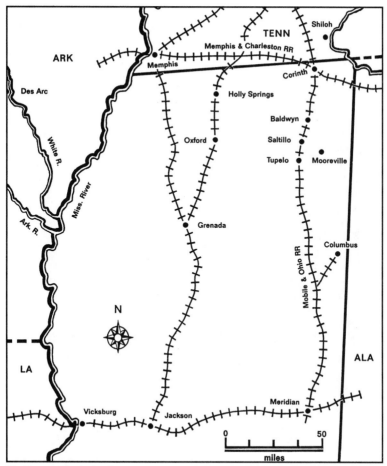

Northern Mississippi

hospital. One man died, but Amos was back driving a company wagon a month later.[9]

The rest of the men enjoyed the sights for a week. Although it rained every day, the privates prowled the busy streets and wharfs. Memphis swarmed with idle soldiers, tradesmen scurrying along the streets, officers in fine uniforms mounted on spirited horses. The country boys from west of the Mississippi were fascinated.[10]

Passes to town ceased Friday, April 25. Each man in the Ninth was issued a hundred rounds of ammunition and ordered to cook five days' rations. They knew they were bound for Corinth to join Gen. Pierre Gustoave Toutant Beauregard, an aristocratic Louisiana Creole and the hero of Fort Sumter. The Union army was inching closer to Corinth, and everyone expected a battle to begin any day. Beauregard had wired

Van Dorn, "Hurry up the movement. Enemy begin to threaten our advance."[11]

The Ninth marched downtown to the Memphis & Charleston depot late in the evening and camped on the platform. The next morning at six

Gen. Pierre G. T. Beauregard

the men loaded their baggage into boxcars and filed onto twenty passenger cars; the wagons and teams would follow by land. An hour later the train rumbled east. After many stops and delays, the regiment reached Corinth, Mississippi, ninety-three miles east of Memphis and twenty-two miles south of Shiloh. The men wrestled their baggage off the train and bivouacked two miles north of the town.[12]

Van Dorn's forty other regiments had already arrived or were on their way. The Sixth Texas spent two days riding twenty flatcars from Memphis in pouring rain. The

Third took the cars—railroad passenger cars. On their thirty-four-hour trip, which should have taken a fourth that long, the decrepit locomotive blew a cylinder head; a coupling broke, leaving the cars in a forty-foot cut; and the train was sidetracked over and over.[13]

At the junction of the east-west Memphis & Charleston Railroad and the north-south Mobile & Ohio Railroad, Corinth was a naturally defensive position on a ridge between two streams, a valuable strategic point, according to Union general U. S. Grant. Oak forests and undergrowth interspersed with houses and clearings covered the surrounding area. The land was low and flat along the Mobile & Ohio.[14]

When the Texans arrived, the town was a teeming mass of soldiers, wagons, mules, headquarters tents, regimental camps, and Shiloh's wounded. For three weeks soldiers had been feverishly throwing up a ring of fortifications a mile and a half beyond the town. Constant rain made every foot of ground a bog. Along muddy roads and through jam-packed streets, teamsters beat and cursed their floundering mules.

Quartermasters, trying to transport ordnance and stores, swore at the congestion. A Texan wrote that the roads were "almost impassable with mud, even for a good horse and rider, and utterly and absolutely impass- able for a wagon . . . the best team we had could not have drawn an empty wagon over the road." Couriers dashed back and forth with orders and messages. In addition, a yellow flag—emblem of a hospital—flew from the top of every large building in town, including the once-comfortable Tisho- mingo Hotel, near the depot.[15]

Railroad Junction at Corinth

Inside the flag-marked buildings lay "gray-haired men, men in the prime of manhood, beardless boys, Federals and all, mutilated in every imaginable way," nurse Kate Cumming wrote in her diary. The foul air from the mass of human beings at first made Cumming giddy and sick.[16]

The Ninth Texas climbed off the train into this morass of mud and misery at 1:00 A.M., Sunday, April 27. A Third cavalryman expressed the Texans' frustrations: "So here we were, without horses, to confront new conditions, under new commanders, constrained to learn the art of war in a different arm of service, and to drill, fight and march with the infantry."[17]

The Ninth set up camp. For the next couple of weeks they drilled and marched. Rain, like the odor of a skunk, hung on and on. Twice the regiment formed in line of battle only to be recalled. The weather was foul, the food horrid, the water worse. When a particularly heavy rain flooded camp, the men lugged all their tents and equipment to higher ground. The dismounted Texans glumly went about their duties, cursing their luck—and Buck Van Dorn.[18]

One event did cheer them. The last day of April the paymaster arrived, set up his portable desk, and counted out a few bills to each soldier. The men were supposed to be paid the last day of every other month, when the rolls were turned in to headquarters. April 30, Reuben received $24, two months' pay. Now that he was in the infantry, he would receive a dollar less per month. Orderly Sergeant Griscom received $20 a month; Captain Berry, $140; and Lieutenant Colonel Quayle, $185 a month plus allowances. Back in Texas, Sims, still on the roster as the Ninth's colonel, received $210 a month plus allowances.[19]

A week later the Ninth was supplied with horses for a mounted reconnaissance. In the saddle, the men felt whole again. Their mounts had been snatched away less than three weeks earlier, but it seemed more like three years. The horsemen galloped southeast "over hills [and] through swamps, without a guide or any knowledge of the country." They wandered around east beyond their entrenchments until they blundered into heavy Union forces near the village of Farmington, four miles east of Corinth. The regiment swung around toward friendly ground and finally stumbled into their own pickets, who supplied them with a guide. Not daring to retrace their route for fear of capture, they followed a circuitous route back to their own lines. The next day they were ordered into Corinth and camped in the streets of town.[20]

The following morning the regiment, reduced by sickness to about five hundred, moved out at sunrise and rode three miles south along the Mobile & Ohio tracks. They were going into camp for rations when ordered to march quick time toward Farmington. General Beauregard, the feisty West Pointer, hoped to cut off and destroy a portion of the Federal army. The Ninth joined their brigade just as the cannonading began.[21]

The brigade, part of the reserve, was under fire for a couple of hours. At 3:30 in the afternoon the enemy fled across a large creek and burned the bridge behind them. Victorious Rebels poured into the captured camp. They rummaged through the Yankees' tents, helping themselves to anything and everything that caught their fancy—boots and pants, coffee and canned food, rifles and saddles. Gris reported that the Ninth seized "much equipage, loads of ammunition & about 3000 knapsacks & blankets & a variety & abundance of Yankee trinkets." H. McBride Pridgen was pawing through the plunder in a tent when he found a treasure. He ran out and yelled to Victor Rose, "By the gods! I have found my blankets I lost at Elkhorn, Arkansas." And indeed, Pridgen held his large, gray double blanket with his name embroidered in crimson letters in one corner.[22]

The Ninth Texas suffered only a single casualty during the battle of Farmington. John Matthew Sloan, the thirteen-year-old in Company C, was shot in the thigh. Because the boy's femur was fractured, Dr. Robertson amputated Sloan's leg near the body.[23]

Two weeks later General Beauregard issued a testimonial:

The commander of the forces desires to call especial attention of the Army to the behavior of Private John Matthew Sloan of the Ninth Texas Volunteers, a lad of only thirteen years of age and having lost his leg in the affair . . . near Farmington exclaimed, "I have but one regret, I shall not soon be able to get at the enemy." That such an example of youthful heroism may not go unrewarded the General Commander will, in person, at a future day to be announced in orders, in the presence of the troops confirm upon Private Sloan a suitable Badge of Merit.[24]

A week later, Sloan was dead.[25]

The day after the battle the Ninth moved camp from north of Corinth to a couple of miles southeast of the town. That same day the regiment received orders to reorganize in accordance with the Conscription Act, which had been passed in April and required that all white males age eighteen to thirty-five serve three years. Any soldier under eighteen or over thirty-five could go home. William Sims, recovering in Texas, was dropped from the roll. William Quayle, having worn himself out, declined reelection and returned to Texas. Major Townes, an ambitious lawyer from Lamar County, vigorously campaigned for the colonelcy of the regiment and won. Lt. Dudley W. Jones, adjutant and twenty-year-old former Titus County student, was elected lieutenant colonel. Another lawyer, tall, dark-eyed J. N. Dodson of Tarrant County, a private in Company A, was elected major.[26]

Company A unanimously reelected Capt. Thomas G. Berry, who had earned the respect and admiration of his men by his bravery and his refusal of any luxury not available to all his men. He declared himself no better than his men, even refusing to take shelter at night in the worst storms unless there was shelter for all. Berry was the only captain in the regiment to remain with his men. One captain in the Ninth was under arrest, and the other eight resigned to go home. Only two departing captains were over thirty-five, but the others chose Texas over the infantry. As officers, they could resign, and the reorganization provided a convenient opportunity to go home.[27]

The new officers were younger than those elected the year before in Texas. Lieutenant Colonel Jones was sixteen years younger than William Quayle, and Lawyer Dodson, at twenty-six, was eight years younger than Townes, the Ninth's original major. Victor Rose of the Third, age twenty, was elected fourth sergeant of his company. In his regiment, the new officers averaged ten years younger than the original officers. Many older men had discovered that riding a horse thirty-six hours straight, sleeping on the ground rolled in a wet blanket, and living on bad beef and cornmeal was for the young.[28]

Stephen M. Hale of the Third, the old captain who had declared the regiment disgraced in the ambush north of Bentonville, could stand the riding but not the marching. At the reorganization, his men begged the trustworthy old man to remain with them. His courage had sustained them since their first moment under fire at the battle of Wilson Creek, back in August. Victor later wrote that when the shot began to fly pretty thick at Wilson Creek

> Captain Hale, who made no military pretensions, called out to his company, "Git in a straight row, here, boys! This is the war you all have hearn talked about! Them's the cannon; them's the muskets; that great big screeching thing is a bung-shell; and them little fellows that sing like bumble-bees are minnie-balls! Git in a straight row; we're gwine to work, now!"

But in Mississippi, Hale told his boys he was too old to make a single day's march with the infantry. His boys took up a collection to purchase their beloved captain a horse and buggy, but Captain Hale went back to Texas.[29]

The privates were as disenchanted with life in the infantry as were the officers. They deplored serving east of the Mississippi, and they mourned the loss of their horses. Moreover, the Conscription Act automatically extended their time of service from one to three years. Many had looked forward to going home in October, when their year was over, but privates could not resign. They were committed, willing or unwilling.[30]

Corinth was a poor place to be introduced to infantry life. A newspaper correspondent reported the water, obtained from shallow holes, "smells so offensively that the men have to hold their noses while drinking it." Nurse Kate Cumming wrote that the men "drank what their horses would turn from in disgust." A member of the Third Texas said his horse refused to drink the "mean, milky looking fluid" and had to be taken to a nearby stream each day. Rations were so poor Beauregard worried about scurvy.[31]

For the next couple of weeks the men picketed in the humid heat and listened to firing coming from the northeast. They lived on a small ration of corn, rancid bacon or lard, and a little molasses. In the evening they boiled sassafras roots in their tin cups of fetid water and pretended it was coffee. They slept on the flea-infested ground and clawed at red, itchy chigger bites circling their waists and other places they would not have discussed with their mothers. They treated the chigger bites with hog fat and went on scratching. A Mississippian wrote home that the chiggers and fleas were of "preponderous size—almost able to shoulder a musket. They hav most Eate me up."[32]

Reuben, protected by his tough Rogers genes, reported for duty every day while twenty-four men in his company fell victim to malaria, dysentery, measles, mumps, and other diseases running rampant through Corinth. Ten company men were sent to hospitals in the area, and four died.[33]

Victor spent his time "drilling, skirmishing and *physicing*, for fully one-half the men were prostrated by dysentery. Disease was the insidious and fatal enemy." Day by day the ranks grew thinner. The hospitals were crowded, and thousands were sent to "asylums far in the rear." By the end of May, only 246 men in the Third Texas were well enough to participate in an engagement. The regiment lost 50 men to disease at Corinth.[34]

David Garrett, Sixth Texas, wrote home that "the mortality in my company has been very great since I came to Corinth. We have pretty rough fare & nothing at all to drink & very hot weather. Water is getting very scarce." Seven men in Garrett's company died of disease, but he continued in good health.[35]

Gris recorded in his diary that health in the Ninth was poor and several men had died at the hospitals. Gris grew up in the more densely settled East, where he was exposed to childhood diseases. At the close of June 1862, he had been present for duty every day since first reporting to Camp Reeves in Texas.[36]

Newton Keen remembered that his regiment's encampment was "in an unhealthy location and the boys began to fall sick right and left." Newt became ill and was confined to his tent for several days. Getting no better, he was "thrown into company with some thirty or more, into a box car and shipped south to Hazlehurst, Mississippi, about a hundred miles." On the trip rain poured through the roof of the car onto the sawdust-covered floor until the "mess and mixture" was inches deep. There was no doctor, no medicine, no rations, and only two men to tend the thirty sick. At a switch the two piled railroad ties on the floor to keep the sick from lying on the mess. Newt was "pretty sick, but not so much so but what I could puke and help work." Three men died on the thirty-six-hour trip. The rest found Hazlehurst full of Corinth's sick and Shiloh's wounded. Newt shared a comfortable room with twenty other men for a month before he was well enough to return to his regiment.[37]

Sul Ross described Corinth as a "malodorous sickly spot, fitten only for alligators and snakes." Half the men in Ross's regiment, including Newt, were unfit for duty. Sul wrote home that he was "very puny and unwell," but he remained on duty. And his duties soon increased. He had been elected colonel of the Sixth at the reorganization and soon was acting brigadier general of his brigade, which included the Ninth.[38]

During May and June the combination of heat and bugs, dysentery and infectious diseases killed as many men at Corinth as had died of bullet wounds in the battle of Shiloh. When it was all over, President Jefferson Davis sent an inspector west with a prepared questionnaire to interrogate the generals. "What was the cause of the sickness at Camp Corinth? Would it have been avoided by occupying the higher ground in front? Has it been corrected?" he demanded. Beauregard, under orders to hold Corinth, had no choice of ground. He knew the sickness was caused by crowding, poor diet, and bad water, yet his repeated requests to Richmond to be allowed to improve and increase the men's rations were denied. Beauregard was on Jefferson Davis's long list of generals he did not like.[39]

Col. Dudley W. Jones

The Ninth's men dragged through the month. May 28, while Rebels and Yankees lobbed shells at each other all day, the Ninth supported two batteries near Chambers Creek, southeast of Corinth near the Memphis & Charleston tracks. A.W.'s friend Old Butch remembered that "shells were bursting in the air and we were discussing their skill in gunnery when a shell stuck the trunnion of one of our pieces, knocking off the trunnion and dismounting the piece. . . ." A fragment struck a shotgun lying on the ground and caused it to discharge its load into Colonel Townes's knee and thigh. The buckshot also hit E. A. Schults of Company A in the right thigh. He was soon back on duty, but Colonel Townes was "taken from us and never again joined his regiment."[40]

Dudley Jones, a lieutenant colonel for only two weeks, assumed command. A veteran recalled that the "boy of scarce twenty years of age was worthy to be the recipient of this very high honor." Jones, a tall, handsome youth, had attended Murray Institute in Coffeeville, Texas, and was studying to become a lawyer at Maury Institute in Columbia, Tennessee, when the war began. He had returned to Texas to join the Titus Grays. His family had migrated to the Lone Star State in 1836, only fourteen years after the arrival of the first Anglo-American settlers. Dud was "scrupulously neat, and very precise in all his communication as well as dress," a soldier remembered.[41]

Despite the loss of Colonel Townes, there were plenty of officers in and around Corinth to keep the privates alert. Many wore elaborate uniforms, "all aglitter with brass buttons and gold lace." Pierre G.T. Beauregard, one of five Confederate full generals, was in overall command. Beauregard, West Point 1838, was among the best known officers in the U.S. Army before the war, and his ability had impressed many Union and Confederate officers, as well as the people of the South. Old Butch also was impressed. He remembered the general's imposing military appearance, saying, "Anyone would have known he was an officer of high rank."[42]

Beauregard's command consisted of Maj. Gen. Earl Van Dorn's Army of the West and Maj. Gen. Braxton Bragg's Army of the Mississippi. Of Van Dorn's forty-two regiments and battalions, ten were dismounted Texas cavalry. The Sixth and Ninth Texas Cavalry were in Maj. Gen. Samuel Jones's Division, the Third and Whitfield's Legion were in Gen. Sterling Price's Division. May 4, 1862, the Ninth reported 657 men present and an aggregate of 869. The men sick in camp were counted among those present. Since the year began, the number present had fallen by 10 despite an increase by enlistment of 156—the men who had ridden up from Texas while the regiment was in Arkansas.[43]

The day after Dud Jones took command, Thursday, May 29, Confederate and Federal cannon along the front lines threw shells at one another. The rumble of guns and spatter of minié balls saturated the hot air. The Federals, outnumbering the 53,244 Confederates by more than two to one, were closing in for the kill.[44]

Beauregard, knowing he was outgunned and outnumbered, valued his army more than he valued the railroad junction. And he was right. Davis and many generals on both sides believed that holding your cities and territory while taking the enemy's would win the war. This ancient strategy, however, had been made obsolete by improved communications and transportation. Beauregard explained his decision to the War Department in his report:

Having ascertained definitely that the enemy had received large accessions to his already superior force, while ours had been reduced day by day by disease, resulting from bad water and inferior food, I felt it clearly my duty to evacuate [Corinth] without delay. . . . The transparent

object of the Federal commander had been to cut off my resources by
destroying the Mobile and Ohio and the Memphis and Charleston
Railroads.[45]

Beauregard laid careful and precise plans for an orderly retreat. His
instructions included such details as the baggage trains must leave their
positions at daybreak and stop six miles out, where the officer in charge
will open his secret orders; no rockets shall be fired; at 3:00 A.M. the
troops will take up the line of march.[46]

At 7:30 that Thursday evening Colonel Jones ordered the Ninth back
from the lines. The teamsters had already started south with the brigade's
trains, the baggage train in the lead, followed by the provision train, then
the ammunition train, and finally the ambulance train, as their orders
required. They had no idea where they were going until they stopped
six miles out. The long line of wagons creaked south along a road that
followed the Mobile & Ohio tracks toward Baldwyn.[47]

When the troops moved out, a few soldiers were left to keep the
usual campfires burning so the Yankees would suspect nothing. The rest
buckled on their cartridge belts, slung their blankets and knapsacks over
their shoulders, and took their places in the ranks. The Ninth fell in
with the rest of Van Dorn's army and trailed along behind the wagons.
The weather was oppressively hot, and the men were already tired after
sleeping in line of battle the night before and being shelled all day.
Marching through the night, they listened to empty trains clattering
north, then rumbling back south with loads of stores, ammunition, and
the wounded. The heavy smell of the Mississippi night mingled with
smoke and cinders from the engines. Overhead, enemy rockets, both
curious and beautiful, looped through the dark sky.[48]

Mile after mile, they marched south on the dusty road. Midnight
came and went. "Close up, men, close up," the officers ordered. As the
men tired, conversation ceased. The jingle of canteens and accoutrements
accompanied the steady tramp of thousands of feet. The soldiers were
dog tired. They wondered where they were going and when they would
stop. No one knew. Sometime before daylight the railroad tracks no
longer vibrated. The last train had left Corinth. Finally the sun climbed
into a dust-filled sky and sent its scorching rays down onto the men's
heads and shoulders.[49]

Wagons jammed the road. Exhausted men—and the usual stragglers—dropped out of column and drifted to the back. An officer reported that the number of stragglers was large. Old Butch and his friend Old Jack had fallen out of rank and were straggling behind when they found a bunch of pigs. They had been ordered not to shoot or make noise. Butch and Jack, hungry for meat, were driving the pigs "along to a place where we could capture one without noise and had them in a lane where a log lay parallel to the fence." Jack was standing at the end of the log with his fixed bayonet and the pigs were between the fence and the log when an officer rode up and snarled, "Move on!"

"We don't belong to your command," Jack said.

"Move on or I will have you arrested," the officer barked.

Butch hurried the pigs and Jack impaled one on his bayonet, then, shouldering the gun with the pig fast on the bayonet, the two marched out at quick time.[50]

The column plodded on through the day. After more than twenty-four hours on the road, the Ninth finally halted. The men were worn out and hungry—except Butch and Jack. The provision wagons were far ahead of the famished men. After a night's rest the regiment moved on south for two more days before making camp to rest and organize the scattered commands.[51]

Beauregard had sneaked away with his entire army, "without confusion or loss of a cartridge," a Texan said. "No artillery of any description was lost; no clothing; no tents worth removal were left standing," Beauregard reported.[52]

When the Federals attacked Corinth the morning after Beauregard left, they found a ghost town defended by only a few Quaker guns, logs of about the diameter of cannon mounted on wheels. The Yanks were angry and horridly embarrassed that the enemy had escaped from right under their very noses. They had labored and sweated for nearly two months to get at the Rebels. In fact, they had already counted their chickens, and now they were furious. Beauregard was gone with every man and every cannon. The Yankees rightfully blamed their commander, overcautious Henry Halleck, for the debacle. The Rebels congratulated Beauregard and themselves on the masterful retreat.[53]

In addition to skillfully laying his plans for retreat, Beauregard had reorganized his two armies before starting south. The Sixth and Ninth

Texas were placed in a brigade commanded by Brig. Gen. Charles W. Phifer. The Third Texas and the First Texas Legion (Whitfield's Battalion, also known as the Twenty-seventh Texas Cavalry) were in another brigade commanded by Col. Louis Hébert, a Louisiana Creole. Old Butch thought the Texas regiments were separated because "the four regiments were too bad to use as soldiers when they were all together."[54]

The Ninth camped south of Booneville to rest and drill for a few days. Several men came down with flu and others were still dragging around with dysentery or other ailments contracted in the pesthole of Corinth. Friday, June 6, the men marched south on a good road running along the railroad's east side toward Saltillo. Three days later they passed through Mooreville and set up camp in a pleasant stand of timber and "fixed for a stay." The fix did not last. They moved a couple of miles the next day and again set up camp, this time on a clear creek, a tributary to the Tombigbee, about a dozen miles west of the Alabama state line.[55]

With camps established, orders were announced establishing strict discipline and regular training, infantry training. The day began with dress parade before sunrise and ended with dress parade at sunset. Companies drilled three hours each morning and battalions drilled three hours each afternoon. Besides regular dress parade, there were reviews and inspections. Saturday afternoons the men were excused from drill to do their washing. On Sunday only dress parade was held.[56]

Dress parades were not always dressy. Sul Ross wrote his wife that his men were "almost in a state of nudity" and that a third of his regiment appeared at a review barefoot. Another group of Ross's men, whose pants had been "expended in the public service," drilled in their underdrawers.[57]

"It was here [near Mooreville] we got our soldiers' schooling," Butch recalled. General Phifer, an old West Pointer, began taming the wild Texas boys. Butch thought Phifer a rigid, hard-nosed taskmaster. Confederate soldiers were peculiar in that they were always ready to fight but never ready to submit to routine duty and discipline. They were determined to be soldiers according to their own notions. Later, Butch said of Phifer, "He worried with us, he stormed at us, he cursed at us, he put us to the severest tests, he punished us." But when the boys had learned, Phifer "rewarded [us] by pronouncing us the best and most efficient brigade in the army."[58]

One day Phifer posted a guard at the creek to keep horses out of the stream where the men got their "using water." To test the guard, Phifer rode down to the creek and started to cross.

The guard languidly rose from his log seat and raised his gun. He commanded, "Halt," and told the general he could not ride into the water.

Phifer glared at the soldier and said, "By whose orders do you presume to halt your commanding officer?"

The Texan drawled, "Don't know, suppose it was old Phifer or some other damned ol' galoot and I'll kill yer if yer go in thar."[59]

Sul Ross felt that Charles Phifer was well qualified to make soldiers out of the wild Texans. And Ross and Phifer were not strangers. As a lieutenant, Phifer had served with Captain Ross and Major Van Dorn at the battle of Washita, back in 1858, when Ross and Van Dorn were wounded. When Phifer was away from the brigade, which happened often, he left Ross in command.[60]

Reuben, healthy as always, served daily guard duty during July and August training. He and the rest of the dismounted Texans marched in the Mississippi heat and learned why their commanding general, Braxton Bragg, was known as a strict disciplinarian, a reputation Bragg brought with him from the U.S. Army. He had taken command when Davis removed Beauregard from command over an infraction.[61]

Braxton Bragg was a dour, terrible-tempered, forty-five-year-old major general who had dyspepsia and an acid personality to match. Six feet tall and slender, with stiff silvered beard and hair, one glance warned of his rigidity. A stern West Pointer, Bragg held a deep dedication to military rules that made him inflexible and often unreasonable. Like many prewar officers, he was eminently capable of training and organizing, but the fog of battle shrouded his nerve.

Few officers or men who served under Bragg had a kind word to say of him. Nurse Kate Cumming wrote, "It is said he makes a perfect pastime of shooting the men, and not long ago he had one shot for killing a pig." A famous tale known throughout the officer corps of both armies relates an incident that happened at a small frontier post before the war. Bragg commanded a company and also served as post quartermaster.

Company commander Bragg sent a requisition to Quartermaster Bragg that Quartermaster Bragg turned down. Company commander Bragg returned his requisition in more demanding form to Quartermaster Bragg, who again turned it down. Unable to resolve the problem, Bragg took the correspondence to his commanding officer for a decision. The officer read the papers, looked up at Bragg, and said, "My god, Mr. Bragg, you've argued with every officer in the army and now you're arguing with yourself."[62]

Bragg's organizational abilities could have served the Confederacy well in another capacity, but like all West Pointers he wanted to command an army in the field, a position he held long after he should have been removed. In Mexico, Bragg's artillery had turned defeat into victory for Col. Jefferson Davis's Mississippi Rifles during the battle of Buena Vista. The victory gained Davis the military fame he coveted and chiseled in granite Davis's debt to the cantankerous officer. And Davis paid his debts with equal ferocity to friend or foe.

In camp at Mooreville the Texans witnessed the results of Bragg's rigid adherence to military law. David Garrett wrote home that the Conscription Act

kicked up a fuss for a while, but since they shot about twenty-five for mutiny and whipped and shaved the heads of as many more . . . everything has got quiet and goes on as usual. The court martial here is in session most of the time & they think no more of shooting a man than we used to do of taking a drink.

Newton, back from the hospital, avoided watching the firing squads execute deserters. "Did not want to," he wrote. Although "they said it was done that discipline might be maintained in the army," Newt was convinced that the "surest, mightiest force with which to maintain discipline is a wise, good general in whom all the soldiers have the utmost confidence . . . the army had no confidence in [Bragg] at all. General Price had few deserters, because his soldiers loved him."[63]

Reuben, with his strong Christian background and the Rogers family trait of frontier independence, was revolted by the whippings and executions, but he grimly did his duty, envying his younger brothers, plowing the good black soil of Tarrant County, where Pa's impatience was the worst threat.

The Ninth was not under the direct supervision of Bragg. Brigadier General Maury, who had served as Van Dorn's adjutant in Arkansas, commanded the division that included the Ninth. He was a charming, urbane Virginia gentleman, a West Pointer who did not take himself too seriously.[64]

Maury later wrote of the Texas cavalrymen in his memoir:

This Texas brigade was one of the finest bodies of men ever seen in any service, but had no idea of accurate discipline. Their colonel [Sul Ross] was a very handsome, poetical-looking young fellow, with voice and manner gentle as a woman's, and the heart of a true soldier of Texas. . . . He had not then the least conception of discipline; so I and my staff devoted ourselves to Ross's brigade, for every potato patch and green apple tree drew them from the ranks until we drove them back again. On the march I usually wore an old suit of corduroy and a light felt hat, and these Texans had never seen me before.

I heard one fellow say, "I wonder who that little fellow is, in that white coat, anyhow? Where did he come from? He's goin' to keep us up close, you bet; he keeps on at it." Another called out to his comrades plundering a melon patch, "Look out, boys! Here comes the pro vo!" A third informed Ross, confidentially, to whom he was giving some green peas just foraged, "If that little fellow don't quit his foolishness, he'll git the stuffin' knocked out of him, first thing he knows."

I devoted especial attention to this brigade for nearly a month, and they hated me accordingly. But after we had been in action together, they used to cheer me . . . and call me "Little Dab". . . they were true men and self-reliant soldiers. Each man with his repeating rifle was a small fortress.[65]

Despite the marching and discipline, the Texans had things to be thankful for. A little mail trickled in from Texas by courier, and rations were better. Baking ovens furnished the novelty of bread. In addition, some men became expert in making light bread and other "little knick knacks" that a cavalryman seldom makes. The ex-cavalrymen learned from the real infantrymen how to make pies, cobblers, and apple dumplings. When the corn filled out, the men fattened on roasting ears. They gorged on peaches and apples after months of living on rancid lard and cornmeal. Water wells dug at the camps furnished good water, a blessing after drinking sludge at Corinth. The boys were feeling good and looked like new men.[66]

Decent food, regular sleep, and pure water improved everyone's health and temper, despite the monotony of camp. Moreover, the men were being paid regularly—a rarity in the Confederate service—and could buy a few knickknacks from the peddlers. In addition, convalescents, including Gus Creed's brother George, were returning from area homes and hospitals. Some men were still sick, but the rage of contagious diseases had abated, and even chronic dysentery had decreased with the better diet. All in all, Gris felt the regiment was doing quite well for infantry. But still, they were infantrymen.[67]

Officers of the four dismounted Texas regiments resented serving in the infantry as much, if not more, than the men. Gris reported, "Every effort is being made to get us again mounted & after sundry applications to Generals Van Dorn & Price there was an order issued to send an officer to Texas to collect them [the horses] & bring them to us." Sul Ross's men were "perfectly intoxicated with delight" at the prospect of getting their horses again, and anticipated "much sport" when again mounted. August 29, Company A's Capt. Thomas G. Berry rode out of camp toward Texas to retrieve the Ninth's mounts.[68]

In addition to the prospect of getting their horses back, war news brightened the men's spirits. In Virginia, Robert E. Lee had thrashed the Yankees twice during the summer, first in front of Richmond at the battle of Seven Days, in June, and again at the second battle of Manassas, the last of August. Victory again perched upon the Confederate banner. Also, Confederate cavalrymen John Hunt Morgan and Nathan Bedford Forrest were leading blue troopers on merry chases around Tennessee and Kentucky.[69]

When the war started, Nathan Bedford Forrest, a rich plantation owner and slave trader, turned his broad back on a million dollars in Mississippi and Tennessee property to join the Confederate army. He was forty years old, tall, lithe, and powerfully built. He entered service as a private, but a month later the two stars of a lieutenant colonel adorned his custom-tailored collar. Shortly after his success at Shiloh, he wore the three wreathed stars of a Confederate brigadier general. For Forrest, decisive and immeasurably practical, instinctively understood what war was about.

During July 1862, Forrest was in Middle Tennessee cutting Federal communication, tearing up railroads, capturing Yankees, and freeing imprisoned Rebels. His uncanny ability to evade every blue detachment sent after him caused smiles and cheers in Mississippi. The dismounted Texas cavalrymen relished Forrest's triumphs and envied his troopers, galloping from success to success.[70]

The Texans felt they too were in good fighting condition and were ready for some victories. David wrote home that the

> boys are in better spirits now than they have been since we left home . . . none of us want to come home until we run the last Fed from our soil. You need not look for me until our little confederacy comes out in flying colors . . . I am content to remain in the army.

Decent food, regular pay, and the prospect of again being mounted cheered the dismounted Texans.[71]

CHAPTER 6

CANNON FODDER

September 4–December 7, 1862

The Texas regiments and their brigades moved a few miles west "to guard against plundering Feds" along the Mobile & Ohio near Tupelo. Braxton Bragg took his Army of Mississippi north to Tennessee, and Earl Van Dorn was transferred to command at Vicksburg. That left Sterling Price in command of the Army of the West, which included seven dismounted Texas, Arkansas, and Missouri cavalry regiments scattered through the army's two divisions. Brig. Gen. Dabney H. Maury commanded one of Price's divisions; Brig. Gen. Henry Little of Missouri commanded the other.[1]

The men from west of the Mississippi River were pleased as a hungry trooper with a pig when bilious old Bragg and vainglorious Van Dorn left them with Price. The westerners believed they had the right to be commanded by one of their own, and they liked and trusted Old Pap. Gris Griscom was sure the Missouri general had the full confidence of all his men.[2]

It was late August 1862. After three months of infantry training, the rowdy Texas boys were getting restless. They were the tough, hardened survivors of Indian Territory, Pea Ridge, Corinth's dysentery, and Braxton Bragg's special variety of discipline. They wanted their horses back, but as long as they had to stay in the infantry they were ready to move. Reuben Rogers, Amos Burgoon, John Dunn, and Gus and George Creed were among the sixty-six restless troopers present for duty in Company A.[3]

Generals in the region, both blue and gray, were also beginning to fidget. The Union's timid commander, Maj. Gen. Henry Halleck, had been transferred to Washington, leaving U. S. Grant in command of the department. Grant, never content to remain inactive, garrisoned Corinth and sent part of his forces to follow Bragg north into Tennessee. Price, in turn, was told to follow Grant's men. The Missourian quickly set his army in motion.[4]

The Ninth received orders Thursday, September 4, to send off all its heavy baggage—everything the men could not carry on their backs or in a few wagons. At 7:00 A.M. Saturday, the regiment took up the line of march north in the direction of Corinth. The temperature soared as the day wore on. Caissons and wagons, marching men and animals pulverized the roads, creating a dense fog of dust. Twelve miles down the road that evening, each step the men had taken registered in their feet and back muscles. Their heels were blistered and their backs ached from shifting knapsacks, haversacks, canteens, guns, cap boxes, and cartridge boxes loaded with forty rounds of ammunition. One Texan said his feet felt as if his shoes were filled with hot embers. Dirt parched their throats, clogged their eyes and ears. Every man in the Ninth sighed with relief when they settled into camp north of Saltillo. They were glad for the next few days' rest while they waited for the balance of the army to catch up.[5]

Price's entire army—artillery, cavalry, wagon trains, and all—arrived four days later, Wednesday, September 10. At noon the next day the army set out northeast toward a Yankee encampment at Iuka, on the Memphis & Charleston twenty miles east of Corinth. Rain and sultry late-summer heat slowed the march. By Friday night Price, unsure of what might lay ahead, was becoming impatient with the army's sluggish progress. At first light the next morning the Ninth moved out at quick time but soon slowed to a crawl when a battery moving toward the front preempted the road. With the road again open, the pace picked up, but it soon slowed again. Under low clouds the men tramped north past houses and farmsteads sacked and burned by the Yankees. A full moon rose on the dust-caked, weary men, but night brought no rest. They trudged on, often standing in line of march when the long column ceased to move for reasons unknown to the privates. They had covered only sixteen miles by dawn. Finally, they halted for an hour to roasted beef and field peas, which they gulped without salt or bread. Eleven miles farther up the road they reached Iuka, a beautiful little resort town known for its

Iuka, Mississippi

mineral springs. It was noon. The men had been on the road over thirty hours.[6]

The lead brigades easily drove off the enemy, who abandoned everything in his haste. The Confederates took possession of the town with its million dollars in U.S. quartermaster and commissary stores, including wagons, flour, crackers, corn, salt, "and many luxuries and plenty of the latter." The regiments that entered the town broke into the sutlers' shops and commissary stores laden with cheese, preserves, mackerel, coffee, canned milk, lager beer, fine wines. Forgetting their fatigue, the hungry troops reveled in the immense stores of Yankee "sow belly and crackers"—bacon and hardtack.[7]

When the wagon trains came up the next day, the infantrymen were ordered to cook two days' rations, but before the food was done orders came to form in line. Grant, wondering what Price was up to, had gathered fifteen thousand men to challenge the Rebels occupying Iuka. The two armies maneuvered and skirmished north of town for the next four days. Rain began to fall, and like the Arkansas winter, it was in no hurry to abandon the area. Food spoiled in the humid heat, and men slept in the mud.[8]

Friday, September 19, dawned warm and clear, good maneuvering weather. At 3:00 P.M., an excited courier dashed up to General Price with the astonishing information that the enemy was advancing from the *south*. Grant had sent Maj. Gen. William S. Rosecrans with two divisions to attack the Rebels' rear. Price ordered out on double quick Louis Hébert's Brigade, which included the Third Texas and the First Texas Legion.[9]

Hurrying along the road, an officer rode up to Hébert and asked, "General, must we fix bayonets?"

"Yes, Sir!" the General barked. "What for you have ze bayonet, if you no fix him? Yes, by gar, fix him, fix him![10]

Hébert ordered his men forward. Victor described the scene:

As the brigade marched with slow and solemn tread down a slight declivity in the direction of the enemy, a little dog . . . trotted along in advance of the line, apparently oblivious to the thunders of artillery, the rattle of rifles, and the whizzing of missiles that literally filled the air.

The opposing lines soon were only three hundred yards apart, so near that men in the Third heard a Federal officer bark, "Double charge with grape and canister!" The Rebels charged.[11]

The double-shotted grape and canister tore huge holes in the Confederate line. The Texans, in the center of the battle, fell by the score before the Federal advance was finally halted. When "night put an end to the carnage," three regiments, the Third, the Legion, and the Third Louisiana, had done most of the fighting, each losing close to a hundred men. Col. Hinchie P. Mabry of the Third had been wounded three times and captured. Col. John W. Whitfield of the Legion had been shot in the shoulder. Their division commander, Brig. Gen. Henry Little, was dead, killed instantly when a bullet crashed into his skull above his left eye.[12]

The Ninth, held in reserve, had watched their fellow Texans charge the Federal cannon and drive back the enemy. Twenty-two men in the Third were killed, 74 wounded—one of four men present and the heaviest losses of any regiment. Iuka had cost Price his friend and division leader, Henry Little, and 1,500 men killed, wounded, or captured. The privates lay on the battlefield that night, the wounded untended, the dead where they had fallen. Long after midnight a few officers, each carrying a flickering candle, buried Henry Little in a cottage garden.[13]

With Grant to the north and Rosecrans to the southwest, Price reluctantly decided to return to Baldwyn and make contact with Van Dorn. Under the bright moon, teamsters started their wagons south at three Saturday morning. The men, rousted from their sleep by equally exhausted officers, set out at first light. Despite numbing fatigue, the lead columns covered fifteen miles by noon. David Garrett wrote home from Tupelo a week later:

> *All our boys are in the retreating order, for I can assure you we have been making it in double quick time on a retreat from Iuka about fifty miles from this place. We marched up to Iuka in double quick and made about 20,000 Feds skedaddle from there and captured about half a million of stores. When we thought we were in the enjoyment of ease & plenty good things the Feds came down from Corinth in force of forty thousand & then you ought to have seen 12,000 Confederates skedaddling down south.*[14]

While the army was on the march, David became ill. He begged to remain with his company, but the surgeon sent him to the hospital in Tupelo. David was more upset over being away from his regiment than being sick. "I am lost when away from my command," he said, and "shall join it as soon as I can get to it."[15]

Newton Keen also was sick during the retreat. He wrote: "I with some thirty others were left sick by the side of the road with the mumps. The whole outfit had them. We constructed a brush arbor and lay under it. We had but little to eat and no medical attention whatever." Newton rejoined his regiment in a few days.[16]

The Ninth tramped the last fifteen miles to Baldwyn the third day after the battle. They remained in camp a couple of days, then set out northwest over unfamiliar country, covering sixteen miles the first day to camp in a creek bottom. At midnight a rainstorm swept through the area, soaking everyone and everything. The men tried to dry their soggy blankets the next morning but were ordered out before the smudgy fires had done their job. When the Ninth and the rest of Price's army reached Ripley the next day, they found Van Dorn and his command waiting. Buck had marched his small army east to join Price.[17]

★   ★   ★

Van Dorn later reported that in southern Mississippi he surveyed "the whole field of operations before me calmly and dispassionately" and "the conclusion forced itself irresistibly upon my mind that the taking of Corinth was a condition precedent to the accomplishment of anything of importance." Therefore, "an attack on Corinth was a military necessity, requiring prompt and vigorous action." With what he called "mature deliberation," he decided to attempt Corinth.[18]

Maj. Gen. Dabney H. Maury

Van Dorn counted 22,000 men available to challenge the railroad junction. Nearly 14,000 were Price's Army of the West, but Major General Van Dorn ranked Major General Price, so there was no question of who was in command. The Sixth and the Ninth Texas Cavalry were in Brig. Gen. C. W. Phifer's Brigade of Brig. Gen. Dabney H. Maury's Division. The First Texas Legion and the Third Texas Cavalry were in Brig. Gen. Louis Hébert's First Division. Van Dorn, "fully alive to the responsibility" of his position as commander of the army, ordered the combined forces out of Ripley on the morning of September 29, on its way Corinth.[19]

At noon that day Col. Dud Jones and his men loaded all but their marching gear into wagons. They hurried to prepare three days' rations but, as usual, were ordered into line before the food was half done. When they passed Van Dorn's headquarters in Ripley, they grudgingly gave the general a war whoop. At least they did not have to stand in the sun and listen to "Behold, your leader!" Unhappy at being under Van Dorn's command again, Newton wrote, "Van Dorn took command, which we all very much regretted . . . we had no confidence in him as a man brave in battle."[20]

The army covered ten miles a day on hot, dusty roads for the next few days. Van Dorn was leading them on a roundabout march to get

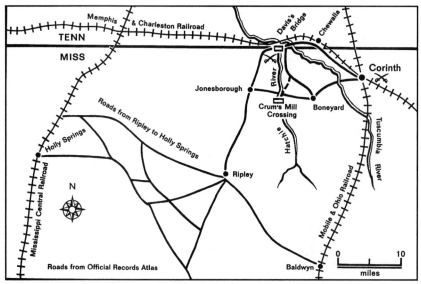

Corinth Campaign—Northeastern Mississippi

north of Corinth in the hope of confusing the Federals. One evening after a long, hot march, the Confederates had a regal feast of muscadine grapes and papaws. When they reached the sixty-foot-wide Hatchie River, they stripped and jumped into deep, sluggish water to wash off fifty miles of sweat and dirt. Shouts and jests mingled with the ring of axes biting into trees. Pioneers were building a rough replacement for Davis's Bridge, which had been destroyed. The infantrymen crossed before daylight the next morning and set out east toward Chewalla, leaving their wagon trains between the Hatchie and the Tuscumbia with the First Texas Legion and two batteries. They marched another ten miles that day.[21]

Reveille brought the soldiers to their feet at 4:00 A.M., Friday, October 3. An hour later they started toward Corinth, only a few miles ahead. The country was dry, water scarce. The temperature rose rapidly, and dust soon filled the air, irritating the men's eyes and parching their throats.[22]

Price deployed his divisions a mile and a half from the enemy's outer ring of fortification between the tracks of the Memphis & Charleston and the Mobile & Ohio. Maury was on the right, Hébert on the left, and two brigades in reserve. The men Van Dorn had brought were right of Price, which placed the Sixth and Ninth Texas in the center of the Confederate line.[23]

The Confederates soon drove the enemy's advance skirmishers into their fortifications surrounding the railroad junction. At 10:00 A.M., Van Dorn ordered his entire line forward. The Ninth, held in reserve north of the Memphis & Charleston during the morning, was ordered into the battle three hours later. Under the blistering sun, double-shotted canister and small arms fire tore into the ranks. The men closed up and steadily pushed the enemy back toward his breastworks. Soon the "bloody battle ground [was] literally strewed with dead from the unerring aim of mus-

Battle of Corinth

kets from 60 to 150 yards distant." The Ninth, with the rest of Maury's Division, had driven the Federals into their main works by 5:00 P.M. When darkness silenced the guns, the hungry Texans searched haversacks of Yankee dead and had a hardy supper by moonlight. Commissary sergeants also brought cooked rations to the extreme front lines.[24]

Sul Ross's Sixth also had driven the Yankees that morning. In the afternoon the Sixth made contact with a Yankee battery of nine guns supported by infantry. They charged through Spanish and post oak timber. Newt remembered:

Our ranks were fearfully thinned, the boys falling in every direction. The trees were tumbling in every direction and the limbs flying through the air. The ground [was] burst into holes and ditches by the mighty force of the cannon balls, but we went through it all up to the very mouth of the battery when the [enemy] gunners and infantry fled. . . . In a moment the whole air seemed to be literally filled with grape shot and shell.

One of Newt's friends was killed by his side, "his blood and brains being scattered all around."[25]

The Confederates held their positions while skirmishing continued in the dark. During the evening Old Butch found a large piece of raw bacon in a Yankee haversack. Lying on his back below the line of fire, Butch sliced off chunks and tossed them to men around him. Lt. J. B. "Buster" Haynes was gnawing off a bite when a bullet struck him in the heart. "Boys, I'm wounded," he said. The boys carried Haynes back a short distance and laid him beside a log. He was dead.[26]

Later that night, after the moon had risen, Butch started to the ordnance wagon in the rear for ammunition. Long before reaching the wagons, he had gathered sufficient ammunition of all calibers from cartridge boxes of the dead.[27]

The Ninth carried their wounded, and many Yankees, to Surgeon James Robertson and his assistants. Still, hundreds of wounded lay groaning on the field. Through the tense night, mournful sounds from bleeding men mingled with

Caring for the Wounded

the distant rattle of railroad cars and the ring of a legion of axes felling timber beyond their front. The men were sure the Federals were being reinforced and adding to their abatis of felled trees with sharpened branches facing toward the Rebels.[28]

Union commander, Brig. Gen. William S. Rosecrans was not being reinforced; he would fight tomorrow with what he had. He spent the night nervously conferring with his four division commanders and seeing that each unit was in place. Exhausted from action and anxiety, the general finally lay down at 3:00 A.M.[29]

An hour later, the Texans moved back four hundred yards and formed in line of battle. Just at daybreak the earth shuddered three times—an earthquake, many men believed, and an obvious sign of impending disaster. Only instants later ten pieces of Price's artillery announced the second day of battle. When Union artillery answered, the Confederate army "rose to its feet as one man."[30]

The scene was grand, a U.S. officer wrote. Sounds of different calibers of guns at various ranges reminded him of "the chimes of Old Rome when all her bells rang out." Newt also was impressed, but he did not hear bells. To him, "the whole heavens lit up like belching volcanoes of fire and smoke."[31]

The Sixth and the Ninth were in the center of Maury's Division, near the center of the Confederate line. Deployed to their right were the Thirty-fifth Mississippi Infantry and the famous Second Texas Infantry, commanded by Col. William P. Rogers. When the artillery duel began, the infantrymen were ordered to lie down in line of battle. Shrieking solid shot tore through the forest, landing behind them. Tall oaks crashed to the ground, throwing limbs and splinters into the air. Although the shells burst harmlessly in the Texans' rear, "it took a steady nerve to lay under such terrific storms of bursting shell and solid shot," Newt said.[32]

Bugles blared at 10:00 A.M. Flags rippled along the entire mile-long battle line, a stirring sight to many. Four columns, including the Sixth and Ninth Texas, and Col. William P. Rogers's Second Texas Infantry, formed in regimental columns, two companies wide and five deep, to advance against a strong work bristling with muskets and cannon, Battery Robinett, which guarded their direct approach to Corinth.[33]

Ohio infantrymen guarding Battery Robinett watched in awe as dense columns of Confederates emerged from the timber. At 11:00 A.M., Maury ordered his men forward. "They started at us," an Ohio captain remembered, "with firm, slow, steady step. In my campaigning I had never seen anything so hard to stand as that slow, steady tramp. Not a sound was heard, but they looked as if they intended to walk over us."[34]

When the Confederates reached a 300-yard abatis protecting the battery, they slung aside branches and scrambled over fallen tree trunks, barely losing their alignment. Two hundred and fifty yards out, Battery Robinett's grape, canister, and cannon balls exploded into the ranks, tearing huge gaps in the columns. The Confederate line quivered but did not falter. "The whole earth trembled and the heavens were filled with the smoke of battle," a Texan remembered.[35]

After clearing the abatis, the Sixth and the Ninth halted a moment to re-form. When bugles again sounded, the Texans' Rebel yell tore through the air. The men fought their way through clouds of gun smoke up a low ridge fifty yards in front of the battery. The nervous Ohioans finally opened fire, mowing down the Texans like "chaff before a gale." When the battery's guns fell silent, no longer able to avoid hitting their own men, the Confederates' superior accuracy gunned down large portions of several Ohio regiments. Three times the Rebels charged, the second time at double quick, the third time at a run. Scaling the high works, they knocked the Federals off the guns with the breeches of their bayonetless muskets and took possession of Battery Robinett, but Union reinforcements poured in, forcing the Texans to retire. By 1:00 P.M., the single gray line was cut to pieces, many men falling among the battery's guns. The valiant Colonel Rogers, determined to make a grade or a grave that day, lay dead on the ramparts of Robinett, his body armor pierced by seven bullets. Maury's men were forced back all along the line while the division to their right mysteriously remained idle.[36]

A Union colonel said the Texans "advanced to the assault with great gallantry." Fighting hand-to-hand, the Sixth had reached to within six or eight yards of the enemy's line when a young Ohio private shot the Texans' color bearer and grabbed the Sixth's flag. "Save the colors!" an officer yelled, and put a bullet into the Ohioan's chest at the same moment. The boy made his way back to his line still clutching the Texans' flag.[37]

The Ninth and the rest of Price's men stumbled back as the murderous fire continued. Tearing their way through the abatis, men crumpled among the logs, bleeding and dying. The survivors staggered back half a mile to re-form in the timber, but they had done all they could. They were beaten and tortured by thirst. The temperature had risen to ninety-four degrees, and the men's canteens had been empty for hours.[38]

Gus and George had been fighting side by side in the trenches when George was shot. With a stab of anguish, Gus realized his brother was dead. In the hurried retreat, none of the Confederates, including Gus, managed to carry out their dead and wounded. The forty-eight hours of fighting cost the Ninth ninety-three men. Sul Ross's Sixth lost fifty killed—more than any other regiment in the Confederate army.[39]

Price's men had fought with extraordinary courage all along the line. Several regiments had forced their way into the center of Corinth before being driven out. Van Dorn reported: "A hand-to-hand contest was being enacted in the very yard of General Rosecrans' headquarters and in the streets of the town. It is impossible for me to do justice to the courage of my troops." Price reported that "the history of this war contains no bloodier page than that which will record this fiercely contested battle." Newt said of the day: "This was war to the knife. In places you could walk on the dead." That night Gris was sure the Ninth, in the center of the line, "bore the brunt of the battle."[40]

The Ninth and all Van Dorn's mangled regiments fell back west six miles to find water—and to get away from the guns. Many seriously wounded men walked the entire distance rather than risk capture. At daylight the next morning, thirty men from the Ninth and men from the other regiments returned to the battlefield under a flag of truce to bury their dead. Perhaps Gus returned to bury his brother and say his lonely farewells. He was six hundred miles and an eternity from home and family. It was Sunday, but nothing about the day would have suggested peace or love to Gus. Later he fell into line and started west with the retreating army. He had no choice.[41]

Van Dorn's army was in full retreat.

The Ninth marched behind their ordnance and supply wagons, their division in the lead. Jones and his men crossed the Tuscumbia River with no interference and marched to Davis's Bridge, spanning the Hatchie, but Federal reinforcements were already there. Ross, in command of Phifer's Brigade because the general was sick, sent his Sixth, the Ninth, and another regiment across the bridge.[42]

Newton Keen later wrote that he was

about half way over the bridge, and the head of Company C had just begun to step off the bridge when this strong force came sweeping up to the bridge. Three regiments were cut off who had gone to the right and up the river. They were forced to swim it while some further up found a foot way over . . . we poured such volleys of lead, grape and shell [on them] that we sent the Yankees flying back over the bridge, leaving the ground covered with their dead. I was down the river about 200 yards from the bridge and had a splendid position behind a large rock

at the edge of the water from which I was enabled to pour in a deadly
fire for some forty minutes or more. . . . We held this position [an
hour] then retreated.[43]

Old Butch was across the Hatchie Bridge that morning when grapeshot struck his gun, knocking him thirty feet. The shock deadened his
arms and hurt his head and chest. Lying beside the road kicking and
grunting, he saw the "Sixth's flag fall and captured, the only flag that
was ever lost by our brigade," he said. When Butch realized the Confederates were falling back in disorder, he leaped to his feet, terrified he
might be captured. Near the river, he saw his friends jumping into the
water to save themselves, but he turned toward the bridge. Fright took
precedence over pain as Butch raced a horseman across, beating him by
a head.

Searching for the regiment, Butch fell in with the enemy's advance.
Hungry, as always, he asked the Yanks for something to eat. "We got
nothing to eat but powder," they growled. Having "partaken of a suffi-
ciency of that article," Butch stepped aside and quickened his pace until
he came up with the Ninth's stragglers.[44]

All day Van Dorn's army passed down the east side of the Hatchie
on the Boneyard Road, seeking a way across the river to safety. Ross,
with parts of the Sixth and Ninth, formed the rear guard. Six miles
below Hatchie Bridge, the bridge at Crum's Mill had been burned, but
Price's cavalrymen had improvised a crossing by pulling down the gable
end of the mill onto the ancient mill dam. By the time the lead units
of the army reached the mill late in the afternoon, the cavalrymen had
smoothed the steep approach to the crude bridge and piled logs on the
bank for a bonfire to light the way after dark.[45]

When the Third Texas reached the rickety bridge that night, a large
bonfire burning on the west bank cast a flicker of light across the unique
bridge. Sterling Price was sitting his horse on the east bank, hurrying
each wagon and piece of artillery across. "Drive up there! Drive up!"
Price shouted to each teamster. The general remained on his horse all
night, urging his men across to safety.[46]

It was near midnight before the last of the Ninth crossed. Jones led
the regiment five miles west toward Jonesborough before daring to stop.
The men dropped to the ground exhausted. They had marched twenty-

five miles that day besides maneuvering and fighting for two hours. Safe from Yankee guns, they slept.[47]

Price's "whole wagon train came off without molestation or loss, except a few wagons that were broken down," the general reported. With the river finally between them and the enemy, "a mighty sigh of relief escaped ten thousand hearts when they realize their escape from the very jaws of destruction," a trooper wrote.[48]

During the battle of Hatchie Bridge the Ninth lost 6 men wounded and 24 missing. The three days around Corinth cost the regiment 149 killed, wounded, or missing out of less than 340 who went into the battle. The four Texas regiments lost 404. Prisoners of war were exchanged a week later and returned to their regiments or were sent to hospitals. Company A's Corp. Alva Knight, captured during the retreat and exchanged, decided enough was enough. He deserted.[49]

Van Dorn reported 505 of his men killed and a total loss of 4,800. Rosecrans reported burying 1,423 Confederates and capturing 2,300, a typical discrepancy of numbers. Rosecrans, of course, had no way of knowing how many wounded Rebels had been carried away. He reported U.S. casualties of 2,500. The butcher's bill was adding up on both sides.[50]

The morning after crossing the Hatchie on the mill dam, the Confederates "fell into the road pell-mell, and moved in any style [they] wished," a soldier said. Only a few Federals harassed the rear of the army. Newton remembered:

We marched until about eight in the morning and stopped to eat breakfast. We hastily made some fires and a few beeves were knocked in the head and each man began to roast him a piece in the fire. [When the Yankees appeared and cannon again began to roar], the breakfast business was smashed into cocks hat [Cox's hat]. I had two good corn dodgers and had succeeded in getting two large ribs of a hog pretty well roasted, that is[,] they had been well salted and burnt black in the fire. . . . I held to my ribs and fought and ate. This was the last time the Yankees disturbed our retreat.

Disheartened and numb with exhaustion, the men staggered toward Ripley, thankful they had saved their trains and that the enemy was content to leave them alone. From Ripley they turned west toward Holly Springs, thirty miles distant.[51]

The Federals did not press Van Dorn's fleeing army because Rosecrans felt his men were too worn from sleepless nights of preparation and three days of battle. Indeed, Rosecrans himself was too exhausted from exertions and apprehension to go any farther. He had allowed his troops a night's sleep before setting out after the Rebels. U. S. Grant was furious with Rosecrans for failing to follow up quickly, but he was miles away and could not see the exhausted Union survivors. By morning it was too late to capture Van Dorn's army, broken and battered though it was. Both armies were spent, but the fox was more motivated than the hounds.[52]

Dud Jones and his men plodded on, first on hot dusty roads, then in drenching rain. October 8, they were issued rations for the first time in five days. The men, however, were not starving. They had supplied themselves with Yankee coffee, bacon, and potatoes from abandoned haversacks on the battlefield. Three days later they made camp a few miles south of Holly Springs on the Mississippi Central Railroad. It had been five weeks to the day since they sent off their heavy baggage and started north toward Iuka and Corinth. Everyone was discouraged, hungry, and threadbare.[53]

Gus shivered in the cold autumn rain, physical exhaustion adding to his sorrow. Pain etched his face when he thought of George, the younger brother he had tried to look after. The severed double iron bonds of brothers and soldiers left Gus feeble with grief and loneliness. It had been a year since the brothers left family and friends in Tarrant County, and now George lay in a makeshift grave so far, so very far, from home.

Home. The men wondered if they ever again would see that cherished place. Around the evening fires, they must have talked of home and discussed their year in the Confederate army. Soldiering was not what they had imagined, especially with Van Dorn. Under Buck's command they had lost two major battles, lost two brigadier generals, lost their colonel, and lost their horses—and Gus had lost George. Serving in the infantry was gruesome work with no rewards. And surely by then they had learned that during the campaign not a single horseman in the two cavalry regiments of their division had been killed and only two had been wounded.[54]

Van Dorn's ranks and reputation were both depleted at Corinth. Others were as disgusted with the useless slaughter as were the privates. Van Dorn was relieved. Lt. Gen. John C. Pemberton would take command in Mississippi. Furthermore, a Missouri brigadier made a formal complaint against Van Dorn for failing to reconnoiter, insufficiently supplying his men with food, "hurling them upon the enemy" when they were exhausted, neglecting the wounded, and "cruel and improper treatment of officers and soldiers under his command"—the identical grievances follow the battle of Pea Ridge. A court of inquiry made up of Van Dorn's peers would exonerate the general, but neither the people of the South nor history would be so understanding.[55]

Two weeks after the army reached safety near Holly Springs, Federal couriers rode in under a flag of truce. They delivered a message to Van Dorn offering "Major-General Rosecrans' compliments to Major-General Van Dorn, commanding officer Confederate forces" and stating that "provision has been made for the burial of the dead, and a soldier's tribute will be paid those who fell fighting bravely, as did many in Maury's division."[56]

Astonished at the message, Gris wrote in his diary, "Quite a new feature in war for our enemy to compliment us." He must not have known that the two major generals, one wearing blue and the other gray, were old friends. Van Dorn, Rosecrans, and fifty-four other young men had spent four years eating and sleeping, drilling and studying together at West Point. They had graduated in 1842, Rosecrans near the top of the class, Van Dorn near the bottom. Now they were on opposite sides of a strange civil war where enemies were truly friends.[57]

Rosecrans also sent a message for Brig. Gen. Dabney Maury: "Tell Maury, with my regards, I never used to think when I taught him, a little, curly-headed boy at West Point, that he would ever trouble me as he has to-day." Awed by the courage displayed at Corinth, Rosecrans wrote in his official report: "I shall leave to pens dipped in poetic ink to inscribe the gorgeous pyrotechny of the battle and paint in words of fire the heroes of this fight."[58]

The Texas troopers, camped a few miles south of Van Dorn's headquarters, did not feel like heroes, and they deplored the infantry. Every mounted officer reminded them of how much easier life had been on horseback. While they sulked around camp, officers began reorganizing the reduced commands. Upon Colonel Jones's recommendation, Gris was assigned to duty as assistant adjutant general of the Ninth, replacing Lt. L. Atkins, who had been killed on top of Battery Robinett. Gris was promoted to first lieutenant, the proper rank of a regimental adjutant. His pay increased from $20 to $110 a month, first lieutenant's pay plus an additional $10 for serving as adjutant. Gris's duties included keeping the regiment's records, muster rolls, copies of orders and reports, and assisting Colonel Jones in the details of duty and discipline.[59]

Gris's rolls were severely reduced by the losses at Iuka and Corinth. The September–October 1862 roll of Company A, Ninth Texas, lists only forty-six men present for duty, 30 percent less than the roll reported the end of August.[60]

In the reshuffling that inevitably follows a change in command, the War Department reminded Pemberton that regiments from the same state should be placed in the same brigade. The Third, the Sixth, the Ninth, and the First Texas Legion (also known as Whitfield's Texas Legion or the Twenty-seventh Texas Cavalry) were brigaded together as Whitfield's Brigade, but they more often were known as the Texas Brigade. Colonel Sul Ross, the ranking officer present, commanded the Texans. Colonel John W. Whitfield, having been shot through the shoulder at Iuka, was on medical leave. The Texans remained in Maury's Division, which was made up of eighteen Texas, Arkansas, and Mississippi regiments. Two weeks after the reorganization Maury was promoted to major general for his valor at Corinth—a well-deserved reward.[61]

During the next couple of weeks the Ninth drilled and stood inspection, often in bitter cold. October 25, a regular Texas wet northerner dumped three inches of snow on the still-green trees. Jones's men were without tents, and a frigid wind bit through their thin clothes. While the cold spell hung on, the Yankees pushed the Rebels out of Holly Springs. The Ninth moved south twenty miles to Abbeyville, but the other three Texas regiments had been remounted and detached from Maury's Division. Through November the Ninth guarded the railroad, played ball, and watched for Tom Berry and the horses.[62]

December 2, the army moved south through Oxford and headed toward Grenada. Four days later a "cold sleety rain fell upon us," Maury later wrote. That night the general, having paid the owner, allowed his men to pull down the rails of a fence to build fires, a rare privilege. Blazing timbers cheered the wet men while the officers dined and slept in a large, comfortable plantation home. A couple of nights later, Maury began waking the men at 2:00 A.M. "I found them peacefully sleeping," he remembered, "the line of white blankets looking weird in the flickering light of the camp-fires." While waking the men, a "fierce old Texan" called out to Maury, "Somebody'll shoot you directly, ef you don't quit goin' about here makin' so much fuss!"[63]

Reuben, Gus, and the fierce old Texan slung their blankets over their shoulders and fell into line of march with Maury's infantry. South of Grenada, they crossed the Yallabusha on a bridge made of old ferryboats and made camp in the mud.[64]

Chapter 7

Horses! Horses!

December 8, 1862–January 7, 1863

Capt. Thomas Berry rode into the Ninth's muddy camp Monday, December 8, 1862. Behind him rode a column of mounted men, each leading four saddled horses. Reuben Rogers's heart surely leaped when he spotted his younger brother Jesse among the riders. They had parted fourteen months before, too long for brothers who had always been close.[1]

Jesse, who had turned eighteen in July, was of medium height and lithe, with a shock of brown hair framing his smooth face. With wide-set blue eyes, he looked innocent and vulnerable next to his tall, muscular, battle-toughened brother. The boys must have pounded each other on the back and both talked at once, laughing and joking to disguise their emotions. Jesse would have had a million questions, anything from where to water the horses to how it felt to be in battle.

Two other brothers pounded one another on the back when the riders arrived. A. W. Sparks had been away with the horses for eight months while John marched with the infantry. John longed to hear about home and the family. How were Ma, Pa, and their sisters? A.W. was eager to learn about John's trip from Arkansas and about serving in the infantry.[2]

Jesse and Reuben, A.W. and John, all the new men and the old, spent the entire day jostling and joking, catching up on the news. They sorted letters and packages from home, tried on new shirts mothers and wives had carefully stitched. Some sneaked off to quiet places to savor letters from their sweethearts. But the horses claimed the day. Laughing and chatting, the men fed and watered, curried and pampered their animals. It was a joyous day.[3]

Jesse and the other recruits had learned a few things about being cavalrymen by the time they reached Mississippi. During the six-hundred-mile, ten-week trip, the returning veterans must have assailed them with cavalry stories, likely of more fabrication than fact. And Berry surely began their training on the trip. The boys, having grown up on the frontier, knew how to ride and shoot, but they knew nothing of military rules and regulations.

Four of Company A's seven men who had taken the horses home returned with Berry. The captain also brought four recruits from around Grapevine, including Jesse Rogers and his sixteen-year-old friend, David Cate. The boys had enlisted in Company A on September 26, when Berry was in northern Tarrant County hunting men to fill his company.[4]

If each of the ten companies brought in only four recruits, the regiment was far short of the number needed to bring it back up to strength. Since the first of the year over fifty men had been killed in battle and seventy-five had been wounded. Another seventy or more had died of disease or returned to Texas.[5]

Around the evening campfires Jesse told Reuben and A.W. told John of their adventures on the trail. A.W. and the other riders who had left Des Arc in April had delivered the horses and visited their homes. In early August they rendezvoused and grudgingly began the march to Mississippi. A.W. later wrote:

> We had been on the march for several days and were encamped on the Red River. The men were in bad spirits, threatening mutiny, when we received orders to return . . . gather up our horses and carry them back to the brigade. There was great joy in the camp.[6]

Back in Texas, Berry ordered men from each company to gather the animals and meet him in a couple of weeks at Mount Pleasant, A.W.'s Titus County home. Meanwhile, Berry scoured North Texas and East Texas for recruits.[7]

The Ninth had advertised across the area for three to five hundred men to fill the ranks, but few Texans were willing to cross the Mississippi River as infantrymen. However, Jesse enlisted when he learned the Ninth was to be remounted. He and David Cate surely left Tarrant County with Berry the day they signed up.[8]

Berry, with his recruits, the veterans, and the Texas mustangs, left Mount Pleasant in late September. The men had rigged the horses to be led by tying the reins or a halter rope of one horse to the tail of the next and stringing the animals out one behind the other. The rider looped the reins or rope of the lead horse around his saddle horn and held the end in his hand. If the string became unruly, the rider could release the guide rope to prevent the string from throwing his mount.[9]

Berry and his men reached Shreveport, then rode on to Monroe and east toward Vicksburg. A few miles west of the river city a Yankee patrol was reported. The column hurried toward the protection of Vicksburg's cannon, each man urging "his four broncos to a quick time march." As the riders struggled to control their charges, a mortar shell ten to twelve inches in diameter struck nearby and rolled along the ground. The men passed "perilously close to these huge iron monsters," but the shells sailed overhead and crashed into the trees. When the column reached the Mississippi River opposite Vicksburg, a steam ferry took them across. A.W., Jesse, and the other riders camped at Vicksburg's fairgrounds that evening. They watched in fascination as exploding shells and rockets arched overhead in the dark sky. Three days later they reached the regiment.[10]

Jesse told Reuben about his trip and how he talked Pa out of a horse and saddle in order to sign up with Berry. He reported that the family was fine but affairs in Tarrant County were far from normal. Comanche raids had increased in neighboring counties since the U.S. Army no longer patrolled. The Federal blockade of the Texas coast had cut off supplies of coffee, paper, ink, cotton cards, baking soda, bootblack, all manufactured goods. People made what they needed or did without. Poll taxes and property taxes had doubled. Prices of grains had quadrupled. Most men—from teenagers to those forty-five years old—were away with the army, throwing the labor of farming on the young and the old, and often the women. The Rogers boys knew their four younger brothers were working from sunup to sundown. Jesse was glad to be in Mississippi with Reuben.[11]

Tuesday morning all the remounted cavalrymen eagerly began oiling saddles and patching together rigging. They stripped unnecessary leather from their cow saddles and improvised carbine slings, rifle rings, missing bridles and halters. Fortunately, their horses were in excellent condition. Tom Berry had done his job well, as always.[12]

The regiment was detached from the infantry that day and reported directly to Maj. Gen. Dabney Maury, who immediately ordered the Ninth to move camp away from the infantry and begin drilling on horseback. The general personally instructed the officers for a few days.[13]

When A.W. saw Maury for the first time, he was unimpressed with the general. He wrote that Maury

> was a small man and did not make the appearance . . . . a Major General should, for he was remarkable plain . . . even his orderly looked more like an officer. But soldiers who pointed him out to me said that in courage and wisdom he was second to no man in the army.[14]

Little Dab, still curly-headed and youthful, had proved his worth.

The Rogers and Sparks boys' regiment was the last of the Texas Brigade to be remounted. A month earlier, when the Confederates were pushed out of Holly Springs, the men of the Third and Sixth decided not to march without their horses, which they knew were near. Victor Rose wrote, "When the drums beat to 'fall in' the sound was absolutely drowned by deafening cries, 'Horses! Horses!' " General Whitfield appealed to the men. They answered, "Horses! Horses!" General Maury appealed to them. "Horses! Horses!" they shouted.[15]

Col. John S. Griffith—who lost a tuft of whiskers on Chustenahlah Creek—ordered his Sixth Texas to fall in. "Horses! Horses!" resounded. Griffith asked the men not to "tarnish their honor, and place a bar sinister upon the escutcheon of Texas." Only one man failed to respond. "Go, sir, and obey orders," Griffith barked at the laggard, "or I will run you through with my saber!"[16]

"My, how bully I felt when I got on my horse," Newton Keen recalled. The Sixth's horses had arrived in Mississippi in poor condition, having been brought from Texas by an officer less capable than Tom Berry. The horn was broken on Newt's saddle, but it did not matter. To Newt "a pair of ribs between ones legs felt very wholesome all the same." David Garrett's horse and saddle arrived without his spurs and bridle, and his captain's horse had died on the trip. The Sixth rode out some fifteen miles that first day to find fodder and corn for their lean horses. They also found pork and sweet potatoes, which the men feasted on that evening.[17]

Monday, December 15, a week after A.W. and Jesse arrived, the Ninth received orders to report to Maj. Gen. Earl Van Dorn at Grenada before daylight the next morning. The troopers hurriedly gathered their gear and prepared to march. By a couple of hours after midnight they were on their way. No one had any idea where they were going, and none of the officers would tell them. The junior officers did not know, and Colonel Jones was not about to tell. Jesse and his friend David Cate had trained with the cavalry only three days, and although they were ignorant of the fact, they were off on a raid—a genuine, first-class, hell-for-leather Confederate cavalry raid.[18]

The expedition had been quickly organized. Gen. U. S. Grant had forced the Rebels south and was moving inexorably toward Vicksburg, the last Confederate stronghold on the Mississippi River. Grant, marching south along the railroad, had reached Oxford. He was supplying his thirty thousand men by rail from Kentucky through Tennessee and into Mississippi. In anticipation of the spring campaign, Grant had built up a huge supply depot at Holly Springs, Van Dorn's old headquarters.[19]

Col. John S. Griffith, commanding the Texas Brigade, knew his men were bored with inactivity and impatient to be off on their horses. He thought about the coming spring campaigns and Grant's tempting depot, less than a hundred miles north. Griffith surmised that with another brigade or two and a daring leader, the depot and the railroad track leading north could be destroyed, thus forcing Grant to retreat. Officers of the four Texas regiments eagerly accepted Griffith's plan and agreed to request Earl Van Dorn as their corps leader. Many Texas officers had known Van Dorn in Texas before the war, and others were aware of his reputation. The Mississippian, then a major in the respected Second Cavalry, had earned a reputation in the Lone Star State as an efficient cavalry officer and brave man of action. The Texans evidently retained their respect for Van Dorn's ability to lead cavalry despite their anger over recent events. And equally important, they surely knew Van Dorn was available. The Texas officers quickly ascribed their names to a letter Griffith dated December 5, 1862, and addressed to Maj. Gen. John C. Pemberton, commanding the department from Vicksburg. They respectfully submitted:

> If you will fit up a cavalry expedition, comprising three or four thousand men, and give us Major-General Earl Van Dorn, than whom no braver man lives, to command us, we will penetrate the rear of the enemy, capture Holly Spring . . . and other points, and perhaps force him [Grant] to retreat.

The letter was signed by Lt. Col. John S. Griffith, commanding Texas Cavalry Brigade, and the commanders of the four Texas regiments: Col. E. R. Hawkins and Maj. J. H. Broocks of the First Texas Legion; Lt. Col. Jiles S. Boggess, commanding the Third Texas Cavalry; Lt. Col. D. W. Jones, commanding the Ninth Texas Cavalry; and Capt. Jack Wharton, commanding the Sixth Texas Cavalry. Colonel Whitfield had gone to Texas to recover, and Colonel Ross had taken his wounded brother to Texas. The major of the Sixth was also absent.[20]

The day after Pemberton received Griffith's letter he answered, "I wish to see you personally, if circumstances will possibly admit of it." Griffith's circumstances admitted. Less than a week later the colonel received orders to report to Van Dorn with the Texas Brigade.[21]

When the Ninth rode out of camp in the middle of the night to join Van Dorn, a cold, brisk December rain wet the men's slickers and boots. Sheets of lightning turned night to day, then made the inky darkness more intense. The clouds blew off toward morning, and bright stars twinkled in a black sky. The cold intensified, forming frost on the wet ground. Jesse surely found it strange that no one knew why they were going to Grenada, yet he was glad to be riding with Reuben. Perhaps they would see some action.[22]

The Ninth rendezvoused at dawn with the Third, the Sixth, and the Legion. The Texas Cavalry Brigade, 1,500 in all, was united at Grenada that morning under the command of Col. John S. Griffith, a thirty-three-year-old merchant-stockman and slaveholder from Kaufman County, Texas. Two other cavalry brigades joined the Texans and Van Dorn early that morning: Col. William H. "Red" Jackson's Tennessee Cavalry Brigade of 1,200 men; and Col. Robert McCullough's Missouri Cavalry Brigade of 800. Each of the 3,500 horsemen drew a hundred rounds of ammunition and rations of ten days' salt only—no bacon, no cornmeal, just salt. One pack mule per company carried two axes, matches, and "all the turpentine they could get." The Texans felt like cheering for the first time since capturing

Night March in the Rain

the Federal battery at Elkhorn Tavern back in March, but they were silent. They had been ordered to be as quiet as possible.[23]

The men stowed their salt and ammunition in gummed haversacks and rolled corn for the horses in their blankets. When they mounted and rode due east, a thrill rippled through the column. Still, no one could tell them where they were going, not even the captains, but everyone was aware that 3,500 horsemen carrying matches and turpentine were not on their way to a division review. They kept moving until late in the afternoon, when a halt was called to feed the horses. Back in the saddle in an hour, they continued east. In midnight darkness, the boys, tired and stiff, dropped off their mounts and stretched their legs. They had been on the move for twenty-four hours and had ridden forty-five miles.[24]

When the sun's dull glow nudged itself over the horizon the next morning, the raiders moved out. Rainstorms and muddy roads slowed the pace. They rode on. At mid-morning they fed and rested the

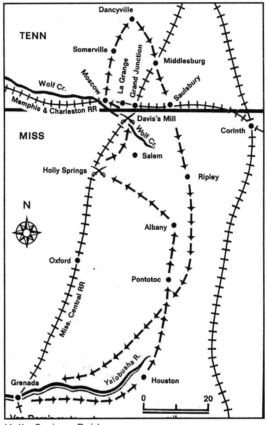

Holly Springs Raid

animals for an hour and a half. On the move again, they passed through the village of Houston and turned north. Van Dorn, mounted on his famous black mare, was leading his raiders around the Federals. They rode steadily until nearly midnight. When the column halted, the men had nothing to eat, but they picked dry corn from a nearby field for the horses. The troopers lay down on the muddy ground for a few hours' sleep.[25]

Van Dorn's famished horsemen rode into Pontotoc Thursday morning in the muted first light of dawn. Townsmen met them with "extravagant demonstrations of joy." The hungry troopers, Victor recalled, were

enthusiastically welcomed by the noble and patriotic citizens . . . trays, dishes and baskets of choicest edibles were offered on all sides, and pitchers of wine and milk as well. No halt was allowed, and the men pursued

their mysterious way munching the welcomed "grub" dispensed by the
fair hand of good and beautiful, and noble heroines. Oh, peerless ladies
of Pontotoc . . . [we] salute you![26]

With the welcome echoing in their heads and their bellies full, the
tired men felt like heroes. They rode on north through New Albany
and crossed Holly Springs Road, three miles north. The column halted
in mid-afternoon, and the men feasted on broiled pork and "luscious
sweet potatoes."[27]

As the sun was coming up Friday morning, guides led the column
off the main road and into the countryside. They rode twenty miles
through creek bottoms and past a few houses. Guards were left at all the
houses along the line of march, and other precautions were taken to
prevent any possibility of the Federals' learning Van Dorn's objective.
The cavalrymen stopped in the late afternoon to feed again. They
mounted after dark and rode in silence to within five miles of Holly
Springs and Grant's tempting depot before quietly bivouacking without
fires. It was "cold as crocus."[28]

At 3:00 A.M., Saturday, December 20, Van Dorn's three brigades
moved in column of fours toward Holly Springs—the Texans in the
center, with Jackson's Brigade on their right and McCullough's on their
left. Every man was alert, his guns ready. They rode slowly and silently.
Van Dorn ordered Griffith to lead the charge into the center of the city
with the Sixth and Ninth. "And take care," Van Dorn added, "that you
do not find a hornet's nest at the square!" Three miles out, Griffith drew
his saber. Galloping at the head of the regiments with his black plume
waving in the breeze, he yelled, "Forward at a gallop!"[29]

The bugle's shrill, harsh blast sounded the charge upon the crisp
morning air, and with a long, wild yell, the Ninth led the horde of
charging Texans into Holly Springs, straight toward the railroad depot.
Van Dorn's other two brigades galloped into town from other directions.
The horsemen rode through and over the unprepared Yankees. Union
infantrymen threw up their hands and surrendered. The depot commander was captured trying to escape out the rear of the depot building.[30]

Near the square, a woman told Pvt. Charlie Carr, Company I, Ninth
Texas, that a Union officer was in a house close by. Carr, a slender,
black-eyed nineteen-year-old, left the ranks and ran to the house with

his long, rusty old musket—Carr never bothered keeping his musket clean. Inside, Carr found the officer and demanded his surrender. The Yankee said it was improper to hand his saber to an inferior in rank.

"What is your rank?" asked Carr.

"I am Colonel _____ of _____ regiment, U.S.A."

"All right, that is my rank; I am Colonel C. C. Carr, Ninth Texas Cavalry, C.S.A.," Charlie politely responded as he reached for the saber with his left hand and kept his rusty musket pointed at the Yank's head with his right hand. "Colonel" Carr turned over his prisoner to the guards.[31]

When part of an Illinois cavalry regiment began forming at the edge of town, Griffith ordered Col. Dud Jones to form the Ninth. Griffith and Jones, riding side by side, led the regiment in a headlong charge. The Illinoisans stood their ground. The Ninth dismounted and fired. They scattered the enemy horsemen, captured their colors, and took several prisoners. With Holly Springs secure, Griffith quickly notified Van Dorn, "The hornet's nest is ours!"[32]

During the charge, Old Butch's horse was shot, and when the bullet struck, Butch said, the horse

jumped as high as [a] ceiling and fell with me in the road and . . . fifty horses at least ran over me before I could roll into the ditch, but none of them hurt me and I jumped up and ran back to some stables where I had noticed some horses and selected me a mule with a good saddle, and while at this I saw a Yankee crouched in one of the stalls[,] and as I ordered him out I saw another and heard something above[,] and called out to them . . . to come out, as I was going to fire the hay.

Butch marched eight prisoners and a prize mule out of the barn.[33]

Citizens of Holly Springs, mostly women and children, thronged the streets, some still in their "dishabilments"—nightclothes. They shouted, "Hurrah for Van Dorn! Hurrah for the Confederacy! Hurrah for Jeff Davis!" Children waved small Confederate flags they had snatched from hiding places. Beautiful young ladies waved handkerchiefs, and matrons "implored the protection of God" on the raiders. "Tears of joy gushed forth from many an eye."[34]

Citizens pointed out the house occupied by Grant's paymaster, his quartermaster, and Mrs. Grant herself. Griffith immediately sent his second in command with a detail of ten men to guarantee that Mrs. Grant and the other ladies be treated with deference and respect. When Griffith reached the house, he found the ladies had refused his men entrance.

Mrs. Grant stepped to the gate and said, "And you, sir, make war upon women, do you?"

John Griffith, raised a Maryland gentleman, removed his hat and bowed. "On the contrary," he said, "we leave that to our enemies!"

The ladies would not allow Griffith's men to search the house. Finally, the colonel said, "Men, offer no rudeness to the

Holly Springs, Mississippi

ladies; if they will not allow you to pass through the gate, tear off a picket from the fence and flank them; if you are denied admittance at the door, go around them and find ingress through a window. You must search the house for concealed prisoners, but do not touch the hem of the garment of one of these ladies." When the soldiers began tearing off the pickets, Mrs. Grant politely invited them in. They found one officer in the house and placed him under guard.[35]

McCullough's Missourians broke into the sutler's store and "commenced an indiscriminate pillage." Griffith appealed to the men to get about their work of burning, but soon Tennesseans, Mississippians, and Texans vied in the work of pillage, the Texans always keeping a sharp lookout for their commanders. The ragged, half-starved men gloried in their loot. They found "plentiful" cigars and kept three thousand puffing.[36]

The cavalrymen's appearance was completely transformed. They donned new pants and overcoats, plumed hats, and glistening leather cavalry boots. They broke open boxes of new Remington and Colt revolvers and carried off two to six each. They gobbled the sutler's canned peaches and oysters, candy and cheese, and stuffed their saddlebags with bacon, pork, hardtack, and coffee. A Third Texas private found

$20,000 in new, crisp U.S. greenbacks, which he traded for five dollars in silver coins.[37]

The indescribable scene of pillage continued. Soon the ecstatic Confederates "inaugurated a jubilee, inspired by the spirit of John Barleycorn, Esq." When they despaired of drinking all the whiskey or carrying it off in their canteens, they knocked in the heads of barrels until whiskey flowed down the streets of the town.[38]

"Release the prisoners from the jail," a trooper yelled. Howling Rebels battered down the doors. Local citizens and others held on various charges poured onto the street and joined their liberators.[39]

Members of the Third Texas recognized B. Thomas—the Texas Irishman who had said he preferred crucifixion to being left afoot in Missouri. Thomas had been discharged for overage and had become the Third's sutler. He had ventured into enemy-held territory seeking a better supply of goods than could be found in Confederate territory. Thomas was under a death sentence for being a spy. "And if ye hadn't a come," he said, "it was shooting me they would the day after the morrow. I'm glad to see yez, boys, and glad yez canteens are full." And Thomas did not exaggerate his case a particle.[40]

Jones kept the Ninth under nominal control, except Charlie and Old Butch. The regiment set about burning Grant's immense stores. They had captured seventy-five fully equipped cavalry horses from the Illinoisans, but Gris complained that other regiments got the sutlers' spoils while the Ninth was obeying orders. Colonel Griffith pleaded with the rowdy gang of looters "not to disgrace the fair fame of the Confederacy." In exasperation he drew his sword and, in language more forceful than polite, drove many men back into the ranks.[41]

When the men were sated they methodically set about applying their turpentine and matches. They burned two complete trains, one loaded with commissary stores, the other with quartermaster stores, both with steam up and bound for the army below. They torched all the depot buildings, the armory, the ordnance buildings, a recently completed two-thousand-bed hospital ready for occupation, thousands of bushels of wheat, two thousand bales of cotton, and one thousand wagons and ambulances. Beef, pork, flour, hard bread, and coffee stacked as high as a man's head and in rows a quarter mile long, great quantities of arms, and ammunition were consumed in the general ruin. They gleefully burned the Yankees' camps, baggage, clothing, tents, even some regimental and company books and papers. The courthouse was the magazine, packed with immense quantities of ordnance stores, bomb-shells, and powder. It was fired moments before the command left the city, setting off a series of explosions that jarred the countryside for twenty-four hours.[42]

With Grant's stores ablaze, Van Dorn paroled the prisoners and ordered his colonels to round up their troopers. The three brigades formed and marched out of the sacked city before noon. The men's outward appearance had been transformed by captured clothing, arms, and accoutrements. Best of all, the pride they took with them from Holly Springs would last a lifetime. Later, when John S. Griffith was asked how he felt after Holly Springs, he replied, "I felt as if I could charge hell and capture the devil, if the Almighty had commanded me to do so."[43]

In addition to their refurbished pride, the troopers rode out of Holly Springs with all the cavalry equipment the U.S. Army could supply. Reuben, Jesse, and Newton—all the Texans—had ridden in that morning on Texas or Mexican saddles with roping horns. They left astride McClellan cavalry saddles. The Ninth's seventy-five captured cavalry horses were equipped with small black leather saddlebags, regulation saddle blankets, carbine buckets, and pistol holsters, all the tack a cavalryman could desire.[44]

The U.S. cavalry saddle had been designed in 1856 by Captain George B. McClellan of the Engineering Corps, a future major general of Lincoln's Army of the Potomac. The saddle was simple, strong, comfortable to both horse and rider, and weighed half what a cow saddle weighed. A short leather underskirt was attached to the saddle's exposed, rawhide-covered tree. Stirrup straps, surcingles, breast straps, cruppers, and equipment straps were of black-dyed leather. Wooden stirrups were standard issue. Besides two holstered pistols worn on the body, many Southern cavalrymen carried two more in saddle holsters. A carbine bucket and snap hook secured the rider's long gun. A full field pack also included a picket rope, a canteen, saddlebags, haversacks, an overcoat strapped in front of the pommel, and blankets strapped behind the cantle.[45]

Six weeks before the Ninth Texas entered Holly Springs, U.S. Maj.

Gen. George B. McClellan had been relieved as commander of the Army of the Potomac after being outgeneraled three times by Robert E. Lee.

At Holly Springs, Earl Van Dorn had bested U. S. Grant. The victory was everything Van Dorn had hoped for—or dreamed of. He had masterfully directed the 120-mile dash from Grenada, reached Holly Springs unmolested, and canceled Grant's plans when the supply depot was reduced to ashes. The handsome, arrogant Mississippian had always sought action and glory, which he found at Holly Springs. Forever the cavalryman, Buck Van Dorn was back where he belonged.

Normally flamboyant and verbose, Van Dorn's terse report reflected a new assurance:

> I surprised the enemy at this place at daylight this morning; burned up all the quartermaster's stores, cotton &c.—an immense amount; burned up many trains; took a great many arms and about 1,500 prisoners. I presume the value of stores would amount to $1,500,000. I move on to Davis' Mill at once.[46]

Grant was furious. The depot ultimately was his responsibility. He had warned the commander at Holly Springs, Col. R. C. Murphy, that a large enemy cavalry force was in the area. "But," Grant reported to headquarters, Murphy "took no steps to protect the place, not having notified a single officer of his command of the approaching danger." Furthermore, the town was taken "while the troops were quietly in their beds." Three days later, Grant, with "pain and mortification," reflected on the disgraceful surrender and blamed Murphy. The unfortunate colonel, the same man who had abandoned Iuka to Price's men back in September, was dismissed for cowardly and disgraceful conduct.[47]

Murphy was not so cowardly as incompetent. The morning of the raid he had scurried around trying to erect barricades and start the trains south, but he was too late. That evening, after the horsemen were gone, he reported to Grant that the enemy had come screaming into town and captured him as he was attempting to reach his infantry. Now there were no supplies for the paroled men and the sick. "What shall be done with them?" Murphy moaned. "My fate is most mortifying. I have wished a hundred times to-day that I had been killed."[48]

Van Dorn, as elated as Murphy was humiliated, led his jubilant and tipsy band northeast toward Salem. The horsemen strung out along the dirt road in their finery. Five hundred head of captured horses and mules added to the length of the column. Butch rode the fleet and intelligent mule he had found in the stable he burned. The old straggler proved an excellent judge of horseflesh—or mule flesh, in this case. When the Ninth stopped ten miles out to feed, Butch began bragging about his splendid mount and did not stop until death closed his mouth decades later.[49]

When Van Dorn finally called a halt that evening, the men unsaddled, fed the horses, and rolled up in their new blankets. It had been a long day, an exciting day. Jesse, David, and the other new recruits must have reflected on their first action with the cavalry and shaken their heads in astonishment. They wanted to talk, but when they calmed down exhaustion washed over them. They slept. In a couple of hours pickets sounded the alarm. The boys jumped up, threw their saddles on their horses, and prepared for action, but the Yanks were not on the prowl that night.[50]

The next day, Sunday, December 21, the column attacked a Federal outpost guarding a railroad trestle over Wolf Creek near Davis's Mill. The Texas Brigade dismounted and charged a blockhouse made of railroad ties and cotton bales that the Union colonel had constructed the night before. A small cannon mounted on a handcar and moving along the tracks for position caused "considerable injury and annoyance." From a distance of only sixty yards, the Federals swept the crossing with gunfire. The Rebels tried to fire the trestle with cotton balls soaked in turpentine, but gunfire from the blockhouse was too hot. Van Dorn decided "to haul off" after two hours, and the cavalrymen "took another gallop."[51]

The battle of Davis's Mill was costly. The Federal colonel, whose resourcefulness had paid off handsomely, reported that the Confederates left twenty-two killed, thirty wounded, and twenty prisoners. Thirteen of the wounded and missing belonged to the Ninth Texas, three to Company A, including new recruit David Cate, who was shot in the right shoulder. A doctor from the Third Texas and a few men remained to tend the thirty dangerously wounded men. Others who were less severely wounded, perhaps two hundred, were carried off in wagons or on horseback. The industrious Yankee colonel, who had taken Grant's warning seriously, had only three men wounded, none killed.[52]

The only records of Van Dorn's wounded come from the bimonthly rolls. Wounded men able to ride with the regiment or taken from the scene in wagons were not noted because they were not listed as absent. David Cate was taken to the U.S. hospital at La Grange, Tennessee. He was not again present for duty with the regiment until the September–October 1863 roll, nine months later.[53]

From Wolf Creek, Van Dorn led his men north into Tennessee. The raiders rode at breakneck speed, stopping only to cut telegraph wires, burn stockades, and tear up the railroads. They ripped up cross ties, set them afire, then heated the rails until they were hot enough to twist around trees. Christmas Eve they captured a Federal regiment's winter quarters and hauled off knapsacks, canteens, blankets, overcoats, shirts, fifty pairs of socks, nine days' rations, and the colonel's horse, overcoat, and dress coat.[54]

That afternoon the Texas Brigade attacked a blockhouse at Middleburg, Tennessee. Griffith dismounted his men and threw the Ninth out front as skirmishers. The blockhouse was a loopholed brick home. After two hours Griffith called off the fruitless fight. The Ninth lost nine more wounded and four missing. The men fed their horses that evening to the accompaniment of the drums at Grand Junction beating the long roll. The Yankees were assembling to pursue the raiders.[55]

Grant ordered out all his cavalry in an effort to capture the marauding gray horsemen, who now were wearing Union blue. Van Dorn turned south toward the protection of his own lines. The column covered thirty-two miles and skirmished with the enemy at dusk. "This is our Christmas," Gris wrote.[56]

The following day the weary cavalrymen pushed their exhausted mounts and the captured animals fifty miles deeper into Mississippi. Cold rain fell during the pitch-black night. December 27, 1862, the men reached their base at Grenada. In another two days, the Ninth joined their trains seven miles south of town and finally got a change of clothes. The few who had remained with the wagons greeted the victors with joy and envy. David Garrett had been on detail shoeing horses twenty miles from camp the day his Sixth left with Van Dorn. He lamented, "I would have given almost anything to have been with them."[57]

★   ★   ★

David and the other Texans soon received news that Nathan Bedford Forrest had been continuing his campaign against Grant's supply line, destroying tracks and trestles, farther north in West Tennessee, while Van Dorn's men were wrecking Federal operations in Mississippi.

On the day after the Texas Brigade joined Van Dorn at Grenada, Forrest had evaded gunboats patrolling the flooded Tennessee River and crossed into West Tennessee. Most of his 2,100 troopers were ill-equipped, poorly mounted, green recruits, many with no arms at all, but for two weeks Forrest led them in a loop through West Tennessee, destroying supplies, railroads, and the reputations of several Yankee colonels. Forrest so thoroughly wrecked the Mobile & Ohio that it was useless to the end of the war. His brigade captured and burned 20 stockades, killed or captured 2,500 Federals, took 10 pieces of artillery, burned hundreds of bales of cotton, and carried off 50 wagons, 10,000 stand of arms, 100,000 rations, 1 million rounds of ammunition, and 500 more Enfield rifles than they needed to arm themselves.[58]

Near Lexington, Forrest captured two rifled three-inch steel Rodman guns from an Indiana battery. He named the Rodmans the "Twins" and used them with deadly effect the rest of the war. Forrest also kept a captured United States Dragoon saber, which he honed razor-sharp and carried until the war ended.[59]

Forrest recrossed the Tennessee River New Year's Day, leaving the incredulous Federals staring at him from the west bank. His force had averaged twenty miles a day and fought or worked to near exhaustion without a single night's uninterrupted sleep. They had returned thoroughly armed and equipped over roads considered impracticable for horsemen, much less artillery and wagons. Now disciplined veterans, they had lost only 173 men. Forrest's genius was becoming more and more apparent—at least to those who were watching.[60]

Van Dorn's and Forrest's Christmas raids forced Grant to retreat and to abandon his planned march down the Mississippi Central to attack Vicksburg. The city was safe from the east, at least for a time. But Grant, always the bulldog, did not give up. If he could not take Vicksburg from the east, there was always the north—or the west, or the south.

On New Year's Day 1863, the Texas Brigade was ordered to Vicksburg. The Ninth's men and horses had rested only two days. In addition, the regiment was depleted by detachments and casualties. Of the seventy-four officers and men in Company A, only fifty were present for duty. Ten men were on detached duty, including five who were with General Whitfield at Yazoo City. Amos Burgoon and another man were detached as teamsters. One man was detached as a regimental butcher, another to brigade ordnance, and another was serving with Van Dorn's bodyguard of fifty.[61]

Five men were in the hospital—three sick and two who had been wounded at Corinth. Another man wounded at Corinth was on medical furlough. Three wounded on the Holly Springs raid and another left to attend them had not returned. Two men captured early in December near Oxford, Mississippi, were prisoners of war. Another pair, captured at the Hatchie Bridge, had been paroled but not exchanged.[62]

The men present for duty were in better health than at any time during their service, thanks to the abundant pork and sweet potatoes in Mississippi. David Garrett wrote home: "I am feeling very well, I have been eating Pork & sweet potatoes & I have got fat. We have less sickness in camp at this time than we have had since we came of Miss."[63]

Samuel Barron, Company C, Third Texas, whose digestive system had been practically in ruin since he came down with measles and typhoid in Arkansas eighteen months earlier, remembered that "the severe horseback service . . . and our diet, principally sweet potatoes, had restored my health completely and my wounds had healed, and I was in good condition to do cavalry service." Sam had also been shot in the right thigh, and a bullet had grazed his face at Holly Springs. Another Texan said every man in his regiment was "entirely cured of the plague, camp dysentery" by their diet of sweet potatoes.[64]

After two years of living on white corn, lard, and rancid salt-cured meat with only occasional variations, the men's reserves of essential nutrients were dangerously depleted, especially vitamins A and C. Vitamin C, which the body does not store, is essential to the cement between the cells, and depletion accentuates other deficiencies. Vitamin A is necessary to the proper function of mucous membranes, which line the entire digestive system. Vitamin A is stored in the liver, and a normal diet provides enough of the nutrient to sustain health for about a year. But white corn contains only a trace of vitamin A, and rancid fat destroys what is available. However, one medium sweet potato per day contains enough of both vitamins for normal body functions. In addition, sweet potatoes are rich in pectin and potassium. They also contain trace elements, fiber, and small amounts of other nutrients, all necessary to good health. The increase in calories alone would have provided energy and added fat to the men's lean bodies.[65]

The specific ingredient in sweet potatoes that helped cure the men's camp dysentery is pectin, the natural substance found in fruits and some vegetables that causes them to jell. In the gut, both fiber and pectin are adsorbents. Pectin is a major ingredient in current diarrhea medicines.[66]

Company A's fifty healthy men who were present for duty marched out of camp the morning of January 2, 1863, with the rest of the Ninth Texas. Rain poured off their shoulders as they rode south-southwest on their tired horses. Deep mud forced the regiment to abandon all but one wagon carrying a few cooking utensils. Every mile of road was floating, many bridges had washed out, and the creek crossings were flooded. The third night out, a courier arrived with a dispatch directing the Texans to "report at Grenada forthwith." The column turned around and headed back the direction it had come.[67]

CHAPTER 8

GLORIOUS TENNESSEE

January 8–May 22, 1863

The Ninth received marching orders at Grenada and set out at 4:00 A.M. Thursday, January 8, 1863. The men rode northeast, the opposite direction of Vicksburg. Pressure on the vital river city had slackened while Grant and his favorite lieutenant, William Tecumseh Sherman, made plans to attack from a different direction, so the Texans were on their way to Middle Tennessee to join Earl Van Dorn's new cavalry corps.[1]

Union and Confederate armies in Tennessee anxiously watched one another along an east-west line some fifty miles south of Nashville. Union commander William S. Rosecrans—Van Dorn's old West Point classmate who had beaten Buck at Corinth—had his headquarters at Nashville. Braxton Bragg, still dyspeptic and cranky, commanded the Confederates from Tullahoma. The two had fought a costly but indecisive battle at Murfreesboro, on Stone's River, as the new year began. Now, neither felt strong enough to start anything.

Both Bragg, in Middle Tennessee, and John C. Pemberton, at Vicksburg, were under the command of Gen. Joseph E. Johnston. In November, Jefferson Davis had sent Johnston to take command in the West—everything west of Virginia to the Mississippi River.

Pemberton had been born and reared in Pennsylvania, had graduated from the Military Academy in 1837, and had won two brevets in Mexico. He had married a Virginian, and when the war began he had resigned from the U.S. Army to serve the Confederacy. He was quarrelsome, often ungracious, and averse to cooperating, but he was counted among that favored group, friends of Jefferson Davis. Joseph E. Johnston was a man of honor, a distinguished soldier and gentleman, a former brigadier general in the U.S. Army, a hero in Mexico and at First Manassas, a friend and West Point classmate of Robert E. Lee, and no friend of Jefferson Davis.[2]

Evidence suggests that Davis's dislike of Johnston began when the two were attending West Point. Cadets Johnston and Lee, both self-assured Virginia aristo-

Gen. Joseph E. Johnston

crats, were exemplary students and close friends. The Mississippian Davis, was sensitive, less than self-assured, quick to take offense, and an indifferent scholar constantly on report. Whatever the source of the friction between Davis and Johnston, it existed before 1861. Early in the war, Davis appointed five full generals and ranked them—Samuel Cooper first, then Albert Sidney Johnston, Robert E. Lee, Joseph E. Johnston, and finally Pierre G. T. Beauregard. Based on his U.S. Army rank and Confederate law, Joseph Johnston felt he deserved to be ranked first. Davis, who jealously guarded his presidential prerogatives and was incapable of setting aside personal feelings, ranked Johnston fourth. And Joe Johnston also could be touchy.[3]

Johnston, barely recovered from a wound received five months earlier at Seven Pines, dutifully went west as ordered. From his headquarters at Chattanooga early in 1863, he looked at Van Dorn's recent success in forcing Grant to pull back from Mississippi and created a cavalry corps for the ambitious Mississippian. Van Dorn was ordered to middle Tennessee to cover Bragg's left and operate against Federal communications.[4]

With his usual verve, Van Dorn plunged into the organization of his new corps. He had no intention of letting this chance for fame and glory slip by for lack of preparation or discipline. He placed Brig. Gen. William H. "Red" Jackson in command of the division that included the Texas Brigade, then issued Special Orders No. 5, setting forth in detail "the minutest rules for the government of his corps," as Victor Rose reported. The general included such items as proper distances to be maintained on the march between companies, regiments, brigades, and divisions; a system of bugle calls; proper challenges and replies of vedettes—sentinels operating four to five hundred yards in advance of the regiment. In his grandiose style, Van Dorn concluded his orders with: "Cavalry knows no danger—knows no failure; what it is ordered to do, it will do."[5]

Brig. Gen. William H. "Red" Jackson

The Texans' attitude toward Van Dorn had changed after Holly Springs. The general "had risen in the estimation of his men as a proficient cavalry commander," according to Newton Keen. Troopers from the Lone Star State, however, were displeased with their new division commander, W. H. Jackson. Brigadier General Jackson, a big burly man with red hair and beard and a round face, was "possessed of a kind of military air that to us Texans was repulsive," a man reported. "He was always accompanied by his Orderly who was to our view a servant." The lowly orderly brushed the general's coat, held his horse, helped the general mount and dismount. The Texans "had no love" for their new general and were indignant that a Tennessean had been placed over them. When they burned Jackson in effigy, the general "was sensible enough to pay no attention to this," Sam Barron noted.[6]

W. H. Jackson had been colonel of the First Tennessee Cavalry at

Holly Springs, where he won the wreathed stars of a Confederate general for his gallantry. He had graduated in the West Point class of 1856 and was a lieutenant in the Mounted Rifles when the war began. The Texans might not have loved Jackson had they known a bit more about him, but they certainly would have respected him. On a frontier campaign against the Comanches with his company, Jackson, then a lieutenant, forbade all hunting and shooting to avoid alerting the Indians to the troopers' whereabouts. When a grizzly bear came down out of the mountains and crossed the column's route, Jackson, armed only with his saber, rode out to meet the beast. Horse and rider closed on the grizzly. When the animal rose up on its hind feet, ready for a fight, Jackson brought his sword down on the bear's head with sufficient force to kill the grizzly. It was an "exploit" that Jackson's commander, Dabney Maury, doubted had been "ever elsewhere attempted or accomplished."[7]

After leaving Grenada, the Texans ferried the Yalobusha, just north of town, and swam three big sloughs before night. For an entire month they slogged across northeastern Mississippi through tremendous rainstorms, mud a foot to three feet deep, snowstorms, and intense cold. They slept on snow-covered ground with no tents, suffering "much from cold both on the march and at night." Two weeks out of Grenada, just south of Coffeeville, Maj. J. N. Dodson, Ninth Texas, quit the column, too ill to ride farther. The next day the men were ordered to send off all their heavy baggage.[8]

It was the first of February before the regiment reached Pontotoc. Townsmen cheered the muddy troopers, waved Confederate flags, and sang patriotic songs. Eighty men who had been picketing at Yazoo City, including five from Company A, joined the brigade the next day. The march was "wearisome in the extreme, devoid of interesting incidents." Hail, sleet, snow, and mud worse than the black prairie gumbo in North Texas continued to slow the column.[9]

Cavalrymen and teamsters urged their animals on. February 9, Van Dorn and the rest of the First Division met the Texans near the Alabama border. Van Dorn had 7,455 men in all: Gen. W. H. Jackson's First Division contained the Texas Brigade, 1,500 men; Col. P. D. Roddey's command of 1,400; eight more regiments; four battalions; and a bodyguard of fifty. John W. Whitfield, the Legion's ambitious colonel, com-

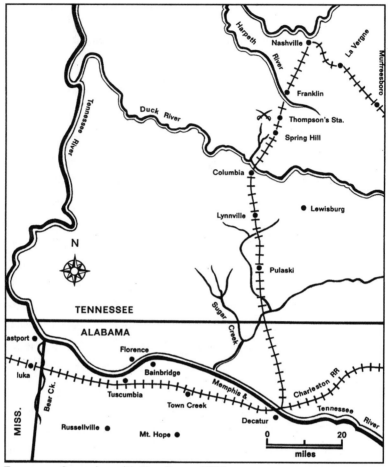

Tennessee Campaign with Van Dorn—1863

manded the Texas Brigade. When they reached Tennessee, Bedford Forrest's division would join Van Dorn's command.[10]

The horsemen and their wagons crossed the Tombigbee on a pontoon bridge made of ferryboats and marched in the rain through poor, hilly country. They crossed into Alabama and rode through the old town of Russellville. It was still raining when they made camp at a ferry landing on the south bank of the Tennessee River, six miles east of Florence. With the bridges burned and the river swollen by recent rains, the command halted for a few days.[11]

Col. Sul Ross, back from Texas, thought of more pleasant times he had spent in northwestern Alabama. Less than four years earlier he had graduated from Wesleyan University in Florence, where he had returned after being shot through the chest by a Comanche. Ross's association with refined society and gentlemen's sons at Wesleyan must have been the source of his gentlemanly manners, which contrasted with his tough frontier heritage.[12]

Besides Ross, other Texans were thinking of home and happier times. Couriers, one man from each regiment, would soon leave with mail for Texas. In camp near Florence on February 14, David Garrett wrote home while his regiment halted to feed. "We are living quite scant at this time, but I hear on the other side of the Tennessee River we will get plenty to eat." Although David was nearly out of clothing, his horse was in good condition—it was the same horse he had ridden from Kaufman County, Texas, eighteen months earlier. David feared that his mount would give out on the trip. If not, David wrote home, "I shall keep him & bring him back home with me & keep him as long as he lives."[13]

Newton Keen had never before been in Alabama, but he would remember the state. He was alone on post duty three hundred yards beyond camp on a clear, moonless night. In hushed silence the stars sparkled like diamonds on black velvet. Newt sat on an old pine log thinking of his dead parents; of his saintly grandparents, who had taken him in as a child; of Grandpa Keen and Uncle John, who were Methodist ministers; of Uncle Billy, an exhorter who "could pray the clap-board off a house." Through the lonely night Newt thought about the war, the killing all around him, the dangers he faced. And he thought about God. He later wrote: "There in my meditation, I made the solemn promise to Almighty God that if spared to get home from the war that I would give my heart to God [,] the remainder of my days to the service of God."[14]

At dawn a couple of days after reaching the banks of the Tennessee, Newt and the other cavalrymen began crossing the half-mile-wide river. They ferried the horses over on the hulk of a river steamer with its upper works burned off, and crossed the wagons on flat boats, which the men drew across the river by hand. As the men rode through Pulaski, Tennessee, three days later, ladies brought the first flowers of spring and "showed every demonstration of joy."[15]

From Pulaski, Van Dorn's corps rode north on the Columbia Pike, one of the macadamized or graveled roads that radiated out of Nashville like spokes of a wheel and were called "pikes" or "turnpikes." Thirty

years earlier the state of Tennessee had undertaken a road-building pro-
gram, and many of these macadamized pikes crisscrossed the area now
in dispute.[16] Reuben and Jesse had never seen hard-surfaced roads, and
even cosmopolitan Gris wrote that the regiment took "the Columbia
Pike."

Riding along the pike, the Rogers boys must have talked of home
and family. Eighty miles east, Grandpa had made gunpowder. As a boy,
Pa had tended the burning charcoal, packed the powder in deerskins,
and peddled it on horseback to settlers and Indians through the mountains
of Marion and Franklin Counties.[17]

Tennessee was home to David Garrett. He was born in 1834 in
Gallatin, thirty miles northeast of Nashville. In the late 1840s, he left the
state with a group of young men determined to make their way in the
West. David settled in Kaufman County, Texas, where he was living
when he mounted his sturdy horse, strapped his double-barreled shotgun
to his saddle, and set out for Dallas to enroll in Company E, Sixth
Texas Cavalry.[18]

From Pulaski, the Texans sat their saddles in cheerless weather several
more days. The animals splashed through puddles on hard-surfaced roads
and bogged to their knees on dirt trails. The Ninth's horses wore out
their shoes, becoming tender-footed long before the regiment ferried the
Duck River, west of Columbia. The Third, the Sixth, and the other
regiments crossed near Columbia on a pontoon bridge. Near Spring Hill,
a dozen miles north of Columbia on the Nashville Pike, the separate
columns came together.[19]

Brig. Gen. Nathan Bedford Forrest reported to Van Dorn with his
brigade. Forrest and many of his Tennesseans knew every foot of the
ground in this part of the state. Forrest had spent his boyhood at Chapel
Hill, twenty-five miles east of Columbia, and one of his officers was
born and raised within a mile and a half of Thompson's Station, a few
miles north of Columbia. Other men in the corps also knew the surrounding country, including Col. Dudley Jones, who had been attending
Maury Institute at Columbia when the war started and he returned to
Texas to join the Titus Grays.[20]

Yankees held the town of Franklin, a dozen miles north of Spring
Hill. On March 4, a week after crossing the Duck River, the Ninth
joined a battalion of sharpshooters and drove in Federal pickets while

Van Dorn rode up the pike toward Franklin on a forced reconnaissance. The general encountered a large body of enemy troops encumbered by a ponderous wagon train. The Union commander at Franklin had sent out the column to challenge the newly arrived Rebels, but he had burdened them with the wagons, which they were to fill with forage. Van Dorn forced the enemy to deploy, then withdrew to Thompson's Station. He reported that "during the night scouts reported the enemy to be a brigade of infantry, two regiments of cavalry, and a battery of artillery, and I determined to give them battle."[21]

Thompson's Station, nine miles south of Franklin, contained a depot, a church, and a few houses. The village lay in a small valley between the Nashville Pike and the Central Alabama tracks. Cedar breaks, open fields of corn, and patches of plum bushes covered the hilly countryside. The Texas Brigade camped on the hills just south of the depot. In their front, a stone fence ran north and south two hundred yards from the railroad tracks.[22]

Bugles blew early the morning of March 5. A.W., whose company was camped near Red Jackson's headquarters, watched the general while waiting for orders. A courier rode up and informed Jackson that the vedettes had been driven in. The general issued a few orders and continued calmly preparing for breakfast while his orderly brushed his coat. In a few minutes another courier galloped up with a message. Jackson spoke a few words to an aide and went on with his meal, his great Russian-style mustache quivering not a twitch. A.W. was impressed. Jackson's "stock in our estimation rose out of sight," he wrote, "for from that day he was so endeared to us that we felt his orderly was occupying a post of honor." Jackson had proved himself a general that morning. The boys were convinced that "there were not enough men north of the Mason and Dixon line to scare him."[23]

At 8:00 A.M., the Ninth Texas left their saddled horses with every eighth man and moved forward to form on the hilltop directly in front of their encampment. The regiment was on the left of the brigade, and forward. Jones ordered Company H and Company A to move out front and form a skirmish line. The Rogers boys cautiously made their way 250 yards beyond the regiment. They stayed in sight of each other. They watched and listened.[24]

The regiment had been in position an hour when the men on the hill were ordered to move up behind the church and form along the stone fence. They stooped to remain out of view as they filed off one at a time to crouch behind the fence. Federal sharpshooters were in sight, but the Confederates had been ordered to hold their fire and not show themselves. Cannon barked from nearby hills.[25]

The Third Texas, the Legion, and the Third Arkansas soon joined the Ninth behind the fence. Firing in their front became lively, tempting the boys to peek over to watch the enemy advancing.

"Keep your heads down," the officers ordered.

"We all wanted to see," the soldiers said. A man near A.W. gouged out a hole in the stone fence and reported what was happening.

"Let me see!" his neighbors insisted. The boys took turns until one refused to yield. The soldier who made the hole demanded his right and struck the usurper a sound blow, which led to a fight. Both were arrested and sent off under a corporal's guard.[26]

The two companies of skirmishers were still out front when enemy infantry advanced from the north through a cedar break and formed behind the depot and some houses. When the Federals began to cross the railroad, they came within range of the Confederates behind the fence. The Texans and Arkansans drove the Yankees back behind the depot and houses. Suddenly, Colonel Jones yelled "Charge! Fire!" With a shout the men leaped the fence. The skirmishers ran to join the regiment. Yelling and firing, the Confederates drove the Yankees across the railroad embankment and half a mile across an open field. Bullets zipped through the air. Men fell with shattered arms or legs, bullet holes through their bodies, or half their brains blown away. The Confederates forced the confused Federals across the field and up a hill into a cedar break. The Yankees stumbled into the timber, where reinforcements stood in line with bayonets fixed.[27]

The bayonets forced the Texans and Arkansans down the hill, across the bloodstained field, and back to the railroad. The day was wearing on; the men were getting thirsty. They re-formed to the right of their original position and charged again. The Yanks stubbornly gave ground, moving back across the same field, up the same hill. When they reached the top, they rallied and pushed the Rebels down the hill to the railroad again. Jones ordered his companies to straighten out their alignment. The troopers were scrambling for position when bugles again sounded the charge. For the third time they charged with a yell, though it was not so loud and the charge was slower. For the third time, the enemy stumbled across the same field, up the same hill, and into the cedar break. The Confederates halted behind a battery to catch their breath.[28]

Smoke obscured the winter sun. It was three in the afternoon, seven hours since the Confederates had formed in line of battle and five hours since the first shots. Cannon continued to roar. Dead and wounded lay along the slope, and the stench of burned black powder filled the air. Twenty-eight Texans lay dead on the field; another 137 were wounded. Behind the battery, men gulped air and wondered, What next?[29]

Colonel Whitfield rode up and asked if the Ninth could go any farther. "Yes!" they yelled, and began to form. Suddenly, the entire Union force surrendered in front of the Texans. Forrest had ridden around the enemy with two mounted regiments and attacked them from the rear.[30]

Van Dorn had ordered Forrest to charge a battery and, if possible, to get in the rear of the enemy. Forrest had taken two of his regiments rapidly across the pike, dismounted the men, and attacked. In the first volley, a lieutenant colonel and a captain were killed. Forrest was unhorsed, and his favorite charger was wounded. With his face the color of heated bronze and his eyes blazing, Forrest led the charge on foot. When his men screamed and charged to within twenty feet of the Federal line, the enemy threw down their arms and surrendered. Forrest conducted the Union commander, Col. John Coburn, to Van Dorn's headquarters.[31]

During the battle Newton's company remained mounted on the extreme left or west, half a mile from both armies. "We loped around to their rear, which put us out of fighting position and yet in plain view of the whole battle," he wrote. "Our forces in front made the attack and as the battle was raging in its fury" Forrest charged the enemy in the rear. "This so non-plused them that they surrendered. This was a regular water haul for us. Only some thirty or forty of them got away." Another Texan said the Federals "dug up more snakes than they could kill."[32]

"The fruits of this *hard fought battle*," according to Gris, were five regiments of infantry with all their field and staff officers. Coburn had started with 1,845 men. His cavalry and artillery had fled early in the battle, but 1,446 Yankees were killed, wounded, or captured. The Confederates, always destitute for clothes, stripped the enemy dead and took arms, accoutrements, and clothing from the captured. Later in the evening victorious Confederates marched Coburn, 72 officers—minus their overcoats—and 1,221 prisoners south to Columbia.[33]

After the prisoners were rounded up the Confederates gathered their dead and helped their 262 wounded men and the wounded Federals to field infirmaries in the rear. The Texas Brigade, in the center of the battle, lost 170 men killed, wounded, or missing. The Third lost 34, the Sixth lost 36, and the Ninth lost 23. Company A, despite their early exposure as skirmishers, suffered no casualties.[34]

The Legion, in the midst of the worst fighting, lost 77 men, a third of those who went into battle. Capt. James A. Broocks, younger brother of Col. John H. Broocks, was killed. As Captain Broocks was dying, he said to his brother, "John, take this sword and tell Father that I died in performance of my duty." Their father had given young James the sword.[35]

The Third Arkansas, fighting with the Texas Brigade, lost their colonel, a captain, and a lieutenant. Several of Sam Barron's friends in the Third Texas were killed or wounded. His regiment also lost a beautiful flag given them by the ladies of Boggy Depot, in Indian Territory. During a charge the flag's shaft was shattered. As the bearer escaped through a plum thicket, the flag was shred into narrow ribbons and left hanging on the bushes.[36]

The Texas cavalrymen and all of Van Dorn's men were deeply saddened over their losses but jubilant over the victory. "With feelings of mingled pride and sadness," they cheered General Van Dorn as he rode along the columns. Buck was elated. Always seeking glory, he loved fighting for its own sake and was insensitive to the death and mangling of battle.[37]

Even General Bragg was pleased, elation being beyond his range of emotions. He expressed "pride and gratification" for the results of "two brilliant and successful affairs recently achieved by the forces of the cavalry of Major General Van Dorn."[38]

The day following the battle both men and horses needed time to recuperate. They had been fighting or marching with only a few days' rest since leaving for Holly Springs eighty-one days earlier. The Ninth remained in camp for the day to help bury the dead, but they saddled up early the next morning and rode until 10:00 P.M. When they reached Spring Hill March 8, the Federals were threatening again. The regiment bivouacked in line of battle with their horses saddled. For two more days they kept the tired animals under saddle, constantly expecting an attack.[39]

The Ninth kept maneuvering until blue cavalry drove all Van Dorn's corps south, across the Duck River. With the swollen river between them and the enemy, the regiment finally had five entire days' rest before the brigade recrossed the river and marched back to their old position, two miles south of Spring Hill.[40]

Neither Bragg nor Rosecrans felt strong enough to push the other, for it took a mighty advantage for either to be willing to start a fight. Each kept his cavalry out front, probing and thrusting. During the following several weeks the Texans became familiar with most of the pikes, trails, fords, and villages from Columbia to Nashville. It was late March, and the lush countryside blazed with peach and cherry blossoms. Most days the boys picketed, skirmished, or formed in line of battle, often waiting for hours and finally returning to camp.[41]

On March 24, vacancies in the regimental field and staff were filled by appointments. The War Department had decreed that vacancies be filled by seniority instead of election. The men resented losing the privilege of choosing their officers but grudgingly accepted the War Department's decree. "Another infringement on our liberties," one said.[42]

The Ninth Texas had been without a colonel since Nathan W. Townes was wounded nearly a year earlier, without a major since J. N. Dodson had left the column north of Grenada in January. Lt. Col. Dudley Jones had been the only regimental field-grade officer present. Jones was promoted to colonel, the position he had been filling. The regiment's senior captain, Company A's Thomas G. Berry, was promoted to lieutenant colonel. The next most senior captain, James C. Bates of Company H, was promoted to major.[43]

Company-grade vacancies were filled by the same method of promotion up the line. The arbitrary system made First Lt. Absalom B. Gant captain of Company A, although Gant was absent on sick leave, had been absent for the past six months, and would never return to the regiment. Second Lt. Thomas Purcell was promoted to first lieutenant and took command of the company. Junior Second Lt. Frank O. Clare was promoted to senior second lieutenant, and Orderly Sgt. James E. Moore of Birdville was promoted to junior second lieutenant.[44]

In addition to new officers, the Ninth was issued a new flag. All the companies in the Fourth Mississippi of General Jackson's Division carried the same flag, and Jackson liked the effect. He had new flags made for his division and issued them when the command returned to their old camps near Spring Hill. The flag, a square of red bunting with white stars on diagonal blue stripes, soon became the Confederate flag, recognized by both North and South. The Ninth furled their old flag of a moon and thirteen stars on a red background and sent it home for safekeeping.[45]

The Texans and the rest of Van Dorn's corps settled into a semblance of routine as pleasant, cool weather ushered in the month of April. Advance guards of the two armies often fought, and "considerable damage was done," Newton wrote. With routine came drills and inspections, reviews and stricter discipline. Roll was called three times a day, "very inconvenient to the soldiers on the line." The reviews were tedious, but both the officers and the men enjoyed the local ladies, who came in their best dresses—the older ladies to watch, the younger ones to be watched. When Bragg inspected the entire corps April 20, ladies attended in force.[46]

Six thousand mounted men and their handsomely turned-out officers paraded for General Bragg, his escort, and the local populace. A Mobile correspondent reported the grand spectacle but was most impressed with the Texans. He wrote:

> Here come those rollicking, rascally, brave Texans; and there at their head is a young man apparently twenty-eight years of age, with wavy black hair, black moustache, an olive complexion, fine expressive features and graceful form. This is Colonel Ross, of the Sixth Texas. . . . What singular looking customers those Texans are, with their large brimmed hats, dark features, shaggy Mexican mustangs, and a lariet . . .

around the pummel of their saddles. They are said to be unmerciful to prisoners, but are a tower of strength when there is a fight on hand.[47]

Ross and the rest of the Texans had to have been pleased. Ross commanded the Texas Brigade because Whitfield had gone to Richmond seeking promotion from his friend, the president.[48] Like Texans of all generations, they took it for granted that their state was unique and made no issue of it at home. Although many of the cavalrymen had lived in the state only a few years, all proudly considered themselves Texans. When they left the Lone Star State, the expectations thrust upon them quickly brought out their prideful arrogance.

Van Dorn had enjoyed lusty, frontier Texas and liked the rambunctious Texans. Later in the month he came out from headquarters to watch the Ninth drill. The regiment performed with precision. Both Gris and Dud Jones wrote in their diaries that Van Dorn said the Ninth Texas had the best horsemen in the world and were inferior to none in drill. Jones savored the compliment from his superior.[49]

April 27, Jones's men were quietly eating breakfast when the bugle blasted Boots and Saddles. They jumped up, ran to the picket lines, and flung the saddles on their horses. Three miles out, they found the Legion's camp destroyed. Yankee cavalry had run over the regiment. Gris described the scene:

The men and horses completely stampeded, 9 officers & 111 men captured & their train burned & 1 man (mere boy) brutally murdered because he was a cripple—The men are scattered to the four winds[,] those that came by our camp being minus hats, coats, blankets & in many instances even saddles & bridles.

The entire brigade struck out after the Yankees. The Texas cavalrymen got close enough to fire on the Federals twice before the Yanks reached safety at Franklin.[50]

The Legion's colonel was humiliated, and rightfully so. The regiment's safety had been his responsibility. Sam Barron wrote:

We all felt a keen sympathy for Colonel Broocks and his men, for no officer in the army would have felt more mortification at such an occur-

rence than the brave, gallant John H. Broocks. It was said that he was so haunted that he was almost like one demented, and that for days and days afterwards he would sit away off alone on some log, with his head down, muttering, "Halt! You d——d Rebel, halt!"[51]

The Federals were also muttering. When Maj. Gen. Gordon Grainger, in command at Franklin, was chided for failing to capture Van Dorn's irksome and dangerous cavalry, he wrote Rosecrans:

You do not seem to understand why it is so difficult to surprise and crush Van Dorn. In the first place, he keeps every road and lane and hill-top for miles picketed; the county people are his friends and are always ready to give information. His policy is to fight when he is sure to win, and always run when his success is doubtful. The nature of his troops being mounted, without baggage or transportation, enables him to do this with great facility; besides, a portion of his troops were [raised] here, and know every road and by-path. . . . I am extremely anxious to whip Van Dorn, and settle up accounts with him contracted at Thompson's Station and Brentwood.[52]

Van Dorn, basking in Fortune's smile, directed operations from a stately brick mansion in Spring Hill. Buck Van Dorn was where he had longed to be all of his life—a soldier earning a reputation in an exciting war. He and his officers enjoyed the warm weather and the hospitality of the Rebel town, including dining and dancing, card games and drinking. Van Dorn, always a ladies' man, particularly enjoyed the company of old Dr. Peters's pretty young wife.[53]

Early the morning of May 7, Dr. Peters loaded his Smith & Wesson and secreted it on his person. He walked a few rods to Van Dorn's office to secure a pass across the lines. With the paper in hand, Dr. Peters turned to leave, whirled, and shot the general in the back of the head. The assassin mounted his horse and galloped north through enemy lines with the pass Van Dorn had just signed. Three hours later. Maj. Gen. Earl Van Dorn, the dashing cavalier, was dead.[54]

The Ninth and the other commands not on picket were ordered out to the funeral that afternoon. Mounted men formed on each side of the street. The general's escort, solemn and near tears, wore black crepe armbands. Two black horses drew the hearse slowly down the street. Victor Rose described the scene:

> *The funeral . . . was very impressive and solemn. The body, in a metallic casket, was laid in the hearse; on the head of the coffin reposed his Mexican sombrero, bearing a gold Texas star; along the breast reposed his gold-hilted sword, a present from the State of Mississippi; at the foot of the coffin stood his military boots. Following the hearse was his horse, bridled and saddled. As the hearse passed down the lines, the officers and men saluted their dead chieftain with the saber; and, though extremest silence reigned, many an eye was moist.[55]*

Van Dorn's death, like his life, generated mixed feelings. To Victor, the death "was a great calamity to the Confederacy." Gris felt "a universal gloom cast over the troops—now beginning to feel his real worth." But Newton wrote, "The Army nor humanity lost nothing." Other enlisted men cheered when they learned Van Dorn was dead.[56]

The next day a small detail, all that could be spared from the front, escorted the casket to Columbia to be deposited in a vault. A few days later the body was taken to Alabama and buried at the home of Van Dorn's father-in-law. Thirty-six years later, Van Dorn's remains were taken home to Port Gibson, Mississippi, where a blond, wavy-haired boy had dreamed of military fame and glory.[57]

Gen. William H. Jackson, the senior brigadier present, assumed command of the corps before the sun set the day Van Dorn was killed. Jackson immediately put the Texans back to work. Colonel Jones wrote in his diary, "Brigade to Columbia and we have constant picket fight for the next ten days."[58]

Two weeks before Van Dorn was shot, Bedford Forrest had raced south into northern Alabama to challenge Union Col. Abel Streight's cavalry raid, directed at the railroad between Chattanooga and Atlanta. In a two-week campaign that ended near Rome, Georgia, Forrest outmaneuvered and outfought Streight. During the final five-day running battle, Forrest and his men averaged forty-one miles a day, fighting several times each day and often at night. Only 500 men were still in their saddles with Forrest when Streight's 1,500 blue cavalrymen surrendered. The citizens of Rome were ecstatic. They strew flowers along the streets when the horsemen entered, then feted and feasted the heroes. The Confederate Congress, Gen. Braxton Bragg, and newspapers across the South praised General Forrest, his officers, and his men for their daring and skill.[59]

Forrest returned to Spring Hill with orders from Bragg to take over Van Dorn's cavalry corps. The Texans had no objection to serving under this Tennessean. Forrest's brilliant and well-known successes—at Fort Donelson, Shiloh, Murfreesboro, in West Tennessee, at Thompson's Station, and now against Abel Streight's powerful raid—had spread Forrest's fame across the South. Cavalrymen all over the West envied the laurels bestowed on Forrest's men wherever they went. The Texans knew Forrest expected a great deal from his troopers and often pushed them beyond normal human limits, but victories would be more than ample reward.[60]

Jones and his men barely had time to absorb the idea that they were part of Forrest's command when the corps was broken up. They were ordered to prepare for a long march back to Mississippi with Jackson's Division.[61]

Two weeks earlier, April 30, Grant had begun ferrying his Union forces from the west bank of the Mississippi River onto dry ground fifty miles south of Vicksburg. He had 33,000 men in the rear of Vicksburg in a week and soon had ferried 10,000 more across the river. Grant set out toward Mississippi's capital of Jackson, Vicksburg's only source of supplies.[62]

Gen. Joseph Johnston was quickly ordered to Mississippi to cooperate with Pemberton, but the two officers' views differed dramatically on how the campaign should be managed. Johnston, convinced they had too few men to save Vicksburg, told Pemberton that if he could not save the city to save his army, but Pemberton marched his men into Vicksburg's fortifications. Grant's soldiers completed the investment of Vicksburg on May 19. Pemberton's 32,000 caged Confederates looked down the muzzles of their cannon at 70,000 Federals.[63]

That same day, the Ninth Texas Cavalry received orders to prepare for a long march. The men were issued a day's rations and set out the next day at noon with Jackson's Cavalry Division. The division consisted of the Texas Brigade, commanded by Colonel Ross; George B. Cosby's Mississippi Brigade; and King's Missouri Battery. They marched through Columbia and onto the Pulaski Pike.[64]

"We reluctantly bade adieu to this beautiful, picturesque middle Tennessee," Sam Barron lamented. Sam had relatives and many friends in the area. To A.W., Tennessee was glorious country where there were "great houses of corn, corn for sale for Confederate money, corn to feed the cavalry horses, corn for the mules, and bacon, shoulders, sides and hams, yes, enough of hams to get a full rations . . . even the privates." Newton remembered turning the horses loose in Tennessee's clover fields. Gris and "many of the boys stopped in town to take leave of their kind friends & acquaintances . . . it feels like leaving home."[65]

Sam, A.W., Gris, Gus, and Jesse would be back in Columbia in a year and a half. But Victor, Newton, Reuben, and Tom Berry said good-bye to glorious Tennessee on May 22, 1863, when they crossed into Alabama.

Chapter 9

Guard Duty

May 23–December 16, 1863

The Ninth Texas cavalrymen pointed their horses south toward Decatur, Alabama, on May 23, 1863, and marched along with Gen. W. H. Jackson's three thousand men in eight regiments. Animals and wagons pounded the dry dirt road to powder that quickly filled the nostrils and reddened the eyes of both man and beast. With handkerchiefs tied over their noses and mouths, the men squinted to see through the roiling dust. There was corn for the horses but little for the men to eat. As usual, the column had set out on a long journey with insufficient food— this time, enough for only one day.[1]

The cavalrymen were returning to Mississippi through western Alabama along a route fifty miles east of the roads they had followed going north a few months earlier. The long column of troopers, artillery, and dirty, canvas-topped wagons, hurrying to join General Johnston near Vicksburg, needed to avoid the Federals occupying northern Mississippi.

The Tennessee River bridge at Decatur had been burned, but three steam ferries were operating. The Ninth waited their turn for the ferries to take the horses and wagons across. With everything over, the regiment moved south two miles to feed the horses a half ration of corn and await the rest of the column. When the last wagon came ashore, Jackson's men formed and rode thirteen miles before dark.[2]

The troopers mounted early each morning for the next several days and remained in their saddles until late at night, with only a short stop in the middle of the day to rest the horses and feed them a few ears of corn or a bundle of fodder, when it could be found. The grimy column skirted the mountains on a wretched road that led through barren country. Out of Mount Hope, the column followed the Great Military Road south toward Columbus, Mississippi.[3]

While crossing the mountains, James C. Thomas, Company A's blacksmith, deserted. Perhaps he had seen too much killing, or maybe he had marched far enough, gone hungry long enough, and said "Yes, sir" as many times as he could tolerate.[4]

The horsemen and their trains hurried on. After ten days on the road they crossed into Mississippi east of Columbus and camped in the valley of the Tombigbee, a lush grain region. Townsmen sent out meat, bread, peas, cabbage, green beans, turnips, and carrots, enough to supply half rations to all the hungry men. Citizens even hauled forage for the cavalrymen's lean animals. After the long march, this unexpected hospitality brought bright smiles to the men's bearded faces. Late in the day they stripped off their dust-coated clothing for a swim in the clear, cool river. A couple of days later, when the column passed through the old Choctaw agency, near Louisville, citizens again stood on the roadside and passed out bread, meat, pies, milk, and water. It was good to be back in Mississippi.[5]

Jackson pushed the column southwest and reached Canton June 3, 1863. The frazzled Texans bedded down, hoping for a little rest, but reveille sounded early the next morning. The boys did their chores and made themselves and their mounts as presentable as they could. Gen. Joseph Johnston had arrived to review their division. After Jackson's eight regiments formed in a field for the formalities, Johnston reviewed the command and accepted the salute. He complimented the men on their "soldierly appearance after so long and fatiguing a march made in so short a time & on part rations." Jackson also praised his men for their rapid 375-mile march across mountains and over bad roads.[6]

The exhausting service in Tennessee and the hurried march back to

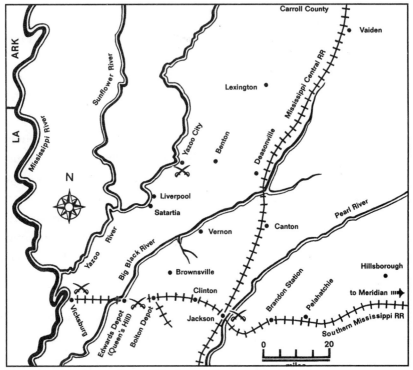

Vicksburg—Jackson—Yazoo City Area—Western Mississippi

Mississippi had been hard on the horses. Many had died, and others were broken down. Around Canton, many animals, starved for anything green, ate "Sneeze Nuratrum weed," causing a malady that resembled what the Texans called "the blind staggers." The poisonous weed caused the animals to have "fits," and they often died. The cavalrymen quickly learned to identify the weed; their horses were difficult to replace and outrageously expensive. Captured horses were issued occasionally, but more often the men had to buy, beg, or borrow to replace their mounts. Lt. Gris Griscom and Sam Barron could afford to purchase horses, but privates could not. Prices had steadily risen since the beginning of the war until a horse valued at $125 two years earlier was selling for $500 to $600. In another nine months, horses would become so valuable that Sul Ross sold his "warhorse" to Gen. Red Jackson for $5,000.[7]

The day after the review the four Texas regiments went back to work under the command of Brig. Gen. John W. Whitfield, recently returned from Richmond with the promotion he had sought. When Whitfield had joined the column on its march from Tennessee, he found

Col. Sul Ross, Sixth Texas, in command of the Texas Brigade. Ross had commanded the brigade during most of their time in Tennessee. Even before Whitfield departed for the Confederate capital, Ross often had been left with the day-to-day responsibilities of the brigade while Whitfield stayed at a hotel in town— "frolicking around seeing his friends," Ross wrote his wife Lizzie. The colonel's performance pleased Generals Johnston and Jackson and the Texas troopers. Whitfield, forty-five years old, over six feet tall, and

Vicksburg, Mississippi

straight as an arrow, looked like a soldier, but in truth he was a politician. Ross, twenty years younger, also tall and straight, *was* a soldier—but he also was a colonel. General Whitfield took command of the Texas Brigade.[8]

June 5, Whitfield led his regiments west from Canton twenty-two miles out on the Yazoo Road. For the next month the Ninth garrisoned the area around Brownsville, the region between the city of Jackson and Federal lines investing Vicksburg. Buglers often sounded Boots and Saddles, and the regiments were constantly in action.[9]

Rations and forage were scarce, but wild berries growing along the roadside were ripe and the corn was ready. Newt recalled:

> *We lived on roasting ears most of the time and on blackberries. One of the finest ways in the world to cook roasting ears is to build a log heap fire, and when it has burned down take your corn with shuck on, and make a large opening in the ashes, and throw in about forty or fifty ears and then cover over with hot embers some six inches deep. In about forty minutes your corn will be done . . . the only difficulty we had was in obtaining wood with which to make fire. We often used [fence] rails.*[10]

The Ninth camped a few days within a hundred yards of a church where a revival was being held. Many men attended the preaching. They needed the comfort of religion and the feeling of normalcy the meetings offered. The weather was hot and dry, and there was little to eat but corn and berries. Skirmishing and picketing in the rough, broken country were dangerous and frustrating. The Texans longed to go home for a few weeks. All mail had ceased except what was sent via hired couriers, who charged a dollar a letter. Union forces investing Vicksburg increased by the day, and the men knew the results of the siege could affect the outcome of the war. Attending church brought a few moments of civility and spirituality.[11]

Perhaps the Rogers boys took advantage of the nearby services. Reuben and Jesse had attended the Methodist church each Sunday as long as they were at home. Pa would have seen to that.[12]

Most citizens around Brownsville were hospitable, although a few were wary of the wild Texas boys. As lieutenants, Gris and Sam were considered gentlemen and had opportunities to visit the ladies and socialize. After one gathering, Gris wrote that a Mississippi colonel's wife expressed "surprise indeed with us Texicans at finding so much *civilization* in our portion of the army." The lady, who thought of all Texans as border ruffians, told Gris she found more intelligence in the Texas army than in others she had encountered.[13]

Certainly, some Texans relished their state's reputation for rowdiness and independence, and few failed to take pride in the recognition the Lone Star State brought them. Texas pride was—and still is—rooted in its history. Only twenty-seven years before Gris's conversation with the colonel's lady, Texans wrested their freedom from Mexico in a short but cruel war and established the Republic of Texas. It was ten years before the Mexican War forced that nation to recognize Texas independence. The war finally persuaded the U.S. Congress that if they continued refusing Texas admission to the Union, Texas would look elsewhere for an alliance.

Although many men in Ross's Brigade had lived in Texas only a few years, all claimed to be Texans, including Gris Griscom, Dud Jones, David Garrett, A.W. Sparks, Gus Creed, the Rogers brothers, and numerous other officers and men in the four regiments.

June 19, the Sixth relieved the Ninth at Brownsville. The regiment reluctantly left the friendly town to move to Bolton, on the Southern Mississippi Railroad, where they joined the rest of the brigade. Long before light the next morning booming artillery at Vicksburg woke everyone in camp. Huge waves of sound rumbled across the countryside from sunup to sundown. The Texans had been hearing cannonading since reaching central Mississippi, but this was heavier. When Sam first had heard the cannonading, he had asked the distance to Vicksburg and was told it was a hundred miles. Dud Jones had written in his diary from Canton, "Again we hear the voice of 'Whistling Dick' as he bellows defiance at Vicksburg near forty miles away."[14]

Artillerymen defending Vicksburg named many of their guns—"Crazy Jane" and "Widow Blakely" and "Lady Davis." But "Whistling Dick" was the most famous. The peculiar, shrill sound of the gun, a rifled 18-pounder, could be heard above all other artillery. Its muzzle had been damaged and about a foot of the barrel had been cut off, which many believed accounted for the unusual whistling. A Mississippi infantryman wondered if the strange shape of the ammunition used in "Whistling Dick" caused its distinctive sound. He described the projectiles as square-cut with pointed ends.[15]

The unusually heavy cannonading heralded increased activities for the Ninth. From Bolton's Depot, the regiment scouted south. June 23, Company A lost two men, one captured and another wounded. The captured man, Alanzo Stephenson was a short, black-haired young man whose luck held throughout the war. He had been captured at Hatchie Bridge back in October but had been released in a few days. Now, the Federals added him to their pen of captured Rebels in Mississippi. In another couple of weeks Alanzo would be paroled and exchanged with the Vicksburg prisoners. He would return to the regiment and serve the rest of the war.[16]

In a few more days the Ninth moved west along a road that paralleled the railroad to Messenger's Ferry, on the Big Black River. From the banks of the river they watched Yankees throwing up earthworks near a battery a mile away. When the Yankees crossed the river July 4, three companies of the Ninth moved out to stall them. The Third and the Legion came up and flanked the Federals, who moved back to their side of the river. A Union officer reported: "Owing to their superior knowledge of the country, it was impossible to surround them and I do not think we succeeded in demoralizing their cavalry much."[17]

That evening the Texans feasted on a fine mess of roasting ears the Yankees had left "ready cooked."[18]

The corn was the only good thing any member of the Texas Brigade remembered about July 4, 1863. John C. Pemberton surrendered Vicksburg to U. S. Grant that day. Neither Gris Griscom nor Dud Jones mentioned the surrender in his diary. Newton Keen did not mention the surrender in his book. Victor Rose's total account of the momentous event was "intelligence came of the surrender." Sam Barron commented, "Vicksburg

Crossing on the Big Black

was surrendered on the 4th, and the 5th our pickets . . ." David Garrett mentioned the surrender in none of his extant letters. It was not a day the Texans wanted to remember.[19]

Pemberton, the 4,000 citizens, and the 31,600 soldiers trapped in the besieged city had hoped and earnestly prayed for forty-seven days that Joseph Johnston would come to their relief. The citizens and soldiers had a right to pray, but Pemberton had chosen to trap himself. President Davis had instructed him to hold the city. Johnston, Pemberton's superior on the field, had told Pemberton that if he had to choose between the city and the army, to save the men.[20]

Pemberton and many citizens blamed Johnston for the loss of Vicksburg, but even housewives in the town knew a city besieged was a city lost. Once Grant completed his investment, it would have taken three times the number of men Johnston had—and there were no more to be found anywhere—to break through the lines and save Pemberton. Johnston had been telling the War Department for a month ". . . my force is too small for the purpose." The War Department answered, "You must rely on what you have." A clerk in Richmond felt that Pemberton's loss of Vicksburg was unpardonable. The accusations and arguments have not ceased to this day.[21]

The Texans, despite their reluctance to mention the catastrophe, were not unaware of the dire consequences. One had written home two weeks earlier: "This fight will tell something of the fate of our beloved country."[22]

The rest of the men soon learned that the Confederacy had taken a double blow on Independence Day. A day earlier, Robert E. Lee, a thousand miles to the east, had lost the battle of Gettysburg. Before 1863, July 4 had been the liveliest, most celebrated holiday in the nation, but it would be more than three quarters of a century before the country's birthday was again celebrated in the Lone Star State.[23]

During the siege the Texas cavalry regiments had picketed and scouted daily, occasionally skirmishing with enemy scouts or foraging parties. Newton remembered: "Everyday more or less we were fighting in what we called skirmish work. There was often from one to two and three men killed and in a month this amounted to considerable loss."[24]

Boots and Saddles woke Jones and his men at 2:30 A.M., July 6 at their Queen's Hill camp, near the Big Black. By the time the boys were on their feet, infantry was already moving through their camp toward a mass of advancing Yankees. With the surrender of Vicksburg, Grant's blue-clad regiments had turned their attention east and were pushing along the railroad toward Mississippi's capital of Jackson. Maj. Gen. William Tecumseh Sherman commanded the U.S. forces.[25]

The Texas cavalrymen moved to the front at seven that morning. In the afternoon the Ninth relieved the Legion at the extreme front and soon came in range of a Federal battery. Companies A, B, D, and E, under the command of Tom Berry, were serving as pickets and skirmishers. Jones and the other companies fell back, fighting every foot of the way. The Yankees flanked Berry's four companies and drove them into a swamp near the Big Black just as a booming thunderstorm hit. Jones and the rest of the regiment were quickly overwhelmed. They fell back east. During the fighting Sgt. John N. Sparks, Company I, was shot through the breast. It was long past midnight before the regiment reached a secure place to feed the horses. John Sparks had been left in critical condition at a field infirmary. The four companies with Berry were still missing.[26]

A. W. Sparks was not with the Ninth but on detail at Jackson when word reached him that his brother had been mortally wounded and was in the hospital at Clinton, between Jackson and Queen's Hill. A.W. went to his temporary commander and asked permission to visit John. The officer refused. The "thought of a Texas mother and sisters and a dying brother flashed like lightning through my mind and set me wild," A.W. later wrote. He told the officer that he "would go if he had to fight his way and spoke in a manner very unbecoming an inferior." When the angry officer placed A.W. under arrest, the young Texan drew his pistol, fired, and bolted out the door.[27]

A.W. flung himself onto his horse and raced ten miles west along the dirt road that followed the railroad tracks to Clinton. At a brush arbor that was serving as a hospital, he found John lying on a cot, pale from loss of blood and dazed by opiates. John recognized him, but Dr. Vandyke forbid A.W. to speak to his brother, who had been shot through the lung. A.W. wrote:

> To look at him was more than I could bear, so I walked out and lay down and then a thousand thoughts passed my sore and troubled mind. I could stay only a few minutes, for the enemy were already in the town and the last line of our army's rear guard was then passing.

A.W. gave the doctor $300 in Confederate money and asked that John be saved, if possible. If not, he asked, would Dr. Vandyke please purchase a coffin and bury John in a well-marked grave. A.W. "fully intended to carry the bones" home to their mother, if he "should ever go to that place." He begged the doctor to let him know how John was doing. After his conversation with Vandyke, A.W. stared at his brother's pale face. Overcome by emotion, he unconsciously called out, "Mother!"

A.W., numbed by grief, remained by John's cot until pounding hoof-beats and whizzing minié balls penetrated his senses. He realized he had no weapons and the Yankees had all the roads. He wandered away from the hospital and into the woods, not knowing or caring where he was. As he was stumbling along in the darkness thick enough to feel, a voice ordered "Halt!"

"A. W. Sparks, Ninth Texas Cavalry," A.W. replied.

"Mark Blair, Third Texas Cavalry," the vedette said. Mark stood guard the rest of the night while A.W. "dozed in a troubled and un-sound sleep."

When Mark was relieved at dawn, he took A.W. to his mess and shared his breakfast of cold bread and raw meat. A.W. soon learned that the Ninth was on another road and would be difficult to find. Determined not to leave the service without letting his messmates and officers know what had happened, he returned to Jackson, where he was arrested immediately and placed under guard for disobedience in the face of the enemy, a capital offense. A.W. was not charged with murder; the bullet had only grazed the officer's arm.

The day after John was shot and the Ninth fell back without Berry and his four companies, the other six companies fed their horses at sunup. They were ordered north to drive off stock the enemy might appropriate and shoot animals in all the pools to spoil the water for the approaching Yanks. Reaching Clinton in the afternoon, they bivouacked in a heavy rainstorm. Berry and his men straggled into camp during the night, tired, muddy, and hungry. They had slogged through swamps and mud for twenty-four hours to avoid blue pickets. They had lost six men.[28]

There was little the Confederates could do to slow Sherman's 16,000 Federals, who were forcing their way toward Mississippi's capital, on the west bank of the clear-running Pearl River. Sherman's purpose was to take the city and drive the Rebels out of the state. The Ninth Texas, along with the rest of General Johnston's army, struggled to stop the blue avalanche descending on them.[29]

July 9, the Third and the Ninth fell back to the fortifications around Jackson. After skirmishing dismounted all day, they moved back to the infantry lines and bivouacked in the streets of the city after dark.[30]

Sam Barron had made his way along the skirmish lines delivering messages during the day. He rode a new horse that he had not tried under fire. He wrote that while riding up the line,

the enemy's skirmishers soon began firing at me, and kept it up until I made the round trip, the minie balls constantly clipping the brush very near me and my horse. This completely demoralized my horse, and he would jump as high and as far as he possibly could every time he heard them. Some horses seem to love a battle, while others are almost unmanageable under fire. The first horse I rode in the army was lazy

and had to be spurred . . . but when we were going into battle and the
firing began he would champ the bits, pull on the bridle, and want to
move up.[31]

While Sam was delivering messages, A.W. was at Jackson under guard
for disobedience in the face of the enemy. He knew that Article 52 of
the Articles of War stated:

Any officer or soldier who shall misbehave himself before the enemy, run
away, or shamefully abandon any fort, post, or guard . . . being duly
convicted thereof, shall suffer death, or such other punishment as shall
be ordered by the sentence of a general court-martial.[32]

A.W.'s general court-martial was set while the Ninth was camped in
Jackson. Pvt. Mortimer Hart, Company E, marched A.W. to the state-
house for arraignment before Gen. William Hardee, Gen. Leonidas Polk,
and another officer. Standing in front of the generals, A.W.'s mind reeled.
He was so agitated he did not comprehend what was being said. About
two minutes after the trial opened he realized the court had issued Mort
an order. A.W. did not understand, but Mort did. He led A.W. out of
the building and finally made him understand that he had been cleared
of all charges.[33]

"Again the spirit of war thrilled my veins," A.W. said, "and again
were vows renewed to fight to the last for the Confederacy." Colonel
Jones disapproved, "but, Colonel Tom Berry was kind enough to say at
my hearing that I was not to blame, and Captain Haynes was ever
afterwards my friend and his sympathy appeared real for he had lost from
his side a noble brother"—J. B. "Buster" Haynes, killed at Corinth.
A.W. returned to his company.[34]

The Ninth and all of Red Jackson's division moved out of the besieged city of Jackson Tuesday, July 14, on their way to Sherman's rear
to disrupt his supplies and communications. The horsemen rode all day
and through the night. Thursday morning at first light they urged their
tired horses through Brownsville and turned south to Bolton's Station,
on the Mississippi Central, halfway between Vicksburg and Jackson. They
had reached Sherman's rear. "A bold scheme," a Union colonel who
had word of them reported to Sherman.[35]

The colonel had learned the Rebel cavalry division's plans from Leroy Carter of the Third Iowa Infantry, U.S.A., who had escaped from Jackson's blacksmith department. Leroy had not been exchanged as punishment for stealing. Leroy also reported the strength of each regiment in the Texas Brigade, a rare account of the number of men on field duty: Third Texas, 400 men; Sixth Texas, 350; Ninth Texas, 300; Texas Legion, 180; for a total of 1,230. The Legion had lost 77 men at Thompson's Station and 120 more when the regiment was run over in Tennessee.[36]

Sherman's rear was no place for a couple of thousand gray cavalrymen whose plans the aggressive officer knew. Jackson's horsemen could only irritate the mass of Yankees pouring east out of Vicksburg. He sent Brig. Gen. George B. Cosby's division of Mississippians toward Clinton on the Vicksburg–Jackson Road and the Texans farther west along the same road. Cosby was quickly pushed back east.[37]

The Third and Ninth Texas rode to Bolton's Station while the Sixth and the Legion moved in the direction of Clinton. When scouts from the Ninth discovered a Federal supply-and-ammunition train two miles south of the depot, they charged the rear of the train while the Third remained in reserve. The Ninth quickly captured sixty mules, eighty-five prisoners, and thirteen wagons and ambulances that were trailing the Federal train, which was too heavily guarded to attack. The Texans' spoils also included rifles, pistols, and "plenty of eatables including coffee." Enemy artillery soon drove them off. They took their prisoners and the spoils, loaded in two ambulances, north through Brownsville and hurried past Vernon before stopping for the night.[38]

The cavalrymen had been in the saddle forty hours and had ridden forty-three miles since sunup. They tended the horses and fell to the ground exhausted. After a few hours' sleep they were back in their saddles. During the middle of the morning two thousand enemy infantry, artillery, and cavalry checked their advance. The Texans skirmished four hours, then fled east across a shallow ford on the Pearl. Five miles beyond the river, they bivouacked for the night. They were out of food but found green corn in the fields along the road.[39]

While Jackson's cavalrymen were trying to harass Sherman, the red-headed Union general drove Joseph Johnston's men out of the city of Jackson and turned the town into "one mass of charred ruins," as Sherman reported. Joe Johnston moved east along the railroad past Brandon and on to Pelahatchie Station in Rankin County, twenty-two miles east of the Mississippi capital. Monday, July 20, Jackson's cavalrymen reached the station after their sweep west. They were worn, dirty, and hungry.

Burning the City of Jackson

Trains rolling into Pelahatchie from the east brought rations, forage, and baggage—even the baggage the Ninth had left near Grenada back in January, or at least part of it. The trunks had been broken open and rifled.[40]

The rainy season had set in, and the hot Southern summer was in full force. In a few days Sherman reported that he had so exhausted the land between the Big Black and the Pearl that no army could exist in the area. Sherman pulled his forces back west of the Big Black. Finally, the Ninth and the rest of Jackson's men had time to cook rations, a feast after fasting.[41]

Dr. Vandyke stopped on his way east to see A.W. The doctor reported that John was still in the hospital at Clinton, then in Federal hands, and that his wounds were "running goodmatter." He assured A.W. that with proper care John's fearful wound would heal.[42]

"Of course to see him was then all my thought," A.W. later wrote. Lieutenant Colonel Berry said A.W. could go to Clinton, but Colonel Jones, saying it was impractical to try, refused to give A.W. a pass. Captain Haynes told A.W. he could not give him a pass over the colonel's objection, but he would not put him on report for being absent for five days.[43]

The Ninth was camped more than thirty miles from Clinton. Without a pass, A.W. would be considered a deserter if caught by Confederates, a spy if caught by the Federals. Either could result in hanging.[44]

Early the next morning A.W. rode out of camp, only two of his messmates knowing where he was going. He followed a farm road west to the Pearl River bottom, five miles south of Jackson, where he stripped and swam his horse across the river. He quickly dressed and started cautiously across country to avoid both blue and gray pickets on the roads. In the afternoon clouds obscured the sun and it began to rain. A.W. lost his bearings. He finally came out on the fenced Jackson–Clinton Road, which he recognized, and started west, but he had gone only a short distance when he spotted two Yankee troopers riding toward him. A.W. wheeled and spurred his horse. To his great relief he found a weak place in the fence and "passed out of the lane into a corn field on a good run." The Yanks did not follow.

"I tied my horse in some woodland and fed him some corn from the field and left him to eat while I went to the top of the hill to reconnoiter," he wrote. Below, he saw the town of Clinton. With the day nearly gone, A.W. decided to wait until dark to move farther. He ate the ration he had in his haversack and lay down for a nap. Raindrops falling in his face woke him at dusk. He mounted and rode back to the road as the rain increased and the night became very dark.

Within sight of the lights of the town, A.W. stopped at a small farmhouse and explained to the owner why he wanted to leave his horse and saddle; he told the farmer that if he did not return by the next night, the horse and saddle were his. The farmer agreed. A.W. tied his horse in the farmer's smokehouse and left his saddle, overcoat, and haversack on the floor. When he returned to the house, the man had supper prepared for him.

The farmer told A.W. that the enemy had taken all the wounded to the college building but that Yankee pickets were near the house, along all the roads, and in every street of the town. A mile and a half away stood the hospital, under constant guard. The farmer also said this was the time of day when the surgeons were in the hospital, but they would all leave later. "I bid him goodbye and shook his hand with the warmth that I felt," A.W. later wrote. A black woman, who was washing dishes, wanted to say good-bye. When A.W. shook her hand, he discovered she was crying. He "felt that she too was a friend."

A.W. set out afoot in the driving rain. He followed a ditch filled with water, then slowly crawled down a hill in the mud. While crossing a shallow creek, the Yankee pickets' relief came down the hill from town. A.W. sat down in the water to hide among some logs. "I took to shivering, not [from] cold," he said, "but shook so bad that I thought

I would die soon, but I looked up the hill and saw the light in a large brick hospital and resolved to go ahead and not shake[,] as I was wet and muddy I felt that I could not be worsted."

It "was raining like blazes." Near the hospital, A.W. crawled along another ditch. "My hand fell on the amputated leg of some poor hospital sufferer, and at once I knew I was crawling through the cess pools of the hospital, and then I realized the sickening stench and it made me very sick, yes, very sick."

When A.W. reached the fence around the hospital he washed as well as he could in the rain and surveyed the building. Guards stood at each gate. Doctors and nurses came and went. At the back of the building he noticed nurses stepping through a low window to dip water from an open cistern a few feet away. He crawled through a broken place in the fence and moved toward the window, then stood against the wall of the building for a long while, watching.

Finally, all the doctors left and the hospital was dark and quiet. Stepping through the window, A.W. "stole along the cots to try and see the face of my brother but all my efforts were in vain." He stepped out the window and lay down in the mud between the sill and the cistern to wait. When a nurse, coming for water, stepped over the windowsill, A.W. gently took hold of the man's foot. The nurse, Joe, stooped and looked down. A.W. quietly asked about John and pleaded to see him.

Joe told A.W. that John was doing well and that he would arrange for A.W. to see his brother. "Later he came for me and led me into his mess room and hastily stripped me and gave me a hospital shirt and drawers." A.W. was surprised when he discovered he still had on his pistol and spurs. The pistol made Joe nervous, but he hid the gun and spurs in a trapdoor beneath his stove.[45]

Joe led A.W. to a ward and put him to bed next to a sleeping man he said was John. A.W. studied the patient's face. "He appeared much older to me . . . his nose was too sharp and his lips too thin and flabby and I fancied his hair was a shade or two too dark . . . he was not the jovial, good natured and lovable brother who was always ready to take hard duty for me"—John was five years older. When the lights dimmed, A.W. fell asleep, still trying to find John in the ugly face.

A.W. awoke when Joe whispered to the patient, "Your brother has come." A.W. looked at the man. "To my joy," he said, "that ghastly look had left him and his open eyes told too well it was my brother. Our hands met. I felt his bony fingers and I knew my brother and his look changed and those fancies were driven away with the first look from his kind eyes."

When the nurse came to carefully sponge John's wounds and replace the oilcloths he lay on, A.W. saw half a pint of "the most offensive pus that I had ever beheld." He was horrified and could not imagine why Dr. Vandyke had said John's wounds were running "goodmatter." Only after a long talk with his brother did A.W. become convinced John was improving.

A.W. kept to his bed all that next day. "When night again came and all was still I left as I had entered and outside in the dark I put on my clothes over the hospital shirt and drawers and had much less difficulty in evading the guards." The farmer's house was dark when he quietly retrieved his horse and saddle. To avoid further endangering the kind man, A.W. rode five or six miles before stopping to sleep. He returned to camp early the next morning and performed extra duty for being absent without leave.

While A.W. was gone, Jackson's tired cavalrymen had remained in camp, a luxury they seldom enjoyed. Forage and *full* rations, another rare luxury, arrived by rail. The mules and horses had been living on cane and a little grass, the men on corn and berries. The weather was intensely hot and it rained daily.[46]

July 27, Special Orders No. 14 arrived from department headquarters granting sixty-day furloughs to one of every twenty-five men present for duty. Everyone was excited, many feeling they would be the lucky ones. After the officers and the men drew lots for the scarce furloughs, winners eagerly filled out their papers.[47]

The day following the drawing for furloughs the men brushed their worn uniforms, curried their thin horses, and marched out to the reviewing field for inspection, this time a Grand Inspection of the entire command. Jackson's Cavalry Division contained Brig. Gen. George B. Cosby's First Brigade of Mississippians and Brig. Gen. J. W. Whitfield's Second Brigade, 4,519 officers and men present, 6,659 aggregate. A Grand Inspection included scrutiny of every man, horse, and department.

Col. Dud Jones reported in his diary the inspection of "the naked horses and equipment." Considering the condition of the men's clothing, some of them must have been nearly naked.[48]

August 1, a Saturday, Jackson ordered the Third and the Ninth on a scout to the west to assess the condition of the railroad and the amount of available forage. Jackson placed the Ninth's Colonel Jones in command, not Brig. Gen. J. W. Whitfield. Jones took the best horses and no wagon train. West of the Pearl, the two regiments crossed the Big Black on one of the few remaining bridges in the area and rode north under the pitiless August sun. They found fruit and forage plentiful in the area. Patriotic citizens cooked for the hungry men and invited them to their homes. Thursday night, at Lexington, "a large concourse of pretty ladies" turned out for nightly dress parade and arranged a dance in the evening.[49]

The scouting party was back at Pelahatchie on August 9, when the official leave and furlough papers arrived. Some had been disapproved and others were for less than sixty days. Moreover, the men could not go home. A provision on the papers, printed in red ink, prohibited them from entering the enemy's lines. With the Federals holding the entire Mississippi River, there was no way to reach home. Colonel Jones, most of the company commanders, and the furloughed men left two days later, traveling east instead of west toward Texas.[50]

The records of Company A show that Pvt. Solon Dunn of Grapevine and Pvt. Joseph H. Simmons of Birdville each received a sixty-day furlough dated August 11, 1863. That same day Dud Jones left with a forty-day leave in his pocket.[51]

Sam Barron had suggested that the officers of his Company C, Third Texas, allow Capt. John Germany the leave, but Germany insisted they draw. "All right, then we'll draw for it, and I will get it," Sam said. Sam did win, but he gave the furlough to Captain Germany, who had relatives all over Mississippi, Alabama, and Georgia. Sam stayed in Mississippi.[52]

Jesse and Reuben, A.W., Victor, Gris, and Gus also remained on duty. Furthermore, according to extant records, none of them would receive a furlough during their entire service. After they rode across the Red River into Indian Territory in the fall of 1861, they would not see home again until the war was over.[53]

★　　★　　★

Soon after the lucky ones left on their furloughs, forage around the railroad station gave out. Jackson took his division west of the Pearl, where Jones had found provisions and forage more available. August 14, the Texas Brigade was ordered north into Carroll County to challenge an enemy cavalry raid bent on gathering up railroad engines and cars to run back to Memphis. Sam Barron wrote:

We were sent after them and had a lively race. As they were about twenty-four hours ahead of us they would have succeeded, doubtless, had not someone burned a bridge across a small creek opposite Kosciusko. As may be imagined, we gave them little time to repair the bridge. We moved about a hundred miles in two days, with no feed for men or horses except green corn from the fields.[54]

When the column reached a village near Vaiden on August 17, "the good ladies had prepared a splendid picnic dinner for us," Sam continued. "But as we could not stop to partake of it," he added, the ladies "lined up on each side of the column as we passed, with waiters loaded with chicken, ham, biscuit, cake, pies and other tempting viands and the men helped themselves as they passed, without halting." The Ninth was in the rear, but their many acquaintances in the area saved choice items for them. The hungry men had been in their saddles since 6:30 that morning and would not stop to feed and rest until 3:00 the following morning.[55]

A week after leaving their wagon trains and dashing north, the Texans returned to their trains, ten miles south of Canton. They rejoined the division and moved west to the Big Black to establish a new picket line on the east side of the river. Jackson ordered out permanent scouts. August 23, the division set up camp a mile from Vernon at the Mount Bluff Church, in Madison County.[56]

The Texans quickly became bored with picketing. They were not protecting their homes, as were the Mississippi regiments in the division. The men were worn out. The horses were worn out. Many officers were on leave, including the Ninth's colonel and most of the company commanders. The Texans had been on nearly constant duty since being remounted the year before. All summer they had marched and fought in muggy heat and constant rain, accomplishing little. Most of the time they depended on citizens' generosity for food or lived on corn from nearby fields.

The Confederate Commissary Department could not feed them, and they had no money to purchase food. Men in the Third had not been paid since May, and those in the Ninth were last paid in June. Inflation made what money they had all but useless. For a private, a pair of boots cost ten months' pay; shoeing a horse required twenty-five days' pay. Peaches cost $1.50 a dozen, a chicken $2, pork $1 a pound, and a watermelon sold for $10. Horses, when they could be found, cost from $600 to $1,000, so much the officers could not afford them, much less the privates. A Texan wrote home, "Everything is out of reason except Confederate money. It is tolerably low down."[57]

Jackson was no happier than his Texans. He must have been tugging his bushy, red mustache and stomping around his tent at midnight in frustration. Both his brigade commanders, George Cosby and J. W. Whitfield, were inefficient leaders. Jackson considered Whitfield "entirely unfit for command," and Cosby's officers and men disliked serving with him. Later in the year Maj. Gen. Stephen D. Lee wrote Cosby that

> *reports concerning a want of confidence on the part of your command toward you [have been made]. . . . It is my belief that there are but few officers or men in your command who have confidence in your judgment and ability on the field, and there is an aversion on their part to go into battle under you. . . . I have yet to find the first officer who is willing to remain with or serve under you.*

Lee suggested Cosby apply for a transfer. His brigade soon came under the command of Brig. Gen. Wirt Adams, a capable Mississippi planter and banker, and a veteran of the Texas war of independence.[58]

Around the middle of August, Brigadier General Whitfield, his health declining and his position deteriorating, resigned as commander of the Texas Brigade. Sam Barron said Whitfield resigned because of failing health. Victor Rose wrote that "Whitfield, whose health was feeble, sought service in the Trans-Mississippi Department." Certainly, campaigning the past three months had been hard service for a forty-five-year-old. Nevertheless, when Whitfield had reported to Gen. Joseph Johnston at Canton, back in June, Johnston had wired Richmond that

W. H. Jackson felt Whitfield unfit for cavalry service and asked that the new brigadier be relieved and Col. Sul Ross be given command of the Texans. The wire continued, "What are your intentions in regard to him [Whitfield]? I am informed that it will be very unfortunate for him to command the brigade to which he has belonged." President Davis, nine hundred miles from the field of action and averse to granting any request from Joe Johnston, gave Johnston no choice. Brigadier General Whitfield, ranking Colonel Ross, took command.[59]

In order not to lose Sul Ross's effectiveness as a brigade leader, Jackson had detached the Texas Ranger and his Sixth and transferred Cosby's First Mississippi Cavalry to Ross. Ross had taken his new brigade on a raid into Tennessee while the rest of the Texans remained in Mississippi.[60]

After Whitfield resigned, Col. Hinchie P. Mabry was given command of the Texas Brigade. Mabry had been severely wounded at Iuka and had only recently returned to duty. An original captain in the Third Texas, he had been elected lieutenant colonel at the first reorganization and soon became colonel of the Third. A Georgian by birth, he moved to Texas as a young man, studied law, and served in the legislature. Gen. S. D. Lee considered Mabry one of the best officers in the army.[61]

August 22, the Ninth received General Orders No. 1 from Maj. Gen. S. D. Lee announcing his assumption of command of all the cavalry in Mississippi. A thirty-year-old West Pointer from South Carolina, Lee had commanded the artillery at Vicksburg and had recently been promoted. His family connections, education, and experience at Vicksburg won him the command, although he lacked cavalry experience.[62]

That same day, Lt. Col. J. N. Dodson appeared in the Ninth's camp to assume his duties. He had been reinstated and promoted by the War Department after being dropped for absence and sickness. None of the officers in the field—Johnston, Lee, or Jackson—had been consulted. Lt. Col. Tom Berry and Maj. James C. Bates both offered to resign. By War Department rules, Berry would become major of the regiment and Bates would go back to his company. Gris wrote in his diary, "trouble anticipated therefrom." Berry and Bates were excellent officers, liked and respected by all. Dodson, evidently feeling the antagonism his appearance created, did not assume command, nor was he ordered to do so.[63]

The Texans began to brood. They were bewildered by all the

changes and infighting among the officers. There was no mail. They were homesick. The Mississippians in the division had been allowed to go home for a couple of weeks. All of Pemberton's men paroled at Vicksburg had been granted thirty-day leaves. If a Texan chanced to get a furlough, he could not go home. They had little to show for their effort and blood. Their colonel was gallivanting around Richmond, buying new clothes and enjoying the entertainment. Furthermore, Company A did not even have a captain. First Lt. Thomas Purcell had been in command of the company since Tom Berry had been promoted back in March. Capt. A. B. Gant had been on sick leave when promoted, was still gone, and would never return. Purcell also was away on leave, and Second Lt. Frank Clare commanded the company. The men liked Clare, Bates, and Berry, and had no objections to their brigade commander or their new corps commander, but the changes caused more disruption. Many Texans had seen all the elephant they were interested in.[64]

Four men from Company H, raised in Lamar County, deserted the night of August 27. During the next few days ten more left. September 4, when morning roll was called, eleven more men from Company H had deserted; a lieutenant and ten men from Company B of Fannin County were gone; and ten from Company G of Hopkins County had left. Rumor suggested that if enough men went west of the "Big Muddy" the brigade would be transferred to Texas. "A general depression of feeling" swept through the regiment, but most of the men were disgusted with the deserters. David Garrett felt a deserter was "a man in form but not acts" and that citizens should "deal out to them disgrace [and] dishonor."[65]

Gen. S. D. Lee, Gen. W. H. Jackson, and their superiors, were startled into action. They ordered daily reviews and drills. Lt. Gen. William Hardee and Maj. Gen. S. D. Lee both came out to Mount Bluff Church for another Grand Review of the entire division. Two weeks later, Gen. Joseph E. Johnston himself reviewed the division. To further dissuade desertion, Maj. J. C. Bates, two lieutenants, and two privates, all of the Ninth, were ordered to Texas to bring back every man from the Texas Brigade that they could find.[66]

Col. Dud Jones returned from leave a week later. With Major Bates on his way to Texas, the regiment needed its colonel. The tall, neat, twenty-one-year-old was the only full colonel present with the Texas

Brigade, and he took his responsibilities seriously. His presence and quick mind had earned his men's respect.[67]

Finally, good news arrived in the cavalrymen's camp late in September. Braxton Bragg, in Tennessee, had beaten the Union army under William Rosecrans at the battle of Chickamauga and forced the Yankees back to Chattanooga. Rosecrans lost 16,000 men killed, wounded, or captured. News of the victory reached Mississippi September 23, three days after the battle. The boys cheered, but the victory was not enough to refurbish their tarnished pride. It did, however, bring immediate results in Mississippi. A week later Grant was ordered to Chattanooga. Sherman and his Vicksburg army started to Tennessee a month later.[68]

The last of September a Yankee regiment crossed the Big Black—the tacit line between the Federals and the Confederates—and gave the Texans something to do besides drill and stand inspection. Boots and Saddles woke everyone at 2:30 A.M. The command was on the move five days, skirmishing and often riding at breakneck speed. They drove away the enemy and returned to the regiment. With forage becoming scarce in the area, the horsemen soon moved camp to Mrs. Tarpley's place, on a creek south of Vernon.[69]

A few days later a party of men from the Third, the Ninth, and the Legion, including Jim and Sam King of the Ninth's Company A, decided to break the monotony of camp life and their diet of corn. The gang slipped off to the woods with their carbines. They were having a great time shooting squirrels when the entire brigade, armed for action, galloped through the trees. The officers were furious. Jim, Sam, and the other hunters were arrested.[70]

The brigade moved camp a mile from Mrs. Tarpley's place to Mrs. Treadwell's place, on the Vernon and Clinton Road in Madison County, where they had camped three weeks earlier. A tributary to the Big Black furnished water, and the site was near the junction of several major roads. Forage, as always, had priority for the cavalry.[71]

Reuben was not in camp at Mrs. Treadwell's place. He and two other men from Company A were with Capt. Hamilton C. Dial and a detachment scouring the countryside for blankets. Winter was coming on, and the men had no tents. The blankets were vital because, with the brigade constantly on the move, the men would not be able to build winter quarters. Later in the fall, General Lee would make a special request for blankets for his horsemen.[72]

October 8, Jesse and his young Tarrant County friend David Cate spent the day preparing for another inspection, this time a Minute Inspection by an officer from Hardee's staff. David had only recently rejoined the regiment after being shot in the shoulder on the Holly Springs raid nine months earlier.[73]

David had much to tell when he returned. After being shot—December 21, 1862, at Davis's Mill, he was taken to the U.S. General Hospital in La Grange, Tennessee. The last of February 1863, he was shipped to the infamous Gartiot Street Federal Military Prison in Saint Louis, then transferred to Alton, Illinois, for shipment to City Point, Virginia, the exchange point for prisoners of war. After being exchanged David entered a hospital. From there he was furloughed until his shoulder was well enough for him to return to his friends in Company A.[74]

The day Jesse and David prepared for the Minute Inspection, the officers also were busy. Adjutant Griscom checked his records and tallied the company rolls. Colonel Jones and General Jackson spent the day preparing.[75]

Dud Jones's black body servant carefully brushed the colonel's new uniform, purchased in Richmond when Jones was on leave. Young Dudley "took pride in his good looks and gloried in his profession as a soldier," one of his troopers wrote. Jones was five-foot-eleven and had brown eyes, dark hair, and a light complexion. He was a bit of a dandy, "scrupulous in dress and communications," according to one of his men. He also was something of a ladies' man. Dud, who loved books and often read the classics in the evening, started a library for his regiment.[76]

While the young colonel prepared for the Minute Inspection, perhaps he thought about his visit to the Confederate capital when he was on leave. He had wanted to go to Texas, but instead he made a loop through the Southern states, traveling by train most of the way. He went to Alabama, then Tennessee and Virginia. He stayed at the Ballard House in Richmond and found the city gay and lively. Sunday, August 23, he attended St. Paul's Church, then visited the War Department the next day. While visiting a hospital in the city, Jones was surprised to find Dr. Dundly of Palestine, Anderson County, Texas, in charge. Jones stopped at the Planter's Hotel in Charleston and visited a nearby powder mill.

He returned west through Atlanta, Montgomery, Selma, and Mobile, reaching Meridian, on Mississippi's eastern border, on September 12. From there the colonel took the Mississippi Central west to Brandon's Station, where the quartermaster furnished him a wagon for the trip to Canton. From Canton he sent to camp for an ambulance and reached his regiment at Mount Bluff Church September 16. Colonel Berry quickly explained the changes in the higher command and the unhappiness of the men. Dud Jones must have thought, Welcome back![77]

A Captain Black of Hardee's staff arrived at the division's encampment at Treadwell's Place October 9, 1863, for yet another inspection. The captain carefully examined every brigade and regimental department. He scrutinized the Ninth's company rolls, which the orderly sergeants had turned in to Gris.[78]

Rain fell for the next five days. Jesse and David must have watched the constant downpour and sullenly thought of home, where the smokehouses were full of bacon and hams and the beds were dry and warm, where there were clean clothes and freshly blackened boots. Their clothes were tattered, their boots muddy, and they were thankful for a handful of cornmeal and a hunk of rancid bacon. Home sounded good, but they would stay.[79]

While the boys moped around, Gris noted the second anniversary of the Ninth's induction into Confederate service, October 14, 1863. Gris made a "Recapitulation of casualties in the Different Battle & Skirmishes that we have lost in the 2 years Campaign":

Killed in action	58 officers & men
Mortally wounded in action	4 officers & men
Wounded in action	128 officers & men
Taken prisoner	64 officers & men
Making a total of	274 officers & men[80]

Many wounded men and those taken prisoner had returned. Gris did not tally the men who had died of disease or who had been dropped from the rolls for illness or inability, nor did he note the men who had deserted, transferred, or left for other reasons.

Half the men who had enlisted in Company A were present for duty, and two thirds were still on the company roll. Sixteen men had died of disease or been discharged because of illness, while nine had been killed in battle and twenty-one wounded. The September–October 1863 roll of Company A shows an aggregate of four officers and sixty-eight men. All four officers and fifty-two men were present for duty. If Company A was representative—and the fifty or so recent desertions are subtracted—the Ninth Texas was down to below 500 men present for duty. The previous tally of the Ninth in the *Official Records* was made May 4, 1862, seventeen months earlier: present for duty, 657; aggregate of 869.[81]

Back in June, Leroy Carter, the Federal prisoner who had escaped from Jackson's blacksmith department, had placed the active force of the Ninth Texas at about 300. The next month Gris, who as adjutant had access to regimental papers, wrote that the regiment contained between 450 and 500 men. Nevertheless, Leroy's estimate of 300 men present on a campaign without wagons or support would be reasonably accurate. Of the fifty-six men present for duty in Company A in October, twenty were away from camp scouting or gathering blankets, under arrest, or on furlough—or the roll does not reveal their activities. Only thirty-two men were in camp and available to ride at a moment's notice.[82]

The day after the Ninth's second anniversary, scouts reported that the enemy had crossed the Big Black again, this time in force. General Jackson sent the wagon trains east and ordered out the entire division. For five days the cavalrymen held off 8,000 Federal cavalry, infantry, and artillery sent out from Vicksburg to tear up the railroad and keep the Rebels busy so they would not be transferred to Chattanooga or Mobile. The brigade, having driven the Yankees back across the river, moved to their old camping grounds at Mrs. Treadwell's. Two men in the Ninth had been severely wounded, including Mortimer Hart, who had taken A.W. to his court-martial.[83]

For the next two months the Texans idled around camp, growing more and more restless. There was little to break the dull monotony of camp life. The brigade moved camp several times, finally settling down a few miles north of Brownsville.[84]

John Sparks was still in the U.S. hospital at Clinton. During the past four months A.W. had gone there several times to see his brother. By then, most wounded at the hospital had recovered or died. Only one doctor remained, and the building was no longer guarded. John was well enough to sit up for a short time. A.W. returned once more. Late in the evening he put John on his horse and "carried him away." The brothers camped for the night a mile or two beyond the hospital. The next day, A.W. stopped often to let John sleep. Eight or ten miles north of Clinton, A.W. left John in the care of a kind family. "He was now much nearer camp and I could visit him often, and in a few weeks he was again in camp," A.W. wrote.[85]

Reuben and Captain Dial's detachment returned November 6 with a hundred blankets after scouring the countryside for a month. The detachment soon learned of the month's activities—the Minute Inspection, the running fight with the Federals up and down the roads from Clinton to Vernon, two weeks of false alarms and boredom. November 11, Reuben's twenty-third birthday, the boys packed up and moved again. They marched through Brownsville and out toward Clinton to set up their encampment near Reynold's Crossroads.[86]

Colonel Mabry was still in command of the brigade. Two weeks later, during a review, the colonel became so angry with a captain that he placed the officer under arrest, likely for insubordination. A few days later Mabry ordered the brigade to saddle up to meet a force of advancing Federals. The horsemen dashed down the road three miles, then returned to camp, thoroughly disgusted with the useless effort. Gris grumpily told his diary that the "imaginary" Federals were not "within 20 M of us." Boredom was turning to fury.[87]

November 25, news reached camp that U. S. Grant had driven Braxton Bragg's Army of Tennessee away from Chattanooga and south into Georgia. "Bad news," Dud Jones told his diary, and one more straw of discontent drifted down on the Texas cavalrymen.[88]

Winter blew in from the north the first week of December in the form of a howling storm that lasted four days. The hundred blankets Reuben had helped find were not enough. The boys huddled morosely by their fires, mulling over their grievances, especially their friends who were under arrest. During the night of December 9, a mob took the balls and chains off several prisoners who had been court-martialed, then threatened Colonel Mabry. The next morning there was a ruckus in camp when the malcontents refused to allow the prisoners to be returned to their guards. After Colonel Jones, with the help of several men, barely managed to halt the mutiny, the brigade was assembled. Mabry addressed the men, noting that their actions would be reported to division headquarters and blaming the row on the Ninth. Gris disagreed, writing that "other regiments are fully as much to blame as any other." Had Nathan

Bedford Forrest been the department cavalry commander, the Texans would have been too busy to mutiny.[89]

Lee and the other generals again were shocked into action. The next day the brigade was assembled and orders were read from General Jackson and Colonel Mabry "denouncing such proceedings." The men were "herded in" and ordered to stack arms, a drastic measure when the enemy might appear at any moment. A camp guard was organized, and no one was allowed beyond the lines without a pass. The troopers were ordered to water the horses by company—no more wandering down to the creek at will. The officers even managed for enough money to pay the regiments.[90]

Brig. Gen. L. S. "Sul" Ross

But the generals continued to fret. Since summer they had been doing everything in their power to have Colonel Ross promoted to brigadier general and placed in command of the Texas Brigade. General Johnston, commanding everything in the West, had written the secretary of war in October urging Ross's promotion.[91]

Down the chain of command, Lt. Gen. S.D. Lee, commanding the cavalry in Mississippi, had written:

> *I earnestly request that Col L.S. Ross Sixth Texas Cavalry be promoted Brigadier General and be assigned command of the Brigade. Col Ross is a good disciplinarian and distinguished on many Battle fields for his gallantry. He has been commanding a Brigade for the last Eight Months by selection, on account of his suitableness for the position. The Texas Brigade as other Troops from West of the Miss. are anxious to cross the River, and in a manner dissatisfied and unless a proper Officer is assigned to their command and one popular with them, they will surely cross the River. . . . Colonel Ross has been recommended repeatedly for promotion.*[92]

Brigadier General Jackson, another step down the chain of command, told the War Department:

I regard Colonel L.S. Ross as one of the best disciplinarians, and one of the most gallant officers, in the Army of the West.[93]

Even Major General Maury, then commanding another department, had written the secretary of war recommending Sul Ross's promotion. Maury also stated:

During the battle of Hatchie, Colonel L.S. Ross commanded his brigade, and evinced such conspicuous gallantry, that, when called upon to report to the War Department the name of the officer who had been especially distinguished there, and at Corinth, I reported the name of Colonel L.S. Ross.[94]

Furthermore, citizens in the area were clamoring for Ross's promotion. Finally, several citizens—or the generals, or both—called on President Davis's older brother, Joseph, at his plantation, south of Vicksburg. Joseph, who had "more influence with Jeff Davis than all the army," wired his brother in Richmond that the interest of the country demanded Ross's promotion. Sul Ross's promotion was assured.[95]

Stephen D. Lee immediately ordered Ross to march from Grenada with his brigade and report to Red Jackson. After the uproar, Ross was instructed to leave his brigade to march on at their leisure and hurry to Reynold's Crossroads.[96]

December 16, 1863, Lawrence Sullivan Ross rode into the Texas Brigade's simmering camp. He knew his fellow Texans welcomed him, and he understood why they were disgruntled. He also knew the wild Texas boys were far from tamed, even after two years in the army. Ross told them, "I will give you something else to do besides guard duty."[97]

CHAPTER 10

A TEXAS RANGER

December 17, 1863–May 14, 1864

Sul Ross had been a captain in the Texas Rangers at age nineteen. Three years later, when Ross was twenty-two, Governor Sam Houston appointed him a colonel of the Rangers. Ross declined the promotion to join the Sixth Texas Cavalry, whose men elected him major of the regiment and later colonel. In 1863, at the age of twenty-five, he wore the three wreathed stars of a Confederate general. Ross was an earnest young man who took his responsibilities seriously, leading his men on the field, not from a hotel. No man doubted his courage. His reputation for daring had followed him from Texas and had increased in Confederate service. Ross was intelligent, honest, self-confident, and possessed of that rarest of traits, common sense. His innate fairness and modest demeanor made him the idol of the brigade. The Texans knew Ross had earned his stars, that he respected them, and that he would look to their safety. Justifiably proud of his promotion, Ross was determined to prove his worth.[1]

The day after Ross took command, December 17, 1863, Gen. Joseph E. Johnston and Lt. Gen. Stephen D. Lee again reviewed Jackson's cavalry at the Reynold's Crossroads camp, near Brownsville. Jackson, un-emotional and professional, must have felt a measure of relief when his division formed with Wirt Adams and Sul Ross in command of his two brigades.[2]

Ross's Sixth Texas rode into camp a few days later. The Third, the Sixth, the Ninth, and the First Texas Legion were back together—and would be separated no more. They immediately began preparing to move out on a new assignment.[3]

Since leaving Arkansas the Texas regiments had spent much of their time in western Mississippi, where the men, especially the young officers, had come to feel at home. Gris recorded in his diary, "All leave this vicinity with deep regret not knowing whether we will ever return." Both he and Sam Barron had dined and danced with the young ladies, and Gris had fallen in love.[4]

Brigadier General Ross—his promotion was dated December 21, 1863—led his brigade and four pieces of artillery due north to the Big Black, which they crossed on a ferry. After lights-out that night, the boys in the Sixth and the Legion became "a little merry" and "cut up a fuss." Aware of their duty to keep order among the perilously disgruntled troops, the officers sorted out their men and marched them back to their camps. The men pouted and grumbled. It was Christmas Eve.[5]

Ross was irate and embarrassed that men from his regiment were among the merrymakers. The following morning, the Ninth marched in the van while the Sixth brought up the rear behind the wagons, punishment for the ruckus the night before. As the boys had complained two years earlier in Indian Territory, they were not even free on Christmas.[6]

This was the Ninth's third Christmas on the march. They had spent Christmas 1861 with the Indians near Tulsey Town. The next year, they had skirmished with Grant's cavalry and ridden thirty-two miles on their way back to Confederate lines after burning Holly Springs. This Christmas they rode farther north and camped without fires to avoid detection by the enemy. And they were not riding toward full rations or a warm camp.[7]

With the Trans-Mississippi Department short of arms, Jackson had asked Ross if his command could put some arms across the Mississippi River at Gaines Ferry, a few miles north of Greenville. Ross had replied,

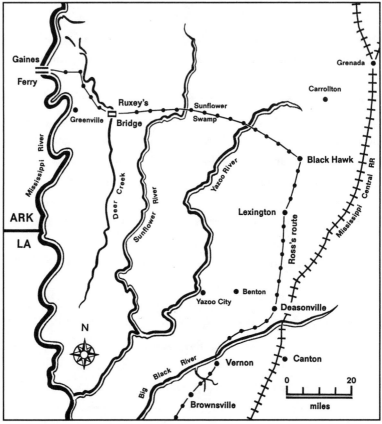

Arms Expedition to Gaines Ferry—Western Mississippi

"We'll try." The ferry was a hundred miles distant, across two major rivers, through swamps and bayous.[8]

For several days the roads had been good and the weather fair, but the day after Christmas, a Saturday, cold rain began to fall from low clouds. The column continued north to southern Carroll County before turning west toward the Mississippi. They reached Murdock's Ferry, on the swift Yazoo River, the next day. Ominous gray clouds blotted out the sun and the temperature dropped. The Legion, impatient with the slow process of crossing the entire brigade on a single ferry, swam their horses over, but the Ninth waited their turn on the ferry. It was nine Monday evening before everything was across. Lt. Col. R. A. Duncan waited on the west bank with the arms for the Trans-Mississippi Department—twenty-three wagons loaded with 3,400 arms packed in wooden crates.[9]

The men saddled their horses in pouring rain Thursday morning. At Garvin's Ferry, on the Sunflower River, they swam the horses across and ferried the saddles, which were hardly less wet than the horses. The boys saddled up and moved two miles up a tributary of the Sunflower to wait for the trains. Windblown, frigid rain whipped the fires through the night.[10]

All the next day, teamsters cursed the weather, the mules, and broken wagon wheels. The cold intensified, and snow began to fall in the afternoon. Ross, who had set up a courier line back to Vaiden, reported:

For 15 miles the road is almost impassable, being covered with water, and the mud is from 2 to 3 feet deep. The train carrying the arms appears to have been selected with a view of having the poorest mules and weakest wagons in the department. The whole outfit is miserably bad.[11]

When Amos Burgoon and Ross's other teamsters finally ferried the Sunflower the next evening, icicles hung from their horses and everything was damp and freezing. Colonel Duncan's arms wagons were scattered back down the road two to eight miles, stuck hard and fast in the icy swamp.[12]

Ross and his men had spent the day struggling to get the arms train to Garvin's Ferry. Ross impressed all the mules in the vicinity and tried to cut another road, but the heavy wagons refused to budge. Duncan declared the road impossible and gave up, but Ross insisted they make an effort—despite, as he reported to Lee that evening, the eight-mile swamp's being "covered with snow and frozen just hard enough to cut and bruise the legs of the animals when they break through."[13]

The night of December 31, ice an inch and a half thick formed on the ponds and along the drowned, rutted road. The men hovered by their fires, their light clothing barely enough to keep them from freezing. Sam Barron wore only a thin homespun gray jean jacket and was without an overcoat. That evening, Sam hung his gloves in front of the fire to dry and they burned to a crisp.[14]

New Year's Day 1864, Sam and the others woke up to a frozen world. They gathered corn from nearby fields to feed the horses and shot hogs in the cane breaks to roast over sputtering fires. Dry corn, parched in the ashes, served as bread. Residents had abandoned the area, leaving the hogs to fend for themselves and thousands of acres of fine corn standing. "We only had to go into the fields and gather what we wanted," a trooper recalled.[15]

Dud Jones held a consultation with his officers after breakfast to discuss the obvious abandonment of the expedition. Feeling their interest in the Trans-Mississippi Department too great to let the effort fail, they agreed to carry the arms to the river on their horses, each officer to carry three, each man two. When consulted, the men quickly agreed. They returned to their fires while the colonel went to see the general. Ross immediately accepted the proposition, complimenting the Ninth on their patriotic suggestion.[16]

Ross talked to the men in the other three regiments. He asked the men of the Third, "What shall we do, give up the expedition or take these guns on our horses and carry them to the river?"

"Carry them through!" they answered. The Sixth and the Legion also agreed.[17]

The next morning the men in the Ninth decided that saddling the horses for the two-mile trip back to Garvin's Ferry was not worth the effort. Certainly, swimming the horses across the Sunflower and back would be too hard on the animals. The regiment marched off early, leaving a small guard at camp. Colonels Jones and Berry took the lead. Company A fell in behind Lt. Tom Purcell to tramp back to the ferry and down the wretched road to the arms wagons.[18]

The regiment crossed the Sunflower on the ferry and started east on the worst roads Gris had ever seen. Arriving first, they broke open the wooden boxes loaded in the wagons closest to the ferry. Each man grabbed his allotment of guns and headed back. When they reached camp, after being gone only four and a half hours, guards had the fires burning.[19]

Sam's Third Texas rode their horses to Garvin's Ferry and left them on the bank. When the ferry nosed up to the opposite bank, a grand race for the wagons began. The Ninth had walked only two miles from the ferry to the first wagons, but the last regiment would have to walk eight miles on the miserable road. Sam was hurrying down the road when Warren Higginbothom, an athletic messmate, dashed past. "Save me some guns from the first wagon," Sam yelled. Warren obliged, and

Sam returned to camp with "the fortunate ones." The last men staggered into camp hours after dark.[20]

The brigade got under way at nine the next morning, the Ninth again in the lead, followed by the other three regiments and one gun with a caisson. A small guard and the men unable to travel remained at the Sunflower with the trains. The thousand horsemen had strapped the extra guns to their saddles and had packed rations in oiled haversacks, but the haversacks used to carry clothing were empty. The men had on everything they owned.[21]

Rain and sleet beat down. Men hunched their shoulders against the unrelenting cold but kept their sense of humor, laughing and joking about the Trans-Mississippi ordnance train. Ten miles out they reached Ruxey's Bridge, over Deer Creek. Ross was relieved to find the bridge still standing. He feared the Federals would burn the bridge when they learned about the Texans' mission, which he was sure they would. The four regiments marched across and strung out along the frozen road.[22]

The Deer Creek area had been known as the garden spot of Mississippi. Now, snow covered the ground and loneliness echoed along the roads and through the abandoned fields. The enemy had taken all the able-bodied slaves, and the plantations were abandoned. Ducks, moving south along the Mississippi flyway, had stopped to winter on the standing corn. "Along the creeks and through the farms there were thousands and thousands of wild ducks," Sam noted. He was sure he saw more ducks at one glance than he had seen in all his life. Perhaps some of the boys roasted plump ducks over their fires in the evening.[23]

Low clouds hugged the snow-covered ground as the north wind rattled dry leaves in the cornfields the next day. The boys gathered corn for the horses before boiling coffee and eating breakfast. During the morning they dried their wet blankets over windblown fires and huddled close to the flames to soak up the warmth. The last regiment dragged into camp red-eyed and weary from a night's march. At 1:30 P.M., the column turned north, into the wind. Blinding sleet drove angry fingers of ice into everyone's eyes. The cold was intense. Men turned down the wide brims of their hats and held their arms close to their bodies to conserve heat. Soon their fingers and toes were numb. Marching slowly along the frozen, rutted road, the horses drove flocks of ducks from their cover. The birds swept into the dull sky with angry protests, the fluorescent green heads of the mallard drakes reflecting the somber light. Ross and his men rode steadily through the afternoon while the cold sliced its way into the cores of their bodies.[24]

Eight miles up Deer Creek Valley the column reached Courtney Plantation. The cavalrymen huddled close to a sturdy oak fence near the slave quarters. Soon blazing piles of rails and a hot meal of pork and potatoes thawed their bodies and spirits. Gris would remember January 4, 1864, as "the most disagreeable day's travel experienced during my campaigning."[25]

The command camped in a dry cypress swamp three miles from Gaines Ferry, on the Mississippi, the next night. Federal gunboats puffed back and forth on the river, looking for the Rebels whose plans they had learned. Ross and his men would have to leave their horses in the cypress trees and pack the guns to the ferry after dark. They found a small flatboat on the riverbank. The men hitched four oxen to the boat and dragged it over a long, ice-covered sandbar to the ferry. After sliding the boat into the water, they loaded 266 guns. Nine volunteers—including Si James, a Choctaw from the Third—pushed the small craft into the choppy water.[26]

The Arkansas shore was iced in, forcing Si and his comrades to wade the last 150 yards several times carrying loads of guns. Wind and current drifted them downriver five miles on the return trip. It was nine the next morning before the boatmen made their way back to camp, exhausted and severely frostbitten. Their clothes were solid ice below the waist, frozen so thick the men could not sit down.[27]

The Confederates fought ice and wind, avoided Yankee gunboats, and waited for their contact on the west bank four more days. Sunday, representatives from the Trans-Mississippi Department were waiting for Ross and his men when they again went to the river, which by then was full of floating ice. The Texans stayed only long enough to watch the Trans-Mississippi men cross the first load of guns. Still, it was dark when they reached their encampment. They had ridden twenty-eight miles on ice that day, and everyone was cold, hungry, and exhausted.[28]

Ice in the bayou was four inches thick. Men and horses had traveled a hundred and twenty-eight miles since first reaching the Sunflower. They were out of rations. The horses had worn out their shoes and their hooves were beginning to split. Some of the men had worn out *their* shoes and were barefoot, their toes frostbitten. By horseback and on foot, they had carried two thousand arms through the ice and mud after the colonel of the ordnance train had given up. Duncan's superior reported that the colonel "seemed to manifest a great indifference, leaving the men and arms to take care of themselves." Ross, his men, and his horses had done all they could.[29]

They started back the next morning, reaching their wagons on the Sunflower January 12. The weather began to moderate, turning the roads from ice to mud. When they crossed the Sunflower, the sun was out, the day beautiful. A week later the horsemen camped near Benton to wait for the wagons to catch up. January 1863 proved to be the coldest month of the war, according to Sam, and "for downright acute suffering from exposure and privation probably no month of our campaign equalled this."[30]

Farriers shod the horses, but there was little the men could do about their tattered shirts and pants. The army occasionally issued a few garments, but the Texas cavalrymen depended on their families for most of what they wore. The North's blockade had stopped the flow of manufactured goods, including cloth, into Texas, but grandmothers across the state had taught the younger women to weave on looms the grandfathers had built. With sawed lumber scarce, the floor of the Masonic Building in Fort Worth had been carefully removed plank by plank to build looms. But in 1863 another shortage stopped the manufacture of fabric. The women's cotton cards were worn out. The men could not make cards, and there were none to purchase. Texas cavalrymen and their families at home were equally threadbare. A.W. and his messmate were down to one decent pair of pants between them, the other pair being worn badly "at the first and second angles." The man on duty wore the decent breeches. When one messmate relieved the other, the boys exchanged pants at the site.[31]

The Ninth had been camped near Benton only one day when orders arrived for the Texas Brigade to guard the area between the Big Black and the Yazoo Rivers. The Federals could easily run transports and gunboats from Vicksburg up the Yazoo to collect slaves, cotton, mules, and forage in the fertile area. Ross, still worrying about discipline and always concerned about forage, ordered his four regiments to camp apart. Pickets and scouts fanned out over the area. The young officers visited friends in nearby towns. A little mail came in from Virginia, and the men wrote letters to their families in Texas, dispatching them by a courier, usually a man unable to stand regular duty. Dodging Yankee patrols, the courier crossed the Mississippi in a small skiff, swimming his horse alongside.[32]

The campaigns of the past year had devastated the countryside between the two rivers, forcing most residents to flee. Slaves had been taken to work elsewhere; mules and horses, pressed by one army or the other. No chicken or pig was safe from the foragers. Yet, seldom did a night pass without skirmishes between scouts and small commands. The four Texas regiments remained alert. Jones's men, camped near an abandoned schoolhouse and church, kept out pickets, or a reserve, four hundred yards in advance of their camp and vedettes another four hundred to five hundred yards beyond.[33]

A.W. and another man were posted as vedettes one night. They took a position back from the road among the trees. The moon had not come up and it was dark and quiet. They were watching, but mostly listening, when a faint noise grabbed their attention. Someone or something was moving toward them. The boys whispered to one another and peered into the darkness.[34]

They sighted a form, fifty yards distant, moving slowly and awkwardly toward them. A.W. squinted to make out the strange object prowling in the night. It was too large and short for a man, too tall to be a pig. He and his comrade cocked their carbines and aimed.

"Halt," one called.

The curious object stopped but did not answer.

"Who comes there?" A.W. said.

"It's me and Major," answered the small voice of a child.

"Well, come here and tell us what you want."

A small, towheaded boy accompanied by a big dog came into view. The boy, about ten or twelve, set down a wooden box. Nodding his chin at the box, the child said, "It's my little brother."

A.W. and his comrade soon learned that the boy and his mother lived seven miles from the church and its graveyard. The father was off to war, and the family owned no animals except the big, trusty dog, who watched the boy with obvious devotion. The boy's little brother had died after a long illness. The mother wanted her child buried in the graveyard near the church, but she was unable to come. She and the boy had placed the small body in a light pine box, and the boy had started with his burden early that morning.

The child had carried the box seven miles through the rough and dangerous countryside. A.W. and his partner explained that they could not leave their post until they were relieved. The boy was concerned that his mother would be worried, but he moved his box to the side of the road and lay down. He and Major curled up together and soon were asleep.

Hours later, when the relief came, A.W. carried the box and the other soldier carried the boy piggyback to camp. Major followed, warily watching the soldiers. At camp the sergeant gave the boy some meat and bread, which the child shared with the dog. The boy and his dog lay down together on a blanket and slept the rest of the night. The next morning, Captain Haynes sent a detail with the boy to bury his little brother. Back at camp, the men found among their meager possessions many small gifts for the child.

Captain Haynes told him, "Go on home now, and stay with your mother." Major and the boy disappeared into the trees in the direction they had come.[35]

While A.W. and other pickets and vedettes guarded the immediate area of camp, scouts ranged along the ridge between the Big Black and the Yazoo. Both rivers flowed southwest into the Mississippi, the Big Black joining the Mississippi south of Vicksburg, the Yazoo joining it north of the city. Plantation landings and small towns were scattered along the navigable Yazoo. In late January a Federal expedition began moving up the Yazoo to occupy the towns and gather the remaining slaves, cotton, forage, horses, mules, and beef cattle left in the valley.[36]

Ross's scouts reported a large Union force moving up the ridge on January 26. Two days later, January 28, scouts spotted enemy boats steaming up the Yazoo. Ross left the Third Texas to guard against a land advance and hurried to the river with the Sixth, the Ninth, the Legion, and the battery.[37]

They found Yankee soldiers loading forage on a transport tied to the opposite bank of the Yazoo while a ten-gun gunboat stood guard. Lieutenant Moore of Capt. Houston King's Missouri Battery unlimbered his two guns and opened fire on the Yankee transport, nine hundred yards away. The transport quickly untied and moved downstream, but not before Moore hit her twenty times. In her haste she left her foragers on shore to "save themselves as best they could," Ross later reported. When a squadron of Federal cavalry, protecting the foragers, rode into range, Moore threw a shell in their midst, unhorsing several and scattering the rest like a covey of quail. The gunboat moved downstream without firing a shot. The Texans, watching the entire affair from the high east bank, were greatly amused.[38]

Sure the gunboats would be back, Ross made ready for them on a high bank between the little river towns of Liverpool and Satartia. Tuesday, February 2, five large side-wheel transports guarded by three formidable-looking gunboats steamed into view, but they remained out of range of Moore's guns all day. The next morning gunboats No. 3, No. 5, and No. 38 moved up and began shelling the Texans while the transports landed three regiments of black and white infantry and cavalry. The Third and the Legion guarded the roads. The Sixth and the Ninth moved out front to challenge the gunboats. Ross reported, "I knew the men in whom I trusted and was not doubtful of the issue."[39]

Colonel Tom Berry, in command of the Ninth, dismounted his men and posted them on a high hill where a depression formed a natural breastworks. Berry and his men drove off several enemy attacks during the next three hours. The Federals then made a most desperate charge. Drawing their six-shooters, the Texans waited. When the enemy advanced to within ten to fifteen paces, the cavalrymen opened fire. The Yankees threw away their guns and equipment and ran back to their boats.[40]

The gunboats moved off late in the evening, leaving their dead and wounded. The Confederates gathered up abandoned guns and accoutrements and brought in the wounded. They counted fifteen dead Yankees and took two prisoners. The Sixth and the battery lost four killed and six wounded. Five men in the Ninth were wounded, including Lt. H. T. Young of Company K, slightly wounded, and Lt. William A. Wingo of Company B, shot in the head. At the field infirmary, Dr. Robertson treated the injured men, leaving Wingo until last because he considered the lieutenant's injury fatal. A bullet had struck Wingo behind the ear, shattering the bone in the mastoid area. Incredibly, the young officer—

he was twenty-three—was still alive when Robertson finished treating the other ten men and Wingo was placed on the scaffold serving as an operating table. There was little Robertson could do beyond extracting the bone fragments and dressing the wound. Wingo and the other seriously wounded were sent to the hospital.[41]

At daylight the next morning the boats were back, but Moore was out of ammunition. The Ninth rode to the river. Leaving their horses with holders, they scattered along the riverbank. When a transport went by, they fired into the men and horses exposed on the decks. Federals hid behind knapsacks and boxes of hardtack, but the Texans killed five and wounded twenty more before the transport could move out of range. Gunboats again appeared the following day. The cavalrymen disabled one and drove off the rest. In the afternoon three Texas regiments rode north to Yazoo City, leaving the Sixth to guard Liverpool. Both Ross and Gris reported that two of the Sixth's pickets were captured and later murdered by black cavalrymen. The Texas cavalrymen, already angered by Federal enlistment of black troops, were enraged. The rest of their time in Mississippi, Ross and his men granted no quarter to black troops.[42]

Friday, gunboat No. 38 came steaming up the river a few miles south of Yazoo City, right into the range of Moore's guns, which had resupplied from the brigade wagon train and were posted on a bluff. The horsemen dismounted and again lined the riverbank. Moore disabled No. 38 with four well-directed shots while sharpshooters kept the Yankee sailors under cover with their ports closed. When the enemy boats moved downstream, the Ninth camped in Yazoo City for the night.[43]

Citizens of the town sent a testimonial of thanks to the "gallant defenders" of their homes. Half the Federal force, as reported by their commanding officer, consisted of "the First Mississippi Cavalry, African descent and the Eighth Louisiana Infantry, African descent." Citizens of Yazoo declared Ross's Brigade worth a whole army for saving them from occupation by their former bondsmen. The townsmen refused to take payment for anything. Sam Barron said that in town

we began to get invitations to dinner. Meeting with a little white boy, he would accost you thus: "Mr. Soldier, Mamma says come and eat dinner with her." Next a little negro boy would run up and say: "Mr.

Soldier, Mistis says come and eat dinner with her." And this kind of
invitation was met on every corner, and between the corners.[44]

The Federal commander of the Yazoo Expedition, who called Ross's
men the Texas Rangers, reported, "I was satisfied that a much larger
force was in position there than was anticipated." Gen. W. H. Jackson,
in his report, wrote, "All praise is due the fighting Texans and King's
battery and their gallant leader, Gen. Ross, for their noble defense of the
Yazoo country."[45]

The Texans enjoyed the grand hospitality of Yazoo City for only three
days before moving east to join the rest of General Jackson's Division
on Monday, February 8. While Ross's Brigade was challenging the gunboats, a Federal force of 35,000 infantry and 12,000 cavalry with twenty
days' rations and sixty-four guns had crossed the Big Black on their way
east along the railroad. Maj. Gen. William T. Sherman had returned to
Vicksburg "to finish cleaning the Rebs out of Mississippi" and to attack
Lt. Gen. Leonidas Polk's headquarters at Meridian, on the eastern border
of the state. Sherman planned to meet a heavy Memphis-based Federal
cavalry column at Meridian. From there, Sherman would move on to
either Mobile or Selma.[46]

Ross and his four regiments, about 1,000 mounted men plus wagons
and support, worked their way southeast as fast as their weary teams
would bear. Out of Canton, they crossed the Pearl River on a pontoon
bridge and turned east. John Dunn of Grapevine wrote in his diary that
the Federals had

swept like a tornado over a comparatively defenseless country at Hills-
borough. We saw the effects of their malignant hatred[,] for houses were
pillaged and burned until it was a heap of ashes. And in like manner
was their track visible on the whole march from Vicksburg to Meridian.[47]

Sherman, disgusted with the South's refusal to see that it could not win
the war, was bent on teaching the Mississippians a lesson.

The brigade caught up with a column of Sherman's men at Marion,
a railroad station five miles north of Meridian. Ross ordered Amos Bur-

goon and the other teamsters to take the trains north. Amos had started driving one of the Ninth's wagons soon after enlisting in Arkansas and had remained with the trains. His mules, thin, slow, and overworked for two months, plodded slowly along the dirt road under a bank of dark clouds.[48]

The cavalrymen, fighting as usual as infantry, skirmished with the Federals but did the enemy little harm. The Texans mounted at sunset and rode back up the road to join their trains, camped in the pine trees. Snow began to fall at midnight.[49]

The bulk of Sherman's infantry was to the south. North of the Texas Brigade, Forrest's cavalry faced the heavy Federal cavalry column on its way from Memphis to join Sherman at Meridian. It was the Texans' responsibility to stop the Federal cavalry if Forrest was unable to drive them back. Ross sent Sam Barron fifty miles north to the little town of Macon, Mississippi, to take charge of the telegraph and keep him informed by courier of Forrest's movements.[50]

Sam set out alone, wearing his jean jacket—no overcoat, no gloves. Heavy dark clouds hung just above the treetops. As the night deepened the temperature dropped. Sam rode north, hoping he was on a road that would take him to Macon. When he reached DeKalb at midnight, snow started falling. Sam had trouble finding someone in the sleepy town to direct him to the Macon Road. He finally roused a man from a warm bed, then rode on feeling lonely and unsure. At daybreak Sam stopped at a house and asked for something to eat. Cold and exhausted, he lay down in front of the fire to sleep while the lady of the house cooked for him.[51]

Just south of Macon he crossed the Noxubee River on a splendid covered bridge that was "filled with tinder that it might be fired if the Federal troops should come in sight." When he rode into town, an excited crowd gathered around. Sam reported what he could and advised the townsmen not to burn the bridge, stating that even if the Yankees appeared, it would slow them but a short time and the destruction of the fine bridge would be a serious loss to the town. The citizens decided Sam must be a spy, and the Texan took charge of the telegraph office under suspicious eyes. After the telegraph operator checked with General Jackson and found that Sam was indeed a Confederate officer, he was treated with great kindness. Sam reported to Ross that Forrest's 2,500 men were falling back before the superior Union force.[52]

The Texas Brigade was ordered north to reinforce Forrest. Sam rejoined his regiment when they passed through Macon. A few days later, north of Starkville, Ross learned that Forrest's renowned cavalrymen had sent the powerful Federal force flying in confusion back toward Memphis. Ross's men were disappointed that they were too late to join Ol' Bedford.[53]

Brig. Gen. William Sooy Smith, commanding the Federal cavalry force, had started from Memphis with twenty pieces of artillery double-teamed, a mule pack train, several ambulances, 7,500 of the best and most experienced troopers in the U.S. service, and Brig. Gen. Benjamin Grierson, Sherman's best cavalry officer. Smith had notified Sherman that he was "resolutely bent on the destruction of the last vestige of Forrest's troublesome little army." Forrest, outnumbered three to one, drew Smith's command deeper and deeper into Mississippi until Smith became so uneasy he turned around. But Forrest was unwilling to let the enemy escape without a battle. He dismounted his troopers, sent one regiment around to attack Smith's rear, and ordered his bugler to sound the charge. When the Federals hurriedly retreated, Forrest remounted his men. The chase was on. Forrest pursued the Yankees until his ammunition gave out, sixty miles in two days. Smith and Grierson hurried back to Memphis.[54]

Sherman, always a realist, had already given up on Smith and their combined advance into Alabama. He had started back to Vicksburg two days before Forrest's attack. The tough, redheaded Yankee was furious with Smith for "allowing General Forrest to head him off and to defeat him with an inferior force." Forrest was beginning to seriously irritate Sherman.[55]

R̲oss's Brigade was ordered back to the Yazoo while the rest of Jackson's cavalrymen followed Sherman on his return to Vicksburg. Sunday morning, February 28, the Texans reached their old camp at the Ponds, four miles west of Benton. Union troops had taken Yazoo City, another eight miles west, the day after the Texans had started east. The Yankee colonel had quickly reported that he had pitched his tents and established camps, and that "everything looks cheering, with enough fighting to create a healthy circulation of the blood." From Yazoo City and other river landings up and down the Yazoo, the Federals had recruited black cavalry and hauled off mules, horses, and 1,728 bales of cotton.[56]

At the Ponds, Ross immediately placed his battery facing down the Plank Road, toward Yazoo City, and sent out pickets and scouts. In a few minutes two of Ross's scouts came clattering into camp chased by a battalion of black cavalry mounted on mules and pouring misdirected fire at the Texans. The battery fired, giving "them a startling salute" and emptying several saddles. Ross mounted his horse and shouted, "Charge them!" The Ninth leaped onto their still-saddled horses and took off at full gallop. The Sixth followed. Jones, riding the fastest horse, took a shortcut "across fences, lanes, ditches, precipices & a boggy creek" to the Plank Road. Jones and three or four men, those whose horses were fast enough to keep up with the colonel, emerged on the road just as the Yankee rear guard was passing. "Halt!" Jones yelled. The enemy refused to stop. The colonel and his men drew their pistols and took dead aim.[57]

When a few more men came up, Jones yelled, "Charge!" He leaped the fence and led his men into the blue cavalry fleeing down the Plank Road. The Sixth Texas gleefully joined the chase. When Jones emptied his pistol, he drew his saber and hacked two Yankees off their horses. Walter Jones of Grapevine wrote home a week later:

> We would charge in amongst them and shoot them off their horses and many would fall off and get on their knees with their hands uplifted and pray for mercy, saying they had not meant to fight the whites, but the response would be only a few curses and the boys would . . . blow their brains out and leave them to wilter in their own blood.[58]

The Texans kept after them for six miles, to the fortifications at Yazoo City. Only the officers and four of the seventy-five black cavalrymen reached their works. "The road all the way to Yazoo City was literally strewed with their bodies," Ross reported. The Sixth had settled the score for their two pickets murdered by black troops earlier in the month. Not a Texan was scratched.[59]

The brigade remained at the Ponds a few days, skirmishing occasionally. Friday, March 4, Brig. Gen. R. V. Richardson of Forrest's cavalry, with his 550-man West Tennessee Brigade and a section of artillery, joined Ross's 1,000 mounted men. Gen. Stephen D. Lee had sent Richardson to help Ross drive the Union troops from Yazoo City.[60]

The Texans were up before dawn the next day. At seven-thirty, they rode down the Plank Road, leading to Yazoo City, where, according to Richardson, the Yankees were "flaunting the U.S. flag." A mile from town Ross dismounted his troopers, leaving the horses with every fourth man. Walter and the rest of the Ninth moved to the left of the road. They drove in the pickets at the base of a hill and captured the fortifications on its crest. In the afternoon they were ordered to a position on the Plank Road a hundred yards in front of a strong redoubt bristling with rifles and one gun. Artillery of both brigades poured shot and shell into the redoubt.[61]

General Richardson, with his men and two of Ross's regiments, advanced through the streets of the town, forcing the enemy back to a couple of brick warehouses near the wharf. Two Yankee gunboats anchored in the middle of the river threw shells into the town.[62]

Rebel artillery enfiladed the strong redoubt on the Plank Road. Walter and all the men in the Ninth kept their heads down and fired into the 400 Illinois and black Mississippi troops trapped in the redoubt. Under a flag, Ross demanded the Federals surrender. "We squabbled about the terms of capitulation," Ross reported, "as I would not recognize negroes as soldiers or guarantee them nor their officers protection as such." Incredibly, the Federal officers argued among themselves before refusing to surrender. When Ross and Richardson decided an assault would cost more men than it was worth, the Tennesseans began to draw off. The Yankees in the redoubt, thinking the Rebels were retreating, "sallied out and attempted to drive the Third and Ninth Texas Regiments from their positions in front, but were quickly and signally repulsed." At sunset Jones's men were nearly out of ammunition. They withdrew and sprinted back to where the horse holders waited. No one in the Ninth was killed, but three were wounded.[63]

In camp that evening Walter Jones and the other privates learned that while their regiment had kept the Federals in the redoubt busy,

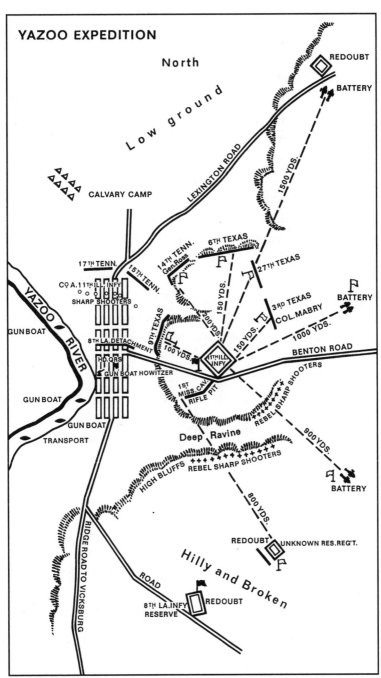

Battle of Yazoo City (*Official Records*, Vol. 32, Part 1)

Richardson's men had taken the town and torched the enemy's quartermaster and commissary stores, as well as a large amount of cotton. The boys also heard that two Federal transports loaded with reinforcements had docked at dusk, just before Jones ordered the retreat.[64]

Richardson wrote in his report: "It gives me great pleasure to commend the gallantry of Brig. Gen. L.S. Ross and his entire brigade of Texans." Richardson also reported capturing mules, horses, clothing, ammunition, and seventeen prisoners. His Tennesseans lost thirty-seven killed and wounded; the Texans, twenty-seven. Again, Jesse and Reuben Rogers, A. W. Sparks, Gris Griscom, Sam Barron, Victor Rose, Newton Keen, and David Garrett were unscratched. Federal casualties, reported by Yazoo City residents, amounted to 243.[65]

The Federals boarded their transports the next morning and went back to Vicksburg. Richardson commented: "It is hoped that he will abandon the idea heretofore entertained of opening the Yazoo River and drawing cotton, negroes, stock and supplies from its rich valley."

The residents of Yazoo City again regarded the men from the Lone Star State as heroes, welcome to anything they wanted.[66]

The day after the battle Ross informed Jackson, "We have a good many prisoners and much plunder now." The plunder was important. During the war Confederate cavalrymen in the West captured more arms and supplies than their commissary department issued to them. At the expense of the Federal government, Confederate troopers filled their empty bellies and replaced their broken-down horses, worn saddles, missing guns, used-up ammunition, captured artillery, and tattered clothing. U.S. equipment, ammunition, food, medicine, and horses were always significant plunder.[67]

After their victory, Ross's Brigade moved back to their old camp east of Benton, midway between the Big Black and the Yazoo, to recruit the men and the horses after ten weeks of constant marching and fighting. The four regiments established camps several miles apart in order to find forage for their thin horses and to stay out of trouble.[68]

The men had little to do during the next month. Sherman had taken his army to Tennessee to prepare for the spring campaign, leaving only a few men to guard the Mississippi River. U. S. Grant had been promoted to lieutenant general and had assumed command of all Federal armies. After Grant and Sherman completed their plans, Grant left for the East to take command of the Army of the Potomac. Not being privy to Grant's and Sherman's plans, the Texans wondered why western Mississippi was quiet.[69]

The Ninth Texas moved camp a few miles each week in search of forage. The men remained in camp, drilling and standing inspection because there was nothing else to do. They were still restless, still unhappy to be on the east side of the mighty river. On March 29, a few men left for Texas on furlough, laden with letters and envied by those still in Mississippi. The furloughed men would have less trouble crossing the river because most of the Federals were gone.[70]

John Sparks was among the men who left for Texas. Soon after his return to the Ninth's camp in October, John had suffered a relapse and had been confined to his room all winter. Nine months after being shot through the lung, he was able to travel. "I was gratified," A.W. said, "that he again did see our mother."[71]

A few days after the men left for Texas the entire brigade was ordered east in anticipation of the spring campaign everyone knew could not be long in coming. Again, the young officers left the area with deep regrets. They had been stationed east of Vicksburg most of the past eighteen months. Gris and Sam had made many friends and felt at home among the Mississippians. The privates also regretted leaving, but for a different reason. They hated being sent farther east, farther from home. Over and over they had been promised furloughs. They even harbored hopes that the entire brigade would be transferred to the Trans-Mississippi Department, but they were marching the wrong direction.[72]

The Texas Brigade rode east with the rest of General Jackson's Division. At Columbus, near the Alabama state line, Lt. Gen. Leonidas Polk, a West Pointer and an Episcopal bishop, addressed the Texas Brigade "in a very flattering speech." Polk, in command of the department, made the Texans the same old promises: clothes and furloughs the moment the present emergency was over. Polk's speech was "altogether a crude specimen of oratory for a Bishop," Gris thought.[73]

The division crossed into Alabama and made camp on the banks of the Black Warrior near Tuscaloosa, where citizens had never seen organized troops. "Their terror and apprehension was amusing," Sam said, "when they learned that a brigade of Texans had arrived. They would not have been surprised if we had looted the town in twenty-four hours." The Alabamians soon discovered that the Texas cavalrymen were as civilized as the Mississippi and Tennessee troops in Jackson's Division.[74]

Jackson's cavalrymen remained in the Tuscaloosa area for a month while the generals waited to see where the Federals would strike when the weather warmed a little more. Joseph Johnston, in northern Georgia; Leonidas Polk, at Columbia, Mississippi; and Dabney Maury, at Mobile; each expected the coming campaign to be directed at him. They had not discovered that Grant and Sherman both would begin their movements south on May 5, Grant toward Richmond, Sherman toward Atlanta. Grant had asked Sherman to keep Joseph Johnston too busy to detach troops to send east. Sherman had told Grant to keep Robert E. Lee busy enough that he could not send troops west. The two Union generals were old and close friends, and despite Grant's now ranking Sherman, the feisty Illinoisan continued to write Grant long letters of advice.

The Confederate generals in Alabama had to keep their men busy while they waited for the inevitable. April 20, Ross sent Dud Jones with a detachment of 300 men north to Marion County, Alabama, to drive out the bushwhackers and Tories—Yankee sympathizers—reported to be in open resistance in the area. Jones discovered that the reports were false, but he found many deserters hiding in the woods.[75]

The deserters had wisely scattered, but the detachment gathered up a few here and there. Their women hid them and freely gave the Rebels "a good large piece" of their minds, often emphasized with clubs. On the evening of April 25, a detachment of cavalrymen knocked on the door of an old schoolhouse being used as a home. A woman whined from behind the locked door that only helpless women occupied the building. The officer assured her they were perfectly safe, but the woman refused to allow him entry. After a couple of men knocked the door from its hinges, two troopers struck a light and went inside with the officer. The single large room contained four beds, each occupied by two persons. Dresses and shoes showed from under the covers, but no pants. The officer mentioned a pair of extra-large shoes. "Them's my shoes and you just leave 'em and get out of here," the woman demanded. The officer insisted they were men's shoes. The woman got out of bed, showed him her shoes, and "dealt him a right-hander full in the face that would have done credit to either Corbett or Fitzsimmons." The officer was dazed. In a moment he quietly "called upon God and all present to witness that he made no war upon women and affirmed that his good right arm should always be used to protect women." Anger, however, quickly overcame his gentlemanly instincts. "Swearing that no living being should treat him thus," the officer "dealt the woman a blow in the pit of the stomach that laid her flat on the floor." Three women and five men were marched back to camp.[76]

The country around Marion County was too poor to sustain Jones's horses more than a few days. He and his men hanged a few deserters and took fifty back to headquarters before returning to their camp near Tuscaloosa.[77]

On May 9, Ross received orders to send to Selma the dismounted men, unfit horses, and all the baggage, including the tents, for a forced march to Rome, Georgia. Sherman had begun his drive south four days earlier, making it clear to the Confederate generals that Atlanta was the Federal objective. A lieutenant started sixty dismounted men and the unfit horses toward Selma while everyone else prepared for the march.[78]

Jackson, still trying to tame the unruly Texas boys, imposed strict discipline on the march east. He kept many men walking, leading their horses as punishment for riding off from the ranks. For three days, A.W. closely observed the soil of eastern Alabama while leading his horse over the poor, rocky country. The column was averaging thirty miles a day.[79]

The afternoon of May 14, Jackson's Division reached Rome, where the Etowa and the Oostanaula join to form the Coosa River. The once-pretty town had been turned into a fort to protect the vital cannon works and machine shops. The Texans camped a mile north along a narrow valley dotted with farms and timber. When the Ninth's wagon train came in at nine that night, the men ate supper and fed their horses. The Texans spread their blankets for their last peaceful night's sleep for months to come.[80]

CHAPTER 11

STALLING SHERMAN

May 15–August 11, 1864

The Texas cavalrymen were up early the morning May 15, 1864, a beautiful late-spring Sunday in the South, cool and mild. The boys looked forward to some rest after a week's forced march, especially A.W., who had led his horse over Alabama's rocky roads. However, when a courier galloped through camp to headquarters, no one was surprised that the bugles soon blared Boots and Saddles with the usual urgency.

Four U.S. cavalry regiments had attacked a Georgia cavalry regiment guarding Farmer's Bridge, over Armuchee Creek, eight miles north of Rome. The Georgians had fallen back nearly to the town. Ross's Brigade mounted and rode north at breakneck speed. The instant they made contact, Ross dismounted the Ninth and sent them to the front. The battery unlimbered and dropped a couple of rounds among the enemy horsemen, who clattered back up the road out of range. The Ninth remounted and set out after them. Jones and his men got close enough to charge the Federals four times during the six-mile chase back to Farmer's Bridge, where Union reinforcements waited. For the Texans, the Georgia campaign had opened.[1]

They were in the saddle before sunup the next two mornings. They were grazing their horses in a clover field ten miles north of Rome at noon Tuesday when a courier on a lathered horse galloped up with news that Rome was under attack. The Texans gathered their horses and hurried back toward town. Two miles out they found a Confederate infantry division holding off a heavy enemy force. Immediately ordered to the front, the men flung themselves off their horses and ran through the startled infantry, bellowing their distinctive Texas Rebel yell. Yankee skirmishers fell back on their main line, but the Texans continued to charge, loading and firing as rapidly as they could. When the enemy's center collapsed, Texans poured through the opening and drove the Yankees back a mile while the Confederate infantrymen watched from their breastworks. Ross suddenly realized he and his men were alone and outnumbered ten to one, with Yankees on their right, on their left, and in their front. Five Texans were dead, fifty wounded. Ross "deemed it prudent to withdraw." The brigade gathered their dead and wounded and withdrew in good order to the breastworks along the road. Rebel infantrymen, astonished to find that cavalry would fight like infantry, gave the Texans a rousing cheer. Ross and his men must have wished the Confederate infantrymen had fought like Texas cavalrymen that afternoon.[2]

The Texans had barely caught their breath when the Federals charged with fixed bayonets and a shout. Newton Keen's blood was up. He glared at the enemy as they approached. When the Yanks were within twenty feet, Newt and the rest of Ross's men drew their six-shooters and fired with the accuracy of long experience. The Yankees "tumbled into piles," Newt said. "Their line came to a dead halt and stood still for at least ten seconds" before "it reeled and fled in great confusion." The Federals retreated to re-form in the woods, but it was getting dark and they would wait until tomorrow.[3]

Sul Ross's Brigade, 1,009 strong, had met the western edge of Sherman's 100,000-man, superbly equipped army. Sherman, fierce determination etched in the wrinkles of his face, was driving toward Atlanta, the industrial hub of the Deep South. Opposing him, Joseph Johnston had 60,000 men, counting his Army of Tennessee and the Army of Mississippi that Leonidas Polk had brought from the West. Johnston's only recourse was to maneuver south until he could catch Sherman's army

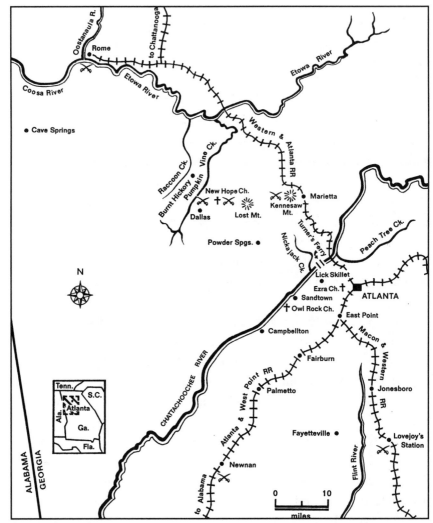

Georgia Campaign

divided or stretch Union supply lines to the breaking point. The Texans trusted Johnston's ability and judgment. They were unhappy about being so far from home, but they would do their duty for Old Joe.[4]

Ross and his men, camped within Rome's fortifications, were ready for action before daylight the next morning. The rest of the Confederate forces had marched out during the night to join the main army, leaving the Texans to slow the enemy's advance and burn the bridges. Rome's merchants, the few who had not fled, opened their doors to the troopers, telling them to take what they needed. A.W. laid in a stock of tobacco while others helped themselves to "a great amount of things that were of no possible use," including stovepipe hats. The men also broke open an army depot and supplied themselves with clothing and commissary goods. When they marched out of Rome, their saddlebags and haversacks were stuffed.[5]

Ross led his men south and east of Rome in stifling heat to Raccoon Creek, a southern tributary of the Etowa. A couple of days later two Federal cavalry regiments attacked Ross's pickets near the river. "The enemy charged twice very boldly, but were so stubbornly resisted by Colonel Jones and his gallant little regiment and [Daniel H.] Alley's scout" that they retired, Ross reported that night. During the fighting, a bullet slammed through Maj. James C. Bates's neck and into his jaw, making a fearful wound. At the brigade field infirmary, Surgeon James Robertson treated the major's wounds before sending him to a hospital in Atlanta.[6]

That same day, Gen. W. H. Jackson was temporarily disabled and command of his cavalry division reverted to Brig. Gen. Frank C. Armstrong. Jackson's Division consisted of Armstrong's Mississippians, Ross's Texans, Brig. Gen. Samuel W. Ferguson's Alabama and Mississippi troopers, and three battalions of artillery, including the Texans' old friend Capt. Houston King and his Missouri battery. Jackson's Division and the rest of the Army of Mississippi Leonidas Polk had brought came under the command of Gen. Joseph E. Johnston and soon became part of the Army of Tennessee.[7]

Ross's men scouted and skirmished along both sides of the Etowa for the next two days. The pleasant weather of the week before gave way to sultry heat. Thousands of Federal infantrymen, marching south on the dry roads, stirred up billowing clouds of dust. The Texans were often so near the enemy they could hear their drums beating. When three separate columns approached Ross's headquarters on Raccoon Creek, he moved south a few miles to the hamlet of Burnt Hickory and camped at a church. Enemy columns followed.[8]

The Texas Brigade rode out to meet an advancing Union column the morning of May 24. When enemy shells began falling into Ross's lines, he handed A.W. his field glasses and sent him up a tree to spot the guns. A Yankee sharpshooter, far out on the flank, fired into the group of officers waiting under the tree, killing Ross's horse. The irate general sent the Ninth's Company I to find the sharpshooter. When they discovered the Federals, a lively skirmish developed. Two hours later, Ross received orders to move south at once to Dallas, a crossroads village west of Marietta. He called in his troops.[9]

The sharpshooter was part of Sherman's 80,000 fighting men moving toward Dallas. Sherman planned to either strike Marietta or cross the Chattahoochee, the last major river protecting Atlanta. He hoped to turn the Confederate right and get between Johnston and Atlanta. Johnston, with his usual perception, discerned Sherman's plan and was falling back to prepared fortifications running eastward from Dallas.[10]

Shells were crashing into the town when the Texans arrived that afternoon. They dismounted and supported an infantry brigade until dark, when they fell back half a mile to bivouac. The men's shoulders drooped from exhaustion. They had been fighting or maneuvering for fifteen hours. While they unsaddled, the men who talked to their mounts must have apologized to the animals for having nothing to feed them. There had been nothing that morning and nothing the night before. The men dropped onto their blankets to sleep a few hours.[11]

At 2:30 A.M. Wednesday, May 25, they were back in their saddles on the way to the front. Federal cavalry were so near the Texans plainly heard Yankee buglers sounding reveille and Boots and Saddles. At first light Jones and his men drove in the enemy pickets and began fighting their advance. When the Legion came up, the two regiments dismounted. Fighting as infantry, they loaded and fired as rapidly as they could manage while trying to keep from getting shot. By 9:00 A.M., six and a half hours after leaving camp, everyone was worn out and hungry. They finally were relieved and ordered to New Hope Church, a few miles east, to feed their famished horses.[12]

The boom of cannon and rattle of small arms grew louder with each step they took toward the church, where Lt. Gen. John Bell Hood's Corps was holding off Sherman's legions. The Texans fed their horses and rested an entire hour before being ordered back to work. West of New Hope Church, they dismounted to skirmish for Hood's infantry. The old Methodist meetinghouse stood on an elevation in a post oak grove. "The cannon balls and minié balls," Newt said, "rattled like hail among the oaks." Bark and splinters flew from the trees onto the sweating men. Shells ripped off tree limbs and sent them crashing to the ground, where acrid gun smoke swirled in the hot air. The old church shuddered and groaned in protest as shell after shell crashed through her roof and into her walls. The building was "bored through and through by cannon shot," and Newt was sure it always did the Yankees good to destroy the Methodists' property.[13]

Five hours later the Texans moved east of New Hope Church to take position on the Confederates' extreme right. They could hear the roar of guns from around the church until long after dark. Again the horses went hungry, but the men were too tired to care. They slept. During the

Rebel Lines South of Atlanta

night, lightning lit up the sky while thunder rolled across the battered land. Pouring rain failed to wake the exhausted men.[14]

The battle around Dallas and New Hope Church raged three more days. Artillery barked a welcome to each sunrise, and the boys from Texas were never idle. The second day the Ninth fought during the morning. At noon Joe Johnston sent them on a reconnaissance to the west, the general himself giving them their instructions. They were back on the line by dark. Skirmishing and fighting continued all night and through the next day.[15]

Saturday, the fourth day of the battle of New Hope Church, the Ninth manned the red dirt trenches along the Confederates' fortified line. They made a charge at 4:00 P.M., then returned to the trenches, where they remained all night. Rations of one pone of corn bread and a small slice of bacon were supposed to be delivered to them in the trenches, but the commissary men did not appear. Everyone was tired and hungry. Mud was six inches deep in the trenches, and the night was dark as pitch. Enemy fire did not cease. When the boys got sleepy, they fired away to keep up the excitement. It was afternoon the next day before the regiment was relieved.[16]

The exhausted cavalrymen retrieved their horses and rode a couple of miles to the rear to camp near Maj. Gen. Patrick Cleburne's infantrymen. After unsaddling their horses, they staked out the hungry animals to graze. It was Sunday, only two weeks since they had arrived in Georgia. The men rested while their horses grazed unsaddled the next day, but Tuesday at noon they were ordered back to the front between Dallas and New Hope Church.[17]

They found the Federal works and encampments around Dallas empty. Sherman was working his army north to flank Johnston out of Allatoona, a strong point on the railroad leading into Atlanta from the north. Bullet-scarred trees bore witness to the fury of the fighting around Dallas. The entire countryside had been turned into a wasteland by spades and hooves and tramping feet. Houses stood empty, bored and reamed by cannon shells.[18]

At Dallas the Yankees had left a hospital full of seriously wounded Confederates who had been captured during the week of fighting. Robertson, now the brigade surgeon, and Assistant Surgeon J. F. March cared for the wounded men with the assistance of their nurses, men from the ranks. Robertson had called for members of the Ninth Texas Cavalry's Infirmary Corps to report to him the first day of the battle of New Hope Church. Jones had organized the Infirmary Corps of ten men, one from each company, earlier in the year. The men remained on active duty with the regiment except when needed at a field hospital. A. W. Sparks, Company I's member, had been ordered to report to Robertson the morning the fighting began around Dallas and New Hope Church.[19]

A.W. had mounted his horse, Mountain Bill, and had ridden a mile and a half beyond the rear of the army to the field infirmary. The moment he dismounted, Mountain Bill was harnessed to one of the ambulances that were already discharging wounded. A.W. reported to Dr. James E. Robertson, a forty-year-old aristocratic Virginian whose arrogant stance and piercing gaze tolerated no challenge. A.W.'s first order was to bury a man. When he asked Robertson how and where, the doctor glared and barked, "Any way decent, any place suitable."

A.W. scratched out a shallow grave in the rocky ground. Before he finished, he was exhausted, his clothes wringing wet. Afterward, he helped build arbors for the wounded and scaffolds for operating tables while others continued the new graveyard. They dug a trench and placed several blanket-shrouded bodies side by side in one end. With great economy of labor, they covered their fallen comrades with earth from the other end of the trench, thereby making room for more burials. During the following three weeks, the trench grew longer and longer until more than seven hundred men were laid to rest in the rude grave.

During A.W.'s first night of medical duty, he awoke to the doctor's insistent call, "Sparks, Sparks, get up and bring a light and let us try to stop the blood from that fellow's leg. Look in the pannier and get me the chloroform. I will fix the bonnet. Hurry up!" A.W. held the light while Dr. Robertson thoroughly examined the wound before shaking his head and saying, "There is nothing we can do." A.W. went back to his blanket beside the doctor's cot.

To his astonishment, A.W. was ordered to assist Robertson at the operating table the next morning. During the amputation of a man's leg, A.W. dripped chloroform on the bonnet placed over the man's nose and mouth. He was watching in fascination as the man's expressions changed when Robertson yelled, "Take it away, you have killed him!" The doctor "laid down his knife and commenced a heavy and rapid manipulation of the patient's stomach" that "restored him," but A.W. "was frightened nearly to death."

The evening of May 26, Wirt Phillips, Third Texas, was brought in with a gunshot wound through the body. When Robertson cut a large ball from Wirt's back, pieces of a leather strap and checkered shirt came with it. Lacking an instrument he needed, Robertson ordered A.W. to ride to the purveyor's office in Marietta for the instrument, adding in his authoritarian tone, "Hurry! Don't stay until they are all dead."

Jack Phillips of the Third—surely Wirt's brother—appeared, leading his fine sorrel horse. He handed A.W. the reins with a single sentence: "He'll last you back." At Marietta the purveyor quickly read Robertson's note and gave A.W. a box of instruments and a cup of whiskey. A.W. reined the sorrel around without dismounting. Near Lost Mountain he rode through battlefield debris of burning wagons and dead horses. Dead and wounded men littered the field. A.W. and the sorrel were tiring, but when an object they rode over moaned, "Oh God! Don't ride over a dying man!" both man and horse were startled into a surge of energy.

A.W. delivered the box to Robertson and March at 11:40 that night after riding fifty miles in five hours. He was paralyzed, unable to move, much less dismount. Men lifted him down, placed him on a blanket, and gave him a dram of whiskey. He was up the next morning, but very stiff and sore.

The wounded able to withstand a wagon or ambulance trip were taken to the hospitals in Atlanta, but several were too desperately injured to be moved. Claib Rigsby, shot through the lung, could not lie down. A.W. rigged "a kind of perch pole" where Claib could lean forward to rest and sleep. From another pole A.W. hung a gourd with a small hole in the bottom to drip water on Claib's bandages. Another man could not swallow. A.W. gave him water and soup through a small piece of bark slipped from a sprout and inserted into the man's stomach. When the brigade left the area, the wounded men who could not be moved were left on their crude beds of leaves and blankets with one of the nurses, who was sure to be captured and sent north to a prison camp. When A.W. suggested he remain, Dr. Robertson would have none of that. "You will go with me," he demanded, and motioned for A.W. to sit beside him in the medicine wagon.

From Dallas and its hospital of wounded, Dud Jones led his regiment east to New Hope Church on June 4. The summer rainy season had set in, turning the torn countryside and churned-up roads to deep mud. At the old Methodist Church, Gris was shocked at the signs of battle. Unburied Union dead lay near their works, soaked and splattered with mud. Dead horses lay about, sprawled in curious positions. The ground was shredded by cannon shot, the trees scarred and torn.[20]

Rain continued to fall, thunderstorms during the days and steady rain through the nights. It was a dismal muddy time, which, according to Gris, "made for altogether unpleasant fighting." Ross reported that "every creek is swimming and the fields and woods very boggy." Off the main roads, animals plunged through knee-deep mud and wheeled vehicles bogged to the axles. Rebels and Yankees alike lay down on wet blankets every night for three weeks. Sherman fumed about the wretched roads and brought up supplies for his next push, while Johnston fortified a line from Lost Mountain to Kennesaw Mountain, in front of Marietta and its vital railroad. The Texans, skirmishing in mud up to their knees and manning the trenches, remained on the Confederate left. Men in both armies dug trenches and threw up breastworks wherever they stopped, but the lines remained virtually unchanged.[21]

The Texas Brigade worked its way farther east to Lost Mountain, halfway between New Hope Church and Kennesaw Mountain, where they relieved General Ferguson's cavalrymen picketing in front of the mountain. The lines were so close together the enemy's reveille woke the Texans on the morning of June 8. Union cavalry and infantry were in plain sight, but no one was in the mood to do much fighting. Stationed on the far left of the brigade, Dud Jones's boys agreed to an armistice with the Yanks in their front. They exchanged Rebel tobacco for Yankee coffee, traded newspapers, and discussed Washington politics. At 3:00 P.M., their conversation and leisure were interrupted by a rainstorm and a group of Yanks making a dash to get around the picket lines.[22]

The evening of June 15, the Ninth fed their horses and left them with holders before occupying a line of trenches when the infantrymen moved out. A.W., who had returned to his company by then, along with his chum Jody Candle and the others, was ordered not to speak above a whisper because the enemy was near. The night was black as a wolf's mouth. Rain poured down, turning the muddy trenches to quagmires. In the middle of the night A.W. and Jody were tired and decided to rest. "I went to sleep," A.W. wrote, "and it seemed to me that during that sleep someone whispered 'Forward to the right,' but I heeded not, sleep was too good." He was "awakened by soldiers coming into the works and talking in low tones." It was 2:00 A.M. A.W. could see nothing, but instinct told him they were Yankees. He jumped up. "Halt! Halt!" a voice cried out. By then A.W. was running. "I knew not where," he wrote, "and the further I ran the more frightened I became." Sprinting through the darkness, he came to a farm where in the dim light of a lantern he saw soldiers issuing ordnance from a wagon. He watched until he was sure they were Confederates. He knew none of them but walked up to a soldier and asked where he could find Ross's Brigade. The man looked at A.W. strangely and said, "Why, have you gone crazy?" In his fright A.W. did not recognize his own messmate.[23]

The rain finally ceased June 22. While Confederate infantrymen waited in their dirt-and-timber fortification on Kennesaw Mountain, Sherman began massing his corps around the base of the mountain. Maj.

Gen. John Schofield's Twenty-third Corps was on the Federal right, maneuvering along the Powder Spring and Marietta Road, where Ross's Brigade stood guard.[24]

Friday, June 24, Ross had his headquarters at Shaw's House, on the extreme left of the Confederate lines, which stretched north to Kennesaw Mountain. Jones's men fortified in infantry style and skirmished all day with Schofield's advance. When the sun set, a full moon rose in the clear sky. To the tune of Schofield's band playing "Dixie," the Texans read their mail and visited with several fur-

Sherman's Lines in Front of Kennesaw Mountain

loughed men who had returned. Others wrote letters. Sam Boaz, Company A, would leave with the mail the next day. Reading their letters and writing their families, the Texans longed for home. A few days later they were again able to send letters to Texas, this time by a member of the Eleventh Texas Cavalry, their old friends from the battle of Pea Ridge.[25]

The enemy advanced in force along a mile-long front near the Texans' position the next day. Shells burst into camp. The Ninth sent their horses to the rear and marched into the trenches, where they "kept up a lively fight all day." Sul Ross maintained his headquarters at Shaw's House, reporting four times during the day that enemy pressure was increasing.[26]

Before daylight the next morning the Texans moved into fortifications at the south end of the line. All hell broke loose at dawn, when Sherman's army struck with massed artillery along the entire Confederate line. With sounds of battle rising like an approaching tornado, A.W. watched from the Ninth's position. Long blue lines came up the slope with colors flying, bands playing, and uniformed soldiers, "their bright guns with fixed bayonets at right shoulder shift," thousands of men moving in line after line "like a blue cloud arising." Rebel rifles replied but had no more effect on the deep blue lines than "a hand full of shot thrown into a stream."[27]

At 5:30 A.M., Ross reported that the regiment on his right was under severe pressure and needed help. If the line broke, Yankees would stream through into the Confederate rear. Ross sent Jones and his Ninth to the regiment's aid. Blue-gray gun smoke clouded the clear sky, turning the sun to a ball of fire. At 8:00 A.M., the enemy breached the lines and soon were within a few hundred yards of the Texans' horses. The troopers ran to rescue their mounts, slung themselves onto their saddles, and fell back half a mile to a hilltop. The Yankees mounted a battery and charged the Texans at noon. They halted the enemy charge only a short time before dropping back again to find a secure place for their horses. Federal cavalry and infantry vedettes held all the roads and trails to the west. Late in the evening, fourteen hours after the battle opened, Ross requested permission "to rest my command a short time, if compatible with the good of the cause." A couple of hours later he threw out a heavy skirmish line and dropped back on the Sandtown Road to unsaddle and "if possible to rest to-night."[28]

That night Gris was pleased to learn from a Federal skirmish officer captured during the day that the Texans had held Schofield's entire corps at bay for the past five days. In contrast, A.W. was depressed. He had watched Schofield drive the Confederates from their fortification with but one of his many lines. A.W.'s only consolation was that he "had really seen an army" for once in his lifetime. Newt shared A.W.'s feelings. "Of course it was quite discouraging to the soldiers," he recounted, "but we did not murmur," for "we had this satisfaction: many of them went to their long home." When the Confederates lost a man, Newt wrote later, "we had no man to take his place, but when the Yankees lost one, they had two to chink the hole with."[29]

After the battle of Kennesaw Mountain, Sherman had 2,500 holes to chink. Joe Johnston's infantry, entrenched on top of the mountain behind log and earthen works, had slaughtered the Yankees with the loss of only 800 of their own. The grim Union general reported his losses and continued to work around behind Johnston. Sherman had been trying since May 5 to bring the Confederates to battle, but Old Joe had skillfully maneuvered his forces closer and closer to Atlanta, always seeking an advantage, despite cries from Richmond and the governor of Georgia to fight an open battle. The integrity of his army was more important to Johnston than territory. Like Beauregard at Corinth, Johnston believed the army had to win the war even at the expense of territory.[30]

Ross's Brigade kept out scouts and skirmishers on the far left of the

Rebel lines. June 30, 1864, the orderly sergeants delivered their company rolls to their adjutants for the bimonthly accounting of the Army of Tennessee. Gen. William H. Jackson's Cavalry Division—Ross, Armstrong, Ferguson, and three batteries—reported an effective total of 3,574. Ross's four

Turner's Mill on Nickajack Creek, near Turner's Ferry

regiments numbered about 1,000, many sick and dismounted men having returned to duty. Two years earlier the four Texas regiments had reported 3,174 men present for duty.[31]

On a warm evening about the time the rolls were taken, an oxcart lumbered into the Ninth's camp. Soldiers gathered around in astonishment. Walking beside the cart was a boy and the nurse who had remained with the seriously wounded when the brigade left the Dallas–New Hope Church area. Claib Rigsby, who had been shot through the lung, and Dave, another Texan, were in the cart. The nurse explained that when the Yankees occupied the area they ignored him and his patients, neither capturing nor paroling them. Two other men, Georgians, had also survived and been placed in nearby homes. For the use of the cart, the nurse paid the boy with stores and utensils left at the field hospital. Claib and Dave were forwarded to Atlanta, and the nurse fell into the ranks.[32]

As July began the Texans were backed up against the last natural barrier in front of Atlanta, the Chattahoochee River. From their position, some ten miles west of Atlanta, the river flowed southwest through rough, timbered country. They skirmished and patrolled along roads and trails that crossed the river at several fords and bridges with names such as

Nickajack Creek, Sweet Water Bridge, Turner's Ferry, Baker's Ferry, and Howell's Ford.[33]

Jones's men moved into the Georgia militia's trenches protecting the river. At mid-morning, July 5, Federals drove them from their lines. The Ninth took new positions three times before noon, but were unable to hold. At 2:30 P.M., they "moved back under a most galling fire from a rifled battery." The men mounted and galloped across the pontoon bridge over the Chattahoochee "in a shower of shells."[34]

Picking Blackberries

They rode southeast a couples of miles to their trains for some food, forage, and a few hours' rest. John Dunn and his comrades soon discovered a patch of luscious blackberries. Starved for fresh fruit, they gobbled berries until their hands and faces dripped purple juice and their stomachs bulged. The berries were in great abundance, and the whole army was well supplied with them, many a blackberry patch being disputed by a sharp skirmish between opposing forces.[35]

In sweltering heat, the Ninth and the rest of the Texans guarded river crossings from Campbellton to Turner's Ferry for the next two weeks. They searched out blackberry patches and occasionally visited friends in the Eighth Texas Cavalry, better known as Terry's Texas Rangers. The enemy was seldom out of sight as artillery on each side of the river threw shells at the other. Ross's scouts roamed up and down the river every hour during the day, every two hours at night. Other Texans dug skirmish pits near the riverbanks to protect themselves from artillery shells.[36]

Often the Yanks and Rebs agreed to a truce—despite orders to the contrary. "Johnnies, let's rest," the Yanks would call across the river. The men swam and played in the water, leaving dirty blue clothes on one bank, tattered gray garments on the other. They dunked their sweaty heads, rubbed dirt and vermin from their bodies. All thoughts of enmity dissolved in the cool water as they swam and splashed one another. When they climbed out onto the banks, they sat around naked, their sun-baked faces and hands contrasting with their pale bodies. Rebels and Yankees traded coffee and tobacco and discussed the coming election between President Abraham Lincoln and Gen. George B. McClellan. When the truce ended the men returned to their guns and began hurling shells at one another.[37]

The firing was too heavy for the Texans to tend their horses in the daytime. After sunset they staked out the animals to graze while they went to the wagon train for grain. A little corn and wheat were available, but often that too stopped, forcing each man to scrounge food for his horse.[38]

Ross and his Texans stayed busy on the Atlanta side of the river, the four regiments taking turns on duty. Sul wrote his wife, Lizzie, early in July that he was worn out and had lost many good men. "Generals Jackson and Johnston have great confidence in my command," Ross told Lizzie, "and they have much cavalry here that is wholly worthless, hence they work me and my men too hard." He also reported that Sherman's men were eleven miles from Atlanta, but he trusted General Johnston, writing, " 'Mars Joe' knows what he is about." The men agreed. They knew Joe Johnston would take care of them.[39]

Sherman agreed with Ross that the Texans were working hard. July 16, he wrote Washington that he did not fear Johnston's infantry if they would take the offensive, but he "recognized the danger arising from my long line and the superiority of the enemy's cavalry in numbers and audacity."[40]

The day Sul wrote Lizzie all was quiet along the Chattahoochee. The Texans peeled off their dirty clothes and waded into the river. They washed their grimy, smelly shirts and pants, then lounged in the sunshine until the clothes dried. The horses, staked in green patches, nibbled the summer grass while the men stuffed themselves with blackberries. Late in the evening, some of the men lounged around their campfires while others cooked, read, or napped under the trees. When artillery shells abruptly began flying into camp, Ross ordered his battery to reply "to the Blue Devils," but the other boys ignored the rude interruption to their quiet evening.[41]

July 17, the Ninth moved five miles up the Chattahoochee to Turner's Ferry, which was eight miles from Atlanta. Jones threw out a heavy skirmish line in infantry rifle pits along the riverbank. When the Ninth was relieved at dark, the regiment encamped at Mason's Church, a mile southeast at a crossroads.[42]

The Ninth was again on duty the next morning. Reuben and Jesse Rogers, John Dunn, and a fourth man were assigned positions entirely exposed to enemy fire, but there had been only sporadic activity along the river for several days. The Rogers boys and the other pair ran across an open field and jumped into their pits without drawing fire. Deciding to make shelters to protect themselves from the sun, the four gathered rails along the riverbank. Not a Yankee was in sight. Nothing stirred. Reuben and Jesse were carrying rails to their pit when a single shot rang out. John said he and his partner "were comfortably fixed in our positions thinking all was quiet," when they heard the shot. Immediately, an excited voice hollered, "John, John, I'm shot!"[43]

The lead bullet, traveling at low velocity, flattened and expanded as it plowed through Reuben's right hand, then tore a large hole in the flesh of his right thigh before burying itself deep. Reuben and Jesse ran to their pit and tumbled in. Reuben grabbed his hand and stared at his leg in horror, sure it was broken and would be amputated as soon as he reached the field infirmary. Doctors routinely amputated limbs with bullet-shattered bones, the only procedure they believed gave the victim a chance of survival.[44]

Reuben had called to John because of the young man's knowledge of medicine. John gave an account in his diary:

I ran to him with all my might and found him bleeding freely from wounds through the hand and thigh. He was very much excited, thinking his leg was broken. His brother was more excited, but when I heard he ran several steps to the pit I laughed at him. After binding up his wounds with my handkerchiefs so as to stop the blood he calmed down and laughed too. From this time on nothing could stir without being shot at.[45]

Shock and excitement would have kept Reuben from feeling pain for a short time. The bullet had bored a clean hole through his hand between the index and third fingers but had carried dirt and fabric from his pants into his leg. John, Jesse, and Reuben crouched in the rifle pit as the fierce southern sun rose higher in the sky. John and Jesse watched across the river for Federals.

Swarms of flies, spawned in the filth of old battlefields, buzzed around the men's sweaty faces and stuck to blood seeping through the handkerchiefs on Reuben's hand and leg. John kept the bandages damp, using as little water as possible. They would have to stay where they were until dark if the firing continued. Morning wore on. Reuben's hand began to feel as if a red-hot poker had been thrust through it, and the poker seemed fastened in his leg. As the sun crawled to its zenith and began dragging its way across the western sky, any visible movement brought fire from across the river. Each minute seemed an hour. While Jesse and John watched, Reuben lay in the pit fouled by weeks of occupation, the stench of sweat and urine rising from the ground.

When darkness enveloped the river, men appeared out of the trees with a stretcher and canteens of water and whiskey. They carried Reuben to the rear. Perhaps Jesse trailed along with his and Reuben's pistols stuck in his belt, two empty canteens slung over his shoulder, a rifle in each hand. The litter bearers took Reuben to Surgeons Robertson and March's field infirmary, several hundred yards behind the church. Reuben was the only man in the Ninth wounded that day, although others in the brigade might have been wounded.[46]

The bearers placed Reuben on a scaffold of oak planks supported by posts set under the trees. Nearby stood the doctors' wagon containing medical supplies. Although the firing had ceased, the woods were alive with nighttime noises—buzzing flies and mosquitoes, the high-pitched drone of cicadas. The smell of chemicals and corruption assaulted Reuben's nostrils as he lay on the plank operating table. He was terrified.[47]

After Robertson examined Reuben's wounds, which had swelled shut during the day, he issued a few instructions. A nurse dripped chloroform on a bonnet placed over Reuben's mouth and nose. Robertson probed with his finger to locate the bullet, then quickly extracted the ball with small pincher-type forceps and trimmed away the damaged tissue. Blood flowed from the newly opened wounds. The doctor placed pieces of lint in the wounds to keep them open, then covered them with clean linen held in place by roller bandages. The procedure took only a few minutes. The nurse began fanning Reuben to purge his lungs of chloroform.

Moving the breath away from the patient's face helped supply a constant flow of fresh air. If a patient was slow to wake, the doctor splashed chloroform on his scrotum. The chemical's quick evaporation produced instant cold, causing the patient to suck in his breath.[48]

Nurses carried Reuben from the operating area and placed him among the other wounded on a bed of leaves covered with a blanket. Sharp, smarting pains radiated from the bullet holes. Reuben might have been given an opium pill and a drink of water. The nurse dampened the dressings with cool water, keeping them constantly wet, the standard treatment.[49]

After leaving his brother, Jesse trudged back toward the Ninth's encampment, fear and loneliness washing over him. Reuben, four years older, had always been his protector and had taught him how to take care of himself in the army. Knowing Rueben soon would be sent to a hospital in Atlanta, Jesse prayed that his brother would be back with the regiment in a few weeks. Perhaps later in the night Jesse returned to sit with Reuben.

At camp, the men were not reading, napping, or writing letters. They sat in small groups, muttering angrily. Joseph Johnston had been relieved as commander of the Army of Tennessee, replaced by John Bell Hood. Jesse was too upset that night to care, but others were concerned. A man in the Sixth Texas said Johnston was "the safest general the Confederacy had." Many considered him not only the safest but the best. Old Joe took care of his men, never wasting their lives in fruitless battle. The men knew little of Hood, only his reputation for rashness.[50]

Jefferson Davis had relieved Johnston for failing to stop Sherman north of the Chattahoochee. The Georgians had been screaming since the armies had been trampling *their* soil and threatening *their* major city. They had demanded that Davis do something. The president and his military adviser, Braxton Bragg, had refused to believe that in mid-July Johnston was outnumbered nearly two to one. They chose Hood to lead the Army of Tennessee.[51]

No one who knew Hood—and there were many in both armies— ever doubted his courage. Many, however, questioned his ability to command. Robert E. Lee had told Davis he feared Hood would lose the army as well as Atlanta. Edmund Kirby-Smith said that Hood "has not the judgment . . . the forethought or the military knowledge or experience of Johnston." Richard Taylor said, "No more egregious blunder was possible than that of relieving [Johnston] from command in front of Atlanta." Three of Sherman's corps commanders, who had known Hood since West Point, told Sherman that Hood was rash, erratic, and headstrong, and that he would come out of his Atlanta fortifications and strike like hell, exactly what Sherman had been trying to get the Confederates to do for two months. Sherman admitted he was pleased.[52]

Dashing and dangerous, Hood was a splendid hero—tall, blond, charming. His daring had cost him a leg at Chickamauga and the use of an arm at Gettysburg. Now, he had to be helped onto his horse and strapped to the saddle. He was often in pain, but he wanted the Army of Tennessee and had jumped the chain of command to complain to Davis of Johnston's timidity.

Men of the Army of Tennessee did not need the blue or gray generals' assessment of the change. A Texas infantryman lamented: "Every soldier's head hung low when we heard that our gallant commander had to give up the command of the Army, for all our hope and confidence was in Gen. Johnston." Another said the replacement "was a death stroke to our entire army." A Texan in a Louisiana infantry regiment said, "Our judgment would not let us admit there was any hope for us now." The men of Ross's Brigade listened to Johnston's farewell with "deep regret."[53]

The day after taking command, Hood began making plans to strike the Federals entrenched along Peach Tree Creek, north of Atlanta. Union artillery along the creek was bombarding the city, and blue-clad troops were closing in from both the east and the west. Only one railroad remained in Confederate control, the Macon & Western, which ran south a few miles from Atlanta before branching off southeast to Macon and southwest into Alabama. Food, fodder, arms, ammunition, and clothing—everything Hood's army lived on—was coming in on the Macon & Western. If Sherman cut that road, Atlanta was dead.

At 4:00 P.M., July 20, Hood's men marched out of the city. Yelling like demons, they surprised the Federals along Peach Tree Creek. The Confederates were repulsed in a fierce, costly struggle. Leaving their dead and wounded on the field, they staggered back into Atlanta's protection.

Two days later they came out again, farther to the right, and caught Sherman's Army of the Tennessee in a movement, unprepared for battle. The Confederates almost succeeded. But almost was not good enough, and again they were forced back into Atlanta. The two battles cost Sherman 3,500 killed, wounded, and missing. Nothing approaching an accurate account of Confederate losses can be found in the *Official Records*. Sherman reported 3,240 dead Confederates on the field. Hood lost at least 8,000, likely more.[54]

Wednesday, July 20, while the battle of Peach Tree Creek raged, the Texas Brigade was off to the southwest at Turner's Ferry. They patrolled as usual but found time that day to graze their horses one regiment at a time. Skirmishing increased in the evening and continued the next morning, but in the afternoon the men again grazed their horses and had time to pick blackberries, the best of the season.[55]

By noon Friday, as Hood's infantry was forming for another attack north of Atlanta, Ross's pickets along the river were driven in by a heavy force. They were forced back under fire a mile to Mason's Church, about two miles from Turner's Ferry. Ross notified General Jackson at 1:00 P.M. that he had sent part of his artillery south to Lick Skillet, a crossroads village in the hills south of the river. Ross stated that he would hold his position until dark—if possible. Four hours later, he reported:

> *The enemy are driving my skirmishers steadily back to this point. One regiment (the Ninth Texas) is skirmishing with them. Their line is a long one, and moves forward without firing a shot, paying no attention to Colonel Jones.*[56]

Jones and his men, accomplishing nothing where they were, formed in the rear as cavalry. The Texans stubbornly held their position around the church. It was nearly dark when Ross was able to form three regiments on foot to support his two pieces of artillery while the Ninth remained mounted in the rear. A half hour of shelling forced the Federals halfway back to the bridge. With an entire regiment, the Ninth, on the picket line between the bridge and the church, the men unsaddled and bivouacked for the night. At 9:11 P.M. Ross informed General Jackson that an intelligent prisoner, a "Dutchman," said all of Brig. Gen. Edward M. McCook's Division was south of the river and would be followed by infantry and artillery. During the night two scouts and two pickets were captured.[57]

The day had been unusually cool and pleasant. After supper the men sat around their fires, cooking, relaxing, enjoying the novelty of a brisk midsummer night, but the flames would not have warmed Jesse's soul. With increased fighting around the city, Dr. Robertson was forwarding his wounded as quickly as possible in case the brigade had to move. Reuben had been sent to Atlanta.[58]

Dawn brought the entire Federal cavalry brigade onto Turner's Ferry Road. The Texas Brigade fell back a couple of miles to Lick Skillet and strengthened their picket lines. The Ninth scouted up and down the river for the next few days. They were eating dinner Thursday, July 28, when heavy firing to the east sent them running for the horses. Hood was attacking Sherman's entrenched infantry near an old meetinghouse called Ezra Church, just outside Atlanta's fortification on the Lick Skillet Road. With the thunder of artillery rumbling through the countryside, squadrons of the Ninth fanned out to picket several roads. The middle of the afternoon the pickets were called in and the entire regiment started toward the firing. Almost immediately they were ordered to turn around. The men were beginning to wonder if anyone knew what was going on.[59]

When General Ross and the three other Texas regiments came up, the brigade set out west. Twelve miles out they reached Owl Rock Church, a couple of miles south of Sandtown, on the Chattahoochee. The men swung off their tired horses to bivouac for the night. It had been a long, muddled day and they were ready to cook and sit. Bacon was sizzling over the fires when Boots and Saddles sounded. The horsemen were off again. Five miles west, near Campbellton, they met Col. Thomas Harrison's Brigade of Wheeler's Cavalry Division, which included the Eighth and Eleventh Texas Cavalry. It was 9:15 P.M. The men were ordered to dismount and stand in the road, bridle in hand. Two hours dragged by. They had been up since 4:30, and now, of all things, they were standing on a road holding their horses. They were grumbling and swearing when information swept down the line that McCook, with a division of 3,500 blue cavalrymen, had flanked the Confederate left and was bound for the Macon & Western Railroad, Atlanta's lifeline.[60]

The Texans' lethargy dissolved in an instant. They were going after the raiders. Each man was issued three days' rations of hard bread and eighty rounds of ammunition. In column of fours, the troopers set out Friday morning at four as the first hint of light appeared on the horizon. Jackson rode with Ross while Harrison took another road. The Texans rode steadily for five hours before stopping to rest on a road lined with apple trees. Forty-five minutes later, stuffed with apples, they remounted.[61]

A.W. and his comrades, picketing down the Chattahoochee that night, had reported every thirty minutes as they watched the Yankees laying their pontoon bridge. By the time he and the other pickets were relieved at 4:00 A.M., the brigade had left, but A.W. was not about to be left behind. He leaped on Mountain Bill and, riding hell-for-leather, soon joined his company.[62]

Two miles from Fayetteville, the brigade "came upon the trail of the foe clearly defined by smoking ashes of burning wagons," Ross wrote in his report. "The sad havoc and destruction of property everywhere visible, and the eagerness of all to overtake and chastise the insolent despoiler was increased two fold." McCook's men,

Capture of a Confederate Wagon Train by Gen. McCook—Fayetteville, Georgia, July 20, 1864

including Col. James P. Brownlow's First Tennessee Cavalry, had captured and burned the main train of the Third Texas Cavalry and Ector's Brigade's quartermaster train. Smoldering wagons—ninety-two belonging to the Third—broken trunks, scattered baggage, quartermasters' desks, tools, and equipment of all kinds littered the road for several miles. The Yankees had captured the Third's teamsters, their chaplain, the blacksmiths, all the train's horses and mules, and, according to Sam Barron, "the usual men who always managed to stay with the train."[63]

Pressing east from Fayetteville, the column passed more burned wagons. They crossed the Flint River and rode toward Lovejoy Station, on the Macon & Western. Dud Jones and the Ninth rode at the head of the column with Ross and Jackson. It was four in the afternoon. Everyone was alert, guns loaded, ready for action. A mile and a half from the station, mounted Yankees, the Eighth Iowa Cavalry, came into sight. Without halting to form, Ross yelled in his clear, ringing voice, "Charge! Charge!" With a piercing yell, the regiment galloped forward in column of fours with pistols drawn, not a man in the regiment having a saber. The Yankees met them halfway, pistols and sabers drawn. Men and horses slammed together. Jones killed a Yankee in a hand-to-hand struggle. While grappling with another, the hammer of Jones's pistol snapped down on an empty chamber. An instant before the Yankee's saber came down on the colonel, T. P. Woods shot the Federal out of his saddle. Sgt. John Grimes fought like a cornered grizzly. The Ninth recoiled and charged again. More Federal horsemen came up and drove the Ninth back.[64]

When the Sixth Texas came up, Ross's and Jackson's escorts and the two regiments formed and charged in column of squadrons, forcing the Federals to give way. By then the Third and the Legion had arrived. Ross dismounted them a hundred yards behind the battle line and called back the Sixth and the Ninth. The Federals also dismounted, formed, and charged. The Texans answered with a hail of lead. Back and forth the battle went for three hours. The Yankees suddenly broke contact, ran to their horses, and left by their flank at double-quick, leaving twenty dead and fifty wounded. Sixteen Texans had been wounded.[65]

Jones led his men to Lovejoy Station to check damage to the railroad while the rest of the brigade "took right in after" McCook. The Ninth met a Confederate infantry brigade on the railroad. Lying on the tracks and embankments were a dozen badly wounded and twenty-five dead Yankees, plus quantities of horses, saddles, arms, and equipment. McCook had struck the railroad six miles south of Lovejoy, torn up two and a half miles of track, and ripped down five miles of telegraph lines. The Eighth Iowa and Brownlow's Tennesseans had burned a hundred bales of cotton and two trains loaded with arms, lard, and tobacco. The tobacco alone was valued at $120,000. The Iowans also burned five hundred wagons and killed eight hundred mules with their sabers, not wanting to waste ammunition. Over four hundred Confederates had been captured, but their infantry had forced the Federals to release the prisoners. The railroad track would be repaired in two days, not what Sherman had in mind.[66]

From Lovejoy Station the Ninth rode west toward Flint River. They picked up John Dunn on the way. Afraid to push his horse because the animal had taken a bullet the day before, John had been struggling to catch up with the regiment. He had been gathering corn for the horses near Campbellton when the command left without him.[67]

A few miles west of Lovejoy Station the Ninth reached the Flint River, where they found Glass's Bridge guarded by two companies of the Eighth Indiana Cavalry waiting behind breastworks. Jones and his men attacked. Gris wrote: ". . . skirmished with them at the bridge all night—a stubborn fight." The Indiana major reported "a terrible fire from both artillery and musketry" and that his men expended five thousand rounds of ammunition during the fight.[68]

Jackson and the other Texas regiments, west a few miles, were on the trail of the rest of McCook's horsemen that night. The Hoosiers burned Glass's Bridge and left at 3:30 A.M. Saturday. With the river too deep to attempt in the dark, the Ninth swam their horses across at daybreak and set out for Fayetteville, four miles west.[69]

At Fayetteville, Jones learned that Ross and the rest of the brigade were hot on the raiders' trail, riding due west on the Newnan Road. Maj. Gen. Joseph Wheeler, cavalry commander of the Army of Tennessee, had swept around from east of Atlanta to help Jackson protect the railroad. Wheeler, with only four hundred men, had passed through Fayetteville on the raiders' trail shortly before the Ninth arrived.[70]

John, Jesse, and A.W.—all Jones's men—had been pushing themselves and their mounts for forty-eight hours. They stopped at the first cornfield on the Newnan Road to feed their horses and rest for an hour. Twenty miles beyond Fayetteville they reached Newnan, a stop on the Atlanta & West Point Railroad, which led to Alabama. Four miles farther west, the Ninth found Ross and the other three regiments fighting the raiders. Wheeler had caught up with Ross out of Fayetteville. "Near Newnan," Ross reported, "after much trouble and delay, the raiders were overtaken and promptly engaged by General Wheeler's advance."[71]

The Federals, deep in Confederate territory, were fighting with desperation. In a dense skirt of timber, Ross ordered his men to dismount and leave the horses with only two men per company. The order to charge rang down the line before the regiments could properly form. "Whooping and running, stooping and creeping" as best they could, the Texans plunged into thick woods and dense undergrowth toward the enemy, the Eighth Iowa, the regiment that had sabered the mules. The men were able to see only a few paces, and the fighting quickly turned into hand-to-hand combat. "Friends and foes were mixed up in the struggle, without regard to order of organization," Ross reported.[72]

Struggling through tangled brush, Sam Barron and another lieutenant were in the advance. The lieutenant suddenly stopped and looked ahead. "I did likewise," Sam said, "casting my eyes to the front, and there, less than twenty-five yards from me, stood a fine specimen of a Federal soldier, behind a black jack tree some fifteen inches in diameter, with his seven-shooting Spencer rifle resting against a tree, coolly and deliberately taking aim at me." Looking down the muzzle of the Spencer's long barrel, "only the man's face, right shoulder, and part of his right breast were exposed. I could see his eyes and his features plainly." Sam threw up his carbine and fired just as the Yankee fired. Both missed, as Sam had hoped. The Federal and his single comrade turned to retreat. "In less time than it takes to tell it two dead bodies lay face downwards, where a moment before, two brave soldiers had stood." Sam walked up to the one who had tried to shoot him, looked at the body, and examined the Spencer. The soldier had fired his last cartridge at Sam. The two Federals had "bravely stood at their post" when their entire line had fallen back, "demoralized by the racket of the charge." Sam was saddened, later saying, "I could not feel glad to see these two brave fellows killed."[73]

The Texans drove the enemy from the woods across an open field. When the Iowans suddenly charged the Texans' left, a regiment of Federals mounted on gray horses, Brownlow's First Tennessee Cavalry, dashed in between the dismounted Texans and their horses. "Without halting to consider," Ross wrote, "I ordered 'bout face." The order was promptly obeyed. The Texans were desperate. They were afoot, fighting mounted men armed with sabers, and their horses were in danger. The Iowa major reported that his men charged through the Texans and drove them back, "clear through and past where their horses were held, capturing at least 500 horses of the brigade" and also capturing General Ross. "The fighting all along the line was terrific," the Iowan continued. With the Yankees too occupied to properly guard their prisoners, Ross managed to escape.[74]

The records, memoirs, and diaries fail to reveal exactly what happened next, neither the Confederates nor the Iowa major caring to discuss the matter further. General Wheeler, in his report, said he "drove off the enemy, capturing a number of prisoners and horses, and recovering all of General Ross' horses." However, Wheeler's report indicates that he, and the few hundred men capable of keeping up with him, cornered and captured McCook's 3,500, while the other Rebel generals and colonels "did not come up . . . rode the wrong direction . . . remained in Newnan . . . took the wrong road . . . had fallen asleep." The colonel of the Eighth Indiana reported that "he held the rear of the column" and "fought Jackson's cavalry all day." Ross reported only that "many instances of capture and recapture occurred during the day, the victor one moment becoming a captive to his prisoner the next." Newton Keen, in his usual terse manner, said, "We fought them from every direction."[75]

Lt. Thomas J. Towles, Third Texas, was seriously wounded during the fighting. He was leaning against a tree, his clothing soaked with blood, when McCook and his staff halted in his front. "Major, you appear to be suffering," McCook said to the Texan. Towles, fearing he was mortally wounded, answered yes and asked for medical aid. McCook said he could not even care for his own wounded and asked what Confederate forces were on the field. When the lieutenant said Wheeler, Jackson, and Roddy, McCook turned to his staff and said, *"We must get out of this!"* and immediately rode away.[76]

The Texas Brigade mounted their recaptured horses at 4:00 P.M. and rode to the enemy's rear while Wheeler prepared to attack their left flank. The Ninth rode at the front of the brigade. Jones's skirmishers quickly freed 250 Confederate captives—teamster, quartermaster and commissary personnel, and others from the rear. When the Texans began to push forward, a considerable force, including the Eighth Iowa, waved a white flag. Ross allowed the enemy to ride out mounted and fitted out. The U.S. cavalrymen were followed by a battery of fine Rodman guns, eleven new ambulances with teams, and portions of several regiments. The moment the Federal troopers laid down their guns and surrendered their horses, A.W. Sparks fell off his horse, fast asleep. It was

5:30 P.M. Saturday. The Texans had ridden, skirmished, and fought three full days and two nights.[77]

Officers and a few men who could still stand sent the prisoners to the rear. Sul Ross had to have been disappointed that Brownlow and the Iowa major, along with two of his officers and ten men, had cut their way out. The Confederates bivouacked on the field. A few of the hardiest were assigned guard duty for the night, but the Yankees needed little guarding. They had ridden and fought as long and hard as the Confederates.[78]

A.W. awoke Sunday morning "in the midst of a dense crowd of sleeping Yankees." He shook his head, wondering where he was. He had his arms on him, but he was famished and his horse was gone. Knowing the Rebels' white canvas haversacks were empty, he found a Yankee haversack of black oilcloth and ate raw bacon and U.S. hardtack for breakfast. He needed a horse and saddle, a Yankee horse, so there would be no question of ownership. Looking over the great number grazing nearby, he chose an officer's mount, fully rigged. A.W. threw away the saber, which he considered "an appendage to dress" rather than "a real implement of war."[79]

Ross and his officers "summed up the fruits of their victory" that morning: "587 prisoners, including 2 brigade commanders, with their staffs, several field and a number of company officers, 2 stand of colors (the Eighth Iowa and the Second Indiana Regiments)," the ambulances and Rodman guns, and a large number of small arms, horses, and horse equipment. Gris reported the capture of 500 stand of arms, 500 pistols, and 1,000 head of stock, including the Texans' horses that the Yankees had carried off the day before. They also recaptured the colors of an Arkansas cavalry regiment and those of another regiment. The chase from Lovejoy Station had cost Ross's Brigade five killed and eleven wounded.[80]

Wheeler did not report the number of men he lost, but he reported taking 950 prisoners and 1,200 horses. He also failed to credit Ross's Brigade with any part in the battle. Gris reported 150 Federals killed and 300 wounded. McCook reported that he, his staff, most of his officers, and 1,200 men cut their way out, leaving the others to their fate: Andersonville.[81]

The Texans armed themselves with Yankee pistols and cavalry guns,

replaced their broken-down horses, replenished their worn horse equipment, and gloated over the two rapid-fire, breech-loading Rodmans—
"dandies," a trooper called them. The captured battery was presented to
Ross's Brigade. Gris said that the Texans got "trophies of all kinds" and
"so much plunder the men are all loaded down." John Dunn was proud
of his good Yankee horse and guns, and Newton Keen said this was "a
magnificent catch for us."[82]

It was Holly Springs all over again. And oh, how the Texas cavalrymen enjoyed the boost to their pride. Since arriving in Georgia, their
only satisfaction had been knowing they were doing their duty—and that
duty had become harder by the day.

Others were also proud of the Texas boys. Brigadier General Ross
addressed his men in the field that Sunday:

> *Soldiers: You have nobly done your duty during the arduous service of
> the last four days, and by your gallantry added new laurels to the already
> wide-extended reputation of the brigade. Through your brigadier-general
> you were highly complimented on the battle-field yesterday by Major-
> General Wheeler, who acknowledged that his success was due chiefly to
> your good fighting. Your brigadier-general is proud of you; proud to
> command such soldiers, and hereby tenders to officers and men his thanks
> for their gallant service.*[83]

In his report, Wheeler did not compliment Ross's Brigade—or anyone
else's.

The men had little time to rest that Sunday. There was work to do.
A.W., again assigned as a nurse, helped carry the wounded to the yard
of a nearby house that had been turned into a hospital. Other men rolled
the dead in their blankets and buried the five Texans in one area, the
Yankees in another. Lt. Sam Barron took a detail to Newnan to guard
the Federal prisoners, held in a large brick warehouse until they could
be forwarded to Andersonville. The stock was gathered. Details dragged
the dead mules and horses from the immediate area, heaved them onto
piles of logs, and burned them. Other men picked up abandoned arms
scattered over the battle area. The vehicles and artillery were parked.[84]

In the evening, several Texans examined the captured Rodmans, the
first rifled, rapid-fire, breech-loading artillery they had seen. McCook's

men had broken off the telescopes and tried to break off the loading cranks, but the Texans used the guns to the end of the war. The Rodmans shot balls about the size of goose eggs, a trooper said, and were true at long range.[85]

The Confederates rested Monday. Tuesday morning, August 2, the Texas Brigade moved northeast up the Atlanta & East Point tracks to Palmetto. A.W. and eight or ten others remained on the field for a week until the wounded could be removed to the army hospital in Newnan. Five Union doctors and ten nurses had stayed to care for their wounded. Doctors in both armies were considered noncombatants, not liable to detention as prisoners of war, an agreement made between the Union and the Confederacy in mid-1862.[86]

The Ninth returned to skirmishing and patrolling south of the Chattahoochee along the Sandtown Road. The men remained in camp a couple of days, inspecting the horses, attending prayer meetings, and reading mail from Mississippi and Alabama. Enemy forces appeared south of the river one day, north the next. Casualties were light, but the loss of each man further depleted the ranks and added one more straw to the Texans' burden of grief.[87]

The dead were buried in their worn blankets, the badly wounded sent to hospitals in Atlanta and Newnan. The slightly wounded were furloughed and sent off to care for themselves. Some remained in Georgia, but many made their way back to Mississippi, where they had friends and acquaintances. A slight wound often became a boon greatly to be prized.[88]

Skirmishing continued through the first half of August, but the Texans remained in camp several days. Mail came in from Texas, and Gris wrote friends in the state, sending the letters off with a civilian he had known in Mississippi. The man likely was a regular courier who had followed his customers to Georgia. The trip to Texas was long and dangerous, but at a dollar a letter it was also profitable. Enemy forces continued to appear, then fade into the trees, as unwilling to start anything as were the Texans. The men, and their generals as well, needed time to catch their breath.[89]

CHAPTER 12

PAYING THE PIPER

August 12–October 24, 1864

Trains on the Macon & Western still rattled into Atlanta loaded with powder and cannon balls, food and fodder, mail and medicine. They chugged the ninety miles back to Macon packed with the wounded and dying.

Johnston's and Hood's efforts to stop the Federals had sent more than eight thousand wounded to hospitals in Atlanta, an important medical center, but the three-month campaign had overburdened the hospitals and the city as well. Sherman was extending his iron trap around Atlanta day by day. With the Georgia capital reduced to one railroad, the possibility of having to evacuate the entire city was becoming more evident. Medical Department officers were forwarding wounded men to Macon as rapidly as possible.[1]

In one of Atlanta's crowded hospitals, Reuben had become sleepless, unable to eat, depressed. His temperature dropped, and he shivered in the summer heat. The wound in his thigh bled when it was dressed and began to redden. In a day or so the edges of the wound turned livid and hard to the touch, the center sunken. Then the pain started—sharp, burning, stinging pain. A layer of gray, ash-colored matter with ragged edges formed in the cavity of the wound, which was seeping watery, bloody matter. The abscessed area enlarged day by day, almost hour by hour. Reuben's suntanned faced turned pale, his pulse rapid. His tongue became covered with a thick, yellow matter, except the tip, which reddened. Extremely anxious and unable to eat, he tossed on his cot through miserably long nights, unable to sleep. Reuben had gangrene. The terrifying infection was running rampant through the Atlanta hospitals.[2]

In one of the many cars on one of the many trips back to Macon, Reuben grimaced in pain. The car rattled along. The rhythmic clackedy-clack of steel wheels passing over track joints drummed in his ears as the car swayed along on the uneven roadbed. Hot air laden with cinders blew through open windows, stirring the fetid odors of infection and death. Attendants, passing through the cars, dampened bandages and offered water. When the train finally arrived at the Macon depot, Reuben was taken to Floyd House Hospital.[3]

Jesse might not have known his brother had gangrene, but either way, he worried. The brothers had shared their food and their blankets, their thoughts and their fears, as they marched and fought across four states for eighteen months. Jesse was left to march on with the regiment, hoping each courier would bring news of Reuben.

By mid-August 1864, Jesse and the rest of the Ninth were picketing in the rough woodlands five miles south of Sandtown. On August 12, the Federals charged the regiment's vedettes on the right center, where Quinton Booth was patrolling on horseback. Quinton, a twenty-six-year-old from Birdville, was tall, well-built, and toughened by three years of active field service. After firing at several of the enemy, he remained mounted, watching and listening. Suddenly, a mounted Federal officer appeared from behind a thicket a short distance away. Both Quinton and the officer put spurs to their horses and charged directly at one another. Quinton raised his pistol and pulled the trigger. The hammer clacked down on an empty chamber. An instant before the horses met, Quinton threw his empty pistol at the Yankee, who fired at the same moment, killing Quinton's horse. As the officer raised his pistol to fire again, Quinton's horse fell forward into the Federal and his horse. When both horses went down, Quinton grabbed the man. The two tumbled to the ground, the Yankee on top. Quinton threw the man over with great force and grabbed him by the throat.

During the struggle, Quinton's right leg struck a sharp rock, cutting a deep gash on the inside of his knee and paralyzing his leg. Blood gushed from the wound, but Quinton choked the officer limp, then wrenched the pistol from the man's hand. He pointed the pistol at the officer's head and said, "My knee's busted. Help me onto your horse and walk in front of me to camp or I'll kill ya." The Yankee entered the Ninth's camp with his own pistol holding him captive and the Rebel mounted on his good Yankee horse.

Quinton's knee was permanently stiff, but he stayed with the regiment, taking charge of the Ninth's ordnance wagon to the end of the war. He must have regretted giving up his horse to become a wagon dog, but his willingness to stay when he could have wandered off with the other wounded surely earned him the respect his dedication deserved.[4]

A few days later, the Ninth rode south toward the railroad junction of Fairburn to challenge a Federal raiding party. Ross and the rest of the brigade joined them, but the Federal cavalrymen were moving so fast that Ross's forward scouts were overrun and the other scouts were unable to report. By the time the Texans reached Fairburn, Yankees were already there. The Confederates charged several times, finally driving the enemy out of town before they could damage the railroad—but not before they burned the depot. Ross sent scouts in every direction, the Ninth out on the Fayetteville Road, the Sixth to Owl Rock Church, two miles south of the Chattahoochee.[5]

It was another couple of days before the situation became clear. Yankee cavalry were again on their way to Atlanta's lifeline. Sherman, who had little faith in cavalry at best, had decided to try one more cavalry raid on the Macon & Western. To command the force, he chose Brig. Gen. Judson Kilpatrick, "a hell of a damned fool," Sherman said, but the kind of daredevil Sherman felt he needed. Kilpatrick was known as "Kil-Cavalry" because of his disregard for the safety of his men and animals. He was vain, flamboyant, and often careless with the truth, yet he was brave and he could be kind.[6]

On the beautiful moonlit night of August 18, Kilpatrick crossed the

Chattahoochee north of Owl Rock Church with six regiments—4,500 cavalrymen, his artillery, ambulances, wagons, a pack train, and even a couple of regimental bands. Two miles south, a detachment of the Sixth held the bridge over Owl Rock Creek, which was a short distance north of the church. The detachment was under the command of Captain Porter, Company A, "an ignorant old goose not having enough sense to command pigs," according to Newton Keen. Porter had stationed six men on the bridge with instructions to fire when the enemy appeared. The rest of the command waited up the road from the bridge on top of a hill.[7]

Newt and others tried to get Porter to let them fill the road with black jack trees, but the captain said, "We will fill the road with dead men and horses, which would be better."

"They'll pass up the road too fast," Newt said.

"I know how to manage the Yankees," Porter barked.

The road, four inches deep in dust, ran through dense black jack brush for over a mile, making it impossible to ride out of the track. At 10:00 P.M., Yankee horsemen stormed across Owl Rock Bridge without pausing and poured down the road, running right through Captain Porter's men. Rebels and Yankees thundered down the road together, whooping and yelling like demons in a dense fog of dust. Only a few shots were fired because no one could tell who was friend and who was foe.[8]

Newt rode a fine mule, black as a crow. The animal was keen and slim, quick as lightning, and he always stayed with the crowd. The dust was so thick Newt could see only a few feet. Riding boot to boot with a trooper, he spotted the soldier's saber and knew he was a Yankee. Half a mile down the road, Newt's mule struck the stump of a fallen oak that projected into the road. The mule went head over heels, throwing Newt ten feet into the dense brush. Newton landed on his back, miraculously unhurt. The mule bounced up and raced on with the crowd.

Newt's gun and ammunition were strapped to his body, but the rest of his accoutrements went back to camp with the black mule. In the bright moonlight, Newt recognized where he was: on the east side of the road, the Yankee side. Enemy troops kept pouring down the road, blocking the way west. Newt walked south two miles, staying in the thick brush well away from the road. When he came to a small field near his camp, he returned to the road and took a good look at the Yankees. They still blocked his way west. He set out through the brush, skirting the field, but had gone only a short distance when he walked into a Federal patrol.

"Give up your gun, Johnny," a Yankee ordered. Newt stopped in his tracks. Instantly understanding that escape was impossible, fear tensed his muscles and knotted his stomach. It took him a moment to force his hand to relax and drop the gun. Newt realized "the jig was up and the dance was over." The Yankees marched him north to Kilpatrick's headquarters.[9]

Kilpatrick's troopers, with the Sixth on their rear, galloped through the darkness. They soon approached the Ninth's camp, bedded down for the night. When pounding hooves and rattling gunfire woke them at midnight, they leaped up. "Our saddles were soon on," John Dunn wrote, "and the riders on them, some not waiting for orders to mount." The regiment formed in column of fours and rode in the direction of the firing. Out on the road, they halted to wait the advance of the enemy when John's mule gave notice of the coming fight with a big, long bray, as was his custom. Horsemen clattering down the road galloped right into the regiment. A few men fired before they realized the horsemen were their own pickets. By the time the pickets turned back down the road to escape the fire of their own men, the Yankees were on them. There was no way to form when the mass of men and horses came together. The Ninth charged down the road among the Yankees. "We fought them so close that the blazes of their guns extended to us," a trooper said. The regiment had been fighting hand-to-hand for an hour when heavy enemy columns began pouring deadly fire down the road. The regiment retreated. John was sure a bullet would strike him in the back of the head at any instant, but he passed out safely. Colonel Jones was knocked from his horse, seriously injured. Two men were wounded. The Legion joined the Ninth just before daylight, and the two regiments fell back to another road.[10]

When Ross, with the Third and the Sixth, came up, the brigade struck out to get in front of the raiders on the road leading south toward Jonesboro. The enemy appeared, cavalry and infantry in separate columns two and a half miles long. Ross's men attacked but were driven farther south, the Yankees right on their rear. A bullet whizzed past John's head, brushing his hair and raising bile in his throat. By the time the Texans reached the bridge over Flint River at 2:00 P.M., "there were some scared men," John wrote, "and nearly every fellow was trying to cross first." When all were safely over, they burned the bridge and pointed their artillery across the river. They were nearly out of ammunition. The troopers threw up breastworks and fed the horses, having no idea what to expect next. Just before night, Ross led his men to Jonesboro. When they reached the town, Federals attacked them with artillery. The Texans dashed down the main street in a near stampede and out into the countryside. Ross threw out a line of pickets for the night so the men could get some rest.[11]

While the rest of the Texans galloped south, two Yanks marched Newt north to Kilpatrick's headquarters. Kilpatrick interviewed the young Texan later in the night. When the general learned that nineteen-year-old Newt had been in the army three years, that he had been born in Indiana, and that his father was a Mason, he offered Newt $300 in cash, a good horse, and a bridle if he would join his command. Newt politely declined. Kilpatrick then offered to send the young Texan west, where there was no war and little danger, but Newt told the general he could not break his oath to the South. Kilpatrick did not give up. He offered to send Newt north to his relatives in Indiana, where he would be safe until the war was over, if he would take the oath of allegiance. Again, Newt's conscience would not allow him to accept. For thirty minutes, Kilpatrick tried to convince Newt to accept his offer and, as Newt later wrote, "certainly tried to do a father's part to me." At Nashville, while Newt was on the way north to prison, an officer once again offered to send him north of the Ohio to kinfolks. "Here is where I let the apple slip," Newt later lamented. He was sent to the North's Andersonville—Camp Douglas, near Chicago.[12]

At first light the next morning, August 20, the brigade cautiously moved back through Jonesboro, stopping only long enough to bury the captain who had been killed the day before. Six miles south at Lovejoy Station, they found Confederate infantry and artillery and Jackson's other cavalry regiments attacking the front of Kilpatrick's column. Near noon, Ross spotted the rear of the Federal column in woods thick with undergrowth. He reported to Jackson from Mrs. Carnes's Gin House, "I have a plain view of at least 4,000 formed in line." Ross dismounted his 400, put his artillery to work, and attacked.[13]

Kilpatrick was getting low on ammunition, and when Ross attacked his rear, the Yankee general realized he was surrounded. He gathered his forces behind the crest of a hill and prepared to cut his way out. In order to reach a road that led to safety, he decided to ride through Ross's Brigade with his advantage of ten to one. Kilpatrick formed three regiments abreast in column of fours and three in close columns with reg- imental front, each regi- ment in line, the men side

Kilpatrick Running over Ross's Brigade

by side, boot to boot. They drew their sabers to avoid firing into their own men.[14]

The Federal cavalrymen trotted to the crest of the hill, then charged at a gallop, leaping fences, ditches, and barricades, seeking safety beyond Ross's dismounted men. Ross's battery fired into them, but they rode straight into the Texans. For an instant Sam Barron watched in astonish- ment, then realized each man was on his own in the melee of plunging horses and slashing sabers. "No order was heard; not a word spoken; every officer and man took in the whole situation at a glance," he said. The men remained in line only long enough to empty their guns. There was no time to reload. They instinctively ran for the horses. Rebel artillerymen fired into the horde of Federals until their last shell was spent before sprinting toward cover. The deafening roar of canister and small arms exploding down a lane caused splinters on the fences to vibrate like the noise of a Jew's harp. John Dunn was sure "the whole of us would go up." On came the Yankees, swinging sabers at everyone within range. Ross's horse holders drove as many horses into the brush as possi- ble. The rest stampeded.[15]

Jesse was running for cover when a Yankee galloped by and swung his saber at Jesse's head. Jesse ducked, but the saber caught him, laying open his scalp. He ran through brush and across gullies, blood pouring down his collar. His company comrades E. J. Brown and J. E. Moore were wounded. E. M. King was captured. The three Perkins boys of Company D were all wounded.[16]

Sam Barron, Capt. S. E. Nobel, and Lt. Tom Soape of the Third ran for a ravine. Nobel jumped across and squatted in tall grass in a fence corner. Soape dropped into the ravine. Sam leaped the ravine, then the fence. Nobel and Soape were captured. Sam had gone fifteen steps when a mounted Yankee was on him. "Surrender, sir!" rang in Sam's ear. The Yankee was standing up in his stirrups with his saber glittering just over Sam's head. Sam hesitated. The man said in a quiet voice, "That is all I ask of you, sir." Sam dropped the carbine he was carrying. "All right," the Yankee said, and spurred his horse to join his friends.[17]

Sam stood still. Columns of Yankees galloped past on each side of him. Artillery burst overhead. When a shell exploded nearby, Sam grabbed his abdomen above his right hip and fell "as long a fall as I could toward the center of a little space between the columns." He was careful to fall on his right side to hide his pistol. He lay still, playing the dead man as best he could while Yankee cavalrymen raced past. Sam could hear their voices, could feel the pounding of hooves near him. He did not move.

The action eventually moved off. In the silence, an awful fear came over Sam that he would be discovered and carried away to prison, "a most horrible consequence." Rain began to fall, rain so hard it made the flesh on his face hurt. Yankee soldiers drove a train of pack mules so near they almost stepped on Sam. He dared not move. Finally, it became so quiet Sam opened his eyes. He slowly raised his head and looked around. Not a man was in sight. He stood. Kilpatrick was gone.

Sam was "no stranger to hardships of a soldier's life." He had "endured the coldest weather with scant clothing, marched day after day and night after night without food or sleep" until his power of endurance was "well-nigh exhausted," but never did he "find anything quite so tedious as playing dead."

Sam started out over the field in search of enough plunder to fit himself out. He was sure Ross's Brigade as an organization was broken up, but he would find another place to serve. He found a completely rigged horse, only slightly wounded, and a pack mule, which he loaded with saddles, bridles, blankets, and oilcloths. Sam even picked up the Sharps carbine he had dropped when he surrendered.

While thinking of which command he would join, a bugle call rent the air, a bugle call Sam instantly recognized. It was Ross's bugler sounding assembly, the sweetest music Sam had ever heard. He rode toward the bugle and found General Ross and his bugler on the highest elevation in the field, calling in the scattered men.[18]

From the dark clouds that had gathered, torrents of rain again began to pour on the exhausted men. Out of the wet timber and brush Texans straggled into camp from every direction, "seeming to come out of the ground." Tom Soape had captured his captors and marched them into the Texans' camp at gunpoint. Other men brought in a prisoner who was so drunk he did not know he had been captured until the next morning. Many of the horses had been saved by being turned into the brush by the holders. Bivouacking on the field that evening, the Texans were "crestfallen and heartily ashamed" of being run over, but they were not seriously damaged.[19]

The next morning men scoured the battlefield for Yankee plunder: horses, saddles, guns, clothing, cooking utensils, food, and most of Kilpatrick's pack train. John's mess gathered enough rations to last a week. Sam's slave came in on his mule, bringing a few of Sam's clothes. The train and "much plunder" were taken by Frank Anderson's Mississippi cavalrymen, who took up the chase after the Federals ran over Ross's men.[20]

Gris and the other regimental adjutants tallied their casualties. Gris discovered that sixty men in the Ninth had been captured, but only four failed to return to the regiment before the week was out. No one in the Ninth was killed when the brigade was run over, but the chase from Owl Creek to Jonesboro had been costly. In addition to the four men captured in the Ninth, two men were killed by shells, another man died of wounds, and twenty-three others were wounded. In the Third, eighty-five men were captured, twenty-three failing to escape. Sgt. Victor Rose, who was wounded during the action, was among those taken north to prison.[21]

From the battlefield the brigade followed the railroad north to West Point the next day. Ross rode to headquarters to report. "General," he told Hood, "I got my brigade run over yesterday."

"General Ross, you have lost nothing by that, sir," Hood assured Ross. "If others, who should have been there, had been near enough to . . . be run over, your men would not have been run over." Ross's conversation with Hood buffed a bit of the tarnish off the Texans' pride. In addition, the men would have been surprised at their fame among the Federals. A courier had raced to Sherman's headquarters to report that Ross's Brigade was broken up. Sherman immediately notified his commanders in the field and wired the good news to Chattanooga and on to Washington.[22]

In spite of the wire to Washington, Sherman was disappointed in the raid, yet Kilpatrick and his troopers had done all they could. Sherman reported that Kilpatrick "had a pretty hard fight" and that the Macon & Western would be disabled for ten days at the most. The raid convinced Sherman that cavalry could not do the job. "I expect I will have to swing around to that road in force to make the matter certain," he told Washington. He soon learned that Hood had sent Wheeler's cavalry north to harass the Federals' only railroad. Sherman reported, "I could not have asked for anything better," and started six corps south down the Sandtown road. Kilpatrick's cavalry led the advance.[23]

Saturday, August 27, the Ninth moved out at noon from their camp at the Fairburn and Sandtown crossroads. They soon clashed with masses of blue infantry and cavalry. The Texans fought through the evening and into the night, constantly falling back toward the railroad. They finally bivouacked for a few hours. Through the night pickets could hear the Federals bringing up wagons and artillery, and tearing up the railroad.[24]

Sunday morning, Colonel Berry, in command since Jones's injury, left a lieutenant and ten scouts to watch the enemy while the regiment moved south ten miles to join the rest of the brigade. They found Ross holding a hilltop protected by a small, swampy stream. The Federals attacked in such numbers that the brigade was forced to fall back several miles. Eight companies of the Ninth remained on the skirmish line that night. Morning brought more Federal infantry into view. When Armstrong's Cavalry Brigade joined Ross and his men, the two brigades fell back another three miles.[25]

The next day official chores took precedence over the enemy. It was August 30, time to report the bimonthly rolls. Before the tallies were finished the Yankees attacked, again in force. Ross and Armstrong fell back together onto the Jonesboro Road and quickly fortified along a creek. The Federals brought up artillery and hammered away. With smoke and dirt filling the air, the Confederates cowered behind piles of rails. A shell burst just as it reached Company K's rail pile. When the timbers flew in every direction, the entire brigade was ready to run. John Dunn feared half the men were killed, but they all crawled out and burrowed deeper behind the scattered timbers. They gritted their teeth and held on.[26]

John and his comrades were lying flat on the ground with their heads behind logs when they felt their stack of logs shudder. A solid shot had passed between two men's heads and within two feet of John's head. No one was hurt, John wrote, but "it made the boys look wild." John felt that Ross was trying to prove that his men were not demoralized after being run over. The Texans did not budge, but when the order to retire finally came they raced to their horses.[27]

They fell back to the Flint River, then farther back to the railroad. At dark, Ross left out an unusually heavy skirmish line half a mile in front of camp. The masses of blue uniforms encountered during the past three days left no doubt in anyone's mind that they were overpowered. The cavalrymen fed the horses and tried to get a little sleep.[28]

The sun brought help. Confederate infantry appeared, regiment after regiment. Hood, finally realizing what was happening, had marched his infantry south all day and all night. The Ninth formed a skirmish line on the infantry's right and waited. Everything was quiet until 4:00 P.M., when Federal infantry struck the railroad two miles north. All that night, John and the other pickets listened to the Yankees chopping up the railroad a short distance away. Small arms fire rattled through the darkness, and every ten minutes a cannon fired. John had no trouble staying awake.[29]

By morning Sherman had his vast corps in place. They had completely destroyed twelve and a half miles of track, burned the ties, heated and twisted the rails, and filled the cuts with tree trunks, rocks, and earth mixed with loaded shells prepared as torpedoes that would explode on contact. Sherman inspected the work, then turned his attention to Hood's army.[30]

Fighting erupted all along the railroad. By noon September 1, the Confederate army was routed and fled the field, leaving their dead and wounded. Jackson posted the Texans four miles out on the Jonesboro and McDonough Road with firm orders to hold the position. They tried. Late in the evening, Colonel Berry, trying to rally his men, yelled, "Hold on!" At that moment, he was struck and thrown from his horse. When Berry went down, the men panicked.[31]

John Dunn and the other pickets met the regiment a few hundred yards from their reserve. "I found the men in a panic," he wrote, and was "mad more at our own men than the Yanks for they were so badly scared" that they were shooting at the enemy through their own ranks. Gris rallied enough men, "under a most galling fire," to reach Berry and bring him out.[32]

Gris treasured his friendship with Berry beyond his relationship with any man in the regiment. He and three other men placed Tom Berry on a blanket and carried him five miles to an ambulance. Gris went with the ambulance carrying Berry to Surgeon Robertson's field infirmary several miles south, near Griffin.[33]

Soon after midnight a courier from Hood passed with information that Atlanta was being evacuated. Deep rumbles of exploding artillery ammunition rolled across the bloodied countryside from the city. When the courier reached headquarters, the Texas regiments were ordered to fall back. The Ninth was ordered to Lovejoy Station to picket the army's right. The Texans had been on the Confederate left since May. Now, they moved only a few miles to reach the right. The entire Confederate army was west of the station, Sherman's army to the east.[34]

Gris stayed at the field infirmary with Tom Berry, his "true friend" and "one of the noblest specimens of God's handiwork." Robertson, who had served with Berry since the regiment was organized, did everything in his power to save the colonel. That night, when Berry realized he was dying, he expressed no fear of death but told Gris, "I am not prepared to die, I have not accomplished all I want to & yet if necessary I can die as well as anyone else but I want to do more before I go!" Stunned and profoundly saddened by the loss of this friend he loved, this "upright man and fearless soldier," Gris told his diary, "All who knew him loved him and mourn his death most sincerely. Surely such men are not unrewarded in the Spirit Land!" September 3, 1864, Lt. Col. Thomas G. Berry, aged thirty-five, was buried in full uniform in the cemetery at Griffin, Georgia, near several other Texans. He was mourned by every man in the Ninth Texas Cavalry.[35]

Gris returned to duty. The regiment remained on the right of the Confederate army for a few more days, but the Yankees had disappeared, causing a strange silence to fall across the land. "We wake up at daylight & could not hear a single gun fired," an infantryman wrote September 7.[36]

"Two tired armies rested," Sam wrote.[37]

Ross and his men moved each day for a week, until they reached Newnan, where they remained in the same camp three entire days. For the first time in four months, the Texans had a full night's uninterrupted sleep. Gris caught up on his paperwork and finished his tally of the Ninth's casualties in the Georgia campaign: six men killed; sixty-two wounded; twenty-two captured; a total of ninety men and sixty-seven horses lost.[38]

Sul Ross also counted his losses and wrote to his father-in-law in Texas:

We are enjoying the rest very much My brigade has been in line of Battle upon an average of once every day for 112 days and has fought eighty six fights. It came to Rome with 1,009, & since then has lost Three hundred & three Killed wounded & missing.[39]

Newton later wrote that "there was not two days but we were in some kind of fight." A. W. Sparks reported the Texans captured three thousand prisoners, four thousand stand of arms, eight pieces of artillery, and twelve stand of colors.[40]

The moment things calmed down, the Texans began agitating for furloughs. Ross told them he would try. General Polk, who had promised them furloughs, had been killed, but Ross pleaded with the division command, Brig. Gen. W. H. Jackson. Jackson assured Ross "that no stone shall be left unturned to secure the permission," and took the

Texans' case to both General Hood and General Beauregard. Ross even wrote to Col. F. R. Lubbock, a former Texas governor, who was at Macon on his way to Richmond. Ross reminded Lubbock that the Texans had originally enlisted for a year, which had been extended to three by an act of Congress, and now the three years were up. "They have despaired of receiving furloughs," he wrote, "and I am convinced beyond a shadow of a doubt that the greater portion of them, if not all, will go to the Trans-Mississippi Department as soon as the enemy ceases to advance in Georgia." Ross told Lubbock he was unsure he could keep his command east of the Mississippi. "Please let me know if anything can be done," he begged.[41]

Ross's pleas came to nothing, but a number of his men furloughed themselves over the next two months. In his diary, Gris did not record any desertions from the Ninth during those weeks, yet surely the regiment was no more immune from desertion than the other Texas regiments. The last surviving rolls of the Ninth were taken June 30, 1864, making it impossible to know the fate of every man. The August 30 muster roll, which was ordered during the last days of fighting to save the Macon Road, did not survive. The June 30 roll of Company A counted twenty-six men present for duty and thirty-one sick, assigned as scouts, or in the rear with the trains or the unfit horses. Nine other men are known from other sources to have been with the company. Three men had deserted since the previous extant roll, made ten months earlier, making a total of sixty-six men remaining in Company A on June 30, 1864. No official count of the Ninth Texas Cavalry appears in the *Official Records*.[42]

Unable to get his men furloughed, Ross did what he could. He sent a courier to Texas with all the mail his horse could safely carry, and instructed him to return as soon as possible. In addition, Lt. Henry G. Haynes was expected to ride in from Texas in another week or two with news and mail.[43]

During the lull, Ross's Brigade was reorganized. Companies, some depleted to as few as eight men present for duty, were consolidated for more efficient service. Extra officers organized themselves into scouting squadrons. Well-armed and well-mounted, they reconnoitered and patrolled—pleasant duty, according to Sam Barron. Col. Dudley Jones visited the Ninth's camp the middle of September, but he was still unfit for duty. He was furloughed for sixty days more. Capt. Hamilton C. Dial, Company K, assumed command of the regiment.[44]

The Texas Brigade gradually worked its way north for the next couple of weeks. The regiments took turns on picket duty, occasionally skirmishing with a few Yankees. Late in September an alarm at midnight woke everyone in the regiment. When the men discovered the source of the firing, they had a good laugh. A picket and a straggler were fighting a duel. September 30, Captain Dial took the Ninth and a squadron of the Third north toward Marietta to destroy the railroad. The guides got lost in a terrific thunderstorm, and the men returned to camp at sunrise tired, wet, and disgusted.[45]

With the onset of fall and another rainy season, officers and men began scrounging for boots and clothing. The officers sent a lieutenant south to buy new uniforms, and Ross ordered fabric from Macon. John Dunn was nearly barefoot. He hurried to a location where a few shoes were for sale, but the place was surrounded by soldiers and John gave up. He later learned the location of a tan yard, but again was too late. Some men were reduced to making moccasins out of hides freshly stripped from beef cattle.[46]

News, mail, and a few supplies were coming in by courier from Macon, still held by the Confederacy. Jesse surely heard from his brother, who was still in the Floyd House Hospital.

When Reuben had reached Macon in late July, the city's eleven military hospitals were filled with wounded men, but the crowding there did not compare to the packed misery of Atlanta's temporary facilities. Fortunately for Reuben, hospitals in Macon were among the best managed in the Confederacy. Early in 1863, an inspector commented on "the perfect cleanliness of each and every part of the establishments," even "the kitchens were free from dirt or disorder," and "no gentleman's residence in the whole South is cleaner or more tidy."[47]

At Floyd House Hospital, in downtown Macon, Reuben was placed in a "gangrene ward"—where air circulation in the hospital was best, or in a tent. He was bathed, clad in clean hospital garments, and given morphine if his pain was intense. As soon as possible, a doctor began treatment. The infection in Reuben's leg had not spread to his hand, but the small bullet wound in his thigh could well have increased to six inches across in a matter of a few days. He likely had malaria, so common in the South that diarists failed to mention it except when they had just suffered a bout of chills. Malaria was known to complicate recovery from gangrene.[48]

Reuben's chances of survival were 50 percent, lower than they would have been had his wound been on his trunk. His prospects, however, were much better than they would have been two years earlier, when doctors were struggling to learn how to treat the infection, which they called a disease. Three other factors were in Reuben's favor: the use of cloth instead of sponges—imported items no longer available; Reuben's positive attitude toward life, which doctors considered worthy of note; and Georgia's abundant blackberries.[49]

The doctor who treated Reuben first anesthetized him with chloroform. Then he thoroughly cleaned away the gray, ash-colored matter and rotting flesh with small cloth swabs. He trimmed the edges of the abscessed area, being sure to excise all pockets of infection. Next, he dipped a clean swab into a bottle of pure nitric acid, which was cautiously held by a nurse, and painted the clean flesh with the acid, again being careful to thoroughly treat the edges.

When Reuben awoke he felt better. Perhaps he asked for something to eat, then slept peacefully for the first time in days. If signs of the infection reappeared, the treatment was repeated. The wound was cleaned daily with a weak solution of nitric acid. Reuben and the others in the ward were given sulfate of quinine, one or two doses of ten grains daily. Special diets for gangrene patients included fruits and vegetables, milk, and eggs. When Reuben's wound showed clear signs of healing, he was transferred to another ward. It would be weeks before his leg healed, but the terrifying threat to his leg and to his life had passed.[50]

The saber cut to Jesse's head had not been serious, and gangrene was no threat. Wounded men who remained in the field did not develop the Civil War's hospital gangrene. The infection, which appeared only in hospitals, was related to trench gangrene of the First World War. Jesse surely had his wound dressed at the field infirmary, then returned to his mess.[51]

★   ★   ★

By the first of October the Ninth was at Powder Spring, midway between Atlanta and Dallas. The countryside, having been fought over for
five months, was desolate. Not a cow, horse, pig, chicken, or goose
remained. Scarcely a bird could be seen in the woods. The fences had
all been torn down for campfires or barricades, leaving the houses looking
forsaken. A few surviving stalks of corn and sorghum had made small
ears and scanty heads, forcing residents to live on corn bread and crudely
made sorghum molasses—with nothing to share with the cavalrymen.[52]

Through this forlorn countryside the Ninth picketed and skirmished
with Federal cavalry. Hood, maintaining his headquarters at Palmetto,
was working his army north toward Sherman's supply line, with Jackson's
cavalry leading the advance. The Ninth was on duty most days, but
neither the Rebels nor the Yankees pushed hard enough to cause
much damage.[53]

The fall rainy season continued with a vengeance. Tremendous
storms pounded the thinly clad Confederates and turned the rutted roads
to deep mud. John was still hunting a pair of boots, and Ross still had
not received his cloth from Macon when a frigid north wind blew in
the night of October 7. Frost decorated the trees and sparkled on the
muddy fields the next morning. Men hovered near their fires, dreading
their turn on picket duty.[54]

By the Ninth's third anniversary, October 14, 1864, the regiment
was at Cave Springs, twenty miles southwest of Rome, where the Atlanta
campaign had begun for them. Rations were short, but the men had
cause to celebrate that day. Lt. Henry Haynes, captain of A.W.'s company, rode in with mail and news from Texas. A few days later the
wagon train came up with supplies and a welcome passenger—Maj. James
C. Bates. Bates had been in the hospital for three months and on medical
leave for two more after being shot in the neck and jaw at Raccoon
Creek. Although Bates had been promoted to lieutenant colonel a month
earlier, he was not well enough to take command of the regiment. Hamilton Dial, recently promoted to major, retained command.[55]

The Ninth and the rest of Ross's Brigade soon received orders to
pack everything and move west as rear guard for the Army of Tennessee.
Hood had decided to leave Atlanta to Sherman and strike north into
Tennessee, where only a handful of Federals guarded Nashville. Perhaps

he could march north as far as the Ohio River and regain a vast area for the Confederacy. It was a bold plan, but he would have to move fast.[56]

The Ninth formed with the rest of their brigade early the morning of October 24 and set out on the Summerville Road at 7:00 P.M.[57] Perhaps Jesse turned in his saddle to gaze across the autumn landscape toward Macon.

The cavalrymen crossed into Alabama at noon, leaving their dead in graves that would forever remain unmarked, their wounded in homes and hospitals scattered across the region. They had no way of knowing, but nothing in the future of the Ninth Texas Cavalry would compare with Georgia.

CHAPTER 13

RIDING WITH FORREST

October 25–December 27, 1864

The Army of Tennessee reached Gadsden, Alabama, on October 20, 1864, where they found abundant supplies waiting, including shoes and clothing. When Ross's Brigade reached the same town, five days later, they found only scanty rations for themselves and their horses. Trailing the army, they crossed the Coosa River on a steamer, climbed to the village of Summit, and marched down to Decatur, on the Tennessee River. Remaining well south of the Union-held town, they made camp. Hood and the infantry were already at Tuscumbia, fifty miles to the west.[1]

The War Department had once again ordered a full general to overall command of the Military District of the West, the system that had failed during the Vicksburg Campaign. Gen. Pierre G. T. Beauregard, whom Old Butch had instantly recognized as an officer of high rank at Corinth, had met Hood in eastern Alabama. Beauregard, agreeing to Hood's plan to invade Tennessee, immediately began funneling to Hood all the men, equipment, and supplies he could wring out of the district. His greatest contribution was Maj. Gen. Nathan Bedford Forrest. Hood was short of

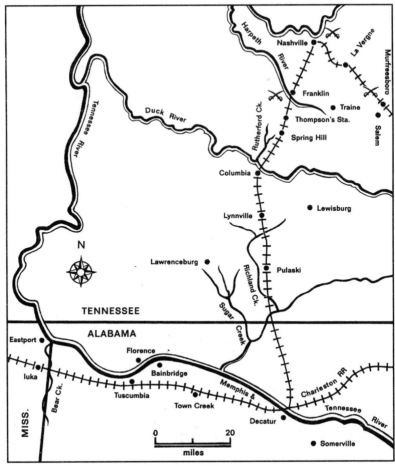

Tennessee Campaign with Forrest—1864

horsemen because Joseph Wheeler's cavalry had been ordered back to Georgia to watch Sherman.[2]

Sherman feared no one in the West except Forrest. During the Atlanta campaign, the tough Yankee had ordered out from Memphis into northern Mississippi three heavy cavalry raids to keep Forrest off the Union's single supply line, running north from Chattanooga. Sherman, who called the Confederate "that Devil Forrest," had ordered his successive Memphis commanders to "send out a force amply supplied to whip him . . . defeat Forrest at all costs . . . keep after Forrest until recalled by either myself or General Grant." Sherman became so exasperated with his cavalrymen's inability to destroy Forrest's command that he wired the secretary of war that he would order out a force sufficient to "follow

Forrest to the death if it costs 10,000 lives and breaks the Treasury." Although the celebrated cavalryman turned back all three raids with spectacular success, Sherman accomplished his goal of holding Forrest in Mississippi.[3]

Forrest was in West Tennessee, where the high command was wasting his talents, when he received Beauregard's orders to report to Hood. Forrest started immediately across the rain-soaked country. Hood rested and refitted his army while waiting for Forrest.[4]

Ross's Brigade, remaining near Decatur under orders to watch Federal movements, soon reported that the enemy was concentrating at the town. The Texans fattened their horses on corn and stuffed themselves with grapes while picketing the roads and occasionally skirmishing with Yankee patrols. One morning at sunrise a strong enemy reconnoitering force, three regiments of infantry with artillery and a battalion of cavalry, attacked the Sixth on the picket line in woods skirting Fox Creek. The Third and the Ninth, galloping toward sounds of firing, soon found their comrades hard-pressed. Hamilton Dial led the Ninth through heavy brush and charged the Federals. Alex Anderson was shot in the arm, and several horses were wounded. The regiment fell back to where their battery was pounding the Yankees. When Ross saw the enemy falter, he ordered the Third and the Ninth to charge on horseback. Yelling and firing in their best style, they forced the enemy back to his works near Decatur.[5]

The Texans were relieved in a few days. They moved down the valley to near Tuscumbia and camped near Town Creek. They did what refitting they could while commissary and ordnance officers issued ammunition, rations, and corn for the horses.[6]

The torrential rains and unusually cold weather that had started in Georgia continued. November 9, a terrific rainstorm flooded Town Creek. Water rose so rapidly the brigade had to move three miles to higher ground. During the night a bitter cold front knifed into the region.[7]

Several men of the Ninth were missing at morning roll call. Angry that they had been promised furloughs over and over and were now expected to move back into Middle Tennessee on another campaign, they had deserted. Three more left a few days later. The majority of the

Texans, disgusted and furious with the deserters, were determined to do their duty regardless of where it led. When scouts captured a deserter later in the month, the men clamored to hang him.[8]

Col. Dud Jones, after an absence of three months, had rejoined his regiment two days before the desertions. Still an invalid on medical leave, Jones remained in camp, watching his men prepare for the coming campaign. After the deserters left, he clenched his jaw and thought of riding with Forrest. When the men began cooking rations and packing corn for the horses, Jones could not bear the thought of being left behind. Friday morning, November 18, when the regiment was ordered north, Jones assumed command and led his Texans across the pontoon bridge spanning the thousand-foot-wide Tennessee River, which had risen eighteen feet during the recent rains. They moved two miles beyond Florence before making camp in pouring rain.[9]

The next day a circular from Forrest was read, announcing his assumption of command and noting the "patient endurance and unflinching bravery" of the troops placed under him, Jackson's Division. The general would review Ross's Texans and Armstrong's Mississippians a couple of days later as they marched along the Lawrenceburg Road. Gris was impressed with being in Forrest's command. He wrote, "[We] are now in *Forrest's Cavalry*." In addition to winning battles, Forrest always took care of his men, their physical comforts, their horses and equipment—and their honor. Hood's infantrymen were also impressed. A Texas infantryman wrote in his diary, "General Forrest is here and we sleep soundly when we know that he is between us and the enemy."[10]

The Texans crossed the state line into Tennessee—Jesse Rogers without his brother Reuben, A. W. Sparks without his brother John, Gus Creed without his brother George, Gris Griscom without his true friend Tom Berry, Dud Jones without his lieutenant colonel or his major (James C. Bates). The regiment counted 110 men present for duty, down from 700 in March 1862. The other Texas regiments were nearly as thin. Lt. Col. Jiles S. Boggess reported 218 men in the Third, and Col. Jack Wharton reported the same number in the Sixth. Col. E. R. Hawkins reported 140 present with the Legion, making a total of 686 in Sul Ross's command.[11]

As usual, the number of mounted men capable of taking the field was far less than those on the rolls. If Company A is representative, the

Ninth's rolls listed many more men than the 110 present for duty. The last extant roll of the company, made four months earlier, reported 26 men present for duty and 31 sick, detached, or absent with permission. Another 9 not reported are known to have been in Georgia with the regiment, making a total of over 66 men remaining in the company. The number of parole papers signed at the end of the war and a few other reports indicate that the Ninth still counted about 500 men in November 1864.[12]

Maj. Gen. Nathan Bedford Forrest

The Army of Tennessee numbered about 30,000, down perhaps 20,000 since Hood had taken command four months earlier. Conflicting reports make an accurate count impossible. Forrest had brought with him Brig. Gen. James R. Chalmers's and Brig. Gen. Abraham Buford's Divisions, about 3,000 men. Jackson's Division—Frank Armstrong's 1,300 and Sul Ross's 686—brought the total number of Forrest's cavalrymen up to around 5,000.[13]

During the two weeks that Hood waited below the river, Sherman had strengthened Tennessee. Before setting out across Georgia toward the coast, Sherman had sent one of his best, Maj. Gen. George Thomas, to take command at Nashville. Sherman was reinforcing Thomas with every man he could squeeze out of the West. Schofield's corps, the Texans' old adversaries, had come up from Georgia to join a corps already at Pulaski. However, Thomas, dependable but always cautious, was not yet ready to tackle the Confederates.[14]

Hood started his infantry north November 22. The fierce wintry weather was still on a rampage. "We marched off from Florence," a Texas infantryman said, "while the snow came down thick." The Army of Tennessee moved north toward Nashville in three columns. In advance of the infantrymen rode Forrest's horsemen, scouting, skirmishing, and gathering supplies as far north as the Duck River.[15]

Ross and Armstrong were forty miles up the road near Lawrenceburg when they ran into their first opposition. The Ninth remained in line while the battery shelled the Federals out of the town at sunset. Ross's men camped on the creek that evening, envying Armstrong's troopers, who remained in town to enjoy forage and supplies left by the Yankees. While the men picketed during the night the temperature plunged, and ice two inches thick formed in the creeks by morning.[16]

When the lazy, late fall sun came up, it was the Texans' turn to take the advance. Ross led them a few miles north from Lawrenceburg, then turned east, toward Pulaski. They soon came upon an abandoned enemy cavalry camp. The men boiled their coffee substitute of parched bran over the still-burning fires and fed their horses Yankee forage. Ten miles up the road that evening, they ran off another party of Federals, again helping themselves to what the blue cavalrymen had left: plenty of potatoes and ample hay for the animals. The men hovered near their fires as the temperature dropped even further during the night.[17]

Again in the advance the next morning, the Ninth followed a trail left by Federal cavalry. Five miles from Pulaski they turned back north, reaching Campbellville at noon. Brig. Gen. Edward Hatch's Union cavalry was drawn up waiting for them. Jackson sent Armstrong around to flank Hatch and ordered Ross forward. Ross sent the Third to the front, dismounted. The battery galloped up, quickly got into position, and began throwing shells at Hatch's men. Ross left the Ninth and the Legion mounted as he watched the battle develop. When he saw the Federals beginning to draw off, he ordered the two mounted regiments after them.[18]

The column galloped forward. Yelling and firing, they cut through the dismounted Yankees and took after the ones on horseback. The Texans charged "through the village [and] fell upon the enemy's moving squadrons with such irresistible force as to scatter them in every direction," Ross reported. Dud Jones emptied his pistol and was grappling with one Yankee when another came up behind him. Jones threw himself off his horse to avoid being shot, but a bullet passed through his hat, clipping off a lock of his hair.[19]

Buford, marching on a parallel road about a mile distant, hit a portion of the Federal cavalry while Armstrong struck Hatch's flank, and the "rout was completed," as Ross reported. "The last of his forces, in full flight, disappeared in the direction of Lynville about sunset." The Texans gleefully gathered their spoils: 200 fully equipped cavalry horses, 125 prisoners, 4 stand of colors, 65 cattle, and several pack mules laden with provisions. The provisions included great treasures—overcoats, blankets, and coffee. None of the Texans were killed and only five were wounded.[20]

A.W., Jesse, Gus, and their comrades sat around their fires near the battleground that night, snug in blue overcoats and sipping real coffee. Middle Tennessee's bare trees, brown fields, and churned-up roads looked nothing like the glorious countryside they had left eighteen months earlier. Nor did the Ninth Texas Cavalry look the same. They were thinner, tougher, and fewer—but "strong in heart and resolved to make up in zeal and courage what was wanting in numbers."[21]

The next morning, November 25, the Texans learned that Schofield was retreating up the Columbia–Nashville Pike and that Hatch's horsemen were demoralized and in full retreat. The Texans marched out onto the pike from Lynville with the rest of Jackson's Division. They were in fine spirits. Forrest was leading them, and the Army of Tennessee was close behind. More victories surely lay ahead.[22]

Three days later, Ross and Armstrong forded the swollen Duck River near a mill nine miles east of Columbia while Forrest's other divisions crossed farther west. The Duck was the only major river on their road to Nashville. The weather remained cold and disagreeably wet.[23]

Moving north-northeast, the Confederates scuffled with Federal cavalry late in the afternoon near the Franklin–Lewisburg Pike. The Ninth was ordered to the right to guard an approach while the rest of the brigade attacked a train of wagons moving up the pike. Ross sent the Yankees galloping north. After dark, when the fleeing Federals blundered into the Ninth, a noisy skirmish erupted. The Texans killed several blue cavalrymen and chased off the others, losing one man killed and another captured. "Quiet was restored," Gris wrote, "after the enemy passed up the pike." The brigade bivouacked at the Federals' abandoned camp, again enjoying Federal fires and forage.[24]

Ross tallied his plunder that evening: an entire company of the Seventh Ohio Cavalry—about eighty men—three stand of colors, several wagons loaded with ordnance, and a number of fully equipped horses. The Texans, always short of mounts and supplies, were adopting Forrest's habit of mounting and supplying at the expense of the U.S. Army. Although many Union cavalry mounts were barely broken, the Texas cavalrymen had been living on horseback for the past three years and could ride anything that was still breathing. They also had become accustomed to hunger, but Yankee bacon, hardtack, and coffee tasted mighty good, they would have said.[25]

As usual, the privates knew little of what was going on beyond their view, especially Old Butch. "My knowledge of military affairs extended little past the regimental limits, and I cared fully as little about them as I knew," he wrote. What the Texans had run into was Schofield's corps hurrying along the pike toward the safety of Nashville.[26]

Schofield's 23,000 men had crossed the Duck the night before. One of his brigades and Hatch's cavalry were trying to hold the pike to Franklin, twenty-six miles north, for the rest of the army. Forrest's three divisions were pushing the Federal cavalrymen away from Columbia and the river, where Hood was crossing his army onto the north bank of the Duck.[27]

The morning of November 29, Forrest ordered Ross's Brigade to move up the pike by way of Hurt's Crossroads toward Franklin, halfway between Columbia and Nashville. Near Thompson's Station, the Ninth charged and stampeded an enemy wagon train. Soon, a railroad train coming from the north rounded a bend and came into view. When the engineer saw the Confederates, he cut loose his engine and raced south. Fifty-eight guards and several other Federals jumped from the stalled cars and surrendered. When the freed cars began rolling toward a blockhouse, the Texans threw obstructions in front of the wheels but were unable to stop the cars before they reached the protection of the blockhouse. While the Ninth guarded the prisoners and burned the railroad bridge, the Third rode into Thompson's Station. Yankees holding the depot burned their papers and other valuables and torched a train of cars loaded with ordnance before they fled. The Third had "a lively time" in the village and "got some booty."[28]

At eleven that fateful night, Forrest, whose other divisions were out of ammunition, ordered Jackson to move Ross's and Armstrong's Brigades onto the pike near Thompson's Station to intercept the enemy, who was moving in full retreat along the Columbia-Nashville Pike. By 3:00 A.M., Ross was on a hill half a mile above the pike. He dismounted three regiments, leaving the Ninth to guard the horses. Armstrong's Brigade was south a mile. The Texans advanced to within a hundred yards of the enemy without being detected. When they heard Armstrong's men begin firing, the Third Texas, having the advance, fronted into line and fired a well-directed volley that killed several Yankees and some mules. The Texans rushed forward with a yell, producing among the teamsters and wagon guards a perfect stampede. "The noise and confusion exceeded all I ever heard," Gris wrote.[29]

The Texans burned thirty-nine wagons, captured several prisoners, and took possession of the pike, which they held for thirty minutes before Federal infantry appeared from both the north and the south. While the Yankees mistakenly fired at one another, the Texans scampered back up the hill. There were more Federals than they could handle. Ross and his men sat their horses on top of the hill and watched until sunrise. Hundreds of wagons, protected on each side by marching infantry, flowed north on the wide, white macadamized turnpike. There was nothing six hundred men could do about the thousands filing past.[30]

What the Texas cavalrymen witnessed that night was Schofield's hairbreadth escape. Forrest had masterfully led the Confederate advance into Tennessee, neutralized the Federal cavalry, and opened the way for Hood, whose men were near, to destroy Schofield's army, strung out on the pike. What went wrong became one of the bitter controversies of the war. Hood blamed his subordinates, as he had at Atlanta, and they in turn blamed him. Only two facts are clear: Hood missed a splendid opportunity to destroy the only army that stood in his way; and Ross's Brigade, holding and blocking the pike for thirty minutes, were the only Confederates to interfere with Schofield's passage to safety the night of November 29, 1864.[31]

At daylight, Forrest borrowed a supply of ammunition from the infantry, then sent Chalmers's Division to the left. The general rode to the right with Buford's and Jackson's Divisions. They moved parallel with the Franklin Pike, pressing the enemy back and clearing the way for Hood's infantry.[32]

Most of Schofield's army had already reached Franklin, on the Harpeth River, before daylight. They immediately began reinforcing an old line of works running along the south edge of town. The last of their wagons reached the town by noon.[33]

As Confederate infantry approached Franklin, Forrest personally reconnoitered the entire Federal line. When Hood arrived, the two generals conferred. Forrest reported what he had seen and advised against a direct assault. He told Hood, "Give me one strong division of infantry with my cavalry, and within two hours' time I can flank the Federals from their works." But Hood's blood was up, and he ordered a frontal assault.[34]

Four miles from Franklin, Ross's Brigade ran into Yankee cavalry drawn up in line of battle south of the Harpeth. The Ninth dismounted and charged, supported by the other three regiments on horseback. They drove the enemy two miles to the bank of the river. The Ninth charged again. The Yankees splashed across the shallow stream and joined several of their squadrons waiting on the north side. The Ninth remounted to form in battle line with the rest of the brigade. From their left came the boom of cannon and the rattle of small arms fire rising in the cold winter air. A general battle had opened along the entire line.[35]

It was 4:00 P.M., only two hours until the sun would set. The Texans, on the south side of the Harpeth, three miles east of Franklin, were on the right of the Confederate line. West of them were Armstrong and Buford with Forrest in immediate command. Across the stream from the Texans, Maj. Gen. James H. Wilson's Union cavalry was posted on a hill, dismounted and drawn up in line of battle. When Forrest ordered the Texans to attack, Ross sent the Third and the Ninth across the river.[36]

At the head of his men, Jones splashed through the shallow water and charged two Federal regiments. The enemy fell back to their main force of two divisions and formed. They charged the Ninth. The struggle quickly degenerated into a hand-to-hand contest. The Third came up in beautiful style and slammed into a mass of gray horses. It was again Brownlow's Tennesseans, the regiment that had burned the Third's train south of Atlanta and had gotten between the Texans and their horses at Newnan. The Ninth disengaged and turned to join the Third. Ross, hurrying forward with the Sixth and the Legion, placed himself at the head of his men. "Stand firm!" he commanded, and ordered the Ninth to rally on him. Standing up in his stirrups, Ross drew his sword. "Forward!" he ordered. The Tennesseans formed and charged, pistols blazing, sabers slashing. The two lines slammed together. Jones ran his sword through a Yankee with such force the blade broke off at the hilt. Tom Cellum killed an enemy officer in single combat, but Cellum received three gunshot wounds during the duel. Gus Creed was wounded. J. J. McDaniel was shot in the arm. F. M. Lewis was shot in the lung and stomach. The Texans were ready to run when Ross, sword in hand and face black with gun smoke, said in his clear, ringing voice, "Boys, if you don't run, they will!" They did.[37]

The Texans took possession of the hill and held it as the short, wintry day came to an end. Wilson advanced his entire line just as the sun set. Armstrong's Mississippians gave way. Ross, unsupported and low on ammunition, withdrew to the south side of the river, leaving Wilson on the north.[38]

Ross wrote in his report:

The gallant bearing of the men and officers of the Third and Ninth Texas on this occasion is deserving of special commendation, and it gives me much gratification to record to the honor of these noble regiments that charges made by them at Harpeth River have never been and cannot be surpassed by cavalry of any nation.[39]

With sounds of firing still rolling in from the west, Ross and Wilson both threw out pickets. The forward men, only half a mile apart, called to each other and agreed to a truce, perhaps instigated by the Texas pickets, who were nearly out of ammunition. The rest of the Texans were glad to catch their breath and gorge on "oodles of apples" an "old citizen" brought to the battlefield. Forrest, having outrun his ordnance train, again borrowed ammunition from the infantry and resupplied Jackson's Division later in the night.[40]

The Yankee pickets left at 3:00 A.M. When the sun rose, the Texans learned what had gone on beyond their view. Hood had attacked before his entire army or any of his artillery were up. Two corps, 16,000 men, had borne the brunt of fighting, leaving the trenches filled with dead men. The reckless slaughter cost the Confederates 6,000 killed or wounded, the bloodiest two hours of the Civil War. Among the casualties were two major generals commanding divisions, ten brigadier generals, and fifty-four regimental commanders. Hood had lost more men than at Peach Tree Creek or Ezra Church, where the entire army had been engaged. The sun had gone down that evening, a soldier wrote, "as if ashamed to witness the scene of slaughter."[41]

Sporadic firing had continued until midnight when Schofield got his men and wagons back on the road to Nashville. Hood was left in posses-

sion of the field, normally a sign of victory, but the battle of Franklin was no triumph. The staggering losses of officers and men had wrecked the gallant Army of Tennessee.

The morning of December 1, Forrest led Jackson's and Buford's Divisions across the Harpeth and rode north toward Nashville. They quickly

Nashville, Tennessee

stampeded the few Federals they met, but the bulk of Schofield's men were already inside the city, one of the best fortified cities north or south. Long after dark, Forrest called a halt six miles out. The men had been in the saddle or on the battlefield for the better part of three days and two nights. They would rest.[42]

At sunrise cold rain was falling. The Ninth mounted and rode east in search of a reported enemy column. Finding no Federals, they rejoined Forrest as he moved north along the pike. When the column drew up within sight of the Capitol in Nashville, Forrest spread out his cavalry to invest the city until the infantry came up. Jackson's and Buford's Divisions guarded the right; Chalmers' Division, the left. Ross's Brigade was posted on a pike three miles east of the city.[43]

Citizens in the area were overjoyed when the gray horsemen appeared. Nashville had been occupied by Federal forces since February 1862, when an unknown colonel named Nathan Bedford Forrest had led the last Confederate regiment out of the city. Ladies, pretty girls, and old men descended on the Texans. They brought joy and enough food for the entire brigade. Girls sang patriotic Southern songs, and citizens did "all in their power to show how hearty a welcome they could give us," Gris wrote that night.[44]

★　　★　　★

When the infantry relieved Forrest's men later in the day, the Texans moved down the pike a couple of miles to feed and bivouac for the night. They fell back another five miles with first light and began preparing for their next assignment. When several infantry forges rumbled into camp, the men went to work shoeing their horses. Fireboxes on the forges glowed through the day and cast flickering shadows into the cold air all night. Forrest had ordered the men to keep at it day and night until every animal was shod. While the blacksmiths, and every man they could use, heated and shaped the horseshoes, farriers and their helpers trimmed hooves and hammered new shoes onto the cavalry mounts and draft animals. The men gorged on potatoes furnished by residents while they cooked five days' rations. Ordnance officers issued a hundred rounds of ammunition to each man.[45]

December 5, at 5:00 A.M., Ross's Brigade moved out under the command of Col. Dudley Jones, with the Ninth commanded by Maj. Hamilton Dial. Ross was not present, evidently too sick to ride. The Ninth took along five empty wagons, a curiosity to Gris. Forrest, with Jackson's and Buford's Divisions, had been ordered to operate against Murfreesboro, thirty miles southeast on the Chattanooga Railroad. Maj. Gen. William B. Bate's infantry division had been assigned to Forrest and would meet the cavalrymen along the road. Eight thousand Federals held the fortified town.[46]

At La Vergne, midway between Nashville and Murfreesboro, the railroad and several pikes and roads converged or crossed. Blockhouse No. 4 guarded the railroad, and a hilltop fort protected the town on the west. Forrest, riding with Buford, attacked the blockhouse and ordered Jackson's Division to attack the fort. Riding ahead, the Texans easily drove the enemy pickets and skirmishers into the fort before Jackson arrived. When the general came up, he demanded the Yankees surrender. After a short parley, a captain and 125 men marched out and stacked arms. The Texans and Armstrong's Mississippians gloated over their loot: "a fine lot of rations," small arms, two pieces of artillery, an ambulance, twenty wagons, twenty-five horses, a few mules, and a large amount of ordnance stores. Gris discovered what the empty wagons were for. Jackson's men loaded their spoils before moving south to rejoin Forrest near Murfreesboro.[47]

They brushed aside the Federal pickets in front of Murfreesboro and invested the town. Forrest sent the Texans south at dark to guard all the approaches to Murfreesboro from the Salem Pike, running southwest from the town, to the Woodbury Pike, running due east of the town, a lot of roads and miles for a few hundred men to guard.[48]

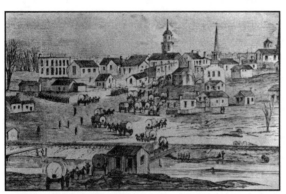

Murfreesboro, Tennessee

With a detachment from the Third, Forrest reconnoitered the enemy's positions and works during the night. The morning of December 7, Forrest watched as Federal infantry, cavalry, and artillery marched out of Murfreesboro onto the Salem Pike to challenge the Confederates. Forrest formed his men on ground of his own choice, the same ground where 100,000 men had fought two years earlier. An occasional human bone protruded from a shallow grave, and rusty muskets, weathered scraps of leather, and rotting haversacks reminded the men of the slaughter that had taken place at the battle of Murfreesboro—or Stones River, as the Yanks called it.[49]

The Ninth had moved out on foot before the sun was up that morning. They remained in line until noon, then maneuvered for two hours. The waiting was getting on everyone's nerves. Finally, at 2:30 P.M., they moved to the front. Bate's infantrymen were formed on the Ninth's right and to their rear. When the Federals gained an open field, they formed in a beautiful line at right shoulder shift and attacked. The cavalrymen fired and fell back on the infantry. When the enemy approached to "within 200 yards [we] turned them over to our infantry who fired a few rounds and fled like turkeys," Gris wrote.[50]

Bate's men, long known for their dependability, had broken in wild disorder. Forrest rose in his saddle to his full six feet, two inches and galloped after the panicked men, swinging his sword and cursing at the top of his lungs. Frantic men dodged Forrest's slashing saber as they scrambled for cover. "I seized the colors of the retreating troops," Forrest reported, "and endeavored to rally them, but they could not be moved by any entreaty or appeal to their patriotism. Major-General Bate did the same thing, but was equally unsuccessful." The privates in the Army of Tennessee had been fought beyond human endurance at Franklin. They could not find within themselves the valor to fight again.[51]

Forrest sent his adjutant racing back to Ross and Armstrong "with orders to say that everything depended on their cavalry." The short afternoon was wearing on. The Texans and Mississippians leaped on their horses. The Ninth galloped to the enemy's flank but was soon overpowered. The men fell back to join the Third and the Legion, then hurried to the Nashville Pike, where the Sixth was heavily engaged. Ross's and Armstrong's men finally drove the enemy into his works as the sun was setting. The cavalrymen had proved, Forrest wrote, "equal to the emergency." Two lieutenants in the Ninth were wounded.[52]

The regiment crossed the West Fork of Stones River and bivouacked. During the night, Thursday, December 8, another bitter cold front came screaming down from the Arctic. Ross's Brigade moved the next morning to a farmstead three miles from Murfreesboro. They set up camp in a cedar break along a creek surrounded by open country. The Texans remained in camp the next two days as the storm raged. Sleet and cold rain fell through the day, then turned to ice during the night. The Texans, whose trains had not come up, used the plentiful local supply of hay to make shelters and warm beds and to feed the horses. They built good fires and sent their rations to nearby houses, where ladies gladly prepared the food. Saturday morning, the ice was an inch thick, the cold intense. Men hovered near their fires all day.[53]

When the sun came out Sunday, the Ninth moved the three miles back to Salem to begin picketing and skirmishing. The brigade's lines still extended around the town from the southwest to the east, covering five roads, their furthermost post being fifteen miles distant. The regiments took turns on picket duty. Monday morning at sunrise, Lt. Gris Griscom led the Ninth on rounds of the picket posts to relieve the Sixth. At the second post the regiment skirmished with a Federal foraging party that had driven off the Sixth's men. Gris reestablished the post and detached a squadron to man it before moving on to the other posts, leaving relief squadrons at each. On the way back to brigade headquarters, Gris and the men relieved from duty ran into the enemy foraging party again. The two columns purposefully ignored one another, the Federals marching into Murfreesboro, Gris and his troopers to their headquarters. The thirty-mile round-trip had taken all day. It was well after dark when Gris reached camp, tired but pleased with himself.[54]

The Texans continued to picket and skirmish with the Federals when they came out of Murfreesboro in search of food and forage. Buford had gone north to picket the Cumberland River while the infantry demolished the railroad from Murfreesboro to La Vergne, which Forrest pronounced "most efficiently done."[55]

Thursday, December 15, the Sixth was picketing seven miles south of Murfreesboro when they spotted a train of fourteen cars coming from the south and guarded by 150 Illinois infantrymen. The pickets sent for help, then devised a means of stopping the train. John Miller, the man who had returned the 1694 British medal and Bible to the Creek woman in Indian Territory, wrote: "We turned a hundred yards of the railroad track over into a ditch full of water. And when the train came up we turned the track over behind them, and so had them trapped."

The action took place at a deserted plantation where the slave quarters were near the railroad tracks. When the rest of the brigade came up, the battery unlimbered, wheeled into position, and began throwing shells at the trapped train. Federal infantrymen fired from the protection of the cars. Miller and two of his company mates were at the corner of one of the quarters. One man was kneeling in front of Miller, the other looking over his shoulder, when a bullet killed the man in front and another grazed Miller's shoulder and killed the man behind. A friend of Miller's was shot in the abdomen "and his bowels ran out on the ground, and while we passed by he called attention to his wound, and was trying to stuff the entrails back."[56]

The Ninth dismounted on the opposite side of the train. They slipped up near the cars and attacked with a fearsome yell. The startled Yankees broke and started running toward a blockhouse a mile away. The Ninth leaped on their horses and took after them as the brigade bugler sounded the charge. Galloping in among the fleeing bluecoats, the Texans captured a hundred of the Illinoisans before they could escape.[57]

The elated Confederates tore open the cars, which they found loaded with 200,000 rations of sugar, coffee, hardtack, and bacon, plus clothing and all manner of tempting supplies. After plundering the cars and carrying off everything possible, they set fire to the train and retired with their booty and prisoners. The booty included enough overcoats to supply the entire brigade. And coffee! The Texans hauled off enough to supply themselves for three weeks, some men carrying away two or three bushels.[58]

The Federal commander in Murfreesboro, in desperate need of the rations, sallied out in hopes of rescuing something. The Confederates drove him back toward the city. "When his anger cooled a little," Gris wrote, he fell back to Murfreesboro without a single cracker.[59]

It was night by the time the Ninth reached the brigade wagon train at Salem with the prisoners and the loaded wagons. In a corral of wagon trains, the men sat around a blazing "log-heap" fire eating Yankee hardtack and drinking real coffee. After camp settled down that evening, Gris tallied the day's casualties. The brigade had lost nine killed in the charge, including one from the Ninth. Three men in the regiment had been seriously wounded, including Gus Creed, who also had been slightly wounded at Franklin. Gus remained with the wagon train, but John H. Watson, shot through the left lung, and W. C. Romines were too dangerously wounded to travel. They were left at a nearby home, where Romines died the next day.[60]

Before Gris finished writing in his journal that night, news arrived that Thomas had struck Hood's army in front of Nashville during the morning. After Forrest had left for Murfreesboro, Hood had spread his thin ranks along the fortified line south of the Tennessee capital. While Hood vainly hoped for reinforcements, his men hovered by fires built on ice-coated ground.[61]

During the two weeks the cavalry had been around Murfreesboro, Thomas had organized his newly arrived troops, finishing mounting 9,000 cavalrymen, and waited out the ice storm. Schofield's men and other troops sent to Nashville had brought Thomas's force up to nearly 60,000. At daybreak, Thursday, December 15, Thomas was ready. Maj. Gen. James H. Wilson's cavalry had opened the battle of Nashville with a smashing attack on Hood's right.[62]

Forrest received notice of the general engagement late that evening. He was ordered to hold himself in readiness to move at any moment. Couriers fanned out to Forrest's scattered commands, ordering them to gather at Wilkinson's Crossroads six miles west of Murfreesboro. The wagon train with the sick and wounded started to Triune, halfway to Columbia. Ross's Brigade reached the crossroads that evening and immediately threw out pickets.[63]

An officer from Hood's staff arrived during the night with information that Hood's army had been disastrously defeated and was falling back on the Columbia–Nashville Pike. Forrest was ordered to move south to Pulaski, seventy-five miles below Nashville. Fortunately for the Army of Tennessee, he had already made his own plans. After his experience with Bate's men, Forrest knew the spirits of the men in the Army of Tennessee were broken and that the retreat could well become a disorganized rout. He would move due west to the Columbia–Nashville Pike and throw his cavalry in the rear of Hood's infantry, where he knew they were needed. His train and the wounded were already at Triune.[64]

About midnight, an aide—Gris was sure he was drunk—roused the Ninth with orders to saddle up and move to brigade headquarters. When they reached headquarters, the entire brigade saddled up and waited for further instructions. None came. The men sat in their saddles for the rest of the night in pouring rain. At first light they learned that Frank Armstrong and Abraham Buford were already on their way to the Columbia–Nashville Pike with their horsemen. The Texans would guard the trains west. They set out toward Triune when the sun was barely up, riding behind the wagons, the artillery, four hundred prisoners, and two brigades of infantry who had been sent to replace Bate's troops after the fight in front of Murfreesboro. The column was further encumbered by several hundred cattle and hogs gathered in the area. Forrest never overlooked the fact that the men had to eat.[65]

Rain pattered down all day as the column worked its way through rocky cedar breaks to Triune and beyond. The roads, alternately soaked and frozen for the past month, were almost impassable. When the short December day came to an end, the column camped in a poplar grove, having covered twenty-five miles on the wretched roads. That evening, Gris, bundled up in overcoat and scarf, rode to Triune to deliver a message. In the town, a citizen gave him a basket of apples, which he carried back to camp to share with his friends. Cold rain fell steadily all night and turned to ice on the ground.[66]

Sunday morning, December 18, Forrest hurried his men on and

reached the rear of Hood's retreating columns on the pike that evening. He rode into Columbia to meet with Hood during the night. Hood felt he could retreat no farther in the dreadful weather and on such miserable roads with broken-down teams. Forrest, sure the entire army would be captured if it remained at Columbia, proposed that with his cavalry and some infantry reinforcement he could hold back the Federals long enough for the army to move eighty miles to the Tennessee River—and escape. Hood agreed and issued the orders Forrest requested.[67]

The Texans and Forrest's other three brigades remained north of the Duck River and Columbia that night. Forrest was back with them when morning came. He immediately ordered his cavalrymen against the enemy. Ross's Brigade rode northwest toward Rutherford Creek, where Armstrong's men were helping hold off the head of Wilson's Union cavalry. When the Texans set out, the horses' iron shoes bit into a glaze of ice on the road. Freezing rain, which had started the evening before, continued to fall. It was miserable. Protected by the heavy wool overcoats they had captured, the Texans rode cautiously along the slick road. They found Rutherford Creek running bank to bank and the bridge destroyed. They fought through the morning, holding Wilson's men on the north bank. The cold rain quickly turned to ice on the horses' rigging and stuck the men's fingers to their carbines and pistols. In the numbing cold, they had to use both hands to cock their pistols. By late afternoon, Hood's columns had crossed the Duck River and reached temporary safety at Columbia. Forrest ordered his men back to the Duck.[68]

The Texans remained north of the flooded river until 10:30 that night, when they finally crossed the fog-shrouded river on a ferry. They passed through Columbia and rode four miles out on the Pulaski Pike before stopping at a farm. It was long past midnight. The men were bone-tired, and there was no forage for their worn, wet horses.[69]

Tuesday morning, Maj. Gen. Edward C. Walthall, Forrest's choice for infantry commander of the rear guard, reported to Forrest with the remnants of eight brigades, 1,900 men. Four hundred of the infantrymen, like many in Hood's army, were barefoot from tramping on ice and coarse, rocky pikes. Bloody footprints marked their passage. Among the chosen units was Ector's Brigade, made up of four Texas and two North Carolina regiments and counting only 341 men present. With the infantrymen and his cavalrymen, Forrest formed a powerful rear guard.[70]

The Texans remained in camp that day; Gris dined with friends in town that evening and regretfully said good-bye. The next morning they rode six miles east in sleet and snow to picket the Duck River. Although every bridge for miles had been destroyed, Forrest wanted the river watched.[71]

During the night Wilson completed his pontoon bridge across the river at Columbia and forced Forrest's rear guard south the next morning. Walthall's infantry and their trains marched on the Pulaski Pike with both Jackson's and Buford's cavalry protecting their rear. After a skirmish three miles south of Columbia, the Confederate cavalry fell back to near Lynville. Citizens along the route bid the Texans "adieu most tearfully." The Ninth bivouacked near the pike that night.[72]

Forrest turned his rear guard back north on Christmas Eve to challenge the Federal advance. He sent the infantry back on the main pike, their flanks protected by the cavalry. Three miles up the road, they engaged the enemy. A heavy force of Wilson's cavalry charged the Legion, threatening to overwhelm them. The Sixth quickly formed and charged. Ross, who had rejoined his brigade that day, later reported: ". . . our columns were all in motion, and it was of the utmost importance to break the charge." The Ninth came into line on double-quick to reinforce the other two regiments. Together, they halted Wilson's advance and held their position for two hours before Forrest ordered them south a couple of miles to where the pike crossed Richland Creek.[73]

Forrest placed his six pieces of artillery on the pike, supported them with Armstrong, and ordered Buford and Chalmers to the left. The Texans were sent to the right to form in the bend of the creek near the railroad tracks. An artillery duel developed to the left of the Texans. When the enemy flanked to both the left and the right, Ross's Brigade was surrounded with no route of escape except across the deep, boggy creek. While bullets flew into their ranks from every direction, the men forced their horses across the frigid stream and galloped to the railroad bridge, which was already ablaze. They dismounted and began firing at the advancing Yankees. The brigade held the enemy in check until the rest of Forrest's cavalry got across the creek. Two hours after the fighting began, Forrest ordered everyone to withdraw.[74]

Forrest reported the loss of one killed and six wounded, including Brig. Gen. Abraham Buford, whose wounds were too severe for him to continue his duty. His brigade was consolidated with that of James Chalmers.[75]

Lt. Sam Barron, Third Texas, and Lt. W. T. McClatchy, Ninth Texas, had reached Pulaski that morning. They had been in northern Alabama with one of the scouting parties made up of extra officers since Ross's Brigade crossed into Tennessee five weeks earlier. Riding north on the pike in search of the brigade, they found their regiments fighting on Richland Creek.[76]

The Confederate horsemen rode south to Pulaski along the pike, which was strewn with abandoned wagons, limbers, small arms, and blankets—all the debris of a routed army. The Texans passed through Pulaski, crossed Richland Creek again, and set up headquarters a mile from town at Mr. Carter's place. When the four regiments were ordered out to watch for the enemy, the Ninth rode four miles along a muddy road to a mill and threw out pickets for the night. There was no forage for the horses, no rations for the men.[77]

In Pulaski that night, Forrest blew up two trains of cars, several locomotives, and the ammunition that could not be carried away. The hard-surfaced pike ended at the town, and the roads beyond were deep mud, floating with ice and water. Hood's artillery, which Forrest had double-teamed with impressed oxen, was ahead, followed by the infantrymen, leaving bloody footprints in the snow as they limped barefoot toward the wide Tennessee and escape.[78]

The Ninth rejoined their brigade five miles south of Pulaski on Christmas morning. While they waited for the wagons to pass, Armstrong and his Mississippians came up. Forrest had left Armstrong at Pulaski to hold back Wilson's cavalry as long as possible and to destroy the covered bridge over Richland Creek after everything had passed. The Mississippians had fought stubbornly until they had to leave at a gallop. When the last troopers dashed across the burning bridge, flames singed their hair and eyebrows.[79]

Ross and Armstrong took turns bringing up the rear. Seven miles down the road, the Texans found Forrest setting a trap for the Federal cavalry. Walthall's infantrymen were formed on Anthony's Hill. Jackson sent Ross to the right, Armstrong to the left. Ross dismounted the Third, the Sixth, and the Legion on the extreme right, leaving the Ninth mounted. The enemy soon advanced on the right flank, straight into the

Ninth. The two mounted forces crashed together. Dud Jones and three others were wounded. Several horses were shot. Ross and the three dismounted regiments hurried to Jones's aid. When Armstrong and Walthall charged into the battle, the Yankees staggered and fell back, abandoning a two-gun battery and enough horses to mount a brigade.[80]

When they were sure the Federals were gone, the cavalry followed the infantry slowly south, remaining alert to further attack. The enemy, however, had been "administered such an effectual check," Ross wrote, "that he did not again show himself that day." Forrest halted that evening on Sugar Creek, a tributary of Elk River, again leaving Ross and Jackson back up the road as rear guard. The Texans finally made camp north of Sugar Creek late in the night and threw out a heavy picket line. There were no other Confederates between them and the Federals.[81]

It was December 25, another Christmas far from home and family. In the past two days, the Ninth had buried two of their men, and five more had been wounded. They were near the Tennessee–Alabama state line, less than forty miles from the river and safety, if they could get across. Rain fell on the ninety or so men left in the regiment while they unsaddled their horses and boiled coffee, real coffee. If Jesse Rogers was not too tired to think, he wondered how Reuben was doing and worried about Gus, farther down the muddy road with the wagons and the wounded. Gus's arm had been severely wounded ten days earlier when the brigade captured the supply train with all its coffee. Jesse also had taken a couple of minor wounds in Tennessee: another saber cut to his head, and a glancing shot in the leg. Neither injury had been serious enough to send him to the rear. He and the other men surely tried to get a little rest. Tomorrow would be another hard day.[82]

The Ninth saddled their horses at daylight. They remained as rear guard while Ross's other regiments took positions down the road. Enemy skirmishers were soon on them. They fired a few shots and fell back on the Legion. Federal cavalry forced the two regiments back to the Third's position. The three regiments were hotly engaged when a courier arrived with orders from Forrest to join him at Sugar Creek.[83]

The general was arranging another ambush for the Federals. The road south from Sugar Creek rose abruptly through a narrow ravine between two steep ridges that united to form a hill, all thickly wooded. Walthall's infantry dug in along the ridges, hastily throwing up log and timber entrenchments. Forrest mounted his guns on top of the hill to sweep the road and the creek crossing. The Ninth and the Legion drew up mounted in a column of fours behind the infantry. The Third and the Sixth dismounted and waited a little farther back. Near noon, "the Yankees, still not satisfied," Ross wrote, "made their appearance." The Second Mississippi, the bait for Forrest's trap, came clattering in, hotly pursued.[84]

There was dense fog along the creek, completely concealing the Confederates waiting on the rough slopes. The Federals, driving the Second Mississippi before them, reached the creek and stopped while the Mississippians galloped up the road as if unsupported. Sensing danger, the Federal commander dismounted several regiments and brought up a gun before moving cautiously forward. His skirmishers were within fifty feet of Walthall's men when the head of his column began crossing the creek, which was saddle skirt deep.[85]

The Confederates waited, nervously tapping their trigger guards. Confederate artillery broke the tension with double-shotted canister. The infantrymen leaped up and charged with a yell. Startled Yankees fled back across the creek in disorder. The Ninth and the Legion trotted through the infantry, crossed the creek at a gallop, and charged, driving the entire enemy force back up the road two miles in utter confusion— "a complete rout," Forrest called it. Forrest ordered back the Texas cavalrymen and held his position for two hours, but the Federals had had enough. Fearing a flank attack in the dense fog, Forrest retired.[86]

The Ninth had captured eight prisoners, several horses, and the usual plunder. Tom Bearcroft had been slightly wounded, the regiment's only casualty. The combined Confederate force killed or wounded 150 Federals and captured 50 men, 300 horses, and a twelve-pound Napoleon gun with its team of 8 horses. The most valuable capture of the day was 300 overcoats. Total Confederate casualties were 15 killed and 40 wounded. The Sixth Texas remained as rear guard, under instruction to stay until 4:00 P.M. Ross took the rest of his brigade south over the wretched, boggy roads as bone-chilling rain and sleet beat down on the men's blue overcoats.[87]

In contrast, Hood's infantrymen were barefoot and threadbare. To cross Shoal Creek, they stripped, tied their clothes to the ends of their gun barrels, and waded across the cold, swift stream.[88]

The Texas Brigade moved southwest across the state line and through Lexington, Alabama, the next morning. They pointed their horses toward Bainbridge Ferry, on the Tennessee River, where a pontoon bridge had been completed the day before, allowing the main army to begin crossing. The Texans stopped on the road to get quarter rations of corn for their horses and reached Bainbridge in the evening without seeing another blue horseman. Hours after sunset, they marched across the pontoon bridge and moved to dry ground, where their wagon train waited. With feelings of relief and pride, tired men boiled coffee and ate their rations of bread at midnight.[89]

During the thirty-eight-day campaign, Forrest's cavalrymen had been engaged every day, often several times. His three divisions had captured and destroyed sixteen blockhouses and stockades; thoroughly wrecked thirty miles of railroad track and twenty bridges; captured twenty yoke of oxen, several hundred horses and mules, four locomotives, 100 railroad cars, 100,000 rounds of ammunition, 200,000 rations; and turned over 1,600 prisoners. They brought out of Tennessee ten more wagons and three more pieces of artillery than they started with—and the drove of cattle and hogs from Murfreesboro. Ross's Brigade had done their share. They had captured two trains—one loaded with ordnance, the other with commissary stores—several hundred fully equipped cavalry horses, enough overcoats and blankets to supply the entire command, forty to fifty wagons, nine stand of colors, and turned over 500 prisoners.[90]

The cavalry commanders also tallied their losses. Forrest, working with incomplete returns, reported a total loss of close to 400 men, 8 percent of those he took into Tennessee. Sul Ross reported the loss of 87 of his troopers, 13 percent of his force. Of these, four men in the Ninth Texas were killed, sixteen wounded, one mortally wounded, and one captured.[91]

Confederate records of casualties are incomplete. But Federal commander Maj. Gen. George Thomas stated in his report that he captured 13,000 Confederates, administered the oath of allegiance to 2,000 more, and captured seventy-two pieces of artillery. No estimate was made of Confederate wounded carried out of Tennessee or of those who died of exposure or slipped off to go home. During the brutal campaign, Hood lost nearly half his army.[92]

The morning after Forrest's cavalrymen crossed the Tennessee to safety, December 28, two hundred of Walthall's infantrymen, left on the north bank as a final rear guard, drove the last guns and wagons—and the cattle and hogs from Murfreesboro—across the river. Just as the pontoon bridge swung onto the south bank, Federal cavalrymen rode up on the opposite side and watched the last of Forrest's rear guard march out of sight.[93]

Chapter 14

Duty Done

December 28, 1864–June 1865

Ross's Brigade started south from Bainbridge, Alabama, the morning of December 28, 1864. With the flooded Tennessee River between them and the Union army, horsemen and teamsters allowed their exhausted animals to move slowly along the heavy road. At Tuscumbia they turned west toward Mississippi. After two weeks of fighting day and night with enemy cavalry seldom out of view, the men kept looking over their shoulders for blue uniforms. No Federals followed them. Thomas's men were as exhausted as the Confederates and his horses as used up.[1]

The perverse winter weather—sleet, snow, and cold rain—continued. Traveling only fifteen miles a day, the Texans followed the stage road along the Memphis & Charleston tracks toward Corinth. Near Iuka, Mississippi, on the night of December 31, 1864, Lt. George "Gris" Griscom sat down by his fire and wrote in his journal: "Moved to vicinity of Iuka & camp—sending 3rd Texas to Eastport, 27th to guard bridge on Bear river." Gris closed his diary for the final time. He had written every day since being elected orderly sergeant of Company D more than three years earlier. New Year's Day 1865, the sun rose in a clear sky, warming the winter earth for the first time in weeks, but Gris could not find the spirit to write more.[2]

He was not alone. John Dunn's diary had stopped in mid-sentence September 26, when the regiment was near Campbellton, on the Chatta-hoochee. Ross and Forrest wrote reports of the cavalry's part in the Tennessee campaign, but Forrest's casualty count was incomplete due to lack of reports from his division commanders. Hood's report, written after much prodding from above, failed to include an accurate account of the casualties. Memoirs by Ross's men tell little or nothing of what happened after the Georgia campaign. Only one of Ross's and one of David Garrett's letters from the time survive.

As Gris noted in his last diary entry, the Third Texas was sent to Eastport, a few miles north of Iuka where the Tennessee turns north. Col. Jiles Boggess threw out his picket lines from the mouth of Bear Creek to the mouth of Yellow Creek to watch for Federals and protect the railroad. Although the bridges had been burned and the river was in flood, an occasional enemy patrol managed to cross. The Legion guarded the vital railroad bridge over Bear Creek, on the Mississippi–Alabama line.[3]

Ross left the brigade wagon train up Bear Creek, where forage was available, and moved his headquarters to Corinth. When Mrs. William M. Inge, wife of a Mississippi cavalry colonel and sister of a friend of the Rosses in Texas, learned that Gen. Sul Ross was in town, she insisted he make his headquarters in her comfortable home. Ross wrote his wife that Mrs. Inge "gave me a magnificent room, and surrounded me with every comfort." Ross needed some comfort. The cold, the constant action, and his heavy responsibility on the retreat from Tennessee had worn and weakened him. He had been bothered with bronchitis since taking the guns to Gaines Ferry, on the Mississippi, a year earlier. In addition, he often suffered from the effects of the Comanche bullet that had ripped through his chest when he was twenty. He also had malaria. Ross, who looked much older than his twenty-six years, was soon forced to his bed at Mrs. Inge's.[4]

He was well enough to assume his duties in a few days. January 12, he wrote his official report of the campaign and a letter to Lizzie. In the report Ross gave an account of the brigade's activities and noted his losses. He concluded with a statement of the condition of the command:

My brigade returned from Tennessee with the horses very much jaded, but otherwise in no worse condition than when it started, its morale not in the least affected nor impaired by the evident demoralization which prevailed to a considerable extent throughout the larger portion of the army.[5]

Gen. George Thomas, in Nashville, agreed with Ross. Forrest's "powerful rear guard," Thomas reported, "was undaunted and firm and did its work bravely to the last," while the rest of Hood's army "became a disheartened and disorganized rabble of half-armed and barefooted men, who sought every opportunity to fall out by the wayside and desert their cause to put an end to their sufferings."[6]

The men in the Army of Tennessee were hungry, bone-tired, ragged, and barefoot. Worse, they had given up. With more sense than the president or the War Department in Richmond, they knew the Confederacy was beaten. Lt. Gen. Richard Taylor, commanding the Department of Alabama, Mississippi, and East Louisiana, reported early in January that the army was useless in its present condition. The exhausted infantrymen's 240-mile trek from Nashville finally ended at Tupelo, Mississippi, 50 miles south of Corinth. They were transported farther south by rail.[7]

Through January, Forrest kept his cavalry between the infantry and the Federals while applying his volcanic energy to the reorganization and recruitment of his command. He scattered his horsemen across northeastern Mississippi, where they could find forage, leaving Ross's Brigade to garrison Corinth. The Texans, taking turns picketing to the northeast, grew increasingly restless. Forrest had furloughed many of his troops from Mississippi, Alabama, and West Tennessee to go home for clothes, mounts, and recruits. Even Frank Armstrong's Mississippians, with whom the Texans had served so long, were going home by turns. The men from Texas remained on duty, being too far from home to go and return, everyone said. Ross apparently was not worried, despite desertions in Georgia and Alabama. He had written Lizzie, "The ragged Texicans are always on hand & ready for a feast or a fight."[8]

The men did not completely give up hope of going home. They knew Hood had telegraphed Jefferson Davis twice requesting permission to furlough the Trans-Mississippi men. "The troops are awaiting the reply with much anxiety and some impatience," Ross wrote. They also had been promised that, at the very least, they would be allowed to go to the rear for some rest by the first of February. After three and a half years without seeing home and nine months of being shot at almost daily, their patience was wearing as thin as their clothes. Ross was sure, however, that by the first of the month another emergency would arise and his troopers would be back in their saddles. "Whenever we grow a little sore and contentious," he wrote, "they feed us on a few high sounding and prettily spilled compliments [and] pat us awhile on the back."[9]

The brigade was soon ordered seventy-five miles south to Egypt Station, on the Mobile & Ohio, located in one of the most fertile black land districts in Mississippi. The area abounded in corn, but also in thick mud. Incessant rain had turned the rich land to gumbo, "very trying on the men in camp."[10]

In addition, the Texans were approaching a state of nudity. They had been unable to replace their boots or clothes and none had been issued. The officers, who usually managed to stay reasonably dressed, were as destitute as their men. When the brigade left Mississippi for Georgia, scarcity of transportation forced the officers to leave their trunks and valises containing their best clothes. A detail of two men, soon reduced to one, had faithfully guarded the baggage for nine months. While the brigade was moving out of Tennessee, the soldier took the baggage north by rail to meet them. "Just before we reached it," Sam Barron wrote, "a small scouting party of the enemy's cavalry swooped down, fired the station, and all our good clothes went up in smoke."[11]

The Texas regiments had been at Egypt Station fattening their horses for a couple of weeks when Ross received orders to start immediately for Canton with wagon train and everything. The orders came from Forrest at the request of Richard Taylor. Taylor had added command of the Army of Tennessee to his department responsibilities after Hood resigned January 13 at Beauregard's request.[12]

With Taylor's assumption of command of the Army of Tennessee, to which Forrest's cavalry belonged, Forrest was placed in command of all cavalry in the department, which stretched from the Chattahoochee to the Mississippi. Forrest was soon promoted to lieutenant general. He and Taylor had liked and respected one another from their first meeting.

The two generals worked together to protect what was left of value in their department. They were sending Ross to patrol an area he and his men knew well, the region around Canton and Jackson. Taylor and Forrest also might have felt that the Texans would be less rebellious patrolling and picketing where they had many friends. They would also be closer to the Mississippi.[13]

But even if the Texans' morale was unaffected by the Tennessee campaign, as Ross had written, their patient waiting for furloughs was near its end. Shortly before starting southwest toward Canton, they learned that Hood's plea that they and other Trans-Mississippi troops be furloughed had been emphatically turned down. Beauregard, who was still in command of the West, and Davis had reacted with horror at the thought of Trans-Mississippi troops being allowed to go home. The general and the president were sure none would return. They were wrong, but the war did not last long enough for them to find out.[14]

From Egypt Station, the Texans moved slowly southwest toward Canton. A few days out, 180 men mounted their horses one morning and started for Texas. They had organized what they called an "owl train," a Western term for being on the run from the law. "Not a harsh word was said to them, nor was any effort made to stop them," Sam Barron wrote. They did not say whether they planned to come back. They simply rode away.[15]

The rest of the brigade was back at Deasonville, between the Big Black and the Yazoo, by mid-February. Dismounted men, others on detached service, and the usual stragglers had rejoined the brigade as it moved through Mississippi. Wounded men scattered from Mississippi to Georgia and Tennessee also returned, happy to again be with their "chums," as they called their friends.[16]

Two men from the Ninth appeared in camp as if from their graves. A bullet had struck Lt. William A. Wingo, Company B, behind the ear a year earlier when Ross's Brigade was fighting gunboats on the Yazoo. When the Texans marched east toward Georgia, Wingo was left in a hospital, his friends sure they would never see him again. A woman took him to her home and nursed him back to health. John W. Watson, Company D, had been shot through the lung during the capture of the coffee-laden train near Murfreesboro the middle of December. Being too dangerously wounded to move, he had been left at a nearby home when

the brigade started toward Columbia the next day with all Forrest's cavalry. Watson had been captured and placed in a Federal hospital. Only
a month later, he and another man escaped. Heading south, the two
evaded capture for twelve days before reaching their own lines south of
the Tennessee River. Watson then made his way back to the regiment.[17]

After the owl train gang left, someone up the line of command must
have realized that the rest of the Texans might desert. By February 20,
Ross had received permission, by authority of Lt. Gen. Richard Taylor,
to furlough half his officers and men for sixty days, the officers to be
responsible for seeing that everyone returned. The troopers were ordered
to recruit men in Texas to fill the ranks by compelling the return of
absentees and deserters. No record has survived of the lucky men in
the Ninth.[18]

Sam Barron and Col. Jiles Boggess were among the fortunate in the
Third. As the senior officer, Boggess would be in command of all the
furloughed men in Texas and on the return trip. The two officers waited
anxiously while their papers were prepared, then set out for Texas the
end of February. Sam and his party, likely all the furloughed men, made
their way north along the route they had followed to Gaines Ferry during
the bitter winter the year before. The weather was not so cold, but rain
was as persistent. Along the way, Sam stopped at homes of friends where
he enjoyed lavish meals and a few hours of shelter. When he and a
companion—the other men in his party had hurried on ahead—reached
the Sunflower Swamp, they found the entire country flooded. In the
evening they cut cane for their horses to stand on and piled more cane
under a tree. "And on that we sat down all night in the rain," he said.[19]

The two ferried the Sunflower River and rode on to Gaines Ferry,
where they found a number of men waiting. The Texans crossed a few
at a time in a skiff, swimming their horses alongside. With the tedious
operation impossible in the dark, the troopers rowed and fought the
current while they worried with the horses and watched for enemy
gunboats.[20]

On the west side, Sam led his wet horse up the bank and over the
levee, then struck out for Texas with four members of his regiment. The
group traveled along the Louisiana–Arkansas border. They crossed a
bayou on a raft of logs, ferried the Ouachita, and swam the rest of the

streams. When Sam's horse gave out in Arkansas, he sold one of his pistols in order to buy another mount.[21]

Sam learned at Shreveport that the owl train gang had been arrested by Confederate authorities at Alexandria, Louisiana, on the Red River, and were being held under guard in Shreveport. Boggess, who had reached Texas ahead of Sam, quickly secured their release, and the men were allowed to go home on sixty-day furloughs. A hundred and eighty experienced troopers were too valuable to court-martial or keep under arrest.[22]

Jesse Rogers might have returned to Texas with the furloughed men. If so, he surely crossed the Mississippi at Gaines Ferry, where so many of the Texans, perhaps all, crossed. When his horse gave out west of the big river, he set out on foot. From Shreveport, on the Texas border, the end of public conveyance, he made his way two hundred miles to Pa's log house, four miles south of Grapevine.[23]

David Garrett had drawn a furlough but remained in Mississippi. Deeply disappointed, he wrote his sweetheart, Mary, "I was never in such a fix in my life when I found I could not get off." He had tried to find a horse until the last moment. David told Mary he thought it too far to walk to Kaufman County, Texas, and back to Mississippi, but he would be ready when the next group was furloughed, likely in June.[24]

The rain that pestered Sam on his way home also poured on David Garrett, Gus Creed, and A. W. Sparks as they settled into a new camp three miles out of Canton, on the Vernon Road. The water was so high and the roads so muddy that the men left in Mississippi could do little. "We could do nothing only go to barbecues & parties that the good people of Yazoo County have given the brigade," David wrote to Mary.[25]

Other officers soon secured leaves to return to Texas. They left loaded with mail and requests to visit families of their homesick men. Ross's precarious health and his deep need to see his wife prompted him to request a leave. He had been telling his darling Lizzie for two years that he surely could get home soon. They had married shortly after he joined the Texas cavalry and had been together only a few precious weeks for the past four years. Brig. Gen. Lawrence Sullivan Ross left for home March 13, 1865.[26]

When the general left, Col. Dudley W. Jones, then twenty-three years old, took command of Ross's Brigade, about 550 strong, the remaining original Texans, and perhaps 100 or more Georgia and Mississippi boys who had eagerly joined the Texas cavalry to avoid being conscripted into the infantry. Maj. James C. Bates, having recovered from the shot through his neck and jaw, returned to duty and assumed command of the Ninth. First Lt. George Griscom, adjutant of the regiment for the past three years, and Capt. James E. Robertson, brigade surgeon, faithfully continued to do their duty. The officers organized drill competitions, kept out squads of pickets and scouts from their camp near Canton, and sent foragers in every direction to find food and fodder. Their major problem, however, was keeping their restless men busy. Everyone knew the war was drawing to a close.[27]

On April 9, Robert E. Lee surrendered to U. S. Grant at Appomattox Courthouse. Nine days later, at Durham, South Carolina, Joseph E. Johnston surrendered the remnant of the Army of Tennessee. In the West, Richard Taylor surrendered his department to Maj. Gen. Edward Canby on May 1, 1865, at Citronelle, a railroad siding thirty miles north of Mobile. The transportation in Taylor's department was so depleted he was pumped on a handcar down the rickety railroad tracks to meet Canby.[28]

All these events remained unannounced to the Texans, camped on the east side of the Big Black, still the demarcation line between them and U.S. forces holding Vicksburg. Confederate prisoners, released and on their way home, told the Texans of Lee's surrender, "which news caused no great sensation," A.W. wrote, "for we all knew the end was near and the terms were the only questions." Yankee pickets along the Big Black shouted across the river news of Johnston's capitulation.[29]

Jones called a meeting of the brigade to discuss the situation. Someone suggested they break up in squads, move to the Trans-Mississippi, and continue a guerrilla war.

"Yes!" shouted Isaac Thompkins, a thirty-five-year-old veteran of the Ninth who was not ready to surrender. "The leaves will soon be green and our horses can live on the grass and this brigade can take all the supplies we want from any corps of Yankees that ever invaded Southern soil. We will fight them to the end, as long as life blood flows in the veins of any man that has followed Ross."

Shouts and cheers rang along the line. When order was established, a staff officer spoke about continuing a guerrilla war from Mexico, an idea that had been circulating throughout the West for some time. The officer also discussed the political turmoil in Mexico, explaining that a war between the United States and France could result and that the Texans owed their allegiance to the United States. "We will take our paroles," he said, "and go home and get ready to fight for our country." The men again shouted their approval.[30]

With the matter settled, officers took the muster rolls to the city of Jackson and soon returned with the paroles, which the men signed May 15. Upon his "solemn Parole of Honor," each man agreed to lay down his arms, take no further military action against the United States, and comply with the laws "in force where he resides." In exchange, the soldiers were promised immunity from prosecution and protection by the Federal government. Cavalrymen were allowed to keep their horses, saddles, and other personal equipment. Officers were allowed to keep their side arms, but the men were supposed to surrender theirs. In addition, the United States would furnish transportation home and provisions on the trip. Ross's men were instructed to embark on a specified day from Vicksburg, less than forty miles west.[31]

Thirty-two of the 111 original Texans in Company A signed their paroles that day, including Gus Creed and Tom Barecroft, who were both wounded in Tennessee; John Estill, who had ridden his fine horse to Camp Reeves; E. A. Schults, who was wounded in the thigh before the retreat from Corinth and was captured at Hatchie Bridge; Hardy Holman, who had been wounded and lost his horse and saddle in Indian Territory; and William Trice, who was present for duty on every extant roll of the Ninth Texas Cavalry. Half the men in Company A had died or been killed, wounded, or captured. Both William Wingo of Company B, who was shot behind the ear, and John Watson of Company D, shot through the lung, signed paroles that day.[32]

The men parked the artillery and stacked their rifles and carbines. They kept their pistols. Sergeants parceled out the remaining commissary stores, only enough to last two or three days. With their duty done, the Texans looked up at their flag, a square of dark red bunting with white stars on diagonal blue stripes and, sewed on the field in white cloth, the names of a few of their battles: Elk Horn, Iuka, Corinth, Hatchie Bridge, Holly Springs, Thompson's Station. They surely thought of other battles:

Round Mountain, Bird Creek, Queen's Hill, Jackson, Yazoo City, Rome, Good Hope Church, Kennesaw Mountain, Lovejoy Station, Franklin, Murfreesboro, and scores of unnamed actions, 108 in Georgia alone. The men stood at attention with lumps in their throats while their flag was lowered for the final time. Ross's Brigade—the Third Texas Cavalry, the Sixth Texas Cavalry, the Ninth Texas Cavalry, and the First Texas Legion—ceased to exist. Not a single Yankee had entered their camp.[33]

With plenty of time to reach Vicksburg by the rendezvous date, the men lolled around camp a few days and visited friends. Nothing much seemed to change—except the officers stopped giving orders. A.W. and four others, two disabled with old wounds, formed into a party and set out together. They learned from other paroled men that guards at the bridge over the Big Black were taking enlisted men's pistols. A.W. and his comrades disassembled their pistols and stowed the parts in their canteens, which they had unsoldered over an open fire and stuck back together. They passed the guards and rode on toward Vicksburg. Before reaching the city, they learned from ex-slaves with black bands around their arms that Abraham Lincoln had been assassinated.[34]

A.W. and his party spent the night at the fairgrounds in Vicksburg, where two and a half years earlier the riders bringing the horses from Texas had watched exploding shells and rockets arch overhead in the dark sky. The rest of Ross's Brigade and other Trans-Mississippi troops filled the fairground. They marched to the pier the next morning to board the *Fairchild*, a Union transport. A barge tied alongside carried the cavalrymen's horses. The perennially hungry Rebels stuffed themselves on Yankee bacon and hardtack, rations their paroles had promised. "Old Glory," as the Texans called the Stars and Stripes, streamed from the front of the steamer that was packed with Confederates, "thick as black birds." Sweating men jostled for space in the heat and humidity of late May. When it began to rain, it was too hot inside and too damp outside.[35]

The Texans, some still untamed by four years of war, unfurled their flag and boldly mounted it on the stern of the steamer. The banner proudly waved in the damp air until several patrolling gunboats persuaded the Confederates they should take down Ross's Brigade flag.[36]

The captain of the *Fairchild* landed the Confederates at Fort Jenicia, up the Red River. The Texans sent the horses overland and forced the crew of an old steamer to take them upriver. They soon found the boat unsafe, as the crew had protested, and hailed the *General Hodges*, coming downstream with a load of seven hundred bales of cotton. When the captain refused to turn around, the boys in ragged gray rolled the cotton onto the riverbank and forced the captain to head upriver. After the captain realized he had no choice, he cheerfully accepted his chore.[37]

Soldiers crowded the rail when the *General Hodges* eased up to the wharf at Shreveport. The moment the gangplank was down, the men, many on crutches, hurried ashore, impatient to be on their way home. A.W. and ten comrades from Titus County hitched a ride with a supply train. When they reached Marshall that afternoon, they learned that the arsenal would be blown up at midnight and that the veterans could draw what they needed. The eleven Titus County boys drew eleven Springfield rifles and a case of one thousand cartridges. They were camped five miles west when the arsenal blew up, sending sound waves reverberating through the green countryside for several minutes.[38]

A.W. tramped the rest of the way home, arriving a few days later, May 27, 1865. John and their other brother were already home. "My mother," A.W. wrote, "in her great joy gathered me about the neck and at the same time her yard dog gathered me by the leg and between the two my reception was full and warm."[39]

Reuben Rogers had remained in Floyd House Hospital in Macon, Georgia, forty days. At the end of the war he was in Minden, Louisiana, thirty-six miles east of Shreveport, where he was paroled May 5, 1865. He reached home later in the month, having served three months short of four years. Jesse and their two young brothers who had served in Texas were already home. When Reuben limped onto the porch, all the Rogers boys were home, their duty done.[40]

Victor Rose, a prisoner of war at Camp Chase, near Columbus, Ohio, was thin and listless when he learned the war was over. He had survived nine months on a starvation diet of three crackers and four ounces of whitefish a day. As the seasons had changed from summer to fall, from winter to spring, Victor and thousands of others had walked aimlessly around inside the tall prison walls like caged animals. We "could not have been treated worse and lived," Victor wrote, "for many absolutely died of starvation." Others' spirits shriveled and died, taking their bodies with them.[41]

Victor's day of exchange finally came late in May. With a group of five hundred, he traveled by rail to Cairo, Illinois, "where kind-hearted citizens vied with each other in their contributions to the necessities of the miserable Southerners." A steamer took Victor and his comrades to New Orleans, then inexplicably turned around and steamed back to Vicksburg, where the men finally disembarked and were paroled. "The noble ladies of Vicksburg" fed, clothed, and pampered the returning men. Victor M. Rose was soon on his way to Victoria County, Texas, the home he had left four years earlier.[42]

Newton Keen was unable to walk when the war ended. For nine brutal months he had been held at Camp Douglas, near Chicago, where Confederate prisoners had frozen to death, been shot and bayonetted by their guards, and had eaten rats to keep from starving. Newt had survived the bitter cold and grinding debasement, but starvation had caused muscle cramps that had drawn Newt's left leg until he could barely touch his toes to the ground. At 10:30 A.M., June 13, 1865, Newt, sick and crippled, was dumped onto the street near Union Depot in Chicago without a cent or a morsel of food.[43]

Newt was hungry and alone, with no idea how he could get home. Rain came down in cold, drifting showers. Having bowed to the rules of prison with "mechanical obedience," Newt found it strange to be able to "go anywhere without running into a bayonet or pistol." A sense of freedom washed over him. He "felt like the playful birds among the limp twigs on a May morning."

Newt hobbled to the sidewalk and sat down on a little box beneath an awning. A farmer offered him a job tending stock, but Newt was sure he would soon be fighting with every Yankee soldier he met. "I was not half whipped," he wrote, "and for the sake of peace I thought it best to return home." Wishing Newt a happy life, the farmer gave him a small bottle of pickles and a pound of crackers, then smiled and turned away. "A piece of bread given to a hungry man always has a ray of sunshine in it."

Newt ate two pickles and four crackers as he pondered his situation. At 4:00 P.M., he limped into Union Depot to read the bulletin board. He chose a train leaving for Cairo at 8:00 P.M. Newt climbed aboard and lay down on a bench in the smoker car. When he awoke the next morning, a shining sliver of sunlight was casting its first rays across a wide, green prairie. "My soul was as much elated as if I were on a great battle field with all things victorious."

Having determined not to lie to the conductor, Newt told his story. The conductor smiled and said, "You shall ride to Cairo." At Cairo, Newt limped to the docks and inquired of a burly Irish workman how he might get home. With a smile and a twinkle in his eye, the Irishman pointed out a boat along the crowded wharf and told Newt what to do.

Newt walked up the gangplank in the evening and slept on the hurricane deck through the night. He went to the captain the next morning to explain his situation, as the Irishman had instructed. The captain said with a smile, "You shall have three square meals a day until we reach Vicksburg," and invited the hungry Rebel into the officers' dining room. Before Newt stood a table—fully twenty-five feet long, he was sure—loaded with foods of all kinds, just as he had dreamed so many starving nights in prison. The food warmed his empty belly, but better yet, the Yankee smiles he had met on his journey warmed Newt's chilled heart.

He drew a week's rations from the U.S. commissary at Vicksburg and soon found a boat going up the Red River. Disembarking at Shreveport, he set out to walk the last two hundred miles home, pleased that his leg was already better and he could hobble along fairly well. Three miles out, a cotton hauler picked him up in a four-mule wagon. The man, an old Southern planter, took Newt home with him. The "magnificent old man" cared for Newt for two weeks, until he was able to travel. The gentleman gave Newt five dollars, a mule, a bridle, and a saddle. At 2:00 P.M., July 8, 1865, Newt rode up to Grandpa's gate a few miles northeast of Dallas, having walked only 3 of the 1,300 miles from Chicago. It had been four years, lacking a month and ten days, since sixteen-year-old Newton Asbury Keen "rode away from the land of peace and plenty to that of blood and trembling."[44]

Samuel B. Barron had rendezvoused with Col. Jiles Boggess to return to Mississippi in April when their furloughs were up. Boggess had heard that the Mississippi River was twenty-five miles wide and they could not cross. He had sent a man to investigate. The colonel told Sam to go home and a courier would contact him when they could return. Sam was waiting at his home in Rusk, Cherokee County, Texas, when he learned that the war was over. With a jumble of thoughts and feelings coursing through him, Sam wrote:

> The four years of war, with all its fun and frolic, all its hardships and privations, its advances and retreats, its victories and defeats, its killing and maiming, was at an end.[45]

EPILOGUE

Sul Ross reached his home in Waco, McLennan County, Texas, near the first of April, 1865. His health slowly improved and he began farming. By 1866, Waco was booming, and with the help of his and Lizzie's parents, Ross began adding to his holdings.[1]

He was elected sheriff of McLennan County in 1873 and was a delegate to the Texas Constitutional Convention two years later. Victor Rose, editor of the *Victoria (Texas) Advocate,* helped organize a campaign that resulted in Ross's election to the state senate in 1880. Six years later, with enthusiastic support of many members of Ross's Brigade around the state, the general was elected governor of Texas by an incredible majority of 73 percent. He was elected to a second term in 1888, once more by an overwhelming majority.[2]

Immediately upon leaving the governor's office, Ross assumed the presidency of Texas A&M, then a small college beset with problems and in danger of failing. Ross's statewide reputation for honesty, courage, and ability increased enrollment dramatically. The general's executive ability and understanding of young men soon transformed A&M into a first-class institution.[3]

Ross remained at A&M until his death January 3, 1898, at the age of fifty-nine. At that time he was the most popular citizen of Texas. The Texas Legislature honored the general in 1917 by naming a new university at Alpine for him. Sul Ross University opened its doors in June 1920.[4]

Lawrence Sullivan Ross was a devoted and caring husband and father, always preferring to be at home with his family. He served his state all his life, first as a Texas Ranger, then as a Confederate general, later as a statesman, and finally as an educator. His name, recognized today by most Texans, is his most famous monument.

George Lewis "Gris" Griscom returned to Dallas and went into the gristmill and flour business. He traveled to Hinds County, Mississippi, in December 1866 to marry Bettie H. Birdsong, who has to be "B.H.B" mentioned many times in his wartime diary. She died of yellow fever in less than a year. Two years later, Gris again traveled to Mississippi to marry Bettie's younger sister, Mary Elizabeth Birdsong.

Gris and his brother Yeamans, the one who fought for the Confederacy, formed a farming partnership at Point Bolivar, near Galveston. In 1884, they moved their families back to North Texas, to Weatherford in Parker County. Gris was active in the Texas ex-Confederate organization and served with Victor Rose on the committee to gather information for a history of Ross's Brigade. Gris, who had become close friends with Sul Ross during the war, actively supported the general in his campaigns for governor. George Griscom died in Weatherford January 25, 1901, at the age of sixty-four. Mary Elizabeth Griscom died in 1925.[5]

Col. Dudley W. "Dud" Jones returned to his home in Titus County, Texas, where he obtained a license to practice law, likely by reading law with an older man. In 1867, he settled in Houston to practice his profession. A couple of years later he was also editing the *Vidette*, one of Houston's first dailies. Jones served in the Texas Constitutional Convention in 1875 but died soon afterward at the age of thirty-five.[6]

Samuel B. Barron made his home in Rusk, Cherokee County, Texas, where he had settled when he moved from his native state of Alabama in 1859. He married Eugenia C. Wiggins, daughter of District Clerk James W. Wiggins, on September 5, 1865. Sam studied law, served as clerk of Cherokee County from 1880 through 1892, and was elected Cherokee County Judge in 1896. He served as a justice of the peace later in his life. Sam was an active member of the Ross-Ector Camp No. 512 of the United Confederate Veterans. He wrote his "recollections of the war between the States" for his children, publishing it under the title *The Lone Star Defenders* in 1908.[7]

Newton Keen stayed with his Keen grandparents along Duck Creek, northeast of Dallas, for a few weeks after he returned from the war. Newt had grown up there when wolves, panthers, and Indians still roamed the area. At age six he had hunted squirrels, prairie chickens, coons, and wild cats with a small shotgun and could ride any animal, wild or gentle, by the time he was nine.

The death of his parents when he was very young, his childhood responsibilities, and four years of war and prison had matured Newt well beyond his twenty years by the time he reached home. But maturity did not bring peace of mind. Soon after his return, Grandpa Keen, who had lost four sons in the war, helped preach a "protracted meeting"—a revival. Newt believed that only the great mercy of God had spared his life during the war, and he felt "overwhelmingly convicted" of his "sins"—the fighting and the killing. He also remembered the promise he had made to God on a starry night in northern Alabama.

After attending the preaching for several evenings, Newt went to the altar and kept his promise to give his heart to God for the remainder of his days. "The change to me was as real as the difference between a live body and a dead one," he wrote, and "I had peace strong and deep," which he still felt when he wrote his story thirty-eight years later.

Newt set out to make his way. He was not sure how, but he "knew work and grit would make it." He rented land and began to court Miss Mary Spillers, daughter of a neighbor. Although he had nothing, he was "happy as a June bug." He and Mary married Christmas Day 1865. He soon traded for his father's old home place and set about improving it at once.

In January 1898, Newt began "The history of Rev. Newton Asbury

Keen's life, written by his own hand," and finished five years later. He gave his manuscript to his son Melvon with instructions that it not be read until the second generation. A granddaughter, Mary Lou Barnes Lawlis, transcribed and published Newt's memoir as *Living and Fighting with the Texas 6th Cavalry* in 1986.[8]

David R. Garrett returned to his 320-acre farm near Cedar Grove in Kaufman County, Texas. He and Mary Elizabeth "Molly" Gibbard, the sweetheart who had waited four years for him, soon married. Four of their seven children reached maturity. David Garrett died April 18, 1892, at the age of fifty-nine and was buried in the Cedar Grove Cemetery. Molly died August 12, 1925, and was buried in the White Rose Cemetery at Wills Point, Van Zandt County, Texas.[9]

Victor Marion Rose returned to his home in Victoria County, where he found his formerly wealthy family nearly destitute. Victor married Julia H. Hardy in the spring of 1866. Julia died of yellow fever the next year, leaving an infant daughter. In 1878, Victor began gathering information from former members to write a history of Ross's Brigade, which was "called for by the dictates of simple justice to the living and dead." General Ross wrote Victor that a trunk containing his orders, private papers, twenty stand of captured colors, and other trophies had fallen into the hands of the enemy while entrusted to Capt. Rufus F. Dunn, Third Texas, who had been detailed to write a history of the brigade. In 1878, Victor made contact with Dunn's widow and received the captain's short manuscript, which Victor referred to a few times in his book. Ross and other officers furnished Victor with the few letters and documents they had.[10]

With his writing experience as owner and editor of the *Victoria Advocate*, Victor published *Ross' Texas Brigade* in 1880. He included sketches of the organization of each of the four regiments and short histories of nine of their officers. He also included accounts of a few of his experiences and stories sent to him by various members of the brigade. His purpose was to "rescue from oblivion" the record of the brigade, which he believed to be as rich "in valor, devotion, and chivalry as ever graced the pages of history."[11]

Victor Rose had returned from college to join Company A, Third Texas Cavalry, in June 1861, when he was eighteen; he returned home a full four years later. He was wounded at the battle of Wilson Creek and at Lovejoy Station when the Texas Brigade was run over by Judson Kilpatrick's forces. In addition to his book on Ross's Brigade, Rose wrote a history of Victoria County, published in 1883. He died ten years later at the age of fifty-one.[12]

Allison Wudville "A.W." Sparks helped organize the Ross Brigade Association. As secretary, A.W. was custodian of the material gathered for a book by the association's historical committee. In 1901, the association asked A.W. to publish the papers the committee had collected. He published *The War Between the States As I Saw It: Reminiscences, Historical and Personal* in 1901. A.W. tells his experiences with the Ninth in the first third of the book. The rest contains information on the organization of each of the four regiments, various stories, and sketches of eighteen officers. Several chapters were taken directly from Victor Rose's book.

On June 24, 1869, A.W. married Fannie T. He remained an unreconstructed Rebel, sure the Southern cause was right and perfectly satisfied that he had done his patriotic duty. A.W. died at the age of seventy-one on November 7, 1912, and was buried in Cypress Cemetery, Franklin County, Texas, a narrow slice of western Titus County that was formed into a separate county in 1875. His brother John Napoleon Sparks, who was shot through the lung during the Vicksburg Campaign, died in 1916 at age eighty and was buried in Weaver Cemetery, Hopkins County, Texas.[13]

John Stanley Dunn and his four older brothers who had also served the Confederacy returned to Texas at the close of the war. John's interest in medicine continued. He attended medical school in Louisville, Kentucky, and continued his studies in Brooklyn, New York. John began his practice in Bee County in South Texas, then settled in Coryell County, between Fort Worth and Austin, where his brother Joseph W. Dunn lived. John and his wife, Josephine Grant, had no children. He died in 1881 at the age of thirty-seven.[14]

John's brother I. P. Solon Dunn, who served in the Ninth with John, returned to Grapevine, Texas, where he became an active and successful businessman. Solon and his wife, Nancy P. Van Zandt, had four children, two of whom reached maturity.[15]

Jesse Evans Rogers put away his pistols and his cavalry boots and re-entered school. He then returned to Mississippi, where he married Jessie Wilder. He surely had met Miss Wilder during the time the Ninth Texas was stationed in the western part of the state. The couple settled in Friars Point, on the Mississippi River, about a hundred miles northwest of Grenada.

During his business life Jesse was a merchant and a planter. He was an active member and served as master of the Blue Lodge No. 104 of Friars Point. Jesse and his wife had no children. When he retired at the age of seventy-five, the couple moved to Venice, California. Jesse was in good health in 1937 at the age of ninety-three when he and his wife returned to Memphis, Tennessee, to visit relatives. He broke his hip in a fall while in Memphis and died there three months later, January 3, 1938.[16]

Neither the official records nor family history reveals Reuben Brawley Rogers' whereabouts after his release from Floyd House Hospital early in September 1864 until May 5, 1865, when he was paroled in Minden, Louisiana. His leg healed, but the damage caused him to limp the rest of his life.[17]

Reuben's Company A friend Augustus Richard "Gus" Creed was paroled with the regiment May 15, 1865. Gus rendezvoused with the other Texans at the fairgrounds in Vicksburg, traveled by steamer to Shreveport, then made his way to his home in Tarrant County.[18]

Feeling that time was slipping away from them, Reuben, then twenty-five, and Gus, age thirty, were eager to start new lives after four years of war. They each began farming and courting the girls. Early in 1866, Reuben married Martha Elizabeth "Mattie" Baker, whose family was among the earliest settlers in Tarrant County. The next day Gus married Reuben's older sister, Martha Jane Rogers. Reuben's stepmother made Jane's wedding dress and, as they said at that time, cut Reuben's wedding suit. The two couples held their infare dinner together, a lavish meal and grand celebration held the day following a wedding.[19]

In 1896, Reuben and Mattie moved to Armstrong County, in the Texas Panhandle, where the first settlers had arrived only two decades earlier. Their farm overlooked the deep Palo Duro Canyon with its red cliffs and steep walls. They raised four sons and three daughters, losing two other children in infancy. Mattie died a few years after the couple celebrated their golden anniversary. Reuben remarried, but his second wife soon died. Reuben lived to the age of ninety-three and a half, dying February 1, 1934. He was mourned by five surviving children, forty grandchildren, and forty-nine great-grandchildren. He and Mattie are buried in the Wayside Cemetery in Armstrong County.[20]

Gus and Martha Jane (Rogers) Creed remained in Tarrant County, farming near the village of Grapevine. They raised four sons and two daughters. Gus, Martha, and Gus's mother, Sally, all died of pneumonia within a single week during December 1884. Gus and Martha were buried in White's Chapel Cemetery, a few miles west of Grapevine.[21]

Reuben, Jesse, Gus, and most of the men who served through the war with the Texas Brigade were proud of their service to Texas and to "their country." That pride increased with the years. Victor Rose wrote in 1880 that he was "prouder of his course during those four years than of any other period in his life." A.W. Sparks wrote in 1901 that he hoped "the children of the Southern States" might realize that they were not descendants of rebels but were "children of patriots" who fought "for liberty and for right and who are proud of their record." Reuben's gravestone is inscribed simply "Reuben B Rogers—CO A 9 Tx Cav CSA," his birth date and date of death not comparing in importance to his time in the Confederate cavalry.[22]

Jesse Rogers lived in northwestern Mississippi after the war and died in Memphis, Forrest's home and territory, where Jesse's service with the famous cavalryman would have eclipsed even the glorious victory at Holly Springs. Jesse was proud of his service with the Ninth Texas beyond everything else in his life. Three quarters of a century after the war, when they laid Jesse Rogers in his grave, the caption on his obituary said it best: "He Rode with Forrest."[23]

Jesse was perhaps the last of the Texas Cavalry Brigade—"The noblest body of men," Gen. Sul Ross wrote, "that ever bared their breasts in defense of a loved land!"[24]

SOURCES

Interviews

Clifton, Bert. Director, Moore County Historical Museum, Dumas, Texas. Comparison of McClellan and cowboy saddles in the museum collection. Interview by author, July 11, 1995.

Hair, Denny. Third Texas Cavalry Reenactment Group, Hockley, Texas. Interviews by author, April 1, July 15, and August 3, 1995; July 12, 1996.

Helm, Virgil. U.S. Department of Agriculture, Soil Conservation Service, Tarrant County, Texas. Interview by author, August 15, 1996.

Lewis, Cora L. Niece of Reuben and Jesse Rogers. Interviews by author, Dumas, Texas, 1962–1988.

Lewis, H. D. Interviews with author, Dumas, Texas, 1970–1980.

Michaelias, Kate Rogers. Half sister of Reuben and Jesse Rogers. Interviews by author, Amarillo, Texas, 1958–1965.

Morgan, Chris. Ranger, Oklahoma Historical Military Park, Oklahoma Historical Society, Fort Gibson, Oklahoma. Telephone interview with author, August 4, 1994.

Wilson, Charles. Great-great-grandson of Reuben Rogers. Interview with author, Canyon, Texas, July 17, 1995.

Wilson, David. Terry's Rangers, Eighth Texas Cavalry Reenactment Regiment. Interviews by author, Hillsboro, Texas, April 1, 1995, and August 1, 1995 (telephone).

Interviews with Combat Veterans

Aldrich, Sam II. Vietnam War. First Lieutenant, U.S. Army Quartermaster Corps, in combat with First and Third Marine Division, 1-5 MAC, for eleven and a half months. Interview by author, Dumas, Texas, August 8, 1994.

McMurry, J. A. World War II. Tail gunner, 338th Bomb Squadron, 96th Bomb Group, 8th Air Force, fourteen missions over Germany. Interview with author, Dumas, Texas, August 5, 1994.

Nevins, Doice. World War II. Rifleman, Fourth Marine Division, invasion of Saipan, seventeen-day battle, June–July 1944; invasion of Tinian, ten-day battle. Interview by author, Dumas, Texas, August 6, 1994.

Phillips, Edward S. World War II. Battalion A, 751st Field Artillery Battalion, February 1944 to January 1946, Omaha Beach to Berlin. Interview by author, Dumas, Texas, October 2, 1994.

Interviews with Cowboys and Cattlemen

Holloway, Glenn. Cowboy. Sneed Ranch, Moore County of Texas Panhandle. Interviews by author, Dumas, Texas, 1994–1996.

Rankin, Rudolph. Owner of Rankin Ranch, Miami, Texas. Cowboy and cowman for fifty years in Roberts County of Texas Panhandle. Interviews by author, Amarillo, Texas, March 7 and 10, 1995.

Record, Tommy Lou. Texas Panhandle cowboy for fifty years. Interviews by author, Dumas, Texas, 1994–1996.

Turner, William J. Texas Panhandle cowboy for forty-nine years. Interviews by author, Dumas, Texas, 1995–1996.

Manuscripts

Bandor, Joseph P. "Memoirs of Tarrant County Confederate Veterans and Others of Post-War Period." Typescript, 1960, in the Fort Worth Public Library.

Banks, William P. "Lt. W. A. Wingo, Ninth Texas Cavalry." Typescript, 1995, in the H. B. Simpson History Complex, Hillsboro, Texas.

Bearss, Edwin C. "The Indians at Pea Ridge." Typescript, Pea Ridge National Military Park, Notes C. IV, n. 1, in W. Craig Gaines, *The Cherokee Confederates,* p. 80.

Coffman, Warren. Letter to Mr. William Coffman, December 7, 1861, from Lochards Mission, Creek Nation, in the Ninth Texas Cavalry files, H. B. Simpson History Complex, Hillsboro, Texas.

Crabb, Martha L. Rogers family historical and genealogical files.

———. Crabb family historical and genealogical files.

Dunn family papers, in the Ninth Texas Cavalry File, H. B. Simpson History Complex, Hillsboro, Texas.

Estill, Weechie Yates. "Grapevine Recollections." Typescript, 1965, in the Amarillo (Texas) Public Library.

Martin, Susan S. Rogers. Rogers family notes, February 22, 1938, author's collections.

———. "The Rogers Family." Manuscript, February 1936, author's collections.

Miller, John A. "A Memoir of the Days of '61." Typescript, n.d, in the H. B. Simpson History Complex, Hillsboro, Texas.

Rogers, Charles E. "The Rogers Family of Ozark, Missouri. Rogersville, Missouri," private publication, 1975.

Shelton, Perry Wayne. "Personal Civil War Letters of Lawrence Sullivan Ross." Master's thesis, Baylor University, Waco, Texas, August 1938. Limited printing, Shelly Morrison, ed., and Richard Morrison, Austin, 1994, in the H. B. Simpson History Complex, Hillsboro, Texas.

Smith, Zoe. "Obituaries Published before 1955 in the *Tulia (Texas) Herald* and the *Happy (Texas) Herald.*" Tule Creek Genealogical Society, 1996, in the Tulia (Texas) Public Library.

———. "Wayside Cemetery, Armstrong County," in *Interments in Swisher County, Texas, and Vicinity 1890–1990.* Tule Creek Genealogical Society, 1990, in the Tulia (Texas) Public Library.

McWhiney, Grady. "General Braxton Bragg." Paper presented at the Confederate History Symposium, April 13, 1996, H. B. Simpson History Complex, Hillsboro, Texas.

Government Documents

Confederate States of America, War Department. *Army Regulations Adopted for the Use of the Army of the Confederate States, also, Articles of War.* Richmond: West & Johnston, Publishers, 1861.

Scott, Major-General [Winfred], by Authority of U.S. Army. *Infantry Tactics, or Rules for the Exercise and Maneuvers of the United States' Infantry.* vol. I., *School of the Soldier and Company.* New York: Harper & Brothers Publishers, 1858.

Tarrant County, Texas, Tax Rolls 1850–1919. Texas/Dallas Collection, Reel #1, Dallas Public Library.

U.S. Army. *The Medical and Surgical History of the War of the Rebellion,* Second Issue. Washington: Government Printing Office, 1883. Reprint. *The Medical and Surgical History of the Civil War.* Wilmington, N.C.: Broadfoot Publishing Company, 1991, vol. 12.

———. *Cavalry Tactics, Second Part, School of the Trooper, or the Platoon, and of the Squadron, Mounted.* Philadelphia: J. B. Lippincott & Co., 1861.

U.S. Bureau of the Census. Seventh Census of United States, 1850, Population Schedule, for Dallas County, Texas, in Amarillo (Texas) Public Library.

———. For Tarrant County, Texas.

———. For Titus County, Texas.

———. For Hunt County, Texas.

———. Eighth Census of United States, 1860, Population Schedule for Dallas County, Texas, in Amarillo (Texas) Public Library.

———. For Titus County, Texas.

U.S. Congress. *Report of Major General William T. Sherman.* Extracted from Joint Committee on the Conduct of the War; Report of Joint Committee on the Conduct to the War 1863–1866. New York: Millwood, Kraus Reprint Co., 1977.

U.S. Department of Agriculture. Susan E. Gebhardt and Ruth H. Matthews, *Nutritive Value of Foods,* Home and Garden Bulletin #72. Washington: Government Printing Office, 1960. Revised 1981.

U.S. Government Printing Office. *Population of the United States in 1860: Compiled from the Original Returns of the Eighth Census.* Washington: Government Printing Office, 1864.

U.S. National Archives. "Compiled Service Records of Confederate Soldiers Who Served in Organizations from the State of Texas," National Archives Microfilm Publication, National Archives and Records Service, General Services Administration, Washington, D.C., 1955, Third, Sixth, and Ninth Texas Cavalry, Series M323, Rolls 18-60, in the Dallas Public Library.

———. Unpublished Military Service Records, Civil War, Ninth Texas Cavalry, Jesse Rogers, Private, Company A.

———. Reuben Rogers, Private, Company A.

———. John Dunn, Private, Company A.

———. Lawrence Sullivan Ross, Sixth Texas Cavalry, Company G.

———. Unpublished Military Service Records, War of 1812, Colonel William Johnson's Regiment East Tennessee Militia (Third Regiment), Captain James Stewart's Company, Corporal Jesse Rogers.

U.S. War Department. *Atlas to Accompany the Official Records of the Union and Confederate Armies.* Washington: Government Printing Press, 1891–1895. Reprint. New York: Thomas Yaseloff, Inc., 1958.

———. *Cavalry Tactics.* Philadelphia: J. B. Lippincott & Co., 1861.

———. *War of the Rebellion: A Compilation of the Official Records of the Union and Confederate Armies,* 129 vols. Washington: Government Printing Press, 1880–1901.

Articles

Barr, Alwyn, ed. "Records of the Confederate Military Commission in San Antonio, July 2, Oct 10, 1862," *Southwestern Historical Quarterly,* Texas State Historical Association, Austin, Texas, vol. 70, no. 1, July 1966, pp. 93–109; no. 2, October 1966, pp. 289–313; no. 4, April 1967, pp. 623–44.

Barron, S. B. "Wade's Supernumary Scouts," *Confederate Veteran,* vol. 2, no. 11, March 1903, p. 115.

Benner, Judith Ann. "Lawrence Sullivan 'Sul' Ross," in *Ten More Texans in Gray,* edited by W. C. Nunn. Hillsboro, Tex.: Hill Junior College Press, 1980.

Blakey, P. A. "Henry Gilbert Haynes," *The Confederate Veteran,* vol. 26, no. 12, December 1918, p. 34.

Bond, John W. "Elkhorn Tavern History," in *The Battle of Pea Ridge 1862.* Rogers, Ark.: Shofner's, n.d., pp. 13–18.

Cawthorn, John A., ed. "Letters of a North Louisiana Private to His Wife, 1862–1865," *Mississippi Valley Historical Review,* March 1944, University of Iowa, Iowa City, Iowa, pp. 533–50.

Coffman, Edward M. "Ben McCulloch Letters," *Southwestern Historical Quarterly,* Texas State Historical Association, Austin, Texas, vol. 60, no. 1, July 1956, pp. 118–22.

"Colonel William Quayle," *Confederate Veteran,* vol. 8, no. 10, August 1902, pp. 372–73.

Commercial Appeal, Memphis, Tennessee, January 6, 1938. Obituary of Jesse Rogers.

Cozzens, Peter. "The Tormenting Flame," *Civil War Times,* April 1996.

Creager, J. A. "Ross's Brigade of Cavalry," *Confederate Veteran,* vol. 28, no. 8, August 1920, pp. 290–92.

Cummins, W. Smith. "A Ruse That Worked Well in Mississippi," *Confederate Veteran,* vol. 21, no. 1, January 1913, pp. 27–28.

Darst, Maury. "Robert Hodges, Jr.: Confederate Soldier," *East Texas Historical Journal,* East Texas Historical Society, Nacogdoches, Texas, vol. 9, no. 1, March 1971, pp. 20–42.

Gage, Larry Jay. "The Texas Road to Secession and War," *Southwestern Historical Quarterly,* Texas State Historical Association, Austin, Texas, vol. 62, no. 2, October 1958, pp. 191–213.

"Griffith, S. A." *Confederate Veteran,* vol. 4, no. 5, May 1896, p. 163.

Hale, Douglas. "Rehearsal for Civil War: The Texas Cavalry in the Indian Territory, 1861," *Chronicles of Oklahoma,* vol. 68, no. 3., Fall 1990, pp. 228–59.

Horton, L. W. "General Sam Bell Maxey: His defense of North Texas and the Indian Territory," *Southwestern Historical Quarterly,* Texas State Historical Association, Austin, Texas, vol. 74, no. 4, April 1971, pp. 505–24.

Jeffries, C. C. "The Character of Terry's Texas Rangers," *Southwestern Historical Quarterly,* Texas State Historical Association, Austin, Texas, vol. 64, no. 4, April 1961, pp. 454–62.

Jones, Allen W. "Military Events in Texas During the Civil War, 1861–1865," *Southwestern Historical Quarterly,* Texas State Historical Association, Austin, Texas, vol. 64, no. 1, July 1960, pp. 64–70.

Mathys, Mary Sue. "Lemuel Jackson Beene—Civil War Questionnaire," *The Bean Stalk,* Southern Bean Association, vol. 14, no. 3, Spring 1986, pp. 93–95.

Martin, Howard N. "Texas Redskins in Confederate Gray," *Southwestern Historical Quarterly,* Texas State Historical Association, Austin, Texas, vol. 70, no. 4, April 1967, pp. 586–92.

McPherson, James M. "Tried by War," *Civil War Times,* vol. 34, no. 5, December 1995, pp. 67–75.

Miller, E. T. "The State Finances of Texas During the Civil War," *Southwestern Historical Quarterly,* Texas State Historical Association, Austin, Texas, vol. 14, no. 1, July 1910, pp. 7–14.

Miller, Thomas L. "Texas Land Grants to Confederate Veterans and Widows," *Southwestern Historical Quarterly,* Texas State Historical Association, Austin, Texas, vol. 69, no. 1, July 1965, pp. 59–65.

Milner, T. J. "Joseph E. Johnston Camp, No. 267, United Confederate Veterans," *Confederate Veteran,* vol. 28, no. 8, August 1920, p. 311.

"Mrs. Bates Wants Her Flag—The Ninth Texas," *Confederate Veteran,* vol. 1, no. 5, May 1893, p. 178.

Newbill, Grace Meredith. "Confederates Buried at Pulaski [Tennessee] in 1863," *Confederate Veteran,* vol. 21, no. 9, September 1913, p. 445.

Oates, Stephen B. "Recruiting Confederate Cavalry in Texas," *Southwestern Historical Quarterly,* Texas State Historical Association, Austin, Texas, vol. 64, no. 4, April 1961, pp. 463–77.

O'Neal, Bill. "The Civil War Memoirs of Samuel Alonza Cooke," *Southwestern Historical Quarterly,* Texas State Historical Association, Austin, Texas, vol. 74, no. 4, April 1971, pp. 533–48.

Page, Mrs. J. H. "Letter of Major J. N. Dodson to Confederate Secretary of War, August 1863," *Confederate Veteran,* vol. 37, no. 11, November 1929, pp. 411–12.

Pollard, Charleen Pulmly. "Civil War Letter of George W. Allen," *Southwestern Historical Quarterly,* Texas State Historical Association, Austin, Texas, vol. 83, no. 1, July 1979, pp. 45–52.

Ray, Johnette Highsmith. "Civil War Letters from Parsons' Texas Cavalry Brigade," *Southwestern Historical Quarterly,* Texas State Historical Association, Austin, Texas, vol. 69, no. 2, October 1965, pp. 210–23.

Rosecrans, Major General William S. "The Battle of Corinth," in *Battles and Leaders of the Civil War,* vol. 2 (New York: E. P. Dutton, 1887–1888. Reprint, Edison, N.J.: Castle, n.d.), pp. 737–56.

Savory, Theodore H. "The Mule," *Scientific American,* August 1967, pp. 102–109.

Simmons, P. B. "The Franklin Fight," *Confederate Veteran,* vol. 1, no. 5, May 1893, p. 163.

Smith, David P., ed. "Civil War Letters of Sam Houston," *Southwestern Historical Quarterly,* Texas State Historical Association, Austin, Texas. vol. 81, no. 4, April 1978, pp. 417–26.

Smyrl, Frank H. "Unionism in Texas, 1856–1861," *Southwestern Historical Quarterly,* Texas State Historical Association, Austin, Texas, vol. 68, no. 2, October 1964, pp. 191–95.

Snead, Thomas L. "With Price East of the Mississippi," in *Battles and Leaders of the Civil War,* vol. 2, (New York: E. P. Dutton, 1887–1888. Reprint, Edison, N.J.: Castle, n.d.) pp. 717–34.

Stevenson, W. R. "The Capture of Holly Springs, Mississippi," *Confederate Veteran,* vol. 9, no. 3, March 1901, p. 134.

"Tarrant County in the War—Lieutenant Colonel William Quayle," *Polignac Gazette,* Arlington, Texas, vol. 2, no. 1, July 1994, p. 9.

Templin, Eleanor. "Making a Road Through the Wilderness," *Franklin County (Tennessee) Historical Review,* vol. 6, no. 2, June 1975, pp. 80–87.

"The Last Roll, Col. N. W. Townes," *Confederate Veteran,* vol. 7, no. 7, July 1900, p. 329.

"The Last Roll, Lieut. William J. Chambers," *Confederate Veteran,* vol. 13, no. 12, December 1905, pp. 515–16.

Vines, Benjamin Rush. Letter to his parents, November 30, 1861. In Virginia Gammons, "A Letter Home from Confederate Soldier Benjamin Rush Vines," *Our Heritage,* February 1991.

Warren, Richard. "Ben McCulloch," in *Ten More Texans in Gray,* edited by W. C. Nunn. Hillsboro, Tex.: Hill Junior College Press, 1980.

Williams, J. W. "The Butterfield Overland Mail Road Across Texas," *Southwestern Historical Quarterly,* Texas State Historical Association, Austin, Texas, vol. 61, no. 1, July 1957, pp. 1–19.

Wooster, Ralph A. "Life in Civil War East Texas," *East Texas Historical Journal,* East Texas Historical Association, Nacogdoches, Texas, vol. 3, no. 2, October 1965, pp. 93–102.

———. "With the Confederate Cavalry in the West: The Civil War Experiences of Isaac Dunbar Affleck," *Southwestern Historical Quarterly,* Texas State Historical Association, Austin, Texas, vol. 83, no. 1, July 1979, pp. 1–28.

Young, H. F. "The Last Roll," *Confederate Veteran,* vol. 7, no. 1, January 1899, pp. 32–33.

Young, J. P. "Hood's Failure at Spring Hill," *Confederate Veteran,* vol. 14, no. 1, January 1908, pp. 25–41.

Books

Adams, George Worthington. *Doctors in Blue.* New York: H. Schuman, 1952. Reprint. Baton Rouge: University of Louisiana Press, 1996, paperback.

Alexander, Edward Porter. *Fighting for the Confederacy.* Chapel Hill: University of North Carolina Press, 1989.

Allardice, Bruce S. *More Generals in Gray*. Baton Rouge: Louisiana State University Press, 1995.

Ambrose, Stephen E., with Edwin C. Bearss, Col. Wilbur S. Nye, Beverly Utley, and Frederic Ray. *Struggle for Vicksburg*. Harrisburg, Pa.: Historical Times, Inc., 1967. Reprint. Eastern National Park & Monument Association, 1994.

Anders, Curt. *Fighting Confederates*. New York: Dorset Press, 1990.

Bailey, Anne J. *Texans in the Confederate Cavalry*. Civil War Campaigns and Commanders Series. Fort Worth: Ryan Place Publishers, 1995.

Barron, S. B. *The Lone Star Defenders: A Chronicle of the Third Texas Cavalry, Ross' Brigade*. New York: The Neale Publishing Company, 1908. Reprint. Waco, Tex.: W. M. Morrison Press, 1964.

Beatty, John. *The Citizen-Soldier, or Memoirs of a Volunteer*. Cincinnati: Wilstach, Baldwin & Co., Publishers, 1879. Reprint. Time-Life Books Inc., 1981.

Benner, Judith Ann. *Sul Ross: Soldier, Statesman, Educator*. College Station: Texas A&M Press, 1983.

Billings, John D. *Hardtack and Coffee*. Boston: George M. Smith and Co., 1887. Reprint. Time-Life Books Inc., 1982.

Blackburn, J. K. P., L. B. Giles, and E. S. Dodd. *Terry Texas Rangers Trilogy*. Austin: State House Press, 1996.

Boatner, Mark M. III. *The Civil War Dictionary*. New York: Vintage Books, First Vintage Civil War Library Edition, 1991.

Broocks, Nathan Covington. *A Complete History of the Mexican War, 1846–1848*. Baltimore: Hutchinson & Seebold, 1849. Reprint. Chicago: The Rio Grande Press, Inc., 1965.

Burton, Benjamin T. *The Heinz Handbook of Nutrition*. New York: McGraw-Hill Book Company, 1965.

Castel, Albert. *General Sterling Price and the Civil War in the West*. Baton Rouge: Louisiana State University Press, 1968. Paperback edition, 1993.

Cater, Douglas John. *As It Was*. William D. Cater, 1981. Reprint. Austin: State House Press, 1990.

Catton, Bruce. *The Coming Fury*. Garden City, N.Y.: Doubleday & Company, Inc., 1961.

———. *Terrible Swift Sword*. Garden City, N.Y.: Doubleday & Company, Inc., 1963.

———. *Never Call Retreat*. Garden City, N.Y.: Doubleday & Company, Inc., 1965.

———. *Grant Moves South*. Boston: Little, Brown and Company, 1960.

———. *Grant Takes Command*. Boston: Little, Brown and Company, 1968.

Cherokee County (Texas) Historical Commission. *Cherokee County History*. Jacksonville, Tex.: 1986.

Cherokee County (Texas) Genealogical Society. *1850 Federal Census, Cherokee County, Texas*. Jacksonville, Tex.: n.d.

————. *1860 Federal Census, Cherokee County, Texas*. Jacksonville, Tex.: n.d.

————. *1870 Federal Census of Cherokee County, Texas*. Jacksonville, Tex.: n.d.

————. *1880 Federal Census of Cherokee County, Texas*. Jacksonville, Tex.; n.d.

Coggins, Jack. *Arms and Equipment of the Civil War*. Wilmington: Broadfoot Publishing Company, 1990.

Cooper, Lenna F., et al. *Nutrition in Health and Disease*. Philadelphia: J. B. Lippincott Co., 1963.

Cotton, Gordon A. *Yankee Bullets, Rebel Rations*. Vicksburg, Miss.: The Office Supply Co., 1989.

————. *Vicksburg: Southern Stories of the Siege*. Vicksburg, Miss.: Private publication, 1988.

Cozzens, Peter. *The Darkest Days of the War: The Battles of Iuka and Corinth*. Chapel Hill: University of North Carolina Press, 1997.

Crabb, Martha L. *Over the Mountain*. Baltimore: Gateway Press, 1990.

Cumming, Kate. *Kate: The Journal of a Confederate Nurse*, edited by Richard Barksdale Harwell. Baton Rouge: Louisiana State University Press, 1959.

Cunningham, H. H. *Doctors in Gray: The Confederate Medical Service*. Baton Rouge: Louisiana State University Press, 1958. Second edition, 1960.

Cutrer, Thomas W. *Ben McCulloch and the Frontier Military Tradition*. Chapel Hill: University of North Carolina Press, 1993.

Dallas Morning News. Texas Almanac 1984–1985. Dallas: A. H. Belo Corp., 1983.

————. *1992–93 Texas Almanac and State Industrial Guide*. Dallas: A. H. Belo Corp., 1991.

Dammann, Gordon, M.D. *Pictorial Encyclopedia of Civil War Medical Instruments and Equipment,* 2 vols. Missoula, Mont.: Pictorial Histories Publishing Company, 1983.

Davis, James Henry. *The Cypress Rangers in the Civil War*. Texarkana, Tex.: Heritage Oak Press, 1992.

Dawson, Francis W. *Reminiscences of Confederate Service 1861–1865*. Baton Rogue: Louisiana State University Press, 1980.

Day, James M., comp. *The Texas Almanac 1857–1873*. Waco, Tex.: Texian Press, 1967.

Eaton, Clement. *Jefferson Davis*. New York: The Free Press, Collier Macmillan Publishers, 1977.

Essin, Emmett M. *Shavetails and Bell Sharps: The History of the U.S. Army Mule*. Lincoln: University of Nebraska Press, 1997.

Fehrenbach, T. R. *Lone Star: A History of Texas and the Texans*. New York: Collier Books, 1985.

Fischer, David Hackett. *Albion's Seed*. New York: Oxford University Press, 1989.

Foote, Shelby. *The Civil War, Fort Sumter to Perryville*. New York: Random House, 1958.

———. *The Civil War, Fredericksburg to Meridian*. New York: Random House, 1963.

———. *The Civil War, Red River to Appomattox*. New York: Random House, 1974.

Foreman, Grant. *Marcy and the Gold Seekers: The Journal of Capt. R. B. Marcy with an Account of the Gold Rush over the Southern Route*. Norman: University of Oklahoma Press, 1939.

———. *The Five Civilized Tribes*. Norman: University of Oklahoma Press, 1934. Eighth printing, 1982.

———. *Fort Gibson: A Brief History*. Muskogee, Okla.: Hoffman Printing Co., n.d.

Frazer, Robert W. *Forts of the West*. Norman: University of Oklahoma Press, 1965.

Fuller, Claud E., and Richard D. Steuart. *Firearms of the Confederacy*. Huntington, W.Va.: Standard Publications, Inc., 1944. Reprint. Fairfax, Va.: The National Rifle Association, 1996.

Gaines, W. Graig. *The Confederate Cherokees*. Baton Rouge: Louisiana State University Press, 1989.

Gallaway, B.P. *The Ragged Rebel, A Common Soldier in W.H. Parson's Texas Cavalry 1861-1865*. Austin: University of Texas Press, 1988.

Garrett, David R. *The Civil War Letters of David R. Garrett, Detailing the Adventures of the 6th Texas Cavalry, 1861–1865,* edited by Max S. Lale and Hobart Key Jr. Marshall, Tex.: Port Caddo Press, 1963.

Garrett, Julia Kathryn. *Fort Worth: A Frontier Triumph*. Austin: Encino Press, 1972.

Gilbert, Paul, and Charles Lee Bryson. *Chicago and Its Makers*. Chicago: Felox Mendelsohn, 1929.

Gluckman, Arcadi. *Identifying Old U.S. Muskets, Rifles and Carbines*. New York: Bonanza Books, 1965.

Goodspeed Publishing Co. *History of Tennessee*. Chicago: 1887. Reprint. Easley, S.C.: Southern Historical Press, 1979.

Govan, Gilbert E., and James W. Livingwood. *General Joseph E. Johnston, C.S.A.* Bobbs-Merrill Company, Inc., 1956. Reprint. New York: Konecky & Konecky, n.d.

Grant, U. S. *Personal Memoirs of U. S. Grant*, edited with notes by E. B. Long. Cleveland: World Publications Co., 1952. Reprint. New York: Da Capo Press, Inc., 1982.

Grayson County Frontier Village. *The History of Grayson County, Texas.* Winston-Salem: Hunter Publishing Company, 1979.

Grimes, Roy. *300 Years in Victoria County.* Austin: Nortex Press, 1986.

Griscom, George L. *Fighting with Ross' Texas Cavalry Brigade, C.S.A.: The Diary of George L. Griscom,* edited by Homer L. Kerr. Hillsboro, Tex.: Hillsboro Junior College Press, 1976.

Hale, Douglas. *The Third Texas Cavalry in the Civil War.* Norman: University of Oklahoma Press, 1993.

Hall, Thomas B., M.D. *Medicine on the Santa Fe Trail.* Morningside Bookshop, 1971. Second edition, revised and corrected, 1987.

Hardee, Brig. Gen. W. J., C.S. Army. *Rifle and Infantry Tactics.* Mobile: S. H. Goetzel & Co., 1861.

Harper, Annie. *Annie Harper's Journal,* edited by Jeannie Marie Deen. Corinth, Miss.: The General Store, n.d.

Hartje, Robert G. *Van Dorn: The Life and Times of a Confederate General.* Nashville: Vanderbilt University Press, 1967.

Havins, Thomas Robert. *Beyond the Cimarron: Major Earl Van Dorn in Comanche Land.* Brownsville, Tex.: The Brown Press, 1986.

Haythornthwaite, Philip. *Uniforms of the Civil War.* New York: Sterling Publishing Co., Inc., 1990.

Hazlett, James C., Edwin Olmstead, and M. Hume Parks. *Field Artillery Weapons of the Civil War.* Newark: University of Delaware Press, 1988.

Henry, Robert Selph. *"First with the Most" Forrest.* Indianapolis: 1944. Reprint. Wilmington, N.C.: Broadfoot Publishing Company, 1987.

Holmes, Maxine, and Gerald D. Saxon, eds. *The WPA Dallas Guide and History.* Dallas: Dallas Public Library, 1992.

Hurst, Jack. *Nathan Bedford Forrest.* New York: Vantage Books, 1994.

Huttash, Ogreta W. *Marriage Records of Cherokee County 1846–1880.* Jacksonville, Tex.: Private publication, 1975. Fifth printing 1965.

———. *Civil War Records of Cherokee County, Texas,* 2 vols. Jacksonville, Tex.: Private publication, 1982. Second printing, 1985.

Jones, John B. *A Rebel War Clerk's Diary,* 3 vols. Philadelphia: J. B. Lippincott & Co., 1866. Reprint. Time-Life Books Inc., 1982.

Jordon, Gen. Thomas, and J. P. Pryor. *The Campaigns of Lieut.-Gen. N. B. Forrest and of Forrest's Cavalry.* New Orleans: 1868. Reprint. Dayton, Ohio: Morningside Bookshop, 1977.

Jurney, Richard Loyall. *History of Titus County, Texas 1846–1960.* Dallas: Royal Publishing Co., 1961.

Kansas State College, School of Home Economics. *Practical Cookery.* New York: John Wiley & Sons, Inc., 1947.

Katcher, Philip. *Civil War Uniforms: A Photo Guide.* London: Arms & Armour Press, 1996.

Keen, Newton A. *Living and Fighting with the Texas 6th Cavalry.* Baithersburg, Md.: Butternut Press, Inc., 1986.

Knight, Oliver. *Fort Worth: Outpost on the Trinity.* Norman: University of Oklahoma Press, 1953.

LaBree, Ben, ed. *Confederate Soldiers in the Civil War.* Louisville: Courier-Journal, 1895.

Lane, Walter P. *The Adventures and Recollections of General Walter P. Lane.* Marshall, Tex.: n.p., 1887. Reprint. Austin: Jenkins Publishing Company, 1970.

Le Grand, Louis. *The Military Hand-Book and Soldiers' Manual of Information.* New York: Beadle and Company, 1861. Reprint. Jacksonville, Ill.: C. W. Heritage, n.d.

Lewis, Lloyd. *Sherman.* Harcourt, Brace and Company, Inc., 1932. Reprint. New York: Konecky & Konecky, n.d.

Lewis Publishing Company. *History of Texas Together with a Biographical History of Tarrant and Parker Counties.* Chicago: Lewis Publishing Co., 1895.

Maury, Dabney Herndon. *Recollections of a Virginian in the Mexican, Indian, and Civil Wars.* New York: Charles Scribner's Sons, 1894.

McCarthy, Carlton. *Detailed Minutia of Soldier Life in the Army of Northern Virginia 1861–1865.* Richmond: Carlton McCarthy and Company, 1882. Reprint. Time-Life Books, 1982.

McClure, Judy Watson. *Confederate from East Texas: The Civil War Letters of James Monroe Watson.* Quanah, Tex.: Nortex Press, 1976.

McPherson, James M. *Drawn with the Sword.* New York: Oxford University Press, 1996.

Mitchell, Reid. *Civil War Soldiers.* New York: Simon & Schuster, Inc., 1988.

Morton, John Watson. *The Artillery of Nathan Bedford Forrest's Cavalry.* Copyright, Mrs. Ellen Morton, 1909. Reprint. Marietta, Ga.: R. Bemis Publishing, Ltd., 1995.

Mullin, Robert N. *Stage Pioneers of the Southwest.* El Paso: University of Texas at El Paso, Southwestern Studies, Monograph No. 17, Texas Western Press, 1983.

Nevins, Allan. *The War for the Union: The Improvised War 1861–1862.* New York: Charles Scribner's Sons, 1959.

———. *The War for the Union: War Becomes Revolution 1862–1863.* New York: Charles Scribner's Sons, 1960.

———. *The War for the Union: The Organized War 1863–1864.* New York: Charles Scribner's Sons, 1971.

———. *The War for the Union: The Organized War to Victory 1864–1865.* New York: Charles Scribner's Sons, 1971.

Nye, Colonel W. S. *Carbine and Lance.* Norman: University of Oklahoma Press, 1937.

Oates, Stephen B. *Confederate Cavalry West of the River.* Austin: University of Texas Press, 1961.

Paddock, Buckley B. *History of Texas, Fort Worth.* Chicago: Lewis Publishing Co., 1922.

Parks, Joseph H. *General Edmund Kirby Smith C.S.A.* Baton Rouge: Louisiana State University Press, 1954.

Parrish, T. Michael. *Richard Taylor: Soldier Prince of Dixie.* Chapel Hill: University of North Carolina Press, 1992.

Parsons, John E. *The Peacemaker and Its Rivals: An Account of the Single Action Colt.* New York: William Morrow and Company, 1950.

Payne, Lillie Ruth, and Iris D. Dunn. *Half Dunn: Once Over Lightly—a History of the John Cartwright Dunn Family.* Corpus Christi: L. R. Payne, 1984.

Peterson, Harold L. *Round Shot and Rammers.* Harrisburg, Pa.: Stackpole Books, 1969.

Porter, Horace. *Campaigning with Grant.* New York: The Century Co., 1897. Reprint. Time-Life Books, Inc., 1981.

Ramsey, J. B. M. *Annals of Tennessee.* Kingsport, Tenn.: n.p., 1853.

Ray, Worth S. *Tennessee Cousins.* Baltimore: Genealogical Publishing Co., 1960.

Rickey, Don Jr. *Forty Miles a Day on Beans and Hay.* Norman: University of Oklahoma Press, 1963.

Roe, Frank Gilbert. *The Indian and the Horse.* Norman: University of Oklahoma Press, 1955.

Rose, Victor M. *Ross' Texas Brigade.* Louisville, Ky.: Courier-Journal Company, 1881. Reprint. Kennesaw, Ga.: Continental Book Company, 1960.

————. *Victor Rose's History of Victoria County [Texas]*. Reprint. Victoria: Book Mart, 1961.

Russell, Traylor. *The History of Titus County*. Waco, Tex.: W. M. Morrision, 1965.

————. *The History of Titus County, Vol. 2*. Waco, Tex.: W. M. Morrision, 1966.

Sears, Stephen W. *George B. McClellan: The Young Napoleon*. New York: Ticknor & Fields, 1988.

Scott, Major-General Winfield. *Infantry Tactics*. New York: Harper & Brothers, Publishers, 1858.

Shea, William, and Earl J. Hess. *Pea Ridge: Civil War Campaigning in the West*. Chapel Hill: University of North Carolina Press, 1992.

Sherman, W. T. *Memoirs of General William T. Sherman*. New York: Library Classics of the United States, Inc., 1990.

Sifakis, Stewart. *Compendium of the Confederate Armies: Texas*. New York: Facts on File, Inc., 1995.

Simpson, Harold B. *Hood's Texas Brigade: Lee's Grenadier Guard*. Waco, Tex.: Texian Press, 1970. Reprint. Gaithersburg, Md.: Olde Soldier Books, Inc., 1994.

Sparks, A. W. *The War Between the States As I Saw It: Reminiscences, Historical and Personal*. Tyler, Tex.: Lee and Burnett, Printers, 1901. Reprint. Longview, Tex.: D & D Printing, 1987.

Spurlin, Charles D., ed. *The Civil War Diary of Charles A. Leuschner*. Austin: Nortex Press, 1992.

Steffen, Randy. *United States Military Saddles*. Norman: University of Oklahoma Press, 1973.

St. Clair, Gladys. *A History of Hopkins County, Texas*. Waco, Tex.: Texian Press, 1965.

Sumrall, Alan K. *Battle Flags of Texas in the Confederacy*. Austin: Eakin Press, 1995.

Texas State Historical Association. *The New Handbook of Texas*, 6 vols. Austin: 1996.

Thomas, Dean S. *Cannon: An Introduction to Civil War Artillery*. Gettysburg: Thomas Publication, 1985.

Thorndale, William, and William Dollarhide. *Map Guide to the U.S. Federal Censuses 1790–1920*. Baltimore: Genealogical Publishing Co., Inc., 1987.

Tuck, June E. *Civil War Shadows in Hopkins County, Texas*. Sulphur Springs, Tex.: Walsworth Printing Company, 1993.

Utley, Robert M. *The Indian Frontier of the American West 1846–1890.* Albuquerque: University of New Mexico Press, 1984.

Vandiver, Frank E. *Rebel Brass: The Confederate Command System.* Baton Rouge: Louisiana State University Press, 1984.

Wallace, Ernest, and E. Adamson Hoebel. *The Comanches, Lords of the Southern Plains.* Norman: University of Oklahoma Press, 1952.

Warner, Ezra J. *Generals in Blue.* Baton Rouge: Louisiana State University Press, 1964. 1977 printing.

———. *Generals in Gray.* Baton Rouge: Louisiana State University Press, 1959. 1978 printing.

Watson, William. *Life in the Confederate Army.* London: Chapman and Hill, 1887. Reprint. Baton Rouge: Louisiana State University Press, 1995.

Waugh, John C. *The Class of 1846.* New York: Warner Books, 1994.

Webb, Walter Prescott, ed. *The Handbook of Texas,* 3 vols. Fort Worth: The Texas State Historical Association, 1952.

———. *The Texas Rangers.* Austin: University of Texas Press, 1935. Paperback edition, 1989.

Wheeler, Maj. Gen. Joseph. *A Revised System of Cavalry Tactics for the Use of the Cavalry and Mounted Infantry, C.S.A.* Mobile: S. H. Goetzel & Co., 1863.

White, Virgil D. transcr. *Index to Texas CSA Pension File.* Waynesboro, Tenn.: The National Historical Publishing Company, 1989.

Wiley, Bell Irving. *The Life of Johnny Reb.* Baton Rouge: Louisiana State University Press, 1943. 1986 printing.

———. *The Life of Billy Yank.* Baton Rouge: Louisiana State University Press, 1952. 1986 printing.

Winick, Myron, M.D., ed. *Columbia Encyclopedia of Nutrition.* New York: G. P. Putnam's Sons, 1988.

Wilson, Eva A., Katherine H. Fisher, and Mary E. Fuqua. *Principles of Nutrition.* New York: John Wiley & Sons, 1967.

Winschel, Terrence J. *Alice Shirley and the Story of Wexford Lodge.* Vicksburg, Tenn.: Eastern National Park and Monument Association, 1993.

Woodward, Grace Steele. *The Cherokees.* Norman: University of Oklahoma Press, 1962.

Wright, Marcus J. *Texas in the War 1861–1865.* Hillsboro, Tex.: Hill Junior College, 1965.

Wyeth, John Allan. *That Devil Forrest: Life of General Nathan Bedford Forrest.* New York: Harper & Brothers, 1959. Reprint. Baton Rouge: Louisiana State University Press, 1989.

Yoakum, H. *History of Texas,* 2 vols. New York: Redfield, 1856.

Young, Charles H., ed. *Grapevine Area History.* Dallas: Grapevine Historical Society, Taylor Publishing Co., 1979.

NOTES

KEY TO ABBREVIATED CITATIONS

O.R. U.S. War Department, *War of the Rebellion: A Compilation of the Official Records of the Union and Confederate Armies,* 129 vols. Washington: 1880–1901. Series 1, unless otherwise noted.

CSR-Texas U.S. National Archives, *Compiled Service Records of Confederate Soldiers Who Served in Organizations from the State of Texas,* National Archives Microfilm Publication, National Archives and Records Service, General Service Administration, Washington, 1955, Series M323, Rolls 18, 41, 56–60, Series M227, Roll 38, Dallas Public Library. Series M323, unless otherwise noted.

Chapter 1: All Afire to Fight

1 Minter's Chapel is in the confines of the Dallas–Fort Worth Airport; *CSR-Texas,* roll 59 for Reuben Rogers; Susan S. Rogers Martin, sister of Reuben and Jesse Rogers, family notes, February 22, 1938, author's collections; Martha L. Crabb, Rogers family data, genealogy, notes, and documents; John Beatty, *The Citizen-Soldier, or Memoirs of a Volunteer* (Cincinnati: Wilstach, Baldwin & Co., Publishers, 1879. Reprint. Time-Life Books Inc., 1981), p. 34. Beatty reported a full moon on July 29, 1861.

2 A. W. Sparks, *The War Between the States As I Saw It: Reminiscences, Historical and Personal* (Tyler, Tex.: Lee and Burnett, Printers, 1901. Reprint. Longview, Tex.: D & D Printing, 1987), pp. 6, 10–13. Sparks states the comet was in the eastern sky; Julia Kathryn Garrett, *Fort Worth: A Frontier Triumph* (Austin: Encino Press, 1972), pp. 175–76, 197–98. Garrett states the comet was in the northwestern sky; Larry Jan Gage, "The Texas Road to Secession and War," *Southwestern Historical Quarterly,* vol. 62, no. 2, October 1958 (Austin: Texas State Historical Association), pp. 191–209; Frank H. Smyrl, "Unionism in Texas, 1856–1861," *Southwestern Historical Quarterly,* vol. 68, no. 2, October 1964 (Austin: Texas State Historical Association), p. 192.

3 Charles H. Young, ed., *Grapevine Area History,* (Dallas: Grapevine Historical Society, Taylor Publishing Co., 1979), pp. 161–62; Crabb, Rogers family data.

The Creed and Rogers families moved to Tarrant County in 1859 from their homes near Springfield, in southwestern Missouri. The battle of Wilson Creek took place August 10, 1861. News of the victory reached Tarrant County, Texas, a few days later; Newton A. Keen, *Living and Fighting with the Texas 6th Cavalry* (Baithersburg, Md.: Butternut Press, Inc., 1986), p. 18; Garrett, *Fort Worth: A Frontier Triumph,* p. 198; Gladys St. Clair, *A History of Hopkins County, Texas* (Waco: Texian Press, 1965), p. 29; David Garrett to William Gibbard, October 27, 1861, in Max S. Lale and Hobart Key Jr., eds., *The Civil War Letters of David R. Garrett, Detailing the Adventures of the 6th Texas Cavalry, 1861-1865* (Marshall, Tex.: Port Caddo Press, 1963), p. 34.

4   Sparks, *The War . . . As I Saw It,* p. 11. See Anne J. Bailey, *Texans in the Confederate Cavalry* (Fort Worth: Ryan Place Publishers, 1995), pp. 13–27, for a discussion of the Texans' enthusiasm for cavalry service.

5   Keen, *The 6th Texas Cavalry,* pp. 4–5, 18–19; Judith Ann Benner, *Sul Ross, Soldier, Statesman, Educator* (College Station: Texas A&M Press, 1983), p. 67; Marcus J. Wright, *Texas in the War 1861–1865* (Hillsboro, Tex.: Hill Junior College, 1965), p. 51; Garrett to William Gibbard, from Camp Davis, Arkansas, October 27, 1861, in Garrett, *Civil War Letters,* p. 34; Ralph A. Wooster, "Life in Civil War East Texas," *East Texas Historical Journal,* vol. 3, no. 2, October 1965 (Nacogdoches, Tex.: East Texas Historical Association), p. 93.

6   U.S. National Archives, Unpublished Military Service Records, War of 1812, Jesse Rogers, Corporal, 3rd Regiment, Captain James Stewart's Co., Col. William Johnson's Regiment of East Tennessee Militia; Crabb, Rogers family files. John Rogers of Wythe County, Virginia, Reuben's grandfather, made gunpowder for the patriots during the Revolution; David Hackett Fischer, *Albion's Seed* (New York: Oxford University Press, 1989), pp. 622–23.

7   Garrett, *Fort Worth: A Frontier Triumph,* p. 202; Young, *Grapevine Area History,* pp. 101–102, 319; Sparks, *The War . . . As I Saw It,* p. 11; "Tarrant County in the War—Lieutenant Colonel William Quayle," *Polignac Gazette* (Arlington, Tex.: Gen. C. J. de Polignac Camp #1648, SCV), vol. 2, no. 1, July 1994, p. 9; Douglas Hale, "Rehearsal for Civil War: The Texas Cavalry in the Indian Territory, 1861," *Chronicles of Oklahoma* (Oklahoma City: Oklahoma Historical Society), vol. 68, no. 3, fall 1990, p. 258; Tarrant County, Texas, tax rolls 1850–1919, Texas/Dallas Collection, Reel #1, Dallas Public Library. Quayle owned 1,344 acres; Lewis Publishing Co., *History of Texas Together with a Biographical History of Tarrant and Parker Counties,* p. 320; "Colonel William Quayle," *Confederate Veteran,* vol. 8, no. 10, August 1902, pp. 372–73; Virgil D. White, transcrib., *Index to Texas CSA Pension File* (Waynesboro, Tenn.: The National Historical Publishing Co., 1989), file #961376 for Thomas H. Cox, file #961380 for William H. Cox, and file #960288 for G. C. Piersall. I have been unable to find the date Quayle began raising his company. However, Thomas H. Cox declared in 1903 that he joined Quayle's company in May 1861, William H. Cox stated he joined in the spring of 1861, and George C. Piersall stated he enlisted in July 1861; *O.R.,* vol. 4, pp. 91–100. William

Quayle must have begun raising his company during the late spring or summer of 1861, certainly before late July, when Governor Edward Clark issued a call for three cavalry regiments to be raised in northeastern Texas. During the late spring and early summer of 1861, Clark had issued calls for cavalry to patrol the state's western Indian frontier and to protect the Lone Star State from invasion from the north and east. Brig. Gen. Earl Van Dorn commanded military affairs in Texas, and Col. Ben McCulloch commanded the state troops. The records do not make clear how men were chosen to raise companies for the cavalry regiments. Perhaps Governor Clark granted authority. Col. W. C. Young of Cooke County was ordered to organize the three regiments, and he might have granted authority to individuals to raise companies. Later in the war authority to raise troops was granted by the Confederate War Department. On July 25, 1861, Governor Clark, convinced that "the integrity of the soil of Texas greatly depends upon the success of the Southern cause in Missouri," issued a call for 3,000 mounted men, three regiments, to be drawn from the seventh, eighth, and ninth Texas Military Districts, the northeastern section of the state. The men were to furnish their own horses and arms. The governor directed that the troops "be governed in all points by the Regulations of the Army of the Confederate States." August 28, 1861, the governor "tendered to the Confederate States the services of four mounted regiments, fully armed and equipped," and ordered Col. W. C. Young to muster three of the regiments into Confederate service.

8   *CSR-Texas,* rolls 18, 41, 56–60; Crabb, Rogers family files; Oliver Knight, *Fort Worth: Outpost on the Trinity* (Norman: University of Oklahoma Press, 1953), pp. 16–17; Walter Prescott Webb, ed., *The Handbook of Texas,* 3 vols. (Fort Worth: The Texas State Historical Association, 1952), vol. 2, pp. 707–708. In 1840, Col. Jonathan Bird and twenty of his Texas Rangers established Fort Bird, later known as Birdville. Johnson's Station, a minor stop on the Butterfield Overland Mail Route, was established in 1847 by M. T. Johnson.

9   Garrett, *Fort Worth: A Frontier Triumph,* pp. 121–22, 125, 212; Knight, *Fort Worth: Outpost on the Trinity,* pp. 25–52. (see p. 24 for a map of Fort Worth in 1853); Webb, *Handbook of Texas,* vol. 2, pp. 707–708. In 1849, the U.S. Army established Fort Worth, named in honor of Mexican War hero Gen. William J. Worth. The town grew up around the fort. In 1857, the population of the town was around a hundred.

10   Garrett, *Forth Worth: A Frontier Triumph,* pp. 202–203; Sparks, *The War . . . As I Saw It,* p. 15; *CSR-Texas,* roll 59.

11   Garrett, *Fort Worth: A Frontier Triumph,* pp. 202–203; *CSR-Texas,* rolls 56–60. The hometowns of only a portion of the men in Company A are noted. Other men from Grapevine were John and Solon Dunn, Phil Greenup, Alex Anderson, J. N. Dodson, Polk Dodson, John Hudgins, and William Trice. Birdville, between Grapevine and Fort Worth, was home to James E. Moore and Jesse Phillips. David and Richard Boaz, Quinton Booth, F. M. Dyer, Hardy Hol-

man, and E. A. Schults were from Fort Worth. Sam Knight and John Parish were from Ashland, and Isaac Davis had ridden south from neighboring Wise County to join the Mounted Riflemen. The 1860 census of Tarrant County, Texas, including the population schedule, the slave schedule, and the agricultural schedule, is lost. Place of residence, age, occupation, number of slaves owned, and composition of family were noted in the 1860 census. The census would reveal much interesting information about the members of Quayle's company.

12 Young, *Grapevine Area History,* pp. 290, 319. Martha (Morehead) Quayle was the wife of Amos Quayle. Jacob L. Morehead was her half brother; Martha's speech is taken from Weeches Yates Estill, "Grapevine Recollections," typescript, 1965, Amarillo Public Library, pp. 18–19; Harold B. Simpson, *Hood's Texas Brigade: Lee's Grenadier Guard* (Waco: Texian Press, 1970. Reprint. Gaithersburg, Md.: Olde Soldier Books Inc., 1994). See pp. 26–28 for a discussion of the presentation of company flags; Alan K. Sumrall, *Battle Flags of Texas in the Confederacy* (Austin: Eakin Press, 1995), pp. 7, 69. The Confederate flag recognized today is a St. Andrew's Cross with a red field and a blue cross edged in white containing thirteen stars. The stars were for the ten Confederate states and the three states the Confederacy claimed—Maryland, Kentucky, and Missouri. This flag was adopted by Gen. Joseph E. Johnston as the official battle flag of the Army of Tennessee in the spring of 1864. However, variations of the flag date from early in the war. The number of stars represented the number of states in the Confederacy at the time the flag was made; Joseph P. Bandor, "Memoirs of Tarrant County Confederate Veterans and Others of the Post-War Period," typescript, 1960, Fort Worth Public Library, p. 16.

13 Garrett, *Fort Worth: A Frontier Triumph,* pp. 203–204; Knight, *Fort Worth: Outpost on the Trinity,* p. 51; Young, *Grapevine Area History,* p. 100–101; S. B. Barron, *The Lone Star Defenders: A Chronicle of the Third Texas Cavalry, Ross' Brigade* (New York: The Neale Publishing Co., 1908. Reprint. Waco: W. M. Morrison Press, 1964), p. 19; Farewell ceremonies for companies leaving for service are discussed in Stephen B. Oates, "Recruiting Confederate Cavalry in Texas," *Southwestern Historical Quarterly,* vol. 64, no. 4, April 1961, pp. 466–70.

14 James Henry Davis, *The Cypress Rangers in the Civil War* (Texarkana, Tex.: Heritage Oak Press, 1992), p. 15, 21–22. Twenty men, calling themselves Cypress Rangers, were sworn into Texas service February 14, 1861. Sixty-four more men joined before the regiment organized. The Cypress Rangers became Company F, Texas Cavalry; Estill, "Recollections," p. 19; Sparks, *The War . . . As I Saw It,* pp. 15–16; *O.R.,* vol. 4, pp. 91, 94–95, 99.

15 George L. Griscom, in Homer L. Kerr, ed., *Fighting with Ross' Texas Cavalry Brigade C.S.A.: The Diary of George L. Griscom, Adjutant, 9th Texas Cavalry Regiment* (Hillsboro, Tex.: Hill Junior College Press, 1976), pp. 1–2. Griscom states that Brinson's company was raised under the call of Texas Governor Edward Clark and was sworn into state service August 19, 1861. Companies commonly were sworn in before gathering to march to training camp; *O.R.,*

vol. 4, pp. 95, 98–99; Garrett, *Fort Worth: A Frontier Triumph,* pp. 203–204. Garrett says Brinson's company left Fort Worth in early September.

16 Griscom, *Fighting with Ross' Texas Cavalry Brigade,* pp. 1–2; Sparks, *The War . . . As I Saw It,* p. 16.

17 U.S. Bureau of the Census, 8th Census of the United States, 1860, Population Schedule, Amarillo (Texas) Public Library, for Titus County, Texas, p. 172, A. W. Sparks's family; Sparks, *The War . . . As I Saw It,* preface, pp. 14–15. In 1897, members of Ross's Brigade Association ordered secretary and member of the historical committee A. W. Sparks to gather and compile "all matter of a reminiscent or historical nature that pertained to the services of Ross' Brigade." At the 1901 meeting, Sparks, as custodian of the historical papers, was ordered to prepare the material and have the book printed; Victor M. Rose, *Ross' Texas Brigade* (Louisville, Ky.: Courier-Journal Co., 1881. Reprint. Kennesaw, Ga.: Continental Book Co., 1960), p. 18.

18 Griscom, *Fighting with Ross' Texas Cavalry Brigade,* p. 2; Oates, "Recruiting Confederate Cavalry in Texas," *Southwestern Historical Quarterly,* pp. 465–66.

19 Griscom, *Fighting with Ross' Texas Cavalry Brigade,* p. 2. See pp. 210–214 for a roster of regimental officers. Company A officers were Capt. Thomas G. Berry, 1st Lt. R. R. Hund, 2nd Lt. James W. Calloway, and 3rd Lt. A. B. Gant. See p. 169, where Griscom stated that Berry was from "Grove Vine Prairie." Griscom, being unfamiliar with Tarrant County, must have meant Grapevine Prairie; Virgil Helm, U.S. Department of Agriculture, Soil Conservation Service, Tarrant County, Texas, interview with author, August 15, 1996. There is no geographical area known as Grove Vine Prairie in Tarrant County. Grapevine Prairie, however, is well-known and has been since the beginning of settlement in Tarrant County; Sparks, *The War . . . As I Saw It,* p. 16. Both Griscom and Sparks state that Sims was elected; *O.R.,* vol. 4, pp. 91, 95. By Confederate War Department rules, company officers were elected. Regimental colonels were appointed by President Jefferson Davis. Sims's regiment was raised by state authority, therefore the men elected their colonel; Hale, "Rehearsal for Civil War: The Texas Cavalry in the Indian Territory, 1861," *Chronicles of Oklahoma,* p. 258. For a complete list of officers and men in the Ninth Texas Cavalry, see Griscom, *Fighting with Ross' Texas Cavalry Brigade,* pp. 209–37.

20 Griscom, *Fighting with Ross' Texas Cavalry Brigade,* pp. ix, 18(n); U.S. Census 1850, Tarrant County, Texas (M. J. Brinson was age twenty-five, making him thirty-five in 1860). Again, the lost 1860 Tarrant County, Texas, census would reveal interesting information about the members of Company D; Knight, *Fort Worth: Outpost on the Trinity,* p. 37. M. J. Brinson was one of the earliest settlers of Johnson's Station; See Garrett, *Fort Worth: A Frontier Triumph* for M. J. Brinson's family connections and contributions to Tarrant County; Barron, *Lone Star Defenders,* pp. 34, 36; Hale, "Rehearsal for Civil War: The Texas Cavalry in the Indian Territory, 1861," *Chronicles of Oklahoma,* p. 258. Com-

pany B of Sims's Regiment was recruited in Fannin County, Company C in Grayson County, Company E in Red River County, Company F in Cass County, Companies G and K in Hopkins County, and Company H in Lamar County. Most men in Company I—including A. W. Sparks and Dudley W. "Dud" Jones, both students—lived in and around Titus County. They and their comrades elected wealthy old Charles Stewart as their captain. Dr. James E. Robertson, regimental surgeon and later brigade surgeon, also lived in Titus County.

21 Sparks, *The War . . . As I Saw It,* p. 16; Davis, *The Cypress Rangers,* p. 26; Oates, "Recruiting Confederate Cavalry in Texas," *Southwestern Historical Quarterly,* p. 470. Names of other companies raised in Texas were more colorful, such as the "Dead Shot Rangers" and the "Texas Hunters" of the Third Texas Cavalry.

22 *CSR-Texas,* rolls 56–60. Ages of 110 of the 125 men who enlisted in Company A are given. William L. Tandy was forty-two and William Greenup was forty-three; Douglas Hale, *The Third Texas Cavalry in the Civil War* (Norman: University of Oklahoma Press, 1993), p. 44; Bell Irving Wiley, *The Life of Johnny Reb* (Baton Rouge: Louisiana State University Press, 1943. 1986 printing), p. 245; Allan Nevins, *The War for the Union: The Organized War 1863–1864* (New York: Charles Scribner's Sons, 1971), p. 130. The average age of Union soldiers at time of enlistment was 25.8 years, with 67 percent under 30. The majority were age 18 to 22.

23 *CSR-Texas,* rolls 56–69; Hale, "Rehearsal for Civil War: The Texas Cavalry in the Indian Territory, 1861," *Chronicles of Oklahoma,* p. 258; H. H. Cunningham, *Doctors in Gray: The Confederate Medical Service* (Baton Rouge: Louisiana State University Press, 1958), p. 165.

24 Dallas Morning News *1992–93 Texas Almanac and State Industrial Guide* (Dallas: A. H. Belo Corp., 1991), pp. 169–71; *Texas Almanac 1857–1873* (Waco: Texian Press, 1967); Exact figures for smaller towns are unavailable because the 1860 census noted total populations of counties but did not record totals for small towns. Paris, in Lamar County, was home to 1,500. The population of Clarksville, in Red River County, was about 400, and that of Grapevine about 200. Sizes of the towns, nonetheless, fail to reflect the density of population in northeastern Texas in 1860. The eight counties that were home to Sims's men had an average population of 8,178. Tarrant County's population was 6,020. More than a century later, ten of fifteen counties in the northern Texas Panhandle had less population per square mile; See Young, *Grapevine Area History,* p. 7, for 1860 population of Tarrant County; Nevins, *The War for the Union,* p. 130. Forty-eight percent of Union soldiers were farmers.

25 Griscom, *Fighting with Ross' Texas Cavalry Brigade,* pp. 210–37. The regimental officers were Col. William B. Sims; Lt. Col. William Quayle; Maj. Nathan W. Townes; 1st Lt. Dudley W. Jones, AAG; Dr. James E. Robertson, Surgeon; Capt. J. W. Sims, Assistant Quartermaster; T. A. Ish of Fort Worth, Chaplain.

Company captains elected at organization were: Company A—Thomas G. Berry, Company B—Gideon Smith, Company C—J. E. McCool, Company D—M. J. Brinson, Company E—Joseph C. Hart, Company F—W. E. Duncan, Company G—L. D. King, Company H—J. D. Wright, Company I—Charles S. Stewart, Company K—James P. Williams; *O.R.*, vol. 4, pp. 91, 99, 122, 144–45; *CSR-Texas,* rolls 56–60; Hale, *The Third Texas Cavalry,* p. 77; Oates, "Recruiting Confederate Cavalry in Texas," *Southwestern Historical Quarterly,* pp. 463–69. The First and Second Texas Cavalry regiments, raised at the request of the governor for frontier service in the state, were sworn into service in April and May 1861. The Third Texas Cavalry, raised by Col. Elkanah Greer with a commission from the Confederate War Department, organized at Dallas in June 1861 and took up the line of march for Missouri, July 9, 1861.

26 *CSR-Texas,* rolls 56–60.

27 See *CSR-Texas,* roll 59, for Reuben Rogers. See roll 60 for pay voucher dated August 9, 1862 to Private William L. Tandy, who was paid $0.10 a mile for traveling 168 miles from Camp Hindman, Texas, to Fort Worth, Texas. His rate of pay was $24 per month, clothing allowance $4.10 per month. Tandy, a carpenter aged forty-four years, was discharged July 16, 1862, "by Virtue of the Conscript Act."

28 *O.R.,* vol. 4, pp. 98–99; *CSR-Texas,* rolls 56–60. The records note values of ninety horses belonging to men who joined Company A during 1861; Garrett, *Fort Worth: A Frontier Triumph,* p. 198. Tarrant County's 1861 tax rolls noted 5,293 horses valued at $206,429.

29 Barron, *Lone Star Defenders,* p. 28; Sparks, *The War . . . As I Saw It,* p. 24.

30 *O.R.,* vol. 1, pp. 516, 635; June E. Tuck, *The Civil War in Hopkins County, Texas* (Sulphur Springs, Tex.: Walsworth Printing Co., 1993), pp. 25–26; Barron, *Lone Star Defenders,* pp. 21, 25, 27. The Third Texas Cavalry was equipped with U.S. Army wagons, mules, tents, camp kettles, and pistols. In addition, each company was furnished with two wagons drawn by six Mexican mules and driven by Mexican teamsters, all from U.S. Army headquarters in San Antonio. A wealthy citizen of Rusk, Texas, furnished a horse and accoutrements for a man who could not afford them; Simpson, *Hood's Texas Brigade,* pp. 14–15. Navarro County appropriated $2,500 for arms and ammunition. Williamson County provided $2,500 for arms. McLennan County supplied $11,000 for uniforms and camp equipment for members of its regiments.

31 Griscom, *Fighting with Ross' Texas Cavalry Brigade,* p. 2; Wright, *Texas in the War 1861–1865,* p. 51; *O.R.,* series 4, vol. 1, p. 128. Section 7 of "An Act for the establishment and organization of the Army of the Confederate States of America," published March 6, 1861, states that a cavalry company shall contain sixty privates; Texas cavalry regiments raised early in the war contained one hundred men per company; Maj. Gen. Joseph Wheeler, *A Revised System of Cavalry Tactics for the Use of the Cavalry and Mounted Infantry, C.S.A.* (Mobile:

S. H. Goetzel & Co., 1863), Part First, p. 1. In 1863, a regulation Confederate cavalry company contained from sixty to eighty privates.

32 Griscom, *Fighting with Ross' Texas Cavalry Brigade,* p. 2; Sparks, *The War . . . As I Saw It,* pp. 16, 18.

33 *O.R.,* sec. 4, vol. 1, p. 130. Colonels, lieutenant colonels, majors, and captains of cavalry were allowed to keep three horses, lieutenants two. All cavalrymen were required to furnish their own mounts throughout the war; *O.R.,* vol. 8, p. 728. The first official record of strength of the Ninth Texas Cavalry, dated December 31, 1861, shows an aggregate of 713 and 677 present; *CSR-Texas,* rolls 56–60. The regiment had gained about as many men as it had lost by the end of 1861; Oates, "Recruiting Confederate Cavalry in Texas," *Southwestern Historical Quarterly,* p. 477. Oates gives the strength of the Ninth Texas as 1,050, which seems high; *O.R.,* vol. 10, pt. 2, p. 489, gives the strength of the Ninth Texas on May 4, 1862, as an aggregate of 869, the highest in the official records; *CSR-Texas,* rolls 50–60, shows the strength of Company A, Ninth Texas Cavalry, as 82 men and 4 officers on October 14, 1861; Sparks, *The War . . . As I Saw It,* pp. 16–18. The Titus Grays, Company I, mustered in 114 men; Davis, *The Cypress Rangers,* p. 25, reports that Company F mustered 85 privates; Garrett, *Fort Worth: A Frontier Triumph,* pp. 203–204. Garrett reports that Brinson's company, which was designated Company D., mustered 70 men; *O.R.,* vol. 4, pp. 144–45.

34 Glenn Holloway, cowboy, Sneed Ranch, Moore County, Texas Panhandle. Interviews by author in Dumas, Texas, 1994–1995. Rudolph Rankin, owner of Rankin Ranch, Miami, Texas, a cowboy and cowman for fifty years in Roberts County, Texas Panhandle. Interview by author in Amarillo, Texas, March 7 and 10, 1995. Tommy Lou Record, full-time Texas Panhandle cowboy for fifty years. Interviews by author in Dumas, Texas, 1994–1995. William J. Turner, full-time Texas Panhandle cowboy for forty-nine years. Interviews by author in Dumas, Texas, 1995.

35 Record, interview with author; Turner, interview with author; Wheeler, *Cavalry Tactics,* Part First, pp. 42–43. The Confederate Cavalry used thirty-eight different bugle calls.

36 W. J. Hardee, Brig. Gen., C.S. Army, *Rifle and Infantry Tactics* (Mobile: S. H. Goetzel & Co., 1861). Hardee's manual became the standard infantry manual in both the Union and Confederate armies; Ezra J. Warner, *Generals in Gray* (Baton Rouge: Louisiana State University Press, 1978 printing), p. 124. Lieutenant Colonel Hardee resigned from the U.S. Army in January 1861 to offer his services to the Confederacy. He rose to the rank of lieutenant general.

37 Griscom, *Fighting with Ross' Texas Cavalry Brigade,* pp. 2–3; Sparks, *The War . . . As I Saw It,* p. 18.

38 Griscom, *Fighting with Ross' Texas Cavalry Brigade,* pp. 2–3; Sparks, *The War . . . As I Saw It,* pp. 18–19.

39   *O.R.,* vol. 8, p. 797; Louis Le Grand, *The Military Hand-Book and Soldiers Manual of Information* (New York: Beadle and Co., 1861. Reprint. Jacksonville, Ill.: C. W. Heritage, n.d.), pp. 7–24; Grant Foreman, *Fort Gibson: A Brief History* (Muskogee, Okla.: Hoffman Printing Co., n.d.), p. 11.

40   Griscom, *Fighting with Ross' Texas Cavalry Brigade,* p. 20(n); Hale, "Rehearsal for Civil War: The Texas Cavalry in the Indian Territory, 1861," *Chronicles of Oklahoma,* p. 258.

41   Griscom, *Fighting with Ross' Texas Cavalry Brigade,* pp. 2–3; Sparks, *The War . . . As I Saw It,* p. 22; *O.R.,* vol. 3, p. 700; *O.R.,* vol. 4, p. 144. November 3, 1861, Young reported to the secretary of war in Richmond that Colonel Sims's regiment "commenced moving on the 28th and on the 30th the entire regiment was *en route* for General McCulloch's command"; Barron, *Lone Star Defenders,* pp. 29–30. The Third Texas crossed the Red River in July 1861. The men rode their horses across, but the wagons were ferried over; W. J. Williams, "The Butterfield Overland Mail Road Across Texas," *Southwestern Historical Quarterly,* vol. 61, no. 1, July 1957 (Austin: Texas State Historical Association), p. 4. The Ninth Texas must have crossed the Red River at Colbert's Ferry, twelve miles north of Sherman in Grayson County. The Butterfield Mail Road, running north from Texas into Indian Territory, crossed the river at the ferry, and the Ninth Texas followed the mail road north.

Chapter 2: Yankee Indians

1   *O.R.,* vol. 4, pp. 144–45: Grant Foreman, *Marcy and the Gold Seekers: The Journal of Capt. R. B. Marcy with an Account of the Gold Rush over the Southern Route* (Norman: University of Oklahoma Press, 1939), pp. 14, 148–49, 402; Robert N. Mullin, *Stage Pioneers of the Southwest* (El Paso: University of Texas at El Paso, Southwestern Studies, Monograph No. 17, Texas Western Press, 1983), pp. 32–37; Griscom, *Fighting with Ross' Texas Cavalry Brigade,* p. 3; Sparks, *The War . . . As I Saw It,* p, 22.

2   Crabb, Rogers family files.

3   Kentucky and Maryland were the other two border states.

4   Crabb, Rogers family files; *CSR-Texas,* roll 59, Jesse Rogers; Charles E. Rogers, *The Rogers Family of Ozark, Missouri* (Rogersville, Mo.: private publication, 1975), p. 2.

5   Sparks, *The War . . . As I Saw It,* p. 22; Griscom, *Fighting with Ross' Texas Cavalry Brigade,* p. 3; *O.R.,* vol. 8, p. 728. The Ninth Texas Cavalry muster rolls taken December 31, 1861, in Indian Territory, reported an aggregate of

713 men; *CSR-Texas,* rolls 56–60. The roll of Company A reported 81 privates and 4 officers; *O.R.,* vol. 8, pp. 718–19, 777. McCulloch had his headquarters at Fort Smith on December 21, 1861. By March 12, 1861, headquarters were in Van Buren.

6   Grant Foreman, *The Five Civilized Tribes* (Norman: University of Oklahoma Press, 1934. 8th printing, 1982), pp. 196–97; Griscom, *Fighting with Ross' Texas Cavalry Brigade,* p. 3.

7   Griscom, *Fighting with Ross' Texas Cavalry Brigade,* pp. 3–4; Sparks, *The War . . . As I Saw It,* p. 22; Rose, *Ross' Texas Brigade,* pp. 49–50; *O.R.,* vol. 8, p. 713; *O.R.,* vol. 7, p. 145. Col. Wm. C. Young reported November 3, 1861, to the War Department in Richmond: "There is considerable dread amongst our people [the Texans] on Red River" because of the threat of Indian depredations coming south out of Indian Territory.

8   Data on Indian Territory and the Five Civilized Tribes from: W. Graig Gaines, *The Confederate Cherokees* (Baton Rouge: Louisiana State University Press, 1989), pp. 1–61; Foreman, *The Five Civilized Tribes*; Grace Steele Woodward, *The Cherokees* (Norman: University of Oklahoma Press, 1962); Robert M. Utley, *The Indian Frontier of the American West 1846–1890* (Albuquerque: University of New Mexico Press, 1984), pp. 72–76. Utley states that no Indians experienced more trauma as a result of the Civil War than the Five Civilized Tribes of Indian Territory. For all the tribes, the war proved a calamity of far-reaching, long-lasting consequences; see Gaines for a discussion of the Cherokees' involvement. Cherokee council leader John Ross was seven-eighths white. The Cherokee Nation had a population in 1859 of 22,000, made up of 4,000 men who were eligible to vote, 4,000 black slaves, 1,000 whites, and the rest women and children. See *O.R.,* vol. 3, pp. 572–698, for military activities in Indian Territory at the beginning of the war.

9   In the *Official Records,* Opothleyohola is spelled Hopoeithleyohola.

10   Gaines, *The Confederate Cherokees,* p. 23; Foreman, *The Five Civilized Tribes,* p. 187; Griscom, *Fighting with Ross' Texas Cavalry Brigade,* p. 3.

11   Warner, *Generals in Gray,* pp. 240–41; *O.R.,* vol. 3, pp. 572–74, 580–81, 587, 623–24.

12   Douglas H. Cooper and Albert Pike served in the Mexican War with the Mississippi Rifles, Col. Jefferson Davis, commanding.

13   Gaines, *The Confederate Cherokees,* pp. 30–37; Woodward, *The Cherokees,* pp. 270–71; *O.R.,* vol. 3, p. 614; *O.R.,* vol. 4, p. 145.

14   Gaines, *The Confederate Cherokees,* p. 35; Utley, *The Indian Frontier of the American West 1846–1890,* pp. 73–74.

15   *O.R.,* vol. 8, p. 5.

16   Griscom, *Fighting with Ross' Texas Cavalry Brigade,* p. 4.

17 Ibid.; Sparks, *The War . . . As I Saw It*, p. 15.

18 Sparks, *The War . . . As I Saw It*, p. 23; Griscom, *Fighting with Ross' Texas Cavalry Brigade*, p. 4; Foreman, *The Five Civilized Tribes*, p. 197; Simpson, *Hood's Texas Brigade*, p. 70. The night of November 12, 1861, there was no moon.

19 Record, interview; a horse walks at about five miles an hour; Jack Coggins, *Arms and Equipment of the Civil War* (Wilmington: Broadfoot Publishing Co., 1990), p. 51. At a walk, cavalry could cover four miles an hour, at a slow trot six, and at an alternate walk and trot six; Wheeler, *Cavalry Tactics*, Part First, p. 37. Paces of horses: "The walk should be at the rate of 3¾ miles an hour, the trot 7½, and the gallop 10 miles an hour." Part Second, p. 77. Twenty-five miles a day was about as far as a cavalry horse could be expected to travel. Comanches and Texas Rangers are known to have covered seventy-five miles in a day. In the 1800s, a poorly mounted Texas Ranger was a dead Ranger, and a poorly mounted Comanche stayed home with the women.

20 Sparks, *The War . . . As I Saw It*, pp. 23–24; Griscom, *Fighting with Ross' Texas Cavalry Brigade*, p. 4.

21 Griscom, *Fighting with Ross' Texas Cavalry Brigade*, p. 4; Sparks, *The War . . . As I Saw It*, pp. 24, 27; Capt. Otis G. Welch commanded Cooper's escort—a Texas cavalry company of about a hundred men; *CSR-Texas*, Ser. M227, roll 38. Otis G. Welch served in Company E of De Morse's Regiment, later the Twenty-ninth Texas Cavalry, he was ranked a lieutenant colonel at the end of the war; Gaines, *The Confederate Cherokees*, p. 37; *O.R.*, vol. 8, p. 5.

22 Clement Eaton, *Jefferson Davis* (New York: The Free Press, Collier Macmillan Publishers, 1977), p. 58. Jefferson Davis commanded the Mississippi Rifles, an elite regiment made up of young gentlemen; Gaines, *The Confederate Cherokees*, pp. 30, 71; Warner, *Generals in Gray*, pp. 61–62.

23 Sparks, *The War . . . As I Saw It*, pp. 24–27; Griscom, *Fighting with Ross' Texas Cavalry Brigade*, p. 4.

24 Sparks, *The War . . . As I Saw It*, pp. 24–27; Griscom, *Fighting with Ross' Texas Cavalry Brigade*, pp. 4–5; Le Grand, *Military Hand-Book*, p. 76.

25 Sparks, *The War . . . As I Saw It*, pp. 25–26; Griscom, *Fighting with Ross' Texas Cavalry Brigade*, p. 4.

26 Robert W. Frazer, *Forts of the West* (Norman: University of Oklahoma Press, 1965), p. 164; Ernest Wallace and E. Adamson Hoebel, *The Comanches, Lords of the Southern Plains* (Norman: University of Oklahoma Press, 1952), pp. ix, 3–4, 8, 288–89; Max L. Moorehead, *The Presidio* (Norman: University of Oklahoma Press, 1975), pp. 29–30, 54, 60.

27 Sparks, *The War . . . As I Saw It*, p. 27; Griscom, *Fighting with Ross' Texas Cavalry Brigade*, p. 213; *CSR-Texas*, roll 58. Records of Edmund M. King, Company A, list him as a bugler on the November–December 1861 roll; John

D. Billings, *Hardtack and Coffee* (Boston: George M. Smith and Co., 1887. Reprint. Time-Life Books Inc., 1982), p. 166. Federal infantry were awakened by assembly call. The only mention Griscom makes in his diary of an awakening call is Boots and Saddles, used in an emergency; Barron, *Lone Star Defenders*, p. 98.

28   Sparks, *The War . . . As I Saw It*, pp. 27–29.

29   Ibid.

30   *O.R.*, vol. 8, p. 5; Griscom, *Fighting with Ross' Texas Cavalry Brigade*, p. 4.

31   Griscom, *Fighting with Ross' Texas Cavalry Brigade*, pp. 4–5; Sparks, *The War . . . As I Saw It*, p. 30; *O.R.*, vol. 8, pp. 5–6.

32   *O.R.*, vol. 8, p. 5; Griscom, *Fighting with Ross' Texas Cavalry Brigade*, pp. 5–6; Sparks, *The War . . . As I Saw It*, pp. 31–33.

33   *O.R.*, vol. 8, pp. 5, 14; Sparks, *The War . . . As I Saw It*, p. 33; Gaines, *The Confederate Cherokees*, p. 39; Wright, *Texas in the War 1861–1865*, plate no. 46.

34   Keen, *The 6th Texas Cavalry*, pp. 20–21; Warren Coffman to William Coffman, from Lochards Mission, Creek Nation, December 7, 1861, in Ninth Texas Cavalry files, H. B. Simpson History Complex, Hillsboro, Texas.

35   Sparks, *The War . . . As I Saw It*, p. 20–21, 32–34.

36   *O.R.*, vol. 8, pp. 5–6; Griscom, *Fighting with Ross' Texas Cavalry Brigade*, p. 5; Richard Loyall Jurney, *History of Titus County, Texas 1846–1960* (Dallas: Royal Publishing Co., 1961), p. 16; Benjamin R. Vines, letter to his parents, November 30, 1861, in Virginia Gammons, "A Letter Home from Confederate Soldier Benjamin Rush Vines, of Company I, Ninth Texas Cavalry," *Our Heritage*, February 1991.

37   *O.R.*, vol. 8, pp. 5–6.

38   Ibid., pp. 5–6, 14–15; Griscom, *Fighting with Ross' Texas Cavalry Brigade*, pp. 5–6.

39   See *O.R.*, vol. 8, pp. 14–15, for the report of Capt. R. A. Young; Benjamin R. Vines to his parents, November 30, 1861, in Gammons, "A Letter Home," *Our Heritage*.

40   Sparks, *The War . . . As I Saw It*, p. 35; *O.R.*, vol. 8, p. 6.

41   *O.R.*, vol. 8, p. 6; Le Grand, *The Military Hand-Book*, p. 118; Griscom, *Fighting with Ross' Texas Cavalry Brigade*, p. 5.

42   Griscom, *Fighting with Ross' Texas Cavalry Brigade*, pp. 5–6; Rose, *Ross' Texas Brigade*, p. 50; Sparks, *The War . . . As I Saw It*, p. 35; Warren Coffman to William Coffman, December 7, 1861, H. B. Simpson History Complex; Barron, *Lone Star Defenders*, p. 43; Edward Porter Alexander, *Fighting for the Confederacy* (Chapel Hill: University of North Carolina, 1989), p. 208. Alexander

wrote: "There is a sort of higher power of sleep, with qualities as entirely different from ordinary sleep as light is from heat. I don't think that mere fatigue, or loss of ordinary sleep, produces this higher power of sleep, because I have never been able to obtain it except in connection with the excitement attendant on a battle."

43 *CSR-Texas,* roll 58. Hardy Holman, age twenty-two, belonged to Company A.

44 *O.R.,* vol. 8, p. 7; *CSR-Texas,* rolls 57–58; Griscom, *Fighting with Ross' Texas Cavalry Brigade,* p. 6. Griscom reported the losses in the Ninth Texas. Men killed were Capt. Charles S. Stewart of Company I, J. H. Crow (age sixteen) of Company D, and James Jackson and E. Reed of Company C. Wounded men were Hardy S. Holman and John C. Friend of Company A.

45 *O.R.,* vol. 8, p. 6. Cooper reported: "Prisoners taken since the battle concur in stating the loss of the enemy to have been about 110 killed and wounded"; Woodward, *The Cherokees,* p. 271. A few Delawares, Kickapoos, Shawnees, and Wichitas also fought with Opothleyohola. See *O.R.,* vol. 8, pp. 5–15, for officers' reports of the battle of Round Mountain.

46 *O.R.,* vol. 8, p. 6; Griscom, *Fighting with Ross' Texas Cavalry Brigade,* p. 6; Sparks, *The War . . . As I Saw It,* p. 36.

47 Sparks, *The War . . . As I Saw It,* p. 36; *O.R.,* vol. 8, p. 6; Griscom, *Fighting with Ross' Texas Cavalry Brigade,* p. 6; Warren Coffman to William Coffman, December 7, 1861, H. B. Simpson History Complex.

48 Sparks, *The War . . . As I Saw It,* pp. 36–37; Griscom, *Fighting with Ross' Texas Cavalry Brigade,* p. 6; Warren Coffman to William Coffman, December 7, 1861, H. B. Simpson History Complex.

49 The battle of Round Mountain also is known as the battle of Red Fork; Sparks, *The War . . . As I Saw It,* pp. 36–37; Russell, *The History of Titus County,* p. 16. Stewart's body remained in the lonesome grave.

50 Griscom, *Fighting with Ross' Texas Cavalry Brigade,* p. 6.

51 Sparks, *The War . . . As I Saw It,* pp. 37–38; Griscom, *Fighting with Ross' Texas Cavalry Brigade,* p. 6; *O.R.,* vol. 8, pp. 6–7; W. J. Lyttle of Welch's squadron and Private Smith of the Creek regiment were severely wounded.

52 Griscom, *Fighting with Ross' Texas Cavalry Brigade,* p. 6; Sparks, *The War . . . As I Saw It,* pp. 37–38; Sparks, *The War . . . As I Saw It,* p. 37. Sparks reported that one man had a broken jaw, but he did not remember the wounded man's name. Sparks did remember that the man "lived for many years after the war." The tone of Sparks's story indicates that the man with the broken jaw was one of the Texans. John Friend was the only Texan severely wounded. Friend's records in *CSR-Texas,* roll 57, show that Friend was furloughed December 18, 1861, at Fort Gibson. He remained in Texas and was discharged on medical disability in August 1862.

53 *O.R.*, vol. 8, p. 7; Gaines, *The Confederate Cherokees*, p. 39; Griscom, *Fighting with Ross' Texas Cavalry Brigade*, p. 6.

54 Griscom, *Fighting with Ross' Texas Cavalry Brigade*, p. 6; Sparks, *The War . . . As I Saw It*, p. 39.

55 Sparks, *The War . . . As I Saw It*, pp. 38–39; Griscom, *Fighting with Ross' Texas Cavalry Brigade*, pp. 6–7; *O.R.*, vol. 8, p. 7. In his report, Cooper stated that the Ninth Texas had gone to "Tallahassa, Missouri." Tullahassee Mission was in Indian Territory.

56 Foreman, *The Five Civilized Tribes*, pp. 179, 194. The Presbyterian Tullahassee Mission was located at the Creek town of Koweta, half a mile east of the Arkansas River and twenty-five miles northwest of Fort Gibson. The imposing three-story brick structure was built in 1850 to house a boarding school for eighty Indian children. It was ninety-four feet long and thirty-four feet wide, with an attached two-story kitchen eighteen feet by thirty feet. Orchards and prosperous farms surrounded the mission; Griscom, *Fighting with Ross' Texas Cavalry Brigade*, pp. 6–7; Kate Cumming, *Kate: The Journal of a Confederate Nurse*, Richard Barksdale Harwell, editor (Baton Rouge: Louisiana State University Press, 1959), p. 18; *CSR-Texas*, rolls 57, 58. Robert R. Fisher of Company A died at the mission December 13, 1861, at the age of twenty.

57 Griscom, *Fighting with Ross' Texas Cavalry Brigade*, p. 7; Sparks, *The War . . . As I Saw It*, p. 40.

58 Gaines, *The Confederate Cherokees*, p. 41; Warren Coffman to William Coffman, December 7, 1861, H. B. Simpson History Complex; *O.R.*, vol. 8, p. 7. Cooper's force consisted of the Choctaw and Chickasaw Mounted Rifles, 430 men; the Choctaw Battalion, 50 men; the First Creek Regiment, commanded by Col. D. N. McIntosh, 285 men; and Capt. James M. C. Smith's 15 Creeks.

59 Woodward, *The Cherokees*, p. 272; Griscom, *Fighting with Ross' Texas Cavalry Brigade*, p. 7; Sparks, *The War . . . As I Saw It*, p. 42; *O.R.*, vol. 8, pp. 7, 18; Gaines, *The Confederate Cherokees*, p. 45.

60 Griscom, *Fighting with Ross' Texas Cavalry Brigade*, p. 8; Sparks, *The War . . . As I Saw It*, pp. 42–43; Gaines, *The Confederate Cherokees*, pp. 45–52 (see pp. 41–54 for this campaign); *O.R.*, vol. 8, pp. 7–8, 18–19.

61 *O.R.*, vol. 8, pp. 9–11, 18–19; Griscom, *Fighting with Ross' Texas Cavalry Brigade*, pp. 8–9; Sparks, *The War . . . As I Saw It*, pp. 43–44.

62 Griscom, *Fighting with Ross' Texas Cavalry Brigade*, p. 8; Eaton, *Jefferson Davis*, pp. 64–65.

63 *O.R.*, vol. 8, p. 10; Sparks, *The War . . . As I Saw It*, p. 43. Sparks had the battles mixed up. He referred to the battle on Bird Creek as the battle of Round Mountain, which was the earlier engagement; *O.R.*, vol. 8, p. 4. In the *Official Records*, the action of December 9, 1861, is noted as "Engagement at Chusto-Talsah (Bird Creek or High Shoal)"; Gaines, *The Confederate Chero-*

kees, p. 52. Gaines calls the engagement the battle of Caving Banks; Griscom, *Fighting with Ross' Texas Cavalry Brigade*, pp. 8–9, 218–19. Griscom recorded in his diary that Company C lost Henry P. Mallory and T. Chaffin, killed, and J. E. Barnett, G. W. Lee, J. Hanson, and Sgt. J. W. Beckett, wounded. Two men in Company A were wounded, David Boaz and John King, for a total loss in the Ninth Texas of two killed and six wounded; *CSR-Texas,* rolls 56, 58. John N. King, age thirty-five, was discharged July 14, 1862. David Boaz, age twenty-three, of Birdville, went home on furlough December 18, 1861, on a certificate of disability. He remained in Texas, unable to serve, and was discharged in September or October 1862; White, *Index to Texas CSA Pension Files,* file #974805. David Boaz lived to the age of sixty-eight; Gaines, *The Confederate Cherokees,* p. 52. Gaines estimates the Federal Indians had two hundred to three hundred wounded and states that Cooper's men buried twenty-seven bodies.

64 *O.R.,* vol. 8, p. 19.

65 *O.R.,* vol. 8, p. 10; Doice Nevins, interview by author, August 6, 1994, at Dumas, Texas. At age eighteen Nevins served in World War II as a rifleman with the Fourth Marine Division in the invasion force at Saipan, June–July 1944, and the invasion force at Tinian. Nevins states that after his second action he thought, "Well, that's over. Now let's see how many of the enemy we can kill and *win* this war! Winning was what was on our minds. We were hardened to the fighting." See Rose, *Ross' Texas Brigade,* p. 46, for a veteran's feeling about killing.

66 Sparks, *The War . . . As I Saw It,* pp. 43–44.

67 Ibid.

68 *O.R.,* vol. 8, p. 7; Griscom, *Fighting with Ross' Texas Cavalry Brigade,* p. 9; Gaines, *The Confederate Cherokees,* p. 44. The deserter from Young's Regiment was Eli Smith.

69 Griscom, *Fighting with Ross' Texas Cavalry Brigade,* p. 9.

70 Ibid.; *O.R.,* vol. 1, p. 637. The U.S. Army abandoned all the forts in Indian Territory in April and May 1861; Foreman, *Fort Gibson,* pp. 11–20; Frazer, *Forts of the West,* pp. 120–21; Gaines, *The Confederate Cherokees,* p. 25; Chris Morgan, ranger at Oklahoma Historical Military Park, Oklahoma Historical Society, Fort Gibson, Oklahoma, interview with author, August 4, 1994. A replica of Fort Gibson was constructed by the Works Progress Administration in the 1930s. The replica is a short distance farther from the river than the original fort.

71 Griscom, *Fighting with Ross' Texas Cavalry Brigade,* p. 9; Foreman, *Fort Gibson,* pp. 22–23. The Cherokees named their town at Fort Gibson Kee-too-wah; Sparks, *The War . . . As I Saw It,* p. 41.

72 Foreman, *Fort Gibson,* pp. 22–23. The stone commissary and barracks were built in the late 1840s; Sparks, *The War . . . As I Saw It,* p. 41; Griscom,

Fighting with Ross' Texas Cavalry Brigade, p. 9; Rose, *Ross' Texas Brigade,* pp. 50–51; Gaines, *The Confederate Cherokees,* p. 40; Morgan, ranger at Fort Gibson, interview with author.

73 Foreman, *Fort Gibson,* pp. 3–5.

74 Thomas B. Hall, M.D., *Medicine on the Santa Fe Trail* (Morningside Bookshop, 1971. Second edition, revised and corrected, 1987), pp. 81–90. In June 1834, Gen. Henry Leavenworth and Col. Henry Dodge, both well-known on the frontier, organized their now-famous Dragoon Expedition at Fort Gibson. While at the fort, many of their men were infected with malaria. On the trail west, the disease devastated the mounted column. Leavenworth died of "a bilious fever" in July at a "sick camp." A hundred men had died before the campaign ended.

75 Griscom, *Fighting with Ross' Texas Cavalry Brigade,* p. 9; Sparks, *The War . . . As I Saw It,* pp. 40–41.

76 Sparks, *The War . . . As I Saw It,* p, 49; *CSR-Texas,* rolls 56–60. R. L. Akers of Company A served as a hospital steward when the regiment was at Fort Gibson. J. F. M. Archer died on December 17, 1861, and a week later M. M. McDaniel died. In another week L. H. Pennington died. D. J. Bradley also died of disease in Indian Territory.

77 Griscom, *Fighting with Ross' Texas Cavalry Brigade,* p. 9; Sparks, *The War . . . As I Saw It,* pp. 41, 43–45.

78 Morgan, ranger at Fort Gibson, interview with author; the description of the old fort is from Griscom, *Fighting with Ross' Texas Cavalry Brigade,* p. 9, and Sparks, *The War . . . As I Saw It,* p. 41.

79 Foreman, *Fort Gibson,* pp. 4–9; Wheeler, *Cavalry Tactics,* Part Third, pp. 23–24. Dragoons were trained to act as both horse and foot soldiers. Technically, regiments of mounted rifles used horses to rapidly reach their objective, then fought on foot. Cavalry fought on horseback. In the antebellum U.S. Army, all three operated in a similar manner.

80 Foreman, *Fort Gibson,* pp. 13–19, 36. Other officers, whose judgments would dramatically affect the Ninth Texas cavalrymen in the Civil War, passed through or served at Fort Gibson, including the famous Second Cavalry's officers, all general officers during the Civil War: Col. Albert Sidney Johnston, Col. Robert E. Lee, Maj. George H. Thomas, Lt. John Bell Hood, and Col. Joseph E. Johnston. All the Second Cavalry officers except George Thomas fought for the Confederacy. Thomas was a Virginian, but he refused to turn against the Union.

81 Griscom, *Fighting with Ross' Texas Cavalry Brigade,* p. 9; Rose, *Ross' Texas Brigade,* p. 41; Cater, *As I Saw It,* p. 101; *O.R.,* vol. 8, pp. 4, 709.

82 Griscom, *Fighting with Ross' Texas Cavalry Brigade,* p. 10; Warner, *Generals in Gray,* pp. 202–203.

83 Warner, *Generals in Gray*, pp. 202–203; Richard Warren, "Ben McCulloch," in W. D. Nunn, editor, *Ten More Texans in Gray* (Hillsboro, Tex.: Hill Junior College Press, 1980), pp. 74, 86. Col. James McIntosh was in command in Arkansas after McCulloch left for Richmond on December 1, 1861, to counter unfavorable reports of his actions circulating in the Confederate capital. McCulloch and President Jefferson Davis had served in the Mexican War together but had been at odds since 1855; Foreman, *Fort Gibson*, p. 34. James A. McIntosh's father, Col. James S. McIntosh of the Seventh Infantry, commanded Fort Gibson in 1838.

84 *O.R.*, vol. 8, pp. 11–12, 713. For McIntosh's report, see pp. 22–25, 30–31. McIntosh reported that his brigade contained five companies of Col. Elkanah Greer's Third Texas, commanded by Lt. Col. Walter P. Lane, the available force of Col. B. Warren Stone's Sixth Texas, commanded by Lt. Col. John S. Griffith, seven companies of Lt. Col. William C. Young's Eleventh Texas, four companies of McIntosh's Second Arkansas Cavalry, Capt. H. S. Bennett's Company of Texas Cavalry from Lamar County, and 220 men in Maj. John C. Whitfield's Battalion, 1,600 total. The name Bennett in the *Official Records* is also spelled Burnett; Gaines, *The Confederate Cherokees*, p. 58. Cooper was camped at Choska, twenty miles north of Fort Gibson. Col. John Drew's First Cherokee Mounted Rifles joined Cooper there; Griscom, *Fighting with Ross' Texas Cavalry Brigade*, p. 10;

85 *O.R.*, vol. 8, pp. 7, 12; Sparks, *The War . . . As I Saw It*, pp. 41–42; Gaines, *The Confederate Cherokees*, p. 32.

86 Griscom, *Fighting with Ross' Texas Cavalry Brigade*, p. 10.

87 Ibid.; Sparks, *The War . . . As I Saw It*, p. 46

88 Sparks, *The War . . . As I Saw It*, pp. 46-47.

89 Griscom, *Fighting with Ross' Texas Cavalry Brigade*, p. 10; Walter P. Lane, *The Adventures and Recollections of General Walter P. Lane* (Marshall, Tex.: n.p., 1887), p. 86; Gaines, *The Confederate Cherokees*, p. 58.

90 Gaines, *The Confederate Cherokees*, p. 58. Chustenahlah was on Hominy Creek, in the Cherokee Cooweescoowee District; Rose, *Ross' Texas Brigade*, pp. 11, 43–44, 127–28. Lt. Col. Walter P. Lane of the Third Texas Cavalry was a Texas Irishman known as a fierce fighter; *O.R.*, vol. 8, pp. 23–24; Lane, *Adventures and Recollections*, p. 87.

91 Rose, *Ross' Texas Brigade*, pp. 128–29; *O.R.*, vol. 8, pp. 23–24. McIntosh reported he killed "upwards of 250" of the enemy.

92 The quotes are from Hale, *The Third Texas Cavalry*, p. 82.

93 Rose, *Ross' Texas Brigade*, pp. 11, 43–45, 48; Roy Grimes, *300 Years in Victoria County* (Austin: Nortex Press, 1985), pp. 96, 204. Victor M. Rose enlisted in June 1861 in Harrison County, Texas, where his wealthy family had connections.

94 John A. Miller, "A Memoir of the Days of '61," typescript, Confederate Research Center, n.d., p. 3.

95   Ibid., pp. 3–4; Rose, *Ross' Texas Brigade,* pp. 44–45.

96   Rose, *Ross' Texas Brigade,* pp. 44–45.

97   *O.R.,* vol. 8, pp. 24, 31; Gaines, *The Confederate Cherokees,* p. 58.

98   *O.R.,* vol. 8, pp. 9–10; Griscom, *Fighting with Ross' Texas Cavalry Brigade,* p. 10.

99   Griscom, *Fighting with Ross' Texas Cavalry Brigade,* p. 10; *O.R.,* vol. 8, pp. 12–13; Lane, *Adventures and Recollections,* p. 89.

100 Lane, *Adventures and Recollections,* p. 89; Rose, *Ross' Texas Brigade,* p. 45.

101 Rose, *Ross' Texas Brigade,* pp. 42; *O.R.,* vol. 8, pp. 12–13; Griscom, *Fighting with Ross' Texas Cavalry Brigade,* pp. 10–11; Sparks, *The War . . . As I Saw It,* p. 47.

102 Sparks, *The War . . . As I Saw It,* p. 47; *O.R.,* vol. 8, p. 13.

103 *O.R.,* vol. 8, p. 13; Sparks, *The War . . . As I Saw It,* p. 47; Griscom, *Fighting with Ross' Texas Cavalry Brigade,* p. 11.

104 Griscom, *Fighting with Ross' Texas Cavalry Brigade,* p. 11.

105 *O.R.,* vol. 8, p. 728; *CSR-Texas,* rolls 56–60. At muster on October 14, 1861, eighty-two men and four officers were on the Company A roll. While the regiment was in Indian Territory, five men enrolled in the company: Frank O. Clare, Robert W. Fisher, Lorenzo Newton, George W. Pointer, and W. Smith Cummings. Six men died of disease: J. F. M. Archer, D. J. Bradley, R. W. Fisher, John P. Hudgins, M. M. McDaniel, and L. H. Pennington. John C. Friend and David Boaz were wounded and furloughed, leaving eighty enlisted men and four officers in the regiment.

106 *CSR-Texas,* roll 56. Records of the Adjutant General's Office, Thomas G. Berry, Capt., Company A, Ninth Texas Cavalry.

107 Griscom, *Fighting with Ross' Texas Cavalry Brigade,* p. 11.

108 Ibid.; *O.R.,* vol. 8, pp. 718–19. On December 21, 1861, Sims's Regiment was ordered to join McCulloch's command at Fort Smith, Arkansas.

Chapter 3: The Seat of War

1   Sparks, *The War . . . As I Saw It,* p. 49; Griscom, *Fighting with Ross' Texas Cavalry Brigade,* p. 11.

2   Griscom, *Fighting with Ross' Texas Cavalry Brigade,* p. 11 ; Rose, *Ross' Texas Brigade,* p. 42. Rose reports that the Third Texas crossed at Van Buren; *O.R.,* vol. 8, p. 728. The Ninth Texas reported 677 men present on December 31, 1861. A few men had been furloughed to go home from Indian Territory.

3   Griscom, *Fighting with Ross' Texas Cavalry Brigade*, p. 11; Sparks, *The War . . . As I Saw It*, p. 49.

4   Griscom, *Fighting with Ross' Texas Cavalry Brigade*, pp. 11–12; Sparks, *The War . . . As I Saw It*, p. 49.

5   Griscom, *Fighting with Ross' Texas Cavalry Brigade*, p. 11, 39(n); Oates, "Recruiting Confederate Cavalry in Texas," *Southwestern Historical Quarterly*, p. 469; Warren, "Ben McCulloch," in Nunn, *Ten More Texas Generals*, p. 86. McCulloch left for Richmond, Virginia, December 1, 1861, leaving Col. James M. McIntosh in command in Arkansas.

6   *O.R.*, vol. 8, p. 728. Field reports of troops stationed in western Arkansas on January 1, 1861, give the present and aggregate: Col. Thomas J. Churchill's First Arkansas Mounted Riflemen, 800-845, McIntosh's Second Arkansas Mounted Riflemen, 820-862, Col. Elkanah Greer's Third Texas Cavalry, listed by its old designation of "South-Kansas-Texas Regt.," 960-1,003, Col. William Sims's Ninth Texas Cavalry, listed by its old designation of "Fourth Texas," 677-713, Col. B. Warren Stone's Sixth Texas Cavalry, 880-927, Burnett's company of Texas cavalry, 79-83, and Whitfield's Battalion of Texas cavalry, 280-297; Rose, *Ross' Texas Brigade*, pp. 40–41; Hale, *The Third Texas Cavalry*, pp. 76; Garrett to William Gibbard, December 14, 1861, from Camp Washington, Maysville, Cherokee Nation, in Garrett, *Civil War Letters*, p. 37; Barron, *Lone Star Defenders*, p. 62. The Third Texas Cavalry's headquarters on Frog Bayou were twelve miles below Van Buren; Douglas John Cater, *As It Was* (William D. Cater, 1981. Reprint. Austin: State House Press, 1990), p. 99.

7   Griscom, *Fighting with Ross' Texas Cavalry Brigade*, p. 11; Sparks, *The War . . . As I Saw It*, p. 49.

8   Griscom, *Fighting with Ross' Texas Cavalry Brigade*, pp. 11–12; Sparks, *The War . . . As I Saw It*, p. 49. Modern Clarksville is fifty-four miles east of Van Buren on Interstate 40. In 1862, the narrow dirt road was several miles longer.

9   Sparks, *The War . . . As I Saw It*, p. 49; Griscom, *Fighting with Ross' Texas Cavalry Brigade*, p. 12.

10 Griscom, *Fighting with Ross' Texas Cavalry Brigade*, p. 12; Sparks, *The War . . . As I Saw It*, p. 49; *CSR-Texas*, rolls 57, 59. Peter S. Moore and Ed Eckhardt of Company A were carpenters; Cater, *As It Was*, p. 99.

11 Griscom, *Fighting with Ross' Texas Cavalry Brigade*, p. 12; Sparks, *The War . . . As I Saw It*, pp. 49–50.

12 Young, *Grapevine Area History*, pp. 15, 236–37. John P. Hudgins's family lived near the Rogerses. Reuben's and John's fathers, both preachers, helped start Minter's Chapel Methodist Church, which is four miles south of Grapevine; *CSR-Texas*, rolls 58, 59.

13 Bell, Irving Wiley, *The Life of Johnny Reb* (Baton Rouge: Louisiana State University Press, 1943. 1986 printing), pp. 256–58; Sparks, *The War . . . As I Saw It,* pp. 49–50.

14 Wiley, *Johnny Reb,* pp. 256–58.

15 Sparks, *The War . . . As I Saw It,* p. 50; Young, *Grapevine Area History,* p. 237; *CSR-Texas,* roll 58. See Garrett, *Fort Worth: A Frontier Triumph,* p. 219, and Griscom, *Fighting with Ross' Texas Cavalry Brigade,* p. 211, for Chaplain T. A. Ish. Ish was appointed chaplain of the Ninth at the regimental organization of October 14, 1861, and resigned August 1, 1862.

16 Hale, *The Third Texas Cavalry,* p. 78; Rose, *Ross' Texas Brigade,* p. 45; *Handbook of Texas,* vol. 1, p. 730. Elkanah Greer, born in 1825, received his colonel's commission in July 1861 from President Jefferson Davis. At the expiration of his first year in service, Greer declined reelection and returned to Texas. He was promoted to brigadier general and served as chief of the Conscription Bureau for the Trans-Mississippi District.

17 Garrett to William Gibbard, October 14, 1861, Maysville, Cherokee Nation, in Garrett, *Civil War Letters,* p. 29, and December 14, 1861, from Camp Washington, p. 37; Barron, *Lone Star Defenders,* p. 59; *CSR-Texas,* rolls 57–60; Hardy Holman was present on the rest of the muster rolls and was paroled at the end of the war; White, *Index to Texas CSA Pension Files,* file #337116, Hardy S. Holman. Holman returned to Tarrant County and lived to age seventy-eight.

18 Griscom, *Fighting with Ross' Texas Cavalry Brigade,* p. 12; Rose, *Ross' Texas Brigade,* p. 41; Garrett to William Gibbard, January 26, 1862, in Garrett, *Civil War Letters,* p. 46.

19 Wiley, *Johnny Reb,* pp. 90–107.

20 Coggins, *Arms and Equipment of the Civil War,* p. 124. One sutler per regiment was appointed either by the governor of the state or by a regimental or brigade officer. A board of officers set prices that could be charged, but sutlers often charged outrageous amounts. The sale of liquor was not allowed; Griscom, *Fighting with Ross' Texas Cavalry Brigade,* p. 12.

21 Sparks, *The War . . . As I Saw It,* p. 50; Cater, *As It Was,* pp. 109–10; *CSR-Texas,* rolls 57–60. Enrollment papers listed the value of each man's horse or horses; Griscom, *Fighting with Ross' Texas Cavalry Brigade,* p. 12.

22 Griscom, *Fighting with Ross' Texas Cavalry Brigade,* p. 12; Rose, *Ross' Texas Brigade,* p. 46.

23 Rose, *Ross' Texas Brigade,* p. 46.

24 *O.R.,* vol. 10, pt. 2, p. 489. On May 4, 1862, the Ninth Texas reported 657 men present and 869 aggregate; *CSR-Texas,* rolls 56–60. Other men in Company A whose names appear on the March–April 1862 roll for the first time

are Quinton Booth, W. R. Carlton, F. M. Dyer, John Grimes, R. William Harrison, Joseph D. Henry, W. Smith Cummings, James P. King, William L. Parker, William Greenup (forty-three years old and likely a brother of Phil), Richard Boaz (whose younger brother, David, was wounded in Indian Territory), and Isaac H. Bradley (surely kin to D. J. Bradley, who died of disease in Indian Territory); White, *Index to Texas CSA Pension Files,* file #961339, Sam Knight.

25 Sparks, *The War . . . As I Saw It,* p. 30; Cater, *As It Was,* p. 113; Henry Morgan to Ellen Morgan, in John A. Cawthorn, editor, "Letters of a North Louisiana Private to His Wife, 1862–1865," *Mississippi Valley Historical Review,* March 1944 (University of Iowa, Iowa City), p. 543.

26 Garrett to Mary E. Gibbard, October 28, 1861, in Garrett, *Civil War Letters,* p. 35.

27 Knight, *Fort Worth: Outpost on the Trinity,* p. 52; Garrett, *Fort Worth: A Frontier Triumph,* p. 220; Garrett to William Gibbard, October 14, 1861, Maysville, Cherokee Nation, in Garrett, *Civil War Letters,* p. 30.

28 Griscom, *Fighting with Ross' Texas Cavalry Brigade,* p. 12.

29 Crabb, Rogers family files; Kate Rogers Michaelias, half sister of Reuben and Jesse Rogers, interviews by author, Amarillo, Texas, 1958–1965.

30 Michaelias, interviews by author. William M. Rogers took a load of supplies to Reuben in Arkansas. The visit took place at Cantonment Slidell, because during the rest of Reuben's time in Arkansas the regiment moved too fast for his father to catch up.

31 Griscom, *Fighting with Ross' Texas Cavalry Brigade,* p. 12; William Shea and Earl J. Hess, *Pea Ridge: Civil War Campaigning in the West* (Chapel Hill: University of North Carolina Press, 1992), pp. 38–39. See *O.R.,* vol. 8, p. 302, for Col. B. Warren Stone's report stating that he was ordered to hurry. Orders to the Ninth Texas to hurry north have not been found.

32 Modern Interstate 44 generally follows the route of the old road; Warner, *Generals in Blue,* p. 107; Shea and Hess, *Pea Ridge,* p. 7.

33 Warner, *Generals in Blue,* pp. 107–108; Shea and Hess, *Pea Ridge,* pp. 2–7; Robert G. Hartje, *Van Dorn: The Life and Times of a Confederate General* (Nashville: Vanderbilt University Press, 1967), p. 112.

34 Warner, *Generals in Gray,* pp. 246–47; Albert Castel, *General Sterling Price and the Civil War in the West* (Baton Rouge: Louisiana State University Press, 1968), pp. 4–5, 69; Shea and Hess, *Pea Ridge,* pp. 15–16.

35 Shea and Hess, *Pea Ridge,* p. 14.

36 Ibid., p. 33; Rose, *Ross' Texas Brigade,* pp. 54–55.

37 Shea and Hess, *Pea Ridge,* pp. 23–24, 34–35.

38 Quote from Shea and Hess, *Pea Ridge,* p. 34.

39 Ibid., pp. 15–19; Warren, "Ben McCulloch," in Nunn, editor, *Ten More Generals in Gray,* pp. 77–86; Castel, *General Sterling Price,* p. 69; *O.R.,* vol. 3, pp. 743–49.

40 Shea and Hess, *Pea Ridge,* p. 19.

41 Walter Prescott Webb, *The Texas Rangers* (Austin: University of Texas Press, 1935. Paperback edition, 1989), pp. 79–96, 84–113; Oates, "Recruiting Confederate Cavalry in Texas," *Southwestern Historical Quarterly,* p. 463.

42 Wright, *Texas in the War 1861–1865,* pp. 11–12; Warner, *Generals in Gray,* pp. 200–201.

43 Hartje, *Van Dorn,* pp. 103–104. See *O.R.,* vol. 3, pp. 734–49, for problems between Price and McCulloch.

Chapter 4: A West Point General

1 Hartje, *Van Dorn,* pp. 106–107.

2 *O.R.,* vol. 8, p. 283.

3 Hartje, *Van Dorn,* pp. 115–16; Dabney Herndon Maury, *Recollections of a Virginian in the Mexican, Indian, and Civil Wars* (New York: Charles Scribner's Sons, 1894), p. 157; Warner, *Generals in Gray,* p. 215.

4 Maury, *Recollections,* p. 161; Hartje, *Van Dorn,* pp. 115–16.

5 Griscom, *Fighting with Ross' Texas Cavalry Brigade,* pp. 12–13.

6 *CSR-Texas,* rolls 57–60.

7 Griscom, *Fighting with Ross' Texas Cavalry Brigade,* p. 12; Rose, *Ross' Texas Brigade,* p. 53.

8 Shea and Hess, *Pea Ridge,* pp. 46, 48; Hale, *The Third Texas Cavalry,* p. 57; Griscom, *Fighting with Ross' Texas Cavalry Brigade,* p. 12; Rose, *Ross' Texas Brigade,* pp. 53–54.

9 *O.R.,* vol. 8, p. 302.

10 John W. Bond, "Elkhorn Tavern History," in *The Battle of Pea Ridge 1862* (Rogers, Ark.: Shofner's, n.d.), pp. 13–14.

11 Shea and Hess, *Pea Ridge,* p. 46; *O.R.,* vol. 8, p. 302.

12 Shea and Hess, *Pea Ridge,* pp. 46–48; L. S. "Sul" Ross to Lizzie Ross, March 1, 1862, in Perry Wayne Shelton, "Personal Civil War Letters of Lawrence

Sullivan Ross." (Waco, Tex.: Master's Thesis, Baylor University, August 1938. Limited printing by Shelly Morrison, ed., and Richard Morrison. Austin: 1994. H. B. Simpson History Complex, Hillsboro, Texas), p. 20.

13 Shea and Hess, *Pea Ridge,* pp. 48, 50; *O.R.,* vol. 8, p. 302; William Watson, *Life in the Confederate Army* (London: Chapman and Hall, 1887. Reprint. Baton Rouge: Louisiana State University Press, 1995), p. 278.

14 Wheeler, *Cavalry Tactics,* Part Third, p. 46. Wheeler states: "When an officer in command of an outpost shall arrive at the position he will immediately throw forward from one third to one half of his command, divided into three or more pickets, a distance of 500 yards. One of these pickets will be placed on the main avenue of approach and the others on its right and left in favorable positions, and each of the pickets will throw forward videttes a still further distance of 400 or 500 yards"; Griscom, *Fighting with Ross' Texas Cavalry Brigade,* p. 12; *O.R.,* vol. 8, p. 303.

15 Shea and Hess, *Pea Ridge,* p. 48; *O.R.,* vol. 8, pp. 297, 303; Griscom, *Fighting with Ross' Texas Cavalry Brigade,* p. 12.

16 Griscom, *Fighting with Ross' Texas Cavalry Brigade,* pp. 12–13.

17 *O.R.,* vol. 8, pp. 302, 763.

18 Griscom, *Fighting with Ross' Texas Cavalry Brigade,* pp. 92–93(n); Rose, *Ross' Texas Brigade,* pp. 61, 147–48. After serving in the Army of the West, the four Texas regiments served in the Army of Mississippi and the Army of Tennessee. The Eleventh Texas Cavalry served in the Army of Tennessee. See Rose, *Ross' Texas Brigade,* p. 64, for feelings of unity among the men in the four regiments. See Hale, *The Third Texas Cavalry,* p. 77; Rose, *Ross' Texas Brigade,* pp. 147–48, 154; and Warner, *Generals in Gray,* pp. 333–34, for John W. Whitfield and his Legion. Whitfield's Legion, earlier known as Whitfield's Battalion and later known as the First Texas Legion, was designated the Twenty-seventh Texas Cavalry Regiment. In 1861, Whitfield raised a battalion of four companies (339 men) in his former state of Kansas. Soon after the battalion fought at Pea Ridge, eight companies of Texans were added to the command, making what was called Whitfield's Legion. A legion contains more than the standard ten companies in a regiment.

19 Lawrence Sullivan Ross preferred to be called "Sul," and through the years Texans have known him by no other name. Few Texans recognize the name L. S. Ross, but most immediately know who Sul Ross was. Sul Ross University is located at Alpine, Texas. Rose, *Ross' Texas Brigade,* p. 63; *CSR-Texas,* rolls 56–60; Sparks, *The War . . . As I Saw It,* p. 178.

20 Ross to Lizzie Ross, March 1, 1862, in Shelton, "Ross . . . Civil War Letters," p. 19; Keen, *The 6th Texas Cavalry,* p. 23; Sparks, *The War . . . As I Saw It,* pp. 51–52; Rose, *Ross' Texas Brigade,* p. 55; Griscom, *Fighting with Ross' Texas Cavalry Brigade,* p. 13.

21 Ross to Lizzie Ross, November 5, 1861, in Shelton, "Ross . . . Civil War Letters," pp. 18–19.

22 Judith Ann Benner, *Sul Ross, Soldier, Statesman, Educator* (College Station: Texas A&M Press, 1983), p. 6.

23 Ibid., p. 8.

24 Ibid., p. 15; *CSR-Texas,* roll 41, L.S. Ross; John E. Parsons, *The Peacemaker and Its Rivals: An Account of the Single Action Colt* (New York: William Morrow and Co., 1950), pp. 5, 8; Coggins, *Arms and Equipment of the Civil War,* p. 54; Arcadi Gluckman, *Identifying Old U.S. Muskets, Rifles and Carbines* (New York: Bonanza Books, 1965), p. 224. During the Civil War, the Colt Armory furnished to the U.S. government 386,417 revolvers, about 7,000 revolving rifles, and 113,908 muzzle-loading rifle muskets. Samuel Colt had obtained a patent on the first practical revolving cylinder in 1836; Griscom, *Fighting with Ross' Texas Cavalry Brigade,* p. 13.

25 Ross to Lizzie Ross, March 1, 1861, in Shelton, "Ross . . . Civil War Letters," p. 19; Keen, *The 6th Texas Cavalry,* p. 23; Benner, *Sul Ross,* p. 72; See *O.R.,* vol. 8, pp. 74–75, for report by Union cavalry colonel. See p. 75 for Curtis's report calling Ross's men Texas Rangers. Curtis wrote: "Major Ross of Sherman, Texas." Ross was from Waco, McLennan County, Texas.

26 Crabb, Rogers family files.

27 Keen, *The 6th Texas Cavalry,* pp. 16, 18, 23–24; Shea and Hess, *Pea Ridge,* p. 54.

28 Keen, *The 6th Texas Cavalry,* p. 24.

29 Ross to Lizzie Ross, March 1, 1862, in Shelton, "Ross . . . Civil War Letters," p. 20; Keen, *The 6th Texas Cavalry,* p. 24; *O.R.,* vol. 8, pp. 74–75.

30 Keen, *The 6th Texas Cavalry,* pp. 24–25.

31 Ross to Lizzie Ross, March 1, 1862, in Shelton, "Ross . . . Civil War Letters," p. 20.

32 Ibid.

33 See *O.R.,* vol. 8, p. 55, for Col. Grenville Dodge's report.

34 *O.R.,* vol. 8, p. 302; Keen, *The 6th Texas Cavalry,* p. 25.

35 *O.R.,* vol. 8, p. 302; Rose, *Ross' Texas Brigade,* p. 55.

36 Griscom, *Fighting with Ross' Texas Cavalry Brigade,* p. 13; Sparks, *The War . . . As I Saw It,* p. 51; *CSR-Texas,* rolls 56–60.

37 Griscom, *Fighting with Ross' Texas Cavalry Brigade,* p. 13; *CSR-Texas,* rolls 56–60. Company A enrolled eighty-two men at Camp Reeves on October 14, 1861. Seven joined the company in Indian Territory and sixteen more joined while the company was in Arkansas.

38 Griscom, *Fighting with Ross' Texas Cavalry Brigade*, p. 13.

39 *O.R.*, vol. 8, p. 283; Warner, *Generals in Gray*, pp. xxvi, 314; Hartje, *Van Dorn*, pp. 118–19; Shea and Hess, *Pea Ridge*, p. 110; Castel, *General Sterling Price*, p. 70.

40 Hartje, *Van Dorn*, pp. 119–21; Watson, *Life in the Confederate Army*, p. 281.

41 Hartje, *Van Dorn*, pp. 31–32; Warner, *Generals in Gray*, p. 118; Webb, *The Texas Rangers*, p. 105; Broocks, *History of the Mexican War*, pp. 167–88; *O.R.*, vol. 4, pp. 91–96.

42 W. S. Nye, *Carbine and Lance* (Norman: University of Oklahoma Press, 1937), pp. 22–24; Benner, *Sul Ross*, pp. 22–32; Rose, *Ross' Texas Brigade*, pp. 158–59, 175–77. Ross later wrote: "I shall never forget the feelings of horror that took possession of me when I saw the arrow sent clear up to the feather into the body of Van Dorn's aide"; Hartje, *Van Dorn*, p. 67; Thomas Robert Harvins, *Beyond the Cimmaron: Major Earl Van Dorn in Comanche Land* (Brownsville, Tex.: Brown Press, 1968), pp. 42, 58–61.

43 Shea and Hess, *Pea Ridge*, p. 56. Van Dorn had a "severe fever" when he reached Strickler's Station; Ross to Dr. R. Tinsley, March 13, 1862, in Shelton, "Ross . . . Civil War Letters," pp. 25–26. Ross wrote: "Gen. Van Dorn did not believe the Federals would fight him—but rather that they would get away."

44 Griscom, *Fighting with Ross' Texas Cavalry Brigade*, p. 13 (see p. 28[n], for the report of Capt. J. M. Brinson of Company D); *O.R.*, vol. 8, pp. 297, 304, 763; Shea and Hess, *Pea Ridge*, pp. 22–23, 62–63.

45 U.S. Army officers regularly used ambulances for personal transportation. Shea and Hess, *Pea Ridge*, pp. 62–63; Sparks, *The War . . . As I Saw It*, p. 172; Watson, *Life in the Confederate Army*, p. 283.

46 Griscom, *Fighting with Ross' Texas Cavalry Brigade*, p. 13; Rose, *Ross' Texas Brigade*, p. 57.

47 Shea and Hess, *Pea Ridge*, p. 64.

48 Ibid., p. 72; Hartje, *Van Dorn*, p. 124; Griscom, *Fighting with Ross' Texas Cavalry Brigade*, p. 13; Watson, *Life in the Confederate Army*, p. 283 (Watson states he had no way to boil the issue of cornmeal); Hartje, *Van Dorn*, p. 124 (Hartje states the infantrymen's rations were coffee substitute and hard bread).

49 Griscom, *Fighting with Ross' Texas Cavalry Brigade*, p. 13; Hartje, *Van Dorn*, pp. 125–26; *O.R.*, vol. 8, pp. 297, 305; Shea and Hess, *Pea Ridge*, pp. 64; Rose, *Ross' Texas Brigade*, p. 56; Watson, *Life in the Confederate Army*, pp. 283–84; Confederate States of America, War Department, *Army Regulations* (Richmond: West & Johnston, Publishers, 1861), p. 65.

50 *O.R.*, vol. 8, pp. 283, 297–98; Griscom, *Fighting with Ross' Texas Cavalry Brigade*, p. 14; Shea and Hess, *Pea Ridge*, pp. 64–65.

51 Shea and Hess, *Pea Ridge*, pp. 71–72; *O.R.*, vol. 8, p. 297; Griscom, *Fighting with Ross' Texas Cavalry Brigade*, p. 14; Sparks, *The War . . . As I Saw It*, p. 53.

52 Griscom, *Fighting with Ross' Texas Cavalry Brigade*, p. 14; Sparks, *The War . . . As I Saw It*, p. 53; Rose, *Ross' Texas Brigade*, p. 56; *O.R.*, vol. 8, p. 297; Barron, *Lone Star Defenders*, p. 64. Barron also comments on the Yankees' "bright guns glistening in the sunshine." Barron wrote that at Corinth, Mississippi, in May 1862, he had seen no uniformed Confederate officers or men west of the Mississippi River; *CSR-Texas*, roll 60. William L. Tandy of Company A, Ninth Texas, was paid a clothing allowance of $4.10 a month for the three months from April 16 to July 16, 1862. Evidently he had drawn no clothing during the three months.

53 Griscom, *Fighting with Ross' Texas Cavalry Brigade*, p. 14; Shea and Hess, *Pea Ridge*, p. 72; *O.R.*, vol. 8, pp. 297–98, 305.

54 *O.R.*, vol. 8, pp. 297–98; Ross to Dr. R. Tinsley, March 13, 1862, in Shelton, "Ross . . . Civil War Letters," p. 24. Ross states there were four thousand cavalry at Pea Ridge, but the Sixth Texas was not with McIntosh north of Bentonville when the column was ambushed. According to Cater, *As It Was*, p. 113, the Texas cavalrymen were riding in fours.

55 *O.R.*, vol. 8, p. 298; Rose, *Ross' Texas Brigade*, pp. 56–57; Griscom, *Fighting with Ross' Texas Cavalry Brigade*, p. 14; Lane, *Adventures and Recollections*, pp. 90–91; Cater, *As It Was*, pp. 112–13. Lt. Col. Walter P. Lane was in command of the Third Texas, Col. Elkanah Greer having remained at winter quarters. Greer joined his regiment that night. Bill Isham and Sam Honey of the Third were killed in the ambush.

56 Cater, *As It Was*, pp. 112–14. Cater's horse ran toward the Federals and Cater's company mate Taylor Brown was thrown; *O.R.*, vol. 8, p. 298; Rose, *Ross' Texas Brigade*, p. 56.

57 Rose, *Ross' Texas Brigade*, p. 57; *CSR-Texas*, roll 20, Capt. Stephen M. Hale; Hale, *The Third Texas Cavalry*, p. 28.

58 Rose, *Ross' Texas Brigade*, p. 56; Cater, *As It Was*, pp. 112–13; Griscom, *Fighting with Ross' Texas Cavalry Brigade*, p. 14; *O.R.*, vol. 8, p. 298.

59 *O.R.*, vol. 8, p. 298.

60 Keen, *The 6th Texas Cavalry*, pp. 4–5, 25–26.

61 *O.R.*, vol. 8, pp. 283, 298; Griscom, *Fighting with Ross' Texas Cavalry Brigade*, p. 14; Rose, *Ross' Texas Brigade*, p. 57.

62 *O.R.*, vol. 8, pp. 22, 286–92; *O.R.*, vol. 23, pt. 1, pp. 819–23; Hartje, *Van Dorn*, p. 163.

63 *O.R.*, vol. 8, p. 287; See *O.R.*, vol. 23, pt. 1, p. 820, for Gen. Albert Pike's report. Pike states that there were nine hundred Cherokees in his Indian bri-

gade. The Choctaw and Chickasaw Regiment came up later with the train. The Creek Regiment had refused to leave Indian Territory; Gaines, *The Confederate Cherokees,* pp. 78–79. Gaines states that Pike's Indian Brigade contained one thousand men; Rose, *Ross' Texas Brigade,* p. 57; the description of Indians at Camp Stevens is from Edwin C. Bearss, "The Indians at Pea Ridge" (Typescript, Pea Ridge National Military Park, Notes C. IV, n. 1), quoted from Gaines, *The Cherokee Confederates,* p. 80.

64 Shea and Hess, *Pea Ridge,* pp. 23–24; *O.R.,* vol. 8, pp. 283, 287, 303, 306, 763; *O.R.,* vol. 13, p. 819.

65 *O.R.,* vol. 8, p. 191; Shea and Hess, *Pea Ridge,* pp. 10, 51.

66 Sparks, *The War . . . As I Saw It,* p. 168.

67 Shea and Hess, *Pea Ridge,* pp. 59, 82.

68 *O.R.,* vol. 8, pp. 281, 283–84; John C. Waugh, *The Class of 1846* (New York: Warner Books, 1994), p. 65. At West Point, Van Dorn's class spent one week studying strategy, tactics, army organization, order of battle, outpost duties, attack, and defense.

69 *O.R.,* vol. 8, pp. 283, 298, 305; Rose, *Ross' Texas Brigade,* p. 57; Ross to Dr. R. Tinsley, March 13, 1862, in Shelton, "Ross . . . Civil War Letters," pp. 22–23; Griscom, *Fighting with Ross' Texas Cavalry Brigade,* p. 14.

70 Ross to Dr. R. Tinsley, March 13, 1862, in Shelton, "Ross . . . Civil War Letters," p. 23.

71 *O.R.,* vol. 8, pp. 283, 287.

72 Ibid., p. 283.

73 Ibid., pp. 191, 281, 287, 298, 303; Gaines, *The Confederate Cherokees,* p. 80; Griscom, *Fighting with Ross' Texas Cavalry Brigade,* p. 14; Keen, *The 6th Texas Cavalry,* p. 27.

74 *O.R.,* vol. 8. pp. 295, 298; Ross to Dr. R. Tinsley, March 13, 1862, in Shelton, "Ross . . . Civil War Letters," p. 23; Keen, *The 6th Texas Cavalry,* p. 27; Griscom, *Fighting with Ross' Texas Cavalry Brigade,* p. 14; Cater, *As It Was,* p. 116.

75 *O.R.,* vol. 8, pp. 115–16, 288, 298, 301, 303; Griscom, *Fighting with Ross' Texas Cavalry Brigade,* p. 14; "S. A. Griffith," *The Confederate Veteran,* vol. 4, no. 5, May 1896, p. 163; Sparks, *The War . . . As I Saw It,* p. 53.

76 Shea and Hess, *Pea Ridge,* p. 99; Rudolph Rankin, interview with author, March 7, 1995; Rose, *Ross' Texas Brigade,* pp. 51, 58.

77 Sparks, *The War . . . As I Saw It,* p. 53; Woodward, *The Cherokees,* pp. 276–77; *O.R.,* vol. 8, pp. 195, 288, 301.

78 Sparks, *The War . . . As I Saw It,* p. 54.

79 Rose, *Ross' Texas Brigade*, p. 58; Sparks, *The War . . . As I Saw It*, p. 54. Thirty years after the event, Sparks wrote of the Red Cross of the South. In the spring of 1862, the Texans likely were still carrying the Stars and Bars; Griscom, *Fighting with Ross' Texas Cavalry Brigade*, p. 14.

80 Sparks, *The War . . . As I Saw It*, p. 54; Shea and Hess, *Pea Ridge*, pp. 101–102; *O.R.*, vol. 8, pp. 194–95, 206–07, 288; Barron, *Lone Star Defenders*, p. 68. Barron reports that the Choctaws scalped the enemy dead; Cater, *As It Was*, pp. 116. Cater wrote: "Gen. Pike's Indian cavalry came upon the field to scalp and plunder."

81 Griscom, *Fighting with Ross' Texas Cavalry Brigade*, pp. 14–15; Rose, *Ross' Texas Brigade*, p. 51.

82 Griscom, *Fighting with Ross' Texas Cavalry Brigade*, pp. 14–15.

83 Sparks, *The War . . . As I Saw It*, p. 53; Griscom, *Fighting with Ross' Texas Cavalry Brigade*, pp. 14–15, 212–36. Casualties among the commissioned and noncommissioned officers at Elkhorn Tavern included: Company A, Lt. Thomas Purcell, wounded; Company B, Lt. Robert P. Tarelton, taken prisoner; Company K, Lt. Charles Mount, mortally wounded, Sgt. J. A. Kiersey, killed; *CSR-Texas*, rolls 56–57. Privates Alex Anderson, David Boaz, and J. N. Dodson of Company A were wounded.

84 Sparks, *The War . . . As I Saw It*, pp. 53–54. When Sparks wrote in the 1890s, the crescent moon flag was in the possession of Maj. Hamilton C. Dial, a lieutenant in Company K at Pea Ridge. See Tuck, *Civil War Shadows in Hopkins County, Texas* (Sulphur Springs, Tex.: n.p., 1993), p. 27, for a photograph of the Company K flag. Tuck states that the flag was presented to "Company K, of the Ninth Texas Infantry that was mustered in at Black Jack Grove (Cumby), Hopkins County, Texas, July 3, 1861 by Miss Texana Trimble, accepted by Mr. Lee P. Green on behalf of the company." Obviously, Tuck means Company K of the Ninth Texas *Cavalry*. Company K was recruited in Hopkins County, which Tuck noted on page 26; Griscom, *Fighting with Ross' Texas Cavalry Brigade*, p. 235. L. P. Green was an original first lieutenant in Company K, Ninth Texas Cavalry; Sumrall, *Battle Flags of Texas in the Confederacy*, p. 42. In 1995, descendants of a Company K cavalryman still possessed the remnants of the crescent moon and thirteen-star flag that A. W. Sparks described in 1901. Van Dorn adopted the flag, with a brighter red background, for his Army of the West early in 1862. The crescent moon and thirteen-star pattern may also have been carried by other Texas regiments during 1862 and 1863.

85 *O.R.*, vol. 8, pp. 293, 299, 301.

86 Ibid., pp. 293, 301, 303; Cater, *As It Was*, p. 116; Shea and Hess, *Pea Ridge*, p. 110; Warner, *Generals in Gray*, pp. 12–13. Warner states that Lt. Frank Crawford Armstrong, Brig. Gen. Ben McCulloch's adjutant, was a few feet away when McCulloch was killed. Armstrong was born in 1835 in Indian

Territory, where his army officer father was stationed. The father died when Frank was very young. Frank's mother soon married Gen. Persifor F. Smith, a hero of the Mexican War. After the battle of Pea Ridge, Frank Armstrong became colonel of the Third Louisiana Infantry and soon commanded cavalry for Maj. Gen. Sterling Price. Brig. Gen. Armstrong commanded a cavalry brigade in Price's army at the battles of Iuka and Corinth. Armstrong's Brigade of Mississippi troopers and Ross's Brigade served together a great deal of the time through the rest of the war.

87 Shea and Hess, *Pea Ridge,* pp. 113–15; Rose, *Ross' Texas Brigade,* p. 59.

88 Rose, *Ross' Texas Brigade,* p. 59; Griscom, *Fighting with Ross' Texas Cavalry Brigade,* p. 15; *O.R.,* vol. 8, pp. 293–94.

89 *O.R.,* vol. 8, pp. 288, 293–94, 300–301, 303–304; Cater, *As It Was,* p. 122; Griscom, *Fighting with Ross' Texas Cavalry Brigade,* p. 15; Shea and Hess, *Pea Ridge,* pp. 210-11; Watson, *Life in the Confederate Army,* pp. 303–304.

90 Watson, *Life in the Confederate Army,* p. 305; Griscom, *Fighting with Ross' Texas Cavalry Brigade,* p. 15; *O.R.,* vol. 8, pp. 294, 300.

91 *O.R.,* vol. 8, pp. 294, 300; *O.R.,* vol. 23, pt. 1, p. 819; Watson, *Life in the Confederate Army,* p. 310.

92 Cater, *As It Was,* pp. 120–21.

93 Griscom, *Fighting with Ross' Texas Cavalry Brigade,* p. 15; Cater, *As It Was,* pp. 121–22.

94 Garrett to William Gibbard, March 20, 1862, from Cantonment Washington, Arkansas, in Garrett, *Civil War Letters,* pp. 49–50; Keen, *The 6th Texas Cavalry,* p. 30; Ross to Lizzie Ross, March 13, 1862, in Shelton, "Ross . . . Civil War Letters," p. 21; *O.R.,* vol. 8, p. 192.

95 Griscom, *Fighting with Ross' Texas Cavalry Brigade,* p. 15; *O.R.,* vol. 8, p. 776. A muster roll of McCulloch's army was taken March 11, 1862, while the men were still scattered across northwestern Arkansas, making an accurate count impossible. "Actual strength present of McCulloch's Division, March 11, 1861" notes 2,894 men. Of McIntosh's original 3,747 cavalrymen, the roll lists only 947 present, with 175 present in the Ninth Texas. See *O.R.,* vol. 8, pp. 300–302, 304, for reports of the other Texas cavalry regiments.

96 *O.R.,* vol. 8, pp. 777–78, 783–84; Griscom, *Fighting with Ross' Texas Cavalry Brigade,* p. 15.

97 Griscom, *Fighting with Ross' Texas Cavalry Brigade,* p. 15; *O.R.,* vol. 8, p. 194.

98 Because McCulloch and McIntosh were killed, there are no battle reports of the cavalry brigade or its division. Neither Sims, Quayle, nor anyone else wrote a report of the Ninth's movements during the month-long campaign. The regiment's activities have been gleaned from other sources and from official

reports of the surviving generals and the other Texas colonels. The *Official Records* of the rest of the war contain few reports from the Texas colonels.

99   Keen, *The 6th Texas Cavalry,* p. 28; Rose, *Ross' Texas Brigade,* p. 61; Garrett to William Gibbard, March 20, 1862, in Garrett, *Civil War Letters,* pp. 49–50; Ross to Dr. R. Tinsley, March 13, 1862, in Shelton, "Ross . . . Civil War Letters," p. 22.

100 Rose, *Ross' Texas Brigade,* p. 61.

101 *O.R.,* vol. 23, pt. 1, pp. 819–23, 955; *O.R.,* vol. 8, pp. 286–92, 302.

102 *O.R.,* vol. 8, pp. 281–86; Shea and Hess, *Pea Ridge,* pp. 214, 239, 268, 307–17.

103 Quote from Shea and Hess, *Pea Ridge,* p. 22.

104 *O.R.,* vol. 53, pp. 796–97. Van Dorn organized Price's and McCulloch's armies into the First Division of the Army of the West. The division included four brigades commanded by Col. Henry Little, Col. Louis Hébert, Brig. Gen. A. E. Steen, and Brig. Gen. Martin Green, with an artillery brigade commanded by Brig. Gen. D. M. Frost. The cavalry was organized into two brigades—the First Cavalry Brigade, commanded by Col. Elkanah Greer, and the Second Cavalry Brigade, commanded by Col. Thomas J. Churchill.

105 The Confederates called the action the battle of Elkhorn Tavern, the Federals called it the battle of Pea Ridge. The battleground is now set aside by the National Park Service as Pea Ridge National Military Park; Griscom, *Fighting with Ross' Texas Cavalry Brigade,* p. 16.

106 *O.R.,* vol. 8, pp. 791–92. Churchill brought with him to Horsehead Creek the Sixth Texas, the Eleventh Texas, and Gates's Battalion of Missouri cavalry.

107 Griscom, *Fighting with Ross' Texas Cavalry Brigade,* p. 16; *CSR-Texas,* roll 56. The Company A muster roll for March–April 1862 shows that J. Amos Burgoon drove a wagon twenty-one days during the two months.

108 *O.R.,* vol. 8, pp. 784, 791–92.

109 Griscom, *Fighting with Ross' Texas Cavalry Brigade,* p. 16.

110 Ibid.

111 Ibid., pp. 16–17.

112 Ibid., p. 17.

113 Ibid.; Theodore H. Savory, "The Mule," *Scientific American,* August 1967, pp. 102–109; Emmett M. Essin, *Shavetails and Bell Sharps: The History of the U.S. Army Mule* (Lincoln: University of Nebraska Press, 1997), pp. 4, 72–75; Beatty, *The Citizen-Soldier,* p. 238.

114 Griscom, *Fighting with Ross' Texas Cavalry Brigade,* p. 17.

115 Ibid., pp. 17, 35.

116 Ibid., p. 35; Rose, *Ross' Texas Brigade*, pp. 63–64; *O.R.*, vol. 17, pt. 1, pp. 374–75; *O.R.*, vol. 13, p. 818. Churchill's command was ordered to Memphis on April 15, 1862.

117 *O.R.*, vol. 53, p. 784. Gov. F. R. Lubbock to Secretary of War J. P. Benjamin, February 12, 1862; Oates, "Recruiting Confederate Cavalry in Texas," *Southwestern Historical Quarterly*, p. 476. In November 1861, Texas Governor Edward Clark worried about the state's inability to raise infantry but noted that any call made for cavalry was "complied with almost instantaneously." There were still organized cavalry companies in the state that had not been called into service. Oates wrote: "Riding to war on a powerful steed certainly was to the Texans much more chivalrous than walking." During 1861, Texas raised seventeen regiments, three battalions, and three companies of cavalry, 17,338 men in all. Before the war closed the state recruited 58,533 cavalrymen in fifty-eight regiments and fifteen battalions, more than the combined totals of the other states in the Trans-Mississippi.

118 Rose, *Ross' Texas Brigade*, p. 64.

119 Sparks, *The War . . . As I Saw It*, p. 146.

120 Griscom, *Fighting with Ross' Texas Cavalry Brigade*, p. 35.

121 Ibid., pp. 35, 84; Sparks, *The War . . . As I Saw It*, p. 56. Each man's horse was taken to his home; Barron, *Lone Star Defenders*, p. 80. The Third Texas sent their horses home from Duvall's Bluff, Arkansas. The riders tied the reins of one horse to the tail of another and "each man riding one horse and guiding the leader of the others, strung out in pairs behind him"; *CSR-Texas*, rolls 56–58, 60. Thomas H. Cox, Isaac J. Curry of Grapevine, F. M. Dyer of Birdville, R. L. Dean, William S. Gray, and William L. Tandy, a forty-four-year-old carpenter from Fort Worth, were among Company A's riders. William R. Allen drove the company wagon loaded with rations, cooking utensils, and other gear; Griscom, *Fighting with Ross' Texas Cavalry Brigade*, p. 84(n). Lt. James W. Calloway commanded Company A's detachment, and Lt. L. D. Miller of Company I commanded the column.

Chapter 5: Infantrymen

1 Griscom, *Fighting with Ross' Texas Cavalry Brigade*, pp. 35–36, 84(n).

2 Ibid., p. 36; Keen, *The 6th Texas Cavalry*, pp. 30–31.

3 Griscom, *Fighting with Ross' Texas Cavalry Brigade*, p. 36.

4 Ibid.; Keen, *The 6th Texas Cavalry*, pp. 30–31.

5 Griscom, *Fighting with Ross' Texas Cavalry Brigade*, p. 36.

6   Ibid.; Keen, *The 6th Texas Cavalry*, pp. 31–32; Hale, *The Third Texas Cavalry*, p. 107.

7   Sparks, *The War . . . As I Saw It*, p. 271.

8   Cunningham, *Doctors in Gray*, pp. 48–49; Benner, *Sul Ross*, pp. 76–77.

9   *CSR-Texas*, rolls 57, 59. Alex Anderson had been wounded at Pea Ridge six weeks earlier. W. L. Parker died of illness in Memphis sometime after the Federals took the city on May 6, 1862.

10   Griscom, *Fighting with Ross' Texas Cavalry Brigade*, p. 36.

11   Ibid.; Warner, *Generals in Gray*, p. 22; *O.R.*, vol. 10, pt. 1, p. 436. Beauregard's wire is dated April 24, 1862.

12   Griscom, *Fighting with Ross' Texas Cavalry Brigade*, pp. 36–37. The trip took eighteen hours; *O.R.*, vol. 10, pt. 2, p. 436.

13   *O.R.*, vol. 10, pt. 2, pp. 462–63; Keen, *The 6th Texas Cavalry*, p. 32; see Barron, *Lone Star Defenders*, pp. 81–83, for a description of the Third's tortuous trip.

14   U. S. Grant, *Personal Memoirs of U. S. Grant, Edited with Notes by E. B. Long* (Cleveland: World Publications Co., 1952. Reprint. New York: Da Capo Press, Inc., 1982), pp. 194–95.

15   *O.R.*, vol. 10, pt. 1, p. 461; Cumming, *Kate, Confederate Nurse*, p. 14; Barron, *Lone Star Defenders*, p. 83.

16   Cumming, *Kate, Confederate Nurse*, pp. 14–15.

17   Griscom, *Fighting with Ross' Texas Cavalry Brigade*, p. 36; Barron, *Lone Star Defenders*, p. 83.

18   Griscom, *Fighting with Ross' Texas Cavalry Brigade*, pp. 36–37; Wiley, *Johnny Reb*, p. 247.

19   *CSR-Texas*, rolls 59–60. Assistant Quartermaster Capt. J. W. Sims signed the pay vouchers for the regiment. Pvt. William Tandy received ten cents per mile for travel; *O.R.*, series 4, vol. 1., pp. 127–31. "An Act for the establishment of the Army of the Confederate States of America," approved March 6, 1861, Sections 17, 22, established the pay of officers and men in the cavalry: colonel, $210 (a colonel of infantry received $195); lieutenant colonel, $185; major, $162; captain, $140; first lieutenant, $100; second lieutenant, $90; adjutant $10 plus his lieutenant's pay; sergeant major, $21; first sergeant, $20; sergeant, $17; corporals, farriers, musicians, and blacksmith, $13; privates, $12. Infantry privates received $11 per month. Section 24 of the act noted that privates were entitled to one ration per day and an annual clothing allowance to be set by the War Department and approved by the president.

20   Griscom, *Fighting with Ross' Texas Cavalry Brigade*, p. 37.

21   Ibid., pp. 37-38.

22 Ibid., p. 38; *O.R.*, vol. 10, pt. 1, pp. 807–10; Rose, *Ross' Texas Brigade,* pp. 61–62.

23 Griscom, *Fighting with Ross' Texas Cavalry Brigade,* p. 38; *CSR-Texas,* roll 60, John M. Sloan; Cumming, Kate, *Kate: Confederate Nurse,* p. 31. Sloan's father nursed him at the hospital established in the Tishomingo Hotel at the railroad junction.

24 *CSR-Texas,* roll 60, John M. Sloan.

25 Ibid. John M. Sloan died May 2, 1862, at a hospital in Oxford, Mississippi.

26 Griscom, *Fighting with Ross' Texas Cavalry Brigade,* pp. 38, 85(n); *CSR-Texas,* rolls 56–60. Lt. L. Atkins of Company E was elected adjutant. In September 1862, a second conscription act extended the upper age of service to forty-five. Men discharged from Company A for being overage were John N. King, William M. Robinson, William L. Tandy, and Lt. R. R. Hund.

27 Griscom, *Fighting with Ross' Texas Cavalry Brigade,* pp. 38, 169. (see pp. 210–37 for officers of the Ninth Texas Cavalry); *CSR-Texas,* rolls 56–60.

28 *CSR-Texas,* rolls 56, 58, 59; Rose, *Ross' Texas Brigade,* p. 65; Hale, *The Third Texas Cavalry,* pp. 29, 115. In the Third Texas, Company B's Capt. Robert Cumby became colonel of the regiment, and Company G's Capt. Hinchie P. Mabry became lieutenant colonel.

29 Rose, *Ross' Texas Brigade,* pp. 30, 57; *CSR-Texas,* roll 20. Hale, captain of Company D, was a planter from Marshall, in Harrison County.

30 *O.R.,* vol. 10, pt. 2, pp. 462–63. Reorganization of Van Dorn's Army of the West on May 29, 1862, included ten dismounted Texas cavalry regiments.

31 Wiley, *Johnny Reb,* p. 247; Cumming, *Kate, Confederate Nurse,* p. 47; Cunningham, *Doctors in Gray,* p. 206; Barron, *Lone Star Defenders,* p. 89; *O.R.,* vol. 10, pt. 2, pp. 571–72.

32 Wiley, *Johnny Reb,* p. 249; *O.R.,* vol. 10, pt. 2, pp. 571–72. Standard rations included: beef or pork; flour, cornmeal or hard bread; beans, dried peas, or rice; coffee; sugar; molasses; vinegar; soap; salt; and candles. Eight ounces of lard could be substituted for the meat ration. In June 1862, General Beauregard ordered that the men be issued bacon or pork two days a week and fresh or salt beef five days. Beauregard also ordered, "The commutation price of rations until further orders will be twenty-five cents"; Watson, *Life in the Confederate Army,* p. 374.

33 *CSR-Texas,* rolls 56–60. The May–June 1862 muster roll for Company A lists twenty-four men sick or in the hospital.

34 Rose, *Ross' Texas Brigade,* p. 65; Hale, *The Third Texas Cavalry,* p. 112.

35 Garrett, fragment of a letter, in Garrett, *Civil War Letters,* pp. 52–53.

36 Griscom, *Fighting with Ross' Texas Cavalry Brigade,* pp. ix, 39.

37 Keen, *The 6th Texas Cavalry,* pp. 33–35.

38 Ross to Lizzie Ross, May 16, 1862, and June 14, 1862, in Shelton, "Ross . . . Civil War Letters," pp. 27–28, 33–34; *O.R.,* vol. 10, pt. 2, p. 489.

39 *O.R.,* vol. 10, pt. 1, pp. 776, 786.

40 Sparks, *The War . . . As I Saw It,* pp. 271–72. In order to fill in the Ninth's activities during the time Sparks was away from the regiment taking the horses to Texas, he visited Old Butch of Company I. The accounts of Butch are taken from Sparks. I have not been able to identify Old Butch or his friend Old Jack; Griscom, *Fighting with Ross' Texas Cavalry Brigade,* p. 39; *CSR-Texas,* roll 59 for Schults, roll 60 for Townes.

41 *CSR-Texas,* roll 58 for Dudley Jones; Rose, *Ross' Texas Brigade,* pp. 149–50; Sparks, *The War . . . As I Saw It,* pp. 66–67; Russell, *The History of Titus County,* p. 189.

42 Sparks, *The War . . . As I Saw It,* p. 272; Barron, *Lone Star Defenders,* p. 83; Warner, *Generals in Gray,* p. 22.

43 *O.R.,* vol. 10, pt. 2, pp. 462–63, 489; *O.R.,* pt. 1, pp. 789–90. June 30, 1862, the Sixth and Ninth Texas Cavalry were in the Third Brigade, commanded by Brig. Gen. C. W. Phifer. The Third Texas Cavalry and the First Texas Legion were in Col. Louis Hébert's Brigade of Brig. Gen. Sterling Price's Division; *O.R.,* vol. 8, p. 728. As of December 31, 1861, the Ninth Texas Cavalry had a total of 677 men present, an aggregate of 713. Each of the ten companies had gained about the same number of men as Company A, which gained sixteen while in Arkansas.

44 Griscom, *Fighting with Ross' Texas Cavalry Brigade,* p. 39; Rose, *Ross' Texas Brigade,* pp. 66–67; *O.R.,* vol. 10, pt. 1, p. 791. Beauregard had 53,244 men present for duty May 28, 1862; Grant, *Personal Memoirs,* p. 195. The Federals had 120,000 men surrounding Corinth.

45 *O.R.,* vol. 10, pt. 1, pp. 762–63.

46 Ibid., pp. 762–65. See pp. 766–70 for Beauregard's orders for the retreat.

47 Ibid., pp. 767–68; Griscom, *Fighting with Ross' Texas Cavalry Brigade,* p. 39.

48 *O.R.,* vol. 10, pt. 1, pp. 767–68; Cumming, *Kate, Confederate Nurse,* p. 41; Griscom, *Fighting with Ross' Texas Cavalry Brigade,* p. 39; Sparks, *The War . . . As I Saw It,* p. 273.

49 Griscom, *Fighting with Ross' Texas Cavalry Brigade,* p. 39; Carlton McCarthy, *Detailed Minutia of Soldier Life in the Army of Northern Virginia 1861–1865* (Richmond: Carlton McCarthy and Company, 1882. Reprint. Time-Life Books, 1982), pp. 52–53.

50 *O.R.,* vol. 10, pt. 2, p. 574; Sparks, *The War . . . As I Saw It,* p. 273; Wheeler, *Cavalry Tactics,* Part First, p. 40. "On foot the common step is at the rate of

90 per minutes; the quick step is at the rate of 110 per minutes; the double-quick step is at the rate of 165 per minute."

51 Griscom, *Fighting with Ross' Texas Cavalry Brigade*, p. 39.

52 Rose, *Ross' Texas Brigade*, p. 65; *O.R.*, vol. 10, pt. 1, p. 764.

53 Grant, *Personal Memoirs*, pp. 197–98; Hale, *The Third Texas Cavalry*, p. 117.

54 Sparks, *The War . . . As I Saw It*, pp. 273–74. A. W. Sparks wrote that Phifer was a major "who was to be respected and obeyed as a brigadier general"; *O.R.*, vol. 10, pt. 2, pp. 548–51; *O.R.*, vol. 17, pt. 2, pp. 728–29. Phifer, an acting brigadier general, was not confirmed by Congress and was relieved of his brigade duty October 16, 1862; Bruce S. Allardice, *More Generals in Gray* (Baton Rouge: Louisiana State University Press, 1995), pp. 181–82.

55 *O.R.*, vol. 10, pt. 2, p. 585; Griscom, *Fighting with Ross' Texas Cavalry Brigade*, pp. 39–40.

56 Griscom, *Fighting with Ross' Texas Cavalry Brigade*, pp. 40–41. Company drill was held from 7:00 to 10:00 A.M., battalion drill from 3:00 to 6:00 P.M.; Keen, *The 6th Texas Cavalry*, p. 36.

57 Ross to Lizzie Ross, June 14, 1862, in Shelton, "Ross . . . Civil War Letters," p. 33.

58 Sparks, *The War . . . As I Saw It*, p. 273; Hale, *The Third Texas Cavalry*, p. 123; Griscom, *Fighting with Ross' Texas Cavalry Brigade*, p. 87.

59 Sparks, *The War . . . As I Saw It*, p. 274. Old Butch told Sparks the story.

60 Benner, *Sul Ross*, p. 80.

61 *CSR-Texas*, roll 59 for Reuben Rogers.

62 Griscom, *Fighting with Ross' Texas Cavalry Brigade*, p. xi; Cumming, *Kate, Confederate Nurse*, p. 48; Grady McWhiney, "General Braxton Bragg," paper presented at the Confederate History Symposium, April 13, 1996, H. B. Simpson History Complex, Hillsboro, Texas.

63 Garrett, letter fragment, June or early July 1862, in Garrett, *Civil War Letters*, p. 53; Keen, *The 6th Texas Cavalry*, pp. 36–37.

64 See Waugh, *The Class of 1846*, for Maury's personality.

65 Quote from Maury, *Recollections*, p. 174.

66 Garrett to William Gibbard, Camp Maury, July 1, August 9, 1862, and Camp Frank Anderson, August 29, 1862, in Garrett, *Civil War Letters*, pp. 56–62; Griscom, *Fighting with Ross' Texas Cavalry Brigade*, p. 40; *O.R.*, vol. 10, pt. 2, p. 576. A scout reported to Beauregard June 3, 1862, that water could be reached by digging twelve to twenty-two feet.

67 Griscom, *Fighting with Ross' Texas Cavalry Brigade*, pp. 40–41; Rose, *Ross' Texas Brigade*, p. 69; *CSR-Texas*, rolls 56–60. The July–August 1862 roll of

Company A, Ninth Texas, lists men sick in camp—W. Smith Cummings, John Dunn, John S. Estill, Isaac S. Tompkins of Grapevine, Ed Cifert, Isaac P. Davis, Joseph S. Lafon, and J. J. Phillips. Thirteen men were hospitalized during the two months—Alex Anderson, in hospital again; George Ayers, still in the hospital; Thomas Barecroft; Richard Boaz; George W. Creed; Green Durham; William R. Harrison, who earlier was sick in camp; Walter N. Jones, in the hospital on the previous roll and remained as nurse after recovering; James J. McDaniel; Lorenzo Newton; William M. Robinson, sick in camp on previous roll and discharged in October 1862; Alonzo L. Stephenson, earlier sick in camp; and James C. Thomas, still in the hospital. Only one man in Company A died during the summer; James Polk "Poke" Dodson, age seventeen, died in the hospital in August. Poke surely was a brother of Maj. J. N. Dodson. Capt. Thomas Berry was granted sick leave from June 2 through July 2, 1862. He reported for duty on June 28, before his leave expired. During the summer and early fall others in Company A were detached for special service. Carpenters E. A. Eckhardt and Peter S. Moore worked on the railroad bridge at Tupelo. Robert Laney was detached as a regimental butcher. Sam and Ed M. King were detached as "pioneers"—construction workers. In October, Orderly Sgt. Joseph D. Henry was detached as assistant ordnance officer of the brigade.

68 Griscom, *Fighting with Ross' Texas Cavalry Brigade,* p. 41; Ross to Lizzie Ross, August 10, 1862, in Shelton, "Ross . . . Civil War Letters," p. 39.

69 Cater, *As It Was,* p. 138.

70 John Allan Wyeth, *That Devil Forrest: Life of General Nathan Bedford Forrest* (New York: Harper & Brothers, 1959. Reprint. Baton Rouge: Louisiana State University Press, 1989), pp. 69–87.

71 Griscom, *Fighting with Ross' Texas Cavalry Brigade,* p. 40; Garrett to William Gibbard, Camp Armstrong, Mississippi, August 29, 1862, in Garrett, *Civil War Letters,* p. 61.

Chapter 6: Cannon Fodder

1 Griscom, *Fighting with Ross' Texas Cavalry Brigade,* p. 40; Hartje, *Van Dorn,* p. 182; *O.R.,* vol. 17, pt. 1, pp. 374–75. Dismounted Texas cavalry regiments were the Third, Sixth, Ninth, and Twenty-seventh (or Whitfield's First Texas Legion) from Texas, the Third Arkansas, and the First and Third Missouri.

2 Griscom, *Fighting with Ross' Texas Cavalry Brigade,* p. xi.

3 *CSR-Texas,* rolls 56–60. Men detached from Company A were J. D. Henry as brigade assistant ordnance officer, Robert Laney as regimental butcher, Walter Jones as a nurse at Okolona, and Sam and Ed King as pioneers.

4   Grant, *Personal Memoirs,* pp. 204, 211–12; Hartje, *Van Dorn,* pp. 208–11; *O.R.,* vol. 17, pt. 1, p. 376.

5   Griscom, *Fighting with Ross' Texas Cavalry Brigade,* p. 41; Barron, *Lone Star Defenders,* p. 104.

6   Griscom, *Fighting with Ross' Texas Cavalry Brigade,* pp. 41–42; Peter Cozzens, *The Darkest Days of the War: The Battles of Iuka & Corinth* (Chapel Hill: University of North Carolina Press, 1997), pp. 52–55.

7   Griscom, *Fighting with Ross' Texas Cavalry Brigade,* p. 42; Rose, *Ross' Texas Brigade,* p. 69; Cozzens, *The Battles of Iuka & Corinth,* p. 57.

8   Griscom, *Fighting with Ross' Texas Cavalry Brigade,* pp. 42–43; Cozzens, *The Battles of Iuka & Corinth,* p. 64.

9   Cozzens, *The Battles of Iuka & Corinth,* pp. 68, 70, 78–79, 96; Rose, *Ross' Texas Brigade,* p. 72.

10 Rose, *Ross' Texas Brigade,* p. 72.

11 Ibid., pp. 70–71; Dean S. Thomas, *Cannon: An Introduction to Civil War Artillery* (Gettysburg: Thomas Publication, 1985), p. 17; Coggins, *Arms and Equipment of the Civil War,* p. 67. Grapeshot consisted of about forty iron balls, usually an inch to an inch and a half in diameter, packed together so as to scatter like shotgun pellets when fired. Canister consisted of a large number of iron balls packed in a different form from grapeshot. They too scattered like shotgun pellets when fired. A twelve-inch Napoleon canister load contained twenty-seven iron balls that were one and a half inches in diameter. "Double shotted" meant two canister or grapeshot shells loaded into the cannon barrel. Canister and grapeshot loads were used at short range, no farther than four hundred yards. Double-shotted loads were used at very close range.

12 Rose, *Ross' Texas Brigade,* pp. 71–72; Griscom, *Fighting with Ross' Texas Cavalry Brigade,* pp. 42–43; Cozzens, *The Battles of Iuka & Corinth,* pp. 88, 96, 99; *O.R.,* vol. 17, pt. 2, p. 709.

13 Griscom, *Fighting with Ross' Texas Cavalry Brigade,* p. 43; *O.R.,* vol. 10, pt. 1, p. 789; Rose, *Ross' Texas Brigade,* pp. 71–72; Hale, *The Third Texas Cavalry,* p. 127; Cozzens, *The Battles of Iuka & Corinth,* p. 121.

14 Griscom, *Fighting with Ross' Texas Cavalry Brigade,* p. 43; Cozzens, *The Battles of Iuka & Corinth,* pp. 116, 122–23; Garrett to William Gibbard, from Tupelo, Mississippi, September 28, 1862, in Garrett, *Civil War Letters,* pp. 65–66.

15 Garrett to William Gibbard, from Tupelo, Mississippi, September 28, 1862, in Garrett, *Civil War Letters,* p. 66.

16 Keen, *The 6th Texas Cavalry,* p. 37.

17 Griscom, *Fighting with Ross' Texas Cavalry Brigade,* pp. 43–44.

18 *O.R.,* vol. 17, pt. 1, pp. 376–78.

19 Ibid., pp. 382–83, 385; *O.R.*, vol. 17, pt. 2, p. 710.

20 Griscom, *Fighting with Ross' Texas Cavalry Brigade*, pp. 43–44; Keen, *The 6th Texas Cavalry*, p. 37.

21 *O.R.*, vol. 17, pt. 1, p. 378; Cozzens, *The Battles of Iuka & Corinth*, pp. 141–42; Rose, *Ross' Texas Brigade*, p. 73; Griscom, *Fighting with Ross' Texas Cavalry Brigade*, p. 44.

22 Griscom, *Fighting with Ross' Texas Cavalry Brigade*, p. 44; *O.R.*, vol. 17, pt. 1, pp. 378, 385–86.

23 *O.R.*, vol. 17, pt. 1, pp. 393–94; See vol. 17, pt. 1, pp. 376–82 for Van Dorn's report, pp. 393–95 for Maury's report, and pp. 385–89 for Price's report; Griscom, *Fighting with Ross' Texas Cavalry Brigade*, pp. 44–45; *CSR-Texas*, roll 56; Maury, *Recollections*, p. 157; Cozzens, *The Battles of Iuka & Corinth*, p. 159; Warner, *Generals in Gray*, pp. 215–16. Col. Dabney H. Maury had been promoted to brigadier general for his service as Van Dorn's adjutant at Pea Ridge.

24 *O.R.*, vol. 17, pt. 1, pp. 378, 386, 393–96; Griscom, *Fighting with Ross' Texas Cavalry Brigade*, pp. 44–45; Wheeler, *Cavalry Tactics*, Part First, pp. 155–56. "The objects of employing skirmishers are to cover movements and evolutions, to gain time, to watch the movements of the enemy, to keep him in check, to prevent his approaching so close to the main body as to line of march, and to weaken and harass him by their fire; to prepare the way for the charge on infantry, by rendering them unsteady, or drawing their fire."

25 Keen, *The 6th Texas Cavalry*, pp. 38–39. Sim Lindsey was killed by Newt's side.

26 Griscom, *Fighting with Ross' Texas Cavalry Brigade*, p. 45; Sparks, *The War . . . As I Saw It*, p. 275.

27 Cozzens, *The Battles of Iuka & Corinth*, p. 221; Sparks, *The War . . . As I Saw It*, p. 275.

28 Griscom, *Fighting with Ross' Texas Cavalry Brigade*, pp. 45–46.

29 Rosecrans, Maj. Gen. William S., "The Battle of Corinth," in *Battles and Leaders of the Civil War*, vol. 2, (New York: E. P. Dutton, 1887–1888. Reprint: Edison, N.J.: Castle, n.d.) p. 748.

30 Griscom, *Fighting with Ross' Texas Cavalry Brigade*, p. 45; Rose, *Ross' Texas Brigade*, pp. 72–73; *O.R.*, vol. 17, pt. 1, p. 379.

31 Shelby Foote, *Fort Sumter to Perryville* (New York: Random House, 1958), p. 723; Keen, *The 6th Texas Cavalry*, pp. 39–40.

32 Cozzens, *The Battles of Iuka & Corinth*, pp. 246–47; Keen, *The 6th Texas Cavalry*, pp. 39–40; Griscom, *Fighting with Ross' Texas Cavalry Brigade*, p. 45.

33 Keen, *The 6th Texas Cavalry*, p. 40; Cozzens, *The Battles of Iuka & Corinth*, p. 255.

34 Cozzens, *The Battles of Iuka & Corinth*, p. 256.

35 Ibid., pp. 258–59; Keen, *The 6th Texas Cavalry*, p. 40.

36 Cozzens, *The Battles of Iuka & Corinth*, pp. 254, 258–61, 265; Rose, *Ross' Texas Brigade*, p. 73; Griscom, *Fighting with Ross' Texas Cavalry Brigade*, p. 46.

37 *O.R.*, vol. 17, pt. 1, pp. 185–86. The Union colonel states that the Ohioan carried off the Ninth's flag. Sparks states that the Ninth never lost their flag and quotes Old Butch as saying the Sixth Texas lost their flag at Hatchie Bridge, the "only flag ever lost by our brigade." The Ninth's Crescent Moon flag was in the possession of Capt. Hamilton Dial's descendants in 1995; Cozzens, *The Battles of Iuka & Corinth*, p. 267. Cozzens states that it was the Sixth Texas that lost their flag. See also Sparks, *The War . . . As I Saw It*, pp. 54, 276; Sumrall, *Battle Flags of Texas in the Confederacy*, p. 42; and Tuck, *Civil War Shadows in Hopkins County, Texas*, p. 27.

38 *O.R.*, vol. 17, pt. 1, p. 169; Rosecrans, "The Battle of Corinth," in *Battles and Leaders*, vol. 2, pp. 750–51; Griscom, *Fighting with Ross' Texas Cavalry Brigade*, p. 46.

39 *CSR-Texas*, roll 56; Griscom, *Fighting with Ross' Texas Cavalry Brigade*, p. 46; *O.R.*, vol. 17, pt. 1, pp. 382–83. The Ninth Texas lost 19 killed, 53 wounded, and 21 missing. In addition to the 50 killed in the Sixth Texas, 59 were wounded and 23 missing—a total of 132; Griscom, *Fighting with Ross' Texas Cavalry Brigade*, p. 46.

40 *O.R.*, vol. 17, pt. 1, pp. 169, 379, 387–88; Keen, *The 6th Texas Cavalry*, pp. 40–41; Griscom, *Fighting with Ross' Texas Cavalry Brigade*, p. 46.

41 Griscom, *Fighting with Ross' Texas Cavalry Brigade*, p. 46; *O.R.*, vol. 17, pt. 1, p. 387.

42 *O.R.*, vol. 17, pt. 1, pp. 378–88, 394–95.

43 Keen, *The 6th Texas Cavalry*, p. 41.

44 Sparks, *The War . . . As I Saw It*, pp. 275–76.

45 *O.R.*, vol. 17, pt. 1, p. 392; Keen, *The 6th Texas Cavalry*, p. 42; Barron, *Lone Star Defenders*, pp. 121–22; Cozzens, *The Battles of Iuka & Corinth*, pp. 291–92.

46 Barron, *Lone Star Defenders*, pp. 122–23.

47 Griscom, *Fighting with Ross' Texas Cavalry Brigade*, p. 47.

48 *O.R.*, vol. 17, pt. 1, p. 388; Rose, *Ross' Texas Brigade*, p. 74; Keen, *The 6th Texas Cavalry*, p. 42.

49 Griscom, *Fighting with Ross' Texas Cavalry Brigade*, pp. 46–47, 90, 220. Griscom's figures of 149 casualties include the Ninth's Company H, which had been detached to Stirman's Sharpshooters in July (see Griscom, p. 40); *O.R.*, vol. 17, pt. 1, pp. 382–83. "Return of Casualties in the Confederate forces,

Maj. Gen. Earl Van Dorn commanding, October 3–5" lists the Ninth Texas losses as 19 killed, 57 wounded, 41 missing, for a total of 117 casualties; Stirman's Sharpshooters, men from several regiments, had 8 killed, 90 wounded, and 77 missing, for a total of 167 casualties; the Sixth Texas, 50 killed, 59 wounded, 23 missing, total 132 casualties; *CSR-Texas*, rolls 56–60. In the Ninth, George Creed, Robert Lanhum, and David Mason were killed. William L. Boyd was mortally wounded and died October 12, 1862. W. Smith Cummings was slightly wounded October 3, was sent to the hospital, and returned to duty in a month. James P. King was wounded October 3, taken prisoner, paroled at Iuka, immediately sent to a hospital, and returned to duty after the first of the year. George C. Piersall was slightly wounded. Lt. Thomas Purcell was severely wounded, taken prisoner, and exchanged at Jackson with the other officers. Purcell returned to duty in January 1863. George Roach was wounded, captured, exchanged, then furloughed for thirty days. Walter N. Leak, Alanzo L. Stephenson, and E. A. Schults were captured during the action at the Hatchie Bridge. Schults had been wounded at Corinth in May. Alva Knight was captured October 6 on the retreat and exchanged with the prisoners of war October 12, 1862. The Union and the Confederacy had agreed to conduct paroles and exchanges of prisoners of war on the basis agreed upon by the United States and Great Britain during the War of 1812. Prisoners of war were paroled within ten days and exchanged man for man, rank for rank. Until a parolee was formally exchanged, he was forbidden to take part in any form of belligerence. Once he was exchanged, he was free to return to active duty.

50 *O.R.,* vol. 17, pt. 1, pp. 173–76, 382. Van Dorn's official report listed 505 killed, 2,150 wounded, and 2,179 missing, for a total of 4,834. Rosecrans reported burying 1,423 Confederates and inscribing the names of 2,268 Rebels on his POW rolls. He reported U.S. casualties of 355 killed, 1,841 wounded, and 324 missing, for a total of 2,520.

51 Barron, *Lone Star Defenders,* p. 123; Griscom, *Fighting with Ross' Texas Cavalry Brigade,* p. 47; Keen, *The 6th Texas Cavalry,* p. 42.

52 *O.R.,* vol. 17, pt. 1, p. 170.

53 Griscom, *Fighting with Ross' Texas Cavalry Brigade,* pp. 47–48.

54 Griscom, *Fighting with Ross' Texas Cavalry Brigade,* p. 47; *O.R.,* vol. 17, pt. 1, p. 382.

55 *O.R.,* vol., 17, pt. 1, pp. 414–59; *O.R.,* vol. 17, pt. 2, p. 728. The Missouri brigadier was John Bowen; Warner, *Generals in Gray,* pp. 29–30.

56 *O.R.,* vol. 17, pt. 1, pp. 173–76; *O.R.,* vol. 17, pt. 2, p. 265; Griscom, *Fighting with Ross' Texas Cavalry Brigade,* p. 48. Rosecrans's official communication is dated October 5, 1862. Griscom reported that it arrived October 20.

57 Griscom, *Fighting with Ross' Texas Cavalry Brigade,* pp. 46, 48; Warner, *Generals in Blue,* pp. 410–11; Warner, *Generals in Gray,* pp. 215–16, 314–15. Brig. Gen. Dabney Maury was promoted to major general for his valor at Corinth. See

Waugh, *The Class of 1846*, for an understanding of the bonds created at West Point. Maury graduated from West Point in the famous class of 1846 with Stonewall Jackson and George McClellan. William S. Rosecrans was one of their instructors. Rosecrans and Van Dorn had graduated from West Point together in 1842. Grant and Sherman had graduated in 1840.

58 Maury, *Recollections*, p. 171; *O.R.*, vol. 17, pt. 1, pp. 173–76, 374–75. Maury's Division, which suffered 52 percent of the casualties at Corinth and Hatchie Bridge, included Alabama and Arkansas regiments, and the Sixth and Ninth Texas; *O.R.*, vol. 17, pt. 1, p. 169.

59 *CSR-Texas*, roll 57; Griscom, *Fighting with Ross' Texas Cavalry Brigade*, pp. ix, 46, 48, 91. George "Gris" Griscom was born April 6, 1837, in Philadelphia County, Pennsylvania. His family moved to Petersburg, Virginia, when Gris was a small child. Gris was educated in Pennsylvania, New Jersey, and Virginia, and had been in Texas only four years when the Civil War began. He and his brother Yeamans fought for the Confederacy. Their brother Ellwood fought for the Union. See *O.R.*, series 4, vol. 1, p. 129, for pay rates; Le Grand, *The Military Hand-Book*, p. 101.

60 *CSR-Texas*, rolls 56–60.

61 *O.R.*, vol. 17, pt. 2, pp. 728–29, 733; Griscom, *Fighting with Ross' Texas Cavalry Brigade*, p. 48; Warner, *Generals in Gray*, p. 215.

62 Griscom, *Fighting with Ross' Texas Cavalry Brigade*, pp. 48–49; Barron, *Lone Star Defenders*, pp. 125, 127.

63 Griscom, *Fighting with Ross' Texas Cavalry Brigade*, pp. 49–50; Maury, *Recollections*, pp. 171–75.

64 Griscom, *Fighting with Ross' Texas Cavalry Brigade*, p. 50.

Chapter 7: Horses! Horses!

1 Griscom, *Fighting with Ross' Texas Cavalry Brigade*, p. 50; Sparks, *The War . . . As I Saw It*, pp. 59–60.

2 1860 U.S. Census, Population Schedule, Titus County, Texas, p. 172. Household of parents of A. W. and John Sparks: James B. Sparks, age fifty-seven, merchant, real estate valued at $6,000, personal property (usually the value of slaves) $5,720; Mary A. Sparks, age forty-six; Mary M. Sparks, age seventeen; Angelina C. Sparks, age fourteen. The census also included A. W. in the household and John in another household.

3 Sparks, *The War . . . As I Saw It*, pp. 59–60; Tuck, *Civil War Shadows in Hopkins County, Texas*, pp. 24, 31–32. Hopkins County issued bonds for clothing and

supplies, and ladies' sewing societies made blankets and clothing for their soldiers—homespun denims for summer wear and thick, heavy woolens for winter.

4   *CSR-Texas,* rolls 56–57, 60. The men in Company A who took the horses to Texas and returned with them were William Allen, Tom Cox, Isaac Curry, and F. M. Dyer. Others remained in Texas: Lt. James Calloway, William L. Tandy, and William S. Gray. E. M. Mitchell of Fort Worth signed up with Berry on September 26, 1862. Veteran Byron Akers, who had gone home in June with typhoid, had reenlisted and returned.

5   *O.R.,* vol. 10, pt. 2, p. 489. The May 4, 1863, roll of the Ninth Texas shows 869 men on the rolls and 657 present for duty. Over 33 men were killed or died of wounds at Iuka and Corinth. This May 1863 roll is the last accounting in the *Official Records* of the number of men in the Ninth Texas Cavalry. After that date the returns list the number of men in the brigade, not in the separate regiments.

6   Sparks, *The War . . . As I Saw It,* p. 58.

7   Ibid., pp. 58–59.

8   Tuck, *Civil War Shadows in Hopkins County, Texas,* p. 31.

9   Sparks, *The War . . . As I Saw It,* pp. 58–59; Barron, *Lone Star Defenders,* p. 80. Sam Barron described the way the Third Texas riders trailed their horses: "They tied the reins of one horse to the tail of another, each man riding one horse and guiding the leader of the others, strung out behind him"; William J. Turner, interview by author. Leading a string of horses tied tail to head with about three feet of rope between is a common practice in Texas cattle country today.

10 Sparks, *The War . . . As I Saw It,* pp. 58–59; Thomas, *Cannon: An Introduction to Civil War Artillery,* p. 49. A ten-inch mortar shell weighed eighty-eight pounds.

11 Crabb, Rogers family files; Wallace and Hoebel, *The Comanches, Lords of the Southern Plains* (Norman: University of Oklahoma Press), p. 305; T. R. Fehrenbach, *Lone Star: A History of Texas and the Texans* (New York: Collier Books, 1985), pp. 360–61; Ralph A. Wooster, "Life in Civil War East Texas," *East Texas Historical Journal,* October 1965, pp. 95–99; E. T. Miller, "The State Finances of Texas During the Civil War," *Southwestern Historical Quarterly,* July 1910, pp. 7–9; Tuck, *Civil War Shadows in Hopkins County, Texas,* pp. 32–38; Maxine Holmes and Gerald D. Saxon, *The WPA Dallas Guide and History* (Dallas: Dallas Public Library, 1992), pp. 56–57.

12 Griscom, *Fighting with Ross' Texas Cavalry Brigade,* p. 50; Denny Hair, Third Texas Cavalry Reenactment Group, Hockley, Texas. Interviews by author, April 1, July 15, and August 3, 1995.

13 Griscom, *Fighting with Ross' Texas Cavalry Brigade,* p. 50; Warner, *Generals in Gray,* p. 215. Dabney H. Maury was appointed major general on November 4, 1862.

14 Sparks, *The War . . . As I Saw It*, p. 60.

15 Rose, *Ross' Texas Brigade*, p. 79.

16 Ibid., pp. 79–80; Keen, *The 6th Texas Cavalry*, p. 44.

17 Keen, *The 6th Texas Cavalry*, pp. 44–45. Newton Keen was from Dallas County, which borders Tarrant County on Dallas County's west boundary. Newton's horse would have traveled about 550 miles to reach Mississippi; Garrett to William Gibbard, Holly Springs, Mississippi, October 21, 1862, in Garrett, *Civil War Letters*, p. 69.

18 Griscom, *Fighting with Ross' Texas Cavalry Brigade*, p. 50.

19 Grant, *Personal Memoirs*, p. 220.

20 Rose, *Ross' Texas Brigade*, pp. 130–32; Benner, *Sul Ross*, p. 88; *CSR-Texas*, roll 41. Sul Ross's brother Peter was wounded in the cheek and wrist at Corinth in October 1862. Peter Ross does not again appear on the rolls until the May–June 1863 roll. In August 1863, Peter was promoted to major of the Sixth Texas. Sul Ross was on detached service beginning November 3, 1862. By the time the January–February 1864 roll was taken, Sul commanded the Texas Brigade.

21 Rose, *Ross' Texas Brigade*, p. 132.

22 W. R. Stevenson, "The Capture of Holly Springs, Mississippi," *Confederate Veteran*, vol. 9, no. 3, March 1901, p. 134. Stevenson belonged to Company F, Third Texas Cavalry; John A. Miller, "A Memoir of the Days of '61," p. 21.

23 Rose, *Ross' Texas Brigade*, pp. 84, 130–35; Griscom, *Fighting with Ross' Texas Cavalry Brigade*, p. 51; Keen, *The 6th Texas Cavalry*, p. 46; Hale, *The Third Texas Cavalry*, p. 143; Garrett to William Gibbard, Grenada, Mississippi, December 20, 1862, in Garrett, *Civil War Letters*, p. 71; See *O.R.*, vol. 17, pt. 2, p. 844, for the strength of the several regiments Van Dorn took on the raid; for information on John S. Griffith, see Rose, *Ross' Texas Brigade*, pp. 123–37, and Webb, editor, *The Handbook of Texas*, vol. 1, pp. 736–37; Crabb, Crabb family files. John S. Griffith was born in Montgomery County, Maryland, in 1829, and moved to East Texas as a child. When the war began, Griffith raised a cavalry company in Kaufman County, Texas. His company joined the Sixth when it was organized, and Griffith was elected lieutenant colonel. He served with the regiment at the battles of Wilson Creek in Missouri, at Chustenahlah in Indian Territory—where a tuft of his whiskers were shot away—at Pea Ridge in Arkansas, and at Iuka, Corinth, Oakland, and Holly Springs in Mississippi. He returned to Texas in June 1863. Griffith was descended from two old Maryland families. Both his grandfathers, Capt. Henry Griffith and Gen. Jeremiah Crabb, served in the Revolutionary army. His mother, Lydia Crabb, was descended from the same Maryland Crabb family as the author's husband.

24 Griscom, *Fighting with Ross' Texas Cavalry Brigade*, p. 51; David Wilson, Terry's Rangers, Eighth Texas Cavalry Reenactment Regiment, interviews by author, April 1 and August 1, 1995.

25 Hartje, *Van Dorn*, p. 257; Griscom, *Fighting with Ross' Texas Cavalry Brigade*, p. 51.

26 Griscom, *Fighting with Ross' Texas Cavalry Brigade*, p. 51; Rose, *Ross' Texas Brigade*, p. 84.

27 Griscom, *Fighting with Ross' Texas Cavalry Brigade*, p. 51; Rose, *Ross' Texas Brigade*, p. 85.

28 Griscom, *Fighting with Ross' Texas Cavalry Brigade*, p. 51; Rose, *Ross' Texas Brigade*, p. 85.

29 Rose, *Ross' Texas Brigade*, pp. 85–86; Griscom, *Fighting with Ross' Texas Cavalry Brigade*, p. 51.

30 Griscom, *Fighting with Ross' Texas Cavalry Brigade*, p. 51; Rose, *Ross' Texas Brigade*, p. 86; *O.R.*, vol. 17, pt. 1, pp. 508–509, 512–13.

31 Sparks, *The War . . . As I Saw It*, pp. 63–64.

32 Rose, *Ross' Texas Brigade*, p. 86; Griscom, *Fighting with Ross' Texas Cavalry Brigade*, p. 51. The Ninth lost one killed, two mortally wounded, and three severely wounded; *O.R.*, vol. 17, pt. 1, pp. 512–13. The Illinoisans belonged to the Second Illinois Cavalry.

33 Sparks, *The War . . . As I Saw It*, p. 277.

34 Rose, *Ross' Texas Brigade*, p. 86.

35 Ibid., p. 87; Griscom, *Fighting with Ross' Texas Cavalry Brigade*, p. 94(n); Miller, "A Memoir of the Days of '61," pp. 21–22; Stevenson, "The Capture of Holly Springs, Mississippi," *Confederate Veteran*, p. 134; Rose, Miller, and Stevenson reported Mrs. Grant's presence at Holly Springs.

36 Rose, *Ross' Texas Brigade*, pp. 87–88.

37 Ibid., pp. 88–89; Griscom, *Fighting with Ross' Texas Cavalry Brigade*, p. 52; Miller, "A Memoir of the Days of '61," pp. 21–22; Stevenson, "The Capture of Holly Springs, Mississippi," *Confederate Veteran*, p. 134.

38 Rose, *Ross' Texas Brigade*, pp. 89–90.

39 Ibid., p. 89.

40 Ibid.

41 Ibid., p. 90; Griscom, *Fighting with Ross' Texas Cavalry Brigade*, p. 52.

42 Griscom, *Fighting with Ross' Texas Cavalry Brigade*, p. 52; *O.R.*, vol. 17, pt. 1, pp. 509–10, 512–15; Rose, *Ross' Texas Brigade*, p. 88.

43 Griscom, *Fighting with Ross' Texas Cavalry Brigade*, pp. 51–52, 94(n). Griscom recorded the capture by the Ninth Texas of "75 cavalry horses with cavalry equipment." According to Kerr, the editor of Griscom's diary, the Holly Springs raid was reported in the *Dallas Herald* on January 14, 1863; Rose, *Ross'*

Texas Brigade, p. 136; Hartje, *Van Dorn,* p. 265. See Allardice, *More Generals in Gray,* pp. 106–107, for Griffith.

44 Wilson, interview by author, April 1, 1995; Coggins, *Arms and Equipment of the Civil War,* pp. 55–57.

45 Stephen W. Sears, *George B. McClellan: The Young Napoleon* (New York: Ticknor & Fields, 1988), pp. 47–48; Randy Steffen, *United States Military Saddles* (Norman: University of Oklahoma Press, 1973), pp. 55–70. Capt. George B. McClellan designed the cavalry saddle in 1856 after returning from a year's study of military systems in Europe. Both his proposed cavalry manual and the saddle were adopted by the U.S. Army. The saddle, McClellan claimed, was based on the Hungarian cavalry saddle with modifications McClellan observed in other European armies. Steffen states: "It is strange to me that no military writer has seen through this bit of subterfuge on McClellan's part and revealed the true source of the McClellan design. Close examination of the . . . Grimsley saddle, the Campbell saddle, the Hope saddle, and the first McClellan saddle reveals that the McClellan saddle incorporates the major features of the Grimsley, the Campbell and the Hope." The Hope or Texas saddle, made in San Antonio, Texas, is a lightweight Texas cow saddle with a horn. It was preferred by many Civil War officers who had served in Texas. Joseph E. Johnston rode a simple, leather-covered Hope—elegant, like the man. Judson Kilpatrick's Hope saddle, with elaborately tooled Texas-style mounting leather, reflected the general's flamboyant personality. The McClellan saddle, with slight modifications, was standard issue from 1859 until the U.S. cavalry was disbanded in 1943 and is still used by ceremonial units; Bert Clifton, Director, Moore County Historical Museum, Dumas, Texas. Examination of two post–Civil War McClellan saddles in the collections of the Moore County Historical Museum.

46 See *O.R.,* vol. 17, pt. 1, p. 503, for Van Dorn's report to Pemberton. I found no other Confederate report of the Holly Springs raid in the *Official Records.*

47 Ibid., pp. 478, 515–17.

48 Ibid., pp. 508–509.

49 Griscom, *Fighting with Ross' Texas Cavalry Brigade,* p. 52; Sparks, *The War . . . As I Saw It,* p. 277. During A. W. Sparks's interview with Old Butch in the 1890s, Butch "lost the thread of his discourse" late in the evening "and fell to telling of the intelligence and fleetness of the mule he got and her pride when arrayed among the cavalry horses—and her the only mule."

50. Griscom, *Fighting with Ross' Texas Cavalry Brigade,* p. 52.

51 Ibid., p. 51; Rose, *Ross' Texas Brigade,* p. 91; Barron, *Lone Star Defenders,* p. 137; *O.R.,* vol. 17, pt. 1, pp. 521–23.

52 *O.R.,* vol. 17, pt. 1, p. 523; Griscom, *Fighting with Ross' Texas Cavalry Brigade,* p. 52; Rose, *Ross' Texas Brigade,* p. 91; *CSR-Texas,* rolls 56–60. William

Tannahill was left wounded and died the next day. David Cate, James McDaniel, and E. A. Eckhardt, the carpenter, were also wounded and left at Davis's Mill. John Grimes remained with Dr. Eugene Blocker of the Third Texas and others to attend to the wounded.

53 *CSR-Texas*, rolls 56–60. McDaniel was present on the March–April 1863 roll, the next extant roll. Eckhardt was taken to the La Grange hospital. He was present for duty on the March–April 1863 roll. Grimes was in a parole camp at Jackson, Mississippi, on the March–April 1863 roll and present for duty on the May–June 1863 roll; James M. Day, compiler, *The Texas Almanac 1857–1873*, p. 504. Robert W. Tannahill was collector for the Confederate Tax District at Forth Worth.

54 Rose, *Ross' Texas Brigade,* p. 91; Griscom, *Fighting with Ross' Texas Cavalry Brigade,* pp. 52–53; Barron, *Lone Star Defenders,* p. 140; *O.R.,* vol. 17, pt. 1, pp. 521–23.

55 *O.R.,* vol. 17, pt. 1, pp. 523–24; Griscom, *Fighting with Ross' Texas Cavalry Brigade,* p. 53.

56 Griscom, *Fighting with Ross' Texas Cavalry Brigade,* pp. 53–54; see *O.R.,* vol. 17, pt. 1, pp. 518–20, for the report of Col. Benjamin Grierson, Sixth Illinois Cavalry, who commanded the Union effort to capture Van Dorn's column.

57 Griscom, *Fighting with Ross' Texas Cavalry Brigade,* pp. 53–54; Sparks, *The War . . . As I Saw It,* p. 61; Garrett to William Gibbard, December 20, 1862, in Garrett, *Civil War Letters,* p. 71.

58 For Forrest's West Tennessee raid, see Wyeth, *That Devil Forrest,* pp. 89–125; Thomas Jordon and J. P. Pryor, *The Campaigns of Lieut.-Gen. N. B. Forrest and of Forrest's Cavalry* (New Orleans and New York: 1868. Reprint. Dayton, Ohio: Morningside Bookshop, 1977), pp. 194–222; and Robert Selph Henry, *"First with the Most" Forrest* (Reprint. Wilmington, N.C.: Broadfoot Publishing Company, 1987), pp. 107–21.

59 Jordon and Pryor, *The Campaigns of Lieut.-Gen. N. B. Forrest,* p. 195; Henry, *"First with the Most" Forrest,* p. 113.

60 Jordon and Pryor, *The Campaigns of Lieut.-Gen. N. B. Forrest,* pp. 221–22. When Forrest crossed into West Tennessee he sank the old flatboat that was raised for the return crossing. The animals were unhitched from the wagons and artillery, and along with the cavalry horses were hurriedly forced into the water and made to swim the six-hundred-yard river. As many as a thousand were in the water at a time. Wagons and artillery were loaded on the flatboat, poled upstream half a mile, and pushed into the current, which took them to the opposite shore. In eight hours Forrest's men crossed five pieces of artillery, six caissons, sixty wagons, and four ambulances.

61 Griscom, *Fighting with Ross' Texas Cavalry Brigade,* p. 54; *CSR-Texas,* rolls 56–60. J. E. Brown was serving with Van Dorn's bodyguard. The accounting

of Company A's 74 men and officers is taken from the November–December 1862 roll. The next extant roll is March–April 1863. The January–February 1863 roll is missing; *O.R.*, vol. 17, pt. 2, p. 844. The "Report of the Inspector-General of the Army of Mississippi," station at and near Grenada, dated January 18, 1863, notes a few cases of smallpox reported. The infantrymen had been vaccinated, but not the cavalrymen. Van Dorn's bodyguard was reported as fifty strong. The two infantry corps of the Army of Mississippi reported 12,058 men present and 8,459 absent; Cawthorn, editor, "Letters of a North Louisiana Private to His Wife, 1862–1865," *Mississippi Valley Historical Review,* March 1944, p. 538. Pvt. Henry Morgan, Thirty-first Louisiana Infantry, was vaccinated for smallpox at Vicksburg in December 1862.

62 *CSR-Texas,* rolls 56–60. George Roach, wounded at Corinth, was on medical furlough.

63 Garrett to William Gibbard, December 20, 1862, in Garrett, *Civil War Letters,* p. 71; Rose, *Ross' Texas Brigade,* p. 85; Keen, *The 6th Texas Cavalry,* p. 44.

64 Barron, *Lone Star Defenders,* p. 144. Sam Barron, born in 1834 in Madison County, Alabama, moved to Nacogdoches County, Texas, in 1859. He enlisted in Company C of the Third Texas in neighboring Cherokee County on June 3, 1861. Barron was elected second sergeant of his company when the Third organized, but he reverted to private in July 1862 because of poor health. After the pork and sweet potatoes restored his health, he was promoted to second lieutenant on March 2, 1863, while the regiment was serving with Van Dorn around Columbia and Spring Hill. Forty years after the war, Samuel Barron wrote a book about his service for his children. Barron's book, A. W. Sparks's book, and many other personal war narratives were written forty years after the war ended. Numerous World War II veterans began to attend reunions, write, and talk about their war experience in the 1980s. It seems to take forty years for many men to begin to emotionally deal with the horrors they witnessed. The more appalling their experiences, the longer it takes. Some never are able to talk about it. Data on Barron is from pp. 11–13, 34, and 147 of his book; *CSR-Texas,* roll 18; and Cherokee County Genealogical Society, *1860 Federal Census, Cherokee County, Texas* (Jacksonville, Texas: nd.), p. 29; Cater, *As It Was,* p. 140.

65 Benjamin T. Burton, *The Heinz Handbook of Nutrition* (New York: McGraw-Hill Book Co., 1965); Eva D. Wilson, et al, *Principles of Nutrition* (New York: John Wiley & Sons, 1967); Lenna F. Cooper, et al, *Nutrition in Health and Disease* (Philadelphia: J. B. Lippincott Co., 1963); Susan E. Gebhardt and Ruth H. Matthews, *Nutritive Value of Foods,* Home and Garden Bulletin #72 (Washington: U.S Department of Agriculture, U.S. Government Printing Office, 1960. Revised 1981), p. 56.

66 Kansas State College, School of Home Economics, *Practical Cookery* (New York: John Wiley & Sons, Inc., 1947), pp. 374–78. A pectin test given in this old college foods text states: "Mix 1 tablespoon of fruit juice to be tested with

1 tablespoon of grain, wood, or denatured alcohol. Do not taste! The last two are poison!! Amount of pectin in juice will be shown by amount of precipitant obtained. If a solid mass is formed, pectin is abundant." I did this test on sweet potatoes using denatured alcohol. A solid precipitant immediately appeared.

67 Griscom, *Fighting with Ross' Texas Cavalry Brigade,* p. 54.

Chapter 8: Glorious Tennessee

1 Griscom, *Fighting with Ross' Texas Cavalry Brigade,* p. 55.

2 Warner, *Generals in Gray,* p. 233; Eaton, *Jefferson Davis,* pp. 144, 181–83; Curt Anders, *Fighting Confederates* (New York: Dorset Press, 1990), pp. 69–73, 84–89; Gilbert E. Govan and James W. Livingwood, *General Joseph E. Johnston, C.S.A.* (Bobbs-Merrill Company, Inc., 1956. Reprint. New York: Konecky & Konecky, n.d.), p. 30.

3 Eaton, *Jefferson Davis,* pp. 3–13, 140; Anders, *Fighting Confederates,* pp. 21–22. Johnston had been severely wounded opposing McClellan's campaign to take Richmond in May 1862. Six months later, when Johnston recovered, Davis sent the general to Tennessee to take command of the Department of the West, partly because Davis had to assign Johnston somewhere; Govan and Livingwood, *General Joseph E. Johnston, C.S.A.,* pp. 28, 30–31, 59–71. Before Joseph Johnston resigned from the U.S. Army, his wife told him, "Jefferson Davis hates you. He has the power and he will ruin you." My view of Jefferson Davis surely is influenced by my concentration on the Confederate West. Concentrating on the East, especially Lee's Army of Northern Virginia, doubtless would result in a more favorable view of Davis.

4 *O.R.,* vol. 23, pt. 2, p. 646; *O.R.,* vol. 17, pt. 2, pp. 832–33, 838.

5 Rose, *Ross' Texas Brigade,* p. 92.

6 Keen, *The 6th Texas Cavalry,* p. 46; Barron, *Lone Star Defenders,* pp. 146–47; Sparks, *The War . . . As I Saw It,* p. 75.

7 Warner, *Generals in Gray,* pp. 152–53; Maury, *Recollections,* p. 124.

8 Griscom, *Fighting with Ross' Texas Cavalry Brigade,* pp. 55–57.

9 Ibid., p. 56; Rose, *Ross' Texas Brigade,* p. 92.

10 Griscom, *Fighting with Ross' Texas Cavalry Brigade,* p. 57; Warner, *Generals in Gray,* p. 262; *O.R.,* vol. 17, pt. 2, pp. 844–47. Van Dorn had left 1,300 cavalry to guard Vicksburg. The Twenty-seventh Texas was still known as Whitfield's Legion or the First Texas Legion and was commanded by Lt. Col. John C. Broocks; Lt. Col. Dudley W. Jones commanded the Ninth, Col. Sul

Ross the Sixth, and Maj. A. B. Stone the Third. The regiments bound for Tennessee were from Mississippi, Tennessee, Arkansas, Alabama, and Texas. The 1,300 left around Vicksburg were Arkansas, Texas, and Missouri regiments.

11 Griscom, *Fighting with Ross' Texas Cavalry Brigade*, p. 57.

12 Benner, *Sul Ross*, pp. 18–21, 34.

13 Griscom, *Fighting with Ross' Texas Cavalry Brigade*, p. 56; Garrett to William Gibbard, February 14, 1863, from camp near Florence, Alabama, in Garrett, *Civil War Letters*, pp. 73–74.

14 Keen, *The 6th Texas Cavalry*, p. 95.

15 Griscom, *Fighting with Ross' Texas Cavalry Brigade*, pp. 57–58.

16 Ibid., p. 58; *History of Tennessee* (Chicago: Goodspeed Publishing Co., 1887. Reprint. Easley, S.C.: Southern Historical Press, 1979), pp. 336–37.

17 Martin, "The Rogers Family," manuscript, February 1936, p. 1.

18 Garrett, *Civil War Letters*, foreword; *CSR-Texas*, roll 38. Garrett enlisted September 7, 1861.

19 Rose, *Ross' Texas Brigade*, p. 92; Keen, *The 6th Texas Cavalry*, p. 46; Griscom, *Fighting with Ross' Texas Cavalry Brigade*, p. 59; *O.R.*, vol. 52, pt. 2, p. 425. Van Dorn reported to Johnston February 22, 1863, from Columbia, Tennessee, stating that his horses needed shoes, and "I am troubled with tender feet, especially in the Texas Brigade."

20 Henry, *"First with the Most" Forrest*, p. 122; Rose, *Ross' Texas Brigade*, p. 149; Russell, *Pioneers of Titus County*, p. 151.

21 Griscom, *Fighting with Ross' Texas Cavalry Brigade*, p. 59; *O.R.*, vol. 23, pt. 1, pp. 77–78, 84, 116.

22 *O.R.*, vol. 23, pt. 1, pp. 116, 123–25; Barron, *Lone Star Defenders*, pp. 148–50.

23 Sparks, *The War . . . As I Saw It*, p. 75.

24 Griscom, *Fighting with Ross' Texas Cavalry Brigade*, p. 59; *O.R.*, vol. 23, pt. 1, pp. 124–25; Miller, "A Memoir of the Days of '61," p. 26; Barron, *Lone Star Defenders*, p. 148.

25 *O.R.*, vol. 23, pt. 1, p. 125; Griscom, *Fighting with Ross' Texas Cavalry Brigade*, p. 59; Sparks, *The War . . . As I Saw It*, p. 76.

26 Sparks, *The War . . . As I Saw It*, p. 76; *O.R.*, vol. 23, pt. 1, pp. 122–23.

27 *O.R.*, vol. 23, pt. 1, pp. 116–25; Barron, *Lone Star Defenders*, pp. 148–49; Sparks, *The War . . . As I Saw It*, p. 76; Griscom, *Fighting with Ross' Texas Cavalry Brigade*, pp. 59–60.

28 *O.R.*, vol. 23, pt. 1, pp. 116–25; Barron, *Lone Star Defenders*, p. 149; Miller, "A Memoir of the Days of '61," pp. 24–25.

29 O.R., vol. 23, pt. 1, p. 119; Barron, *Lone Star Defenders,* p. 149; Rose, *Ross' Texas Brigade,* p. 93.

30 Rose, *Ross' Texas Brigade,* p. 93; Griscom, *Fighting with Ross' Texas Cavalry Brigade,* p. 60; O.R., vol. 23, pt. 1, pp. 120, 125; Barron, *Lone Star Defenders,* p. 149.

31 O.R., vol. 23, pt. 1, p. 120; Wyeth, *That Devil Forrest,* p. 141; Jordan and Pryor, *Campaigns of . . . N. B. Forrest,* pp. 236–37.

32 Keen, *The 6th Texas Cavalry,* p. 48; Miller, "A Memoir of the Days of '61," p. 23.

33 Griscom, *Fighting with Ross' Texas Cavalry Brigade,* p. 60; O.R., vol. 23, pt. 1, pp. 74–75, 85–93, 109. The Federal prisoners were transported in boxcars to Richmond and exchanged in May. Coburn wrote his report in August.

34 O.R., vol. 23, pt. 1, pp. 109, 119; Rose, *Ross' Texas Brigade,* p. 93; Griscom, *Fighting with Ross' Texas Cavalry Brigade,* p. 60.

35 Rose, *Ross' Texas Brigade,* p. 93 (see pp. 152–56 for the history of Col. John H. Broocks).

36 O.R., vol. 23, pt. 1, p. 119; Barron, *Lone Star Defenders,* pp. 33, 150–51. In Sam Barron's Third Texas Cavalry, Beecher Donald, Moses Wyndham, and Drew "Redland Bully" Polk were killed. The *Official Records* notes only one officer in the Third, Lt. R. S. Tunnell, killed at Thompson's Station. See Rose, *Ross' Texas Brigade,* p. 19, for presentation of the flag to the Third Texas in Indian Territory.

37 Rose, *Ross' Texas Brigade,* pp. 93–94; Hartje, *Van Dorn,* p. 290.

38 O.R., vol. 23, pt. 1, p. 118. The Ninth participated in no other battle that was covered as thoroughly in the *Official Records* and other primary sources. The *Official Records,* vol. 23, part 1, pp. 115–27, contains reports and comments on the battle of Thompson's Station by the Ninth Texas Cavalry's regimental commander, Col. Dudley Jones; the regiment's brigade commander, Col. John W. Whitfield; the brigade's division commander, Brig. Gen. William H. Jackson; the division's corps commander, Maj. Gen. Earl Van Dorn; the corps' army commander, Gen. Braxton Bragg; and the army's department commander, Gen. Joseph E. Johnston. Lengthy reports from twelve Federal generals and colonels and a captain are included in the *Official Records,* plus detailed casualty reports of both Confederate and Union losses. During the Ninth's service in Indian Territory and Arkansas, when the war had first started, Confederate regimental colonels often filed reports that were forwarded to the War Department. Later, when the command situation became more structured, most battle reports were made by brigadier and major generals. As was mentioned before, Confederate records are considerably more fragmented than Union records. However, Federal forces also lost their papers and records when they were overrun. In addition to the reports in *Official Records,* the battle of Thompson's Station is discussed in the following primary sources used in this

book: Rose, Barron, Griscom, Sparks, Miller, Keen, and Jordon and Pryor. The more reports I read, the less I understood exactly what happened.

39 Rose, *Ross' Texas Brigade,* p. 98; Griscom, *Fighting with Ross' Texas Cavalry Brigade,* p. 60.

40 Griscom, *Fighting with Ross' Texas Cavalry Brigade,* p. 61.

41 Ibid., pp. 60–62; Beatty, *The Citizen-Soldier,* p. 233.

42 Griscom, *Fighting with Ross' Texas Cavalry Brigade,* pp. 60–61; McCarthy, *Detailed Minutia of Soldier Life,* p. 38; *CSR-Texas,* roll 56. James C. Bates's records show the Ninth's officers were appointed by order of Brig. Gen. William H. Jackson.

43 Griscom, *Fighting with Ross' Texas Cavalry Brigade,* pp. 59, 61. See *CSR-Texas,* roll 56, for Thomas Berry and James C. Bates, roll 48 for Dudley Jones, roll 60 for Capt. J. W. Sims, AQM, assigned by Van Dorn as corps paymaster on February 28, 1863; Griscom, *Fighting with Ross' Texas Cavalry Brigade,* p. 66. Griscom wrote on May 18, 1863, "Reorganized the Regiment according to rank of Captains"; *CSR-Texas,* roll 56. Thomas G. Berry's records state, "Promoted to Lt. Colonel, Ninth Texas Cav., 24 March 1863." Data in his file and in James C. Bates's file also include: "Register of Appointments: 2 Oct 1863 date to take rank; 3 Sept 1864 date of appointment; 5 January 1865 date of confirmation." These dates reflect the sluggish administrative processes in Richmond. Another card in Berry's file reads: "25 Sept 1861—G.O. #29— 1st Lt. Thomas G. Berry, Corps of artillery, is appointed Aide de camp to Brigadier General Lewiston." This must be another Thomas G. Berry, because the Ninth's Thomas G. Berry was sergeant of Quayle's Mounted Riflemen before the unit left Fort Worth, and on October 14, 1861, Berry was elected captain of Company A, Ninth Texas Cavalry.

44 *CSR-Texas,* rolls 56–60, March–April 1863 report. Roll 57, Company A: Pvt. F. M. Dyer of Birdwell had been serving as temporary orderly sergeant; Roll 56, F. O. Clare; Roll 57, A. B. Gant's health did not permit him to return to active service; Roll 59, James E. Moore and Thomas Purcell; Roll 57, Sgt. Phil Greenup of Grapevine was on special detail after deserters, by order of Colonel Jones; Roll 57, R. William Harrison was at a camp of dismounted men at Columbia; Roll 60, Isaac S. Thompkins of Grapevine was at Columbia with the dismounted men; Roll 57, Capt. Absalom B. Gant, age thirty-one, resigned November 21, 1863. Affidavit by Surgeon J. E. Robertson states Gant had suffered from chronic rheumatism and nephritis for more than twelve months.

45 Sparks, *The War . . . As I Saw It,* p. 78. The wording in Sparks's book fails to make clear what the new flag looked like. He wrote: "On our return to the old camp near Spring Hill Gen. Jackson had new flags made for his division and they were given to us near Spring Hill. The 4th regiment's flags were all alike and were adopted by order of Gen. Jackson and the same is now seen at our reunions and the flag of the Ninth Texas is now in the hands of John

Moreland at Cumby, Texas, held as custodian by order of the survivors of the brigade"; *O.R.,* vol. 24, pt. 3, p. 947. The organizational chart shows that the only "4th regiment" in Jackson's Division was the Fourth Mississippi; see "Mrs. Bates Wants Her Flag—The Ninth Texas," in *Confederate Veteran,* vol. 1, no. 5, May 1893, p. 178, for a description of the flag; see Tuck, *Civil War in Shadows, Hopkins County, Texas,* unnumbered pages in back of book, for a picture of the Ninth's flag with battle credits in white cloth.

46   Beatty, *The Citizen-Soldier,* p. 243. Beatty reported from Winchester, Tennessee, a full moon and a pleasant, cool, clear day on April 1, 1863; *CSR-Texas,* roll 59. George Roach of Company A, Ninth Texas, was killed in private difficulty at Lewisburg, Tennessee, on April 6, 1863; Griscom, *Fighting with Ross' Texas Cavalry Brigade,* pp. 63–64; Sparks, *The War . . . As I Saw It,* p. 68; Keen, *The 6th Texas Cavalry,* p. 46.

47   Griscom, *Fighting with Ross' Texas Cavalry Brigade,* p. 63; quote from Benner, *Sul Ross,* p. 91.

48   Ross to Lizzie Ross, April 12, 1863, in Shelton, "Ross . . . Civil War Letters," p. 49.

49   Griscom, *Fighting with Ross' Texas Cavalry Brigade,* p. 64; Sparks, *The War . . . As I Saw It,* p. 68. Portions of Dudley W. Jones's diary are quoted or paraphrased by Sparks. The diary begins April 23, 1863, and ends in mid-sentence January 15, 1864.

50   Griscom, *Fighting with Ross' Texas Cavalry Brigade,* p. 64; Barron, *Lone Star Defenders,* pp. 154–55.

51   Barron, *Lone Star Defenders,* p. 154.

52   *O.R.,* vol. 23, pt. 2, p. 233.

53   Hartje, *Van Dorn,* pp. 306–307.

54   Barron, *Lone Star Defenders,* pp. 154–55; Griscom, *Fighting with Ross' Texas Cavalry Brigade,* p. 65. For several versions of what happened that morning, see Hartje, *Van Dorn,* pp. 307–27. See Rose, *Ross' Texas Brigade,* pp. 99–100, for Victor Rose's account of the shooting and of Dr. Peter's arrest by a lieutenant of the Third Texas.

55   Sparks, *The War . . . As I Saw It,* p. 69; Rose, *Ross' Texas Brigade,* p. 102.

56   Rose, *Ross' Texas Brigade,* p. 102; Griscom, *Fighting with Ross' Texas Cavalry Brigade,* p. 65; Keen, *The 6th Texas Cavalry,* p. 47; Hartje, *Van Dorn,* p. 325.

57   Hartje, *Van Dorn,* pp. 322–23; Griscom, *Fighting with Ross' Texas Cavalry Brigade,* p. 65.

58   Griscom, *Fighting with Ross' Texas Cavalry Brigade,* pp. 65–66, 96; *O.R.,* vol. 52, pt. 2, pp. 467–68; Sparks, *The War . . . As I Saw It,* p. 69; Henry, *"First with the Most" Forrest,* p. 161.

59 Henry, *"First with the Most" Forrest*, pp. 144–61; Jordon and Pryor, *The Campaigns of . . . N. B. Forrest*, pp. 250–78; Wyeth, *That Devil Forrest*, p. 197. Capable military critics consider the pursuit and capture of Colonel Streight's command as one of Forrest's most brilliant achievements and one of the most remarkable performances known to warfare.

60 Jordon and Pryor, *The Campaigns of . . . N. B. Forrest*, pp. 277-78, 283-84; Henry, *"First with the Most" Forrest*, p. 161.

61 Griscom, *Fighting with Ross' Texas Cavalry Brigade*, p. 66.

62 Grant, *Personal Memoirs*, pp. 252, 278. Grant began landing his men on the east side of the Mississippi River April 30, 1863.

63 *O.R.*, vol. 24, pt. 1, pp. 244-45; Grant, *Personal Memoirs*, pp. 252, 278.

64 Griscom, *Fighting with Ross' Texas Cavalry Brigade*, p. 66; *O.R.*, vol. 24, pt. 3, p. 947. Abstract of return of Brig. Gen. W. H. Jackson's Cavalry Division, June 4, 1863, aggregate present: Field and staff 7; Escort 60 men; Brig. Gen. George B. Cosby's Brigade of the First, the Fourth, and Twenty-eighth Mississippi, 1,048 men; Clark's (Missouri) Artillery; Brig. Gen. Whitfield's Brigade of 1,815 men; King's Missouri Battery of 89 men, for a total of 3,019 men present out of an aggregate of 4,713 men. Whitfield's Brigade contained the Third Texas Cavalry, commanded by Lt. Col. J. S. Boggess; the Sixth Texas Cavalry, commanded by Col. L. S. Ross; the Ninth Texas Cavalry, commanded by Col. D. W. Jones; and the First Texas Legion, commanded by Lt. Col. J. H. Broocks.

65 Barron, *Lone Star Defenders*, p. 155; Sparks, *The War . . . As I Saw It*, p. 74; Keen, *The 6th Texas Cavalry*, p. 46; Griscom, *Fighting with Ross' Texas Cavalry Brigade*, p. 66.

Chapter 9: Guard Duty

1 Keen, *The 6th Texas Cavalry*, p. 49; Griscom, *Fighting with Ross' Texas Cavalry Brigade*, pp. 67–68; *O.R.*, vol. 24, pt. 3, p. 947.

2 Griscom, *Fighting with Ross' Texas Cavalry Brigade*, p. 67.

3 Ibid, pp. 67–78. The column moved through Courtland and Mount Hope, then along the northwestern edge of what is now the William S. Bankhead National Forest in Alabama; *O.R.*, vol. 24, pt. 3, p. 699.

4 *CSR-Texas*, roll 60. Thomas deserted May 28, 1863; was captured by Federal authorities December 30, 1863; and was soon exchanged. He did not return to the regiment.

5   O.R., vol. 24, pt. 3, p. 699; Griscom, *Fighting with Ross' Texas Cavalry Brigade,* p. 68. Miss M. L. Donor presented the Ninth with the Texas flag.

6   Griscom, *Fighting with Ross' Texas Cavalry Brigade,* p. 69. See Wheeler, *Cavalry Tactics,* Part First, pp. 13–19, for "Compliments by cavalry under review."

7   Griscom, *Fighting with Ross' Texas Cavalry Brigade,* pp. 69–70. June 14, 1863, the quartermaster secured some horses from mounted infantry pickets to re- mount men in the Ninth Texas Cavalry; Sparks, *The War . . . As I Saw It,* p. 288; Rose, *Ross' Texas Brigade,* p. 122; Barron, *Lone Star Defenders,* pp. 159–61, 276. By 1864 decent horses were selling for $1,000 to $2,000; Ross to Lizzie Ross, March 19, 1864, in Shelton, "Ross . . . Civil War Letters," p. 62.

8   Griscom, *Fighting with Ross' Texas Cavalry Brigade,* p. 69; Rose, *Ross' Texas Brigade,* pp. 147–48; Benner, *Sul Ross,* pp. 89–91; Ross to Lizzie Ross, April 12 and June 9, 1863, in Shelton, "Ross . . . Civil War Letters," pp. 49, 53; O.R., vol. 52, pt. 2, p. 497; O.R., vol. 24, pt. 1, p. 225. General Johnston wrote Richmond June 5, 1863: "Brigadier-General Whitfield, who was or- dered to report to me when I was in Tennessee, but could not, has just done so. What is your intention in regard to him? I am informed that it will be very unfortunate for him to command the brigade to which he has belonged."

9   Griscom, *Fighting with Ross' Texas Cavalry Brigade,* pp. 69–72.

10 Ibid., p. 70; Keen, *The 6th Texas Cavalry,* p. 49.

11 Griscom, *Fighting with Ross' Texas Cavalry Brigade,* p. 70; Keen, *The 6th Texas Cavalry,* pp. 49–50; Garrett to M. E. Gibbard, July 28, 1863, from Telehatchie [Pelahatchie] Station, in Garrett, *Civil War Letters,* p. 79; James Monroe Watson to Father, July 22 and August 1, 1863, in Judy Watson McClure, *Confederate from East Texas: The Civil War Letters of James Monroe Watson* (Quanah, Tex.: Nortex Press, 1976), pp. 14–19.

12 Crabb, Rogers family files.

13 Griscom, *Fighting with Ross' Texas Cavalry Brigade,* p. 70.

14 Ibid.; Barron, *Lone Star Defenders,* p. 162; A. A. S. McDougal to William Gibbard, June 21, 1863, from Brownsville, Mississippi, in Garrett, *Civil War Letters,* p. 77; Sparks, *The War . . . As I Saw It,* pp. 69, 78. Sparks wrote that the artillery at Vicksburg was heard in Titus County, Texas, a distance of at least three hundred miles; O.R., vol. 52, pt. 2, p. 497.

15 Stephen E. Ambrose with Edwin C. Bearss, et al, *Struggle for Vicksburg* (Harris- burg, Pa.: Historical Times, Inc., 1967. Reprint. Eastern National Park & Monument Association, 1994), p. 56; Gordon A. Cotton, *Yankee Bullets, Rebel Rations* (Vicksburg: The Office Supply Co., 1989), p. 34.

16 Griscom, *Fighting with Ross' Texas Cavalry Brigade,* pp. 71–72; *CSR-Texas,* roll 60. The wounded man, George W. Pointer, appears on no further rolls. Alanzo

Stephenson was back with the regiment when the May–June 1864 roll was taken.

17 *O.R.,* vol. 30, pt. 2, p. 806; *O.R.,* vol. 24, pt. 3, p. 989; Griscom, *Fighting with Ross' Texas Cavalry Brigade,* p. 72.

18 Griscom, *Fighting with Ross' Texas Cavalry Brigade,* p.72.

19 Griscom, *Fighting with Ross' Texas Cavalry Brigade,* p. 72; Sparks, *The War . . . As I Saw It,* p. 69; Keen, *The 6th Texas Cavalry,* pp. 50–51; Barron, *Lone Star Defenders,* p. 162; Garrett, *Civil War Letters.*

20 Ambrose et al, *Struggle for Vicksburg,* p. 27. Ambrose gives the population of Vicksburg as 4,600, taken from the 1860 census; Grant, *Personal Memoirs,* p. 299. Pemberton surrendered to Grant 31,600 men, 172 cannon, 60,000 muskets, and a large amount of ammunition; Davis and Johnston both contributed to the command problems. Davis should have directed Pemberton's and Bragg's communications through Johnston. Johnston had the authority to command both Pemberton and Bragg, but his communications with them were most often suggestions. The concept of a theater commander, which in essence was Johnston's position, was new to the Confederate army. The full general and the two major generals were accustomed to independent command, and the new arrangement put each officer in an awkward position.

21 *O.R.,* vol. 24, pt. 1, p. 224; Cotton, *Yankee Bullets, Rebel Rations,* p. 3; John B. Jones, *A Rebel War Clerk's Diary* (Philadelphia: J. B. Lippincott & Co., 1866. Reprint. Time-Life Books Inc., 1982), vol. 2, p. 20. Jones in Richmond viewed Pemberton's loss of Vicksburg as unpardonable; *O.R.,* vol. 24, pt. 3, p. 1043. Pemberton was relieved from command and sent to Demopolis, Alabama, to command the parole camps set up for his Army of Mississippi.

22 A. A. S. McDougal to Gibbard, June 21, 1863, from Brownsville, Mississippi, in Garrett, *Civil War Letters,* p. 77.

23 H. D. Lewis, born in Cherokee County, Texas, in 1895, said that when he was growing up in East Texas there were no Fourth of July celebrations because Independence Day was considered a Yankee holiday. Firecrackers were reserved for Christmas.

24 Keen, *The 6th Texas Cavalry,* p. 49.

25 Griscom, *Fighting with Ross' Texas Cavalry Brigade,* pp. 72–73; *O.R.,* vol. 24, pt. 3, pp. 988–89.

26 Griscom, *Fighting with Ross' Texas Cavalry Brigade,* pp. 72–73.

27 Sparks, *The War . . . As I Saw It,* pp. 247–56. Part of the time Sparks tells this story in first person and part of the time in third person. I changed a few quotes to first person for easier reading.

28 Griscom, *Fighting with Ross' Texas Cavalry Brigade,* pp. 73, 98; *CSR-Texas,* rolls 58, 60. Capt. D. C. Whiteman, Company E, was among the captured men.

The May–June 1863 roll shows J. W. Hutton, bugler with Company A, captured near Jackson on either July 7 or July 11, 1863. Three months later, September 11, 1863, Hutton escaped from the Federal prison camp at Morton, Illinois, and was not heard from again.

29 Grant, *Personal Memoirs,* pp. 301–302; *O.R.,* vol. 24, pt. 2, pp. 534–35.

30 Griscom, *Fighting with Ross' Texas Cavalry Brigade,* pp. 73-74; Barron, *Lone Star Defenders,* p. 163.

31 Barron, *Lone Star Defenders,* p. 164.

32 Sparks, *The War . . . As I Saw It,* p. 249; Le Grand, *The Military Hand-Book,* p. 15.

33 Sparks, *The War . . . As I Saw It,* p. 249; Griscom, *Fighting with Ross' Texas Cavalry Brigade,* p. 224. Pvt. M. C. Hart belonged to Company E, Ninth Texas Cavalry.

34 Sparks, *The War . . . As I Saw It,* p. 249; Griscom, *Fighting with Ross' Texas Cavalry Brigade,* p. 233. Henry G. Haynes, the senior lieutenant in Company I, was acting captain of the company. Sparks mentions "Captain Haynes" several times after Henry's brother, Capt. J. B. "Buster" Haynes, was killed at Corinth in October 1862.

35 Griscom, *Fighting with Ross' Texas Cavalry Brigade,* pp. 74–75; Barron, *Lone Star Defenders,* p. 164; Sparks, *The War . . . As I Saw It,* p. 79; *O.R.,* vol. 24, pt. 2, pp. 535, 554.

36 *O.R.,* vol. 24, pt. 2, pp. 226, 554–55. Leroy Carter reported that he belonged to the Third Iowa Infantry, Lauman's Division, and had been taken prisoner January 4, 1863, near Lexington, Mississippi, before W. H. Jackson's Division left for Tennessee. Carter "was detained because he was caught plundering." He had been kept under guard and attached to the blacksmith or farrier departments. "So much for his reliability," the Federal general reported. Carter reported that W. H. Jackson's Division consisted of: Cosby's Brigade, 400 men; First Mississippi, 400 men; Fourth Mississippi, 200 men; Starke's Regiment, 800 men; Wirt Adams's Brigade, 1,000 men; Ross's detachment, Sixth Texas, 350 men, and Bridge's Battalion, 200 men; Whitfield's Brigade, Ninth Texas, 300, Third Texas, 400, and Texas Legion, 180 men—for a total of 4,230 in Jackson's Division; *O.R.,* vol. 30, pt. 4, p. 656. Abstract from the return of Jackson's Cavalry Division, dated September 16, 1863, lists the strength of Whitfield's Brigade as 1,421 officers and men present with an aggregate of 1,774, and Ross's Brigade of the Sixth Texas and First Mississippi with 1,103 present and an aggregate of 1,351. Leroy's accounting of the strength of the Texas regiments was reasonably accurate. The Texans and the First Mississippi, 2,524 men present for duty, would have been able to put about 1,600 men in the field. The other 1,000 were dismounted or occupied with the duties and detachments required to maintain 3,200 men, their guns, mounts, commissary, wagons, headquarters, camps, and other support.

37 O.R., vol. 24, pt. 2, pp. 535, 660.

38 Ibid., p. 535; Griscom, *Fighting with Ross' Texas Cavalry Brigade*, p. 75; Sparks, *The War . . . As I Saw It*, p. 79.

39 Sparks, *The War . . . As I Saw It*, p. 79; O.R., vol. 24, pt. 3, p. 1016.

40 O.R., vol. 24, pt. 3, p. 1017; O.R., vol. 24, pt. 2, p. 536; Griscom, *Fighting with Ross' Texas Cavalry Brigade*, pp. 75–76.

41 O.R., vol. 24, pt. 2, p. 537; Griscom, *Fighting with Ross' Texas Cavalry Brigade*, p. 76.

42 Sparks, *The War . . . As I Saw It*, pp. 250–56.

43 Again, A.W. tells the story in first person part of the time and in third person part of the time.

44 Spies and deserters were more often hanged than shot.

45 Joe's "forebodings" at handling A.W.'s gun indicates he was a Yankee. However, he could have been a Confederate. After the battle at Davis's Mill, north of Holly Springs, Dr. Eugene Blocker of the Third Texas and Pvt. John Grimes of Company A, Ninth Texas, remained at the Federal hospital to care for the wounded Confederates.

46 Griscom, *Fighting with Ross' Texas Cavalry Brigade*, p. 76.

47 Ibid., pp. 76, 78; Sparks, *The War . . . As I Saw It*, p. 69; Barron, *Lone Star Defenders*, p. 165; Garrett to M. E. Gibbard, June 28, 1863, from Telehatchie [Pelahatchie] Station, in Garrett, *Civil War Letters*, p. 79.

48 Griscom, *Fighting with Ross' Texas Cavalry Brigade*, p. 76; Sparks, *The War . . . As I Saw It*, p. 71; O.R., vol. 24, pt. 3, pp. 1039–42. Abstract of Lt. Gen. William Hardee's Army of Mississippi and Eastern Louisiana, July 30, 1863. Hardee had 30,429 officers and men present for duty and 53,999 present and absent. Gen. Joseph E. Johnston was in command of the Department of the West.

49 Griscom, *Fighting with Ross' Texas Cavalry Brigade*, pp. 76–78.

50 Ibid., p. 78; Sparks, *The War . . . As I Saw It*, p. 69; Barron, *Lone Star Defenders*, p. 165; CSR-Texas, roll 58. Dudley Jones was granted a forty-day leave from August 11, 1863; CSR-Texas, roll 57. Capt. Hamilton C. Dial, Company K, was on leave from August 11 to September 19, 1863; CSR-Texas, roll 59. Lt. Thomas Purcell, commanding Company A, was on forty-day leave from August 11, 1863.

51 CSR-Texas, rolls 57, 58, 60; Barron, *Lone Star Defenders*, p. 165. Barron wrote that the furloughs were for thirty days.

52 Barron, *Lone Star Defenders*, p. 165; CSR-Texas, roll 18. Sam Barron's records show he received a forty-day leave; Martha L. Crabb, *Over the Mountain* (Balti-

more: Gateway Press, 1990), pp. 275–328. Capt. John Germany, a Texas resident in 1861, was a member of the large and prolific Germany family of Georgia, Mississippi, and Texas; *CSR-Texas,* roll 19. John Germany was born in 1830 in Georgia and enrolled in Company C, Third Texas Cavalry, on June 3, 1861, in Cherokee County, Texas. He gave his address in June 1862 as New Salem, Texas.

53 *CSR-Texas,* rolls 22, 56, 60.

54 Griscom, *Fighting with Ross' Texas Cavalry Brigade,* pp. 77–79; Barron, *Lone Star Defenders,* pp. 165–66; *O.R.,* vol. 30, pt. 2, pp. 811–817.

55 Barron, *Lone Star Defenders,* p. 166; Griscom, *Fighting with Ross' Texas Cavalry Brigade,* p. 79.

56 Griscom, *Fighting with Ross' Texas Cavalry Brigade,* pp. 79–80.

57 Hale, *The Third Texas Cavalry,* p. 193; James Monroe Watson to Father, August 1, 1863, in McClure, *Confederate from East Texas,* p. 23; Barron, *Lone Star Defenders,* pp. 160, 276. Sam Barron had paid $300 for a horse in mid-1863. Early in 1864 a decent horse was worth $1,000, and Capt. John Germany's bay was valued at $2,000; *CSR-Texas,* rolls 56–60. Reuben Rogers, Jesse Rogers, J. Amos Burgoon, and Augustus R. Creed were paid regularly every two months, on the last days of February, April, June, and August 1862. They were not paid again until June 30, 1863, ten months later. After the October 1863 payment, the records show the men were not again paid through June 30, 1864. The May–June 1864 roll is the last surviving roll. There are no extant records of the men in the Ninth Texas after that roll, which was taken "In the field near Marietta, Georgia." For an account of inflation in Richmond, Virginia, see Jones, *A Rebel War Clerk's Diary,* vol. 2, pp. 8, 56, 89, 97.

58 Griscom, *Fighting with Ross' Texas Cavalry Brigade,* p. 80; *O.R.,* vol. 31, pt. 3, p. 841; Warner, *Generals in Gray,* pp. 2–3, 64. Cosby was born in 1830 in Kentucky and graduated from the Military Academy in 1852.

59 Griscom, *Fighting with Ross' Texas Cavalry Brigade,* p. 79; Barron, *Lone Star Defenders,* p. 171; Rose, *Ross' Texas Brigade,* pp. 103, 147–48; Benner, *Sul Ross,* p. 91; *O.R.,* vol. 24, pt. 1, p. 225; *O.R.,* vol. 52, pt. 2, p. 497.

60 Benner, *Sul Ross,* p. 92; Rose, *Ross' Texas Brigade,* pp. 121–22; *O.R.,* vol. 52, pt. 2, p. 497; *O.R.,* vol. 24, pt. 3, p. 1041. Abstract of return, Organization of the Army of the Department of Mississippi and Eastern Louisiana, July 30, 1863: Whitfield's Brigade contained Third Texas Cavalry, Ninth Texas Cavalry, First Texas Legion, and Bridges's Battalion. The Sixth Texas Cavalry, commanded by Maj. Jack Wharton, was detached to Col. L. S. Ross's Brigade; *O.R.,* vol. 30, pt. 4, pp. 656, 704. September 16, 1863, Ross's Brigade consisted of the First Mississippi, Col. R. A. Pinson commanding, and the Sixth Texas, Capt. P. R. Ross, Sul's older brother, commanding. On September 26, 1863, Ross's Brigade reported 1,094 officers and men present for duty and an

aggregate of 1,351. On the same date, Whitfield's Brigade reported 1,320 present for duty and an aggregate of 1,644.

61 From early 1864 to the end of the war, Mabry commanded a Mississippi cavalry brigade; Hale, *The Third Texas Cavalry*, pp. 29, 115, 121, 188; Allardice, *More Generals in Gray*, pp. 146–47; Rose, *Ross' Texas Brigade*, pp. 142–46. Mabry studied at the University of Tennessee at Knoxville before moving to Jefferson, Texas. Rose wrote that Mabry was "absolutely fearless, and cool to indifference in the midst of danger." Mabry remained a colonel but commanded a brigade, despite his superiors' continuing efforts to secure his promotion to brigadier general.

62 Griscom, *Fighting with Ross' Texas Cavalry Brigade*, p. 80; Warner, *Generals in Gray*, pp. 183–84.

63 Griscom, *Fighting with Ross' Texas Cavalry Brigade*, p. 80; *CSR-Texas*, roll 57, J. N. Dodson's records. The roll of March–April 1863, taken in Tennessee, notes that Dodson was "Dropped from the Rolls by order of General Bragg." On August 10, 1863, "Letter to James A. Seddon, Sec. of War, from John H. Reassain [surely John H. Reagan of Texas, Postmaster General of the Confederacy] states that J. N. Dodson was dismissed from the service for being absent without leave." Dodson submitted an application to the War Department for reinstatement and promotion. October 2, 1863, Dodson resigned. Later in the fall, he applied for and received payment for a shotgun, a horse, and rigging lost at the battle of Elkhorn Tavern.

64 Sparks, *The War . . . As I Saw It*, pp. 69–71; *CSR-Texas*, rolls 56–58; see Allan Nivens, *The War for the Union: The Organized War 1863–1864* (New York: Charles Scribner's Sons, 1971), vol. 3, pp. 117–19, for discouragement throughout the Confederacy. See pp. 374–412 for a discussion of Southern morale in late 1863; *O.R.*, vol. 24, pt. 3, p. 1014. Paroled Confederates from Vicksburg were granted a month's leave. The officers knew the men were going home, with or without permission; Jones, *A Rebel War Clerk's Diary*, vol. 1, p. 391. On July 31, 1863, Jones wrote that in Mississippi "the people are fast losing hope."

65 Griscom, *Fighting with Ross' Texas Cavalry Brigade*, pp. 80–81, 100; Garrett to William Gibbard, from Benton, Mississippi, July 23, 1864, in Garrett, *Civil War Letters*, pp. 88–89. Although the letter is dated July 1864, the incidents reported indicate it was written in February or March 1864. The Sixth Texas was in Georgia in July 1864; Jones, *A Rebel War Clerk's Diary*, vol. 2, pp. 3–5, 8. Desertions in the East reflected the general gloom felt in Richmond. Aside from battlefield losses, the Confederate dollar continued to fall in value. August 4, 1863, a gold dollar was worth $12 to $15 in Confederate paper. Flour sold for $40 a barrel and four days later had gone up to $45.

66 Griscom, *Fighting with Ross' Texas Cavalry Brigade*, pp. 80–82. The first Grand Review was held on September 9, the second on September 26, 1863. Lts.

Henry G. Haynes, Company I, and Macum Russell, Company G, went with Bates to Texas.

67 Ibid., p. 81; Sparks, *The War . . . As I Saw It*, p. 67; *O.R.*, vol. 31, pt. 3, p. 746. Abstract of Return, S. D. Lee's Cavalry, November 23, 1863, lists Jones as a lieutenant colonel; *CSR-Texas*, roll 58. Jones was promoted to colonel on March 24, 1863. It often took many months for promotions to clear the morass of paperwork in Richmond.

68 Grant, *Personal Memoirs*, pp. 310–13; Griscom, *Fighting with Ross' Texas Cavalry Brigade*, p. 81.

69 Griscom, *Fighting with Ross' Texas Cavalry Brigade*, pp. 82–83.

70 Ibid., p. 83; *CSR-Texas*, roll 58, for James P. King and Samuel D. King.

71 Griscom, *Fighting with Ross' Texas Cavalry Brigade*, p. 83; Mrs. Treadwell's Place was noted as being on Bogue Chito Creek, shown in U.S. War Department, *Atlas to Accompany the Official Records*, Plate CLV, as an eastern tributary to the Big Black, due north of Clinton. Plate CLV also shows another Bogue Chitto Creek in the southern part of the state, south of Brookhaven; William Thorndale and William Dollarhide, *Map Guide to the U.S. Federal Censuses 1790–1920* (Baltimore: Genealogical Publishing Co., Inc., 1987), p. 185. The county lines in this part of Mississippi have not changed since 1860.

72 *CSR-Texas*, rolls 57–58. Hamilton C. Dial was mustered in on October 14, 1861, as a third lieutenant and was promoted to captain at the May 26, 1862, reorganization when the regiment was serving as infantry at Corinth; Reuben's company mates Jim McDaniel and Levi Leonard were also with Dial's detachment hunting blankets; Sparks, *The War . . . As I Saw It*, p. 71. Jones noted in his diary that Dial's detachment returned on November 6, 1863; *O.R.*, vol. 31, pt. 3, pp. 748–49. A month later, Gen. S. D. Lee wrote from Grenada to headquarters: "The cavalry are much in need of blankets, they have no tents, and as it is not expected that they should have them, I request that they be furnished before other troops, as they have not the advantage of being stationary to make themselves comfortable by temporary shelters."

73 Griscom, *Fighting with Ross' Texas Cavalry Brigade*, p. 83; *CSR-Texas*, rolls 56, 57.

74 *CSR-Texas*, roll 56; Young, *Grapevine Area History*, p. 142. David Cate was born in 1845 in Missouri and died in 1926 in Justin, Texas.

75 Sparks, *The War . . . As I Saw It*, p. 70.

76 Ibid., pp. 67, 70.

77 Ibid., pp. 67, 69–70; Griscom, *Fighting with Ross' Texas Cavalry Brigade*, p. 81.

78 Griscom, *Fighting with Ross' Texas Cavalry Brigade*, p. 83; *CSR-Texas*, roll 56, "Stations of Field & Staff, Sept/Oct 1863, the Ninth Texas at Treadwell's Place." Griscom's diary shows the Ninth camped at Mrs. Treadwell's on Octo-

ber 7 through 9, when the Minute Inspection was held, and were again at Treadwell's from October 20 through November 6, 1863. The roll was likely taken at the end of October.

79 Crabb, Rogers family files.

80 Griscom, *Fighting with Ross' Texas Cavalry Brigade,* p. 83: *CSR-Texas,* rolls 56–80. The *Official Records* does not note the Ninth's strength, only that of the brigade. The numbers could be ascertained by tallying each of the ten companies. By October 9, 1863, Company A had enlisted a total of 114 men. Since the first of 1863, James C. Thomas had deserted, George Roach was killed in private difficulty in Tennessee, and Jonathan W. Hutton was taken prisoner while on a scout near Jackson on July 11, 1863. Company A had gained 4 men during the year—J. E. Brown had been transferred back to the company from Van Dorn's bodyguard, and three Mississippians had joined: Sam F. Boaz, T. T. Dew, and B. F. Passmere. The roll shows that Company A had lost a total of 44 men—6 killed, 2 mortally wounded, 21 wounded in action, 14 taken prisoner, and one had deserted. Solon Dunn had returned from leave, but Joseph Simmons was still absent. Richard Boaz, wounded on the Holly Springs Raid, was still in the Texas General Hospital at Quitman, Mississippi. David Cate, also wounded on the famous raid, had just returned. E. A. Eckhardt, wounded on the raid, had returned. Three men were sick in camp, and Amos Burgoon, John Mullins, F. M. Lewis, Isaac Bradley, and John Dunn were in the hospital. John Dunn's files in the National Archives note that he was "Absent, Sick in the hospital Oct. 12, 1863"; Payne and Dunn, *Dunn Family,* pp. 148–63. John Dunn's diary states that he returned to duty January 1, 1864, "after being absent some time on account of a fractured limb." Later, Dunn mentions his leg; Young, *Grapevine Area History,* pp. 183–86. John Dunn was from Grapevine, Tarrant County, Texas.

81 *CSR-Texas,* rolls 56–60; *O.R.,* vol. 10, pt. 2, p. 489.

82 *O.R.,* vol. 24, pt. 2, p. 555; Griscom, *Fighting with Ross' Texas Cavalry Brigade,* p. 78; *CSR-Texas,* rolls 56–60.

83 Griscom, *Fighting with Ross' Texas Cavalry Brigade,* pp. 101–102. See *O.R.,* vol. 30, pt. 2, pp. 802–17, for reports of the Messenger's Ferry expedition. In the Ninth Texas, M. C. Hart and J. R. Cantrill were wounded.

84 Griscom, *Fighting with Ross' Texas Cavalry Brigade,* pp. 102–103; Rose, *Ross' Texas Brigade,* p. 103.

85 Sparks, *The War . . . As I Saw It,* p. 256.

86 Ibid., p. 71; Griscom, *Fighting with Ross' Texas Cavalry Brigade,* p. 102.

87 Griscom, *Fighting with Ross' Texas Cavalry Brigade,* p. 102.

88 Sparks, *The War . . . As I Saw It,* p. 72.

89 Griscom, *Fighting with Ross' Texas Cavalry Brigade,* p. 103.

90 Ibid.; *O.R.,* vol. 30, pt. 2, p. 816. On October 15, 1863, Col. Wirt Adams was commanding General Cosby's Brigade.

91 Ross to Lizzie Ross, June 9 and August 25, 1863, in Shelton, "Ross . . . Civil War Letters," pp. 53, 55.

92 Rose, *Ross' Texas Brigade,* p. 168; Griscom, *Fighting with Ross' Texas Cavalry Brigade,* pp. 117–18.

93 Rose, *Ross' Texas Brigade,* p. 168.

94 Ibid. Ross furnished copies to Victor Rose of the letters from Johnston, Lee, Jackson, and Maury. Maury was commanding the Department of the Gulf.

95 Ross to Lizzie Ross, December 16, 1863, in Shelton, "Ross . . . Civil War Letters," p. 59.

96 *O.R.,* vol. 31, pt. 3, p. 794; Benner, *Sul Ross,* p. 97.

97 *O.R.,* vol. 52, pt. 2, p. 577; Griscom, *Fighting with Ross' Texas Cavalry Brigade,* p. 103. The exact quote from Griscom's diary is: "He makes a speech and says he will give them something else to do but guard duty"; *CSR-Texas,* roll 41. L. S. Ross was promoted to brigadier general December 21, 1863.

Chapter 10: A Texas Ranger

1 Benner, *Sul Ross,* pp. 3, 24–25, 90. Ross was born September 27, 1838; Ross to Lizzie Ross, December 16, 1863, in Shelton, "Ross . . . Civil War Letters," pp. 58–59; Rose, *Ross' Texas Brigade,* p. 103.

2 Griscom, *Fighting with Ross' Texas Cavalry Brigade,* p. 103; *O.R.,* vol. 52, pt. 2, pp. 640–41. April 14, 1864, the official name of the Texas Brigade was changed from Jackson's Second Brigade to Ross's Brigade.

3 The Twenty-seventh Texas Cavalry was still known as the First Texas Legion; Griscom, *Fighting with Ross' Texas Cavalry Brigade,* p. 103.

4 Griscom, *Fighting with Ross' Texas Cavalry Brigade,* pp. xiii, 103. George Griscom returned to Mississippi and married Bettie H. Birdsong on December 20, 1866.

5 *CSR-Texas,* roll 41; Griscom, *Fighting with Ross' Texas Cavalry Brigade,* pp. 103–104; see Sparks, *The War . . . As I Saw It,* p. 72, for the diary of Colonel Jones; *CSR-Texas,* roll 56. December 24, 1863, J. H. Bunch of Lexington, Mississippi, enlisted in Company A, Ninth Texas.

6 Griscom, *Fighting with Ross' Texas Cavalry Brigade,* p. 104.

7 Ibid.

8   *O.R.*, vol. 31, pt. 3, pp. 841–42; *O.R.*, vol. 34, pt. 2, p. 999; Barron, *Lone Star Defenders*, p. 173.

9   Barron, *Lone Star Defenders*, p. 173; Griscom, *Fighting with Ross' Texas Cavalry Brigade*, p. 104; Sparks, *The War . . . As I Saw It*, p. 72; *O.R.*, vol. 34, pt. 2, p. 999; *O.R.*, vol. 53, p. 925. Maj. Gen. Richard Taylor, commanding the Trans-Mississippi Department, wrote on January 9, 1864, that the shipment contained 3,400 stand of arms; Hale, *The Third Texas Cavalry*, p. 198, states that the arms trains of 23 wagons contained 2,000 rifles.

10 Griscom, *Fighting with Ross' Texas Cavalry Brigade*, p. 104; Barron, *Lone Star Defenders*, p. 174.

11 Barron, *Lone Star Defenders*, pp. 173–74; *O.R.*, vol. 31, pt. 3, pp. 879–80; *O.R.*, vol. 32, pt. 2, pp. 823–24; Sparks, *The War . . . As I Saw It*, p. 72.

12 *O.R.*, vol. 31, pt. 3, pp. 879–80; *O.R.*, vol. 32, pt. 2, pp. 823–24; Barron, *Lone Star Defenders*, pp. 173–74; Sparks, *As I Saw It*, p. 72.

13 Barron, *Lone Star Defenders*, p. 173; *O.R.*, vol. 32, pt. 2, p. 823.

14 Barron, *Lone Star Defenders*, p. 174; Griscom, *Fighting with Ross' Texas Cavalry Brigade*, p. 104.

15 Barron, *Lone Star Defenders*, p. 176.

16 Griscom, *Fighting with Ross' Texas Cavalry Brigade*, pp. 104–105; *O.R.*, vol. 32, pt. 2., pp. 825–26; Sparks, *The War . . . As I Saw It*, p. 72. There is disagreement on the number of guns each man carried. In his diary, Colonel Jones said three each. Rose, *Ross' Texas Brigade*, p. 104, says two. Barron, *Lone Star Defenders*, p. 174, says "usually four apiece." Griscom, *Fighting with Ross' Texas Cavalry Brigade*, pp. 104–105, says the officers carried three and the men two.

17 Barron, *Lone Star Defenders*, p. 174.

18 Griscom, *Fighting with Ross' Texas Cavalry Brigade*, p. 105; Sparks, *The War . . . As I Saw It,* p. 72.

19 Griscom, *Fighting with Ross' Texas Cavalry Brigade*, p. 105; Rose, *Ross' Texas Brigade*, p. 104; Barron, *Lone Star Defenders*, pp. 174–75.

20 Barron, *Lone Star Defenders*, p. 174.

21 Griscom, *Fighting with Ross' Texas Cavalry Brigade*, p. 105; Sparks, *The War . . . As I Saw It,* p. 72.

22 Sparks, *The War . . . As I Saw It*, p. 72; Barron, *Lone Star Defenders*, pp. 174–75; Griscom, *Fighting with Ross' Texas Cavalry Brigade*, p. 105; *O.R.*, vol. 31, pt. 3, p. 880. The number of men who rode from the Sunflower to the Mississippi is not given in any source I have found. My estimate of 800 to 1,000 is based on earlier accounts of brigade strength given by Ross and by General Richardson, and on the number of guns delivered to Gaines Ferry (2,000).

23 Barron, *Lone Star Defenders*, p. 176.

24 Griscom, *Fighting with Ross' Texas Cavalry Brigade*, pp. 105–106; Barron, *Lone Star Defenders*, pp. 175–76.

25 Griscom, *Fighting with Ross' Texas Cavalry Brigade*, pp. 105–106. Griscom wrote that it was twelve miles from Ruxey's Bridge to Courtney Plantation; Sparks, *The War . . . As I Saw It*, p. 72. Jones wrote in his diary that it was eight miles from the bridge to the plantation.

26 Barron, *Lone Star Defenders*, p. 175; *O.R.*, vol. 32, pt. 1, pp. 66–67; *O.R.*, vol. 34, pt. 2, p. 1000; Sparks, *The War . . . As I Saw It*, p. 72; Hale, *The Third Texas Cavalry*, p. 199.

27 Barron, *Lone Star Defenders*, p. 175; Griscom, *Fighting with Ross' Texas Cavalry Brigade*, p. 105.

28 Griscom, *Fighting with Ross' Texas Cavalry Brigade*, p. 107; Sparks, *The War . . . As I Saw It*, pp. 72–73; *O.R.*, vol. 32, pt. 1, pp. 66–67; *O.R.*, vol. 34, pt. 2, p. 862.

29 Griscom, *Fighting with Ross' Texas Cavalry Brigade*, pp. 106–108; Sparks, *The War . . . As I Saw It*, p. 73; Barron, *Lone Star Defenders*, p. 176; *O.R.*, vol. 53, p. 925. The number of arms carried across the river is stated as 2,000 by Ross (*O.R.*, vol. 32, pt. 1, pp. 66–67), as 2,000 by Barron (*Lone Star Defenders*, p. 173), as 1,500 by Richard Taylor (*O.R.*, vol. 34, pt. 2, p. 1000, and vol. 53, p. 925), and by Adjutant Thomas E. Vick as about 1,500 (*O.R.*, vol. 53., p. 925).

30 Griscom, *Fighting with Ross' Texas Cavalry Brigade*, p. 108; Barron, *Lone Star Defenders*, p. 173; *O.R.*, vol. 34, pt. 2, p. 862. The brigade had been ordered back to Benton.

31 Sparks, *The War . . . As I Saw It*, pp. 82–83, 246; Garrett, *Fort Worth: A Frontier Triumph*, p. 214.

32 *O.R.*, vol. 32, pt. 1, pp. 387–88; *O.R.*, vol. 32, pt. 2, pp. 514, 824–25, 832; Griscom, *Fighting with Ross' Texas Cavalry Brigade*, p. 108; Cater, *As It Was*, pp. 176–77.

33 Sparks, *The War . . . As I Saw It*, p. 263; Wheeler, *Cavalry Tactics*, Part Third, p. 46.

34 Sparks, *The War . . . As I Saw It*, pp. 263–65.

35 Ibid., pp. 263–64.

36 *O.R.*, vol. 32, pt. 1, pp. 315–18.

37 *O.R.*, vol. 32, pt. 1, pp. 387–88; *O.R.*, vol. 32, pt. 2, pp. 826–27; Griscom, *Fighting with Ross' Texas Cavalry Brigade*, p. 109.

38 Griscom, *Fighting with Ross' Texas Cavalry Brigade,* p. 109; *O.R.,* vol. 32, pt. 1, pp. 333, 370, 387–88; *O.R.,* vol. 32, pt. 2, pp. 826–27.

39 *O.R.,* vol. 32, pt. 2, pp. 826–27; *O.R.,* vol. 32, pt. 1, pp. 388–89; Griscom, *Fighting with Ross' Texas Cavalry Brigade,* p. 110.

40 Griscom, *Fighting with Ross' Texas Cavalry Brigade,* p. 110; *O.R.,* vol. 32, pt. 1, pp. 388–89; *O.R.,* vol. 32, pt. 2, pp. 827–28, 830.

41 *O.R.,* vol. 32, pt. 1, pp. 388–89; *O.R.,* vol. 32, pt. 2, pp. 828–29, 831; Griscom, *Fighting with Ross' Texas Cavalry Brigade,* p. 110. Lt. William A. Wingo of Company B was severely wounded in the head. J. H. Smith of Company B was wounded in the foot. T. G. Coleman of Company D was shot in the arm. G. T. Moore of Company G was slightly wounded in the head. Lt. H. T. Young of Company K was slightly wounded; Banks, William P. Jr., "William Anderson Wingo, Lieutenant, C.S.A.," typescript (Hillsboro, Tex.: H. B. Simpson History Complex, 1995). Wingo's records show he was sent to the hospital immediately after his injury. There are no further records of Wingo after the May–June 1864 roll taken in Georgia, which noted simply that he was "in the hospital." Family stories state a woman cared for him in Mississippi. Wingo's wound healed, and he was paroled May 15, 1865, with the regiment.

42 *O.R.,* vol. 32, pt. 1, pp. 317, 389; *O.R.,* vol. 32, pt. 2, pp. 826–37, 830–31; Rose, *Ross' Texas Brigade,* pp. 104–105; Griscom, *Fighting with Ross' Texas Cavalry Brigade,* p. 110; Sparks, *The War . . . As I Saw It,* p. 232.

43 Sparks, *The War . . . As I Saw It,* p. 232; Griscom, *Fighting with Ross' Texas Cavalry Brigade,* p. 110; *O.R.,* vol. 32, pt. 1, p. 389; *O.R.,* vol. 32, pt. 2, p. 831; Payne and Dunn, *Dunn Family,* p. 149, John Dunn's diary.

44 *O.R.,* vol. 32, pt. 1, p. 315; *O.R.,* vol. 32, pt. 2, p. 832; Griscom, *Fighting with Ross' Texas Cavalry Brigade,* p. 111; Barron, *Lone Star Defenders,* p. 177.

45 *O.R.,* vol. 32, pt. 1, pp. 318, 370.

46 Griscom, *Fighting with Ross' Texas Cavalry Brigade,* p. 111; *O.R.,* vol. 32, pt. 1, pp. 358, 389–90; *O.R.,* vol. 32, pt. 2, pp. 340–41, 693; Grant, *Personal Memoirs,* pp. 354–55.

47 Payne and Dunn, *Dunn Family,* p. 149; Griscom, *Fighting with Ross' Texas Cavalry Brigade,* p. 111; *O.R.,* vol. 32, pt. 1, p. 390.

48 *O.R.,* vol. 32, pt. 1, p. 390; *CSR-Texas,* roll 56; Griscom, *Fighting with Ross' Texas Cavalry Brigade,* p. 111.

49 Barron, *Lone Star Defenders,* pp. 178–79; Griscom, *Fighting with Ross' Texas Cavalry Brigade,* p. 111; *O.R.,* vol. 32, pt. 1, p. 390.

50 Barron, *Lone Star Defenders,* pp. 178–79.

51 Ibid., p. 179.

52 Ibid., pp. 179–80; Henry, *"First with the Most" Forrest,* p. 222.

53 Henry, *"First with the Most" Forrest*, pp. 224–25; Griscom, *Fighting with Ross' Texas Cavalry Brigade*, p. 112; *O.R.*, vol. 32, pt. 1, p. 390.

54 Henry, *"First with the Most" Forrest*, pp. 217–32.

55 Ibid., p. 233.

56 *O.R.*, vol. 32, pt. 1, pp. 318–20, 370, 390.

57 Ibid., p. 390; Griscom, *Fighting with Ross' Texas Cavalry Brigade*, pp. 112–13; Rose, *Ross' Texas Brigade*, p. 105.

58 Griscom, *Fighting with Ross' Texas Cavalry Brigade*, pp. 112–13; Young, *Grapevine Area History Book*, p. 103. Walter Leake Jones belonged to Company A; Barron, *Lone Star Defenders*, pp. 181–82; *O.R.*, vol. 32, pt. 1, p. 390.

59 *O.R.*, vol. 32, pt. 1, p. 390; Griscom, *Fighting with Ross' Texas Brigade*, p. 113.

60 *O.R.*, vol. 32, pt. 1, pp. 367, 385, 390; Griscom, *Fighting with Ross' Texas Cavalry Brigade*, p. 113.

61 Griscom, *Fighting with Ross' Texas Cavalry Brigade*, pp. 113–14; Barron, *Lone Star Defenders*, p. 182; *O.R.*, vol. 32, pt. 1, pp. 383, 390.

62 *O.R.*, vol. 32, pt. 1, p. 383; Griscom, *Fighting with Ross' Texas Cavalry Brigade*, p. 113.

63 *O.R.*, vol. 32, pt. 1, pp. 384–85, 387–88, 390–91; Griscom, *Fighting with Ross' Texas Cavalry Brigade*, pp. 113–14. Griscom reported the Confederates lost 8 killed and 52 wounded with the Texans losing 3 killed and 25 wounded. In the Ninth Texas, George W. Pointer was shot in the shoulder, Lt. C. Duncan was shot in the thigh, and J. W. Winton was also wounded.

64 *O.R.*, vol. 32, pt. 1, pp. 384, 391.

65 Ibid., pp. 384–85.

66 Ibid., pp. 384–85, 391; Barron, *Lone Star Defenders*, p. 184.

67 *O.R.*, vol. 32, pt. 1, p. 386.

68 Griscom, *Fighting with Ross' Texas Cavalry Brigade*, p. 114. The Ninth remained at Benton; the Third was sent to Pritchett's Crossroads, the Sixth to Richland, and the Legion to Deasonville.

69 Ibid., pp. 114–15.

70 Ibid.

71 Sparks, *The War . . . As I Saw It*, p. 256. John Sparks was shot July 6, 1863; *CSR-Texas*, roll 60. Records of Sgt. John Napoleon Sparks state he was captured June 10, 1864, at Garvin's Ferry, on the Sunflower River, was exchanged at Vicksburg July 29, 1864, and was paroled with the regiment May 18, 1865; White, *Index to Texas CSA Pension Files*, file #974777. John N. Sparks died on February 10, 1916, at the age of eighty-one.

72 Griscom, *Fighting with Ross' Texas Cavalry Brigade,* p. 115.

73 Ibid., pp. 138, 174; Ross to Lizzie Ross, April 26, 1864, in Shelton, "Ross . . . Civil War Letters," p. 63.

74 Barron, *Lone Star Defenders,* pp. 186–87.

75 Ibid., p. 188; Griscom, *Fighting with Ross' Texas Cavalry Brigade,* p. 139; *O.R.,* vol. 32, pt. 1, pp. 671–72; Ross to Lizzie Ross, April 26, 1864, in Shelton, "Ross . . . Civil War Letters," pp. 62–63.

76 Sparks, *The War . . . As I Saw It,* pp. 80–81; Griscom, *Fighting with Ross' Texas Cavalry Brigade,* p. 140.

77 Ross to Lizzie Ross, April 26, 1864, in Shelton, "Ross . . . Civil War Letters," pp. 62–63; Griscom, *Fighting with Ross' Texas Cavalry Brigade,* pp. 139–40; *O.R.,* vol. 32, pt. 1, pp. 671–72.

78 *O.R.,* vol. 38, pt. 4, p. 691. Sixty men, under the command of Lt. M. M. Scoggins (or Scroggins), Company E, Ninth Texas, were sent to Selma; Griscom, *Fighting with Ross' Texas Cavalry Brigade,* p. 141.

79 Griscom, *Fighting with Ross' Texas Cavalry Brigade,* pp. 141–42; Sparks, *The War . . . As I Saw It,* p. 82.

80 Griscom, *Fighting with Ross' Texas Cavalry Brigade,* p. 142. The division traveled to Rome by way of Jacksonville, Alabama, and Cave Springs, Georgia; *O.R.,* vol. 38, pt. 3, p. 704.

Chapter 11: Stalling Sherman

When Ross's Brigade reached Georgia, Lt. George L. Griscom, Adjutant, began noting in his diary the men in the Ninth Texas Cavalry who were killed, wounded, or captured. I have listed the names in these notes because I am aware of no other source where this information can be found. The last rolls of the four Texas regiments were taken on June 30, 1864, "In the field near Marietta," nearly a year before the men were paroled.

1 Griscom, *Fighting with Ross' Texas Cavalry Brigade,* p. 150; *O.R.,* vol. 38, pt. 3, pp. 962–63; *O.R.,* vol. 38, pt. 5, pp. 811, 816; *O.R.,* vol. 38, pt. 1, p. 701; *O.R.,* vol. 38, pt. 4, p. 714.

2 *O.R.,* vol. 38, pt. 3, pp. 899, 962–63; Griscom, *Fighting with Ross' Texas Cavalry Brigade,* p. 143; Keen, *The 6th Texas Cavalry,* p. 55; Barron, *Lone Star*

Defenders, p. 235. Barron states that the Yankees could identify Ross's Texans by their distinctive yell.

3 Keen, *The 6th Texas Cavalry,* p. 56; *O.R.,* vol. 38, pt. 3, p. 963.

4 *O.R.,* vol. 38, pt. 3, pp. 675–77; Grant, *Personal Memoirs,* p. 380; U.S. Congress, *Report of Major General William T. Sherman* (Report of Joint Committee on the Conduct of the War 1863–1866. Millwood, N.Y.: Kraus Reprint Co., 1977), p. 72; Ross to Dr. Tinsley, September 14, 1864, in Shelton, "Ross . . . Civil War Letters," p. 68.

5 Griscom, *Fighting with Ross' Texas Cavalry Brigade,* pp. 143–44; Sparks, *The War . . . As I Saw It,* p. 84; *O.R.,* vol. 38, pt. 1, p. 701.

6 *O.R.,* vol. 38, pt. 4, pp. 729, 731–32; Griscom, *Fighting with Ross' Texas Cavalry Brigade,* p. 144; *CSR-Texas,* roll 56.

7 *O.R.,* vol. 38, pt. 3, pp. 653–54, 673, 675, 677.

8 *O.R.,* vol. 38, pt. 4, pp. 734, 737; *O.R.,* vol. 38, pt. 3, pp. 985–87; Griscom, *Fighting with Ross' Texas Cavalry Brigade,* pp. 144–45.

9 Sparks, *The War . . . As I Saw It,* p. 85.

10 U.S. Congress, *Report of Major General William T. Sherman,* pp. 72–75; *O.R.,* vol. 38, pt. 3, p. 985.

11 *O.R.,* vol. 38, pt. 3, p. 987; Griscom, *Fighting with Ross' Texas Cavalry Brigade,* p. 145.

12 Griscom, *Fighting with Ross' Texas Cavalry Brigade,* p. 145.

13 Keen, *The 6th Texas Cavalry,* p. 57; Sparks, *The War . . . As I Saw It,* p. 85; Griscom, *Fighting with Ross' Texas Cavalry Brigade,* p. 145.

14 Griscom, *Fighting with Ross' Texas Cavalry Brigade,* p. 145.

15 Ibid., pp. 146–47.

16 Payne and Dunn, *Dunn Family,* p. 151; Griscom, *Fighting with Ross' Texas Cavalry Brigade,* p. 146.

17 Griscom, *Fighting with Ross' Texas Cavalry Brigade,* pp. 146–147; *O.R.,* vol. 38, pt. 3, p. 647. Abstract of Return, June 10, 1864. Smith's Brigade of Maj. Gen. Patrick Cleburne's Division contained eight Texas infantry and dismounted cavalry regiments.

18 William T. Sherman, *Memoirs of General William T. Sherman* (New York: Library Classics of the United States, Inc., 1990), p. 515; Griscom, *Fighting with Ross' Texas Cavalry Brigade,* pp. 147–48.

19 Griscom, *Fighting with Ross' Texas Cavalry Brigade,* p. 147; Sparks, *The War . . . As I Saw It,* pp. 86–93. Sparks tells the following story of "Blank" and his experiences with Dr. Robertson. Details of activities, names of the wounded,

and the vivid descriptions of events and feelings attributed to "Blank" leave no doubt that Sparks is telling his own story; John Dunn, Company A, was known for his interest in medicine. After the war he became a physician. Surely he was Company A's member of the Infirmary Corps; see Tuck, *Civil War Shadows in Hopkins County, Texas,* p. 361, for Dr. James Robertson; see Rose, *Ross' Texas Brigade,* p. 97, for Jack Phillips, Company A, Third Texas Cavalry; Hale, *The Third Texas Cavalry,* p. 222. Wirt Phillips survived and returned to Texas, where he lived to old age.

20 Griscom, *Fighting with Ross' Texas Cavalry Brigade,* p. 148. See *O.R.,* vol. 38, pt. 3, p. 687, for casualties at New Hope Church.

21 Griscom, *Fighting with Ross' Texas Cavalry Brigade,* pp. 147–51; Barron, *Lone Star Defenders,* p. 197; U.S. Congress, *Report of Major General William T. Sherman,* p. 83; *O.R.,* vol. 38, pt. 4, pp. 780, 783; Charles D. Spurlin, ed., *The Civil War Diary of Charles A. Leuschner* (Austin: Nortex Press, 1992), p. 37.

22 *O.R.,* vol. 38, pt. 4, pp. 764–65; Griscom, *Fighting with Ross' Texas Cavalry Brigade,* pp. 148–49.

23 Sparks, *The War . . . As I Saw It,* p. 96; Griscom, *Fighting with Ross' Texas Cavalry Brigade,* p. 150.

24 U.S. Congress, *Report of Major General William T. Sherman,* p. 90; *O.R.,* vol. 38, pt. 4, pp. 785–87.

25 *O.R.,* vol. 38, pt. 4, p. 790; U.S. War Department, *Atlas to Accompany the Official Records of the Union and Confederate Armies,* Plate 50; Peter Cozzens, "The Tormenting Flame," *Civil War Times,* vol. 35, no. 1, April 1996, p. 54; *CSR-Texas,* roll 58; Griscom, *Fighting with Ross' Texas Cavalry Brigade,* pp. 152–53.

26 Griscom, *Fighting with Ross' Texas Cavalry Brigade,* p. 152; *O.R.,* vol. 38, pt. 4, pp. 792–93.

27 Griscom, *Fighting with Ross' Texas Cavalry Brigade,* pp. 152–53; Sparks, *The War . . . As I Saw It,* p. 97; *O.R.,* vol. 38, pt. 4, p. 799.

28 *O.R.,* vol. 38, pt. 4, pp. 799–801; Griscom, *Fighting with Ross' Texas Cavalry Brigade,* pp. 152–53; Sparks, *The War . . . As I Saw It,* p. 97.

29 Sparks, *The War . . . As I Saw It,* pp. 97–98; Griscom, *Fighting with Ross' Texas Cavalry Brigade,* p. 153; Keen, *The 6th Texas Cavalry,* pp. 58, 63.

30 Lloyd Lewis, *Sherman* (New York: Harcourt, Brace and Company, Inc., 1932. Reprint, New York: Konecky & Konecky, n.d.), p. 378.

31 *CSR-Texas,* rolls 56–60; Griscom, *Fighting with Ross' Texas Cavalry Brigade,* pp. 153–54; *O.R.,* vol. 38, pt. 3, pp. 653, 678; *O.R.,* vol. 38, pt. 5, p. 878. On July 13, 1864, Johnston reported to Richmond the strength of Brig. Gen. W. H. Jackson's Brigade as 3,574; *O.R.,* vol. 10, pt. 2, pp. 489–91. On the roll date of May 4, 1862, the Third Texas (then Greer's Regiment) had 707

present for duty, Sixth Texas (Stone's Regiment) 803, Ninth Texas (Sims's Ninth Regiment) 657, and First Texas Legion (Whitfield's Legion) 1,007.

32 Sparks, *The War . . . As I Saw It*, p. 95.

33 *O.R.*, vol. 38, pt. 5, pp. 860–64; Griscom, *Fighting with Ross' Texas Cavalry Brigade*, pp. 154–55. Casualties in the Ninth Texas that are not listed in any other known source: July 3, 1864, slightly wounded, Orderly Sgt. R. C. Guinness of Company A, John McDonnell of Company C, Joe Toliver of Company D, M. L. Cloninger of Company F, W. H. H. Saunders of Company I; July 4, 1864, R. Jones of Company F, severely wounded in the knee; T. D. Wilkerson of Company I, slightly wounded.

34 *O.R.*, vol. 38, pt. 5, p. 866; Barron, *Lone Star Defenders*, pp. 197–98; Sparks, *The War . . . As I Saw It*, p. 100; Griscom, *Fighting with Ross' Texas Cavalry Brigade*, pp. 153–55.

35 Griscom, *Fighting with Ross' Texas Cavalry Brigade*, p. 155; Payne and Dunn, *Dunn Family*, p. 155.

36 Griscom, *Fighting with Ross' Texas Cavalry Brigade*, pp. 156–58; *O.R.*, vol. 38, pt. 3, p. 647. The Eighth Texas was in Smith's Brigade of Cleburne's Division.

37 Griscom, *Fighting with Ross' Texas Cavalry Brigade*, pp. 156–58; Barron, *Lone Star Defenders*, p. 198; Ross to Lizzie Ross, July 19, 1864, in Shelton, "Ross . . . Civil War Letters," pp. 65–66; Payne and Dunn, *Dunn Family*, pp. 155–56.

38 Payne and Dunn, *Dunn Family*, p. 156; Griscom, *Fighting with Ross' Texas Cavalry Brigade*, p. 155.

39 Ross to Lizzie Ross, July 7, 1864, in Shelton, "Ross . . . Civil War Letters," p. 64.

40 U.S. Congress, *Report of Major General William T. Sherman*, p. 127.

41 Ross to Lizzie Ross, July 7, 1864, in Shelton, "Ross . . . Civil War Letters," p. 64; Griscom, *Fighting with Ross' Texas Cavalry Brigade*, p. 156.

42 U.S. War Department, *Atlas to Accompany the Official Records of the Union and Confederate Armies*, Plates 58, 62; Griscom, *Fighting with Ross' Texas Cavalry Brigade*, p. 158.

43 Payne and Dunn, *Dunn Family*, p. 156; Griscom, *Fighting with Ross' Texas Cavalry Brigade*, p. 158.

44 Cunningham, *Doctors in Gray: The Confederate Medical Service*, pp. 220–21; George Worthington Adams, *Doctors in Blue* (New York: H. Schuman, 1952. Reprint. Baton Rouge: Louisiana State University Press, Paperback edition, 1996), p. 114.

45 Payne and Dunn, *Dunn Family*, p. 156.

46 Griscom, *Fighting with Ross' Texas Brigade*, p. 158.

47 Payne and Dunn, *Dunn Family*, p. 156; Sparks, *The War . . . As I Saw It*, p. 87.

48 Sparks, *The War . . . As I Saw It,* p. 90; Gordon Dammann, M.D., *Pictorial Encyclopedia of Civil War Medical Instruments and Equipment* (Missoula, Mont.: Pictorial Histories Publishing Company, 1983), vol. 1, pp. 3–5; Cunningham, *Doctors in Gray,* pp. 225–26; Adams, *Doctors in Blue,* pp. 220–21; U.S. Army, *The Medical and Surgical History of the War of the Rebellion* (Second Issue, Washington: Government Printing Office, 1883. Reprint, *The Medical and Surgical History of the Civil War,* Wilmington, N.C.: Broadfoot Publishing Company, 1991), vol. 12, p. 867.

49 Cunningham, *Doctors in Gray,* pp. 231–33.

50 Griscom, *Fighting with Ross' Texas Cavalry Brigade,* p. 158; Miller, "A Memoir of the Days of '61," p. 50; *O.R.,* vol. 38, pt. 5, p. 887.

51 *O.R.,* vol. 38, pt. 4, p. 805.

52 Shelby Foote, *The Civil War: Red River to Appomattox* (New York: Random House, 1974), p. 420; Eaton, *Jefferson Davis,* pp. 254–55; Joseph H. Parks, *General Edmund Kirby Smith C.S.A.* (Baton Rouge: Louisiana State University Press, 1954), p. 254; T. Michael Parrish, *Richard Taylor: Soldier Prince of Dixie* (Chapel Hill: University of North Carolina Press, 1992), p. 411: Lewis, *Sherman,* p. 382.

53 Spurlin, *The Civil War Diary of Charles A. Leuschner,* p. 43; Bill O'Neal, ed., "The Civil War Memoirs of Samuel Alonza Cooke," *Southwestern Historical Quarterly,* Texas State Historical Association, Austin, Tex., vol. 74, no. 4, April 1971, p. 543; Cater, *As It Was,* p. 186; Griscom, *Fighting with Ross' Texas Cavalry Brigade,* p. 158.

54 U.S. Congress, *Report of Major General William T. Sherman,* pp. 132–33, 138; *O.R.,* vol. 38, pt. 1, p. 702. Lt. Gen. William J. Hardee stated in his report of the Atlanta Campaign that Hood said the Army of Tennessee lost 5,247, but Hardee stated that his corps alone lost 7,000; *O.R.,* vol. 38, pt. 1, p. 85. Sherman reported taking 12,983 prisoners and deserters; *O.R.,* vol. 38, pt. 2, p. 81. Maj. Gen. John A. Logan reported July 25, 1864, that he had buried or delivered to the Confederates 3,220 dead, sent 1,071 north, was holding 1,000 wounded prisoners, and estimated the Confederate loss as at least 10,000.

55 Griscom, *Fighting with Ross' Texas Cavalry Brigade,* pp. 158–59; Payne and Dunn, *Dunn Family,* p. 157. Dunn wrote that the Ninth was at Baker's Ferry, which is down the Chattahoochee, near Sandtown.

56 *O.R.,* vol. 38, pt. 5, p. 901; Griscom, *Fighting with the Texas Cavalry Brigade,* p. 159.

57 *O.R.,* vol. 38, pt. 5, p. 901; Griscom, *Fighting with Ross' Texas Cavalry Brigade,* p. 159. Captured men were Terrell Woodson of Company A, H. Fuzzle of Company B, H. R. Rogers of Company H, and Ben R. Vines of Company I; *CSR-Texas,* roll 60. Terrell Woodson was captured on July 23, 1864, near

Atlanta, and was taken to Camp Chase, where he died of pneumonia on Christmas Day 1864.

58 Griscom, *Fighting with Ross' Texas Cavalry Brigade,* p. 159.

59 Griscom, *Fighting with Ross' Texas Cavalry Brigade,* pp. 158–60; *O.R.,* vol. 38, pt. 5, pp. 907, 911–12, 915, 923; *O.R.,* vol. 38, pt. 1, pp. 77–78.

60 *O.R.,* vol. 38, pt. 5, p. 923; *O.R.,* vol. 38, pt. 3, pp. 632, 666, 688, 963. Colonel Harrison's Brigade was made up of the Eighth and Eleventh Texas Cavalry, the Third Arkansas Cavalry, and the Fourth Tennessee Cavalry; J. K. R. Blackburn, L. B. Giles, and E. S. Dodd, *Terry's Texas Rangers* (Austin: State House Press, 1996), p. 14. Thomas Harrison of Waco, Texas, was the original major of the Eighth Texas Cavalry, Terry's Texas Rangers, and served as colonel of the regiment before becoming a brigade commander under Wheeler; Griscom, *Fighting with Ross' Texas Cavalry Brigade,* p. 160; Keen, *The 6th Texas Cavalry,* p. 64; Barron, *Lone Star Defenders,* p. 199; U.S. Congress, *Report of Major General William T. Sherman,* p. 142.

61 Payne and Dunn, *Dunn Family,* p. 157; *O.R.,* vol. 38, pt. 3, p. 963; Griscom, *Fighting with Ross' Texas Cavalry Brigade,* p. 160.

62 Sparks, *The War . . . As I Saw It,* pp. 100–101.

63 *O.R.,* vol. 38, pt. 3, p. 963; *O.R.,* vol. 38, pt. 2, p. 878; Griscom, *Fighting with Ross' Texas Cavalry Brigade,* p. 160. Color Sgt. W. L. Murray, Company E, was wounded, his leg amputated; Sparks, *The War . . . As I Saw It,* p. 101; Barron, *Lone Star Defenders,* p. 200.

64 Griscom, *Fighting with Ross' Texas Cavalry Brigade,* pp. 160–61; *O.R.,* vol. 38, pt. 1, p. 774; *O.R.,* vol. 38, pt. 3, pp. 963–64; *O.R.,* vol. 38, pt. 2, pp. 776–77.

65 *O.R.,* vol. 38, pt. 3, p. 964; Griscom, *Fighting with Ross' Texas Cavalry Brigade,* p. 161. At Lovejoy Station, the Ninth's casualties were Lt. J. C. Garrett of Company K, Lt. R. W. Gallaher of Company C, and C. E. Orr of Company F, severely wounded. Samuel H. McClatchy of Company K was slightly wounded.

66 U.S. Congress, *Report of Major General William T. Sherman,* p. 148; *O.R.,* vol. 38, pt. 1, p. 775; *O.R.,* vol. 38, pt. 2, p. 776; *O.R.,* vol. 38, pt. 3, p. 964; *O.R.,* vol. 38, pt. 5, p. 929; Griscom, *Fighting with Ross' Texas Cavalry Brigade,* p. 161.

67 Payne and Dunn, *Dunn Family,* p. 161.

68 *O.R.,* vol. 38, pt. 2, pp. 878, 883; Sparks, *The War . . . As I Saw It,* p. 101; Griscom, *Fighting with Ross' Texas Cavalry Brigade,* p. 161.

69 Griscom, *Fighting with Ross' Texas Cavalry Brigade,* p. 161; *O.R.,* vol. 38, pt. 3, pp. 954, 964; *O.R.,* vol. 38, pt. 5, p. 932.

70   O.R., vol. 38, pt. 3, pp. 688, 953–54, 964; O.R., vol. 38, pt. 5, pp. 927, 932; Griscom, *Fighting with Ross' Texas Cavalry Brigade*, p. 161.

71   Payne and Dunn, *Dunn Family*, p. 157; Griscom, *Fighting with Ross' Texas Cavalry Brigade*, pp. 160–61; O.R., vol. 38, pt. 3, p. 964.

72   O.R., vol. 38, pt. 3, p. 964; Barron, *Lone Star Defenders*, pp. 200–201.

73   Barron, *Lone Star Defenders*, p. 201.

74   O.R., vol. 38, pt. 3, p. 964; O.R., vol. 38, pt. 2, pp. 776–77; Griscom, *Fighting with Ross' Texas Cavalry Brigade*, p. 162; Rose, *Ross' Texas Brigade*, p. 118; Barron, *Lone Star Defenders*, p. 202. Col. James P. Brownlow's First Tennessee Cavalry were known as the Gray Horse Regiment. The Texans would again encounter them in Tennessee.

75   Griscom, *Fighting with Ross' Texas Cavalry Brigade*, p. 162; O.R., vol. 38, pt. 3, pp. 953–57, 964; O.R., vol. 38, pt. 2, pp. 776–77, 879; Keen, *The 6th Texas Cavalry*, pp. 65–66.

76   Rose, *Ross' Texas Brigade*, pp. 112–13; Barron, *Lone Star Defenders*, p. 203.

77   O.R., vol. 38, pt. 3, pp. 956, 965; Sparks, *The War . . . As I Saw It*, p. 101; Griscom, *Fighting with Ross' Texas Cavalry Brigade*, pp. 161–62.

78   Griscom, *Fighting with Ross' Texas Cavalry Brigade*, p. 161; O.R., vol. 38, pt. 3, p. 964; O.R., vol. 38, pt. 2, p. 777.

79   Sparks, *The War . . . As I Saw It*, pp. 101–102.

80   Griscom, *Fighting with Ross' Texas Cavalry Brigade*, p. 162; O.R., vol. 38, pt. 3, p. 965. The Arkansas cavalry regiment mentioned by Ross must have been the Second Arkansas Mounted Rifles, Dismounted, which was serving in the area.

81   O.R., vol. 38, pt. 3, pp. 689, 956, 965; see pp. 953–56, for Wheeler's report of the McCook raid, which often varies with Ross's report, with Griscom's diary, and with the Union cavalry officers' reports. In his report, Wheeler criticized Jackson and several of his own officers and took personal credit for the success; O.R., vol. 38, pt. 2, pp. 776–77, 878–79; Griscom, *Fighting with Ross' Texas Cavalry Brigade*, p. 162; Barron, *Lone Star Defenders*, p. 203.

82   Griscom, *Fighting with Ross' Texas Cavalry Brigade*, p. 162; Sparks, *The War . . . As I Saw It*, p. 102; Payne and Dunn, *Dunn Family*, p. 157; Keen, *The 6th Texas Cavalry*, p. 66.

83   O.R., vol. 38, pt. 5, p. 936; O.R., vol. 38, pt. 3, pp. 956–57.

84   Barron, *Lone Star Defenders*, pp. 203–204; Sparks, *The War . . . As I Saw It*, p. 102.

85   Sparks, *The War . . . As I Saw It*, p. 102.

86   Ibid.; Cunningham, *Doctors in Gray*, pp. 130–31. The Union and Confederate

governments signed an agreement June 6, 1862, to view doctors as noncombatants and not liable to detention as prisoners of war.

87 Griscom, *Fighting with Ross' Texas Cavalry Brigade,* pp. 162–63; Barron, *Lone Star Defenders,* p. 204; *CSR-Texas,* roll 58. Walter N. Leak, Company A, Ninth Texas, was captured August 8, 1864, near Canton, Georgia.

88 Barron, *Lone Star Defenders,* p. 204.

89 Griscom, *Fighting with Ross' Texas Cavalry Brigade,* pp. 162–63.

Chapter 12: Paying the Piper

1 Cunningham, *Doctors in Gray,* pp. 60–61.

2 *CSR-Texas,* roll 59, Reuben Rogers; for a description of the symptoms and treatment of the Civil War's hospital gangrene see U.S. Army, *Medical-Surgical History,* pp. 824–36. Rogers likely did not exhibit all the symptoms; Cunningham, *Doctors in Gray,* pp. 60, 239–41. Cunningham wrote in 1960, "No one even today can speak with certainty and authority as to the 'hospital gangrene' of the Civil War." The Civil War's hospital gangrene was not related to dry gangrene, but likely was related to the gas gangrene of the First World War; Adams, *Doctors in Blue,* pp. 144–45. In 1914, a Civil War Union surgeon said of hospital gangrene, "We shall never know with certainty" which bacteria caused hospital gangrene.

3 Cunningham, *Doctors in Gray,* pp. 95–96; *CSR-Texas,* roll 59, Reuben Rogers.

4 Griscom, *Fighting with Ross' Texas Cavalry Brigade,* pp. 163–64; *CSR-Texas,* rolls 56, 59. Both Quinton Booth and Lorenzo Newton of Company A were injured on August 12, 1864.

5 *O.R.,* vol. 38, pt. 5, pp. 968, 971; Griscom, *Fighting with Ross' Texas Cavalry Brigade,* p. 164; Keen, *The 6th Texas Cavalry,* p. 67.

6 U.S. Congress, *Report of Major General William T. Sherman,* p. 146; Lewis, *Sherman,* p. 405; Barron, *Lone Star Defenders,* p. 205.

7 Barron, *Lone Star Defenders,* pp. 206, 217, 222–23; Keen, *The 6th Texas Cavalry,* pp. 68–69; *O.R.,* vol. 38, pt. 2, p. 858.

8 *O.R.,* vol. 38, pt. 2, p. 858; Keen, *The 6th Texas Cavalry,* pp. 71–72.

9 Keen, *The 6th Texas Cavalry,* p. 73.

10 Griscom, *Fighting with Ross' Texas Cavalry Brigade,* p. 165. Smith Compton of Company H and Lee Perkins of Company D were wounded; Payne and Dunn,

Dunn Family, pp. 158–60; Barron, *Lone Star Defenders,* p. 206; *CSR-Texas,* roll 58; *O.R.,* vol. 38, pt. 2, p. 858.

11   Griscom, *Fighting with Ross' Texas Cavalry Brigade,* p. 165. Capt. A. R. Wells, Company G, was killed. Lt. J. E. Moore of Company A, W. P. Reece of Company D, and J. A. Vines of Company I were wounded; Payne and Dunn, *Dunn Family,* pp. 159–60; Barron, *Lone Star Defenders,* p. 206; *O.R.,* vol. 38, pt. 2, pp. 813, 858; *O.R.,* vol. 38, pt. 5, pp. 976, 978.

12   Keen, *The 6th Texas Cavalry,* pp. 73–75.

13   Griscom, *Fighting with Ross' Texas Cavalry Brigade,* pp. 165–66; Barron, *Lone Star Defenders,* pp. 207–208; Payne and Dunn, *Dunn Family,* p. 161; Barron and Dunn both state that Ross's Brigade had about four hundred men in the field that day; *O.R.,* vol. 38, pt. 2, pp. 814, 825; *O.R.,* vol. 38, pt. 5, p. 981.

14   *O.R.,* vol. 38, pt. 2, pp. 814–825; Barron, *Lone Star Defenders,* pp. 222–33.

15   *O.R.,* vol. 38, pt. 2, pp. 814–825, 858, 863–64, 903; Barron, *Lone Star Defenders,* pp. 211, 208–209 (see pages 216–27 for a vivid account of the raid written by a lieutenant of the Fourth U.S. Cavalry, one of Kilpatrick's lead regiments); Payne and Dunn, *Dunn Family,* p. 160; Griscom, *Fighting with Ross' Texas Cavalry Brigade,* p. 166.

16   Griscom, *Fighting with Ross' Texas Cavalry Brigade,* p. 166.

17   Barron, *Lone Star Defenders,* pp. 209–10.

18   Ibid., pp. 211–13.

19   Ibid., pp. 213–14, 124; Payne and Dunn, *Dunn Family,* p. 161; Hale, *The Third Texas Cavalry,* p. 241; Griscom, *Fighting with Ross' Texas Cavalry Brigade,* p. 166.

20   Griscom, *Fighting with Ross' Texas Cavalry Brigade,* p. 166; Payne and Dunn, *Dunn Family,* p. 161; Barron, *Lone Star Defenders,* p. 213.

21   Barron, *Lone Star Defenders,* pp. 213–14; Rose, *Ross' Texas Brigade,* p. 179; Hale, *The Third Texas Cavalry,* p. 241; Payne and Dunn, *Dunn Family,* p. 161; Griscom, *Fighting with Ross' Texas Cavalry Brigade,* p. 166. Gris reported the Ninth's casualties as 2 killed, 20 wounded (1 mortally), and 4 captured, but he listed the names of 24 wounded. Killed and mortally wounded: Capt. A. R. Wells of Company G, W. L. Goodwin of Company D, and Cpl. C. Deeds of Company F. Wounded were: Company A—Lt. J. E. Moore, E. J. Brown, and Jesse Rogers; Company C—Sgt. B. O'Reiley, J. A. Hogue, G. W. Sloan, and H. C. Sears; Company D—W. P. Reece, A. Perkins, L. F. Perkins, Tom Perkins, and J. T. Turner; Company F—M. L. Cloninger, J. J. Weatherall, and J. D. Pruitt; Company H—Sgt. S. Dider and Cpl. Smith Compton; Company I—J. H. Caudle, M. Miller, and John Vines; Company K—R. C. Johns, Martin Williams, and G. T. Richardson. Captured: Company A—Edmund M. King; Company E—Bugler Daniel S. Alvey, Samuel T. Butler, and Sgt. Lemuel A. Porter. Griscom also listed the wounded in the Twenty-eighth Artillery—

Sloan and M. Miller. Griscom states in his diary that only three men failed to rejoin the regiment, but his company records verify that King, Alvey, Butler, and Porter were all captured; *CSR-Texas,* roll 22, Victor Rose; *CSR-Texas,* roll 58. Edmond M. King was released from Camp Chase on June 10, 1865; Barron, *Lone Star Defenders,* p. 214.

22 Griscom, *Fighting with Ross' Texas Cavalry Brigade,* pp. 166–67; Barron, *Lone Star Defenders,* pp. 214–15; *O.R.,* vol. 38, pt. 5, pp. 628, 629, 630, 634.

23 *O.R.,* vol. 38, pt. 5, p. 628; *O.R.,* vol. 38, pt. 1, p. 79; *O.R.,* vol. 38, pt. 2, p. 860; Barron, *Lone Star Defenders,* p. 227.

24 *O.R.,* vol. 38, pt. 5, pp. 995–96; Ross to Dr. D. A. Tinsley, September 14, 1864, in Shelton, "Ross . . . Civil War Letters," p. 66; Payne and Dunn, *Dunn Family,* p. 162; Griscom, *Fighting with Ross' Texas Cavalry Brigade,* p. 167.

25 Griscom, *Fighting with Ross' Texas Cavalry Brigade,* p. 167; *O.R.,* vol. 38, pt. 1, p. 706.

26 Griscom, *Fighting with Ross' Texas Cavalry Brigade,* pp. 167–68; Payne and Dunn, *Dunn Family,* pp. 162–63.

27 Payne and Dunn, *Dunn Family,* p. 162; Griscom, *Fighting with Ross' Texas Cavalry Brigade,* p. 167.

28 Griscom, *Fighting with Ross' Texas Cavalry Brigade,* pp. 167–68; Payne and Dunn, *Dunn Family,* p. 162.

29 Payne and Dunn, *Dunn Family,* p. 163; Spurlin, *The Civil War Diary of Charles A. Leuschner,* p. 46; Griscom, *Fighting with Ross' Texas Cavalry Brigade,* p. 168.

30 *O.R.,* vol. 38, pt. 1, pp. 80–81.

31 Griscom, *Fighting with Ross' Texas Cavalry Brigade,* p. 168; Barron, *Lone Star Defenders,* p. 229; Payne and Dunn, *Dunn Family,* p. 163.

32 Payne and Dunn, *Dunn Family,* p. 163; Griscom, *Fighting with Ross' Texas Cavalry Brigade,* p. 168.

33 Griscom, *Fighting with Ross' Texas Cavalry Brigade,* pp. 168–69, 218, 225. Capt. W. E. Alderson of Company F, Capt. J. W. Beckett of Company C, and Orderly Sgt. J. B. Scroggins of Company E helped carry Berry to the ambulance; Payne and Dunn, *Dunn Family,* p. 163.

34 Barron, *Lone Star Defenders,* pp. 229–30; Griscom, *Fighting with Ross' Texas Cavalry Brigade,* p. 169; *O.R.,* vol. 38, pt. 1, p. 81.

35 Griscom, *Fighting with Ross' Texas Cavalry Brigade,* pp. 169–70.

36 Ibid., p. 170; Spurlin, *The Civil War Diary of Charles A. Leuschner,* p. 47.

37 Barron, *Lone Star Defenders,* p. 230.

38 Griscom, *Fighting with Ross' Texas Cavalry Brigade,* pp. 170–71.

39 Ross to Dr. D. A. Tinsley, September 14, 1864, in Shelton, "Ross . . . Civil War Letters," p. 68.

40 Keen, *The 6th Texas Cavalry,* p. 56; Sparks, *The War . . . As I Saw It,* p. 83.

41 Payne and Dunn, *Dunn Family,* pp. 164–65; Brig. Gen. W. H. Jackson to Ross, October 23, 1864, in Shelton, "Ross . . . Civil War Letters," p. 98; *O.R.,* vol. 38, pt. 5, pp. 1026–27.

42 *CSR-Texas,* rolls 56–60. Other sources include Griscom's and Dunn's diaries, and later notations on a few men's records. The inaccuracy of the records is illustrated by the June 30, 1864, roll that notes Thomas G. Berry "present: stationed near Spring Hill, Tennessee," and George Griscom "present: Adj., stationed at Corinth, Mississippi." Both, of course, were in Georgia with the regiment; Griscom, *Fighting with Ross' Texas Cavalry Brigade,* p. 171; Hale, *The Third Texas Cavalry,* p. 250, states that fifty-seven men in the Legion had deserted by October 5, 1864, and seven in the Ninth Texas are known to have deserted by then.

43 Griscom, *Fighting with Ross' Texas Cavalry Brigade,* pp. 171, 173. The courier, J. G. McDade, Company B, Ninth Texas, left on September 27.

44 *O.R.,* vol. 38, pt. 5, pp. 995–97 (see pt. 3, pp. 668–75, 682–83, for August 31, 1864, Abstract of Return); *CSR-Texas,* roll 57, for Hamilton Dial, and roll 58, for Dudley W. Jones; Barron, *Lone Star Defenders,* pp. 230–32; Griscom, *Fighting with Ross' Texas Cavalry Brigade,* p. 171.

45 Griscom, *Fighting with Ross' Texas Cavalry Brigade,* pp. 171–72; Payne and Dunn, *Dunn Family,* pp. 164–65.

46 Ross to Lizzie Ross, October 23, 1864, in Shelton, "Ross . . . Civil War Letters," p. 69; Payne and Dunn, *Dunn Family,* p. 165; Griscom, *Fighting with Ross' Texas Cavalry Brigade,* p. 171; Cater, *As It Was,* p. 196.

47 Cunningham, *Doctors in Gray,* pp. 89, 288–89.

48 U.S. Army, *Medical-Surgical History,* pp. 823–49.

49 Ibid., p. 824. Statistics are from Federal records. No Confederate records are available.

50 U.S. Army, *Medical-Surgical History,* pp. 823–49; Cunningham, *Doctors in Gray,* pp. 60, 240; *CSR-Texas,* roll 59. The file of Reuben Rogers states: "Record of Medical Examining Board, Aug. 29, 1864, Appears on Register of Floyd House Hospital, Disease—G.S.W. [gunshot wound] right hand & lower 3rd right thigh (flesh) has had gangrene."

51 Cunningham, *Doctors in Gray,* pp. 239–41.

52 Griscom, *Fighting with Ross' Texas Cavalry Brigade,* pp. 172–73; Barron, *Lone Star Defenders,* pp. 231–32.

53 *O.R.,* vol. 39, pt. 1, pp. 725–27, 729; Griscom, *Fighting with Ross' Texas Cavalry Brigade,* pp. 172–73.

54 Griscom, *Fighting with Ross' Texas Cavalry Brigade,* pp. 172–73; Spurlin, *The Civil War Diary of Charles A. Leuschner,* p. 48; Cater, *As It Was,* p. 194.

55 Griscom, *Fighting with Ross' Texas Cavalry Brigade,* pp. 173, 187; *CSR-Texas,* roll 56. See *O.R.,* vol. 52, pt. 2, pp. 754, 759–61, for Ross's reports.

56 *O.R.,* vol. 39, pt. 3, p. 842; *O.R.,* vol. 45, pt. 1, p. 767; *O.R.,* vol. 52, pt. 2, p. 768.

57 Griscom, *Fighting with Ross' Texas Cavalry Brigade,* p. 187.

Chapter 13: Riding with Forrest

1 Griscom, *Fighting with Ross' Texas Cavalry Brigade,* pp. 187–88; *O.R.,* vol. 39, pt. 1, pp. 802, 808; *O.R.,* vol. 45, pt. 1, pp. 767–68.

2 *O.R.,* vol. 45, pt. 1, pp. 647–48; *O.R.,* vol. 39, pt. 3, p. 874.

3 *O.R.,* vol. 38, pt. 4, p. 480; U.S. Congress, *Report of Major General William T. Sherman,* pp. 84, 122, 129, 139.

4 *O.R.,* vol. 45, pt. 1, pp. 751–52.

5 Ibid., p. 768; *O.R.,* vol. 39, pt. 3, pp. 671, 874, 883; Griscom, *Fighting with Ross' Texas Cavalry Brigade,* pp. 187–88. Alexander Anderson belonged to Company A, Ninth Texas. The Sixth Texas lost two men.

6 Griscom, *Fighting with Ross' Texas Cavalry Brigade,* p. 188; *O.R.,* vol. 45, pt. 1, p. 768.

7 *O.R.,* vol. 45, pt. 1, p. 768; Griscom, *Fighting with Ross' Texas Cavalry Brigade,* p. 188.

8 Griscom, *Fighting with Ross' Texas Cavalry Brigade,* pp. 188–89.

9 Ibid.; *CSR-Texas,* roll 58; *O.R.,* vol. 45, pt. 1, pp. 887, 1217.

10 Griscom, *Fighting with Ross' Texas Cavalry Brigade,* p. 189; Jordon and Pryor, *Campaigns of Forrest,* p. 612; Cater, *As It Was,* pp. 198–99.

11 *O.R.,* vol. 45, pt. 1, pp. 768, 1221. Charges had been preferred against Col. Jack Wharton on March 24, 1864, by men in the Sixth who objected to his commanding the regiment. Wharton was acquitted of the charges and his record was cleared. November 18, 1864, Brig. Gen. W. H. Jackson issued General Orders No. 29, stating, "Wharton will assume command." Ross's brother Peter, whom the men liked, reverted to second in command.

12 *CSR-Texas,* rolls 56–60.

13 *O.R.,* vol. 45, pt. 1, p. 664; Jordon and Pryor, *Campaigns of Forrest,* p. 611 (they place Forrest's strength at 5,000); Henry, *"First with the Most" Forrest,* p. 384 (places Forrest's strength at less than 6,000); Wyeth, *That Devil Forrest,* p. 471 (also lists the command's strength at 5,000).

14 *O.R.,* vol. 45, pt. 1, pp. 32–34.

15 Griscom, *Fighting with Ross' Texas Cavalry Brigade,* p. 189; Jordon and Pryor, *Campaigns of Forrest,* p. 612; Spurlin, *The Civil War Diary of Charles A. Leuschner,* p. 49; Henry, *"First with the Most" Forrest,* pp. 384–85; *O.R.,* vol. 45, pt. 1, p. 768.

16 *O.R.,* vol. 45, pt. 1, p. 768; Griscom, *Fighting with Ross' Texas Cavalry Brigade,* p. 189. W. G. Springer of Company K deserted.

17 Griscom, *Fighting with Ross' Texas Cavalry Brigade,* p. 189; *O.R.,* vol. 45, pt. 1, p. 768.

18 *O.R.,* vol. 45, pt. 1, p. 768; Griscom, *Fighting with Ross' Texas Cavalry Brigade,* p. 189.

19 Griscom, *Fighting with Ross' Texas Cavalry Brigade,* pp. 189–90; *O.R.,* vol. 45, pt. 1, p. 768.

20 Jordon and Pryor, *Campaigns of Forrest,* pp. 617–18; *O.R.,* vol. 45, pt. 1, pp. 768–69; Griscom, *Fighting with Ross' Texas Cavalry Brigade,* p. 190. J. M. Brinney of Company H and J. H. Smith of Company B were slightly wounded, neither leaving the field.

21 *O.R.,* vol. 45, pt. 1, p. 768.

22 Griscom, *Fighting with Ross' Texas Cavalry Brigade,* p. 190; Jordon and Pryor, *Campaigns of Forrest,* pp. 617–18.

23 Griscom, *Fighting with Ross' Texas Cavalry Brigade,* p. 190. Ross and Armstrong crossed at Wallace's Mill.

24 Griscom, *Fighting with Ross' Texas Cavalry Brigade,* pp. 190–91. Cpl. B. C. Childers of Company E was killed, and Cpl. Gentry of Company C was captured; Jordon and Pryor, *Campaigns of Forrest,* p. 620; *O.R.,* vol. 45, pt. 1, p. 769.

25 *O.R.,* vol. 45, pt. 1, p. 769; Griscom, *Fighting with Ross' Texas Cavalry Brigade,* p. 191; Jordon and Pryor, *Campaigns of Forrest,* p. 620.

26 Sparks, *The War . . . As I Saw It,* pp. 271–72; *O.R.,* vol. 45, pt. 1, p. 33.

27 *O.R.,* vol. 45, pt. 1, pp. 33, 752–53; Henry, *"First with the Most" Forrest,* p. 385.

28 Griscom, *Fighting with Ross' Texas Cavalry Brigade,* p. 191; *O.R.,* vol. 45, pt. 1, pp. 769–70.

29 *O.R.,* vol. 45, pt. 1, pp. 753, 770; Griscom, *Fighting with Ross' Texas Cavalry Brigade,* p. 191.

30 Griscom, *Fighting with Ross' Texas Cavalry Brigade,* p. 191; *O.R.,* vol. 45, pt. 1, p. 770; Henry, *"First with the Most" Forrest,* pp. 393–95.

31 *O.R.,* vol. 45, pt. 1, p. 770. Ross's report is the only Confederate report of what happened on the pike that night; *O.R.,* vol. 45, pt. 1, p. 753. Forrest reported that his other divisions were out of ammunition and that Ross and Armstrong, receiving no support, were compelled to retreat.

32 *O.R.,* vol. 45, pt. 1, pp. 753–54, 770; Griscom, *Fighting with Ross' Texas Cavalry Brigade,* p. 191; Henry, *"First with the Most" Forrest,* pp. 396–97.

33 Henry, *"First with the Most" Forrest,* pp. 396–97.

34 Ibid., p. 397; Griscom, *Fighting with Ross' Texas Cavalry Brigade,* p. 191; Wyeth, *That Devil Forrest,* p. 480.

35 *O.R.,* vol. 45, pt. 1, p. 770; John Watson Morton, *The Artillery of Nathan Bedford Forrest's Cavalry* (Copyright, Mrs. Ellen Morton, 1909. Reprint. Marietta, Ga.: R. Bemis Publishing, Ltd., 1995), pp. 273–74; Griscom, *Fighting with Ross' Texas Cavalry Brigade,* p. 191.

36 Griscom, *Fighting with Ross' Texas Cavalry Brigade,* p. 191; Wyeth, *That Devil Forrest,* pp. 480–81; *O.R.,* vol. 45, pt. 1, pp. 754, 770.

37 *O.R.,* vol. 45, pt. 1, p. 770; Griscom, *Fighting with Ross' Texas Cavalry Brigade,* pp. 191–92; Rose, *Ross' Texas Brigade,* pp. 118–19; Hale, *The Third Texas Cavalry,* p. 260. Sgt. Tom Cellum of the Third Texas; Sparks, *The War . . . As I Saw It,* p. 281; *CSR-Texas,* rolls 56–58. Creed, McDaniel, and Lewis belonged to Company A; J. W. Duese, slightly wounded, to Company H.

38 Griscom, *Fighting with Ross' Texas Cavalry Brigade,* p. 192; *O.R.,* vol. 45, pt. 1, pp. 770–71.

39 *O.R.,* vol. 45, pt. 1, p. 770.

40 Ibid., p. 754; Griscom, *Fighting with Ross' Texas Cavalry Brigade,* p. 192.

41 *O.R.,* vol. 45, pt. 1, p. 35. Thomas reported burying 1,750 Confederates, capturing 702, and placing 3,800 wounded in hospitals around Franklin. Confederate casualty reports are incomplete; *O.R.,* vol. 45, pt. 1, pp. 754, 771; Griscom, *Fighting with Ross' Texas Cavalry Brigade,* p. 192; Henry, *"First with the Most" Forrest,* pp. 398–400; Rose, *Ross' Texas Brigade,* p. 116; Cater, *As It Was,* p. 201.

42 *O.R.,* vol. 45, pt. 1, p. 754; Griscom, *Fighting with Ross' Texas Cavalry Brigade,* p. 192.

43 Griscom, *Fighting with Ross' Texas Cavalry Brigade,* p. 192; *O.R.,* vol. 45, pt. 1, p. 754. The Texans were posted on the Nolansville Pike.

44 Griscom, *Fighting with Ross' Texas Cavalry Brigade*, p. 192.

45 Ibid., pp. 192–93.

46 *O.R.,* vol. 45, pt. 1, p. 771. Ross's report, written mostly in the first person, indicates he was not present with his brigade for several days. From December 5 through December 23, the report is in the third person, but changes back to first person December 24; Benner, *Sul Ross,* pp. 115–16. Ross suffered throughout his life from the wounds he received at the hands of the Comanches in 1858. During his service, which was severe by any standard, Ross often suffered from severe colds, bronchitis, and malaria; Griscom, *Fighting with Ross' Texas Cavalry Brigade,* pp. 191–95. Griscom stated on December 4 that Colonel Jones was in command of the brigade, and he does not mention Ross by name until December 25, 1864; *O.R.,* vol. 45, pt. 1, pp. 36, 755.

47 *O.R.,* vol. 45, pt. 1, pp. 755, 771; Griscom, *Fighting with Ross' Texas Cavalry Brigade,* p. 193.

48 *O.R.,* vol. 45, pt. 1, pp. 755, 771.

49 Ibid., p. 755; Henry, *"First with the Most" Forrest,* p. 404.

50 Griscom, *Fighting with Ross' Texas Cavalry Brigade,* pp. 193–94.

51 Henry, *"First with the Most" Forrest,* pp. 390, 404–405; Morton, *The Artillery of Nathan Bedford Forrest's Cavalry,* pp. 281–84; *O.R.,* vol. 45, pt. 1, p. 755.

52 *O.R.,* vol. 45, pt. 1, p. 755; Griscom, *Fighting with Ross' Texas Cavalry Brigade,* pp. 193–94, 212, 233. Lt. H. F. Young of Company K and Lieutenant Moore were slightly wounded. Lt. James E. Moore served with Company A, Lt. J. W. Moore with Company I.

53 Griscom, *Fighting with Ross' Texas Cavalry Brigade,* p. 194.

54 Ibid.

55 *O.R.,* vol. 45, pt. 1, p. 756.

56 Miller, "A Memoir of the Days of '61," pp. 59–60. Miller's wounded friend was Henry Crawford; *O.R.,* vol. 45, pt. 1, pp. 756, 771; Griscom, *Fighting with Ross' Texas Cavalry Brigade,* p. 195.

57 Griscom, *Fighting with Ross' Texas Cavalry Brigade,* pp. 195–96; *O.R.,* vol. 45, pt. 1, pp. 756, 771.

58 *O.R.,* vol. 45, pt. 1, p. 771; Griscom, *Fighting with Ross' Texas Cavalry Brigade,* pp. 195–96.

59 Griscom, *Fighting with Ross' Texas Cavalry Brigade,* p. 195.

60 Miller, "A Memoir of the Days of '61," p. 60; Griscom, *Fighting with Ross' Texas Cavalry Brigade,* p. 196. In the Ninth, Sgt. James Bellah of Company K was killed. Sgt. James H. Watson, commanding Company D, and W. C. Romines of Company G were severely wounded. Romines died at a Mr. Fletcher's

home; *History of Texas Together with a Biographical History of Tarrant and Parker Counties* (Chicago: Lewis Publishing Co.), p. 5; *CSR-Texas*, roll 56.

61 Griscom, *Fighting with Ross' Texas Cavalry Brigade*, p. 196; Henry, *"First with the Most" Forrest*, pp. 405–407.

62 Henry, *"First with the Most" Forrest*, p. 407; *O.R.*, vol. 45, pt. 1, pp. 37–38.

63 *O.R.*, vol. 45, pt. 1, p. 756; *O.R.*, vol. 45, pt. 2, p. 693; Griscom, *Fighting with Ross' Texas Cavalry Brigade*, p. 196; Morton, *The Artillery of Nathan Bedford Forrest's Cavalry*, p. 285.

64 *O.R.*, vol. 45, pt. 1, p. 756.

65 Ibid.; Griscom, *Fighting with Ross' Texas Cavalry Brigade*, p. 196; Henry, *"First with the Most" Forrest*, p. 411.

66 *O.R.*, vol. 45, pt. 1, p. 756; Griscom, *Fighting with Ross' Texas Cavalry Brigade*, p. 196.

67 Jordon and Pryor, *Campaigns of Forrest*, pp. 645–46.

68 Henry, *"First with the Most" Forrest*, pp. 411–12; *O.R.*, vol. 45, pt. 1, p. 756; Jordon and Pryor, *Campaigns of Forrest*, p. 646; Griscom, *Fighting with Ross' Texas Cavalry Brigade*, p. 196.

69 Griscom, *Fighting with Ross' Texas Cavalry Brigade*, p. 196.

70 *O.R.*, vol. 45, pt. 1, pp. 42, 726, 729, 756–57; *O.R.*, vol. 49, pt. 2, pp. 852, 855; Ector's Brigade included the Tenth, Fourteenth, and Thirty-second Texas Cavalry, Dismounted, and the Ninth Texas Infantry; Wyeth, *That Devil Forrest*, p. 502.

71 Griscom, *Fighting with Ross' Texas Cavalry Brigade*, p. 197; Morton, *The Artillery of Nathan Bedford Forrest's Cavalry*, p. 293.

72 *O.R.*, vol. 45, pt. 1, p. 757; *O.R.*, vol. 45, pt. 2, p. 726; Griscom, *Fighting with Ross' Texas Cavalry Brigade*, p. 197.

73 Griscom, *Fighting with Ross' Texas Cavalry Brigade*, p. 197; *O.R.*, vol. 45, pt. 1, pp. 757–58, 771.

74 Griscom, *Fighting with Ross' Texas Cavalry Brigade*, p. 197. Avery Couch and Sergeant Curry of Company D were killed, and J. Howard of Company C was wounded; *O.R.*, vol. 45, pt. 1, pp. 757–58, 771.

75 *O.R.*, vol. 45, pt. 1, pp. 756–57; Griscom, *Fighting with Ross' Texas Cavalry Brigade*, p. 197.

76 Barron, *Lone Star Defenders*, p. 251.

77 Griscom, *Fighting with Ross' Texas Cavalry Brigade*, p. 197; *O.R.*, vol. 45, pt. 1, p. 771.

78 *O.R.*, vol. 45, pt. 1, p. 758; Wyeth, *That Devil Forrest*, p. 505; Henry, *"First

with the Most" Forrest, p. 414; Morton, *The Artillery of Nathan Bedford Forrest's Cavalry,* p. 293.

79 Griscom, *Fighting with Ross' Texas Cavalry Brigade,* p. 197; Henry, *"First with the Most" Forrest,* p. 414; *O.R.,* vol. 45, pt. 1, p. 758.

80 *O.R.,* vol. 45, pt. 1, pp. 758, 771–72; Griscom, *Fighting with Ross' Texas Cavalry Brigade,* pp. 197–98. Col. D. W. Jones was slightly wounded. Capt. W. E. Alderson of Company F, Lt. J. T. R. Jouett of Company B, and Ransom Russell of Company A were wounded.

81 Griscom, *Fighting with Ross' Texas Cavalry Brigade,* pp. 197–98; *O.R.,* vol. 45, pt. 1, pp. 758, 771–72.

82 Griscom, *Fighting with Ross' Texas Cavalry Brigade,* pp. 196–98; *The Commercial Appeal,* Memphis, Tenn., January 6, 1938, obituary of Jesse Rogers.

83 Griscom, *Fighting with Ross' Texas Cavalry Brigade,* p. 198; *O.R.,* vol. 45, pt. 1, pp. 758, 782.

84 *O.R.,* vol. 45, pt. 1, pp. 727–28, 772; Griscom, *Fighting with Ross' Texas Cavalry Brigade,* p. 198; Jordon and Pryor, *Campaigns of Forrest,* pp. 649–50.

85 Jordon and Pryor, *Campaigns of Forrest,* pp. 650–53; Barron, *Lone Star Defenders,* p. 252.

86 Barron, *Lone Star Defenders,* pp. 252–53; Griscom, *Fighting with Ross' Texas Cavalry Brigade,* p. 198; *O.R.,* vol. 45, pt. 1, p. 758; Morton, *The Artillery of Nathan Bedford Forrest's Cavalry,* p. 299; Jordon and Pryor, *Campaigns of Forrest,* pp. 650–51.

87 *O.R.,* vol. 45, pt. 1, pp. 758, 772; Jordon and Pryor, *Campaigns of Forrest,* p. 651; Griscom, *Fighting with Ross' Texas Cavalry Brigade,* p. 198. Wounded: Thomas L. Bearcroft of Company A.

88 Cater, *As It Was,* p. 203.

89 Griscom, *Fighting with Ross' Texas Cavalry Brigade,* p. 198; *O.R.,* vol. 45, pt. 1, pp. 674, 772; *O.R.,* vol. 45, pt. 2, p. 384.

90 *O.R.,* vol. 45, pt. 1, pp. 772, 758; Jordon and Pryor, *Campaigns of Forrest,* p. 654.

91 *O.R.,* vol. 45, pt. 1, pp. 760–63, 772.

92 Ibid., pp. 35, 46; *O.R.,* vol. 45, pt. 2, p. 780. Beauregard reported on January 13, 1865, that the Army of Tennessee could muster only 15,000 men.

93 *O.R.,* vol. 45, pt. 1, p. 728; Wyeth, *That Devil Forrest,* p. 507.

Chapter 14: Duty Done

1   Griscom, *Fighting with Ross' Texas Cavalry Brigade*, p. 198.

2   Ibid. If Griscom continued his diary into 1865, it has not been found; Barron, *Lone Star Defenders*, p. 267; Cater, *As It Was*, p. 204.

3   *O.R.*, vol. 45, pt. 1, p. 748. Forrest had ordered Jackson to leave Ross at Iuka, sending one regiment to Eastport to picket the Tennessee River and another to guard the bridge over Bear Creek; *O.R.*, vol. 45, pt. 2, p. 773. January 9, 1865, Col. Jiles Boggess, Third Texas, wrote Ross from Burnsville asking that his regiment be relieved.

4   *O.R.*, vol. 45, pt. 2, p. 748; Benner, *Sul Ross*, pp. 115–16; Rose, *Ross' Texas Brigade*, p. 174; Ross to Lizzie Ross, January 12, 1865, in Shelton, "Ross . . . Civil War Letters," pp. 69–70. William M. Inge was colonel of the Twelfth Mississippi Cavalry.

5   Ross to Lizzie Ross, January 12, 1865, in Shelton, "Ross . . . Civil War Letters," pp. 69–70; *O.R.*, vol. 45, pt. 1, p. 772.

6   *O.R.*, vol. 45, pt. 1, p. 42.

7   *O.R.*, vol. 45, pt. 2, p. 785. January 9, 1865, Taylor reported to Davis that if the Army of Tennessee were moved in its present condition its destruction would be completed; Parrish, *Richard Taylor*, pp. 428, 472.

8   Ross to Lizzie Ross, January 15, 1865, in Shelton, "Ross . . . Civil War Letters," pp. 69–70; *O.R.*, vol. 45, pt. 2, pp. 751–52, 756, 763, 770, 773; *CSR-Texas*, roll 59. George C. Piersall of Company A was captured at Iuka, January 18, 1865. He had blue eyes, dark hair, and a florid complexion.

9   *O.R.*, vol. 45, pt. 2, p. 770; Ross to Lizzie Ross, January 15, 1865, in Shelton, "Ross . . . Civil War Letters," pp. 69–70.

10 *O.R.*, vol. 45, pt. 2, p. 756; Barron, *Lone Star Defenders*, pp. 267–68.

11 Barron, *Lone Star Defenders*, p. 268.

12 *O.R.*, vol. 49, pt. 1, pp. 952–53.

13 *O.R.*, vol. 49, p. 972; Parrish, *Richard Taylor*, p. 408; Warner, *Generals in Gray*, p. 92. Forrest's commission as a lieutenant general was dated February 28, 1865.

14 *O.R.*, vol. 45, pt. 2, pp. 757–58, 770–72, 778.

15 Barron, *Lone Star Defenders*, pp. 268–69.

16 *O.R.*, vol. 49, pt. 1, p. 998.

17 Banks, "William Anderson Wingo, Lt. C.S.A.," n.p.; Lewis Publishing Co.; *History of Texas Together with a Biographical History of Tarrant and Parker Counties*, p. 5; Griscom, *Fighting with Ross' Texas Cavalry Brigade*, p. 196.

18 *O.R.*, vol. 48, pt. 1, pp. 1394–95; *O.R.*, vol. 49, pt. 1, pp. 998–99. The brigade was near Deasonville, in Yazoo County; Barron, *Lone Star Defenders*, p. 274. Although no record remains of the men furloughed from the Ninth, the twenty-nine who signed Paroles of Honor on May 15, 1865, were the half who remained in Mississippi.

19 Barron, *Lone Star Defenders*, pp. 271–72.

20 Ibid., p. 272.

21 Ibid., p. 273.

22 Ibid., p. 274. The owl train gang was arrested at Alexandria, Louisiana, on the Red River; *O.R.*, vol. 48, pt. 2, pp. 92–93. Lt. Gen. Simon Buckner, Adjutant of the Trans-Mississippi, granted the men sixty-day furloughs; *O.R.*, vol. 48, pt. 1, p. 1199. A Union officer reported on March 5, 1865, that the owl train had passed through Port Gibson, Louisiana.

23 Zoe Smith, "Obituaries Published before 1955 in the *Tulia (Texas) Herald* and the *Happy (Texas) Herald* (Tulia, Tex.: Tule Creek Genealogical Society, 1996), in the Tulia Public Library, Tulia, Texas, pp. 152–53; Martin and Rogers family notes; *CSR-Texas*, roll 59. Paroles are not noted in the files of Reuben Rogers or Jesse Rogers.

24 Garrett to Miss M. E. Gibbard, March 14, 1865, in Garrett, *Civil War Letters*, p. 90.

25 Ibid.

26 Rose, *Ross' Texas Brigade*, p. 174; Benner, *Sul Ross*, p. 113. Ross's leave was for ninety days.

27 *CSR-Texas*, rolls 56–59; *O.R.*, vol. 49, pt. 2, p. 1277; Sparks, *The War . . . As I Saw It*, p. 116. For correspondence from Jones to headquarters, see *O.R.*, vol. 49, pt. 2, p. 1221. April 8, 1865, the brigade, with 550 men present, was camped three miles out of Canton on the Vernon Road.

28 Parrish, *Richard Taylor*, p. 439.

29 Sparks, *The War . . . As I Saw It*, p. 116.

30 Ibid., pp. 116–17.

31 Ibid., p. 117; Parrish, *Richard Taylor*, p. 441.

32 *CSR-Texas*, rolls 56–60. Regimental officers Col. Dudley W. Jones, Lt. Col. James C. Bates, and Surgeon James E. Robertson signed paroles. The original Texans in Company A who signed paroles were Lt. F. M. Dyer, Lt. Frank O. Clare, Lt. James E. Moore, Alexander Anderson, George A. Ayers, Thomas L. Bearcroft, David Boaz, Richard Boaz, E. J. Brown, William Cox, Augustus R. Creed, W. Smith Cummings, Isaac J. Curry, Isaac P. Davis, John S. Estill, Phil C. Greenup, H. S. Harrison, T. J. Harvell, Hardy S. Holman, Walter N. Jones, Samuel Knight, Peter Moore, John M. Parish, J. J. Phillips, George W. Pointer, Oscar B. Ruley,

E. A. Schults, Joseph H. Simmons, James L. Tinsley, Isaac S. Tompkins, William L. Trice, and M. L. Wolf. Eight men who had joined east of the Mississippi River were paroled with Company A; Hale, *The Third Texas Cavalry*, p. 273. Two hundred and six men in the Third Texas signed paroles; Griscom, *Fighting with Ross' Texas Cavalry Brigade*, pp. 208–37. Thirty-nine percent of the officers and men on Adjutant Griscom's rolls died of disease or were killed, wounded, or captured. Others unfit for service were discharged. Company D lost 50 percent, Company E 53 percent, and Companies B and F each lost over 45 percent.

33   Sparks, *The War . . . As I Saw It,* p. 117; "Mrs. Bates Wants Her Flag— The Ninth Texas Cavalry," *Confederate Veteran,* vol. i, no. 5, May 1893, p. 178.

34   Sparks, *The War . . . As I Saw It,* pp. 117–20.

35   Ibid., pp. 118–20.

36   Ibid., pp. 120–21.

37   Ibid., p. 121.

38   Ibid., pp. 123–24.

39   Ibid., pp. 122–23.

40   Martin and Rogers family notes; Smith, "Obituaries Published before 1955 in the *Tulia (Texas) Herald* and the *Happy (Texas) Herald,*" pp. 152–53.

41   Rose, *Ross' Texas Brigade,* pp. 180–83.

42   Ibid., p. 183.

43   Keen, *The 6th Texas Cavalry,* pp. 73–101; Mary Sue Mathys, "Lemuel Jackson Beene—Civil War Questionnaire," *The Bean Stalk,* Southern Bean Association, vol. 14, no. 3, spring 1986, pp. 93–95; Paul Gilbert and Charles Lee Bryson, *Chicago and Its Makers* (Chicago: Felox Mendelsohn, 1929), p. 437.

44   Keen, *The 6th Texas Cavalry,* pp. 73–101.

45   Barron, *Lone Star Defenders,* pp. 274–75.

Epilogue

1   Benner, *Sul Ross,* pp. 117–21.

2   Ibid., pp. 126, 141–47, 152–54, 157; Rose, *Ross' Texas Brigade,* pp. 170–71, 173.

3   Benner, *Sul Ross,* pp. 198–217.

4   Ibid., pp. 231–33.

5   Griscom, *Fighting with Ross' Texas Cavalry Brigade,* pp. xiii–xiv; White, *Index to Texas CSA Pension File,* file #969099, George Lewis Griscom. Griscom married Mary Elizabeth Birdsong on May 13, 1868.

6   Rose, *Ross' Texas Brigade,* pp. 149–50. Rose states that Jones died in 1875; Russell, *Pioneers of Titus County,* pp. 151–52; Sparks, *The War . . . As I Saw It,* pp. 66–67. Sparks states that Jones died in July 1869. However, other dates in Sparks's book, provided to him by a half sister of Jones, are in error. Jones would not have represented Titus County in the 1875 Texas Constitutional Convention if he were living in Houston, but would have served from there. Neither could he have died in 1869 and taken part in the convention, as both Sparks and Rose state.

7   Ogreta W. Huttash, *Marriage Records of Cherokee County 1846–1880* (Private publication, Jacksonville, Tex., 1975. 5th printing 1965), p. 4; Cherokee County (Texas) Historical Commission, *Cherokee County History* (Jacksonville, Tex.: 1986), pp. 86–98; Ogreta W. Huttash, *Civil War Records of Cherokee County, Texas* (Private publication, 1982. Reprint, 1985), vol. 1, pp. 74–75.

8   Keen, *The 6th Texas Cavalry,* pp. 8–14, 95–101.

9   Garrett, *Civil War Letters,* pp. ix–x, 103–104.

10 Rose, *Ross' Texas Brigade,* pp. 5–6; Grimes, *300 Years in Victoria County,* pp. 377, 412; Victor M. Rose, *History of Victoria County* (Reprint. Victoria: Book Mart, 1961), p. 13.

11 Rose, *History of Victoria County,* p. 176; Rose, *Ross' Texas Brigade,* pp. 5–6.

12 *CSR-Texas,* roll 22; Rose, *Ross' Texas Brigade,* p. 11; Benner, *Sul Ross,* p. 140; Sparks, *The War . . . As I Saw It,* preface; Grimes, *300 Years in Victoria County,* pp. 377, 412.

13 Sparks, *The War . . . As I Saw It,* preface; White, *Index to Texas CSA Pension File,* file #97451; Ninth Texas Cavalry file, H. B. Simpson History Complex, Hillsboro, Texas.

14 Ninth Texas Cavalry file, H. B. Simpson History Complex, Hillsboro, Texas; Payne and Dunn, *Dunn Family,* p. 145; Young, *Grapevine Area History,* p. 183.

15 Young, *Grapevine Area History,* pp. 184–85.

16 *The Commercial Appeal,* January 6, 1938. Obituary of Jesse Rogers.

17 Smith, "Obituaries Published before 1955 in the *Tulia (Texas) Herald* and the *Happy (Texas) Herald,*" pp. 152–53; Cora L. Lewis, interviews.

18 *CSR-Texas,* roll 56, Augustus Creed.

19 Michaelias, interviews.

20 Smith, "Obituaries Published before 1955 in the *Tulia (Texas) Herald* and the *Happy (Texas) Herald*," p. 152; Zoe Smith, "Wayside Cemetery, Armstrong County," in *"Interments in Swisher County, Texas, and Vicinity 1890–1990,"* pp. 235–79 (Tulia, Tex.: Tule Creek Genealogical Society, 1990), in the Tulia Public Library, p. 245; Charles Wilson, interview with author, Canyon, Texas, 1995.

21 Young, *Grapevine Area History*, pp. 161–62; Crabb, Rogers family files.

22 Rose, *Ross' Texas Brigade*, p. 11; Sparks, *The War . . . As I Saw It*, p. 8; Smith, "Wayside Cemetery, Armstrong County," p. 245.

23 *The Commercial Appeal*, January 6, 1938. Obituary of Jesse Rogers.

24 Rose, *Ross' Texas Brigade*, p. 13.

Illustration Credits

Map content provided by the author and illustrated by Myles Sprinzen. Grateful acknowledgment is given to the following for permission to reproduce illustrations:

97   H. B. Simpson History Complex

109   H. B. Simpson History Complex, from *Harper's Weekly*, September 13, 1862

112   Maury, *Recollections of a Virginian*, 1894

114   LaBree, ed., *Confederate Soldiers in the Civil War*, 1895, drawing by Henry Lovie

115   H. B. Simpson History Complex, from *Harper's Weekly*, October 29, 1864

131   H. B. Simpson History Complex, from *Harper's Weekly*, January 16, 1864

135   H. B. Simpson History Complex, from *Harper's Weekly*, January 10, 1863

145   Anne S. K. Brown Military Collection, Brown University Library

146   Jordon & Pryor, *Campaigns of Lieutenant-General N.B. Forrest*, 1868, engraved by G. E. Perime & Co. N.Y.

165   H. B. Simpson History Complex, from *Harper's Weekly*, July 25, 1862

168   H. B. Simpson History Complex, from *Harper's Weekly*, June 27, 1863

174   H. B. Simpson History Complex, from *Harper's Weekly*, May 15, 1863

188   H. B. Simpson History Complex

217   *Atlas to Accompany the Official Records*, 1891–1895 plate 128

222   H. B. Simpson History Complex, from *Harper's Weekly*, July 30, 1864

224   H. B. Simpson History Complex, from *Harper's Weekly*, August 13, 1864

225   LaBree, ed., *Confederate Soldiers in the Civil War*, 1895

233   H. B. Simpson History Complex, from *Harper's Weekly*, September 3, 1864

247   H. B. Simpson History Complex, from *Harper's Weekly*, January 14, 1865

263   Alabama Department of Archives and History, Montgomery, Alabama

270   LaBree, ed., *Confederate Soldiers in the Civil War*, 1895

272   LaBree, ed., *Confederate Soldiers in the Civil War*, 1895

INDEX

Page numbers appearing in italics refer to illustrations.

413